ALL TI
TOP 1000
ALBUMS

COLIN LARKIN

GUINNESS PUBLISHING

DEDICATED TO BEN LARKIN

WHO LOVED A LOT OF THE MUSIC IN THIS BOOK

FIRST PUBLISHED IN 1994 BY
GUINNESS PUBLISHING LTD
33 LONDON ROAD, ENFIELD, MIDDLESEX EN2 6DJ, ENGLAND
ALL EDITORIAL CORRESPONDENCE TO SQUARE ONE BOOKS

GUINNESS IS A REGISTERED TRADEMARK OF GUINNESS PUBLISHING LTD

BRITISH LIBRARY CATALOGUING-IN-PUBLICATION DATA
A CATALOGUE RECORD FOR THIS BOOK IS AVAILABLE FROM THE BRITISH LIBRARY

ISBN 0-85112-786-X

PRODUCED BY
SQUARE ONE BOOKS LTD
IRON BRIDGE HOUSE, 3 BRIDGE APPROACH, CHALK FARM, LONDON NW1 8BD

CONCEIVED, DESIGNED & EDITED BY COLIN LARKIN
EDITORIAL AND PRODUCTION: ALEX OGG, SUSAN PIPE AND JOHN MARTLAND
SPECIAL THANKS: DIANA NECHANICKY, MARK COHEN,
DAVID ROBERTS, SALLIE COLLINS, SARAH SILVÉ, FRANCIS LASS,
KEITH ALLISON OF MRM GRAPHICS AND GUY BIRCHALL OF L & S COMMUNICATIONS

IMAGE SET BY L & S COMMUNICATIONS LTD
ORIGINATION BY MRM GRAPHICS LTD

PRINTED AND BOUND IN GREAT BRITAIN BY THE BATH PRESS

CONTENTS

ACKNOWLEDGEMENTS

My grateful thanks to everybody who submitted lists and offered opinions. Those who were particularly helpful were, in no particular order: Rick Christian, Simon Jones, Neil Slaven, Jeff Tamarkin, Bill Ruhlmann, Al Kooper, Brian Hogg, John Myer, Roy Sheridan, Pete Nickols, Alex Ogg, Hugh Wilson, Spencer Leigh, Tony Clayton-Lea, Bruce Crowther, John Tobler, Linton Chiswick, John Martland, Harry Hawke, Steve Smith, David MacDonald, John Child, Ben Larkin and the legendary Fred Dellar.

Those valued and reasonably talented colleagues who helped me write the brief overviews: Neil Slaven, Brian Hogg, John Martland, Johnny Black, Roy Sheriden, Simon Jones, Bruce Crowther, Linton Chiswick, Spencer Leigh, Alex Ogg, Harry Hawke and Phil Wilding.

Further thanks for help in assembling the albums and researching, and most importantly to those who parted with their prized possessions to allow them to be photographed: Peter Doggett, Mark Simpson, Trevor Dann, John Myer, Tony Russell, the Richard Cook Collection and Richard himself, Harry Shapiro, Alex Ogg, Pete Nickols, Hugh T. Wilson, William McEwan, Harry Hawke, the John Tobler Collection, the Colin Larkin Collection, Linton Chiswick, Joel and Kim Whitburn, Phil Wilding and Mike Chapman from Rock It, in Croydon.

Two further second hand record shops were especially helpful; Terry Jones from The Spinning Disc in the High Road, Chiswick, London. Beanos in Surrey Street, Croydon, Surrey is the largest second hand record store in Britain and is a real serious haven for collectors. Adrian the manager and David Lashmar the owner allowed me to raid their racks one afternoon. Towards the end things became desperate as albums that we thought everybody had, suddenly became as rare as rocking horse droppings. Phil Wilding and Nick Rabin were poached from BBC GLR to attempt to find some albums, Brian Hogg sent down his gems from Scotland and Steve Harrison failed miserably in finding items from the BBC library. The record companies were the last resort, but first you have to convince the press office that you are not just another blagger. Andrea and Phil Knox-Roberts from WEA always believe me and have so far, never let me down, Lesley from EMI Strategic Marketing, Adrian from EMI, Judy from Phonogram Records, Jane at Trojan, Kay at One Little Indian, Lorraine Bromley at Sony Jazz, Tony at 4AD, Andy Saunders at Creation Records, Regine and Sandra of RMP, Miles and Peter at Topic, Cooking Vinyl Records, Lesley Bleakley at Beggars Banquet, Dress Circle Records in Covent Garden, Roxy Mead of Scott Riseman Lipsey Meade, Tony Morley, Berni Kilmartin at Chrysalis Records, Andrea Britton at Polydor and Harmonia Mundi. Phil Wilding thanks Mogwai, Mike, Zaki Boubs, Anthony Noguera, Dave Mack, Joel at Steve Sounds, Neil Lach-Szyrma, Andrew Bass, Jamie and Darryl at Rough Trade, Neil Brown at Sister Ray, John Dryland and Rays Record Shop. General help and encouragement was received from Timothy Martland, Teddy Warwick, Martin Allerton from Mole Jazz, Kersten and Steve at New Note, Diana Luke, Simon Barnett, John Cavannah, Kip Trevor, David Roberts and Mark Cohen. Susan Pipe is always there and never panics. I'm sorry if I have missed others out, please forgive me.

Colin Larkin, the night before final press day

INTRODUCTION

The All-Time-Top 1000 albums. Oh yeah, who says so?

Well, first and foremost, I do not say so. As much as I would love to indoctrinate the rest of the world with my personal choice I feel that the opinion of others is of more importance and interest.

During 1993, in my capacity as editor of the *Guinness Encyclopedia Of Popular Music,* I was asked by *Today* newspaper if I would assemble the top 100 albums of all time. This was in anticipation of *BBC Radio 1 FM's* 100 top albums that was about to be broadcast, after compiling listeners' votes. I was already aware of many lists that had been published over the years. Magazines, radio stations and notable writers had already produced fine attempts. The most recent was published in *The Times,* and compiled by the anonymous Vulture.

Paul Gambaccini has already published two editions of the excellent *Top 100 Albums.* Paul plans to produce a new edition every 10 years to reflect our fickle tastes. The next edition is due in 1997 and I look forward to an invitation to vote for my 10 indispensable items. That book reflected the opinions of musical writers, journalists and broadcasters but it did not consult the person in the street or the growing number of musical train spotters, obsessives and vinyl junkies.

Tom Hibbert, who now writes with great humour in Q magazine produced *The Perfect Collection* in 1982. Excellent though it is, I am sure that he would have to own up to a little personal bias in arriving at this list. While I broadly share his view over the vast majority selected I would suggest that *Blues Helping* by Love Sculpture or *Contact High With the Godz* by the Godz would not be on the tip of everybody's tongue.

Many of us are fascinated by lists and charts and both those books and others remain a fascinating read. The *Guinness British Hit Singles, British Hit Albums* and Joel Whitburn's Record Research titles based on *Billboard* charts may be as indispensable as they are addictive, but it is still possible for a classic album to be omitted from their pages because it never reached the best-selling charts.

The lists are arranged by genre, and I have added a few extra charts for sections that often get forgotten, and to lighten the atmosphere. At the end of the book the 1000 are listed in an overall chart of charts. This sets out to answer the inevitable question of how the different genres fair against almighty rock and pop, and this if anything will clearly demonstrate the strong and the weak genres. I have placed albums in their closest genre, so there will be R&B in the blues section, country rock in country and folk rock in folk. Pigeonholing artists in this way will always lead to problems: is Elvis Costello pop or punk, are the Everly Brothers country or rock 'n' roll?

This book has taken over a year to compile. The results are as close as any book has come in finding out what people really think. I was determined not to accept the cognoscenti view without thorough investigation. I contacted hundreds of people who I knew had a serious interest in popular music. Many contributors to the *Guinness Encyclopedia* proffered their lists, usually by genre and usually in lists of 50 or 100. I read and digested thousands of reviews culled from the music press over the past 40 years. I consulted musicians, songwriters and record producers, the most efficient being Al Kooper who faxed me his fascinating list less than 12 hours after hearing of my request. It can be revealed that the former Bob Dylan session man and founder of Blood Sweat And Tears appears on at least five of the albums in the book - making his musical contribution quite considerable, even though none of his solo work is represented. Al's favourite albums include those by the Rotary Connection, Larry Carlton, Little Beaver and Robert Palmer - none appear in the final listing. John Child, our Latin music expert, sent his choice which had *They Just Don't Makim Like Us Anymore* by the Alegre All-Stars at the top. Sadly the Latin section was just outside the final crop. Pete Nickols, one of our soul contributors, placed *I'm Just A Prisoner* by Candi Staton as his all-time favourite - this also failed to make the final 1000. Jeff Tamarkin, the Editor of *Goldmine* magazine in New York had many of the final selection even though his overall number two, *Argent,* did not make it. His colleague, the American writer William Ruhlmann, had the same number one, together with many others, yet his choice of *Seductive Reasoning* by Maggie and Terre Roche did not appear. Their valued opinions did however, help to shape the final list and made it a bit more international.

I also consulted the record buying public who maybe acquire a dozen albums a year, and are often very fastidious even if their selection may well be a highly popular item such as *Brothers In Arms* or *Hotel California*. In accepting their nomination and banishing elitism I hope that they will consider my own opinion in recommending *Making Movies* and *Desperado* by the same bands as far superior albums. That is as far as I could go in influencing this book less we end up having the lists dominated by Poco's entire catalogue, almost

every note sung by John Martyn, Dusty Springfield and Bonnie Raitt followed by three albums from the Keef Hartley Band (Miller Anderson, your time is still to come).

OK, twist my arm and I will tell you that my five greatest albums of all time are:

If I Could Only Remember My Name - David Crosby;
Forever Changes - Love;
Grace And Danger - John Martyn;
Kind Of Blue - Miles Davis;
Buffalo Springfield Again - Buffalo Springfield.

That could change at any time because my three greatest albums of all time, this week, are those from Ian McNabb, the Subdudes and the Crash Test Dummies. Such is the ever evolving face of popular music and our own flighty nature. Three weeks ago, when listening to Sinatra's catalogue, I could easily have been swayed into the MOR camp.

It was not punishing to listen to 926 of the final 1000 albums over the past 12 months, it was revealing, irritating, frustrating but mostly a glorious experience.

I don't expect everybody to agree with this list, any selection is subjective, but it is honest and deeply trawled from a wide river of music. I look forward to your own lists, suggestions and complaints with anticipation. Until the next edition, this *really* is the Top 1000 albums of all time.

Colin Larkin, August 1994

THE TOP 250
ROCK AND POP ALBUMS

THIS IS THE DOG THAT WAGS THE TAIL AND THE GENRE THAT ALMOST EVERYTHING COULD FIT INTO. THIS PROVOCATIVE LIST CONTAINS NO REAL SURPRISES OTHER THAN GLARING OMISSIONS. THERE ARE NO ALBUMS BY XTC, SURELY THE WORLD HAS GONE MAD? THERE IS NO BARBRA STREISAND, NEIL DIAMOND, TOM JONES OR JETHRO TULL. THE DIVISION BETWEEN THE 'CLASSIC ROCK ALBUM' IS NARROWING YEAR BY YEAR - AS *BRIDGE OVER TROUBLE WATER* DROPS DOWN, SO *BOOKENDS* GAINS. SPRINGSTEEN'S LOFTY DOMINATION IS OVER AS R.E.M. AND U2 MOVE IN. NINE ALBUMS IN THE LIST BY FRANK SINATRA MUST DEMONSTRATE THAT WE ARE A WORLD OF HOPELESS ROMANTICS AFTER ALL.

1. SGT. PEPPERS LONELY HEARTS CLUB BAND
Beatles

The album that revolutionized, changed and re-invented the boundaries of modern popular music. 27 years on and now re mastered for the digital age this 4-track recording is still a masterpiece. Equal credit is now justifiably placed with George Martin, the producer in addition to the world's most famous quartet. He shaped glorious songs, fantazmagorical lyrics with melody and harmony and pushed recording technique into unknown waters. Much of late 60s pop was fashioned out of this one record, a whole gamut of tangerine chocolate bicycle sunshine groovy getting high crapollino followed. Nothing came near it. Unlikely to be toppled in our lifetime.

Sgt. Pepper's Lonely Hearts Club Band; With A Little Help From My Friends; Lucy In The Sky With Diamonds; Getting Better; Fixing A Hole; Being For The Benefit Of Mr. Kite; Within You Without You' When I'm Sixty Four; Lovely Rita; Good Morning Good Morning; Sgt. Pepper's Lonely Hearts Club Band (Reprise); A Day In The Life.

First released 1967
UK peak chart position: 1
USA peak chart position: 1

2. HIGHWAY 61 REVISITED
Bob Dylan

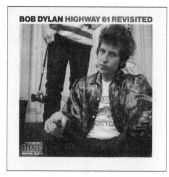

Dylan's first fully-fledged electric album engendered considerable controversy. Folk purists were alarmed at its undiluted power but rock had become the metier through which the singer could now best express his vision. Session organist Al Kooper and blues guitarist Michael Bloomfield were among those providing free-spirited accompaniment to a collection of songs which redefined pop music. Wrapped in a raw, driving sound, Dylan's lyrics - part Beat Poet, part Symbolist, part Concrete - ensured that contemporaries could no longer rely on traditional forms, an influence immediately apparent on contemporaries the Beatles and the Rolling Stones.

Like A Rolling Stone; Tombstone Blues; It Takes A Lot To Laugh, It Takes A Train To Cry; From A Buick Six; Ballad Of A Thin Man; Queen Jane Approximately; Highway 61 Revisited; Just Like Tom Thumb's Blues; Desolation Row.

First released 1965
UK peak chart position: 4
USA peak chart position: 3

3. PET SOUNDS
Beach Boys

The Beach Boys, and more specifically, their acknowledged leader Brian Wilson worked too hard to make this the greatest pop record of all time. At the time of recording Brian was experiencing a creative growth which he never recovered from. The intense beauty of this record grows with age and Wilson should not feel any failure or under achievement against the four moptops from Liverpool. They had a George Martin, Brian had only himself, some rival siblings and a cousin to deal with. The orchestral arrangements remain magnificently lush but never sickly, yet how can this masterpiece be given such a pedestrian cover.

Wouldn't It Be Nice; You Still Believe In Me; That's Not Me; Don't Talk (Put Your Head On My Shoulder); I'm Waiting For The Day; Let's Go Away For Awhile; Sloop John B; God Only Knows; I Know There's An Answer; Here Today; I Just Wasn't Made For These Times; Pet Sounds; Caroline, No.

First released 1966
UK peak chart position: 2
USA peak chart position: 10

4. BLONDE ON BLONDE
Bob Dylan

A year after *Highway 61 Revisited* Dylan repeated the act with further epitaphs of creative malarkey and intrigue. We were spoilt with a double album, longer than anything we had ever heard yet still destined to endure. The punishing touring and high profile drove Dylan to be creative beyond belief as he scribbled these gems in his hotel rooms. Surrounding himself with the likes of Al Kooper, Robbie Robertson, Charlie McCoy and Kenny Buttrey - seasoned musicians who gave this album relaxed confidence, unlike the youthful energy of *Highway 61 Revisted* which is ahead by a whisker.

Rainy Day Woman Numbers 12 & 35; Pledging My Time; Visions Of Johanna; One Of Us Must Know (Sooner Or Later); Most Likely You Go Your Way And I'll Go Mine; Temporary Like Achilles; Absolutely Sweet Marie; Fourth Time Around; Obviously Five Believers; I Want You; Stuck Inside A Mobile With The Memphis Blues Again; Leopard-skin Pill-box Hat; Just Like A Woman; Sad-eyed Lady Of The Lowlands.

First released 1966
UK peak chart position: 3
USA peak chart position: 9

5. REVOLVER
Beatles

Music critics have always preferred *Revolver* to its more famous successor while fans were at first a little wary of the brilliantly bizarre 'Tomorrow Never Knows', the eastern promise of 'Love You To' or the good time brass of 'Got To Get You Into My Life'. Years of repeated listening unfolds quiet gems such as Harrison's exceptional 'I Want To Tell You' and Lennon's wondrously hazy 'I'm Only Sleeping'. McCartney was also on a creative roll with the unabashed and brave romanticism of 'Here There And Everywhere and the classical sadness of 'Eleanor Rigby'. Subtly original and beautifully recorded.

Taxman; Eleanor Rigby; I'm Only Sleeping; Love You To; Here There And Everywhere; Yellow Submarine; She Said She Said; Good Day Sunshine; And Your Bird Can Sing; For No One; Dr. Robert; I Want To Tell You; Got To Get You Into My Life; Tomorrow Never Knows.

First released 1966
UK peak chart position: 1
USA peak chart position: 1

6. DARK SIDE OF THE MOON
Pink Floyd

An album that is destined to always be sold to and recommended by lovers of 'grown up rock' music. Now over 20 years old it still sets standards of recording excellence for today's digitally minded customers. Dave Gilmore's piercing guitar solo on 'Money' will still make you shiver, Clare Torry's wailing vocal on 'The Great Gig In The Sky' is still remarkable and Water's lyrics remain relevant in the 90s. Once the album coveted by cosy 70s couples as an essential purchase for their new home but now recognised by succeeding generations as a monster of a record.

Speak To Me; Breathe; On The Run; Time; The Great Gig In The Sky; Money; Us And Them; Any Colour You Like; Brain Damage; Eclipse.

First released 1973
UK peak chart position: 2
USA peak chart position: 1

7. ASTRAL WEEKS
Van Morrison

Cited, recommended and worshipped by the cognoscenti for over 20 years, this underground masterpiece has now become part of the establishment. It cries to be listened to with uninterrupted ears, which may explain why it failed to make either the UK or US charts. It wanders and weaves repeating themes and lyrics as if one song, yet we never tire of 'gardens wet with rain', 'champagne eyes' or the illusion of how Morrison can make a place like Ladbroke Grove seem so hauntingly evocative. The record is also a great educator in opening our eyes beyond pop to soul and jazz and although Morrison continues to return to its themes, this is his core.

In The Beginning; Astral Weeks; Beside You; Sweet Thing; Cyprus Avenue; Afterwards; Young Lovers Do; Madame George; Ballerina; Slim Slow Slider.

First released 1968
UK peak chart position: did not chart
USA peak chart position: did not chart

8. LET IT BLEED
Rolling Stones

The last Rolling Stones album to have the presence of the band's creator Brian Jones was a brilliant culmination of all their musical influences over the past monumental decade. The power of the opening track 'Gimmee Shelter' will haunt many of us forever with the memory of the Altamont murder, Jagger's top hat and scarf and the death of the 60s. The repeated line 'Its just a shot away' compliments the repetition of the album's last track's naively profound lyric 'you can't always get what you want'. The filling in between, like the layered cake on the cover is equally delectable.

Gimmee Shelter; Love In Vain; Country Honk; Live With Me; Let It Bleed; Midnight Rambler; You Got The Silver; Monkey Man; You Can't Always Get What You Want.

First released 1969
UK peak chart position: 1
USA peak chart position: 3

9. RUBBER SOUL
Beatles

The album that put the Beatles into the hearts and minds of middle class quality Sunday newspaper readers. The working class lads won over a new audience with a mature collection of songs that belied their age. As the art and literary world moved away from polo necked bohemian jazz, the Beatles wooed them with simple melodies and clever lyrics. This album also demonstrated that the Beatles were not without their own demons as unparalleled success took its toll alongside Lennon's illicit affair in 'Norwegian Wood', Paul's profound 'I'm Looking Through You' and Harrison's continuing growth with the thoughtful 'Think For Yourself'. Lennon owned the jewel however with the prophetic 'In My Life'.

Drive My Car; Norwegian Wood; You Won't See Me; Nowhere Man; Think For Yourself; The Word; Michelle; What Goes On; Girl; I'm Looking Through You; In My Life; Wait; If I Needed Someone; Run For Your Life.

First released 1965
UK peak chart position: 1
USA peak chart position: 1

10. STICKY FINGERS
Rolling Stones

The cheek and arrogance of the Stones came of age with this work, complete with zip fly cover and up yours tongue and lips. Crushing any doubts that they had gone soft with *Satanic Majesties* the guitars of Keef and Mick Taylor rocked together while Jagger spat out some of his foxiest lyrics. Never had they sounded so loose, yet together with examples such as 'Bitch', 'Sister Morphine', the country tinged 'Wild Horses' and the perennial 'Brown Sugar'. Dirty rock like this has still to be bettered and there is still no rival in sight.

Brown Sugar; Sway; Wild Horses; Can't You Hear Me Knocking?; You Gotta Move; Bitch; I Got The Blues; Sister Morphine; Dead Flowers; Moonlight Mile.

First released 1971
UK peak chart position: 1
USA peak chart position: 1

11. OUT OF TIME
R.E.M.

The highest ovewall position for a recent album illustrates the importance of R.E.M. as America's greatest post-Springsteen export. Michael Stipe's thinking persons lyrics are almost buried by the band's Byrdslike arrangements of the notable 'Radio Song' and 'Shiny Happy People'. There are those that now criticise R.E.M. for stepping out of a parochial indie scene, but their impact in the 90s was as welcome as the Sex Pistols were in the 70s. Their catalogue is destined to endure as critics reluctantly accept their considerable importance in the history of rock. Their anonymity is the only thing that holds them back.

Radio Song; Losing My Religion; Low; Near Wild Heaven; Endgame; Shiny Happy People; Belong; Half A World Away; Texarkana; Country Feedback; Me In Honey.

First released 1991
UK peak chart position: 1
USA peak chart position: 1

12. THRILLER
Michael Jackson

The finest example of perfect disco pop that should be prescribed to musical snobs and manic depressives. The record is a true ambassador of what pop music can be. Jackson whoops and dances through a suite of unforgettable melodies that are meant to be danced to with a smile on your face. While many of us will lapse into Lenny Henry's Aston Villa lyric to replace 'thriller' we are all touched by this quite magnificent record. Each track offers at least one musical hook, whether its the beauty of 'Human Nature' (who can resist the dada dada da da da) or the whoo whoo of 'Billie Jean'. Its all too good.

Wanna Be Startin' Somethin'; Baby Be Mine; The Girl Is Mine; Thriller; Beat It; Billie Jean; Human Nature; PYT (Pretty Young Thing); The Lady In My Life.

First released 1982
UK peak chart position: 1
USA peak chart position: 1

13. WHITE ALBUM
Beatles

Whilst this has often been mooted that this could have been edited to make the greatest single album instead of a double, we did at least get the efforts of four different, yet troubled individuals. The Beatles demonstrated that they could be way above our heads with items such as 'Revolution No. 9' and downright kitsch with 'Martha My Dear' and 'Good Night'. Above all they showed that they could really play, as displayed by 'Helter Skelter' and 'Back In The USSR'. even though they enlisted Eric Clapton for support on 'While My Guitar Gently Weeps'.

Back In The USSR; Dear Prudence; Glass Onion; Ob-La-Di, Ob-La-Da; Wild Honey Pie; The Continuing Story Of Bungalow Bill; While My Guitar Gently Weeps; Happiness Is A Warm Gun; Birthday; Yer Blues; Mother Nature's Son; Everybody's Got Something To Hide Except Me And My Monkey; Sexy Sadie; Helter Skelter; Long, Long, Long; Martha My Dear; I'm So Tired; Blackbird; Piggies; Rocky Raccoon; Don't Pass Me By; Why Don't We Do It In The Road?; I Will; Julia; Revolution One; Honey Pie; Savoy Truffle; Cry Baby Cry; Revolution No. 9; Good Night.

First released 1968
UK peak chart position: 1
USA peak chart position: 1

14. BORN TO RUN
Bruce Springsteen

Springsteen's standing as 'the future of rock 'n' roll' has taken a battering in recent times as his elevation and greatness is questioned. This much hyped album however should be the one that stands. The title track still makes hairs stand on end as the images conveyed in the lyrics have lasting power. Saxophones came back into fashion thanks to the blistering Clarence Clemons, as did forgotten 50s images of cars and drive-ins. Springsteen meanwhile exhumed his youth and reminded us of ours with honest tales of growing up in post-Eisenhower America.

Thunder Road; Tenth Avenue Freeze-out; Night; Backstreets; Born To Run; She's The One; Meeting Across The River; Jungleland.

First released 1975
UK peak chart position: 17
USA peak chart position: 3

15. RUMOURS
Fleetwood Mac

The reviewers tell us what to buy, but the public actually part with the cash. Twenty four million people cannot be wrong, as Peter Green's creation became the prime example of AOR in the 70s. The inner strife and turmoil of the band is credited as having helped to make this many headed beast into such a success. Christine sparred with John and Stevie scrapped with Lindsay. Mick Fleetwood held the emotional mess together with confidence steadiness as demonstrated in his drumming throughout the record. Nicks' fiery vocals on 'Go Your Own Way' complimented McVie's beautifully understated 'You Make Loving Fun'. The people have chosen.

Second Hand News; Dreams; Never Going Back Again; Don't Stop; Go Your Own Way; Songbird; The Chain; You Make Loving Fun; I Don't Want To Know; Oh Daddy; Gold Dust Woman.

First released 1977
UK peak chart position: 1
USA peak chart position: 1

16. UNFORGETTABLE FIRE
U2

The title of this album is taken from an exhibition of paintings by survivors of Hiroshima and Nagasaki. It confirmed U2 as one of the handful of bands able to tackle such vast and emotive subjects with dignity and musical integrity. There are few artists capable of writing about religion, war, race, the Irish problem and Life with such ferocity and with global commercial success. 'Pride (In The Name Of Love)', a hymn to Martin Luther King, was a worldwide hit, and almost every track is an anthem sung by millions. The production by Brian Eno and Daniel Lanois was a taste of things to come.

A Sort Of Homecoming; Pride (In The Name Of Love); Wire; The Unforgettable Fire; Promenade; Fourth Of July; Bad; Indian Summer Sky; Elvis Presley And America; MLK.

First released 1984
UK peak chart position: 1
USA peak chart position: 12

17. THE RISE AND FALL OF ZIGGY STARDUST AND THE SPIDERS FROM MARS
David Bowie

David Bowie's penchant for re-invention has allowed the singer to follow a fascinating career. The blend of rock star persona and alien creature defining *Ziggy Stardust* was arguably his finest creation. Buoyed by the support of guitarist Mick Ronson, Bowie produced some of his finest songs, from the raucous 'Suffragette City' to the prophetic 'Rock'n'Roll Suicide' - the singer would famously declare Ziggy dead during a live concert. Androgyny and science fiction combined with the artist's love of theatre to bring a visual nature to an album which remains central to Bowie's wide-ranging canon.

Five Years; Soul Love; Moonage Daydream; Starman; It Ain't Easy; Lady Stardust; Star; Hang On To Yourself; Ziggy Stardust; Suffragette City; Rock'n'Roll Suicide.

First released 1972
UK peak chart position: 5
USA peak chart position: 75

18. VELVET UNDERGROUND AND NICO
Velvet Underground

This dark, decadent and steamy album failed to sell when it was first released in deference to what was happening on the hippie laden east coast of America. Andy Warhol's pets unconsciously produced one of the most influential rock albums of all time. Openly addressing drugs, sex and everything that was sub-culture, this album still smells bad. Reeds brilliantly uncompromising lyrics together with the band's sloppy sexuality continues to influence. 'Venus In Furs', 'Heroin', 'The Black Angel's Death Song' and the magnificent 'I'm Waiting For The Man', its all here in 45 minutes of untouchable debauchery.

Sunday Morning; I'm Waiting For The Man; Femme Fatale; Venus In Furs; Run, Run, Run; All Tomorrow's Parties; Heroin; There She Goes Again; I'll Be Your Mirror; The Black Angel's Death Song; European Sun To Delmore Schwartz.

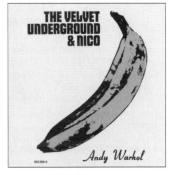

First released 1967
UK peak chart position: did not chart
USA peak chart position: 171

19. SONGS FOR SWINGING LOVERS
Frank Sinatra

The highest Sinatra in this listing and unquestionably his most perfect work. No album could begin to encapsulate quality 50s pop more than this. Quite apart from his graceful vocals the orchestral arrangements are immaculate and fresh almost 40 years on. The band conducted by Nelson Riddle gave Sinatra such space and freedom that he was able to make already established songs his own. The 15 songs contained on this record should serve to educate elitists that pop music has to swing before it rocks. Nobody should be too proud to have this indispensable record in their collection.

Too Marvellous For Words; Old Devil Moon; Pennies From Heaven; Love Is Here To Stay; I've Got You Under My Skin; I Thought About You; We'll Be Together Again; Makin' Whoopee; Swingin' Down The Lane; Anything Goes; How About You; You Make Me Feel So Young; It Happened In Monterey; You're Getting To Be A Habit With Me; You Brought A New Kind of Love To Me.

First released 1958
UK peak chart position: 8
USA peak chart position: 2

20. BAD
Michael Jackson

Jackson's domination of the world record market continued following *Thriller*, although by comparison it was an almighty flop with only 12 million sales. Like the Pink Floyd and Dire Straits, one album can go completely haywire, without not necessarily being any better. The title track and the gorgeous 'Man In The Mirror' were substantial hits but quality stuff such as 'Dirty Diana' and 'Liberian Girl' bolster a strong album. Jackson also seemed to have found the romance he seeks in 'I Just Can't Stop Loving You' and 'The Way You Make Me Feel'. However history shows him, he has made a lot of people very, very happy.

Bad; The Way You Make Me Feel; Speed Demon; Liberian Girl; Just Good Friends; Another Part Of Me; Man In The Mirror; I Just Can't Stop Loving You; Dirty Diana; Smooth Criminal.

First released 1987
UK peak chart position: 1
USA peak chart position: 1

21. BEGGARS BANQUET
Rolling Stones

The Rolling Stones emerged into the post-flower power age with this declamatory selection. Producer Jimmy Miller was instrumental in rekindling a musical power which possessed renewed forcefulness and focus. R&B remained rooted at the group's core - their reading of Robert Wilkins' 'Prodigal Son' is enthralling - while menace and anger ooze from what remains some of their finest compositions. Lascivious, malevolent, even politically impotent, they articulate a group freed from indecision and assured of direction. Their career as 'the world's greatest rock 'n' roll band' began with this release.

Sympathy For The Devil; No Expectations; Dear Doctor; Parachute Woman; Jig-Saw Puzzle; Street Fighting Man; Prodigal Son; Stray Cat Blues; Factory Girl; Salt Of The Earth.

First released 1968
UK peak chart position: 3
USA peak chart position: 5

22. PRIVATE DANCER
Tina Turner

Enlisting the help the help of notable producers such as Joe Sample, Martin Ware and Rupert Hine, Tina out-performed even the original artists as she strutted her way into rock music, having been on the edge for years with her screaming R&B and her ex-husband's strong influence. Al Green's 'Let's Stay Together' is made her own and even without the thin sounding organ on the Anne Peebles original her interpretation of 'I Can't Stand The Rain' is wholly acceptable. Mark Knopfler's standing benefited from having written the title track and if that isn't enough there is also 'What's Love Got To Do With It'.

I Might Have Been Queen; What's Love Got To Do With It; Show Some Respect; I Can't Stand The Rain; Private Dancer; Let's Stay Together; Better Be Good To Me; Steel Claw; Help; 1984.

First released 1984
UK peak chart position:2
USA peak chart position: 3

23. AUTOMATIC FOR THE PEOPLE
R.E.M.

Only two years old and already established as a classic of modern rock. Released soon after *Out Of Time* it shows the band on a creative roll with no shortage of original ideas. Bold songs such as 'Drive' and 'Everybody Hurts' demonstrated that the band were not reluctant to experiment, while 'The Sidewinder Sleeps Tonite' and Stipe's magnificent hair-lip Elvis on 'Man On The Moon' were as good as anything they have recorded. It is already anticipated that this record will find its way to a higher position in the future.

Drive; Try Not To Breathe; The Sidewinder Sleeps Tonite; Everybody Hurts; New Orleans Instrumental No. 1; Sweetness Follows; Monty Got A Raw Deal; Ignoreland; Star Me Kitten; Man On The Moon; Nightswimming; Find The River.

First released 1992
UK peak chart position: 1
USA peak chart position: 2

24. GOODBYE YELLOW BRICK ROAD
Elton John

An ambitious and bold attempt to produce a double album with no fillers, and Elton succeeded better than anybody. His formidable list of albums has a surprisingly small number of entries in the listings but those that are in will endure and be recommended for centuries to come. This is a brilliant package of sadness and pathos notably; 'Funeral For A Friend', 'Love Lies Bleeding', 'Candle In The Wind' and 'Goodbye Yellow Brick Road'. Both Taupin and John were able to change mood for the perennial encore 'Benny And The Jets' which is usually followed by 'Saturday Night's Alright For Fighting'.

Funeral For A Friend; Love Lies Bleeding; Benny And The Jets; Candle In The Wind; Goodbye Yellow Brick Road; This Song Has No Title; Grey Seal; Jamaica Jerk Off; I've Seen That Movie Too; Sweet Painted lady; Ballad Of Danny Bailey; Dirty Little Girl; All The Girls Love Alice; Your Sister Can't Twist (But She Can Rock 'N' Roll); Saturday Night's Alright For Fighting; Roy Rogers; Social Disease; Harmony.

First released 1973
UK peak chart position: 1
USA peak chart position: 1

25. Forever Changes
Love

The high position of this gem is no fluke. Its universal appeal to rock critics earns this position even though its total sales have yet to break a million. The enigmatic Arthur Lee created the perfect hippie album, with joyous acoustic melody, strings and occasional biting guitars. The paradox was for Lee to sing a line such as 'oh the snot has caked against my pants, it has turned to crystal' and sound absolutely right and sincere. The equally arresting 'Alone Again Or' has the line 'I could be in love with almost everyone' somehow avoids to sound like a hippie cliché. For anybody not familiar with this record it is urgently recommended.

Alone Again Or; A House Is Not A Motel; Andmoreagain; The Daily Planet; Old Man; The Red Telephone; Between Clark And Hilldale; Live And Let Live; The Good Humor Man; Bummer In The Summer; You Set The Scene.

First released 1967
UK peak chart position:24
USA peak chart position: 154

26. HUNKY DORY
David Bowie

David Bowie's most eclectic album acknowledged 60s' mentors and prepared the artist for subsequent musical directions. Andy Warhol, Bob Dylan and the Velvet Underground were illiberally canonised, a veneer of menace bubbled beneath the surface of several sweet pop songs while the subject matter embraced transexuality, Nitszche and science fiction. Guitarist Mick Ronson proved a sympathetic foil amid a support cast understanding Bowie's chameleon-like qualities and reacting accordingly. The singer's expansive interests have never been captured to succinctly.

Changes; Oh! You Pretty Thing; Eight Line Poem; Life On Mars?; Kooks; Quicksand; Fill Your Heart; Andy Warhol; Song For Bob Dylan; Queen Bitch; The Bewley Brothers.

First released 1972
UK peak chart position: 3
USA peak chart position: 93

27. THE BAND
The Band

Initially renowned as Bob Dylan's backing group, the Band emerged from the singer's shadow to proclaim a distinctive talent. Drawing upon a musical canon embracing soul, country, folk and rock 'n' roll, the quintet created a unique sound that was quintessentially American. Its rustic qualities were enhanced by principle songwriter Robbie Robertson who created vistas suggestive of a pre-industrial age and as such captured the restlessness of the late 60s without the need for explicit manifestos. Expressive singing, sublime melodies and telepathic musicianship instils *The Band* with quality, but its adult themes and perspectives ensures an absolute timelessness.

Across The Great Divide; Rag Mama Rag; The Night They Drove Old Dixie Down; When You Awake; Up On Cripple Creek; Whispering Pines; Jemima Surrender; Rockin' Chair; Look Out Cleveland; Jawbone; The Unfaithful Servant; King Harvest (Has Surely Come).

First released 1970
UK peak chart position:25
USA peak chart position: 9

28. IMPERIAL BEDROOM
Elvis Costello

Elvis clearly had a lot to get off his chest with this album dealing with emotional turmoil. Whilst much of its lyrical brilliance deals with his thoughts a small percentage slipped through for us mortals to relate to. Now having shown us he can deal with humour, politics and romance like no other, *Imperial Bedroom* is his most substantial album because the issues covered will always be relevant and important. Chris Difford pitched in with one composition 'Boy With A Problem', maybe Elvis found it too painful to write so directly about himself? Every track is powerful, simply read the list. A gigantic record.

Beyond Belief; Tears Before Bedtime; Shabby Doll; The Long Honeymoon; Man Out Of Time; Almost Blue; And In Every Home; The Loved Ones; Human Hands; Kid About It; Little Savage; Boy With A Problem; Pidgin English; You Little Fool; Town Crier; The Only Flame In Town; Room With No Number; Inch By Inch; Worthless Thing; Love Field; I Wanna Be Loved; The Comedians; Joe Porterhouse; Sour Milk Cow Blues; The Great Unknown; The Deportees Club; Peace In Our Time.

First released 1982
UK peak chart position:6
USA peak chart position: 30

29. ARE YOU EXPERIENCED
Jimi Hendrix

By 1967 Jimi Hendrix was feted as a genius by audience and contemporary musicians alike. His innovative, evolving guitar prowess was captured to perfection on this, his album debut. At times audacious, at others lyrical, Hendrix brought new perspectives to whichever style he chose to play; be it blues, pop or psychedelia. *Are You Experienced* contains a wide range of material, on which Noel Redding (bass) and Mitch Mitchell (drums) provide the ideal springboard for the guitarist's flights. Each format offered avenues for experiment, none more so than the vibrant 'Red House', on which the standard 12-bar blues is teased and twisted to new heights. Hendrix is clearly enraptured by a newfound artistic freedom, a joy which pervades this entire album.

Foxy Lady; Manic Depression; Red House; Can You See Me; Love Or Confusion; I Don't Live Today; May This Be Love; Fire; Third Stone From The Sun; Remember; Are You Experienced.

First released 1967
UK peak chart position:2
USA peak chart position: 5

30. CROSBY STILLS AND NASH
Crosby Stills And Nash

The finest example of 'wooden music' is enjoying a deserved re-appraisal after being abused for many years in favour of the more varied *Déjà Vu*. Although the badly recorded bass still booms throughout, the quality of the harmonies remain breathtaking. Three youthful men singing songs about relationships and changing partners with a fair degree of regularity, in those days. They sing as if they mean it, even if it is sometimes coy. Graham Nash's delicate 'Lady Of The Island' (about Joni Mitchell), Stills' opus-like 'Suite: Judy Blue Eyes' (about Judy Collins) and a slim Crosby singing of his sadly deceased sweetheart Christine on 'Guinevere'.

Suite: Judy Blue Eyes; Marrakesh Express; Guinevere; You Don't Have To Cry; Pre-paid Downs; Wooden Ships; Lady Of The Island; Helplessly Hoping; Long TIme Gone; 49 By Pass.

First released 1969
UK peak chart position: 25
USA peak chart position: 6

31. PURPLE RAIN
Prince

A soundtrack to a movie so appalling that it's infinitely wiser to let the record stand on its own merits. While Prince cavorted in purple kitchen foil and rode his Harley in high heels, the real star of the film, the music, was doing the real talking. A knit of funk and rock, a heavily stylised Hendrix guitar lick here and there, and a wilfully danceable backbeat all made for a huge commercial smash and the first real international introduction for many people to a star in waiting. 'Darling Nikki' accidentally set the PMRC ball rolling, but the heady lilt of the title track and the crushing, 'When Doves Cry' can forgive him that.

Let's Go Crazy; Take Me With U; The Beautiful Ones; Computer Blue; Darling Nikki; When Doves Cry; I Would Die 4 U; Baby I'm A Star; Purple Rain.

First released 1984
UK peak chart position:7
USA peak chart position: 1

32. MY AIM IS TRUE
Elvis Costello

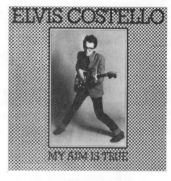

'Oh I used to be disgusted, and now I try to be amused' sang a youngish Costello in 1977 as he opened what for many is his best album. The pent-up frustration of the first album was mixed with melancholy for this, his second offering. 'Alison' is a beautiful love song and could be (and should be) covered by Tony Bennett and Barbra Striesand, in the way that McCartney's 'Yesterday' became universal. Elsewhere the wonderful Attractions support class songs such as 'Mystery Dance', 'Red Shoes' and the paradoxical 'I'm Not Angry'. I wonder if Costello knew how significant both he and this album would become?

Welcome To The Working Week; Miracle Man; No Dancing; Blame It On Cain; Alison; Sneaky Feelings; (The Angels Wanna Wear) My Red Shoes; Less Than Zero; Mystery Dance; Pay It Back; I'm Not Angry; Waiting For The End Of The World.

First released 1977
UK peak chart position: 14
USA peak chart position: 32

33. THE JOSHUA TREE
U2

After their arresting appearance at Live Aid, U2 album sales went berserk across the globe, and the world waited impatiently for their next release. *The Joshua Tree* arrived, and the world was not disappointed. There are few weaknesses, musical or lyrical, in this album. The pure power of the music and patent honesty of the lyrics steer the band clear of whimsy and self-indulgence. The anguish and questioning is shot through with faith as they chant and stomp and batter their way through instant classics like 'Where The Streets Have No Name' and 'With Or Without You', leaving the listener bruised but elated.

Where The Streets Have No Name; I Still Haven't Found What I'm Looking For; With Or Without You; Bullet The Blue Sky; Running To Stand Still; Red Hill Mining Town; In God's Country; Trip Through Your Wires; One Tree Hill; Exit; Mothers Of The Disappeared.

First released 1987
UK peak chart position: 1
USA peak chart position: 1

34. STARS
Simply Red

Mick Hucknall is one of the most prodigious talents in the music business; anyone who disputes this statement need only listen without prejudice to *Stars*. His voice has a range, sensitivity and accuracy which puts others to shame, and enables him to journey between soul, hip hop and jazz with alacrity. As if that were not enough, he has an almost Mozartian ability to compose melodies woven from the very essence of music. On *Stars* he left behind much of the narcissism of previous albums, gave the band quality material to develop and produced an enduring classic.

Stars; Thrill Me; Your Mirror; Model; Something Got Me Started; She's Got It Bad; For Your Babies; Freedom; Wonderland; How Could I Fall.

First released 1991
UK peak chart position: 1
USA peak chart position: 76

35. NEW BOOTS AND PANTIES
Ian Dury And The Blockheads

Ian Dury's one great album, so good that it overtakes major stars and million selling supergroups. Dury portrayed the Essex man before Essex man was thought of, and brilliantly satirized it in 'Billericay Dickie' and 'Clevor Trever'. It's hard to imagine Dury the romantic but there is a romantic in 'Wake Up And Make Love To Me' and 'I'm Partial To Your Abracadabra' there is also sadness and regret in the beautiful 'My Old Man'. He must be remembered for his dynamite band the Blockheads and this necessary album - not his gold radio station albatross 'Hit Me With Your Rhythm Stick'.

Sweet Gene Vincent; Wake Up And Make Love With Me; I'm Partial To Your Abracadabra; My Old Man; Billericay Dickie; Clevor Trever; If I Was With A Woman; Plaistow Patricia; Blockheads; Blackmail Man.

First released 1977
UK peak chart position: 5
USA peak chart position: 168

36. SWING EASY
Frank Sinatra

For many Sinatra devotees this remains the best album above the populist *Songs For Swingin' Lovers*. Sinatra started 'swingin'' with this collection, albeit in a more relaxed mode akin to 40s dance bands rather than the brassy 50s orchestration. Nelson Riddle is present here adding golden touches to Cole Porter's' 'Just One Of Those Things' in addition to further quality songs, chosen with care. Everybody knew Sinatra could sing, he just needed to find the right songs and the right arranger. This album together with its sister *Songs For Young Lovers* (included on the CD version) started it all.

Jeepers Creepers; Taking A Chance On Love; Wrap Your Troubles In Dreams; Lean Baby; I Love You; I'm Gonna Sit Right Down And Write Myself A Letter; Get Happy; All Of Me; Why Should I Cry Over You; Sunday; Just One Of Those Things.

First released 1960
UK peak chart position: 5
USA peak chart position: did not chart

37. NEVERMIND
Nirvana

Historically, America's north-west coast has produced edgy, rebellious music, of which grunge was one manifestation. An offspring of punk, speed metal and the 'slacker' lifestyle, it found an apotheosis in Nirvana, who combined such elements with a faultless grasp of hooklines. On *Nevermind* group leader Kurt Cobain unleashed frustrated alienation, his ravaged rasp and bone-crunching guitar soaring through a tight, intensive sound, courtesy of former hardcore producer Butch Vig. Cobain's solipsism proved tragically prophetic and his suicide elevated him to cultural icon status. This should not obscure the singer's empathy for the mechanics of classic rock, reworked and breathed with new life on this emphatic statement.

Smells Like Teen Spirit; In Bloom; Come As You Are; Breed; Lithium; Polly; Territorial Pissings; Drain You; Lounge Act; Stay Away; On A Plain; Something In The Way.

First released 1991
UK peak chart position: 33
USA peak chart position: 1

38. ABBEY ROAD
Beatles

The product of the Beatles' last recording session, *Abbey Road* transcends the internecine strife gripping its participants. Individuality triumphs on side one as each group member pursues specific callings, be it classic rock 'n' roll, Lear-like nonsense verse, riff-laden cris de coeur or simple sumptuous pop. Side two offers collectively where partworks and fragments are fused together to perfection to construct a breathtaking suite. Characters are cast and melodies envelop until the final experience is of a seamless whole, a proclamation of the ultimate joy of pop itself.

Come Together; Something; Maxwell's Silver Hammer; Oh! Darlin; Octopus's Garden; I Want You (She's So Heavy); Here Comes The Sun; Because; You Never Give Me Your Money; Sun King; Mean Mr. Mustard; Polythene Pam; She Came In Through The Bathroom Window; Golden Slumbers; Carry That Weight; The End; Her Majesty.

First released 1969
UK peak chart position: 1
USA peak chart position: 1

39. THE DOORS
Doors

The Doors were the antithesis of windblown Californian pop. Dark, brooding and alienated, every element of the quartet's metier was unveiled on their debut album. In Jim Morrison they possessed one of rock's authoritative voices, while the group's dense instrumental prowess reflected his lyrical mystery. Highly literate, they wedded Oedipean tragedy to counter-culture nihilism and, in 'Light My Fire', expressed erotic images unheard of in pop. Howlin' Wolf and Brecht and Weill are acknowledged as musical reference points, a conflict between the physical and cerebral which gives *The Doors* its undiluted tension.

Break On Through; Soul Kitchen; The Crystal Ship; Twentieth Century Fox; Alabama Song; Light My Fire; Back Door Man; I Looked At You; End Of The Night; Take It As It Comes; The End.

First released 1967
UK peak chart position: 43
USA peak chart position: 2

40. DISRAELI GEARS
Cream

The power trio's perfect studio album which captured the dayglo spirit of psychedelic London as no other record could. As their blues influence waned the hippie lyrics of Pete Brown came to the fore as the confident voice of Jack Bruce fused with Clapton's stinging guitar and Baker's polyrythmic drums. 'Tales Of Brave Ulysees', 'SWLABR' and 'Strange Brew' remain classics of their era whilst 'Sunshine Of Your Love' has become one of rock's most imitated opening riffs. The Martin Sharpe album sleeve completes the package and displays Eric Clapton with the finest perm of 1967.

Strange Brew; Sunshine Of Your Love; World Of Pain; Dance The Night Away; Blue Condition; Tales Of Brave Ulysses; We're Going Wrong; Outside Woman Blues; Take It Back; Mother's Lament; SWLABR.

First released 1967
UK peak chart position: 5
USA peak chart position: 4

41. IMAGINE
John Lennon

Lennon's solo debut although powerful did not have the universal appeal as this album. Lennon veered from spitting anger in 'How Do You Sleep?', 'Give Me Some Truth' and cruel humour with 'Crippled Inside', yet the man was capable of intense romanticism as highlighted in 'Jealous Guy' and 'Oh My Love'. Those who resented John for being part of the Beatles break up finally forgave him and began to love him again with this collection. The title track will stand as a classic of popular song and one that should be made part of the national curriculum.

Imagine; Crippled Inside; Jealous Guy; It's So Hard; I Don't Want To Be A Soldier; Give Me Some Truth; Oh My Love; How Do You Sleep?; How?; Oh Yoko!.

First released 1971
UK peak chart position: 1
USA peak chart position: 1

42. THIS YEARS MODEL
Elvis Costello

Yet another collection from Elvis, surely the most prolific quality lyricist of the past decade or two. This is a young angry and inexperienced Costello. He shouts and spits but always retains irrisistible melody. 'Pump It Up' contains driving pop with a fine example of 'cheesy' organ, and is a high point. The Attractions sound like the best backing band in the world and it is staggering to think that Costello had so much more bursting to get out when many of us would have been happy with this one album. Anyone who can rhyme Chelsea with Elsie and still sound cool has got to be a bit special.

No Action; This Year's Girl; The Beat; Pump It Up; Little Triggers; You Belong To Me; Hand In Hand; (I Don't Want To Go To) Chelsea; Lip Service; Living In Paradise; Lipstick Vogue; Night Rally.

First released 1978
UK peak chart position: 4
USA peak chart position: 30

43. BROTHERS IN ARMS
Dire Straits

The album many critics hate to love. Mark Knopfler's multi-million seller was the success story of the 80s in the same way that *Dark Side Of The Moon* was in the 70s. The doubters of its greatness argue that it was no better than the debut album, *Love Over Gold* or *Making Movies* a few years later. The public clearly disagreed and it continues be a steady seller. 'Money For Nothing' and 'Walk Of Life' were perfect songs for 80s mainstream rock radio, yet it was the undeniable beauty of Knopfler's playing on tracks such as 'Brothers In Arms' that give credence to its phenomenal success.

So Far Away; Money For Nothing; Walk Of Life; Your Latest Trick; Why Worry?; Ride Across The River; The Man's Too Strong; One World; Brothers In Arms.

First released 1985
UK peak chart position: 1
USA peak chart position: 1

44. ELECTRIC WARRIOR
T. Rex

Marc Bolan emerged from the petals of Britain's Underground scene to become one of the 70s bona fide stars. *Electric Warrior* followed the pattern of his group's highly successful singles wherein every track boasted nagging hooklines and incessant charm. Bolan understood pop history and his work drew on the immediacy of classic rock 'n' roll and the charm of its icons. He infused his music with an ebullient energy impossible to ignore while offering a mythology to enhance its appeal. The antithesis of contemporaneous progressive rock, *Electric Warrior* was fresh and uncluttered and therein lies its continued attraction.

Mambo Sun; Cosmic Dancer; Jeepster; Monolith; Lean Woman Blues; Get It On; Planet Queen; Girl; The Motivator; Life's A Gas; Rip Off.

First released 1971
UK peak chart position: 1
USA peak chart position: 32

45. BORN IN THE USA
Bruce Springsteen

Springsteen purists may well bemoan his overtly commercial stance taken on this record but its catchiness, high toe-tapping factor and damn good songs cannot be denied. 'Darlington County' and 'Working On The Highway' are familiar Springsteen themes but it is the incredible power of the title track's riff and the euphoria that 'Dancing In The Dark' still manages to convey a decade later. It is felt that he peaked with this record, and his commercial standing has dipped but *Born In The USA* still sparkles and above it still sounds like a great rock album.

Born In The USA; Cover Me; Darlington County; Working On The Highway; Downbound Train; I'm On Fire; No Surrender; Bobby Jean; I'm Goin' Down; Glory Days; Dancing In The Dark; My Hometown.

First released 1984
UK peak chart position: 1
USA peak chart position: 1

46. FACE VALUE
Phil Collins

The risk that Phil Collins took in displaying painful lyrics at an obviously harrowing time could have been taken as self-indulgent but almost 15 years on this album is seen as his best and most assured. The Genesis drummer displayed dynamic arrangements ('In The Air Tonight'), melancholy piano ('You Know What I Mean') and Philadelphia soul ('I Missed Again') and wrapped up with a cover of 'Tomorrow Never Knows' that even John Lennon would have tipped his hat to. After this album Collins embarked on an extraordinarily busy career that included a rejuvenated Genesis, film roles and huge solo success. This will always be the album closest to his heart.

In The Air Tonight; This Must Be Love; Behind The Lines; Roof Is Leaking; Droned; Hand In Hand; I Missed Again; You Know What I Mean; I'm Not Moving; If Leaving Me Is Easy; Tomorrow Never Knows; Thunder And Lightning.

First released 1981
UK peak chart position: 1
USA peak chart position: 7

47. ELECTRIC LADYLAND
Jimi Hendrix

The last official Experience band contained contributions from both Traffic and Jefferson Airplane. An unrivalled collection of songs including a brilliant renditioning of Dylan's, 'All Along The Watchtower', an interpretation that Dylan was later to adopt live. While, 'Crosstown Traffic', 'Gypsy Eyes', and 'The Burning Of The Midnight Lamp', as well as the posthumous number one, 'Voodoo Chile' (Slight Return), showed an incredible clarity in Hendrix's musical thinking. His vision already moving beyond the musical confined of the trio. A brilliant and still somehow contemporary record.

And The Gods Made Love; Electric Ladyland; Crosstown Traffic; Voodoo Chile; Rainy Day, Dream Away; 1983 (A Merman I Should Turn To Be); Moon, Turn The Tide...Gently Gently Away; Little Miss Strange; Long Hot Summer Night; Come On; Gypsy Eyes; The Burning Of The Midnight Lamp; Still Raining Still Dreaming; House Burning Down; All Along The Watchtower; Voodoo Chile (Slight Return).

First released 1968
UK peak chart position: 6
USA peak chart position: 1

48. SO
Peter Gabriel

So consolidated Gabriel's reputation as an original and exciting composer, capable of projecting sophisticated lyrics on accessible melodies. 'Sledgehammer' was a massive hit (number one in the USA), as was 'Don't Give Up', with Kate Bush's vocals adding extra pathos. 'This Is The Picture' clearly shows the slightly surreal influence of co-writer Laurie Anderson, and the whole is given flight by Daniel Lanois' impeccable production. The towering achievement, though, is 'Mercy Street', a sparely orchestrated and perfectly constructed tribute to the late poet Anne Sexton.

Red Rain; Sledgehammer; Don't Give Up; That Voice Again; In Your Eyes; Mercy Street; Big Time; We Do What We're Told; This Is The Picture.

First released 1986
UK peak chart position: 1
USA peak chart position: 2

49. THE STRANGER
Billy Joel

During the late 70s many bemoaned the fact that Mr Joel spent hours on our radio and years in the charts. Alexi Sayle even used his name in vain on 'Hello John Got A New Motor'. Two of his other albums *An Innocent Man* and *52nd Street* just failed the listings, but this monster of smooth AOR is the industry standard Joel album of which no comprehensive collection should be without. Lots of rich Fender Rhodes piano and crystal clear vocals and 15 million worldwide sales, even though Barry White did a better version of 'Just The Way You Are'.

Movin' Out (Anthony's Song); The Stranger; Just The Way You Are; Scenes From An Italian Restaurant; Vienna; Only The Good Die Young; She's Always A Woman; Get It Right The First Time; Everybody Has A Dream.

First released 1978
UK peak chart position: 25
USA peak chart position: 2

50. SIGN O' THE TIMES
Prince

A gleefully adventurous double album from Prince. Thought in some quarters as a little too ambitious at the time, it has come in time to be regarded as probably his greatest album. Drawing on just about every influence he'd toyed with before in his career, here he wove them together and created a pallet rich with colour, style and life. The title track a snapshot of modern life and its slow erosion. 'Starfish And Coffee', a precise and neat piece of storytelling. 'U Got The Look', all swagger and poise, Prince verbally jousting with Sheena Easton. Magnificent, and one album he's yet to come close to since.

Play In The Sunshine; Housequake; Ballad Of Dorothy Parker; It; Starfish And Coffee; Slow Love; Hot Thing; Forever In My Life; U Got The Look; If I Was Your Girlfriend; Strange Relationship; I Could Never Take The Place Of Your Man; The Cross; It's Gonna Be A Beautiful Night; Adore.

First released 1987
UK peak chart position: 4
USA peak chart position: 6

51. ONCE UPON A TIME
Simple Minds

Simple Minds gained belated US chart success with '(Don't You) Forget About Me' and a distinctly transatlantic burr covered this, the ensuing album. Producers Jimmy Iovine and Bob Clearmountain sculpted an unambiguous sound where crowd-pleasing anthems invoked a genuine excitement. Loud, forthright and shorn of subtlety, *Once Upon A Time* shows the group's core trio - Jim Kerr (vocals), Charlie Burchill (guitar) and Mick McNeil (keyboards) - working together with genuine empathy, while a revamped rhythm section underpins the material with sinewy precision. They combine to create what many consider is Simple Minds' most exciting and exhilarating release.

Once Upon A Time; All The Things She Said; Ghostdancing; Alive And Kicking; Oh Jungleland; I Wish You Were Here; Sanctify Yourself; Come A Long Way.

First released 1985
UK peak chart position: 1
USA peak chart position: 10

52. BLUE
Joni Mitchell

Joni Mitchell's fourth album maintained the confessional style of its predecessors, but her biographical epistles were here infused with greater maturity. Although her lyrics remained personal, Mitchell drew upon their described scenarios to express a greater context. Stephen Stills and James Taylor added sympathetic accompaniment, but the album's musical textures were defined by the singer's use of guitar, piano or dulcimer. Mitchell's showed a new depth and range than on earlier work, emphasising *Blue*'s important place in her maturation as an artist.

All I Want; My Old Man; Little Green; Carey; Blue; California; This Flight Tonight; River; A Case Of You; The Last Time I Saw Richard.

First released 1971
UK peak chart position: 3
USA peak chart position: 15

53. BAT OUT OF HELL
Meat Loaf

Pomp and circumstance of the grandest order for the multi-platinum Meat Loaf and his songwriting mentor, Jim Steinman. The grandiose intro to the title track was indication enough of the tone of album. Songs stretching out over what at times seemed like musical infinity. While Steinman set his songs in evocative wastelands populated by full orchestras and small town weirdos. 'Paradise By The Dashboard Light' a entire two handed play in itself. 'Two Out Of Three Ain't Bad', an overblown symphony of regret and unrequited love. Between them, they pretty much gave the balance of the album. A huge success only to be repeated by its follow up last year.

You Took The Words Right Out Of My Mouth; Heaven Can Wait; All Revved Up With No Place To Go; Two Out Of Three Ain't Bad; Bat Out Of Hell; For Cryin' Out Loud; Paradise By The Dashboard Light; Praying For The End Of Time; Man And Woman; Dead Ringer For Love.

First released 1977
UK peak chart position: 9
USA peak chart position: 14

54. OFF THE WALL
Michael Jackson

The album that moved Jackson out of juvenile pop, even though the suit he wears on the cover belies his still tender years untouched by facial butchery. Is it really 15 years ago that along with the Clash, Jackson was deemed OK. The Quincy Jones production was immaculate and totally sympathetic to the 90s sound. Virtually the whole album holds up with a thumbs down for 'Burn This Disco Down', but remember this does contain the perfection of 'Rock With You', the angst of 'She's Out Of My Life', McCartney's 'Girlfriend' and the abandon of 'Get On The Floor/Off The Wall'. Absolutely harmlessly brilliant.

Don't Stop 'Til You Get Enough; Rock With You; Working Day And Night; Get On The Floor; Off The Wall; Girlfriend; She's Out Of My Life; I Can't Help It; It's The Falling In Love; Burn This Disco Down.

First released 1979
UK peak chart position: 5
USA peak chart position: 3

55. GRACELAND
Paul Simon

Through the mist of subsequent pale imitations, it is difficult now to recall the enormous impact of this trans-cultural album. The mold-breaking blend of rock and African rhythms is exemplified by 'Homeless', an exquisitely melancholic evocation of African beauty and desolation. The stirring harmonies of Ladysmith Black Mambazo illuminate 'Homeless' and 'Diamonds On The Soles Of Her Shoes'. The element of humour in the latter is echoed in 'You Can Call Me Al', a hit single. The lyrics are finely-crafted and the result is a structure of impeccable proportions. There are angels in the architecture.

The Boy In The Bubble; Graceland; I Know What I Know; Gumboots; Diamonds On the Soles Of Her Shoes; You Can Call Me Al; Under African Skies; Homeless; Crazy Love Volume Two; All Around The World Or The Myth Of Fingerprints.

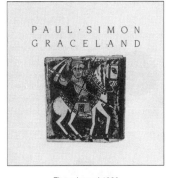

First released 1986
UK peak chart position: 1
USA peak chart position: 3

56. TRANSFORMER
Lou Reed

Having quit the Velvet Underground, a disillusioned Lou Reed came to Britain to rethink his musical career. A low-key solo debut was followed by this highly successful release, which combined the artist's narrative compositions with the lure of contemporaneous fashions, glam-rock and androngony. Long-time fan David Bowie co-produced the set which emphasised the commercial nature of Reed's work without sacrificing his individuality or authenticity. Members of Andy Warhol's entourage were described graphically in 'Walk On The Wild Side' which broke taboos on lyrical content when issued as a single. Its Top 10 place ensured Reed's long-awaited commercial approbation.

Vicious; Andy's Chest; Perfect Day; Hangin' Around; Walk On The Wild Side; Make Up; Satellite Of Love; Wagon Wheel; New York Telephone Conversation; I'm So Free; Goodnight Ladies.

First released 1972
UK peak chart position: 13
USA peak chart position: 29

57. ROXY MUSIC
Roxy Music

Totally original and a breath of bizarre air when released in 1972 and it put Brian Ferry and Eno at the forefront of the art-rock movement. The sheer style of the band gave rock music a powerful injection after years of meandering British prog and American west coast lethargy, brilliantly. From the opening bars of 'Re-Make/Re-Model'; the bitter end of 'Bitters End' the album enthrals and hold the listener. You can almost believe that Ferry is sincere when he states 'I would climb mountains, walk a thousand miles and put roses around our door' almost, but not quite.

Bitters End; The Bob; Chance Meeting; If There Is Something; Ladytron; Re-Make/Re-Model; 2HB; Would You Believe?; Sea Breezes.

First released 1972
UK peak chart position: 10
USA peak chart position: did not chart

58. BRIDGE OVER TROUBLED WATER
Simon And Garfunkel

The measured beauty of its opening title track set the tone for this album's quiet authority. International acclaim immediately ensued and the duo's passage from folk act to popular singers was confirmed through a series of stellar, Simon-penned compositions. Alternately reflective, then bubbling, the collection revealed a growing maturity and, in 'El Condor Pasa', the first flowering of his infatuation with world music styles. Art Garfunkel's angelic tenor was never so perfect; when combined with Simon's lower register it created a seamless resonance, redolent of the Everly Brothers. It is no surprise this album ends with a rendition of the latter's 'Bye Bye Love'.

Bridge Over Troubled Water; El Condor Pasa; Cecilia; Keep The Customer Satisfied; So Long, Frank Lloyd Wright; The Boxer; Baby Driver; The Only Living Boy In New York; Why Don't You Write Me; Bye Bye Love; Song For The Asking.

First released 1970
UK peak chart position: 1
USA peak chart position: 1

59. BLOOD ON THE TRACKS
Bob Dylan

No word other than 'masterpiece' can describe this album. Where Dylan had once obscured personal feelings in simile and metaphor, here he articulates disintegrating relationships with a painful, almost harrowing, honesty. There are fleeting moments of optimism, but overall the atmosphere is of loss and the quest to come to terms with it. Lyrically, Dylan takes the specific to declare the universal, no more so than on 'If You See Her, Say Hello', one of the saddest love songs in rock's entire canon. The set, however, is far from maudlin. Its regrets, while intense, are passing and a sense of survival in spite of trauma permeates each selection. Few albums, even in Dylan's catalogue, come close to matching it.

Tangled Up In Blue; Simple Twist Of Fate; You're A Big Girl Now; Idiot Wind; You're Gonna Make Me Lonesome When You Go; Meet Me In The Morning; Lily, Rosemary And The Jack Of Hearts; If You See Her, Say Hello; Shelter From The Storm; Buckets Of Rain.

First released 1975
UK peak chart position: 4
USA peak chart position: 1

60. WITH THE BEATLES
Beatles

Released as its creators evolved from pop group to phenomenon, *With The Beatles* both affirmed promise and proclaimed genius. A slew of memorable Lennon/McCartney compositions embraced pop at its most multi-facetet; robust, melancholic, excited or wistful. Their grasp of melody and harmony startled, yet for every unusual chord sequence employed, the Beatles' vigour and sense of purpose remained true. Influences and mentors were acknowledged by a handful of cover versions, but the strength of the album lies in the group's own creations. *With The Beatles* freed artists to record their own material, and the course of pop was irrevocable changed.

It Won't Be Long; All I've Got To Do; All My Loving; Don't Bother Me; Little Child; Till There Was You; Please Mister Postman; Roll Over Beethoven; Hold Me Tight; You Really Got A Hold On Me; I Wanna Be Your MAn; Devil In Her Heart; Not A Second Time; Money.

First released 1964
UK peak chart position: 1
USA peak chart position: 1

61. ELTON JOHN
Elton John

Still learning his craft as a songwriter this is the album that really made us take notice. Although recording techniques now make this (even on CD) sound dated, the quality of the songs and the mood they convey still have the ability to move us all. 'Your Song' will perennially be in the top 100 singles of all time. 'Border Song' and 'No Shoestrings On Louise' will always show that Bernie Taupin should have been born in the mid-west and romantics will still see the logic of 'I Need You To Turn To'. A little gem that needs to be remembered.

Your Song; I Need You To Turn To; Take Me To The Pilot; No Shoestrings On Louise; First Episode At Heinton; 60 Years On; Border Song; Greatest Discovery; The Cage; The King Must Die.

First released 1970
UK peak chart position: 11
USA peak chart position: 4

62. LIKE A VIRGIN
Madonna

The title track, which combined with her overt sexuality, caused waves of controversy at the time. But with time has now become part of movie folklore with director Quentin Tarantino letting his brutish cast mull over the meaning of its lyrics for the opening sequence of the film *Reservoir Dogs*. It's somehow gratifying that the Madonna album that unleashed her on the world should now become a cultural icon and reference point for the 80s. A telling blend of lush pop songs and street suss; the snappy come on of, 'Into The Groove', the Monroe pastiche for, 'Material Girl'. The dancing went on all through the night.

Material Girl; Shoo-bee-doo; Pretender; Stay; Angel; Like A Virgin; Over And Over; Love Don't Live Here Anymore; Into The Groove; Dress You Up.

First released 1984
UK peak chart position: 6
USA peak chart position: 1

63. WAR
U2

U2's strident march into rock 'n' roll legend took its first true steps with this record. *Boy* and *October* had given them an audience of hardcore devotees, but *War* was to give them the full and rapt ear of the world. Their case was made with a record of contrasting moments, it's interesting to note that the lyrics printed on the gatefold sleeve are done so selectively. Though, when this record breaks the silence, it roars. U2's now familiar outcry making itself apparent through dogmatic, but insatiable appeal. While, 'Drowning Man' hinted at the texture and depth of work they'd someday reach.

Sunday Bloody Sunday; Seconds; Like A Song; New Years Day; Two Hearts Beat As One; The Refugee; Drowning Man; Red Light; '40'; Surrender.

First released 1983
UK peak chart position: 1
USA peak chart position: 12

64. AFTER THE GOLDRUSH
Neil Young

Young's first solo release since joining Crosby, Stills And Nash, *After The Goldrush* confirmed the singer's talent in the full glare of the public eye. His most eclectic set to date encompassed the delicate wistfulness of 'I Believe In You' and 'Only Love Can Break Your Heart', as well as the vitriol of 'Southern Man', a raging tour de force which captured the special tension generated between Young and backing group Crazy Horse. Stephen Stills and Nils Lofgren also provided support on an album consolidating a talent while extending its range. The transformation of Don Gibson's 'Oh Lonesome Me' from canter to ballad confirmed an original musical vision, but the album's continued strength is due to Young's own remarkable compositions.

Tell Me Why; After The Goldrush; Only Love Can Break Your Heart; Southern Man; Till The Morning Comes; Oh Lonesome Me; Don't Let It Bring You Down; Birds; When You Dance I Can Really Love; I Believe In You; Cripple Creek Ferry.

First released 1970
UK peak chart position: 7
USA peak chart position: 8

65. COME FLY WITH ME
Frank Sinatra

A concept album that has lasted, with a choice of songs that takes you around the world in 45 minutes. Some of Sinatra's finest moments are on this album, notably with Sammy Cahn and Jimmy Van Heusen's uplifting 'Come Fly With Me' and 'It's Nice To Go Trav'ling'. This was Sinatra's first album arranged and conducted by Billy May, a relationship that produced further classic orchestrations. Once again the CD purchaser will greatly benefit from three bonus tracks with Nelson Riddle in charge; 'Chicago' South Of The Border' and 'I Love Paris'. Happy go lucky stuff that we all need from time to time.

Come Fly With Me; Around The World; Isle Of Capri; Moonlight In Vermont; Autumn In New York; On The Road To Madalay; Let's get Away From It All; April In Paris; London By Night; Brazil; Blue Hawaii; It's Nice To Go Trav'ling.

First released 1958
UK peak chart position: 2
USA peak chart position: 1

66. PARALLEL LINES
Blondie

Madonna and Michael Jackson aside, this is supreme pop music and as good as the genre can ever get. Everybody loved Blondie; fans, children, critics, other musicians and senior citizens - and not just because the pouting little Debbie Harry was its frontperson. This is an unintentional greatest hits record that never lets up until the last note of 'Just Go Away' has died. If one wanted to carp you could have asked for 'Denis' and 'Call Me' to have been included, but that would be just plain greedy. One of the greatest 'up' records of all time.

Fade Away; Hanging On The Telephone; One Way Or Another; Picture This; Pretty Baby; I Know But I Don't Know; 11.59; Will Anything Happen; Sunday Girl; Heart Of Glass; I'm Gonna Love You Too; Just Go Away.

First released 1978
UK peak chart position: 1
USA peak chart position: 6

67. PRETZEL LOGIC
Steely Dan

Donald Fagen and Walter Becker were session musicians and staff songwriters prior to founding Steely Dan in 1972. Their highly inventive music relied on a synthesis of styles, heard to perfection on this, their third album. Jazz, baion-based R&B and sumptuous west coast pop were fused together to create a sound greater than the sum of its parts and one that was uniquely 'Steely Dan'. Crafted session musicians brought a technical excellence to the set, but the strength of the duo's vision ensured that sterility did not supplant inspiration. Gorgeous melodies interweave with expertise to create a sumptuous tapestry satisfying head and heart.

Rikki Don't Lose That Number; Night By Night; Any Major Dude Will Tell You; Barrytown; East St. Louis Toodle-oo; Parker's Band; Thru With Buzz; Pretzel Logic; With A Gun; Charlie Freak; Monkey In Your Soul.

First released 1974
UK peak chart position: 37
USA peak chart position: 8

68. L.A. WOMAN
Doors

The final Doors album to feature vocalist Jim Morrison reaffirmed the quartet's grasp of blues/rock. Beset by personal and professional problems, they retreated to a rehearsal room, cast such pressures aside and recorded several of their most memorable compositions. The musicianship is uniformly excellent, the interplay between guitarist Robbie Krieger and keyboard player Ray Manzarek exudes confidence and empathy, while the strength and nuances of Morrison's voice adds an unmistakable resonance. His death within weeks of the album's completion inevitably casts a pall over its content, but the artistry contained within is undeniable.

Changeling; Love Her Madly; Been Down So Long; Cars Hiss By My Window; LA Woman; L'America; Hyacinth House; Crawling King Snake; The WASP (Texas Radio And The Big Beat); Riders On The Storm.

First released 1971
UK peak chart position: 28
USA peak chart position: 9

69. HELP
Beatles

Signs that the loveable moptops were human after all began to show on this, their fifth album. Lennon was hiding his love away and crying out, but nobody was listening; 'help I need somebody, help, not just anybody'. Harrison was in love as heard on 'I Need You' and 'You Like Me Too Much' and McCartney in addition to 'The Night Before' dashed off two minutes of perfection with 'Yesterday'. This album often gets overlooked in the Beatles pantheon but it contains some of their finest songs in addition to a definitive Lennon vocal as he tears into 'Dizzy Miss Lizzy'.

Help; The Night Before; You've Got To Hide Your Love Away; I Need You; Another Girl; You're Going To Lose That Girl; Ticket To Ride; Act Naturally; It's Only Love; You Like Me Too Much; Tell Me What You See; I've Just Seen A Face; Yesterday; Dizzy Miss Lizzy.

First released 1965
UK peak chart position: 1
USA peak chart position: 1

70. SYNCHRONICITY
Police

Fancy knowing you were going to break-up and yet be able to record and produce this masterpiece. The world domination of the Police was calculated and planned as was their departure. Each of the albums in between have something special but the power of tracks such as 'Synchronicity II' the haunting quality of 'Every Breath You Take' (you really believe Sting when he says 'I'll be watching you') give this record the edge. The only tracks less than brilliant are Andy and Stewart's offerings, something they must all have been aware of. They got out while they were winning.

Synchronicity; Walking In Your Footsteps; O My God; Mother; Miss Gradenko; Synchronicity II; Every Breath You Take; King Of Pain; Wrapped Around Your Finger; Tea In The Sahara.

First released 1983
UK peak chart position: 1
USA peak chart position: 1

71. EXILE ON MAIN STREET
Rolling Stones

The Rolling Stones entered the 70s as 'the world's greatest rock 'n' roll band', an epithet this album confirmed. Where its predecessor, *Sticky Fingers*, boasted a clear production, this rampaging double set offered a thick, muddy mix which adds an air of mystery to the proceedings. Up-tempo material, laden with riffs ('All Down The Line', 'Happy', 'Soul Survivor') contrast loose, unhinged performances drawn form the rich textures of delta blues. Hedonism and bacchanalia ooze from every pore, emphasising an air of degeneracy encapsulating the Rolling Stones' appeal. This expansive album is now rightly regarded as the pinnacle of their career.

Rocks Off; Rip This Joint; Shake Your Hips; Casino Boogie; Tumbling Dice; Happy; Turd On The Run; Ventilator Blues; I Just Want To See His Face; Let It Loose; Sweet Virginia; Torn And Frayed; Sweet Black Angel; Loving Cup; All Down The Line; Stop Breaking Down; Shine A Light; Soul Survivor.

First released 1972
UK peak chart position: 1
USA peak chart position: 1

72. HARVEST
Neil Young

Only after the release of *Harvest Moon* in 1993 did the Young aficionados reluctantly admit that this was a superlative album in deference to *Tonight's The Night* and *On The Beach*. Young knew he had a winner when he recorded it and revisited it 20 years later. Using the Stray Gators as his foils and even recording two tracks in Barking Town Hall, Essex, Young sounds wonderfully old before his time. Introspective and pleading he has to remind us in 'Old Man' that he is 'twenty four and there's so much more'. Another 24 glorious albums to be precise.

Out On The Weekend; Harvest; Man Needs A Maid; Heart Of Gold; Are You Ready For The Country?; Old Man; There's A Word; Alabama; Needle And The Damage Done; Words Between The Lines Of Age.

First released 1972
UK peak chart position: 1
USA peak chart position: 1

73. BE YOURSELF TONIGHT
Eurythmics

This album replays like a greatest hits package, such is the content of full blown memorable pop songs. The list is almost endless as this album is a chilling reminder of how good pop can get and how well Lennox and Stewart worked together. Even without the legendary Aretha Franklin on 'Sisters Are Doing It For Themselves' there is the pace and guts of 'I Love You Like A Ball And Chain' or the numerous confessional 'I'll be's' of 'It's Alright (Baby's Coming Back)'. This album stands up to repeated plays and will continue to improve with age. What perfection.

It's Alright (Baby's Coming Back); Would I Lie To You; There Must Be An Angel (Playing With My Heart); I Love You Like A Ball And Chain; Sisters Are Doing It For Themselves; Conditioned Soul; Adrian; Here Comes That Sinking Feeling; Better To Have Lost In Love Than Never To Have Loved At All.

First released 1985
UK peak chart position: 3
USA peak chart position: 9

74. ABRAXIS
Santana

Even though Santana now rarely roll off our tongues, their initial trio of albums still sound incredibly alive and exciting. *Abraxis* is the best of the three as it combines the Latin fusion of their debut with smooth edges. The relaxed opening elegantly slips into 'Black Magic Woman' the finest interpretation of a Peter Green song. 'Se A Cabo', 'El Nicoya' and the memorable 'Oye Como Va' give us our quota of Latin rock. The album's star turn is the beautifully erotic 'Samba Pa Ti', which features a superb guitar solo that oozes the sexuality that the Mati cover illustration blatantly depicts.

Singing Winds; Crying Beasts; Black Magic Woman; Gypsy Queen; Oye Como Va; Incident At Neshabur; Se A Cabo; Mother's Daughter; Samba Pa Ti; Hope You're Feeling Better; El Nicoya.

First released 1970
UK peak chart position: 7
USA peak chart position: 1

75. A SWINGIN' AFFAIR
Frank Sinatra

A further sequence of immaculate songs, chosen with uncanny knowledge that they could be adapted for 'swingability' (my word). Four songs by Cole Porter, including 'Night And Day' and 'You'd Be So Nice To Come Home To' and further gems from Richard Rodgers and Lorenz Hart ('I Wish I Was In Love Again'), the Gershwin brothers and Duke Ellington's glorious 'I Got It Bad And That Ain't Good'. Those who will buy this in the age of the CD will find the bonus of 'The Lady Is A Tramp'. All 15 tracks once again beautifully Nelson Riddled, giving space for the strings, trumpets and bassoons. For swingin' romantics only.

Night And Day; I Wish I Was In Love Again; I Got Plenty O' Nuttin'; I Guess I'll Have To Change My Plan; Nice Work If You Can Get it; Stars Fell On Alabama; No One Ever Tells You; I Won't Dance; Lonesome Road; At Long Last Love; You'd Be So Nice To Come Home To; I Got It Bad And That Ain't Good; from This Moment On; If I Had You; Oh Look At Me Now.

First released 1957
UK peak chart position: did not chart
USA peak chart position: 2

76. MORRISON HOTEL
Doors

Feted first as underground heroes, then reviled as teenybop stars, the Doors threw off such conundrums with this magnificent release. *Morrison Hotel* reaffirmed their blues' roots, opening with the powerful 'Roadhouse Blues' before unfolding through a succession of songs showcasing all the group's considerable strengths. Distinctively tight instrumental playing underscores memorable material, while Jim Morrison's authoritative vocal ranges from the demonstrative ('Maggie McGill') to the melancholic ('The Spy'). Despite contemporary problems, the Doors emerged with an album the equal of their first two stunning releases.

Roadhouse Blues; Waiting For The Sun; You Make Me Real; Peace Frog; Blue Sunday; Ship Of Fools; Land Ho; The Spy; Queen Of The Highway; Indian Summer; Maggie McGill.

First released 1970
UK peak chart position: 12
USA peak chart position: 4

77. TEN
Pearl Jam

Formed from the ashes of Seattle's Band-Most-Likely-To, Mother Love Bone who fell quietly to pieces after the untimely OD of vocalist Andrew Wood. Stone Gossard and Jeff Ament unearthing vocalist Eddie Vedder and rescuing him from a job as an all night petrol pump attendant. The result was a most curious multi-platinum album, that, like its predecessors attempts, drew on 70s rock as a major influence. While Vedder's lyrical insights were as beguiling as they were obtuse. Though, they captured a disenchanted nation's imagination and success came running.

Once; Even Flow; Alive; Why Go; Black; Jeremy; Oceans; Porch; Garden; Deep; Release; Master; Slave.

First released 1992
UK peak chart position: 18
USA peak chart position: 2

78. RUST NEVER SLEEPS
Neil Young

Neil Young's lengthy recording career contains several landmark albums of which *Rust Never Sleeps* is one of the most vital. Half-acoustic, half-electric, it is bookended by contrasting versions of the same song which pays homage to Sex Pistols' vocalist, Johnny Rotten. Longtime associates Crazy Horse support Young on the electric selections which exude white-noise power, marrying savage guitar work with emphatic lyrics. The remaining selections offer a pastoral atmosphere. Part country, part folk, their gentle qualities invoke the atmosphere of Young's best-seller, Harvest, completing a set which provides a scintillating précis of the artist's canon.

My My, Hey Hey (Out Of The Blue); Thrasher; Ride My Llama; Pocohontas; Sail Away; Powder Finger; Welfare Mothers; Sedan Delivery; Hey Hey, My My (Into The Black).

First released 1979
UK peak chart position: 13
USA peak chart position: 8

79. WISH YOU WERE HERE
Pink Floyd

Pink Floyd reaped considerable commercial acclaim with *Dark Side Of The Moon*, but it was on *Wish You Were Here* that the quartet reached an artistic maturity. The album revolves around 'Shine On You Crazy Diamond', a lengthy suite devoted to founder member Syd Barrett, whose fragile ego snapped at the earliest whiff of success. This in mind the group address music business exploitation in 'Welcome To The Machine', particularly pithy given their new-found status. A quiet determination marks this set. Roger Waters contributes some of his most openly heartfelt lyrics, while guitarist Dave Gilmour proved both economical and incisive. Free of the self-indulgence marking later work, Pink Floyd emerge as thoughtful technocrats, amalgamating and contextualising new possibilities, rather than being swamped by them.

Shine On You Crazy Diamond (Parts 1-9); Welcome To The Machine; Have A Cigar; Wish You Were Here.

First released 1975
UK peak chart position: 1
USA peak chart position: 1

80. MAKING MOVIES
Dire Straits

The last album of their career that sounded as if they were trying to play, instead of going through the motions. David Knopfler had already departed the band and brother Mark had a free rein clear from any sibling rivalry. Every song stands up apart from the dreadful 'Les Boys' hardly one of their show-stoppers. 'Solid Rock', 'Tunnel Of Love', Romeo And Juliet' and 'Skataway' would be on any decent greatest hits package. Following this artistic triumph they went and released *Love Over Gold*, and we all know what album followed that, don't we. Ho hum.

Tunnel Of Love; Romeo And Juliet; Skataway; Expresso Love; Hand In Hand; Solid Rock; Les Boys.

First released 1980
UK peak chart position: 4
USA peak chart position: 19

81. AJA
Steely Dan

This is pinnacle of Steely Dan's gradual transition from rock band to their own brand of jazz-influenced white soul. Guitars were replaced by keyboards, and saxophones became more common. Walter Becker and Donald Fagen were only interested in spending time in the recording studios, while the fans pined and waited. The result set new standards in recorded excellence, and is regularly used as a hi-fi shop demonstration. The music cannot be faulted, the ambitious title track, the two overtly accessible tracks 'Josie' and 'Peg' and the song we have to blame for Deacon Blue.

Black Cow; Aja; Deacon Blue; Peg; Home At Last; I Got The News; Josie.

First released 1977
UK peak chart position: 5
USA peak chart position: 3

82. SURREALISTIC PILLOW
Jefferson Airplane

One of a handful of albums epitomising the 'Summer of Love', *Surrealistic Pillow*'s strengths lie in a gorgeous cross-section of folk, blues and acid-rock. Vocalists Grace Slick and Marty Balin interwove over a seamless instrumental section in which Jack Cassady (bass) and Jorma Kaukonen (guitar) enjoyed an almost telepathic understanding. The scope of the material is breathtaking, be it science fiction, Lewis Carrol or a succession of haunting, fragile love songs. Restrained when required, animated at others, but always challenging the album succeeds through a collective determination.

She Has Funny Cars; Somebody To Love; My Best Friend; Today; Comin' Back To Me; 3/5 Mile In 10 Seconds; D.C.B.A-25; How Do You Feel; White Rabbit; Plastic Fantastic Lover; Embryonic Journey.

First released 1967
UK peak chart position: did not chart
USA peak chart position: 3

83. LOVE IS THE THING
Nat 'King' Cole

Released in the days when albums were not promoted by extracting individual tracks and issuing them as singles, this was the first opportunity that young record-buyers had of hearing Nat Cole sing 'When I Fall In Love' and 'Stardust', songs which would forever be identified with him. Composer Hoagy Carmichael, who wrote 'Stardust' with Mitchell Parish, always maintained that this version, complete with the lovely verse, was his personal favourite. Of all the singer's varied albums - jazz, 'soft' country, easy listening - *Love Is The Thing*, which spent 55 weeks in the US Top 40, was the only one that went to number 1 where it stayed for eight weeks.

When I Fall In Love; The End Of A Love Affair; Stardust; Stay As Sweet As You Are; Where Can I Go Without You; Maybe It's Because I Love You Too Much; Love Letters; Ain't Misbehavin'; I Thought About Marie; At Last; It's All In The Game; When Sunny Gets Blue; Love Is The Thing.

First released 1957
UK peak chart position: did not chart
USA peak chart position: 1

84. NOTORIOUS BYRD BROTHERS
Byrds

Building on the maturity of their previous effort *Younger Than Yesterday*, the Byrds delivered a suite of songs that naturally flow into one another with uncanny ease. It is one of the few vinyl releases that both sides would always get played, and 26 years later it begs to be played uninterrupted as individually the songs lose their power. This was an artistic triumph and a commercial disappointment as the memory of Crosby faded only to be allegedly replaced by a horse on the album sleeve. The Byrds moved on to their country phase and numerous line-ups but they were never to sound so perfect again.

Artificial Energy; Goin' Back; Natural Harmony; Draft Morning; Wasn't Born To Follow; Get To You; Change Is Now; Old John Robertson; Tribal Gathering; Dolphins Smile; Space Odyssey.

First released 1968
UK peak chart position: 12
USA peak chart position: 47

85. REMAIN IN LIGHT
Talking Heads

Led by the animated David Byrne and held together musically by a mathematically precise rhythm section of Tina Weymouth (bass) and Chris Frantz (drums), Talking Heads articulated America's post-60s' cultural malaise. *Remain In Light*, their fourth album, consolidated a relationship with composer/producer Brian Eno, incorporating horns and guest performers to their intellectually-based muse. Compositions and styles are deconstructed, then reassembled afresh, no more so than on the exquisite 'Once In A Lifetime', which suggests a pan-international sound without expressing it aurally. Post-modern alienation was never so danceable.

The Great Curve; Cross-eyed And Painless; Born Under Punches (Heat Goes On); Houses In Motion; Once In A Lifetime; Listening Wind; Seen And Not Seen; Overload.

First released 1980
UK peak chart position: 21
USA peak chart position: 19

86. THE PRETENDERS
Pretenders

Former rock critic Chrissie Hynde launched the Pretenders with an engaging, yet passive, version of the Kinks' 'Stop Your Sobbing'. She unveiled her own persona fully on *The Pretenders*, which contains a series of excellent compositions marked by her sensual vocals and brilliant sense of dynamics. An understanding of pop's structures allow Hynde to exploit them to her own ends while sympathetic support, particularly that of guitarist James Honeyman-Scott, uses the excitement of rock without reference to its cliches. Tough and opinionated, Chrissie Hynde's first declaration of independence established the formula she continued to follow.

Precious; The Phone Call; Up The Neck; Tattooed Love Boys; Space Invader; The Wait; Stop Your Sobbing; Kid; Private Life; Brass In Pocket; Lovers Of Today; Mystery Achievement.

First released 1980
UK peak chart position: 1
USA peak chart position: 9

87. LAYLA AND OTHER ASSORTED LOVE SONGS
Derek And The Dominos

Studying the photographs inside of the fold-out sleeve makes you question how such a wrecked bunch of musos could make such a great record. Excess was obviously the order of the day, yet excel was what they did. Everybody knows that 'Layla' is one of the best rock songs ever written, here is the chance to strike a blow for Duane Allman's consistent guitar, especially on lost gems such as 'Anyday' and 'Key To The Highway'. Did anybody also notice how good Jim Gordon's drumming was? And the CD age means we can skip 'Thorn Tree In The Garden'.

I Looked Away; Bell Bottom Blues; Keep On Growing; Nobody Knows You; I Am Yours; Anyday; Key To The Highway; Tell The Truth; Why Does Love Got To Be So Sad; Have You Ever Loved A Woman; Little Sing; It's Too Late; Thorn Tree In The Garden; Layla.

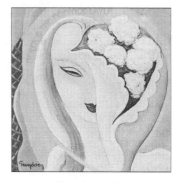

First released 1970
UK peak chart position: did not chart
USA peak chart position: 16

88. THE RIVER
Bruce Springsteen

Only Springsteen could have got away with releasing a double album with 19 tracks of basically the same song. Such was his standing that he did, and it worked like a dream. Almost all the tracks hit you in the stomach with burning saxophone from Clarence Clemons and piercing wurlitzer organ. Bruce meanwhile sings of cars and girls and girls and cars but at no stage does he forget that this is rock 'n' roll. With this release Springsteen completed a rite of passage. Described as 'the new Dylan' early in his career, the singer proved this tag a fallacy, drawing on Dansette pop - Phil Spector, Gary US Bonds, Mitch Ryder - rather than the folk tradition. The singer articulated the dilemmas of America's blue-collar workforce, encapsulating a generation trapped in a post-60s' malaise. He does so with sumptuous melodies which draw in, rather than confront, the listener and show not just Springsteen a magnetic showman, but a pensive, literate songwriter.

The Ties That Bind; Sherry Darling; Jackson Cage; Two Hearts; Independence Day; Hungry Heart; Out In The Street; Crush On You; You Can Look (But You'd Better Not Touch); I Wanna Marry You; The River; Point Blank; Cadillac Ranch; I'm A Rocker; Fade Away; Stolen Car; Ramrod; The Price You Pay; Wreck On The Highway.

First released 1980
UK peak chart position: 2
USA peak chart position: 1

89. WHO'S NEXT
Who

Following *Tommy* would always provide Pete Townshend with an artistic dilemma, and two years would pass before the Who unleashed their next studio album. The wait proved worthwhile and taking the best from the aborted Lifehouse project, Townshend added a handful of urgent new songs to create one of his group's finest releases. Synthesiser obligattos and acoustic guitars provide occasional counterpoints to the quartet's accustomed power, a contrast emphasising their sense of dynamics. 'Won't Get Fooled Again', 'Behind Blue Eyes' and 'Baba O'Reilly' were each destined to become integral parts of the Who's 70s' lexicon, as vital as 'My Generation' had proved from the previous decade. *Who's Next* set a hard rock standard even its creators struggled to emulate.

Baba O'Riley; Getting In Tune; Love Ain't For Keeping; My Wife; Song Is Over; Bargain; Going Mobile; Behind Blue Eyes; Won't Get Fooled Again.

First released 1971
UK peak chart position: 1
USA peak chart position: 4

90. WORLD MACHINE
Level 42

Although it looks like Level 42 will never make another great album at least we have one which seems destined to endure. Mark King had already proved he could slap his bass almost better than anybody, now it was his turn to demonstrate his prowess as a classy songwriter. He succeeded in buoyant fashion with every track, very funky, very poppy and at times upliftingly wonderful, especially 'Something About You' and 'Coup D'etat'. The winner for emotion however is the heartfelt 'Leaving Me Now'. Perfection made for the age of the CD.

World Machine; A Physical Presence; Something About You; Leaving Me Now; I Sleep On My Heart; It's Not The Same For Us; Good Man In A Storm; Coup D'etat; Lying Still; Dream Crazy; Something About You.

First released 1985
UK peak chart position: 3
USA peak chart position: 18

91. FLY LIKE AN EAGLE
Steve Miller Band

Miller forsook his love for the blues for this and its sister project *Book Of Dreams*. In turning to mainstream pop/rock he became a huge star and developed the knack of delivering quality three-minute songs that were perfect for FM Radio. The album is linked by Miller's fascination with electronic sounds, sandwiched between the irresistible title track, the Bonnie and Clyde tale of 'Take The Money And Run', the irritatingly simple 'Rock 'n' Me' and the subdued 'The Window' with its quirky lyric 'ask my baby what she want's to be, she says a monkey in a tree'. After all it was Miller who rhymed 'northern California' with 'girls are warm yeah'.

Blue Odyssey; Dance, Dance, Dance; Fly Like An Eagle; Mercury Blues; Rock 'n' Me; Serenade; 2001; Sweet Marie; Take The Money And Run; Sild Mountain Honey; The Window; You Send Me.

First released 1976
UK peak chart position: 11
USA peak chart position: 3

92. COURT AND SPARK
Joni Mitchell

Court And Spark continued Joni Mitchell's transition from folk singer to sophisticated rock auteur. Crafted songs are bathed in a warm, textured backing, courtesy of Tom Scott's L.A. Express, a sinuous jazz-based combo. Her expressive voice weaves in and around engaging melodies which support and enhance the imagery suggested by evocative, personal lyrics. The title track alone is worth the price of admission, but the gorgeous lilt of 'Help Me' or elegant sweep of 'Free Man In Paris' shows an artist in firm control of her craft. A measured, thoughtful album, *Court And Spark* confirmed Mitchell as one of rock's most important and subtle talents.

Court And Spark; Help Me; Free Man In Paris; People's Parties; The Same Situation; Car On A Hill; Down To You; Just Like This Train; Raised On Robbery; Trouble Child; Twisted.

First released 1974
UK peak chart position: 14
USA peak chart position: 2

93. TRAFFIC
Traffic

On their second album the cottage dwellers from Berkshire refined their hippie pop into a looser and vastly mature work. Evocative tales of nonsense in the beautiful '40,000 Headmen', joyful malarkey with Mason's 'You Can All Join In' and one of his finest songs 'Feelin Alright' which was a signpost to masons imminent departure. Throughout the record Capaldi's understated yet steady drums demonstrate just what a great rock drummer should do and Chris Wood's sound is everywhere with trills on flute and blasts on saxophone. A record that will always be meant for glorious sunny days.

You Can All Join In; Pearly Queen; Don't Be Sad; Who Knows What Tomorrow May Bring; Feelin Alright; Vagabond Virgin; 40,000 Headmen; Cryin' To Be Heard; No Time To Live; Means To An End.

First released 1968
UK peak chart position: 9
USA peak chart position: 17

94. YOUNGER THAN YESTERDAY
Byrds

With this album the Byrds proclaimed fully their musical oeuvre. Distinctive three-part harmonies and chiming 12-string guitars affirmed the quartet's unique sound as a succession of superior compositions embraced folk, pop or country styles. Beguiling melodies nestled alongside experiment as the principals asserted an individuality while remaining aware of the strength of the whole. The acerbic wit of 'So You Wanna Be A Rock'n'Roll Star', showed a group aware of commercial entrapment. On this set the Byrds rejected such advances and offered a beautiful altruism.

So You Want To Be A Rock'n'Roll Star; Have You Seen Her Face; CTA; Renaissance Fair; Time Between; Everybody's Been Burned; Thoughts And Words; Mind Gardens; My Back Pages; Girl With No Name; Why.

First released 1967
UK peak chart position: 37
USA peak chart position: 24

95. OUTLANDOS D'AMOUR
Police

It is hard to imagine after the sophistication of *Synchronicity* and Sting's excellent solo work together with the new age/prog direction that Andy has taken that the Police debut is a bit punky. This writer saw one of their first gigs supporting hippie darlings Spirit. They were energetic and raw but when they did 'So Lonely', 'Next To You' and 'Roxanne', you realised the potential of something really special. This album is underproduced and raw but it retains a quality that cannot be quantified. This is the real inventors of white reggae-flavoured punk pop. Derivative but innovative.

Next To You; So Lonely; Hole In My Life; Roxanne; Peanuts; Can't Stand Losing You; Truth Hits Everybody; Born In The 50s; Be My Girl - Sally; Masoko Tango.

First released 1979
UK peak chart position: 6
USA peak chart position: 23

96. MOONDANCE
Van Morrison

Where on previous recordings Van Morrison had implied soul and R&B roots, on *Moondance* he set them free. He had rarely sounded so relaxed, whether on the bubbling joy of 'And It Stoned Me', the finger-popping ease of the title track or the celebratory bliss of 'Caravan'. Morrison revelled in the music's tight arrangements, clearly enjoying the punchy horn section ('Glad Tidings') or empathising with quieter, acoustic settings ('Warm Love'). Where *Astral Weeks* was a cathartic stream-of-consciousness, *Moondance* shows an artist enraptured by a new-found musical freedom, which is used herein to telling effect.

And It Stoned Me; Moondance; Crazy Love; Caravan; Into The Mystic; Come Running; These Dreams Of You; Brand New Day; Everyone; Glad Tidings.

First released 1970
UK peak chart position: 32
USA peak chart position: 29

97. DIVA
Annie Lennox

None of us know if Annie Lennox can follow this outstanding solo debut, her whole solo career stands before her. After contributing to the Tourists and being 50% of the Eurythmics she could be forgiven for getting writers block, but no. This record is already a classic work, barely two years old. Annie's emotions pour forth in 'Why?', she reminds us to be wary on 'Walking On Broken Glass' and reaffirms the cliche on; 'Money Can't Buy It'. While all this is going on we are adoring her talent, integrity and fantastic voice. Phew!

Why?; Walking On Broken Glass; Precious; Legend In My Living Room; Cold; Money Can't Buy It; Little Bird; Primitive; Stay By Me; Gift.

First released 1992
UK peak chart position: 1
USA peak chart position: 23

98. NEW GOLD DREAM (81,82, 83, 84)
Simple Minds

Simple Minds began their career indebted to Roxy Music, David Bowie and Magazine, but over successive releases emerged as a distinctive act. On *New Gold Dream* the group's ambitions came to full fruition, the awkward dissonance of early recordings replaced by a warm, textured sound. The content ranged from brash stadium rock to melodic ballad, but a singleness of purpose ensured such contrasts enhanced the set's overall cohesion. The quintet had never sounded so confident or assured and the resultant lush textures launched them into the international arena, fulfilling their undoubted promise.

Someone, Somewhere In Summertime; Colours Fly And Catherine Wheel; Promised You A Miracle; Big Sleep; Somebody Up There Likes You; New Gold Dream; Glittering Prize; Hunter And The Hunted; King Is White And In The Crowd.

First released 1982
UK peak chart position: 3
USA peak chart position: 69

99. DIAMOND LIFE
Sade

Sade snuck up on us when we were least expecting it. 'Your Love Is King' was a pretty mature record for the singles market and one that opened the door to smooth soul-based pop. This album proved that she was no fluke and it became one of the most acclaimed debuts of all time. Sade rode out the publicity and coped with everything, for once the music did the talking, 'Smooth Operator' put her back in the pop charts but it was the overall class and confidence of the whole album that makes it so darn good. Her reading of Timmy Thomas' 'Why Can't We Live Together' is phenomenal.

Smooth Operator; Your Love Is King; Hang On To Your Love; When Am I Gonna Make A Living; Frankie's First Affair; Cherry Pie; Sally; I Will Be Your Friend; Why Can't We Live Together.

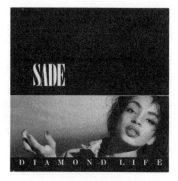

First released 1984
UK peak chart position: 2
USA peak chart position: 5

100. DEJA VU
Crosby, Stills, Nash And Young

With the inspired decision to add Neil Young to the ranks CSNY became one America's biggest attractions. While the results on this excellent record show four individuals, rather than the unity of the debut, it still holds up to repeated listening. Young contributed 'Country Girl', with a wonderful John Sebastian harmonica added, and the aching 'Helpless'. His colleagues pitched in with notable songs from Crosby ('Almost Cut My Hair'), Stills ('Carry On' and '4+20') and Nash who has just about been forgiven for 'Our House' and 'Teach Your Children' with Jerry Garcia's piercing but beautiful pedal steel guitar.

Carry On; Teach Your Children; Almost Cut My Hair; Helpless; Woodstock; Deja Vu; Our House; 4+20; Country Girl; Everybody I Love You.

First released 1970
UK peak chart position: 5
USA peak chart position: 1

101. MOBY GRAPE
Moby Grape

Time and time again this album is cited as the finest debut of all time. But who were Moby Grape? They were a stellar San Francisco rock band who became appalling victims of record company hype followed by their own excesses as they were lulled into believing they were more than they were. Loopy Skip Spence, growling Bob Mosely and talented bluesman Jerry Miller were but three fifths of a great band. Every track could have been pulled as a single, which is exactly what CBS did when they released five on the same day, with disastrous results. An indispensable collection.

Hey Grandma; Mr. Blues; Fall On You; 8.05; Come In The Morning; Omaha; Naked, If I Want To; Someday; Ain't No Use; Sitting By The Window; Changes; Lazy Me; Indifference.

First released 1967
UK peak chart position: did not chart
USA peak chart position: 24

102. BOOKENDS
Simon And Garfunkel

Over the years the overblown acclaim of *Bridge Over Troubled Water* has lessened as the credibility of Bookends has grown. The gap is set to narrow in future years as listeners discover some of Simon's most entertaining lyrics in 'Fakin' It', 'Punky's Dilemma' and 'Save The Life Of My Child' not to forget for God's sake 'Mrs Robinson' and the evocative 'America'. Sadly there is nothing to be done about still having to sit through 'Voices Of Old People', although CD technology makes this less painful. Almost a perfect album, apart from the last mentioned turkey.

Bookends; Save The Life Of My Child; America; Overs; Voices Of Old People; Old Friends; Fakin' It; Punky's Dilemma; Hazy Shade Of Winter; At The Zoo; Mrs. Robinson.

First released 1968
UK peak chart position: 1
USA peak chart position: 1

103. ACHTUNG BABY
U2

From their Trabant period, this is U2 at their most powerful and eloquent. The production (Daniel Lanois, Steve Lillywhite and Brian Eno) is raw and uncompromising. On the opening track 'Zoo Station' the VU meters are driven mercilessly into the red by Larry Mullen's percussive attack. The words are equally potent, creating the lyrical equivalent of an Hieronymous Bosch painting; a tangled steel web of tortured love and urban nightmare. *Achtung Baby* spawned numerous hit singles, including 'Even Better Than The Real Thing', 'One', 'The Fly', 'Mysterious Ways' and 'Who's Gonna Ride Your Wild Horses'.

Zoo Station; Even Better Than The Real Thing; One; Until The End Of The World; Who's Gonna Ride Your Wild Horses; So Cruel; The Fly; Mysterious Ways; Tryin' To Throw Your Arms Around The World; Ultra Violet (Light My Way); Acrobat; Love Is Blindness.

First released 1991
UK peak chart position: 2
USA peak chart position: 1

104. MUSIC FROM BIG PINK
The Band

The Band emerged from months of seclusion with this enthralling debut album. It followed a lengthy spell accompanying Bob Dylan, which culminated in sessions known as The Basement Tapes. Three songs herein were revived from those recordings, and the remainder showed a similar pastoral spirit. Where contemporaries sought expression in progressive music, the Band were largely reflective, creating atmosphere from traditional forms and distilling the results in an economic style. Their ensemble playing and rural voices were best captured on 'The Weight', an elliptical composition which displayed their craft to perfection. Americana of every hue can be gleaned from this collection, the depth of which left a marked impression on audiences and musicians alike.

Tears Of Rage; To Kingdom Come; In A Station; Caledonia Mission; The Weight; We Can Talk; Long Black Veil; Chest Fever; Lonesome Suzie; Wheels On Fire; I Shall Be Released.

First released 1968
UK peak chart position: did not chart
USA peak chart position: 30

105. A NIGHT AT THE OPERA
Queen

The album that gave the world the inimitable, 'Bohemian Rhapsody', and its pioneering video, is still a record that has every aspect of a true and timeless classic to it. Queen's collective and quite sheer inventiveness, collective contribution and the original verve and displays of ingenuity that they brought to this album were immense. The dramatic and quite theatrical strut of, 'Death On Two Legs (Dedicated To...)', the graceful, 'Love Of My Life', the ritz and panache of, 'I'm In Love With My Car'. Without measure or equal, or boundaries. Every home should have one.

Death On Two Legs (Dedicated To...); Lazing On A Sunday Afternoon; You're My Best Friend; I'm In Love With My Car; Sweet Lady; Seaside Rendezvous; Good Company; '39; The Prophet's Song; Love Of My Life; Bohemian Rhapsody; God Save The Queen.

First released 1975
UK peak chart position: 1
USA peak chart position: 4

106. WOODFACE
Crowded House

The third and best album to date from the finest rock band Australia has yet produced. A good second would have been Split Enz, but they split up to become errr . . . Crowded House. The Finn brothers have been writing songs for many years and it is encouraging to see that their lyrics are a sharp, fresh and perceptive as ever. The opener 'Chocolate Cake' starts with 'not everyone in New York would pay to see Andrew Lloyd Webber, may his trousers fall down as he bows to the Queen and the crown'. Nothing lapses, no standards are dropped. No worries.

Chocolate Cake; It's Only Natural; Fall At Your Feet; Tall Trees; Weather With You; Whispers And Moans; Four Seasons In One Day; There Goes God; Fame Is; All I Ask; As Sure As I Am; Italian Plastic; She Goes On; How Will You Go.

First released 1991
UK peak chart position: 6
USA peak chart position: 83

107. CAN'T BUY A THRILL
Steely Dan

Even the debut from Becker and Fagen put them stylistically a cut above the others. Played alongside the Doobie Brothers and the Eagles on FM radio Steely Dan were linked immediately to the west coast music scene, a fact that was utterly wrong. This was and is an east coast album, it is also assured, laid back and layered with jazz and soul influences that made their special kind of rock. Jeff 'Skunk' Baxter added the metal and David Palmer added pop vocal - but, from this sparkling debut we can clearly see Becker and Fagen in immaculate control.

Do It Again; Dirty Work; Kings; Midnite Cruiser; Only A Fool; Reelin' In The Years; Fire In The Hole; Brooklyn (Owes The Charmer And Me); Change Of The Guard; Turn That Heartbeat Over Again.

First released 1972
UK peak chart position: 38
USA peak chart position: 17

108. JOHN WESLEY HARDING
Bob Dylan

Bob Dylan's eighth album followed a lengthy hibernation in which the singer re-evaluated his art. He emerged with a set of stark simplicity and heartfelt intensity. Neither folk, nor rock, nor country, the selection boasts elements of all three, slipping into consciousness with a mesmerising power belying its setting. A biblical purity encompasses the collection as Dylan paints graphic portraits of the disenfranchised - hobo, immigrant, drifter, messenger - articulating the uncertainty of the times. The mood lifts for the final track, a beautifully tender love song, suggesting that there is where salvation lies. *John Wesley Harding* repays repeated play with ever-unfolding metaphor and interpretation.

John Wesley Harding; As I Went Out One Morning; I Dreamed I Saw St. Augustine; All Along The Watchtower; The Ballad Of Frankie Lee And Judas Priest; Drifter's Escape; Dear Landlord; I Am A Lonesome Hobo; I Pity The Poor Immigrant; The Wicked Messenger; Down Along The Cove; I'll Be Your Baby Tonight.

First released 1968
UK peak chart position: 1
USA peak chart position: 2

109. HOTEL CALIFORNIA
Eagles

A steady growth suddenly mushroomed into a monster as the Eagles, along with Fleetwood Mac, epitomised AOR in the early 70s. This record is supposedly a concept album but most of the purchasers merely enjoyed the accessible songs while driving in their Volkswagen Caravanettes with 2.4 children. Joe Walsh was added to give gutsy guitar in the wake of the country-flavour of Bernie Leaden, while Randy Meisner grew in stature as a writer with 'Try And Love Again' and 'New Kid In Town'. The title track still bites as Henley's voice blends with Walsh's epic solo.

Hotel California; New Kid In Town; Life In The Fast Lane; Wasted Time; Wasted Time (Reprise); Victim Of Love; Pretty Maids All In A Row; Try And Love Again; The Last Resort.

First released 1976
UK peak chart position: 2
USA peak chart position: 1

110. DAMN THE TORPEDOES
Tom Petty And The Heartbreakers

It is encouraging to note that in compiling the superlative recent *Greatest Hits* four tracks from this blinder of an album are included, more than any other. This is the ideal starting point for Petty students, and then you can acquire all his other albums. For those unaware, he is a rock 'n' roll Roger McGuinn. Those who are already aware of him will already know he has the knack of writing some of the best middle eight hooks ever heard, he has an addictive voice and a knock-out supporting band. Is that enough?

Refugee; Here Comes The Girl; Even The Losers; Century City; Don't Do Me Like That; What Are You Doin' In My Life?; Louisiana Rain.

First released 1979
UK peak chart position: 57
USA peak chart position: 2

111. SWORDFISHTROMBONES
Tom Waits

Tom Waits' early recordings cast him as a bohemian sage. Part Kerouac, part Bukowski, he infused Beat culture with the sweep of Hollywood movie soundtracks and the precision of a Tin Pan Alley songsmith. Aware of stylistic straightjacket, he cast it aside and produced this challenging album. Eschewing a traditional back-up group, Waits opted for a percussive sound based around marimbas, woodblocks and ever shifting rhythm patterns. Elements of Captain Beefheart and *avant garde* composer Harry Parch can be heard as the singer roars, barks and growls through a series of adventurous compositions reliant on impression and suggestion for effect. Uncompromising and exciting, *Swordfishtrombones* is a remarkable achievement from an already unconventional artist.

Underground; Shore Leave; Dave The Butcher; Johnsburg, Illinois; 16 Shells From A 30.6; Town With No Cheer; In The Neighbourhood; Just Another Sucker On The Vine; Frank's Wild Years; Swordfishtrombones; Down, Down, Down; Soldier's Things; Gin Soaked Boy; Trouble's Braids; Rainbirds.

First released 1983
UK peak chart position: 62
USA peak chart position: 167

112. STRANGER IN TOWN
BOB SEGER

Although this can be perceived as a dated album it is in the listings because of the importance it had in epitomising American rock in the 70s. Seger had been around for some time making his first record in 1965, treading the boards and must have found it mildly amusing to have such a colossal hit on his hands. As Seger was around first it is insulting to say he sounds like Springsteen, both in voice and in melody, but he does. 'Still The Same' still makes you melt and 'We've Got Tonight' is for those grown up macho hopeless romantics who like motorbikes.

Stranger In Town; Hollywood Nights; Still The Same; Old Time Rock 'n' Roll; Till It Shines; Feels Like A Number; Ain't Got No Money; We've Got Tonight; Brave Strangers; The Famous Final Scene.

First released 1978
UK peak chart position: 31
USA peak chart position: 4

113. THE WALL
Pink Floyd

There are hidden depths to this remarkable album which fans and critics have at times dismissed. It is not the concept of tearing down the wall, of opposition to the educational system or even Roger Waters becoming intolerable for the others to work with. It is a double album that contains some outstanding songs. For example; 'Nobody Home' highlights the frustration of Waters rock star lot, but for all the luxury we can sense his appalling frustration at finding nobody home. Similarly the epic 'Comfortably Numb'; 'the child is gone, the dream is gone, and I have become comfortably numb'. These are just two tracks!

In The Flesh; Thin Ice; Happiest Days Of Our Lives; Another Brick In The Wall (Part 2); Mother; Goodbye Blue Sky; Empty Spaces; Young Lust; One Of My Turns; Don't Leave Me Now; Another Brick In The Wall (Part 3); Goodbye Cruel World; Hey You; Is There Anybody Out There?; Nobody Home; Comfortably Numb; Show Must Go On; Run Like Hell; Waiting For The Worms; Stop; The Trial; Outside The Wall.

First released 1980
UK peak chart position: 3
USA peak chart position: 1

114. SURFS UP
Beach Boys

Surf's Up established the Beach Boys as an 'albums' band without sacrificing their individuality. The group's harmonies are as peerless as ever, their grasp of evocative melody unerring, particularly on Bruce Johnson's 'Disney Girls'. The ecological tenor of several tracks was politically shrewd and by opting to revive the title song from the unit's fabled Smile project, the Beach Boys reminded the outside world of their innovative past. Carl Wilson emerged a fine composer, ''Till I Die' showed Brian Wilson's gifts intact and the result was an artistic triumph, enabling the group to progress unfettered by artistic preconceptions.

Long Promised Road; Take A Load Off Your Feet; Disney Girls; Students Demonstration Time; Feel Flows; Lookin' At Tomorrow; A Day In The Life Of A Tree; 'Till I Die; Surf's Up; Don't Go Near The Water.

First released 1971
UK peak chart position: 15
USA peak chart position: 29

115. PARADE
Prince

Another soundtrack that fared more favourably than the movie, 'Under The Cherry Moon', from which it came. It was also the record that marked Prince's return to the live arena. The record itself came with a high camp video and guaranteed hit in the shape of, 'Kiss', which Tom Jones and the Art Of Noise would later collaborate together to cover. A delightfully, funky little number that the world threatened to dance around. Elsewhere, both, 'Girls And Boys' and 'Anotherloverholenyohead', charted. While the lifting strains of, 'Sometimes It Snows In April' rounded off a wonderfully whole album, but couldn't quite save the film.

Christopher Tracey's Parade; New Position; I Wonder U; Under The Cherry Moon; Girls And Boys; Life Can Be So Nice; Venus De milo; Mountains; Do U Lie; Kiss; Anotherloverholenyohead; Sometimes It Snows In April.

First released 1986
UK peak chart position: 4
USA peak chart position: 3

116. DON'T SHOOT ME I'M ONLY THE PIANO PLAYER
Elton John

In writing reviews it is impossible to refer to this artist as John, it fits for some but this subject is Elton, which immediately endears him to us. He is one of the best liked personalities in the music business, not renowned to leave any prisoners. This album more than any makes him loved. The happiness/sadness of 'Daniel' we all relate to, 'Teacher' is in all of us. He rocks out and induces warmth with 'Crocodile Rock' (we hate to love it), and on and on with 'Elderberry Wine'. Elton is seen as a good bloke which sometimes clouds his genius.

Daniel; Teacher I Need You; Elderberry Wine; Blues For My Baby And Me; Midnight Creeper; Have Mercy On The Criminal; I'm Going To Be A Teenage Idol; Texan Love Song; Crocodile Rock; High Flying Bird.

First released 1973
UK peak chart position: 1
USA peak chart position: 1

117. TAPESTRY
Carole King

During the 60s Carole King was renowned for composing a succession of classic pop songs. A low-key recording career blossomed with the release of this album which successfully married this skill with the contemporary singer/songwriter movement. *Tapestry* comprises of self-penned material and collaborations with either ex-husband Gerry Goffin or lyricist Toni Stern. King's unfussy vocal style enhances the simply-stated yet astute material and in 'It's Too Late' the singer expresses the break-down of a relationship with percipient incisiveness. Such a skill ensures the album's lasting popularity.

I Feel The Earth Move; So Far Away; It's Too Late; Home Again; Beautiful; Way Over Yonder; You've Got A Friend; Where You Lead; Will You Love Me Tomorrow; Smackwater Jack; Tapestry; (You Make Me Feel Like) A Natural Woman.

First released 1971
UK peak chart position: 4
USA peak chart position: 1

118. THE LOW SPARK OF HIGH HEELED BOYS
Traffic

The wandering jazzy music that Traffic gradually flowed into hit a peak with this exceptional recording. The title track, with its perplexing lyrics reaches numerous musical heights during its 12 minutes or life as it repeatedly comes back to Steve Winwood's accomplished vocal. Equally impressive, although shorter, is 'Hidden Treasure', highlighting what a good musician the late Chris Wood was. Finally, the band's loyal anchor, 'Gentleman' Jim Capaldi takes lead on the cheeky (and sexist) 'Light Up Or Leave Me Alone'. The power of Traffic was in the atmosphere and space they created, this captures it.

Hidden Treasure; The Low Spark Of High Heeled Boys; Light Up Or Leave Me Alone; Rock 'N' Stew; Many A Mile To Freedom; Rainmaker.

First released 1971
UK peak chart position: did not chart
USA peak chart position: 7

119. GET HAPPY!
Elvis Costello

This album highlights the fine line between Elvis' brand of pop/punk and R&B and soul. The impression is that he wrote, recorded and produced an album whilst on a creative roll of short, snappy, simple songs which go straight to the heart. Both he and his band played with fiery energy without losing a great sense of melody. The contrast is great with lyrical ingenuity of 'New Amsterdam' to the pace of 'I Stand Accused' and 'High Fidelity'. A record to lie down and have a rest after digestion. Quite magnificent.

Love For Tender; Opportunity; Imposter; Secondary Modern; King Horse; Possession; Man Called Uncle; Clowntime Is Over; New Amsterdam; High Fidelity; I Can't Stand Up For Falling Down; Black And White World; Five Gears In Reverse; B Movie; Motel Matches; Human Touch; Beaten To The Punch; Temptation; I Stand Accused; Riot Act.

First released 1980
UK peak chart position: 2
USA peak chart position: 11

120. NICE 'N EASY
Frank Sinatra

The perfect Sinatra album that bridged both swing and gentle ballads and yet another successful collaboration with Nelson Riddle and producer David Cavanaugh at Capitol Records. It is remarkable that ol' Blue Eyes continued to find exquisite songs to fill an album and not have to resort to any fillers that often occurred when deadlines loomed. The title track sets the mood and he tackles 'Fools Rush In', 'Try A Little Tenderness' and Johnny Mercer's 'Dream'. Many of these songs were previously recorded when Sinatra was with Columbia as he began to prepare to depart for his own company Reprise.

Nice 'n Easy; That Old Feeling; How Deep Is The Ocean; I've Got A Crush On You; You Go To My Head; Fools Rush In; Nevertheless (I'm In Love With You); She's Funny That Way; Try A Little Tenderness; Embraceable You; Mam'selle; Dream.

First released 1960
UK peak chart position: 4
USA peak chart position: 1

121. DESPERADO
Eagles

Drawing from a previous experience as hired musicians, the Eagles quickly became one of America's leading country-rock attractions. *Desperado*, their second release, was an ambitious concept album wherein the outlaw was used as a metaphor for the rock performer. Recorded in London under the aegis of Glyn Johns, the set was marked by the quartet's highly-measured playing and distinctive harmonies. Described at their inceptions as the 'new Buffalo Springfield', the Eagles certainly drew on Californian musical heritage, but on this album they proclaimed an original identity.

Doolin Dalton; 21; Out Of Control; Tequila Sunrise; Desperado; Certain Kind Of Fool; Outlaw Man; Saturday Night; Bitter Creek.

First released 1973
UK peak chart position: 39
USA peak chart position: 41

122. GREEN
R.E.M.

The album that found the band sandwiched between being an important cult band on the verge of major success and being the world's most successful rock band of the 90s. A tricky one, but this album did it and mighty Warner Brothers were behind it. R.E.M. were able to get their folky mandolin material like 'You Are Everything' accepted on equal footing with great pop such as 'Stand' or 'Pop Song 89' (which could have been written by Jim Morrison and titled 'Hello I Love You'). 'Orange Crush' is already an FM radio favourite, and the rest is all recent history.

Pop Song 89; Get Up; You Are Everything; Stand; World Leader Pretend; The Wrong Child; Orange Crush; Turn You Inside Out; Hairshirt; I Remember California; Untitled Song.

First released 1988
UK peak chart position: 27
USA peak chart position: 12

123. HOT RATS
Frank Zappa

Having temporarily disbanded the Mothers Of Invention, Frank Zappa recorded this exceptional solo album. His group was renowned for musical satire, but here the artist opted to showcase his prowess on guitar. 'Willie The Pimp' apart, which features a cameo vocal by Captain Beefheart, the set comprises of instrumentals. The players, which include Don 'Sugarcane' Harris, Jean-Luc Ponty and Ian Underwood, are uniformly excellent, combining to provide a solid jazz-rock platform for Zappa's always compulsive soloing. He relishes a freedom which, while acknowledging past achievements, prepared new territories for exploration. *Hot Rats* is a pivotal release in Zappa's career.

Peaches En Regalia; Willie The Pimp; Son Of Mr. Green Genes; Little Umbrellas; The Gumbo Variations; It Must Be A Camel.

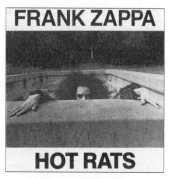

First released 1969
UK peak chart position: 9
USA peak chart position: 173

124. THERE GOES RHYMIN' SIMON
Paul Simon

Was it really the tail end of the 60s that Simon gave us this little gem? After he parted from Garfunkel, Simon wrote songs without having to consider two part harmonies and this in turn gave his music a freer and less of a folk/rock flavour. 'American Tune' remains one of his greatest compositions and would make a better alternative to 'America The Beautiful' as the national anthem. Simon had to wait a long time before he topped this record artistically, but he did it in style with *Graceland*. This is the other Paul Simon album to own.

Kodachrome; Tenderness; Take Me To The Mardi Gras; Something So Right; One Man's Ceiling Is Another Man's Floor; American Tune; Was A Sunny Day; Learn How To Fall; St. Judy's Comet; Loves Me Like A Rock.

First released 1973
UK peak chart position: 4
USA peak chart position: 2

125. AXIS, BOLD AS LOVE
JIMI HENDRIX

Live performances and the brilliant *Are You Experienced* established Jimi Hendrix as a guitarist nonpareil. This second set was largely less demonstrative, focusing on the artist's gifts as a songwriter. It included several reflective compositions, notably the haunting 'Little Wing'. This did not represent a radical change of emphasis - many of the tracks were actually recorded at sessions producing its predecessor - and the set simply offered another side to his talent. The guitarist's sonic creativity underscored 'If Six Was Nine' and 'Spanish Castle Magic' and although sometimes eclipsed by the albums issued on either side of it, *Axis, Bold As Love* brims with the same inventiveness.

Experience; Up From The Skies; Spanish Castle Magic; Wait Until Tomorrow; Ain't No Telling; Little Wing; If Six Was Nine; You've Got Me Floating; Castles Made Of Sand; She's So Fine; One Rainy Wish; Little Miss Lover; Bold As Love.

First released 1968
UK peak chart position: 5
USA peak chart position: 3

126. IN THE WEE SMALL HOURS
Frank Sinatra

As ever Sinatra's collaboration with Nelson Riddle on this album is wholly successful, this time a magnificent statement in understated orchestration. Emotional and romantic Sinatra gently eases himself through another 16 classics of American popular song. Although he fails to swing he never ceases to move the listener and images of comfy sofas, scotch on the rocks and radiograms spring to mind as we hear songs by Ellington, Rodgers and Hart, Van Heusen, Arlen and Harburg, and Porter. Mellow, rich and pure but not to follow Jimi Hendrix in playing order.

In the Wee Small Hours Of The Morning; Glad To Be Unhappy; I Get Along Without You Very Well; Deep In A Dream; I See Your Face Before Me; Can't We Be Friends; When Your Lover Has Gone; What Is This Thing Called Love; I'll Be Around; Ill Wind; It Never Entered My Mind; I'll Never Be The Same; This Love Of Mine; Last Night When We Were Young; Dancing On The Ceiling.

First released 1955
UK peak chart position: did not chart
USA peak chart position: 2

127. CALYPSO
Harry Belafonte

Belafonte's third and most successful chart album was full of the kind of folksy and calypso-style songs that made him one of the show-business sensations of the 50s. Two of them, 'The Banana Boat Song (Day-O)' and 'Jamaica Farewell', were singles hits as well. The album itself spent 72 weeks in the US Top 40, 31 of them at number 1, and made history by becoming the first 33 1/3 rpm record by a solo artist to sell a million copies. It was only the beginning of Belafonte's phenomenal career on records, television and films.

The Banana Boat Song (Day-O); Jack-ass Song; Hosanna; Come Back Liza; I Do Adore Her; Dolly Dawn; Jamaica Farewell; Will His Love Be Like His Rum?; Man Smart; Star O; Brown Skin Girl.

First released 1956
UK peak chart position: did not chart
USA peak chart position: 1

128. VELVET UNDERGROUND
Velvet Underground

Now affectionately known as 'the third album' it forms part of a catalogue which contains some of the most influential music since time began. Not even getting its money back when released, nor making the charts, it is astonishing how this important band have seeped into our minds. Every track has huge merit, whether its Maureen's innocent voice or Lou's drawl, even the enthrallingly bizarre 'The Murder Mystery' still baffles. Like the cover, dark and decadent, like Lou Reed on the back cover, out of his head and upside down.

White Light; White Heat; What Goes On; Venus In Furs; That's The Story Of My Life; Here She Comes Now; Beginning To See The Light; Jesus; Run Run Run; Some Kinda Love; The Gift; I'm Set Free; I Heard Her Call My Name.

First released 1969
UK peak chart position: did not chart
USA peak chart position: did not chart

129. REVENGE
Eurythmics

Having now made the transition into a full bloodied band that rocks, Lennox and Stewart could do no wrong and must be seen as one of the musical highlights of the 80s. To maintain such a high standard through six albums in four years takes some doing, yet here they go again, each time growing musically and adding that little extra, for example the meaty harmonica opening on 'Missionary Man', bringing a harder drum sound on all tracks and finally Stewart back to playing lots of guitar and sounding as though he is having fun. Hypnotic bouncy music.

Let's Go; Take Your Pain Away; A Little Of You; Thorn In My Side; In This Town; I Remember You; Missionary Man; The Last Time; When Tomorrow Comes; The Miracle Of Love.

First released 1986
UK peak chart position: 3
USA peak chart position: 12

130. AVALON SUNSET
Van Morrison

Any one of a dozen Morrison titles should have figured in this listing, so why this one? Maybe a few extra sales were made by having Cliff Richard as co-vocalist on the overtly Christian 'Whenever God Shines His Light On Me'. The overall themes are the same, the songs have that glorious quality of melancholy and Morrison sings as well as ever. The religion and spiritualism that has become a strong part of his work is here in large doses. The real success is behind the lyrics, where the private man lets us find a bit more about him.

Whenever God Shines His Light; Contacting My Angel; I'd Love To Write Another Song; Have I Told You Lately; Coney Island; I'm Tired Joey Boy; When Will I Ever Learn To Live In God; Orangefield; Daring Night; These Are The Days.

First released 1989
UK peak chart position: 13
USA peak chart position: 91

131. PET SHOP BOYS ACTUALLY
Pet Shop Boys

Reappraisal always reveals, good or bad. In the case of this the great revelation is the magnificent orchestration, even though it is created by fairlights and keyboards. 'One More Chance' is blissfully symphonic and the favourite hits are still irritatingly effective. The production is shared between Julian Mendelsohn, David Jacob, Shep Pettibone and Stephen Hague and is mixed to digital perfection. Ultimately this album succeeds in delivering 'pop' exactly as it should be, but played too often it will begin to grate on your friends, because you will end up humming it all day and drive them to despair.

One More Chance; Shopping; Rent; Hit Music; What Have I Done To Deserve This?; It Couldn't Happen Here; It's A Sin; I Want To Wake Up; Heart; King's Cross.

First released 1987
UK peak chart position: 2
USA peak chart position: 25

132. WAITING FOR THE SUN
Doors

The Doors' third album is one of contrast, capturing brash commerciality and political militancy. It survives the artistic dilemma this poses through a succession of excellent songs and many of singer Jim Morrison's most explicit lyrics. 'The Unknown Soldier' and 'Five To One' capture the Doors at their most politically strident, wherein music and image compliment each other perfectly. Other selections show the quartet playful ('Hello I Love You'), wistful ('Summer's Almost Gone') or even peculiar ('My Wild Love'), but in each case the Doors proved themselves as intriguing as ever.

Hello I Love You; Love Street; Not To Touch; The Earth; Summer's Almost Gone; Winter Time Love; The Unknown Soldier; Spanish Caravan; My Wild Love; We Could Be So Good Together; Yes, The River Knows; Five To One.

First released 1968
UK peak chart position: 16
USA peak chart position: 1

133. ALL THINGS MUST PASS
George Harrison

A preponderance of timeless Lennon/McCartney songs ensured that George Harrison's contribution to the Beatles' catalogue was held in check. This backlog ensured that his 'official' debut set was teeming with strong material. 'Isn't It A Pity' and 'My Sweet Lord' are among his finest songs, despite the charge of plagiarism directed at the latter. A suitably lush Phil Spector production cocooned Harrison's sometimes one-dimensional voice, creating a tapestry enhanced by contributions by Eric Clapton and the group which would later become Derek And The Dominoes. Three albums made up a set which showed Harrison's gifts mature and indicated that his talents had been too long obscured.

I'd Have You Anytime; My Sweet Lord; Wah-wah; Isn't It A Pity; What Is Life; If Not For You; Behind That Locked Door; Let It Down; Run Of The Mill; Beware Of Darkness; Apple Scruffs; Ballad Of Sir Frankie Crisp (Let It Roll); Awaiting On You All; All Things Must Pass; I Dig Love; Art Of Dying; Isn't It A Pity; Hear Me Lord; Out Of The Blue; It's Johnny's Birthday; Plug Me In; I Remember Jeep; Thanks For The Peperoni.

First released 1970
UK peak chart position: 4
USA peak chart position: 1

134. FLEETWOOD MAC
Fleetwood Mac

The loss of founding member Peter Green dealt a blow to Fleetwood Mac which took five years to assimilate. Numerous changes in personnel robbed them of focus until Californian singer/songwriters, Stevie Nicks and Lindsay Buckingham, joined the ranks. The duo introduced a new dynamism to the group, their bright, melodious compositions offsetting the earthier muse of pianist/vocalist Christine McVie. Buckingham's quicksilver guitar work energised the group's pulsating rhythm section, regaining, at last, the sense of purpose marking early releases. Titling the album *Fleetwood Mac* suggested a new beginning, which indeed it was. This set saved the group from ignominy, and turned them into one of the world's leading rock bands.

Monday Morning; Warm Always; Blue Letter; Rhiannon; Over My Head; Crystal; Say You Love Me; Landslide; I'm So Afraid; World Turning; Sugar Daddy.

First released 1975
UK peak chart position: 23
USA peak chart position: 1

135. LOW
David Bowie

The first, *Heroes* and *Lodger* would follow, of Bowie's three Berlin albums. Living there as a semi-recluse for three years, he worked with Svengali/producer Brian Eno and the results of their collaborations helped change the face of the European mainstream. Artists from Gary Numan, Ultravox and OMD were indebted to the sound Bowie had created with the synthesiser to build a somewhat terse wall of sound. Critically acclaimed, but a relative commercial failure, apart from the surprise 'Sound And Vision' hit single. It remains, however, as a pertinent reminder of Bowie's ability to surprise and enlighten.

Speed Of Life; Breaking Glass; What In The World; Sound And Vision; Always Crashing In The Same Car; Be My Wife; A New Career In A New Town; Warszawa; Art Decade; Weeping Wall; Subterraneans.

First released 1977
UK peak chart position: 2
USA peak chart position: 11

136. PRETENDERS II
Pretenders

The band look magnificent on the cover as they pose with make-up or heavily retouched faces. They look confident, knowing that their follow-up is almost as good as the debut. Chrissie and Ray Davies were stepping out at this time, hence the opening track 'The Adultress' as Hynde whispers her confession over a furious wall of sound to be immediately followed by her reminding us that 'Bad Boys Get Spanked'. If only Chrissie, if only. The album drives and dives, pausing for 'I Go To Sleep', an old Ray Davies song. There is not a dud track in sight.

The Adultress; Bad Boys Get Spanked; Messages Of Love; I Go To Sleep; Birds Of Paradise; Talk Of The Town; Pack It Up; Waste Not, Want Not; Day After Day; Jealous Dogs; English Rose; Louie Louie.

First released 1981
UK peak chart position: 7
USA peak chart position: 10

137. OUT OF THE BLUE
Electric Light Orchestra

Leader Jeff Lynne took his Lennon/Beatles sound to the extreme by giving us a double album of Beatlesque pop. Hit after hit followed and its fair to say that radio overplay made us sick of the sound of ELO. This is totally unfair because Lynn is a master songwriter and this album is crammed full of great melodies and 'interesting twiddly bits'. Rather than recall the hits let us recall other corkers; 'Jungle', 'Standing In The Rain' and 'Birmingham Blues'. Who will own up to building the impossible cardboard cut-out space ship that came with the original?

Turn To Stone; It's Over; Sweet Talkin' Woman; Across The Border; Night In The City; Starlight; Jungle; Belive Me Now; Steppin' Out; Standing In The Rain; Summer And Lightning; Mr. Blue Sky; Sweet Is The Night; The Whale; Wild West Hero; Birmingham Blues.

First released 1977
UK peak chart position: 4
USA peak chart position: 4

138. TUBULAR BELLS
Mike Oldfield

Still a firm favourite of the class of 1973 which was given a huge lease of life in 1993 with the dreaded sequel/new version. The original is always the best statement can be applied here as Virgin Records V2001 set Richard Branson down a very lucrative road. Try as you may it is an excellent piece of instrumental music. The inspired choice of using Viv Stanshall as the orchestra master gives the album greater strength. Studying the credits we are reminded that Edgar Broughton's brother Steve plays drums. Oldfield meanwhile plays every instrument he can get his hand on.

Tubular Bells Part I; Tubular Bells Part II.

First released 1973
UK peak chart position: 1
USA peak chart position: 3

139. FREAK OUT
Frank Zappa/Mothers Of Invention

Led by the irascible Frank Zappa, the Mothers Of Invention were outsiders, even on this, their debut album. Older than most contemporaries, they brought a cynicism to their work which celebrated joys without recourse to nostalgia. Telling parodies of pop forms were as engaging as those they drew upon, while experimental pieces, drawn on *avant garde* compositions by Edgar Varese and Stravinsky, took the notion of 'rock' into uncharted territory. Zappa's overview allowed such contrasting elements to function without disengagement, his skills as musician and engineer ensuring the innovative nature of this creation.

Hungry Freaks, Daddy; I Ain't Got No Heat; Who Are The Brain Police?; Go Cry On Somebody Else's Shoulder; Motherly Love; How Could I Be Such A Fool; Wowie Zowie; You Didn't Try To Call Me; Any Way The Wind Blows; I'm Not Satisfied; You're Probably Wondering Why I'm Here; Trouble Every Day; Help, I'm A Rock; The Return Of The Son Of Monster Magnet.

First released 1967
UK peak chart position: did not chart
USA peak chart position: 130

140. TODAY
Beach Boys

Although other Beach Boys albums have received greater critical acclaim *Today* is almost unbeatable for its content of two-minute quality songs that are unpretentious and infectious. Their rock 'n' roll roots are revisited with 'Do You Wanna Dance' and 'The Girl From New York City'. 'Dance, Dance, Dance' and 'Good To My Baby' are two underrated Brian Wilson songs and he compliments them with more of his gorgeous ballads in 'She Knows Me Too Well and 'Please Let Me Wonder'. The seeds of *Pet Sounds* were sewn with this impressive record.

Do You Wanna Dance; Good To My Baby; The Girl From New York City; Don't Hurt My Little Sister; When I Grow Up; Help Me, Ronda; Dance, Dance, Dance, Please Let Me Wonder; I'm So Young; Kiss Me Baby; She Knows Me Too Well; In The Back Of My Mind; Bull Session With The Big Daddy.

First released 1965
UK peak chart position: 6
USA peak chart position: 4

141. STRANGE DAYS
Doors

The Doors' second album redefined their uncompromising art. The disturbing timbre of Ray Manzarek's organ work provided the musical cloak through which guitarist Robbie Kreiger and vocalist Jim Morrison projected. Few singers in rock possessed his authority, where every nuance and inflection bore an emotional intensity. *Strange Days* contains some of the quartet's finest work, from the apocalyptical vision of 'When The Music's Over' to the memorable quirkiness of 'People Are Strange' and 'Moonlight Drive'. The graphic 'Horse Latitudes' meanwhile confirms Morrison's wish to be viewed as a poet, a stance ensuring the Doors were always more than just another rock band.

Strange Days; You're Lost; Little Girl; Love Me Two Times; Unhappy Girl; Horse Latitudes; Moonlight Drive; People Are Strange; My Eyes Have Seen You; I Can't See Your Face In My Mind; When The Music's Over.

First released 1963
UK peak chart position: did not chart
USA peak chart position: 3

142. EVERYBODY KNOWS THIS IS NOWHERE
Neil Young

Neil Young's second album introduced his longstanding relationship with backing group Crazy Horse. Their partnership allowed the singer greater musical flexibility and the understanding generated gave a unique synergy to his work. The combination could be concise, as on the vibrant 'Cinnamon Girl', but the pivotal selections are the lengthy, guitar-based workouts, 'Down By The River' and 'Cowgirl In The Sand'. The group goad Young into textured, improvised playing, the appeal of which never palls. Elsewhere the singer revisits his folk past and embraces country rock, but a determined unity of purpose allows these disparate elements gell to perfection.

Cinnamon Girl; Everybody Knows This Is Nowhere; Round And Round; Down By The River; The Losing End; Running Dry (Requiem For The Rockets); Cowgirl In The Sand.

First released 1969
UK peak chart position: did not chart
USA peak chart position: 34

143. TOUCH
Eurythmics

This came at the end of 1983, a particularly prolific period for Stewart and Lennox - they already had spent most of the year in the chart with *Sweet Dreams*, released at the beginning of the year. This album shows less reliance on programmed instrumentation and a less 'Germanic' feel to the production. 'The First Cut' and "Right By Your Side' indicate a loosening up and a more rootsy approach as Lennox discovers she has a great R&B/soul voice. 'Here Comes The Rain Again' and 'Who's That Girl?' are the more familiar haunting Eurythmics sound.

Here Comes The Rain Again; Regrets; Right By Your Side; Cool Blue; Who's That Girl?; The First Cut; Aqua; No Fear, No Hate, No Pain (No Broken Hearts); Paint A Rumour.

First released 1983
UK peak chart position: 1
USA peak chart position: 7

144. AGAIN
Buffalo Springfield

A year after *Sgt Pepper* came America's possible answer, both with the formidable talent within the band, including Stephen Stills, Richie Furay and Neil Young and the varied content of folk, rock, country, soul and mild psychedelia. The strong egos within made their future an impossibility as the leaders went on to major success with CSNY and Poco. Hearing this record made David Crosby want to join them while the UK rock cognoscenti prayed for them to stay together long enough to tour over here. It was not to be but this was a document to their great potential.

Mr. Soul; A Child's Claim To Fame; Everydays; Expecting To Fly; Bluebird; Hung Upside Down; Sad Memory; Good Time Boy; Rock 'N' Roll Woman; Broken Arrow.

First released 1967
UK peak chart position: did not chart
USA peak chart position: 44

145. Stage Fright
The Band

The third Band album reflected their transformation from studio ensemble to that appearing live. Several selections, notably the title track, articulated disquiet this engendered. The set still offered the quintet's mesmerising cross-section of American music - soul, country R&B and pop - but where previous releases took a largely historical perspective, this collection brings together the past and present. Thus the ribald, carnival atmosphere of 'W.S. Walcott Medicine Show' is set against 'The Rumor', in which songwriter Robbie Robertson sculpts a chilling portrait of the Nixon era. This ambitious panorama results in a pivotal early 70s' release.

Strawberry Wine; Sleeping; Just Another Whistle Stop; All La Glory; The Shape I'm In; The W.S. Walcott Medicine Show; Daniel And The Sacred Harp; Stage Fright; The Rumor; Time To Kill.

First released 1970
UK peak chart position: 15
USA peak chart position: 5

146. COME DANCE WITH ME
Frank Sinatra

On Sinatra's great records of the 50s and early 60s equal billing should be given to the conductor/arrangers. Sinatra was able to let loose and blossom with the confidence that the great song he had chosen, together with his voice would be enhanced by the orchestration. This album is another in a series of quite brilliant arrangements giving new life to Johnny Mercer's 'Something's Gotta Give' Irving Berlin's 'Cheek To Cheek' and George Weiss' 'Too Close For Comfort'. In keeping with other reissues the CD has four bonus tracks including 'It All Depends On You'.

Come Dance With Me; Something's Gotta Give; Just In Time; Dancing In The Dark; Too Close For Comfort; I Could Have Danced All Night; Saturday Night Is The Loneliest Night Of The Week; Day In, Day Out; Cheek To Cheek; Baubles, Bangles And Beads; The Song Is You; Last Dance.

First released 1959
UK peak chart position: 2
USA peak chart position: 2

147. DARKNESS AT THE EDGE OF TOWN
Bruce Springsteen

Springsteen rarely figures in favourite albums nowadays, his moon seems to have waned. This was the album before the famous Jon Landau statement came to pass, and although there are still lots of references to cars and girls it is a blistering album. It has a similar energy that was later to be found on *The River*. He states in 'Something In The Street', 'soon as you've got something they send someone to try and take it away'. He repeated the themes again and again, and we loved it, maybe his fall from grace is because we ultimately only need one song about cars and girls.

Badlands; Adam Raised A Cain; Something In The Street; Candy's Room; Racing In The Street; Promised Land; Factory; Streets Of Fire; Prove It All; Darkness On The Edge Of Town.

First released 1978
UK peak chart position: 16
USA peak chart position: 5

148. ARMED FORCES
Elvis Costello

Only recently has this album been re-appraised favourably - this was after all his most commercial offering, yet its lowly position still indicates some resistance. Its political content should have given it credibility, lyrically it is as powerful as anything Costello has written, even the overtly radio friendly 'Oliver's Army' delivered some pretty uncompromising words. That seems to be Costello's strength dressing up a statement under the guise of a pop song. 'Green Shirt', 'Accidents Will Happen' and 'Goon Squad' are all as important as a pop song can get. Costello rarely wastes a lyric, this album is no exception.

Senior Service; Oliver's Army; Big Boys; Green Shirt; Party Girl; Goon Squad; Busy Bodies; Sunday's Best; Chemistry Class; Two Little Hitlers; Accidents Will Happen.

First released 1979
UK peak chart position: 2
USA peak chart position: 10

149. A DAY AT THE RACES
Queen

Another UK number 1 for Queen. *A Day At The Races* celebrating their diversity and colourfully flamboyant sense of the unreal. Stylistically, the adoption of any one musical form over the other was simply beneath them. They flirted with a passion, dipping and whimsical with, 'Good Old Fashioned Lover Boy', grand, entranced and eloquent with, 'Somebody To Love', while, 'Tie Your Mother Down', with its sense of mischief, scathing wit and a shrill, delighted laugh, put its foot through the floor and a fist through the ceiling. To paraphrase *The Times*, a work of sheer bloody poetry.

Long Away; The Millionaire Waltz; You And I; Somebody To Love; White Man; Good Old Fashioned Lover Boy; Drowse; Teo Torriate (Let Us Cling Together); Tie Your Mother Down; You Take My Breath Away.

First released 1976
UK peak chart position: 1
USA peak chart position: 5

150. WHITE LIGHT WHITE HEAT
Velvet Underground

The difficult second album from one of rock's greatest influences was dusted off with little regard to trying to sell records. Blissfully unaware of how important this band was to become, their label Verve must have torn their hair out when they were presented with John Cale telling the story of Waldo over a guitar backdrop on the eight minute plus 'The Gift' or 17 minutes of chunking and distorted heaven with 'Sister Ray' and Lou Reed extolling the virtues of 'searching for his mainline' or 'oh man I haven't got the time time, too busy sucking on his ding dong'.

White Light; White Heat; The Gift; Lady Godiva's Operation; Here She Comes Now; I Heard Her Call My Name; Sister Ray.

First released 1968
UK peak chart position: did not chart
USA peak chart position: 171

151. ST DOMINIC'S PREVIEW
Van Morrison

The cover depicts a troubled soul sitting on the church steps strumming his Martin guitar, probably unaware of his P.J. Proby split in his pants. The music inside is varied, as if Van is still feeling his way. He places soul/jazz with 'Jackie Wilson Said' and 'I Will Be There' next to delicious acoustic ramblings of 'Almost Independence Day' and 'Listen To The Lion'. It is the latter two that make this album so special. Van can knock off a soul song every time he opens his mouth but 'Listen To the Lion' opens his soul.

Jackie Wilson Said; Gypsy; I Will Be There; Listen To The Lion; St. Dominic's Preview; Redwood Tree; Almost Independence Day.

First released 1972
UK peak chart position: did not chart
USA peak chart position: 15

152. REGGATTA DE BLANC
Police

The career of the Police was planned, controlled and timed to perfection. The three talented individuals probably always knew they would attempt to conquer and then disappear to their own musical interests. This is the second of their five albums and contains two number 1 hits. Both are interesting little vignettes from the mind of Sting; 'Walking On The Moon' where he pleads 'I hope my legs don't break' and 'Message In A Bottle' which has a similarly desperate Sting observing 'seems I'm not alone in being alone, 100 billion castaways looking for a home'. Stings' theories do still hold water.

Message In A Bottle; Reggatta De Blanc; It's Alright For You; Bring On The Night; Deathwish; Walking On The Moon; On Any Other Day; The Bed's Too Big Without You; Contact; Does Everybody Stare; No Time This Time.

First released 1979
UK peak chart position: 1
USA peak chart position: 25

153. FEATS DON'T FAIL ME NOW
Little Feat

If albums could be rolled and smoked, this would be one to keep for a special occasion, passed from friend to friend in a grin-inducing haze of contentment. Everything, from the Neon Park artwork to the sleevenotes, is goodtime. The line-up of the band on *Feats Don't Fail Me Now* works equally well on composition and playing. The songs, from the rhythmically chunky 'Rock And Roll Doctor' to the sprawlingly energetic 'Cold Cold Cold/Tripe Face Boogie' roll along without looking to left or right, and the arrangement is so tight you couldn't slide a Rizla in sideways. Country funk at its best, by George.

Rock and Roll Doctor; Cold Cold Cold; Tripe Face Boogie; Fan; Oh Atlanta; Skin It Back; Down The Road; Spanish Moon; Feats Don't Fail Me Now.

First released 1974
UK peak chart position: did not chart
USA peak chart position: 36

154. RECKLESS
Bryan Adams

Bryan Adams was played a lot on the radio in 1984/5, his music was the most radio friendly rock that had been heard in a long time. Revisiting this album a decade later still confirms this, if anything hearing him less makes you like him more. The hit singles still sound consistently good; 'Somebody', 'Summer Of '69' and 'Run To You', but although he has a clearly recognisable style and sound all the other tracks sound fresh. Adams never needs to top this record as there is enough grist on this to keep him playing them live for ever.

The Only One; Take Me Back; This Time; Straight From The Heart; Cuts Like A Knife; I'm Ready; What's It Gonna Be; Don't Leave Me Lonely; The Best Was Yet To Come; One Night Love Affair; She's Only Happy When She's Dancin'; Run To You; Heaven; Somebody; Summer Of '69; Kids Wanna Rock; It's Only Love; Long Gone; Ain't Gonna Cry.

First released 1984
UK peak chart position: 7
USA peak chart position: 1

155. DOCUMENT
R.E.M.

R.E.M's later albums have sold by the millions but they needed to make albums like this to build a fan-base that got them noticed. a number of critics place this record as their best. The band do sound as though they are having to work to be heard, there is much more energy in 'Finest Worksong' and their Byrdslike 'Welcome To The Occupation'. Its been a while since Michael Stipe had so many words to say as he did in 'It's the End Of The World As We Know It' and 'The One I Love' has to be one of their top five songs of all time.

Finest Worksong; Welcome To The Occupation; Exhuming McCarthy; Disturbance At The Heron House; Strange; It's The End Of The World As We Know It (And I Feel Fine); The One I Love; Fireplace; Lightnin' Hopkins; King Of Birds; Oddfellows Local 151.

First released 1987
UK peak chart position: 28
USA peak chart position: 10

156. ALF
Alison Moyet

Poor Alison Moyet may end up cursing this album for the rest of her career. Finding yourself with one of the year's biggest triumphs and rewarded by your record company with a large advance to put in your deposit account may sound satisfying, but for Alf it has not been an easy ride. The crisp Jolley/Swain production aided its success, and Moyet delivered a stunning voice to match strong material. Together they composed all the tracks bar one, Lamont Dozier's 'Invisible', the third hit single following on from 'Love Resurrection' and 'All Cried Out'. Powerful quality pop.

Love Resurrection; Honey For The Bees; For You Only; Invisible; Steal Me Blind; All Cried Out; Money Mile; Twisting The Knife; Where Hides Sleep.

First released 1984
UK peak chart position: 1
USA peak chart position: 45

157. HELLO I MUST BE GOING
Phil Collins

The omnipresent Phil took two years to follow *Face Value*, which cynics believed to be a fluke and fans willed him to repeat. This album rocketed him back to the top together with a number 1 single 'You Can't Hurry Love', and a superb video with Phil in triplicate with a tonic mohair suit and shades. The rest is in a similar vein to his debut, albeit with a happier theme running through. The album's finale is the touching 'Why Can't It Wait 'Til Morning', a sentence we have all used at some time in our life, in the same way.

I Don't Care Anymore; I Cannot Believe It's True; Like China; Do You Know, Do You Care?; You Can't Hurry Love; It Don't Matter To Me; Thru' These Walls; Don't Let Him Steal His Heart Away; The West Side; Why Can't It Wait 'Til Morning.

First released 1982
UK peak chart position: 2
USA peak chart position: 8

158. AMERICAN BEAUTY
Grateful Dead

Following on from their beautiful country-tinged exercise in sounding like Crosby Stills And Nash, the Dead gave us an even mellower set with the exemplary record. The albums stand out track is the introspective 'Ripple', for once Jerry Garcia actually sings one of Robert Hunter's lyrics as though he means it. Other excellent supporting numbers are 'Box Of Rain' and the overwhelmingly sad 'Attics Of My Life'. Although the Grateful Dead remain a mellow band, they have yet to record another album that is so light and emotional. There are no overlong solo's on this absolutely charming record.

Box Of Rain; Friend Of The Devil; Operator; Sugar Magnolia; Ripple; Brokedown Palace; Till The Morning Comes; Attic Of My Life; Truckin'.

First released 1970
UK peak chart position: did not chart
USA peak chart position: 30

159. YOUNG AMERICANS
David Bowie

David Bowie abandoned the glam/sci-fi personae of *Ziggy Stardust, Aladdin Sane* and *Diamond Dogs* with this radical departure. Recorded at Sigma Sound Studios, the home of Philadelphia International, it featured the labels' crack houseband and, as a result, confirmed the singer's growing love of soul and R&B. Pulsating dance grooves abound, in particular on the disco-influenced 'Fame', which topped the US singles' chart. The song was co-written with John Lennon, a compliment Bowie repaid by reinventing the Beatles' 'Across The Universe' as a dancefloor classic. Such self-confidence abounds throughout this album which shows the singer firmly in command of yet another musical direction.

Young Americans; Win; Fascination; Right; Somebody Up There Likes Me; Across The Universe; Can You Hear Me; Fame.

First released 1975
UK peak chart position: 2
USA peak chart position: 9

160. SAILIN' SHOES
Little Feat

A band that received nothing but praise and is rightly remembered with great affection. The reformed version of the 90s with Craig Fuller does not come near the magical unit led by the late Lowell George. Many of their albums were nominated and three made the listings. 'Easy To Slip' opens with George smacking chords from his acoustic guitar as his partners fall in line, loose yet totally together. Little Feat were one of the finest band's of the 70s - only now do we really appreciate just how great they were. And yes, this is the one that has 'Willin' on it.

Easy To Slip; Cold Cold Cold; Trouble; Tripe Face Boogie; Willin'; Apolitical Blues; Sailin' Shoes; Teenage Nervous Breakdown; Got No Shadows; Cat Fever; Texas Rose Cafe.

First released 1972
UK peak chart position: did not chart
USA peak chart position: did not chart

161. ALADDIN SANE
David Bowie

Aladdin Sane was released as its creator's star was firmly ascending. A sprawling US tour inspired much of its content, particularly 'Drive In Saturday' and 'Panic In Detroit', but such images are infused with Bowie's contemporary interest in science-fiction-styled alter-egos. Regular backing group, the Spiders From Mars, which included guitarist Mick Ronson, fuelled the compositions with an intuitive punch, although the diverse nature of the material showed Bowie's ever-present desire to challenge. Futuristic vistas are even harnessed to vintage R&B, as evinced on 'Jean Genie', which inspires comparisons with the Yardbirds and a reworking of the Stones' 'Let's Spend The Night Together'. The singer disbanded his group following this album, and *Aladdin Sane* thus marks a watershed in his inventive career.

Watch That Man; Aladdin Sane; Drive In Saturday; Panic In Detroit; Cracked Actor; Time; The Prettiest Star; Let's Spend The Night Together; Jean Genie.

First released 1973
UK peak chart position: 1
USA peak chart position: 17

162. AFTERMATH
Rolling Stones

The fourth Rolling Stones LP was the first to comprise solely of Jagger/Richard compositions. As such it reflected a switch from pure R&B, although the group's roots are still to the fore, particularly in Brian Jones' slide guitar work. The same musician was also responsible for introducing exotica to the quintet's overall sound; marimbas, dulcimer, harpsichord and sitar being added at his behest. The result is a selection of unrivalled scope, where the Knightsbridge chic of 'Lady Jane' sits beside C&W ('High And Dry') and improvised workouts ('Goin' Home'). The desultory 'Under My Thumb' would meanwhile remain an integral part of the Stones' lexicon throughout the subsequent two decades. *Aftermath* confirmed that the directions suggested by 'The Last Time' and 'Satisfaction' could be successfully sustained.

Mother's Little Helper; Stupid Girl; Lady Jane; Under My Thumb; Doncha Bother Me; Goin' Home; Flight 505; High And Dry; Out Of Time; It's Not Easy; I Am Waiting; Take It Or Leave It; Think; What To Do.

First released 1966
UK peak chart position: 1
USA peak chart position: 2

163. SMILEY SMILE
Beach Boys

The aborted Smile project was replaced with a perplexing release which lost the band surf and hot rod fans but endeared them to people who smoked funny cigarettes. Rumour has it that the band were so high they had to stay low, and record this album lying on the floor. Van Dyke Parks wove his wackiness around 'Heroes And Villains', 'Vegetables' and 'She's Going Bald'. The monumental 'Good Vibrations' was thrown in for good measure in glorious stereophonic sound. Now regarded as a classic and the album that Brian Wilson would never recover from and be the same again.

Heroes And Villans; Vegetables; Fall Breaks And Back To Winter; She's Goin' Bald; Little Pad; Good Vibrations; With Me Tonight; Wind Chimes; Gettin' Hungry; Wonderful; Whistle In.

First released 1967
UK peak chart position: 9
USA peak chart position: 41

164. THE LEXICON OF LOVE
ABC

ABC are frequently described as purveyors of high quality pop music, but this undervalues the elegance and attention to detail of their work. Although they have failed to repeat the success of *Lexicon Of Love*, it nevertheless represents an achievement to which many other artists can only aspire. The maturity of Trevor Horn's production created a remarkable debut album, yielding hits in 'Tears Are Not Enough', 'Poison Arrow', 'The Look Of Love' and 'All Of My Heart', with Martin Fry's talent as songwriter and vocalist delivering the goods with consistent aplomb.

Show Me; Poison Arrow; Many Happy Returns; Tears Are Not Enough; Valentine's Day; The Look Of Love (Part 1); Date Stamp; All Of My Heart; 4 Ever 2 Gether; The Look Of Love.

First released 1982
UK peak chart position: 1
USA peak chart position: 24

165. SEPTEMBER OF MY YEARS
Frank Sinatra

Released shortly before Frank Sinatra's 50th birthday, this album predictably found the singer in a warm and reflective mood. Conductor-arranger Gordon Jenkins provided a string-laden setting for a mixture of songs old and new, including Sammy Cahn and Jimmy Van Heusen's specially written title number. Released in the middle of the beat boom, it was awarded Grammys for album of the year and Sinatra's best male vocal performance on one of the tracks, 'It Was A Very Good Year' (Erwin Drake), and provided a great deal of musical comfort for many middle-aged, former 'Swingin' Lovers'.

Septmeber Of My Years; How Old Am I; Don't Wait Too Long; It Gets Lonely Early; This Is All I Ask; Last Night When We Were Young; The Man In The Looking Glass; It Was A Very Good Year; When The Wind Was Green; Hello Young Lovers; I see It Now; Once Upon A Time; September Song.

First released 1965
UK peak chart position: did not chart
USA peak chart position: 5

166. PLASTIC ONO BAND
John Lennon

Now referred to as the primal scream album, Lennon allowed his tonsils and heart to bleed in a powerful exhumation of many of his demons. The plea for his lost mother in 'Mother' is as desperate as his realisation expressed in 'I Found Out', with 'I've had religion from Jesus to Paul'. His Yoko songs are also a reassurance that throughout this therapy his Yoko was always there, and history has shown that it was his Yoko that got him through. 'Working Class Hero' is another equally powerful track, even though John was not. Essential listening for Beatles students with strong hearts.

Mother; Hold On; I Found Out; Working Class Hero; Isolation; Remember; Love; Well Well Well; Look At Me; God; My Mummy's Dead.

First released 1970
UK peak chart position: 11
USA peak chart position: 10

167. THE LAST RECORD ALBUM
Little Feat

Many of us remembered Little Feat albums by the wonderful Neon Park cover paintings. The famous giant jelly graces this one. The music within is equally delectable the horizontal mambo on 'Romance Dance' and 'All That You Dream' as they celebrate by singing 'I've Been Down But Not Like This Before'. The album's star is the tear jerking beautiful ballad 'Long Distance Love'. Very probably Lowell's greatest song, its gentle understatement and simplicity is pure genius. An essential Little Feat album. The CD reissue contains two extra tracks from the live album *Waiting For Columbus*.

Romance Dance; All That You Dream; Long Distance Love; Day Or Night; One Love; Down Below The Borderline; Somebody's Leavin'; Mercenary Territory.

First released 1975
UK peak chart position: 36
USA peak chart position: 36

168. 461 OCEAN BOULEVARD
Eric Clapton

It's really only 'Give Me Strength' which provides a hint of the emergence from anguish and peril which *461 Ocean Boulevard* represents. Clapton had descended into the depths of a terminal heroine habit, invisible to the world for two years until Pete Townshend organised his come-back concert at the Rainbow. 461 followed, and showcases a relaxed Clapton, drawing as much on his songwriting ability and gentle vocal style as on his legendary guitar skills. Marley's 'I Shot The Sheriff' was a worldwide hit, and 'Let It Grow' and 'Get Ready' (written with Yvonne Elliman) are still regular concert favourites. This was Clapton's new dawn.

Get Ready; Give Me Strength; I Can't Hold Out Much Longer; I Shot The Sheriff; Let It Grow; Mainline Florida; Motherless Children; Please Be With Me; Steady Rollin' Man; Willie And The Hand Jive.

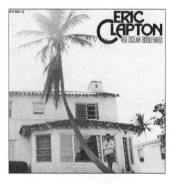

First released 1974
UK peak chart position: 3
USA peak chart position: 1

169. VIVA HATE
Morrissey

When internal strife killed off the Smiths, attention focused on ex-lead singer Morrissey. His response was a self-assured debut album in which echoes of his former group, notably on 'Suedehead', largely gave way for softer, orchestrated material. Aided by Durutti Column guitarist Vini Reilly and sometimes Smiths' producer Stephen Street, Morrissey crooned in now-accustomed fashion, toying with melody lines and articulating high-camp angst for a wan generation. The ambition of 'Late Night, Maudlin Street' is balanced by the crispness of 'Everyday Is Like Sunday' and for those worried that Morrissey would flounder without Smiths' foil Johnny Marr, *Viva Hate* is a singularly confident riposte.

Alsation Cousin; Little Man, What Now?; Everyday Is Like Sunday; Bengali In Platforms; Angel, Angel, Down we Go Together; Late Night, Maudlin Street; Suedehead; Break Up The Family; The Ordinary Boys; I Don't Mind If You Forgive Me; Dial A Cliche; Margaret On The Guillotine.

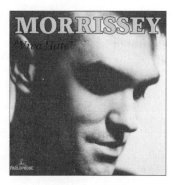

First released 1988
UK peak chart position: 1
USA peak chart position: 48

170. FOR YOUR PLEASURE
Roxy Music

The second album from the purveyors of art and glamour and three out of five members appear left handed, according to the inner sleeve. This put them way out of balance from the rest of the world, and for a while their wondrously inventive music put them out of step with the music being fed to us. The energy of tracks such as 'Editions Of You' still incites the need to dance. And how many times did you wait patiently for Ferry to get to the 'but you blew my mind' bit in 'Every Dream Home A Heartache' just so you could hear Manzanera's excellent phased guitar.

Do The Strand; Beauty Queen; Strictly Confidential; Editions Of You; Every Dream Home A Heartache; The Bogus Man; Grey Lagoons; For Your Pleasure.

First released 1973
UK peak chart position: 4
USA peak chart position: 193

171. A KIND OF MAGIC
Queen

Produced, in part, for the film, *Highlander*, *A Kind Of Magic* celebrated Queen as intelligent, speculative travellers, utilising newfound technology with their instantly recognisable body of harmony and pointed arrangements. The title track, with its accompanying part animated/part action video, was a finger clicking build that spiralled gorgeously into whoops of sheer delight. 'One Vision' celebrated their dazzling, show stealing set at Live Aid. while, 'Who Wants To Live Forever' yearned majestically. 'Friends Will Be Friends' a guaranteed, arm-waving, crowd pleaser. A gracious and graceful pleasure.

Princes Of The Universe; A Kind Of Magic; One Year Of Love; Pain Is So Close To Pleasure; Friends Will Be Friends; Who Wants To Live Forever; Gimme The Prize; Don't Lose Your Head; One Vision.

First released 1986
UK peak chart position: 1
USA peak chart position: 46

172. THE KICK INSIDE
Kate Bush

Discovered and nurtured by Pink Floyd's Dave Gilmour, Kate Bush burst into an unsuspecting world with the dramatic 'Wuthering Heights'. The ambitiousness of this startling single was carried over into the singer's debut album where already imaginative compositions were enriched by her evocative falsetto. Bush's intonation expressed a variety of emotions. Alternately coy, playful or sensual, she uses her voice to swoop and glide around the material, enhancing the imagery posed by graphic lyrics. Sympathetic accompaniment added weight to a collection in which the artist's purposeful single-mindedness was already apparent.

Moving; Saxophone Song; Strange Phenomena; Kite; The Man With The Child In His Eyes; Wuthering Heights; James And The Cold Gun; Feel It; Oh To Be In Love; L'amour Looks Something Like You; Them Heavy People; Room For The Life; The Kick Inside.

First released 1978
UK peak chart position: 3
USA peak chart position: did not chart

173. Rock 'N' Roll Animal
Lou Reed

Lou turned from the minimalist fuelled on anger and betrayal to full blown, heavy metal superstar for this album. A gloriously live revamping and workout of his older hits filled with a strutting confidence that reed's audience had never fully experienced before. Ferocity was at an optimum with tough reworkings of, 'White Light', 'White Heat,' 'Sweet Jane' and 'Lady Day' among others, all recorded as part of a set at New York's Academy Of Music. The following year, 1974, *Lou Reed Live* appeared, culled from the same set. Purists may have been galled by his approach, but . . . *Animal* was to earn Reed his first gold disc.

Intro; Sweet Jane; White Light; White Heat; Heroin; Lady Day; Rock And Roll.

First released 1974
UK peak chart position: 26
USA peak chart position: 45

174. Arc Of A Diver
Steve Winwood

With a glorious voice that sounds as if he's just swallowed something terminally sticky, Winwood has the advantage of instant recognition. Add to this a musicianship which has been employed in sessions for most major recording artists and the result is a prodigious talent which runs like a vein of gold through rock music since the mid-60s. *Arc Of A Diver*, released at the end of 1980 after a long period of self-imposed retreat, is a triumphant resurgence. With lyrical contributions by Viv Stanshall (the rich imagery of the title track) and Will Jennings, Winwood never falls into the trap of shaming the music with sub-standard words. Another musical genius.

While You See A Chance; Second Hand Woman; Slowdown Sunset; Spanish Dancer; Night Train; Dust; Arc Of A Diver.

First released 1980
UK peak chart position: 13
USA peak chart position: 3

175. Autobahn
Kraftwerk

Germanic in approach and delivery this record gets under the skin and infuriates as you find yourself compelled to hum the melodies. A significant record in the development of electronic music, and not to be confused with other 'kraut rock' efforts from the school of mid-70s prog. This is where countless bands borrowed riffs - passages of the Cure, Depeche Mode, Joy Division, New Order are to be found amongst the five lengthy tracks. Don't be fooled Kraftwork were there at least five years in advance. Great for driving on the motorway!

Autobahn; Kometenmelodie 1; Kometenmelodie 2; Mitternacht; Morgenspaziergang.

First released 1975
UK peak chart position: 4
USA peak chart position: 5

176. ESCAPE
Journey

One of America's biggest rock bands. Journey managed to achieve a perfect blend of spirited and soulful AOR that brought them both commercial and critical success. With Steve Perry's blistering vocal range and Neal Schon's colourful shading of sounds, they created an album that was neither understated or overblown. Their songwriting skill as a band was extraordinary, passing quickly from fond balladeering to hard rock in an assured instant. From the astounding, 'Don't Stop Believing' to the quiet sanctity of, 'Open Arms', their all round ability still astounds.

Don't Stop Believing; Stone In Love; Who's Crying Now; Keep On Running; Still They Ride; Escape; Lay It Down; Dead Or Alive; Mother, Father; Open Arms.

First released 1981
UK peak chart position: 32
USA peak chart position: 1

177. HEART
Heart

The Wilson sisters strode wilfully back into the international charts with their self-titled debut for Capitol Records. Drawing on outside writers to help develop the project, they created an album of enormous musical wealth that charted internationally with a host of successful spin-off singles. With Ron Nevison's lush production and the Wilsons soulful vocals, tracks such as 'What About Love', 'Never', and the yearning 'These Dreams' were guaranteed sellers. while the band still rocked majestically for, 'If Looks Could Kill', and 'Wolf' especially.

If Looks Could Kill; What About Love; Never; These Dreams; Wolf; All Eyes; Nobody Home; Nothin' At All; What He Don't Know; Shellshock.

First released 1985
UK peak chart position: 19
USA peak chart position: 1

178. IN MY TRIBE
10,000 Maniacs

Natalie Merchant is one of those writers with an uncanny ability to portray the minutiae of life with pinpoint accuracy and detached humour. The songs on *In My Tribe* cover the difficulty of getting up in the morning ('Like The Weather'), her sister's wedding ('My Sister Rose') and childhood holidays ('Verdi Cries'), as well as relationships, drinking, corporal punishment and soldiering. Merchant writes free-flowing prose songs and performs them impeccably, ably assisted by the other Maniacs and the production of Peter Asher. All slightly off-the-wall, but none the worse for that.

What's The Matter Here?; Hey Jack Kerouac; Like The Weather; Cherry Tree; Painted Desert; Don't Talk; Peace Train; Gun Shy; My Sister Rose; Campfire Son, A; City Of Angels; Verdi Cries.

First released 1987
UK peak chart position: did not chart
USA peak chart position: 37

179. BLOOD AND CHOCOLATE
Elvis Costello

This time around the Attractions are fronted by Napoleon Dynamite and perform with him as if they have known him for years. Napoleon trots out another powerful stream of angst, emotion and vitriol. Costello has so much lyrical frustration, he should be commissioned to write the entire top 40. 'I Want You' is one of the most powerful songs he has ever written, Elvis really opens up his soul and makes a public statement over a simple melody accompanied by Nick Lowe on acoustic guitar. The album has a similar in feel to Imperial Bedroom and one that needs the lyric sheet to be read, digested and acted upon. Costello might end up working for Relate.

Uncomplicated; I Hope You're Happy Now; Tokyo Storm Warning; Home Is Anywhere You Hang Your Head; I Want You; Honey Are You Straight Or Are You Blind?; Blue Chair; Battered Old Bird; Crimes Of Paris; Poor Napoleon; Next Time Around.

First released 1986
UK peak chart position: 16
USA peak chart position: 84

180. DIRE STRAITS
Dire Straits

They do look happy and innocent on the back of the sleeve, blissfully unaware of the mantle they would be thrown on and of the millions they would be expected to please. This for many, is the only Dire Straits album, yet it appears way down the listing compared to its famous 'brother'. Knopfler sounded like he meant it on 'Sultans Of Swing' and who can forget the cheek of his lyric in the melancholic 'Wild West End'? 'I saw you walking out Shaftsbury Avenue, excuse me talking, I wanna marry you'. I hope Mr Knopfler has not forgotten this album.

Down To The Waterline; Water Of Love; Setting Me Up; Six Blade Knife; Southbound Again; Sultans Of Swing; Wild West End; In The Gallery.

First released 1978
UK peak chart position: 5
USA peak chart position: 2

181. THE PRETENDER
Jackson Browne

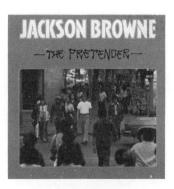

Jackson Browne's literate Californian music reached a creative peak with this exceptional release. A pensive, introspective songwriter, he combines a poetic perceptiveness with subtle melodies, resulting in an engaging music reliant on suggestion, rather than power. *The Pretender* contains several of his finest songs, particularly the lengthy title track and the melancholic 'Here Come Those Tears Again'. Superb support from guitarist David Lindley emphasises the nuances in Browne's work, gently adding to its poignancy. Recorded following the suicide of the singer's wife, *The Pretender* provided Browne with an artistic carthesis which never slips into self-pity.

The Fuse; Your Bright Baby Blues; Linda Paloma; Here Comes Those Tears Again; Only Child; Daddy's Time; Sleep's Dark And Silent Gate; Pretender.

First released 1976
UK peak chart position: 26
USA peak chart position: 5

182. IF ONLY I COULD REMEMBER MY NAME
David Crosby

Although this was a highly successful album Crosby was later accused of being self-indulgent throughout. In recent years that has reversed as the amount of space he allowed fellow musicians is seen as a wholly unselfish record. The cream of San Francisco assembled, and in no particular order we can pick out Jerry Garcia, Phil Lesh, Jack Casady, Paul Kantner, Joni Mitchell and Grace Slick. Crosby moves from the humour in his modern day Jesse James story 'Cowboy Movie' to wondrous spiritual voice excursions in 'I'd Swear There Was Somebody Here' and 'Tampalpais High'. The playing is faultless throughout.

Music Is Love; Cowboy Movie; Tamalpais High; Laughing; What Are Their Names; Traction In The Rain; Song With No Words; Tree With No Leaves; Orleans; I'd Swear There Was Somebody Here.

First released 1971
UK peak chart position: 12
USA peak chart position: 12

183. SINGS FOR ONLY THE LONELY
Frank Sinatra

Asked to reveal the mood of this album prior to it's release, Frank Sinatra (tongue in cheek) said: 'Put it this way - we discarded 'Gloomy Sunday' (the 'suicide' song) because it was too swingin'!' Bleak, it certainly is, but with the singer at the height of his powers singing a classy set of saloon songs superbly arranged and conducted by Nelson Riddle, this is still the number 1 album of all-time for many a Sinatra aficionado. Even in the 90s he is compelled to include one of the tracks, 'One For My Baby', complete with the distinctive piano introduction, in every concert performance. The album's cover, with it's sad clown-face picture, won a Grammy Award.

Only The Lonely; Angel Eyes; What's New?; It's A Lonesome Old Town; Willow Weep For Me; Good-bye; Blues In The Night; Guess I'll Hang My Tears Out To Dry; Ebb Tide; Spring Is Here; Gone With The Wind; One For My Baby.

First released 1958
UK peak chart position: 5
USA peak chart position: 1

184. RAIN DOGS
Tom Waits

Tom Waits discarded his bohemian sage persona with the radical *Swordfishtrombones* and this follow-up release synthesised and developed themes from that groundbreaking album. Ever-shifting percussive textures are supported, where applicable, by horns or Farfisa organ and several guest musicians, including Rolling Stone Keith Richards, contribute to its melange. Waits' bourbon-laced voice is as riveting as ever, intoning lyrics which are, at various times, touching, evocative, sly or simply funny. His off-kilter perceptions encompass country, polkas and heart-rendering ballads, each of which he expresses with consummate ease. *Rain Dogs* is yet another strong statement from a highly innovative artist.

Singapore; Clap Hands; Cemetary Polka; Jockey Full Of Boubon; Tango Till They're Sore; Big Black Maria; Diamonds And Gold; Hang Down Your Head; Time; Rain Dogs; Midtown; Ninth And Headpin; Gun Street Girl; Union Square; Blind Love; Walking Spanish; Downtown Train; Bride Of Raindog; Anywhere I Lay My Head.

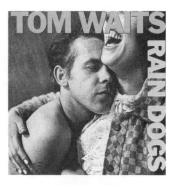

First released 1985
UK peak chart position: 29
USA peak chart position: 181

185. STEPHEN STILLS
Stephen Stills

This outstanding solo debut came at a particularly successful and creative time for Stills. in the space of couple of years he made two solo albums, released the superb Manassas double album and was part of CSNY. He was also living in England, which explains the appearance of many England-based musicians from Eric Clapton to Ringo Starr and even Jimi Hendrix. This varied set shows Stills to be precociously talented as he tackled memphis soul, folk, blues, rock and good time pop with the still fresh-sounding 'Love The One You're With'. Equally arresting is 'Black Queen' allegedly recorded after Stills had downed a bottle of tequila, and was 'drunk as a skunk'.

Love The One You're With; Do For The Others; Church (Part Of Someone); Old Times, Good Times; Go Back Home; Sit Yourself Down; To A Flame; Black Queen; Cherokee; We Are Not Helpless.

First released 1970
UK peak chart position: 30
USA peak chart position: 3

186. BAD COMPANY
Bad Company

This is not heavy metal, this is not rock, this is heavy rock. There is a difference and Bad Company were it. Coming out of the blues-based band Free, Paul Rodgers immediately found good company with the talented Mick Ralphs. Although subsequent albums reworked the same basic theme, this is the standard by which *Bad Company* should be judged. Tightly structured songs, driving beat, immaculate guitar and of course the definitive vocals of Rodgers. Just replay 'Can't Get Enough', 'Bad Company' and 'Ready For Love' as a reminder and finish with the gentle 'Seagull', one of Rodgers/Ralphs' finest compositions.

Can't Get Enough; Rock Steady; Ready For Love; Don't Let Me Down; Bad Company; The Way I Choose; Movin' On; Seagull.

First released 1974
UK peak chart position: 3
USA peak chart position: 1

187. LIKE A PRAYER
Madonna

Madonna's exquisite sense of the pop song and suitably stylish aesthetic to match, was pushed to the hilt for 1989's *Like A Prayer*. Sporting a bare midriff and a stylishly dark bob, she immediately set the Moral Majority up in arms with the title track's video depicting, among other things, a negro Christ and a hillside of burning crosses. The song though, was as strong and as dazzling as the images. Before deciding on utilising a constant barrage of public sexuality over songs, Madonna made great records. Highlights here include the sexy bubblegum of, 'Cherish' and the delightful, 'Express Yourself'. Great pop to go.

Like A Prayer; Love Song; Promise To Try; Dear Jessie; Keep It Together; Act Of Contrition; Express Yourself; Till Death Us Do Part; Cherish; Oh Father; Spanish Eyes.

First released 1989
UK peak chart position: 1
USA peak chart position: 1

188. LETS DANCE
David Bowie

Bowie's best work since *Heroes* at that time, and the critics responded with relief as much as anything else. The Nile Rogers production was an inspired partnership as Bowie entered another phase in his chameleon-like career - this time rock/disco. Even the late Stevie Ray Vaughan was added to sharpen the guitar parts, although the overall impression is that this is not a guitar album. Had that been the case then surely Mick Ronson would have been hired. Rarely has an album opened with three blockbuster tracks, 'Modern Love', 'China Girl' and the title track.

Modern Love; China Girl; Let's Dance; Without You; Ricochet; Criminal World; Cat People (Putting Out Fire); Shake It.

First released 1983
UK peak chart position: 1
USA peak chart position: 4

189. PEARL
Janis Joplin

Released posthumously in 1971, *Pearl* is a startling, multi-coloured portrait of major artist bestriding her material with consumate ease. From the chugging 'Move Over' to the portentous 'Get It While You Can' the power never wavers. 'Me And Bobby McGee' leaves all other versions at the starting blocks (it was a number one in the USA), while the a cappella 'Mercedes Benz' demonstrates that she only needed the Full Tilt Boogie Band to add colour, not depth. The balance is perfect on 'Half Moon', which sounds like Little Feat backing Grace Slick with laryngitis. If only there was more.

Move Over; Cry Baby; A Woman Left Lonely; Half Moon; Buried Alive In The Blues; Me And Bobby McGee; Mercedes Benz; Get It While You Can; Trust Me.

First released 1971
UK peak chart position: 50
USA peak chart position: 1

190. SAILOR
Steve Miller Band

Long before Miller discovered the art of writing great short pop songs with infectious guitar licks he had a dynamite band that featured Boz Scaggs. This incandescent album was their last together and for the vast majority of Miller followers it remains the pinnacle. Sandwiched in between their love for the blues and R&B with 'Gangster Of Love' and 'You're So Fine' are great rock tracks; 'Living In The USA' and 'Dime-A-Dance Romance. the desert island choice however is the imaginative instrumental 'Song For Our Ancestors', close your eyes and actually hear ferry boats entering the harbour, without artificial stimulants.

Song For Our Ancestors; Dear Mary; My Friend; Living In The USA; Quicksilver Girl; Lucky Man; Gangster Of Love; You're So Fine; Overdrive; Dime-A-Dance Romance.

First released 1968
UK peak chart position: did not chart
USA peak chart position: 24

191. CLOSE TO THE EDGE
Yes

Taken as a musical whole this suite of three parts is very sound, what does begin to jar are some of the lyrics. In the 90s, even with the hippie revival and new age travellers lyrics such as 'my eyes convinced eclipsed with the younger moon attained with love' do make you shake your head. What on earth are they going on about? Yes have been shabbily treated by the press over the years and the appearance of two of their albums in the list is in some way a forgiveness. Steve Howe's guitar sounds great, Squire's bass punches through, but what makes the album so good is the melodic theme that runs through.

Solid Time Of Change; Total Mass Retain; I Get Up, I Get Down; Seasons Of Man; And You And I; Cord Of Life; Eclipse; The Preacher; Teacher; Siberian Khatru.

First released 1972
UK peak chart position: 4
USA peak chart position: 3

192. DAYDREAM
Lovin Spoonful

At least one album from this stellar new York pop band should be in every collection and *Daydream* narrowly pipped *Do You Believe In Magic* and *Hums Of.* John Sebastian was a lyrical craftsman and master of short humorous love songs. Lengthy titles that said exactly what they meant, 'Didn't Want To Have To Do It' or 'You Didn't Have To Be So Nice' (an unforgettable intro), both glorious. Sebastian, Boone, Yanovsky and Butler were no slouches at good time blues either, for example 'Bald Headed Lena' and 'Jug Band Music'. It is however the title track that brings the biggest smiles and happiest memories.

Daydream; There She Is; It's Not Time Now; Warm Baby; Day Blues; Let The Boy Rock & Roll; Jug Band Music; Didn't Want To Have To Do It; You Didn't Have To Be So Nice; Bald Headed Lena; Butchie's Tune; Big Noise From Speonk.

First released 1966
UK peak chart position: 8
USA peak chart position: 10

193. STRANDED
Roxy Music

Roxy Music subverted a jaded progressive rock scene with an original blend of science fiction imagery, art-school nonce and eccentric music. Vocalist Bryan Ferry sang in a camp-styled croon, part Noël Coward, part Lou Reed, and having dismissed leadership rival Brian Eno, assumed full control of artistic direction for the group's third album. *Stranded* introduced violinist Eddie Jobson whose contributions slotted perfectly alongside reed player Andy Mackay and guitarist Phil Manzanera. A sense of cohesion permeates the set, group members contribute lyrically, but there was no denying that Roxy Music here represent Ferry's vision. Melodically strong, the album provides an ideal structure for his quirky intonation, resulting in a heady mix of experimentation and commercial acumen.

Street Life; Just Like You; Amazon; Psalm; Serenade; Song For Europe; Mother Of Pearl; Sunset.

First released 1973
UK peak chart position: 1
USA peak chart position: 186

194. NIGHT AND DAY
Joe Jackson

Jackson's great New York album, full of atmosphere, quality musicianship and mature arrangements that put him way beyond the pop of his first two albums. The cosmopolitan flavour is captured on the latin styled 'Cancer', Jackson's romantic nature is exposed on the beautiful 'Would You Be My Number Two' and the album's headliner is the modern classic 'Steppin' Out' with its unforgettable bass and piano intro. this album should have been a platform to make Jackson an international artist, for some reason his career faltered and was eventually dropped by his record company. Repeated radio play of 'Steppin' Out' should keep this album in print.

Another World; Chinatown; TV Age; Target; Would You Be My Number Two; Steppin' Out; Breaking Us In Two; Cancer; Real Men; Slow Song.

First released 1982
UK peak chart position: 3
USA peak chart position: 4

195. BAND ON THE RUN
Wings

Paul McCartney's immediate solo career was largely viewed as lightweight. This album restated artistic strengths missing from earlier releases, reclaiming the artist's grasp of pop's dynamics and hooklines. From the pulsating abandonment of 'Jet' to the measured control of 'Let Me Roll It', *Band On The Run* is a tight, disciplined collection, full of contrast and commitment. McCartney's unfettered self-confidence permeates a selection which not only forced commentators to revise their views, but also asserted the singer's individual identity, rather than that of ex-Beatle.

Band On The Run; Jet; Bluebird; Mrs. Vanderbilt; Let Me Roll It; Mamunia; No Words; Picasso's Last Words; 1985.

First released 1973
UK peak chart position: 1
USA peak chart position: 1

196. POCKET FULL OF KRYPTONITE
Spin Doctors

The Steve Miller Band of the 90s has made a huge impression with this irresistible package. Crammed full of great riffs and licks, tight playing and singing with enthusiasm. The title track together with the wry 'Little Miss Can't Be Wrong' were both hit singles in the wake of the excellent 'Two Princes'. One of the few occasions where the cliche of rhyming 'baby' with 'maybe' is completely acceptable. On the European edition the three extra tracks show off their ability as a live band. Unpretentious rock music for the 90s and a memorable debut.

Jimmy Olsen's Blues; What Time Is It?; Little Miss Can't Be Wrong; Forty Or Fifty; Refrigerator Car; Two Princes; Off My Line; How Could You Want Him (When You Could Have Me?); Shinbone Alley; Yo Mamas A Pajama; Sweet Widow; Stepped On A Crock.

First released 1992
UK peak chart position: 2
USA peak chart position: 3

197. SOME GIRLS
Rolling Stones

One of the few latter period Stones albums that stands up to any real scrutiny in light of their magnificent catalogue. Strolling out as the 70s were diminishing and punk was beginning to inflict a stranglehold and cultivate a disdain for anything over 30, the Stones once more enlivened their audience with the ability to surprise. Disdaining the contemporary mood and their earlier R&B leanings, which they'd later readopt again, for funkier ground. Irresistible undercurrents of rock 'n' roll patiently rumbled still and, 'Miss You' and the especially excellent, 'Beast Of Burden', showed them still capable of greatness.

Miss You; When The Whip Comes Down; Just My Imagination; Some Girls; Lies; Faraway Eyes; Respectable; Before They Make Me Run; Beast Of Burden; Shattered.

First released 1978
UK peak chart position: 2
USA peak chart position: 1

198. I WANT TO SEE THE BRIGHT LIGHTS TONIGHT
Richard And Linda Thompson

The debut album from Richard and Linda started a career that has placed Thompson in the 'forever to be a huge cult figure' bracket. They did everything on this album, bar make the charts and sell records. Folk, rock, country and pop are brilliantly covered in a tasteful and controlled package which is a delight from beginning to end with Linda singing beautifully. Concert favourites such as 'Calvary Cross' and 'When I Get To the Border' are to be found here. It is not flippant to say that Richard Thompson is a world class songwriter and guitarist, albeit totally under appreciated.

When I Get To The Border; The Calvery Cross; Withered And Died; I Want To See The Bright Lights Tonight; Down Where The Drunkards Roll; We Sing Hallelujah; Has He Got A Friend For Me?; The Little Beggar Girl; The End Of The Rainbow; Great Valerio.

First released 1974
UK peak chart position: did not chart
USA peak chart position: did not chart

199. CLIFF SINGS
Cliff Richard

Britain's greatest hitmaker has never been critically acclaimed for making a great album and Cliff's monumental contribution is for dozen's of memorable pop singles. It is fitting to note that this is his second album, and strangely his most appealing. This is Cliff, the cute sneering rocker whizzing through tried and tested rock 'n' roll classics. This falls into the pop category because the tracks sound like 'beat group' music and images of bad British B-movies spring to mind. Lots of Bigsby tremelo arms and echo from the Drifters make this a timeless period piece, even though the title is lame.

Blue Suede Shoes; The Snake And The Bookworm; Here Comes Summer; I'll String Along With You; Embraceable You; As Time Goes By; The Touch Of Your Lips; Twenty Flight Rock; Pointed Toe Shoes; Mean Woman Blues; I'm Walking; I Don't Know Why; Little Things Mean A Lot; Somewhere Along The Way; That's My Desire.

First released 1959
UK peak chart position: 2
USA peak chart position: did not chart

200. TOYS IN THE ATTIC
Aerosmith

A truly inventive Aerosmith album. Still suffused with a gloriously raspy sense of the blues, but quietly evocative in its timbre and approach. Tyler working out lyrics that were so much more than simple cars and girls fodder, 'Adam's Apple' theorising that creation could quite possibly have occurred with an alien mothership landing on earth and setting the wheels of the human race in motion. 'Sweet Emotion' throbbed slowly into life, 'Big Ten Inch Record', a salty R&B workout, while 'You See Me Crying' was heightened and given body by a warm orchestration. A clear steeple of great work among a skyline of repeating successes.

Toys In The Attic; Uncle Salty; Adam's Apple; Walk This Way; Big Ten Inch Record; Sweet Emotion; No More No More; Round And Round; You See Me Crying.

First released 1975
UK peak chart position: did not chart
USA peak chart position: 11

201. EVERY PICTURE TELLS A STORY
Rod Stewart

Rod Stewart's third solo album brought the singer long-awaited commercial acclaim. Its combination of strong, original songs and plum cover versions was finely judged as the artist paid tribute to mentors and declared his own craft. Members of Stewart's regular group, the Faces, provide intuitive support without the sense of compromise apparent on their own recordings. The singer's voice was rarely better; his interpretation of the Temptations '(I Know I'm) Losing You' brought new dimensions to a Tamla/Motown classic. The highlight is, inevitably, 'Maggie May', one of pop's immutable anthems, but the remaining selections contain a similar sense of purpose. This consistency gives the set its lasting value.

True Blue; You Wear It Well; I Don't Want To Discuss It; You're My Girl; Sweet Little Rock 'N' Roller; Sailor; Dixie Toot; Street Fighting Man; Every Picture Tells A Story; Seems Like a Long Time; That's Alright; Amazing Grace; Tomorrow Is Such A Long Time; Henry; Maggie May; Mandolin Wind; (I Know I'm) Losing You; Reason To Believe.

First released 1971
UK peak chart position: 1
USA peak chart position: 1

202. QUEEN 2
Queen

The first of two Queen albums released in 1974 that elevated them high into the British consciousness. As mystically embracing as their self-titled debut, references to Ogres and Fairies and, unsurprisingly, Queens, abounded. But it was their sense of musical adventure. May's evocative guitar sound, and daring arrangements, combined with Mercury's sense of the grandiose and unique vocal style that indicated early on that they weren't a band who were afraid of innovation. 'Funny How Love Is', and the successful, 'Seven Seas Of Rhye', hinted at an album and band quite capable of changing the face of musical history.

Procession; Father To Son; White Queen (As It Began); Some Day One Day; The Loser In The End; Orge Battle; The Fairy Feller's Master Stroke; Nevermore; The March Of The Black Queen; Funny How Love Is; Seven Seas Of Rhye.

First released 1974
UK peak chart position: 5
USA peak chart position: 49

203. Twelve Dreams Of Dr Sardonicus
Spirit

The charismatic and legendary Randy California starred alongside his step-father Ed Cassidy with the bare chested and handsome Jay Ferguson. Together with Mark Andes and pianist John Locke this west coast band were one of the finest to come out of the late 60s. This is such an excellent album its hard to imagine that Spirit were not huge band. They hit a peak with this suite of songs right from the word go, 'Nothing To Hide' tells us he's married to the same bride, on to 'Nature's Way' who's telling us something's wrong. This is the concept album we never understood what the concept was.

Nothing To Hide; Nature's Way; Animal Zoo; Love Has Found A Way; Why Can't I Be Free; Mr. Skin; Space Child; When I Touch You; Street Worm; Life Has Just Begun; Morning Will Come; Soldier; We've Got A Lot To Learn; Potatoland (Theme); Open Up Your Heart; Morning Light; Potatoland (Prelude); Potatoland (Introduction); Turn To The Right; Donut House; Fish Fry Road; Information; My Friend.

First released 1970
UK peak chart position: did not chart
USA peak chart position: 63

204. Fire And Water
Free

Free emerged from the British blues' boom with a tight, muscular style which framed Paul Rodgers' throaty voice. Guitarist Paul Kossoff provides the perfect foil with incisive, measured solos exemplified by his contribution to 'All Right Now'. This successful single transformed the group from club to star status. Free's unhurried, careful intensity is captured perfectly on this album's title track and 'Oh I Wept', two songs charged with emotion. Where many contemporaries tended towards excess, Free implied a resonant power, particularly through Andy Fraser's liquid bass work, which weaves between the melody lines, rather than asserting them. *Fire And Water* is a high spot in rock; rather than merely asserting masculine qualities, this album also shows a rare vulnerability.

Oh I Wept; Remember; Heavy Load; Fire And Water; Mr. Big; Don't Say You Love Me; All Right Now.

First released 1970
UK peak chart position: 2
USA peak chart position: 17

205. Shoot Out The Lights
Richard And Linda Thompson

The world's most underrated man, although Thompson must tire of hearing it so often. Together with his ex-wife Linda they made a series of quite brilliant albums that garnered heaps of praise and minimal sales. This is another slice of perfection that veers from whimsical fun in 'Wall Of Death' to desperate emotions in 'Shoot Out the Lights' which features the definitive Thompson guitar solo. Critics have often been accused of hyping artists, try as they may they can't do it with this one. Time will tell but this album should be a hundred places higher.

Man In Need; Walking On A Wire; Don't Renage On Our Love; Just The Motion; Shoot Out The Lights; Backstreet Slide; Did She Jump Or Was She Pushed?; Wall Of Death.

First released 1982
UK peak chart position: did not chart
USA peak chart position: did not chart

206. FULL MOON FEVER
Tom Petty

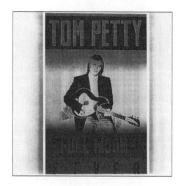

This album is just damn good fun - a great collection of easy-going rock songs, crafted not to change the world, but certainly to make it just a little brighter. Petty's first solo project (without the Heartbreakers), *Full Moon Fever* shares the good-time feel of the Traveling Wilburys' contemporary 'Handle With Care'. This is not altogether surprising; Jeff Lyne co-produced and George Harrison and Roy Orbison guest. The only non-Petty composition is a Byrd-bettering version of 'Feel A Whole Lot Better', while 'Zombie Zoo', a bewildered parent's diatribe on the kids of today, comes perilously close to social commentary.

Free Fallin'; I Won't Back Down; Love Is A Long Road; Face In The Crowd, A; Runnin' Down A Dream; Feel A Whole Lot Better; Yer So Bad; Depending On You; Apartment Song, The; Alright For Now; Mind With A Heart Of It's Own, A; Zombie Zoo.

First released 1989
UK peak chart position: 8
USA peak chart position: 3

207. BREAKFAST IN AMERICA
Supertramp

Often forgotten, and when finally remembered it is usually for the often tedious, but huge selling *Crime Of The Century*. This record cuts away the pomp and keeps it comparatively simple with some memorable songs and lyrics, for example in the title track a simple statement 'take a look at my girlfriend, she's the only one I've got', or the ridiculous simple rhymes in 'The Logical Song'. the painful truth of 'Goodbye Stranger' and 'Take The Long Way Home' are further irritatingly catchy songs. Sadly Supertramp were not able to build on this excellent collection.

Gone Hollywood; The Logical Song; Goodbye Stranger; Breakfast In America; Oh Darling; Take The Long Way Home; Lord Is It Mine; Just Another Nervous Wreck; Casual Conversation; Child Of Vision.

First released 1979
UK peak chart position: 3
USA peak chart position: 1

208. DUKE
Genesis

Surprisingly the only Genesis album to make the listings, trailing in the wake of Philip Collins. *Duke* was the record that shed their 'heavy prog' image and found them beginning to loosen up. Phil had grown in confidence following Peter Gabriel's departure and the band immediately became much tighter musically. In addition to the hit singles 'Dutchess', the buoyant 'Turn It On Again' and realism of a situation in 'Misunderstanding', there is the painful honesty of 'Please Don't Ask'. There have been bigger Genesis albums, but none have anywhere near as much heart.

Behind The Lines; Duchess; Guide Vocal; Man Of Our Time; Misunderstanding; Heathaze; Turn It On Again; Alone Tonight; Cul-de-sac; Please Don't Ask; Duke's End; Duke's Travels.

First released 1980
UK peak chart position: 1
USA peak chart position: 11

209. AVALON
Roxy Music

Like the Police, Roxy Music never outstayed their welcome and got out while on top. Their farewell album leaves a good taste in the mouth when remembering the doyens of art/rock. By the time of this album they had become immaculate smoothies, Ferry had taken to suits, Eno had long gone and Andy Mackay had kept his quiff but grown an extra chin. Appearances aside this is a lasting record and it proved to be one their most successful. 'More Than This', 'Take A Chance With Me' were both hit singles as was the title track on which Ferry at his most seductive informs us 'now the party's over, I'm so tired'. A most agreeable exit.

More Than This; The Space Between; India; While My Heart Is Still Beating; Main Thing; Take A Chance With Me; Avalon; To Turn You On; True To Life; Tara.

First released 1982
UK peak chart position: 1
USA peak chart position: 53

210. GREEN RIVER
Creedence Clearwater Revival

Creedence Clearwater Revival were part of a second wave of San Francisco groups, but unlike their geographical contemporaries, the quartet offered a disciplined music, indebted to 50s rock 'n' roll and southern 'swamp' styles. Leader, singer and songwriter John Fogerty possesses one of rock's most distinctive voices, his hoarse, urgent intonation matched by his group's mathematically precise drive. *Green River*, their third album, includes two million-selling singles, the title track and 'Bad Moon Rising', both of which encapsulate the Creedence metier. Remaining selections expose a similar economy, crammed with punchy hooklines, tight playing and incisive lyrics, taking inspiration from traditional styles, but in the process creating something unique.

Bad Moon Rising; Cross-tie Walker; Sinister Purpose; Night Time Is The Right Time; Green River; Commotion; Tombstone Shadow; Wrote A Song For Everyone; Lodi.

First released 1969
UK peak chart position: 20
USA peak chart position: 1

211. ME AND MY SHADOWS
Cliff Richard

By the time this album was released Cliff had name-changed his Drifters to the Shadows and they were seen as a permanent recording unit. He had also abandoned the American rock 'n' roll cover versions and started down the path of straight pop. His Shadows were unknowingly about to become the most famous instrumental group in the world with their own records. This is the best example of Cliff being 'backed by a beat combo'. The recording although primitive is quite perfect and demonstrated what a tight unit they were until strings and orchestration eclipsed their later recordings.

I'm Gonna Get You; You And I; I Cannot Find A True Love; Evergreen Tree; She's Gone; Left Out Again; You're Just The One To Do It; Lamp Of Love; Choppin' 'N' Changin'; We Have It Made; Tell Me; Gee Whizz It's You; I Love You So; I'm Willing To Learn; I Don't Know; Working After School.

First released 1960
UK peak chart position: 2
USA peak chart position: did not chart

212. SWEET DREAMS
Eurythmics

Still finding their way after a disjointed debut album following the break-up of the Tourists, Annie and Dave found commercial success with this, their 'programmed' album. the electronic drums and keyboards fit well into the eerie and mysterious qualities of the songs (Edward de Bono is thanked on the sleeve). For those that thought synthesizer pop was the answer during the lull of the 80s then the Eurythmics were it, they did it better than most. It will be good to see these songs performed by a performing band when they eventually reform, maybe in the 21st century.

Love Is A Stranger; I've Got An Angel; Wrap It Up; I Could Give You (A Mirror); The Walk; Sweet Dreams (Are Made Of This); Jennifer; This Is The House; Somebody Told Me; This City Never Sleeps.

First released 1983
UK peak chart position: 3
USA peak chart position: 15

213. CHEAP THRILLS
Big Brother And The Holding Company

This ramshackle, sparkling and ear-shattering album from the band 'featuring' their lead vocalist Janis Joplin came out of the San Francisco rock scene in 1968. The full blown vocals from Janis sparred with the loose electric guitar of Sam Andrew and the finger picking-style of James Gurley and kept them apart from other bands in the area who courted folk and psychedelia. Both 'Piece Of My Heart' and 'Ball And Chain' are classics of their time and place and although the recording is flawed the atmosphere Joplin creates is riveting.

Combination Of The Two; I Need A Man To Love; Summertime; Piece Of My Heart; Turtle Blues; Oh Sweet Mary; Ball And Chain.

First released 1968
UK peak chart position: did not chart
USA peak chart position: 1

214. FACE TO FACE
Kinks

Sadly, the long and magnificent career of one of the finest songwriters of our age, Ray Davies, is not truly represented on album, other than greatest hits packages. While many Kinks albums appeared when compiling this book, the surprisingly low positions gained are due to having so many albums with butter spread thinly. This record summed up swinging London in the 60s and like its successor *Something Else* contained Ray's observations of ordinary people and situations. The album is strengthened by the classic 'Sunny Afternoon' but perceptive tracks such as 'Fancy', 'Dandy', 'Session Man' and 'Most Exclusive Residence For Sale' are gentle satires that give the record its heart.

Party Line; Rosy Won't You Please Come Home; Dandy; Too Much On My Mind; Session Man; Rainy Day In June; House In The Country; Holiday In Waikiki; Most Exclusive Residence For Sale; Fancy; Little Miss Queen Of Darkness; You're Looking Fine; Sunny Afternoon; I'll Remember.

First released 1967
UK peak chart position: 12
USA peak chart position: 135

215. BLOOD, SWEAT AND TEARS
Blood, Sweat And Tears

Their finest moment and a testimony to the best of the jazz/rock movement. Created by the legendary Al Kooper, the band were one of the major attractions throughout 1969. The album is bold, brassy and adventurous. Interpretations of Eric Satie music is followed by Traffic's 'Smiling Phases'. Hit singles galore were culled from this record; 'Spinning Wheel', You've Made Me So Very Happy', and 'And When I Die', not to forget a superb rendition of Billie Holiday's 'God Bless The Child'. And where is the superb voice of David Clayton-Thomas to be found today?

Variations On A Theme By Eric Satie (1st & 2nd Movement); Smiling Phases; Sometimes In Winter; More And More; And When I Die; God Bless The Child; Spinning Wheel; You've Made Me So Very Happy/Blues Part II; Variations On A Theme By Eric Satie (1st Movement).

First released 1969
UK peak chart position: 15
USA peak chart position: 1

216. INGÉNUE
k. d. lang

Emerging from her ambivalent affair with country music, lang assembled a solid collection of material for Ingénue, her most commercially successful album. The opening lines 'Save me/Save me from you/But pave me/The way to you' introduce a recurring theme – the agonising conflict between the pain and the ecstasy of love. This is serious stuff; anthems of introspection and cries for honesty illuminated with startling imagery. There are lighter moments too, particularly in 'Miss Chatelaine', and the omnipresent Ben Mink ensures that the country influence is not totally abandoned.

Save Me; The Mind Of Love; Miss Chatelaine; Wash Me Clean; So It Shall Be; Still Thrives This Love; Season Of Hollow Soul; Outside Myself; Tears Of Love Is Recall; Constant Craving.

First released 1992
UK peak chart position: 3
USA peak chart position: 18

217. COSMO'S FACTORY
Creedence Clearwater Revival

Described as the consummate singles' act, Creedence Clearwater Revival enhanced this reputation when three of the tracks included herein, 'Travelin' Band', 'Up Around The Bend' and 'Looking Out My Back Door', each achieved gold status. Such recordings fully captured the group's exciting brand of 50s-oriented rock 'n' roll, its urgency enhanced by the expressive voice of lead singer/songwriter John Fogerty. His ability to harness traditional pop but express it in a contemporary manner had been established over four previous albums and *Cosmos Factory* was no exception. Two extended selections, 'Ramble Tamble' and 'I Heard It Through The Grapevine', show a penchant for guitar workouts unexplored since the quartet's debut album and the combination of economy and experimentation captures an act at a creative peak.

Ramble Tamble; Before You Accuse Me; Lookin' Out My Back Door; Run Through The Jungle; Up Around The Bend; My Baby Left Me; Who'll Stop The Rain; I Heard It Through The Grapevine; Long As I Can See The Light; Travelin' Band; Ooby Dooby.

First released 1970
UK peak chart position: 1
USA peak chart position: 1

218. EAST SIDE STORY
Squeeze

In one of the smartest free transfer deals ever, Squeeze were able to plug the massive midfield gap left by the departing Jools Holland with the nimble fingered Paul Carrack. They gained an extra vocalist, and maybe there was no room for Carracks underrated and expressive voice. For many the album's best track was 'Tempted', with Carrack taking lead vocal (with help from producer Elvis Costello). Close behind in the queue is 'Someone Else's Bell', 'Is That Love', 'In Quintessence' – in fact the entire except maybe the uncomfortable chord/key change of 'F-Hole', which leads into 'Tempted'. Deserves a higher place.

In Quintessence; Someone Else's Heart; Tempted; Piccadilly; There's No Tomorrow; A Woman's World; Is That Love; F-hole; Labelled With Love; Someone Else's Bell; Mumbo Jumbo; Vanity Fair; Messed Around.

First released 1981
UK peak chart position: 19
USA peak chart position: 44

219. HOLLAND
Beach Boys

Having finally rid themselves of a jejune image with *Surf's Up*, the Beach Boys continued the process with this ambitious album. The entire group had decamped to the titular country to record much of its content, a decision adding an emotional fission to its 'California Saga' trilogy. Although Brian Wilson's contribution was limited to two excellent songs, siblings Dennis and Carl rose to the occasion, with the latter's particularly impressive 'Trader'. The group's harmonies remain as distinctive as ever, while two recent additions to the line-up, Blondie Chaplin and Ricky Fataar, increased the vocal range and added new instrumental muscle. This became their best selling album for six years, *Holland* prepared the way for the Beach Boys 70s' comeback.

Sail On Sailor; Steamboat; California Saga; Big Surf; Beaks Of Eagles; The California Trader; Leaving This Town; Only With You; Funky Pretty; I'm The Pied Piper; Better Get Back In Bed; Magic Transistor; Radio Kingdom.

First released 1973
UK peak chart position: 20
USA peak chart position: 36

220. OGDENS NUT GONE FLAKE
Small Faces

Having begun a career as the archetypal Mod band, the Small Faces latterly embraced traces of flower-power's whimsy. Astute enough not to sacrifice their identity, the quartet retained a distinctive perspective, as evined by a string of superb pop singles, including 'Here Comes The Nice' and 'Itchycoo Park'. A sense of pop melody and adventurism culminated on this album which encompassed tongue-in-cheek fun ('Lazy Sunday') and passionate love songs ('Afterglow'). Steve Marriott's voice remains completely self-assured and the group's characteristic organ-based swell is often enhanced by P.P. Arnold's emotional backing vocals. Eccentric comedian Stanley Unwin narrates the concept suite 'Happiness Stan', but the music is strong enough to withstand the novelty tag. *Ogdens Nut Gone Flake* would be the Small Faces' swan-song, at least until an ill-starred reunion, but it proved a fitting end to a golden era.

Ogden's Nut Gone Flake; Afterglow Of Your Love; Long Agos And Worlds Apart; Rene; Son Of A Baker; Lazy Sunday; Happiness Stan; Rollin' Over; The Hungry Intruder; The Journey; Mad John; Happy Days Toy Town; Tin Soldier (live).

First released 1967
UK peak chart position: 1
159

221. VILLAGE GREEN PRESERVATION SOCIETY
Kinks

Although Pete Townshend's *Tommy* is seen as the first rock opera, Ray Davies actually conceived the idea with *Arthur* and this album. Taking the theme of England and its quaint Englishness, *Village Green* addresses Beeching's barbaric railway closures with 'The Last Of The Steam Powered Trains', and nostalgia in the title track; 'god bless strawberry jam, vaudeville and variety'. 'Picture Book' describes growing old and 'Animal Farm' is a wonderful plea for rural sanity. The commercial failure of the album was in not having one outstanding song, but as a concept the collection is true delight.

Village Green Preservation Society; Do You Remember Walter; Picture Book; Johnny Thunder; The Last Of The Steam Powered Trains; Big Sky; Sitting By The Riverside; Animal Farm; Village Green; Starstruck; Phenomenal Cat; All My Friends Were There; Wicked Annabella; Monica; People Take Pictures Of Each Other.

First released 1968
UK peak chart position: did not chart
USA peak chart position: did not chart

222. SCOTT 2
SCOTT WALKER

Although it opens with the up-tempo strains of 'Jackie', Scott Walker's second solo album generally courts the dark existentialism of its predecessor. Four enigmatic original songs, of which 'The Bridge' is particularly dramatic, match the moody intensity of the singer's Jacques Brel interpretations. Walker's reading of 'Next', the tale of a mobile army brothel, is particularly riveting. He invests material by Tim Hardin and Burt Bacharach with the same dark power, using his deep, resonant voice to majestic effect, buoyed by imaginative orchestral arrangements from, among others, Peter Knight and Reg Guest. *Scott 2* is an astonishing work, confirming Walker as one of the finest singers in pop.

Jackie; Best Of Both Worlds; Black Sheep Boy; The Amorous Humphrey Plug; Next; The Girls From The Street; Plastic Palace People; Wait Until Dark; Windows Of The World; The Bridge; Come Next Spring.

First released 1968
UK peak chart position: 1
USA peak chart position: did not chart

223. ROCKS
Aerosmith

One of the reasons why Aerosmith, after a number of creatively lean years, are still given legendary credence and an eager ear with each new release. *Rocks* encapsulated the very essence of rock 'n' roll. They may have suffered detractors who still pinned them as nothing more than a poor man's Rolling Stones, but *Rocks* pioneered a strength and swagger and real depth that remains very nearly unsurpassed. From the slowly escalating, 'Back In The Saddle'. to the dying strains of, 'Home Tonight' this album held the full spirit and soul of Aerosmith in both hands.

Back In The Saddle; Last Child; Rats In The Cellar; Combination; Sick As A Dog; Nobody's Fault; Get The Lead Out; Lick And A Promise; Home Tonight.

First released 1976
UK peak chart position: did not chart
USA peak chart position: 3

224. 12 SONGS
Newman, Randy

Newman began his career as a contract songwriter, before embarking on a recording career renowned for sardonic wit. On this, his second album, the singer opted for simple accompaniment, his ragged voice and stylised piano supported largely by a crisp backing group which included Byrds' guitarist Clarence White. Superb melodies were matched by an intense lyricism which embraced sometimes disquieting images unheard of in rock. Cynicism, bitterness and sexual perversion are unleashed in turn as Newman adopts different roles and personae. His dispassionate delivery demands decisions from the listener, an interaction that is as compulsive as it is disquieting.

Have You Seen My Baby; Let's Burn Down The Cornfield; Mama Told Me Not To Come; Suzanne; Lover's Prayer; Lucinda; Underneath The Harlem Moon; Yellow Man; Old Kentucky Home; Rosemary; If You Need Oil; Uncle Bob's Midnight Blues.

First released 1970
UK peak chart position: did not chart
USA peak chart position: did not chart

225. DARE
Human League

The acceptable face of computerised pop, were you aware that four out of the six members were playing synthesizers. *Dare* was a one-off and apart from one or two excellent singles the Human League never came near to equalling such a collection of instantly recognisable melodies. 'Mirror Man' and 'Human' were classy songs but every track on this winner had you dancing or singing along. This was one of Martin Rushent's finest productions and its a pity that the Human League are not around our turntables any more. Maybe the fear of giving up all those synthesizers was intolerable.

Things That Dreams Are Made Of; Open Your Heart; The Sound Of The Crowd; Darkness; Do Or Die; Get Carter; I Am The Law; Seconds; Love Action (I Believe In Love); Don't You Want Me.

First released 1981
UK peak chart position: 1
USA peak chart position: 3

226. THE YES ALBUM
Yes

OK, so much of Yes's output was pretentious, over-blown and over-long. But that doesn't detract from the volume of adventurous and technically brilliant work which lies buried beneath the less-enduring (and endearing) stuff. The Yes Album benefits from having been recorded before Jon Anderson's lyrics became embarassingly obtuse, and before the producers lost the use of their fader fingers. The album opens with a storming 'Yours Is No Disgrace', Steve Howe excels on 'The Clap', the band take 'Starship Trooper' into orbit, and we all sing along to 'I've Seen All Good People'. It's really quite good fun.

Yours Is No Disgrace; The Clap; Starship Trooper; Life Seeker; Disillusion; Wurm; I've Seen All Good People; Your Move; All Good People; A Venture; Perpetual Change.

First released 1971
UK peak chart position: 7
USA peak chart position: 40

227. THE B-52'S
B-52's

Formed in Athens, Georgia, the B-52's emerged from this nominal outback with 'Rock Lobster', a quirky pop song which drew critical praise and engendered a major recording deal. *B-52's* maintained the originality of that debut single, with staccato voices, cheesy organ, vox guitar and surreal lyrics. Drawing on 60s kitsch ephemera, both aurally and visually, the quintet created a unified image, but one reflecting post-modernism rather than nostalgia. A cracked sense of humour lay at the core of this album, but the group's infectious joy and sense of purpose blends with danceable rhythms to ensure a quality more than mere wackiness.

Planet Claire; 52 Girls; Dance This Mess Around; Rock Lobster; Lava; There's A Moon In The Sky (Called Moon); Hero Worship; 6060-842; Downtown.

First released 1979
UK peak chart position: 22
USA peak chart position: 59

228. HOUNDS OF LOVE
Kate Bush

Though not the most prolific of album artists, Bush's works make up in impact what they lack in frequency. Her style and material has always been unique, eccentric even, but *Hounds Of Love* is probably the strongest mix of controlled musical experimentation and lyrical expression. It deals with big issues - childhood fantasy and trauma, conflict, sexuality - but rarely lapses into pretention. The intense arrangements are perfectly matched to the subjects: 'Running Up That Hill' climactically erotic, 'Cloudbusting' broodingly triumphant, 'The Big Sky' just… big. And it's all her own work.

Running Up That Hill; Hounds Of Love; The Big Sky; Jig Of Life; Mother Stands For Comfort; Cloudbusting; And Dream Of Sleep; Under Ice; Waking The Witch; Watching You Without Me; Hello Earth; Morning Fog.

First released 1985
UK peak chart position: 1
USA peak chart position: 30

229. JAILBREAK
Thin Lizzie

Not true heavy metal perpetrators, more out-and-out rocker hence their appearance on this list. The late Phil Lynott has a growing core of younger fans, has word is passed down that even though he had his demons he was an outstanding performer. This is their best studio album and it contains two classics; 'The Boys Are Back In Town' and the title track. Both spit and crackle, bass and lead guitar burst out of the speaker at loud volume, and all the while the gentle laconic voice of Lynott delivers his poetry.

Angel From The Coast; The Boys Are Back In Town; Cowboy Song; Emerald; Fight Or Jail; Jailbreak; Romeo And The Lonely Girl; Running Back; Warriors.

First released 1976
UK peak chart position: 10
USA peak chart position: 18

230. THE MONKEES
Monkees

Created to fulfil roles in a television series, the Monkees were greeted with scepticism by certain sections of the rock fraternity. The quartet may not have played the instruments on their debut album; this does not diminish the appeal of its content. Excellent songs by Tommy Boyce and Bobby Hart formed its core, while contributions by Carole King, David Gates and group member Mike Nesmith ensures that the quality remains constantly high. Mickey Dolenz possesses the ideal pop voice and the enthusiasm generated on each performance is completely captivating. The Monkees' grasp of teen angst and melodrama is sure and, now divorced from contemporary travails, this album stands as one of the era's most entertaining debuts.

Theme From The Monkees; Saturday's Child; I Wanna Be Free; Tomorrow's Gonna Be Just Another Day; Papa Gene's Blues; Take A Giant Step; Last Train To Clarksville; This Just Doesn't Seem To Be My Day; Let's Dance On; I'll Be True To You; Sweet Young Thing; Gonna Buy Me A Dog.

First released 1966
UK peak chart position: 1
USA peak chart position: 1

231. THE ROLLING STONES
Rolling Stones

A lowly position gained presumably because new product pushes it down the listings. It was, is and should always be a great white R&B record. Recorded swiftly and simply it smells of the London club scene of 1963. Admittedly crude by the Stones later high standards it is still a vital and historically important album. They attempt Muddy Waters, 'I Just Want To Make Love To You', Jimmy Reed, 'Honest I Do', a frantic Chuck Berry, 'Carol' and even Marvin Gaye's 'Can I Get A Witness'. They even do a better whistle than Rufus Thomas on 'Walking The Dog'. Primitive but dazzling.

Route 66; I Just Want To Make Love To You; Honest I Do; I Need You Baby; Now I've Got A Witness; Little By Little; I'm King Bee; Carol; Tell Me (You're Coming Back); Can I Get A Witness; You Can Make It If You Really Try; Walking The Dog.

First released 1964
UK peak chart position: 1
USA peak chart position: 11

232. JESUS OF COOL
Nick Lowe

In America, presumably objecting to the title, they put out this record with the title *Pure Pop For Now People*. in 1994 us 'now people' can continue to enjoy this little masterpiece. After serving his apprenticeship in Brinsley Schwarz, Lowe debuted during punk's heyday. He was feted by the cognoscenti and his face regularly graced the pages of the UK music press. A 'surprise' hit single put Nick on *Top Of The Pops*, and the masses saw him only as the man who sang 'I Love The Sound of Breaking Glass'. It was a pity because overlooked were gems such as 'So It Goes', 'Little Hitler' and the perceptive 'Music For Money'.

Music For Money; I Love The Sound Of Breaking Glass; Little Hitler; Shake And Pop; Tonight; So It Goes; No Reason; 36-inches High; Marie Provost; Nutted By Reality; Heart Of The City.

First released 1978
UK peak chart position: 22
USA peak chart position: 127

233. NO JACKET REQUIRED
Phil Collins

No Jacket Required reached number 1 in more countries than you can shake a drumstick at, and shows Collins at his most mature and versatile. 'Sussudio' opens the album with the familiar death-by-drums intro, setting the pattern of strong arrangements and attacking vocals. 'Only You Know And I Know' and 'Who Said I Would' explore this territory with the vibrant assistance of the Phoenix Horns, while the massive 'One More Night' provides an elegant contrast. Surely the strongest track, though, is the elegiac 'Long Long Way To Go', which brought tears to a billion pairs of eyes as one of the highlights of Live Aid.

Sussudio; Only You Know And I Know; Long Long Way To Go; Don't Want To Know; One More Night; Don't Lose My Number; Who Said I Would; Doesn't Anybody Stay Together Anymore?; Inside Out; Take Me Home.

First released 1985
UK peak chart position: 1
USA peak chart position: 1

234. STARSAILOR
Tim Buckley

Tim Buckley's work was always challenging, developing from that of a superior folksinger to one encompassing many forms of expression. A growing jazz influence came to full fruition on *Starsailor*, which embraced the radical avant garde aspects of John Coltrane and Ornette Coleman. On several tracks the singer largely eschewed melody, giving full rein to his astonishing range, turning his voice into another instrument. Yet there were equal moments of gorgeous melancholia, no more so than on 'Song To The Siren', later popularised by This Mortal Coil. Supported only by muted electric guitar and eerie sound effects, Buckley sings with heartfelt emotion, resulting in one of his finest-ever performances. The contrast between its ethereal atmosphere and the dense textures elsewhere results in a enthralling, intense collection.

Come Here Woman; I Woke Up; Montreux; Moulin Rouge; Song To The Siren; Jungle Fire; Starsailor; The Healing Festival; Down By The Borderline.

First released 1970
UK peak chart position: did not chart
USA peak chart position: did not chart

235. 5TH DIMENSION
Byrds

The legendary Byrds pose on the cover, minus Gene Clark, on a magic carpet and the music within is often magical as McGuinn bends his Rickenbacker around 'raga rock'. The influential 'Eight Miles High' with its breathtaking solo and title track show just how important this band were and still are. McGuinn's lyric on the latter is often overlooked 'and I saw the great plunder my teachers had made, scientific, delirium, madness'. Crosby also dealt with important issues on 'I Come And Stand At Every Door' and 'I See You'. A wonderful electric and eclectic timeless flight.

5D; Wild Mountain Thyme; Mr. Spaceman; I See You; What's Happening?; I Come And Stand At Every Door; Eight Miles High; Hey Joe; Captain Soul; John Riley; 2-4-2 Foxtrot (The Lear Jet Song).

First released 1966
UK peak chart position: 27
USA peak chart position: 24

236. HERE COME THE WARM JETS
Brian Eno

Having left Roxy Music, (Brian) Eno began his solo career with this idiosyncratic album. Robert Fripp, Paul Thompson and Phil Manzanera are among those appearing on a set of songs exhibiting a mischievous love of pure pop music. Macabre lyrics constantly subvert the quirky melodies, a feature fully expressed on 'Baby's On Fire', while the singer's cheeky vocals exaggerates the ambiguity. Savage guitar lines, erratic synthesiser and pounding drums provide exciting textures to a collection as beguiling as it is invigorating.

Needles In The Camel's Eye; The Paw Paw Negro Blowtorch; Baby's On Fire; Cindy Tells Me; Driving Me Backwards; On Some Faraway Beach; Black Frank; Dead Finks Don't Talk; Some Of Them Are Old; Here Comes The Warm Jets.

First released 1974
UK peak chart position: 26
USA peak chart position: 151

237. MORE OF THE MONKEES
Monkees

Clearly they were not America's answer to the Beatles, even though at the time moptop fans seethed and decided to boycott them. They were the best manufactured pop group ever and in Michael Nesmith had a semi musical genius. Their second album apart from the wretched 'Your Auntie Grizelda' carries on from their debut. It contains the mantric '(I'm Not Your) Steppin' Stone', Neil Diamond's chunka chunka chunk 'Look Out (Here Comes Tomorrow)', the funky 'Mary Mary' and the paragon, 'I'm A Believer', also written by Neil Diamond. Euphoric and nostalgic and completely marijuana free.

When Love Comes Knockin' (At Your Door); Mary, Mary; Hold On Girl; Your Auntie Grizelda; (I'm Not Your) Steppin' Stone; Look Out (Here Comes Tomorrow); The Kind Of Girl I Could Love; The Day We Fall In Love; Sometime In The Morning; Laugh; I'm A Believer.

First released 1967
UK peak chart position: 1
USA peak chart position: 1

238. ELECTRIC MUSIC FOR THE BODY AND MIND
Country Joe And The Fish

A lynchpin release in 1967, this album defined the genre known as acid-rock. Led by former folk musician Joe McDonald, the quintet combined engaging melodies with sharp, satirical lyrics encompassing different facets of the counter-culture. Drugs ('Bass Strings'), sex ('Porpoise Mouth') and politics ('Superbird') were detailed to pinpoint accuracy while the group contributed exquisite, subtle support. Guitarist Barry Melton brought shimmering majesty to the instrument, cutting through the verse with mercurial insight and soloing to perfection. The quiet power of this album continues to enthral.

Flying High; Not So Sweet Marsha Lorraine; Death Sound Blues; Happiness Is A Porpoise Mouth; Section 43; Superbird; Sad And Lonely Times; Love; Bass Strings; The Masked Marrader; Grace.

First released 1967
UK peak chart position: did not chart
USA peak chart position: 39

239. NICK OF TIME
Bonnie Raitt

Although famed primarily for her interpretation of compositions by the likes of Joni Mitchell, John Hiatt, James Taylor and Paul Brady, Nick Of Time includes two fine Raitt-penned songs. 'The Road's My Middle Name' is an up-tempo blues number, harking back to her early career performing alongside Son House and Mississippi Fred McDowell. The title track is one of her best, a sensitive examination of the traumas of ageing. Throughout the album her voice is haunting and controlled, bringing new meaning and depth to a varied range of material. Bonnie turned 40 gracefully with this album. *Luck Of the Draw* just missed the list.

Nick Of Time; A Thing Called Love; Love Letters; Cry On My Shoulder; Real Man; Nobody's Girl; Have A Heart; Too Soon To Tell; I Will Not Be Denied; I Ain't Gonna Let You Break My Heart Again; The Road's My Middle Name.

First released 1989
UK peak chart position: 51
USA peak chart position: 1

240. TANGO IN THE NIGHT
Fleetwood Mac

Not having the mega multi million sales of *Rumours* allows this record greater credibility - you have the choice of discovering it on your own. A worthy entrant in the listing, even though it was now two million miles away from the monster Peter Green created. It showed a much happier and cleaner Fleetwood Mac, having put a lot of their emotional baggage in the cupboard. Some of their strongest material is found here, Lindsay Buckingham's ambitious 'Big Love', Christine's beautiful 'Everywhere' and close second 'Little Lies'. Reappraising this record gives you a further chance to work out if a rude word is repeated throughout 'Family Man'.

Big Love; Seven Wonders; Everywhere; Caroline; Tango In The Night; Mystified; Little Lies; Family Man; Welcome To The Room...Sara; Isn't It Midnight?; When I See You Again; You And I (Part Two).

First released 1987
UK peak chart position: 1
USA peak chart position: 7

241. TOMMY
Who

The definitive rock opera, *Tommy* liberated the Who from a 'singles' band' stigma, and made them an international attraction. Composer Pete Townshend had flirted with the genre on two previous releases, here his vision was spread over two ambitious albums which played to all his group's strengths. Memorable songs were matched by pulsating musicianship, which emphasised the Who's internal kineticism, while the cast of characters unleashed revealed an unconventional imagination. Townshend even incorporates 'Eyesight To The Blind', first recorded by Sonny Boy Williamson, to his fable about the 'deaf, dumb and blind kid', a rare, but successful, reference to the past in what is a forward-looking achievement.

Overture; It's A Boy; 1921; Amazing Journeys; Sparks; Eyesight To The Blind; Miracle Cure; Sally Simpson; I'm Free; Welcome; Tommy's Holiday Camp; We're Not Gonna Take It; Christmas; Cousin Kevin; The Acid Queen; Underture; Do You Think It's Alright; Fiddle About; Pinball Wizard; There's A Doctor; Go To The Mirror; Tommy Can You Hear Me; Smash The Mirror; Sensation.

First released 1969
UK peak chart position: 2
USA peak chart position: 4

242. SCOTT
Walker, Scott

Vocalist Scott Walker left the Walker Brothers in the hope of ridding himself of pop star trappings. His first solo album drew featured songs brimming with alienation and doomed romanticism. Walker's moody, introspective muse brought heartfelt resonance to several Jacques Brel compositions while his own material, principally 'Montague Terrace (In Blue)' and 'Such A Small Love', draw from the same stylistic well. Wally Stott's imaginative orchestral arrangements enhanced the singer's gorgeous voice. Love, death and existentialism have never been sung so elegantly, nor with such understated power.

Mathilde; Montague Terrace (In Blue); Angelica; The Lady Came From Baltimore; When Joanna Loved Me; My Death; The Big Hurt; Such A Small Love; You're Gonna Hear From Me; Through A Long And Sleepless Night; Always Coming Back To You; Amsterdam.

First released 1967
UK peak chart position: 3
USA peak chart position: did not chart

243. DAVID ACKLES
David Ackles

David Ackles' first album announced the arrival of an original songwriting talent. Drawing from previous experience in film and theatre, he produced a highly literate music in which stories unfolded with vivid detail. His dispassionate vocal encouraged songs to unfold with brooding intensity, but unlike many contemporaries, Ackles was not confessional composer. He spoke for the rootless drifter ('The Road To Cairo'), the unrequited lover ('Down River') or the dreamer whose hopes were inevitably dashed ('When Love Is Gone'). Backing group Rhinocerous provide intuitively understanding support in a set which continues to grow in stature.

The Road To Cairo; When Love Is Gone; Sonny Come Here; Blue Ribbons; What A Happy Day; Down River; Leissez-Faire; Lotus Man; His Name Is Andrew; Be My Friend.

First released 1968
UK peak chart position: did not chart
USA peak chart position: did not chart

244. FUNHOUSE
Stooges

The Stooges minimalist approach to rock erupted fully on this, their second album. Simple riffs and splattered chords echo primitive R&B and provide a basic framework over which vocalist Iggy Pop tore the notion of 'singer' apart. Impulsive yelps and orgasmic moans punctuate a delivery that thrills and surprises in equal measure. Conventional structure disintegrates as the set progresses, culminating in the mayhem of a cacophonous finale into which recent addition, saxophonist Steve Mackay, adds a stream of notes implicit of Bedlam. Deranged yet free, *Funhouse* destroyed preconceptions of 60s music and prepared a path for 70s punk.

Down On The Street; Loose; TV Eye; Dirt; 1970; Fun House; LA Blues.

First released 1970
UK peak chart position: did not chart
USA peak chart position: did not chart

245. ANTHEM OF THE SUN
Grateful Dead

Although much of this seminal record was taken from 15 live gigs it counts as a studio album because of the studio content and the remarkable tape splicing that removes any audience participation. 'The Faster We Go, The Rounder We Get' is one track and the older we grow the easier it gets, is how we now view this work. Quite why it works is perplexing but there is incredible depth in the instrumentation, which reveals new facets after hundreds of plays. There is also a haunting beauty about the overall sound. It is an astonishingly good record that begs concentration.

That's It For The Other One; Cryptical Envelopment; Quadlibet; For Tender Feet; The Faster We Go, The Rounder We Get, We Leave The Castle; Alligator; Caution (Do Not Stop On The Tracks).

First released 1968
UK peak chart position: did not chart
USA peak chart position: 87

246. STEVE MCQUEEN
Prefab Sprout

While many felt that *Jordan: The Comeback* was their creative peak this remains the most popular choice. Recorded before the band's creative force Paddy MacAloon was hyped as the next big thing, it stands as a truly great pop album with enough complexity to make it special. The hit single 'When Love Breaks Down' opened doors to a wider market and 'Faron Young' reawakened interest in the country music star of the same name. The jury is still out on their long-term prospects after so much promise and we await to see if MacAloon can surpass the quality of *Steve McQueen.*

Faron Young; Bonny; Appetite; When Love Breaks Down; Goodbye Lucille; Hallelujah; Moving The River; Horsing Around; Desire As; Blueberry Pies; When The Angels.

First released 1985
UK peak chart position: 21
USA peak chart position: 178

247. THE CAPTAIN AND ME
Doobie Brothers

Boasting three strong vocalists, two expert guitarists and a brace of rhythmic drummers, the Doobie Brothers burst to national prominence with a sound crossing AM pop-rock, soul-tinged R&B and strong musicianship. Traces of Moby Grape, whom the group adored, can be heard in their vibrant harmonies and flowing hooklines, but *The Captain And Me* showed an act of singular purpose. The effervescent urgency propelling 'Long Train Running' and 'China Grove' into the US singles' charts is apparent on every selection where melody combines with twin-lead arpeggios emphasise to create an undoubted excitement. The unified sound emerging from this cross-section provides this album with its lasting strength.

Natural Thing; Long Train Running; China Grove; Dark-eyed Cajun Woman; Clear As The Driven Snow; Without You; South City Midnight Lady; Evil Woman; Busted Down Around O'Connelly Corners; Ukiah; The Captain And Me.

First released 1973
UK peak chart position: did not chart
USA peak chart position: 7

248. HEJIRA
Joni Mitchell

Joni Mitchell draws freely on her heroes and influences, and in her turn inspires and informs the work of countless others; thus are the genes of our musical heritage passed on to new generations. The love of jazz glimpsed in *Court And Spark* and *The Hissing Of Summer Lawns* is wanton in *Hejira*. The arrangements are loose and the melodies seductively free-flowing. The lyrics, too, have broken free of rigid verse and rhyme structures and tend towards prose poetry. The cloak of introspection which weighs down on much of her work is lighter here; though far from mainstream, Hejira is an engaging and approachable collection.

Coyote; Amelia; Furry Sings The Blues; Strange Boy; Hejira; Song For Sharon; Black Crow; Blue Motel Room; Refuge Of The Road.

First released 1976
UK peak chart position: 11
USA peak chart position: 13

249. ARGYBARGY
Squeeze

Squeeze played real instruments, made mistakes and were often sloppy on stage. What fantastic failings, they were the lone true beat group of the 80s; a little punk, a little pop and a lot of humour. They were successful because they refused to take themselves seriously and became the antithesis of pomp. Tilbrook, Holland and Difford never denied how much they loved the Beatles, Byrds and Beach Boys and they wrote their own equivalent, 'Farfisa Beat', 'Pulling Mussels (From The Shell)', 'Another Nail In My Heart'. Tilbrook can be forgiven for sometimes stretching outside his octave range, because it was his voice that made Squeeze very special.

Pulling Mussels (From The Shell); Another Nail In My Heart; Seperate Beds; Misadventure; I Think I'm Go-go; Farfisa Beat; Here Comes That Feeling; Vicky Verky; If I Didn't Love You; Wrong Side Of The Moon; There At The Top.

First released 1980
UK peak chart position: 32
USA peak chart position: 71

250. GOODBYE AND HELLO
Tim Buckley

Initially a folksinger, Tim Buckley quickly defied stylistic categorisation. *Goodbye And Hello* offers a rich musical vocabulary, from plaintive love song to hints of the free-form expressionism of his later work, with its core the artist's remarkable voice. Buckley glides and swoops around the melody, colouring his material with raw emotion. His range is startling, from sonorous baritone to wild falsetto, but the intonation is never gratuitous The beautiful 'Morning Glory' is on this album and its worthy of noting three other Buckley albums were just outside this listing, *Sefronia, Blue Afternoon* and *Look At The Fool*. The haunting beauty of Tim Buckley's work is caught to perfection herein and continues to influence.

No Man Can Find The War; Carnival Song; Pleasant Street; Hallucinations; I Never Asked To Be Your Mountain; Once I Was; Phantasmagoria In Two; Knight-Errant; Goodbye And Hello; Morning Glory.

First released 1967
UK peak chart position: did not chart
USA peak chart position: 171

THE TOP 100 JAZZ ALBUMS

IN GIVING JAZZ THE SECOND LARGEST CATEGORY WE ATTEMPTED TO
IGNORE THE JAZZ BUFFS, NEVER KNOWN FOR THEIR TOLERANCE OF
OTHER FORMS OF MUSIC. JAZZ, LESS WE FORGET, IS POPULAR MUSIC
AND THE APPEARANCE OF PAT METHENY, JOHN SCOFIELD AND
JIMMY SMITH ALONGSIDE ALBERT AYLER AND ANTHONY BRAXTON IS
POSITIVELY UPLIFTING. JAZZERS MAY DISAGREE
BUT THE PEOPLE HAVE CHOSEN WELL.

1. KIND OF BLUE
Miles Davis

All the many corners of jazz will argue their point, some with bigoted passion and
self righteousness - a trait that has been known to follow jazz buffs. But, when
you get jazzers, rock and popular music followers actually unanimously united
over one record, then you know something must be right. This album contains
only five tracks, Julian Adderley; alto, John Coltrane; tenor, Bill Evans; piano,
Paul Chambers; bass, James Cobb; Drums and Miles on trumpet. This is the
greatest jazz album in the world ever, so what, just accept it.

So What; Freddie Freeloader; Blue In Green; Al Blues; Flamenco Sketches.

First released 1960
UK peak chart position: did not chart
USA peak chart position: did not chart

2. THE BLANTON-WEBSTER YEARS
Duke Ellington

A special kind of magic surrounds the Ellington band which featured Ben Webster and Jimmy Blanton. The former's tenor solos, breathily romantic or fiercely swinging; the latter changing the role of the bass in jazz. Yet these two were far from being the only stars. Not least amongst others were the liquid beauty of Johnny Hodges's alto and Cootie Williams's plangent trumpet. And there was always the arranging-composing skills of Billy Strayhorn, another new arrival, and the maestro himself. Together, they brought to eternal life masterpieces such as 'Just A-Settin' And A-Rockin'', 'Ko-Ko', 'Jack The Bear', 'Cotton Tail' and 'Concerto For Cootie'.

First released 1987 rec. 1940-42
UK peak chart position: did not chart
USA peak chart position: did not chart

You, You Darlin'; Jack The Bear; Ko Ko; Morning Glory; So Far, So Good; Conga Brava; Concerto For Cootie (Do Nothin' Till You Hear From Me); Me And You; Cotton Tail; Never No Lament; Dusk; Bojangles; A Portrait Of Bert Williams; Blue Goose; Harlem Air Shaft; At A Dixie Roadside Diner; All Too Soon; Rumpus In Richmond; My Greatest Mistake; Sepia Panorama; There Shall Be No Night; In A Mellow Tone; Five O'clock Whistle; Warm Valley; The Flaming Sword; Jumpin' Punkins; Across The Track Blues; John Hardy's Wife; Blue Serge; After All; Chloe; Bakiff; Are You Sticking?; I Never Felt This Way Before; Just A-Settin' And A-Rockin'; The Giddybug Gallop; The Sidewalks Of New York; Chocolate Shake; Flamingo; I Got It Bad (And That Ain't Good); Clementine; Brown Skin Gal; The Girl In My Dreams Tries To Look Like You; Jump For Joy; Moon Over Cuba; Take The 'A' Train; Five O'clock Drag; Rocks In My Bed; Blip Blip; Chelsea Bridge; Raincheck; What Good Would It Do?; I Don't Mind; Someone; My Little Brown Book; Main Stem; Johnny Come Lately; Hayfoot Strawfoot; Sentimental Lady; A Sip Of The Lip (Can Sink A Ship); Sherman Shuffle.

3. A LOVE SUPREME
John Coltrane

John Coltrane's great masterpiece and one of the most profoundly moving records in all of jazz, *A Love Supreme* was recorded in 1964 by Coltrane's classic quartet (with pianist McCoy Tyner, bassist Jimmy Garrison and drummer Elvin Jones). It is a brilliantly integrated jazz suite looking at four distinct stages of spiritual development, represented by four movements, entitled 'Acknowledgement', 'Resolution', 'Pursuance' and 'Psalm'. The music is intense and gripping, and builds to a head on the fast and aggressive 'Pursuance' before the beautiful and soothing 'Psalm'. *A Love Supreme* is without doubt one of the most profound statements of religious conviction to come from this century.

Part 1 Acknowledgement; Part 2 Resolution; part 3 Puruance; Part 4 Psalm.

First released 1967
UK peak chart position: did not chart
USA peak chart position: did not chart

4. BIRTH OF THE COOL
Miles Davis

Although this is generally credited to Miles, the importance of Gerry Mulligan's playing and especially his stellar compositions 'Jeru', 'Rocker' and the gorgeous 'Venus De Milo' make this album special. Only a few paces behind *Kind Of Blue*, yet in some ways more important. It would be churlish to say this was the birth of the cool, but the songs recorded by the legendary nonet and collected together here as an album are certainly the birth of something. Hearing all the tracks on CD makes it more complete, and more necessary than ever. Again in dispensable.

Move; Jeru; Moon Dreams; Venus De Milo; Budo; Deception; Godchild; Boplicity; Rocker; Israel; Rouge.

First released 1950
UK peak chart position: did not chart
USA peak chart position: did not chart

5. CHARLIE PARKER ON DIAL VOLS 1-6
Charlie Parker

Alto saxophonist Charlie Parker turned jazz on its head in the years following World War II, playing a thoroughly original and highly demanding music that furthered the emphasis on improvisation, and gave jazz a greater technical complexity and psychological depth. His numerous sides for the west coast Dial label began in 1946, and represent one of the greatest bodies of work to be found anywhere in the music. The six volumes available today represent the complete works, and feature contributions by a host of leading musicians of the time, including Dizzy Gillespie, Miles Davis, Lucky Thompson, Errol Garner, Duke Jordan, Max Roach, Teddy Wilson, Red Norvo, and J.J. Johnson.

First released 1974
UK peak chart position: did not chart
USA peak chart position: did not chart

Volume 1 - Diggin' Diz; Moose The Mooche (three takes); Yardbird Suite (two takes); Ornithology (three takes); The Famous Alto Break; Night In Tunisia (two takes); Max Making Wax; Loverman; The Gypsy; Bebop. Volume 2 - This Is Always (two takes); Bird's Nest (three takes); Cool Blues (four takes). Volume 3 - Relaxin' At Camarillo; Cheers; Carvin' The Bird; Stupendous Theme Cooking (three takes). Volume 4 - Dexterity (two takes); Bongo Bop; Dewey Square (three takes); The Hymn (two takes); Bird Of Paradise (three takes); Embraceable You (two takes). Volume 5 - Bird Feathers; Klart-oveeseds-tere (two takes); Scapple From The Apple; My Old Flame; Out Of Nowhere (three takes); Don't Blame Me; Moose The Mooche; Dark Shadows; Hallelujah. Volume 6 - Drying On A Reed (three takes); Quasimodo (two takes); Charlie's Wig (three takes); Bongo Beep; Crazeology (two excerpts); How Deep Is The Ocean (two takes).

6. LADY IN AUTUMN
Billie Holiday

Without question the greatest jazz singer there has ever been (or ever will be), Holiday's unmistakable sound, her inimitable phrasing, her faultless sense of what was right, helped mould an artist unique in the history of popular music. In the early years her joyous, youthful voice was backed by soloists of the calibre of Buck Clayton, her close friend Lester Young, and her ideal arranger, pianist Teddy Wilson. Towards the end of her life her voice was a flaking, fractured caricature of itself but her commanding artistry and musical integrity lent dignity and poignancy to her recordings.

Body And Soul; Strange Fruit; Trav'lin' Light; All Of Me; (There Is) No Greater Love; I Cover The Waterfront; These Foolish Things (Remind Me Of You); Tenderly; Autumn In New York; My Man; Stormy Weather; Yesterdays; (I Got A Man, Crazy For Me) He's Funny That Way; What A Little Moonlight Can Do; I Cried For You (Now It's Your Turn To Cry Over Me); Too Marvelous For Words; I Wished On The Moon; I Don't Want To Cry Anymore; Prelude To A Kiss; Nice Work If You Can Get It; Come Rain Or Come Shine; What's New?; God Bless The Child; Do Nothin' Till You Hear From Me; April In Paris; Lady Sings The Blues; Don't Explain; Fine And Mellow; I Didn't Know What Time It Was; Stars Fell On Alabama; One For My Baby (And One More For The Road); Gee Baby, Ain't I Good To You; Lover Man (Oh, Where Can You Be?); All The Way; Don't Worry 'bout Me.

First released 1973
UK peak chart position: did not chart
USA peak chart position: did not chart

7. GENIUS OF MODERN MUSIC VOLS 1 & 2
Thelonious Monk

Taken as a body of work these are two of the most important jazz albums of all time. Over the years Monk's importance grows, yet when these sessions were recorded his reputation was of cult status only. Monk has given us some outstanding compositions, and many are contained here. Naturally the most recorded jazz song of all time 'Round Midnight' is present, but so is the evergreen 'Ruby My Dear' and 'Monk's Mood'. And so on and so on, it reads like a greatest hits package. The CD versions are indispensable as there are many additional alternate takes.

Volume 1 - Round Midnight; Off Minor; Ruby My Dear; April In Paris; In Walked Bud; Thelonius; Epistrophy; Misterioso; Well You Needn't; Introspection; Humph/Volume 2 - Carolina Moon; Homin' In; Skippy; Let's Cool One; Suburban Eyes; Evonce; Straight No Chaser; Four In One; Nice Work If You Can Get It; Monk's Mood; Who Knows; Ask Me Now.

rec. 1947-52
UK peak chart position: did not chart
USA peak chart position: did not chart

8. MILES SMILES
Miles Davis

This was the last Miles album before his next plateau (or his next album), an occurrence that happened throughout his career. This is the quintet that moved into electronic music with *Bitches Brew*, Herbie Hancock, Wayne Shorter, Tony Williams, Ron Carter, an astonishing line-up and surely Miles' best post Coltrane group. This is like music for the last supper, they all knew that Fender Rhodes piano's and Precision bass's were coming and this is a superb farewell to acoustic jazz. All six tracks are rewarding, all different, yet the sound is the same. Much more appreciated than when it was first released.

Orbits; Circle; Footprints; Dolores; Freedom Jazz Dance; Ginger Bread Boy.

First released 1966
UK peak chart position: did not chart
USA peak chart position: did not chart

9. THE HOT FIVES AND SEVENS 1-7
Louis Armstrong

Almost 70 years on and still these recordings are breathtaking. The audacity of the virtuoso trumpeter, captured in the first full flush of his realization that he was the greatest, makes clear why Armstrong in the 20s was the first true genius of jazz. An innovator, a pathfinder, not yet showman but with all the showman's qualities on tap, he surges triumphantly through a succession of masterpieces, minor and major. And above even these superlative surroundings is 'West End Blues' - endlessly imitated, never equalled. A monumental performance by a giant. Unmistakable, irreplaceable, unmissable, eternal music.

including - Memories Of You; You're Lucky To Me; Sweethearts On Parade; You're Drivin' Me Crazy; The Peanut Vendor; Just A Gigolo; Shine; Walkin' My Baby Back Home; I Surrender Dear; When It's Sleepytime Down South; Blue Again; Little Joe; I'll Be Glad When You're Dead; You Rascal You; Them There Eyes; When Your Lover Has Gone; Lazy River; Chinatown, My Chinatown; My Heart; (Yes!) I'm The Barrel; Gut Bucket Blues; Come Back, Sweet Papa; Georgia Grind; Heebie Jeebies; Cornet Chop Suey; Oriental Strut; You're Next; Muskrat Ramble; Don't Forget To Mess Around; I'm Gonna Gitcha; Dropppin' Shucks; Who' Sit; King Of The Zulus; Big Fat Ma And Skinny Pa; Willie The Weeper; West End Blues; Wild Man Blues; Chicago Breakdown; Alligator Crawl; Potato Head Blues; Melancholy Blues; Weary Blues; Twelfth Street Rag;

rec. 1925-28
UK peak chart position: did not chart
USA peak chart position: did not chart

10. MILESTONES
Miles Davis

The third Davis album to appear in the listings and another that has matured with age. Featuring the classic sextet with the personnel of Coltrane, Cannonball Adderley, Red Garland, Philly Joe Jones and Paul Chambers it hints at what was to come with *Kind Of Blue* the following year. The modal jazz period was germinated here, particularly with 'Sid's Ahead' featuring one of Miles' finest solos, a tribute to late night New York disc jockey Symphony Sid. Elsewhere the pace is swing and cool, a unique drum sound on 'Billy Boy' and it closes with a superior reading of Monk's 'Straight No Chaser.

Doctor Jekyll; Sid's Ahead; Two Bass Hits; Miles; Billy Boy; Straight No Chaser.

First released 1958?
UK peak chart position: did not chart
USA peak chart position: did not chart

11. BODY AND SOUL
Coleman Hawkins

The high position overall is enhanced by having one of the most beautiful interpretations of the title track. Hawkins did not write it, but embossed his own soul into it, and by rights he should own it. However he played it, however or wherever it was recorded, the sparse breathy tone is, well, breathtaking. Without wishing to denigrate the other tracks on this record the title track remains as important as *Kind Of Blue* in assembling a record collection. Beautifully preserved from 10-inch disc and recorded in 1939, also contained is the 1956 recording, where you can here the subtle click of the saxophone keys.

Meet Doctor Foo; Fine Dinner; She's Funny That Way; Body And Soul; When Day Is Done; The Sheik Of Araby; My Blue Heaven; Bouncing With Bean; Say It Isn't So; Spotlight; April In Paris; How Strange; Half Step Down Please; Jumping For Jane; I Love You; There Will Never Be Another You; Little Girl Blue; Dinner For One, Please James; I Never Knew; His Very Own Blues; Thirty Nine Inches; Bean Stalks Again; I'm Shooting High; Have You Met Miss Jones?; The Day You Came Along; The Essence Of You.

First released 1958
UK peak chart position: did not chart
USA peak chart position: did not chart

12. COMPLETE BENNY GOODMAN VOL 1-7
Benny Goodman

Although there were jazzier bands than Goodman's, more musical and more creative bands, and bands that swung more, none had the popular and commercial appeal his enjoyed for two or three glorious years in the 30s. After his breakthrough appearance at the Palomar Ballroom in Los Angeles on 21 August 1935 nothing could stop him. Labelled the 'King of Swing', Goodman offered the public what it wanted: punchy dance music, soloists like Harry James, magnetic showmen like Gene Krupa, and his own impeccable clarinet playing. The personnel was ever-changing thanks to Goodman's irascibility but the band thundered unmistakably on.

including- He Ain't Got Rhythm; Never Should Have Told You; This Year's Kisses; You Can Tell She Comes From Dixie; Goodnight My Love; I Want To Be Happy; Chloe; Rosetta; Ida, Sweet As Apple Cider; Tea For Two; Runnin' Wild; Peckin'; Can't We Be Friends; Sing, Sing, Sing; Roll 'Em; When It's Sleepytime Down South; Afraid To Dream; Changes; Avalon; Handful Of Keys; The Man I Love; Smiles; Liza (All The Clouds Will Roll Away); Bob White; Sugarfoot Stomp; I Can't Give You Anything But Love Baby; Minnie The Moocher's Wedding Day; Let That Be A Lesson To You; Can't Teach My Old Heart New Tricks; I've Hitched My Wagon To A Star; Pop Corn Man.

rec. 1935-39
UK peak chart position: did not chart
USA peak chart position: did not chart

13. THE BLACK SAINT AND THE SINNER LADY
Charles Mingus

In many ways the essential Mingus album, *Black Saint* is a rich and powerful suite, embracing in one work the elements of blues, gospel, funk and Latin music that infused Mingus's sound and made it what it was. As well as featuring some of the best group arrangement outside the work of Ellington, it boasts superb contributions by pianist Jaki Byard and alto saxophonist Charlie Mariano. Black Saint is also revealing for its early use (in jazz) of studio dubbing, heard on the occasions when Mariano can be identified in the ensemble at the same time he is soloing.

Solo Dancer (Stop! Look! And Listen, Sinner Jim Whitney); Duet Solo Dancers (Heart's Beat And Shades In Physical Embraces); Group Dancers ([Soul Fusion] Freewoman); Trio And Group Dancers (Stop! Look! And Sing Songs Of Revolutions!); Single Solos And Group Dance (Saint And Sinner Join In Merriment On Battle Front); Group And Solo Dance (Of Love, Pain, And Passioned Revolt, Then Farewell, My Beloved).

First released 1963
UK peak chart position: did not chart
USA peak chart position: did not chart

14. GERRY MULLIGAN MEETS BEN WEBSTER
Gerry Mulligan & Ben Webster

This album combines the talents of two jazz giants. Saxophonist Ben Webster was one of the instrument's most influential exponents, primarily through his work with Duke Ellington. Mulligan, meanwhile, was an integral part of the 50s' west coast movement and this set represents the confluence of two different generations. The featured quintet includes drummer Mel Lewis and bassist Leroy Vinnegar (who later played on the Doors' *The Soft Parade*), but the six tracks are noteworthy for the splendid empathy struck by Mulligan (baritone) and Webster (tenor). One of several collaborations between the former and notable guest artists, *Gerry Mulligan Meets Ben Webster* is a fine example of how two seemingly disparate musicians can perform together superbly.

Chelsea Bridge; Cat Walk; Sunday; Who's Got Rhythm?; Tell Me When; Go Home.

First released 1960
UK peak chart position: 15
USA peak chart position: did not chart

15. THE COMPLETE SAVOY SESSIONS
Charlie Parker

Although they do not contain the number of classic sides found within the Dial collection, the importance of Charlie Parker's Savoy recordings is more than justified by the involvement of bebop piano genius Bud Powell (perhaps the only other true bebopper playing with the level of invention and profundity of Parker himself) and the fascinating play-off between a young and troubled Miles Davis and his own hero Dizzy Gillespie. The Savoy records include the legendary 'KoKo' (a breakneck torrent of improvisation based around the tricky 'Cherokee' chord sequence), and two classic blues in F major: 'Billies Bounce' and 'Now's The Time'.

including - Billie's Bounce; Now's The Time i; Now's The Time ii; Thriving On A Riff i; Thriving On A Riff ii; Meandering; Koko; Dizzy Boogie i; Dizzy Boogie ii; Flat Foot Floogie i; Flat Foot Floogie ii; Popity Pop; Slim's Jam.

First released 1982
UK peak chart position: did not chart
USA peak chart position: did not chart

16. GIANT STEPS
John Coltrane

As influential upon contemporaries and successors as were Armstrong and Parker, Coltrane divided critical comment. For his supporters he was both high priest of contemporary jazz and prophet of what was yet to come. The ultimate statement of Coltrane's early obsession with chord progressions, this album marks the moment before he changed direction. *Giant Steps* is a vibrant demonstration of his inventive, dazzling and relentless playing of bop. Hereafter, Coltrane sought and found an avenue for his restless exploratory zeal in modal jazz. The album is therefore both landmark and turning point and is still a textbook for many young musicians.

Giant Steps; Cousin Mary; Countdown; Spiral; Syeeda's Song Flute; Mr. P.C.; Naima.

First released 1959
UK peak chart position: did not chart
USA peak chart position: did not chart

17. Out To Lunch
Eric Dolphy

Although a difficult album for those not seeped in jazz, it is still regarded as a milestone of recorded jazz. Featuring Freddie Hubbard, trumpet; Bobby Hutcherson, vibes; Tony Williams, drums and Richard Davis, bass show a unit hellbent on pushing forward the perimeters of jazz, with extraordinary success. Dolphy various saxophones, flute and chilling bass clarinet are literally all over the place without ever taking over from the quite outstanding performances from his supporting musicians. Although it won't be played as often as *Kind Of Blue* your collection would be all the poorer without it.

Hat And Beard; Something Sweet, Something Tender; Gazzelloni; Out To Lunch; Straight Up And Down.

First released 1964
UK peak chart position: did not chart
USA peak chart position: did not chart

18. Our Man In Paris
Dexter Gordon

One of the most successful of Blue Notes 'blue' period and an album that remains his finest work. Although his tenor sax occasionally grates, this is a brilliant example of late bebop. Supported by Bud Powell, piano; Kenny Clarke, drums and Pierre Michelot, bass the simple quartet sound coolly in control. 'Willow Weep For Me' is played with great beauty and 'A Night in Tunisia' is yet another well crafted version. The wonderful bonus of 'Our Love Is Here To Stay' and 'Like Someone In Love' (from Powell's Alternate Takes) on the CD reissue puts this album in the first division.

Scrapple From The Apple; Willow Weep For Me; Stairway To The Stairs; A Night In Tunisia; Our Love Is Here To Stay; Like Someone In Love; Broadway.

First released 1963
UK peak chart position: did not chart
USA peak chart position: did not chart

19. My Favorite Things
John Coltrane

One of John Coltrane's (many) extraordinary talents was his ability to drastically transcend the material he chose to play, and often infuse the trivial or frivolous with something altogether very profound. Under the spell of the quartet (with pianist McCoy Tyner, temporary bassist Steve Davis and drummer Elvin Jones), My Favorite Things becomes an almost religious celebration of life, brought to a series of ecstatic climaxes by Coltrane's nasal, Eastern-sounding soprano saxophone and Jones's propulsive, 6/8 clatter. This popular album also contains 'But Not For Me', a break-neck version of 'Summertime' and a beautiful 'Every Time We Say Goodbye'.

My Favorite Things; Everytime We Say Goodbye; Summertime; But Not For Me.

First released 1960
UK peak chart position: did not chart
USA peak chart position: did not chart

20. THE ORIGINAL AMERICAN DECCA RECORDINGS
Count Basie

These sides capture all the fire, energy and raw excitement of the Basie band as it roared out of Kansas City to startle the jazz world. Talented players occupy every chair, many of them awesome soloists: Buck Clayton, Harry Edison, Dicky Wells, Earle Warren, Herschel Evans, and the sublime and trend-setting Lester Young. And all were buoyed and spurred along by the All-American Rhythm Section of Basie, Freddie Green, Walter Page and Jo Jones. If this were not enough the band singer was the great Jimmy Rushing. Not surprisingly, after this big band jazz was never quite the same again. Indeed, it might even be argued that later Basie bands never quite recaptured this early magic.

including: Honeysuckle Rose; Pennies From Heaven; Swinging At The Daisy Chain; Roseland Shuffle; Exactly Like You; Boo Hoo; Glory Of Love; Boogie Woogie (I May Be Wrong); Smarty (You Know It All); One O'clock Jump; Listen My Children And You Shall Hear; Jon's Idea; Goodmorning Blues (1st take); Goodmorning Blues (2nd take); Our Love Was Meant To Be; Time Out; Topsy; I Keep Remembering; Out Of The Window; Don't You Miss Your Baby; Let Me Dream; Georgianna; Blues In The Dark; Sent For You Yesterday; Every Tub; Now Will You Be Good?; Swingin' The Blues; Mama Don't Want No Peas 'N' Rice 'N' Coconut Oil; Blue And Sentimental; Doggin' Around; Stop Beatin' Around The Mulberry Bush (1st take); Stop Beatin' Around The Mulberry Bush (2nd take); London Bridge Is Falling Down; Texas Shuffle.

rec. 1937-39
UK peak chart position: did not chart
USA peak chart position: did not chart

21. SONNY ROLLINS VOL 2
Sonny Rollins

The famous Harold Feinstein cover borrowed by Joe Jackson ('how dare he' said the purists) for *Body And Soul* also announces 'Monaural' Sonny Rollins. Did we ever have a 'Stereophonic' Charlie Parker, do we care? This is a blisteringly good album that never once loses pace. The formidable line-up is Jay Jay Johnson, trombone; Horace Silver and Thelonious Monk, piano; Art Blakey, drums and Paul Chamber, bass. Wonderful versions of Monk's 'Misterioso' and 'Reflections' are included plus Rollin's own 'Why Don't I' and 'Wail March'. The finest 'monaural' record Rollins ever made.

Why Don't I; Wail March; Misterioso; Reflections; You Stepped Out Of A Dream; Poor Butterfly.

First released 1957
UK peak chart position: did not chart
USA peak chart position: did not chart

22. THE SHAPE OF JAZZ TO COME
Ornette Coleman

As the 50s ended, Ornette Coleman became the new herald of the future of jazz surpassing even John Coltrane. Intent on feeling and with often scant regard for technique, he plunged headlong into a musical form that defied categorization and dismayed orthodox musicologists. Especially aware of the blues, Coleman eschewed the rigid structure of music and favoured instead explorations of its poetic content. Free jazz to Coleman and his followers was jazz freed not only from musical restraints but also from sociological and cultural parameters. This album demonstrates his radicalism and his awareness of both past and future jazz.

Lonely Woman; Eventually; Peace; Focus On Sanity; Congeniality Chronology.

First released 1960
UK peak chart position: did not chart
USA peak chart position: did not chart

23. COLTRANE JAZZ
John Coltrane

Released shortly after the ground-breaking *Giant Steps*, *Coltrane Jazz* features a number of takes from the 'Naima' session, with Wynton Kelly, Paul Chambers and Jimmy Cobb, as well as a track with Cedar Walton and Lex Humphries and an early outing by his newly formed quartet featuring pianist McCoy Tyner, Steve Davis and Elvin Jones. Whilst lacking the conceptual strength of many of Coltrane's greatest works, *Coltrane Jazz* captures the saxophonist during one of his interesting periods of change, and includes some memorable original tunes. Particularly worth investigating are 'Harmonique', an unusual theme involving polyphonics (more than one note played simultaneously) and a beautiful ballad performance of 'I'll Wait And Pray'.

Little Old Lady; Village Blues; My Shining Hour; Fifth House; Harmonique; Like Sonny; I'll Wait And Pray; Some Other Blues.

First released 1961
UK peak chart position: did not chart
USA peak chart position: did not chart

24. TIME OUT
Dave Brubeck

Second only to *Jazz Samba* by Stan Getz, as the most commercially successful jazz record of all time (it even contained a single for the pop charts, Paul Desmond's magnificent 'Take Five'). Brubeck brilliantly popularised jazz and gave it as a palatable alternative to Bobby Vee. This album sold by the trunkload and made Brubeck a popular star. Those jazz critics who shunned him for becoming too commercial must eat their words for this is a monumental album of the finest modern jazz. 'Blue Rondo A La Turk' and 'Kathy's Waltz' demonstrate this mans graceful nonchalant class.

Blue Rondo A La Turk; Strange Meadow Lark; Take Five; Three To Get Ready; Kathy's Waltz; Everybody's Jumpin'; Pick Up Sticks.

First released 1959
UK peak chart position: 11
USA peak chart position: 2

25. THE LOUIS ARMSTRONG STORY 1-7
Louis Armstrong

Legendary New Orleans trumpeter and vocalist Louis 'Satchmo' Armstrong was jazz's first instrumentalist soloist. An immensely gifted technician with a profoundly lyrical melodic conception and ringing, celebratory tone, he broke away from the entirely polyphonic New Orleans tradition to play a music that shifted the emphasis onto his (and sometimes others') individual solos. This skilfully compiled seven volume set starts in November 1925 and ends in March 1931, and features his celebrated Hot Fives and Hot Sevens recordings, his brilliant early big band work, and the start of the concurrent interest in his extraordinary vocals.

including: When You're Smiling; Some Of These Days; On The Sunny Side Of The Street; Solitude; When The Saints Go Marching In; Ain't Misbehavin'; Jeepers Creepers; I Want A Little Girl; Someday You'll Be Sorry; Lazy River; I Love Jazz; Mack The Knife; Muskat Ramble; Tiger Rag; When It's Sleepy Time Down South; Cabaret; Volare; Indiana; A Kiss To Build A Dream On; Hello Dolly; Blueberry Hill; St. James Infirmary; Tenderly; You'll Never Walk Alone; Mop Mop.

First released 1988
UK peak chart position: did not chart
USA peak chart position: did not chart

26. ART BLAKEY'S JAZZ MESSENGERS WITH THELONIOUS MONK
Art Blakey

It is interesting to wonder whether, if this record was played anonymously to a major record company today, anyone there would have the foresight, understanding or courage to take it on – incredibly, this daring and advanced album was recorded in 1957. Its illustrious personnel consists of fast-fingered, prolific saxophone virtuoso Johnny Griffin, fiery trumpeter Bill Hardman, bassist Spanky DeBrest, the quirky and brilliant pianist Thelonious Monk and thunderous drummer Art Blakey, and the material features mainly Monk originals, played with as much guts, gumption and originality as ever. Monk's piano work is particularly full of thrilling, fascinating surprises.

Evidence; In Walked Bud; Blue Monk; I Mean You; Rhythm-A-Ning; Purple Shades.

First released 1957
UK peak chart position: did not chart
USA peak chart position: did not chart

27. IMPRESSIONS
John Coltrane

So this is where the Byrds borrowed 'Eight Miles High' from. Yes, on 'India'. Coltrane managed to continue to influence and break barriers both within his own highly fickle cognoscenti and outside in the rock world during the mid-60s as contemporaries of his would cite his massive influence. Four exquisite excursions with McCoy Tyner, piano; Jimmy Garrison and Reggie Workman, bass; Elvin Jones and Roy Haynes, drums and Eric Dolphy playing some extraordinary bass clarinet on the previously mentioned 'India'. The other tour de force is the similarly explorative 'Impressions'. Not easy but absolutely worthwhile.

India; Up Against The Wall; Impressions; After The Rain.

First released 1963
UK peak chart position: did not chart
USA peak chart position: did not chart

28. SAXOPHONE COLOSSUS
Sonny Rollins

A truly flawless album representing everything bop was at its best, *Saxophone Colossus* is a quartet recording from 1956 led by the great Sonny Rollins on tenor saxophone and featuring pianist Tommy Flanagan, bassist Doug Watkins and drummer Max Roach. The record opens with the original, catchy and rousing version of Rollins's much-loved Caribbean-flavoured standard 'St. Thomas', and includes a richly emotional 'You Don't Know What Love Is' and a superbly angular, side-long blues entitled 'Blue Seven'. Few musicians ever spoke the bebop language with such consistent inspiration and flair.

Moritat; Blue Seven; Strode Rode; St. Thomas; You Don't Know What Love Is.

First released 1956
UK peak chart position: did not chart
USA peak chart position: did not chart

29. THE THUNDERING HERDS 1945-1947
Woody Herman

Of all the big band leaders, Herman was one of the most committed to jazz. Hardly ever concerning himself with commerciality, happily ranging from blues to bop,. a striking array of jazz soloists adorned his 'Herds'. Whether playing loose-limbed charts by Ralph Burns, the tightly-structured arrangements of Jimmy Giuffre, or the rampaging 'heads' by the band, Herman, as soloist, vocalist, leader, catalyst and talent finder, was one of the all-time jazz greats. All these qualities, together with soloists like Sonny Berman, Bill Harris, Flip Phillips, Red Norvo and Stan Getz, appear on this album which covers his greatest years.

Woodchopper's Ball; Apple Honey; Goosey Gander; Northwest Passage; The Good Earth; A Jug Of Wine; Your Father's Moustache; Bijou; Wild Root; Panacea; Backtalk; Non-alcoholic; Blues Are Brewin'; The Goof And I; Four Brothers; Blue Flame.

First released 1953
UK peak chart position: did not chart
USA peak chart position: did not chart

30. JAZZ GIANT
Benny Carter

One of a very small number of jazz musicians to have enjoyed successful careers playing both trumpet and saxophone, Benny Carter was already firmly established as an important swing name when, in 1958, he recorded this superb small group album. Accompanied by tenor saxophone legend Ben Webster, Stan Kenton-trombonist Frank Rosolino, pianists André Previn and Jimmie Rowles, swinging West Coast guitarist Barney Kessel, bassist Leroy Vinnegar and top West Coast drummer Shelly Manne, Carter proves he was as great a jazz improviser as big band composer and arranger, on a selection of standards and two original compositions.

Old Fashioned Love; I'm Coming Virginia; A Walkin' Thing; Blue Lou; Ain't She Sweet; How Can You Lose; Blues My Naughty Sweetie Gives To Me.

First released 1958
UK peak chart position: did not chart
USA peak chart position: did not chart

31. IN A SILENT WAY
Miles Davis

Miles Davis's hushed masterpiece *In A Silent Way* was pieced together in the studio from a series of long stretches of quiet and intense collective improvisation. Masterfully demonstrating to the jazz world that rock's electronic instruments were not necessarily harsh and noisy creatures, he again proved his creative and conceptual genius, fashioning the sound of fusion, with the aid of Herbie Hancock, Chick Corea and Joe Zawinul on electric pianos and organ, John McLaughlin on electric guitar, Wayne Shorter on soprano saxophone, British bassist Dave Holland and drummer Tony Williams. This is a the delicate and beautiful thing that has rarely been repeated.

Ssh Peaceful; In A Silent Way; It's About That Time.

First released 1969
UK peak chart position: did not chart
USA peak chart position: 134

32. COLEMAN HAWKINS ENCOUNTERS BEN WEBSTER
Coleman Hawkins

Although both Hawkins and Webster could play with power and authority, the two men shared a love for rhapsodic and romantic music. Teaming them for a session of gorgeous ballads proved to be a wise decision. Fluid, graceful, rich in promise and fulfilment, these are solos and duets that are echoed every time two tenor saxophonists play together. Only rarely does any other pairing reach these heights and never have they been surpassed. Hawkin's barrel-chested muscular sound and Webster's breathy sensuality bring to the songs they perform profound depths of emotional understanding. This is jazz balladry at its very best.

Blues For Yolande; It Never Entered My Mind; Rosita; You's Be So Nice To Come Home To; Prisoner Of Love; Tangerine; Shine On Harvest Moon. (1958)

First released 1959
UK peak chart position: did not chart
USA peak chart position: did not chart

33. OUT OF THE COOL
Gil Evans

A much admired and loved man, of all the many brilliant orchestration projects this was his finest in his own right. He teases us with the opening of 'La Nevada' until the gorgeous repeated four bar riff finally bursts on our ears with orgasmic delight. There are wonderful brass solos from John Coles, Tony Studd and Budd Johnson and a bass showcase for Ron Carter. As the opening track peters out after 15 minutes the listener has the smug realisation that there are a further four outstanding pieces to come. Too much of Evans' fame came through Miles Davis and Jimi Hendrix.

La Nevada; Where Flamingoes Fly; Bilbao Song; Stratusphunk; Sunken Treasure.

First released 1960
UK peak chart position: did not chart
USA peak chart position: did not chart

34. THE BLUEBIRD SESSIONS
Sidney Bechet

An unashamed romantic, Bechet was a balladeer with a majestic playing style. He commanded attention on clarinet and soprano saxophone. On the former instrument he ranked with the best; on the latter there was simply no competition during his lifetime. Bechet soars gloriously over his accompanists, receiving all the attention his full-blooded, heart-on-sleeve romanticism demands. Swinging remorselessly, he demonstrates over and over again that his was a talent unique amongst his contemporaries. Although he had a handful of disciples, hardly anyone followed Bechet's path - a fact which makes his work even more worthy on interest today.

including: Sweetie Dear; I Want You Tonight; I've Found A New Baby; Lay Your Racket; Maple Leaf Rag; Shag; Ja Da; Really The Blues; When You And I Were Young Maggie; Weary Blues; Oh, Didn't He Ramble; High Society; I Thought I Heard Buddy Bolden Say; Winin' Boy Blues; Indian Summer; One O'clock Jump; Preachin' Blues; Sidney's Blues; Shake It And Break It; Old Man's Blues; Nobody Knows The Way I Feel This Morning; Wild Man Blues; Make Me A Pallet On The Floor; St. Louis Blues; Blues In Thirds; Blues For You, Johnny; Ain't Misbehavin'; Save It Pretty Mama; Stompy Jones; Muskat Ramble; Coal Black Shine; Egyptian Fantasy; Baby Won't You Please Come Home; Slippin' And Slidin'; The Sheik Of Araby; Blues Of Bechet; Swing Parade.

rec. 1932-43
UK peak chart position: did not chart
USA peak chart position: did not chart

35. HELIOCENTRIC WORLDS OF SUN RA VOL 1
Sun Ra

Cult bandleader, black activist and self-proclaimed space traveller Sun Ra left such a rich recorded legacy on planet Earth, each album with its fair share of magic, that to choose a top handful is a gruelling task. But the records he made for the forward-thinking, musician-managed ESP (short for Esperanto) label during the '60s are surely outstanding for the concentrated and consistently powerful music they contain. Recorded before the days of the space chants and chaotic swing standards, *Heliocentric Worlds* contains long and cacophonous group improvisations, breath-taking in execution and ecstatic in conception. They also contain some of the most exciting and spirited keyboard work Sun Ra ever put to vinyl.

The Sun Myth; House Of Beauty; Cosmic Chaos.

First released 1965
UK peak chart position: did not chart
USA peak chart position: did not chart

36. SOMEDAY MY PRINCE WILL COME
Miles Davis

Quintessional Miles, laid back, confident and spacious together with for many his best musical unit of John Coltrane, Wynton Kelly, Paul Chambers and Philly Joe Jones, further augmented by Hank Mobley, tenor and Jimmy Cobb. Although Coltrane was only guesting his strong spirit is felt and his vignettes are faultless. The title track builds beautifully until a wonderful drone-like booming bass line closes it. The other stand out tracks are 'Pfrancing', with some glorious light fingers from Kelly and on 'Teo the groove is very much in the *Kind Of Blue* mould. This an exceptional Miles album that often gets overlooked.

Someday My Prince Will Come; Old Folks; Pfrancing; Drad-Dog; Teo; I Thought About You.

First released 1961
UK peak chart position: did not chart
USA peak chart position: did not chart

37. MODERN ART
Art Farmer

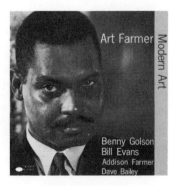

Trumpet and flugelhorn player Art Farmer is a warm and lyrical improviser, capable of creating stunningly original and carefully structured solos. This fascinating 1958 Blue Note date brings Farmer together with the highly-regarded swing-led tenor saxophonist Benny Golson (and prolific jazz composer, most notably of 'I Remember Clifford') a year before they would form the lastingly popular Jazztet. The amazing Bill Evans, on loan at the time from Miles Davis's Sextet, fills the piano chair, while Art's twin brother Addison plays bass, and Dave Bailey is on drums.This is swinging and melodic modern mainstream jazz at its very best.

Mox Nix; Fair Weather; Darn That Dream; The Touch Of Your Lips; Jubilation; Like Someone In Love; I Love You; Cold Breeze.

First released 1958
UK peak chart position: did not chart
USA peak chart position: did not chart

38. BITCHES BREW
Miles Davis

A thoroughly unsaintly concoction of jazz experimentation and rock psychedelia, *Bitches Brew* took the loose, exploratory, collective improvisation and rock beat approach that Miles Davis had developed on *In A Silent Way*, but painted it a slightly harsher and more sinister hue. This is a long work, sold as a double album, with a mesmerising feel to its collection of strange funk-rock grooves. Benny Maupin's bass clarinet adds an unnerving dimension to the group's sound, creaking threateningly from deep within, while Davis himself plays lean, but fragmented, trumpet lines. An inspired and intense work, *Bitches Brew* dramatically influenced the course of jazz history, and ushered in the fusion movement.

Pharaoh's Dance; Bitches Brew; Spanish Key; John McLaughlin, Miles Runs Down The Voodoo Down; Sanctuary.

First released 1970
UK peak chart position: 71
USA peak position: 35

39. MINGUS AH UM
Charles Mingus

One of the five essential Mingus albums to own, and even if you are not a jazz fan this is still worthy of being in any comprehensive collection. The opening track 'Better Git It In Your Soul' rushes along at a furious pace and then there is a wonderful change of tempo into an a cappella and hand clap pause. It rolls on of course, but the nature of this track is very much the nature of Mingus who never failed to experiment (even though sometimes he failed). The personnel comprises; John Handy III, Shafi Hadi and Booker Ervin, saxophones; Horace Parlan Jr, piano; Willie Dennis and James Knepper, trombones and Charles Richmond on drums. Mingus whoops, shouts and holds it all together and then turns the pace majestically on numbers such as 'Goodbye Pork Pie Hat'.

Better Git It In Your Soul; Goodbye Pork Pie Hat; Boogie Stop Shuffle; Self-Portrait In Three Colours; Open Letter To Duke; Bird Calls; Fables Of Faubus; Pussy Cat Dues; Jelly Roll

First released 1960
UK peak chart position: did not chart
USA peak chart position: did not chart

40. BLUES AND THE ABSTRACT TRUTH
Oliver Nelson

Beautifully recorded and easily the best album of his career, which early on included stints with Louis Jordan, Quincey Jones and conducted and arranged for Jimmy Smith (notably 'Walk On The Wild Side'). The personnel on this album is formidable and probably enhances the albums high standing; Eric Dolphy, alto and flute, Bill Evans, piano, Roy Haynes, drums, Freddie Hubbard, trumpet, George Barrow, baritone and Nelson, alto, tenor and writer/arranger. Its hard to imagine that the man wholly behind this exceptional album is responsible for the 'Six Million Dollar Man' television series theme.

Stolen Moments; Hoe Down; Cascades; Yearnin'; Butch And Butch; Teenie's Blues.

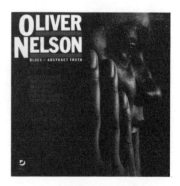

First released 1961
UK peak chart position: did not chart
USA peak chart position: did not chart

41. NEW TIJUANA MOODS
Charles Mingus

The third of only three Mingus albums in the listings, *Mingus Mingus Mingus Mingus Mingus* and *Pithecanthropus Erectus* were surprisingly just outside the 100. The original sessions were held in 1957 and released as *Tijuana Moods*, the bonus of the CD age gives us additional alternate versions which benefit from digital remastering. It is glorious stuff with Mingus leading strong musicians on his personal favourite recording. Mingus acts like a kindly father allowing his offspring to shine, without taking over or showing off, that alone is sure sign of his greatness as a musician and band leader.

Dizzy Moods; Ysabel's Table Dance; Tijuana Gift Shop; Los Mariachis; Flamingo; Dizzy Moods; Tijuana Gift Shop; Los Mariachis II; Flamingo.

First released 1986
UK peak chart position: did not chart
USA peak chart position: did not chart

42. THE SIDEWINDER
Lee Morgan

Simple and direct and somewhat of a runt album in the history of jazz. The solos on Art Blakey's recording of Bobby Timmons 'Moanin' is Morgan, as is 'A Night In Tunisia'. By the time he came to record this album he had simplified his style which appealed to the soul/jazz lovers of the 60s. To use the ultimate cliche this is groovin' music, it rolls it bops, it makes you feel good and its success is that it is refreshingly uncomplicated. Supported by Joe Henderson, tenor; Billy Higgins, drums; Barry Harris, piano and Bob Cranshaw, bass.

The Sidewinder; Totem Pole; Gary's Notebook; Boy, What A Night!; Hocus Pocus.

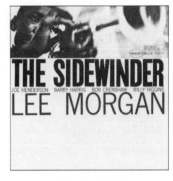

First released 1964
UK peak chart position: did not chart
USA peak chart position: 25

43. SPIRITS REJOICE
Albert Ayler

Recorded on the forward-thinking, musician-controlled ESP (short for Esperanto) label in 1965, *Spirits Rejoice* is a free jazz masterpiece – a riotous, hugely emotional and astonishingly creative celebration of the urge to make noise, recorded when the 'new thing' was still genuinely new. This is Ayler at his very best: playing his gospel-soaked themes with a poignant dignity, and a sad introspection that is liable at any time to tumble into chaotic aggression, before being saved by a beautiful, if mournful, resolution. He is joined by trumpeter Albert Ayler, saxophonist Charles Tyler, bassists Henry Grimes and Gary Peacock, harpsichordist Call Cobbs and drummer Sunny Murray.

Spirits Rejoice; Holy Family; D.C.; Angels; Prophet.

First released 1965
UK peak chart position: did not chart
USA peak chart position: did not chart

44. ESP
Miles Davis

Probably the best of a number of edgy and exciting albums recorded during one of Miles Davis's most creative periods, *ESP* dates from 1965 and features one of his greatest bands. The daring, youthful sense of adventure that tenor saxophonist Wayne Shorter, pianist Herbie Hancock, bassist Ron Carter and drummer Tony Williams brought to Davis helped relaunch his career and put him in touch with the experimental jazz spirit of the period. The new music was looser, freer, and featured abrupt changes of direction and rhythm, as the musicians responded to each other as much as to any preset scheme.

ESP; Eighty One; Little One; RJ; Agitation; Iris; Mood.

First released 1965
UK peak chart position: did not chart
USA peak chart position: did not chart

45. OFFRAMP
Pat Metheny

If it isn't jazz what is it? Where do we place Metheny apart from being a comparatively recent musical genius? This album is one of a dozen of his albums which came close to qualifying, his music is uplifting, emotional, clever and often breathtaking. 'Are You Going With Me' is the finest example of Metheny music. It slowly builds on a hypnotic beat until his guitar synthesizer is unleashed to a fitting climax. 'James' (dedicated to Mr Taylor) demonstrates that beauty and simplicity can go together. Metheny has to be seen as one of the most important musical figures over the past 20 years.

Barcorolle; Are You Going With Me; Au Lait; Eighteen; Offramp; James; The Bat (Part Two).

First released 1982
UK peak chart position: did not chart
USA peak chart position: 50

46. BIG BAND BOSSA NOVA
Stan Getz

Stan Getz's name is synonymous with the *bossa nova* movement. A profoundly lyrical tenor saxophonist, full of melodic surprises and aide by a flawless, virtuoso technique, he was, along with guitarist Charlie Byrd and the Gilbertos, one of the key figures fusing bossa with jazz in the 60s. This 1962 Verve big band date (recorded a year before the hugely successful 'The Girl From Ipanema') features four classic compositions by Bonfa, Gilberto and Jobim, and four authentic-sounding original tunes by arranger Gary McFarland. Getz is on inspired form throughout, and there is a characteristically beautiful contribution by guitarist Jim Hall on the opening 'Manha De Carnival'.

Manha De Carnival; Balanco No Samba; Melancolico; Entre Amigos; Chega De Sandade; Noite Triste; Samba De Uma Nota So; Bim Bam.

First released 1962
UK peak chart position: did not chart
USA peak chart position: 13

47. WALTZ FOR DEBBY
Bill Evans

Redcorded on the same night as *Sunday At The Village Vanguard*, *Waltz For Debby* captures one of the most important and well-integrated piano trios in the history of jazz, working on a superbly inspired night. It is clear, listening to this record, that bassist Scott Lafaro had a very special rapport with Evans, and drummer Paul Motian's subtle, improvised accompaniments and eccentric, quirkily quiet swing was the perfect engine for this subtle, impressionistic pianist. Check out the lovely, gentle 'My Foolish Heart', and the lively 'Milestones' and, of course, 'Waltz For Debby'.

My Foolish Heart; Waltz For Debby; Detour Ahead; My Romance; Some Other Time; Milestones.

First released 1961
UK peak chart position: did not chart
USA peak chart position: did not chart

48. BELONGING
Keith Jarrett

The spine on the CD states Keith Jarrett, but many of us regard this as a Jan Garbarek album. Jarrett was the non-Scandinavian in a superb quartet that comprised Garbarek, saxophones; Pelle Danielson, bass and Jon Christensen, drums. Garbarek and Jarrett constantly interplay offering melancholy, romance, sadness and emotional musical bliss on 'Spiral Dance' and 'Blossom' and manages to groove along with the out of character 'Long As You Know You're Living Yours'. One of the finest moments from ECM's exceptional and now sizeable catalogue. Maybe Jarrett and Garbarek need to work with each other sporadically to recharge each other.

Spiral Dance; Blossom; Long As You Know You're Living Yours; Belonging; The Windup; Solstice.

First released 1974
UK peak chart position: did not chart
USA peak chart position: did not chart

49. DIZ AND GETZ
Dizzy Gillespie & Stan Getz

A meeting of two giants can often be a disaster, especially with two quite different characters musically and personally, both used to having a lot of the solo limelight. The fusion works to perfection, alone but totally together. The recording level, even on the CD puts Getz a few watts behind. In 1953 they forgot to balance the harshness of Dizzy's trumpet against the smoothness of Getz's tenor, a minor gripe on a fine recording. The line-up is faultless as it is impressive; Oscar Peterson, piano; Herb Ellis, guitar; Ray Brown, bass; Max Roach, drums play on all tracks except 'One Alone' which is supported by Hank Mobley, tenor; Wade Legge, piano; Lou Hackney, bass; Charlie Persip, drums. Its all very amiable and solid.

It Don't Mean A Thing (If It Ain't Got That Swing); I Let My Heart Go Out Of My Heart; Exactly Like You; It's The Talk Of The Town; Impromptu; One Alone; Girl Of My Dreams; Siboney (Part I), Siboney (Part II).

First released 1955
UK peak chart position: did not chart
USA peak chart position: did not chart

50. JAZZ SAMBA
STAN GETZ

The album that launched Jobim's now classic 'Desafinado', Jazz Samba was released in 1962, in the early days of America's bossa nova craze and before the music lost its charm to cliché. Joined by fellow Latin jazz pioneer Charlie Byrd on classical guitar, and a discreet bass and drums team, tenor saxophonist Getz makes light and elegant music out of a collection of catchy bossas and sambas. His virtuosity, bluesy drive and smooth, soft tone make the music cook like bossa jazz rarely has since. There are still enough surprises to make this record more than just a period piece, but a fine example of one of Getz's lyrical genius.

Desafinado; Samba Dees Days; O Pato; Samba Triste; Samba De Uma Nota So; E Luxo So; Baia.

First released 1962
UK peak chart position: 15
USA peak chart position: 1

51. NEW CONCEPTS OF ARTISTRY IN RHYTHM
STAN KENTON

When West Coast big band leader Stan Kenton recorded this 1952 masterpiece, his powerful and versatile 21-piece featured bebop trumpet virtuoso and high note specialist Maynard Ferguson, trombonists Frank Rosolino and Bill Russo, the brilliant and advanced alto saxophonist Lee Konitz, Sal Salvador on guitar and the subtle swing of drummer Stan Levey. It is a typically dramatic production – dissonant and experimental, and thunderous in a similar way to the Hollywood film music of the time. Highlights include a fascinating introduction ('This Is An Orchestra') featuring Kenton as narrator and, amongst the CD's extra tracks, a brilliantly out rearrangement of 'You Go To My Head'.

Prologue (This Is An Orchestra!); Portrait Of A Count; Young Blood; Frank Seaking; 23 Degrees North - 82 Degrees West; Taboo; Lonesome Train; Invention For Guitar And Trumpet; My Lady; Swing House; Improvisation; You Go To My Head.

First released 1952
UK peak chart position: did not chart
USA peak chart position: did not chart

52. FREE JAZZ
Ornette Coleman

The revolutionary Free Jazz features Coleman's Double Quartet which included Eric Dolphy (bass clarinet), trumpeters Don Cherry and Freddie Hubbard, bassists Charlie Haden and Scott La Faro, drummers Billy Higgins and Ed Blackwell and the ensemble leader on alto saxophone. Brief written parts aside, which introduced each soloist, the piece is completely improvised, without editing or overdubs. Set free to follow artistic inclinations, the musicians respond to their own imagination, or react to those around them, resulting in a fervid collectivity. The ambition of the concept is rewarded with exceptional playing, at times lyrical, at other intense, but always inventive and challenging. The results were a landmark in the development of jazz.

Free Jazz (Part One); Free Jazz (Part Two).

First released 1960
UK peak chart position: did not chart
USA peak chart position: did not chart

53. CONFERENCE OF THE BIRDS
David Holland

A challenging but hugely rewarding ECM label classic, *Conference Of The Birds* is a delicate balance of Ornette Coleman-influenced free improvisation with rhythm and more fragmented response playing. Sam Rivers and Anthony Braxton share the dynamic front line, both playing assorted reeds and flute, whilst drums, percussion and marimba are provided by Barry Altschul. Dave Holland has always been a fine composer, and his distinctive tunes and rich, resonant and flawlessly accurate bass playing stamp a subtle identity on this work. The title track is in particular a sombre and painfully beautiful masterpiece, shifting gently on a tapestry of flute, soprano saxophone and marimba.

Four Winds; Q&A; Conference Of The Birds; Interception; Now Here (Nowhere); See-Saw.

First released 1972
UK peak chart position: did not chart
USA peak chart position: did not chart

54. CHANGE OF THE CENTURY
Ornette Coleman

Listening to these pioneering free-jazz sessions a quarter of a century later, it is hard to understand the violently outraged responses Coleman received at the time. Gentle, spacey, melodic and certainly very beautiful, his piano-less quartet, with trumpeter Don Cherry, bassist Charlie Haden and drummer Billy Higgins, ran a quirky, blues-oriented groove with grace and wit. This is music that swings as hard as any jazz, but harmonically follows its own spontaneous laws, relying on Haden's astonishing versatility and quick thinking to establish its order.

Ramblin'; Free; The Face Of The Bass; Forerunner; Bird Food; Una Muy Bonita; Change Of The Century.

First released 1960
UK peak chart position: did not chart
USA peak chart position: did not chart

55. MIDNIGHT BLUE
Kenny Burrell

From the sight of Reid Miles' brilliant typography on the cover you know what you are getting. Smooth smootchy jazz guitar played at the pace of a slow loris - quite magnificent in its sparing qualities. Mr Burrell together with Grant Green and Wes Montgomery defined this style. 'Chitlins Con Carne' is a late night feast while 'Midnight Blue' is smokey and soulful and yes, Van Morisson did borrow the intro for 'Moondance'. There is subtle support from Major Holley Jnr., bass; Bill English, drums; Ray Barretto, conga and lustrous understated tenor from the omnipresent Stanley Turrentine.

Chitlins Con Carne; Mule; Soul Lament; Midnight Blue; Wavy Gravy; Gee Baby Ain't I Good To You; Saturday Night Blues.

First released 1963
UK peak chart position: did not chart
USA peak chart position: did not chart

56. ELLA FITZGERALD SINGS THE COLE PORTER SONG BOOK
Ella Fitzgerald

One of Fitzgerald's great assets was also, paradoxically, one of her failings as a jazz singer. Throughout her long career her voice was that of an innocent girl. This immaturity of sound, allied as it was to consummate musical mastery, weakened her jazz performances, especially the blues where emotional intensity is of paramount importance. As if sensing this, Norman Granz heard in Ella's voice the ideal vehicle for a selection of readings from the Great American Songbook. Her coolly detached approach to lyrics is nowhere better displayed than on this album of songs by one of the most sophisticated American songwriters.

All Through The Night; Anything Goes; Miss Otis Regrets; Too Darn Hot; In The Still Of The Night; I Get A Kick Out Of You; Do I Love You; Always True To You In My Fashion; Let's Do It; Just One Of Those Things; Every Time We Say Goodbye; All Of You; Begin The Beguine; Get Out Of Turn; I Am In Love; From This Moment On; I Love Paris; You Do Something To Me; Riding High; Easy To Love; It's Alright With Me; Why Can't You Behave; What Is This Thing Called Love; You're The Top; Love For Sale; It's D'Lovely; Night And Day; Ace In The Hole; So In Love; I've Got You Under My Skin; I Concentrate On You; Don't Fence Me In.

First released 1956
UK peak chart position: did not chart
USA peak chart position: 15

57. AND HIS ORCHESTRA
Dizzy Gillespie

Dizzy Gillespie is usually remembered as one of a handful of musicians who led a the way to a new small group sound in the post-war period, when the swing big bands were suffering economical problems. Along with Charlie Parker, Thelonious Monk and Bud Powell, Gillespie helped revolutionise and complicate the music, with an extended harmonic vocabulary and, most strikingly, an incredible virtuoso technique. But Gillespie's own bebop-based big band work resulted in some of the most exciting dates of his career, providing a climactic background for his own trumpet fireworks, and a good place for him to test his burgeoning interest in Latin American musics.

A Night In Tunisia; Ol' Man Rebop; Ow; Oop-Pop-A-Da; Two Bass Hit; Stay On It; Algo Bueno; Overtime; Manteca; Good Bait; Cool Breeze; Cubana Be; Cubana Bop; Minor Walk; Swedish Suite; Victory Ball.

rec. 1946-49
UK peak chart position: did not chart
USA peak chart position: did not chart

58. RETURN TO FOREVER
Chick Corea

'Return To Forever' became the name keyboardist Chick Corea gave to a series of three different fusion projects during the '70s. But coined originally here in 1972, it was a stunning Latin-influenced jazz/rock quintet, featuring the now celebrated vocals and percussion team of Flora Purim and Airto Moreira, flautist/saxophonist Joe Farrell and virtuoso bassist Stanley Clarke. The eerie and distinctly 'trippy' title track that opens the album is a breathtaking lesson for fusion rhythm sections, as Corea, Clarke and Moreira surge forward on something close to telepathy, while Purim adds mesmeric and disturbing shrieks and cries across the top. This is a fusion classic and 45 minutes of genius.

Return To Forever; Crystal Silence; What Game Shall We Play Today; Sometime Ago - La Fiesta.

First released 1971
UK peak chart position: did not chart
USA peak chart position: did not chart

59. GUITAR FORMS
Kenny Burrell

An extraordinarily varied record that moves away from jazz to encompass classical Spanish guitar, bossa nova, pop and blues. The key to its success is that the whole package is conducted and arranged by Gil Evans. He enables quite different styles to come together and sound cohesive with his remarkable vision of musical shape and form. The personnel is lengthy and includes Ron Carter, bass; Steve Lacy, saxophone; Lee Konitz, saxophone; Elvin Jones and Charlie Persip, drums and Jimmy Cleveland, trombone. Evans' mixes Burrell's lone Spanish guitar against 16 other musician with absolute confidence and dedication to make it work like a dream.

Greensleeves; Last Night When We Were Young; Breadwinner; Downstairs; Lotus Land; Prelude Number Two; Moon And Sand; Loie; Terrace Theme.

First released 1965
UK peak chart position: did not chart
USA peak chart position: did not chart

60. MEDITATIONS
John Coltrane

One of John Coltrane's classic religious suites, *Meditations* is a long and complex work from a period late in his career, when he was beginning to break his ties with the classic quartet, and augment the band with new members. Pianist McCoy Tyner, bassist Jimmy Garrison and drummer Elvin Jones are joined by tenor saxophonist Pharoah Sanders on the front line and drummer Rashied Ali. In five-parts, joined by long improvised linking passages, *Meditations* is an intense, emotional and difficult work, and signalled the beginning of a fiercely challenging final period for Coltrane.

Love; Consequences; Serenity; The Father And The Son And The Holy Ghost; Compassion.

First released 1966
UK peak chart position: did not chart
USA peak chart position: did not chart

61. ELLA FITZGERALD SINGS THE RODGERS AND HART SONGBOOK
Ella Fitzgerald

Richard Rodger's tuneful music and Lorenz Hart's wittily amusing lyrics form a very special part of America popular music. So too does Ella Fitzgerald and their meeting - under the benign influence of Norman Granz - is a highwater mark in the story of popular singing. The singer's unworldly and ingenuous charm suits the material and transports the listener to times without care; until, that is, the occasional tartness of a Hart lyric reminds us that life is not always a song. Along with the rest of the Songbook series, this is popular music at its best and sets standards never previously attained.

Have You Met Miss Jones?; You Took Advantage Of Me; Ship Without A Sail; To Keep My Love Alive; Dancing On The Ceiling; The Lady Is A Tramp; With A Song In My Heart; Manhattan; Johnny One Note; I Wish I Were In Love Again; Spring Is Here; It Never Entered My Mind; This Can't Be Love; Thou Swell; My Romance; Where Or When; Little Girl Blue; Give It Back To The Indians; Ten Cents A Dance; There's A Small Hotel; I Don't Know What Time It Was; Everything I've Got; I Could Write A Book; Blue Room; My Funny Valentine; Bewitched; Mountain Greenery; Wait Till You See Her; Lover; Isn't It Romantic?; Here In My Arms; Blue Moon; My Heart Stood Still; I've Got Five Dollars.

First released 1957
UK peak chart position: did not chart
USA peak chart positiion: 11

62. UNITY
Larry Young

During the mid-60s the Hammond organ was having a particularly popular time, especially with the host of soulful jazz organists. The leaders were Jimmy Smith and Jimmy McGriff, and they were followed by John Patton, Lonnie Smith and for many the best of all Larry Young. *Unity* his second Blue Note album and features Woody Shaw, trumpet; Joe Henderson, tenor and Elvin Jones on drums. The playing is polished, clever an occasionally breathtaking. Young never came near the quality of this album again, even though he went on to work with Miles Davis and John McLaughlin. He died at the age of 38.

Zoltan; Monk's Dream; If; The Moontrane; Softly As A Morning Sunrise; Beyond All Limits.

First released 1966
UK peak chart position: did not chart
USA peak chart position: did not chart

63. ORGAN GRINDER SWING
Jimmy Smith

'Incredible', 'fantastic', 'legendary' or just plain 'good', the man who made the Hammond organ acceptable and in turn became its most famous user rightly appears in this chart. Smith and his disciples nurtured and monopolised the late night soul/jazz sound with a series of landmark albums during the 60s. This highly successful album co-stars guitarist Kenny Burrell and Grady Tate on drums. The bouncing title track has been used many times by disc jockeys as a perfect programme opener. 'Oh No Babe' is a lengthy slow blues which allows the trio to stretch out and relax. Groovy and still exciting.

The Organ Grinder's Swing; Oh No Babe; Blues For J; Greensleeves; I'll Close My Eyes; Satin Doll.

First released 1965
UK peak chart position: did not chart
USA peak chart positiion: 15

64. BIRDS OF FIRE
John McLaughlin And The Mahavishnu Orchestra

The seminal jazz/rock band, The Mahavishnu Orchestra was formed by John McLaughlin shortly after the virtuoso guitarist's brilliant contributions to Miles Davis's fusion masterpiece *Bitches Brew*. Orchestral in power, but in fact just a five-piece, the first Mahavishnu featured keyboardist Jan Hammer, violinist Jerry Goodman, bassist Rick Laird and the advanced drumming of Billy Cobham, and established the fusion vocabulary of noisy, electric virtuosity and complex time signatures. Highlights of *Birds Of Fire* include the climactic and funky 'One Word', featuring a mesmerising bass figure and an exciting three-way improvisation, and the subtle groove on 'Miles Beyond'.

Birds Of Fire; Miles Beyond (Miles Davis); Celestial Terrestial Commuters; Sapphire Bullets of Pure Love; Thousand Island Park; Hope One Word; Sanctuary; Open Country Joy; Resolution.

First released 1973
UK peak chart position:20
USA peak chart position: 15

65. THE GEORGE AND IRA GERSHWIN SONGBOOK
Ella Fitzgerald

The paradox of Ella Fitzgerald's prominence in the history of jazz singing and her lack of emotional intensity is much less apparent in this album. George Gershwin's affinity with jazz, and the corresponding delight jazz musicians take in performing his material, allows the singer to fly with the music. As for brother Ira's lyrics, they receive their due as cheerful, tender and always delightful examples of the lyricist's art. The Songbook series remains one of Ella Fitzgerald's major contributions - amongst many - to American popular music and this particular is one of the best of the bunch.

including: Sam And Delilah; But Not For Me; My One And Only; Let's Call The Whole Thing Off; I've Got Beginners Luck; Lady Be Good; Nice Work If You Can Get It; Things Are Looking Up; Just Another Rhumba; How Long Has This Been Going On; S'wonderful; Man I Love; That Certain Feeling; By Strauss; Who Cares; Someone To Watch Over Me; Real American Folk Song; They All Laughed; Looking For A Boy; My Cousin From Milwaukee; Somebody From Somewhere; Foggy Day; Clap Yo' Hands; For You, For Me, Forever More; Stiff Upper Lip; Strike Up The Band; Soon; I've Got A Crush On You; Bidin' My Time; Aren't You Kind Of Glad We Did; Of Thee I Sing; Half It Dearie Blues; I Was Doing It Right; He Loves And She Loves; Love Is Sweeping The Country; Treat Me Rough; Love Is Here To Stay; Slap That Bass; Isn't It A Pity; Shall We Dance;

First released 1959
UK peak chart position: did not chart
USA peak chart position: 111

66. HEAD HUNTERS
Herbie Hancock

Head Hunters has spawned a thousand copies and copyists, but is only strengthened through comparison. One of the most enduring works of the 70s' jazz/funk legacy, and surely one of Herbie Hancock's most enjoyable and infectious recordings, the album was released in the deeply groovy days of 1973, an soon became the best-selling record in jazz history. Loping along on a glorious bed of springy wah-wah and synth bass, the group used all the new technology of the time, and Hancock himself seemed to revel (as he still does) in the latest keyboard sounds available to him. Jazz/funk has never sounded so exciting and dangerous since.

Chameleon; Watermelon Man; Sly; Vein Melter.

First released 1974
UK peak chart position: did not chart
USA peak chart position: 13

67. BLUE TRAIN
John Coltrane

Although it would seem that Alfred Lion's Blue Note label would have been the perfect home for a Bluetrane this is his only record for the label. Notwithstanding it shows a confident Coltrane before he became a giant. The opening track is the leader, although a straightforward blues it is a warming and familiar song. He is supported adequately by Lee 'Sidewinder' Morgan, trumpet; Kenny Drew, piano; Paul Chambers, bass; Curtis Fuller, trombone and Philly Joe Jones, drums. Coltrane may have made more important albums, but none swung as much as this one.

Blue Train; Moments Notice; The Locomotion; I'm Old Fashioned; Lazy Bird.

First released 1957
UK peak chart position: did not chart
USA peak chart position: did not chart

68. SOULVILLE
Ben Webster

Ben Webster's breathy and romantic tenor saxophone tone was one of the best loved, and widely imitated, sounds in all of jazz. This flawless 1957 date features pianist Oscar Peterson's celebrated trio as the rhythm section, with guitarist Herb Ellis and bassist Ray Brown, as well as Stan Levey behind the kit. The title track is a slow, mellow blues, but the record's highlight is probably the short but breathtakingly beautiful 'Time On My Hands' - one of Webster's wonderful ballad performances. Interestingly, the CD reissue ends with three tracks of Webster playing an exuberant and appealingly clumsy stride piano - the only surviving examples of him at the keyboard.

Soulville; Late Date; Time On My Hands; Lover Come Back To Me; Where Are You; Makin' Whoopee; Ill Wind.

First released 1958
UK peak chart position: did not chart
USA peak chart position: did not chart

69. THE BIG GUNDOWN
John Zorn

New York-based alto saxophonist, composer and controversial avant gardist John Zorn recorded this tribute to the brilliant soundtrack composer Ennio Morricone (the man behind the music in Sergio Leone's westerns) in 1984/5, and called upon a huge and disparate roster of musicians to give the record its stunning sense of variety. There are appearances by fellow experimenters Bobby Previte (drums), Wayne Horvitz (piano), Tim Berne (alto saxophone) and Christian Marclay (turntables), as well as more mainstream stars, like Toots Thielemans (harmonica) and Big John Patton (organ), but these powerful revisions of Morricone's often disturbing and trippy themes clearly comes out of Zorn's own wacky, off-beat and thoroughly original vision.

The Big Gundown; Peur Sur La Ville; Poverty (Once Upon A Time In America); Milano Odea; Erotico (The Burglars); Battle Of Algiers; Giu La Testa (Duck, You Sucker!); Metamorfosi (La Classe Operaia Va In Paradiso); Tre Nel 5000; Once Upon A Time In The West.

First released 1986
UK peak chart position: did not chart
USA peak chart position: did not chart

70. MAIDEN VOYAGE
Herbie Hancock

Probably the best in Herbie Hancock's series of fine Blue Note albums from the 60s, *Maiden Voyage* finds him in what is basically the Miles Davis band of the time, with Miles replaced by the young Freddie Hubbard. Hancock has always been fine composer, but *Maiden Voyage* contains two classic compositions in particular - the beautiful 'Dolphin Dance', and the atmospheric and popular title track. Saxophonist George Coleman, bassist Ron Carter and drummer Tony Williams play as well as they have ever played throughout, and the whole record is marked with a timeless freshness and sense of creative tension.

Maiden Voyage; The Eye Of The Hurricane; Little One; Survival Of The Fittest; Dolphin Dance.

First released 1964
UK peak chart position: did not chart
USA peak chart position: did not chart

71. SONG FOR MY FATHER
Horace Silver Quintet

Yet another jazz steal, this time, Steely Dan borrowed the title track for their 'Rickki Don't Lose That Number'. Horace Silver should take heart, this is his most successful album and one that finds its way on many recommended lists, not just for the jazz fraternity. Its strength is its acessability, and in keeping with many piano leader albums Silver does not seek to dominate. The quintet is completed by Carmell Jones, trumpet; Joe Henderson, tenor; Teddy Smith, bass and Roger Humphries, drums. The reissued CD versiion contains four extra tracks from the same sessions 1963/4.

Song For My Father; The Natives Are Restless Tonight; Calcutta Cutie; Que Pasa; Kicker; Lonely Woman.

First released 1965
UK peak chart position: did not chart
USA peak chart position: 95

72. THE FIFTH POWER
Lester Bowie

Trumpeter Lester Bowie was born in St. Louis, but he remains closely associated with the jazz developments of '60s Chicago, where he moved in 1962. Along with saxophonists Joseph Jarman and Roscoe Mitchell, and bassist Malachi Favors, musicians he had met through Chicago's Association For The Advancement Of Creative Music, he formed the famous Art Ensemble Of Chicago. This 1978 date was recorded in Italy, and once again features bassist Favors, as well as Chicago saxophone talent Arthur Blythe, pianist/vocalist Amina Myers and drummer Philip Wilson, playing slightly more orthodox, but no less exciting, music.

Sardegna Amore (New Is Full Of Lonely People); 3 In 1 (Three In One); BBB (Duet); God Has Smiled On Me (Traditional Gospel); The 5th Power (Finale).

First released 1978
UK peak chart position: did not chart
USA peak chart position: did not chart

73. IDLE MOMENTS
Grant Green

Guitarist Grant Green's bright but bluesy sound and infectious swing have been featured on massive number of Blue Note albums. During the label's soul-jazz trend, Green was a true stalwart, touching each session with a certain spirited brilliance. Probably his best date, *Idle Moments* is marked by a more serious, introspective quality, and features vibraphone by Bobby Hutcherson, tenor saxophone by a young but already undeniably exceptional Joe Henderson and underrated pianist and composer Duke Pearson. The long, intimate title track is a particular highlight, and deserves to be played again and again.

Idle Moments; Jean De Fleur; Django; Nomad.

First released 1963
UK peak chart position: did not chart
USA peak chart position: did not chart

74. AMERICAN GARAGE
Pat Metheny

Purists may wince but this excellent album is in the jazz category, like it or not. As previously discussed Metheny's importance in popular music is significant as he is able to transcend barriers. This is the closest he came to rock music, yet it is still a mile away. The group on this record in addition to the ever present keyboard player Lyle Mays are Mark Egan, bass and Dan Gottlieb, drums. The music is played with great ease and sounds like it was made during positive times. Metheny utilizes the acoustic 12-string that he used to great effect on *New Chautauqua* in addition to his regular hollow bodied Gibson.

(Cross The) Heartland; Airstream; The Search; American Garage; Epic.

First released 1979
UK peak chart position: did not chart
USA peak chart position: 53

75. TUTU
Miles Davis

Where else can you put Miles? Folk? Soul? Rap? This is funky and very electronically tested with synthesizers evrywhere, and is one of Miles' least jazzy albums. Marcus Miller played most of the instruments and arranged where the syn drums would go. So far this sounds like a put down, but no, this is a hypnotic and brilliant record that seeps into you after one or two plays - once you accept that this is light years away from even *Bitches Brew*. It wanders and flows like one long suite and Miles, although unwell at this time plays with class that we took for granted. In building a Miles Davis collection this is the best of his later work, but it ain't no *Kind Of Blue*.

Tutu; Tomaas; Portia; Splatch; Backyard Ritual; Perfect Way; Don't Lose Your Mind; Full Nelson.

First released 1986
UK peak chart position: 74
USA peak chart position: 141

76. PORTRAIT OF SHEILA
Sheila Jordan

One of a (perhaps disappointingly small) number of jazz vocalists to break out of the cabaret ghetto and make a real contribution to jazz and the vocalist's art, Sheila Jordan was influenced as much by instrumentalists, and Charlie Parker in particular, as by vocalists. Her sparse, understated style and empathy for the musicians who work with her have resulted in collaborations with some of the most original and striking contemporary jazz players around. *Portrait Of Sheila* features guitarist Barry Galbraith, bassist Steve Swallow and drummer Denzil Best; in 1962, making subtle, interesting music.

Falling In Love With Love; If You Could See Me Now; Am I Blue?; Dat Dere; When The World Was Young; Let's Face The Music And Dance; Laugh Clown Laugh; Who Can I Turn To Now; Baltimore Oriole; I'm A Fool To Want You; Hum Drum Blues; Willow Weep For Me.

First released 1962
UK peak chart position: did not chart
USA peak chart position: did not chart

77. EVIDENCE
Steve Lacy

Without doubt one of jazz's true originals, Steve Lacy was an early modern jazz disciple of the soprano saxophone – he is said to be the man who introduced it to John Coltrane, and remains one of its few practitioners to play it without combining it with another instruments. He is almost as well known for his fruitful fascination with the music of Thelonious Monk, whose tunes he had continuously studied and with whom he worked in 1960. *Evidence* features four Monk compositions and two tunes by Ellington, performed with the help of free jazz trumpet legend Don Cherry, bassist Carl Brown and flawless drummer Billy Higgins.

The Mystery Song; Evidence; Let's Cool One; San Francisco Holiday; Something To Live For; Who Knows.

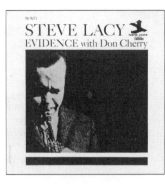

First released 1962
UK peak chart position: did not chart
USA peak chart position: did not chart

78. OPEN SESAME
Freddie Hubbard

Trumpeter Freddie Hubbard had an amazing gift for being around at just the right time, appearing on countless modern jazz classics, and recording some of the Blue Note label's greatest albums of the '60s. *Open Sesame* was his very first Blue Note release as leader, and features bluesy tenor saxophonist Tina Brooks, pianist McCoy Tyner (who had recently joined John Coltrane), bassist Sam Jones and drummer Clifford Jarvis. A fiery, but superbly controlled, trumpeter who never, even at this stage in his career, sounds stretched or short of an idea, Hubbard would become one of the most profound trumpet talents in post-war jazz.

Open Sesame; But Beautiful; Gypsy Blue; All Or Nothing At All; One Mint Julep; Hub's Nub.

First released 1960
UK peak chart position: did not chart
USA peak chart position: did not chart

79. CREATIVE ORCHESTRA MUSIC 1976
Anthony Braxton

One of the avant-garde's eccentric trail-blazers, Anthony Braxton is a virtuoso reeds and flute multi-instrumentalist, and one of a number of leading experimental musicians to have developed out of Chicago's AACM hot-house during the second half of the '60s. His innovations have included the first ever album of improvisations performed on solo saxophone, unorthodox techniques for naming compositions (including algebraic formulae or, in this case, diagrams) and a clever balance between large group composition and improvisation. *Creative Orchestra Music 1967* consists of compositions for a number of large groups, and features bassist Dave Holland, pianist Muhal Richard Abrams, saxophonist Roscoe Mitchell and trumpeters Kenny Wheeler, Jon Faddis and Leo Smith.

Piece One; Piece Two; Piece Three; Piece Four; Piece Five; Piece Six.

First released 1977
UK peak chart position: did not chart
USA peak chart position: did not chart

80. DIALOGUE
Bobby Hutcherson

Vibraphone player Bobby Hutcherson is another gifted contemporary jazz musician associated with the Blue Note label scene of the '60s. His incredible versatility left him uniquely at home on both gentle, mellow grooves and more robust and demanding avant-garde dates (see *Out To Lunch*). *Dialogue* is from the more modern end of the spectrum, and is a six-way musical give and take, featuring a group of the best new players on the label. Freddie Hubbard takes care of trumpet, the underrated Sam Rivers is on saxophones, bass clarinet and flute, the brilliant Andrew Hill plays piano, bass is by Richard Davis and Joe Chambers is behind the kit.

Catta; Idle While; Les Noirs Marchent; Dialogue; Ghetto Lights.

First released 1965
UK peak chart position: did not chart
USA peak chart position: did not chart

81. JAZZ IN SILHOUETTE
Sun Ra

This 1957 Sun Ra album is perhaps surprisingly orthodox for what we have come to expect of an Arkestra outing. Speaking a language grounded in bop, a superb 10-piece of Sun Ra's finest players work through some inspired tunes and arrangements with an unusual flair and consistency – baritone saxophonist Pat Patrick and tenor genius John Gilmore soloing with particular strength. Breaking the mould, and in many ways a glimpse of what was to come, 'Ancient Aiethopia' is a mesmerising percussion-based composition with chanting, displaying an unusual freedom and featuring superbly compelling solo contributions by trumpeter Hobart Dotson and pianist Ra himself.

Enlightenment; Saturn; Velvet; Ancient Aiethopia; Hours After; Horoscope; Images; Blues At Midnight.

First released 1959
UK peak chart position: did not chart
USA peak chart position: did not chart

82. EMPYREAN ISLES
Herbie Hancock

The early 60s were another Golden Age for the Blue Note label, due, in part, to the work of a creative pool of young but conceptually advanced musicians, who constantly reappeared on each other's records, bringing an enthusiasm and creative flair each time they played. This Herbie Hancock quartet session features trumpeter Freddie Hubbard, and Hancock's regular rhythm section partners bassist Ron Carter and drummer Tony Williams working together so closely they might have been joined at the hip. Although best known for the popular and funky 'Cantaloupe Island', *Empyrean Isles* has its best moments on a long and free track entitled 'The Egg'.

One Finger Snap; Oliloqui Valley; Cantaloupe Island; The Egg.

First released 1964
UK peak chart position: did not chart
USA peak chart position: did not chart

83. SOUL
Coleman Hawkins

The opening track starts with a typical Ray Bryant piano boogie roll, akin to 'Little Susie'. The groove starts and is joined by the familiar tone of Kenny Burrell's guitar. Hawkins comes in late and takes control with some of his sweetest ever tenor playing. We are still discussing the first track 'Soul Blues', but in reality this is the benchmark for the whole session. 'Groovin' highlights the ease and rapport the musicians have with each other. Wendell Marshall, bass and Osie Johnson on drums never dominate, they merely embellish. The CD reissue is crystal clear.

Soul Blues; I Hadn't Anyone Till You; Groovin'; Greensleeves; Sunday Mornin'; Until The Real Thing Comes Along; Sweetnin'.

First released 1959
UK peak chart position: did not chart
USA peak chart position: did not chart

84. STILL WARM
John Scofield

Scofield has really come of age since this album was released, winning awards and nominations galore and in doing so has become one of the world's leading jazz guitarists. His popularity expanded with this record as his funk and rock influence shone through. 'Techno' is the type of music we would have imagined Hendrix to be playing had he lived. The title track is both romantic and highly erotic, the rhythm is almost Latin and the song builds continuously as the musical scale ascends, yet the listener is completely fooled because the climax is only one octave. It is a brilliant piece of music.

Techno; Still Warm; High And Mighty; Protocol; Rule Of Thumb; Picks And Pans; Gil B 643.

First released 1987
UK peak chart position: did not chart
USA peak chart position: did not chart

85. WE FREE KINGS
Roland Kirk

Kirk bought an exciting and original sound to jazz during the early 60s and was quietly influential. Sadly in recent years his standing has lessened. This is a very 60s jazz album, and one that found imitators in numerous musical scores for dreadful b-movies. Although it sounds dated, Kirk plays his heart out and gives variation by playing flute, stritch, manzello and siren. Kirk looked outrageously awesome, was courted by the rock world and could play three wind instruments at the same time. 'The Haunted Melody' demonstrates his clean blowing style whilst 'We Free Kings' allows him to blast into the freer form that gained him such a following. He was an innovator.

Three For The Festival; Moon Song; Haunted Melody; Blues For Alice; We Free Kings; You Did It, You Did It; Some Kind Of Love; My Delight.

First released 1962
UK peak chart position: did not chart
USA peak chart position: did not chart

86. ESCALATOR OVER THE HILL
Carla Bley

Escalator Over The Hill is the product of a vibrant musicians' co-operative. Arranged and composed by pianist Carla Bley, with lyrics by poet Paul Haines, it takes the form of an avant garde opera. Bley's innovative and imaginative score is central to this exceptional recording, but equally crucial are contributions by Don Cherry, Gato Barbieri, Roswell Rudd, Charlie Haden and Jack Bruce. Brilliant playing at the cutting edge of free jazz underscores Bruce's emphatic vocals, resulting in passages of ravaged intensity and lyric beauty. Together they bring an urgency to a composition already charged with musical insight and adventure.

Hotel Overture; This Is Here; Like Animals; Escalator Over The Hill; Stay Awake; Ginger And David; Song To Anything That Moves; Eoth Theme; Businessmen; Ginger And David Theme; Why; Detective Writer Daugter; Doctor Why; Slow Dance (transductory Music); Smalltown Agonist; End Of Head; Over Her Head; Little Pony Soldier; Say Can You Do; Holiday In Risk; All India Radio; Rawalpindi Blues; End Of Rawalpindi; End Of Animals; . . .And It's Again.

First released 1971
UK peak chart position: did not chart
USA peak chart position: did not chart

87. THERE GOES THE NEIGHBORHOOD
Gary Bartz

Recorded live at New York's famous Birdland Club in November 1990, *There Goes The Neighborhood* is a vivid record of one of modern jazz's most intense and exciting living saxophonists, playing at his peak. Pianist Kenny Barron, bassist Ray Drummond and drummer Ben Riley offer firm support for Bartz's powerful, plaintive alto, as he powers his way through a well-chosen programme of standards and original tunes. Bartz by this time had got over his bland jazz/pop flirtation, and was playing an intense combination of neo-bop and heavy, Coltrane-influenced shapes. Check out the inspired version of 'Impressions'.

Racism (Blues In Double Bb Minor); On A Misty Night; Laura; Tadd's Delight; Impressions; I've Never Been In Love Before; Flight Path.

First released 1990
UK peak chart position: did not chart
USA peak chart position: did not chart

88. KELLY BLUE
Wynton Kelly Trio & Sextet

From the opening flute played by Bobby Jasper, the listener is immediatly hooked and welcomed, Kelly's piano floats in, his fingers landing like a butterfly. The title track opens this album, and although all the other tracks are excellent, the album is worth the price of this one piece. The cool support in addition to Jasper comes from; Nat Adderley, cornet; Benny Golson, tenor; Paul Chambers, bass; Jimmy Cobb, drums. This is an amaxingly relaxed album with Kelly at times just breathing on the keys. The CD reiussue has the bonus of the third take of 'Keep It Moving'. Serious buffs only will notice the difference. An essential album, often overlooked by the populist vote.

Kelly Blue; Soflty, As In A Morning Sunrise; Do Nothin' Till You Hear From Me; On Green Dolphin Street; Willlow Weep For Me; Keep It Moving (take four); Keep It Moving (take three); Old Clothes.

First released 1960
UK peak chart position: did not chart
USA peak chart position: did not chart

89. FACING YOU
Keith Jarrett

The ECM debut that unleashed one of the greatest musical talents of our time. Using jazz as an excuse Jarrett initiated and indoctrinated us with improvised solo piano, something we would become used to over the next three decades. Facing You is boogie woogie, country hoedown, blues, folk, rock 'n' roll flavoured jazz. It is an astonishing album, still. The music press at the time of issue were bereft of ideas where to place him, it would have been much simpler just to wallow in the music. Much of Jarrett and Manfred Eicher's future musical philosophy started out with this important record.

In Front; Ritooria; Lalene; My Lady: My Child; Landscape For Future Earth; Starbright; Vapallia; Semblence.

First released 1972
UK peak chart position: did not chart
USA peak chart position: did not chart

90. LOST AND FOUND
Sheila Jordan

Sheila Jordan is commonly regarded as the finest contemporary singer working within the jazz field. With a musical grounding in the bebop language of the late 40s, she single-mindedly developed her own demanding and complex style of improvisation, based on what she learned from Charlie Parker, but with a freer and more dramatic edge that suits the vocalist's art. This highly acclaimed 1990 date features the fabulous piano of Kenny Barron, her long-standing musical partner Harvie Swartz on bass and ex-Thelonious Monk drummer Ben Riley, and helped put Jordan back firmly in the limelight.

Good Morning Heartache; Anthropology; I Concentrate On You; The Water Is Wide; Alone Together; The Very Thought Of You; Lost In The Stars; My Shining Hour/We'll Be Togther Again

First released 1990
UK peak chart position: did not chart
USA peak chart position: did not chart

91. MACHINE GUN
Peter Brotzman

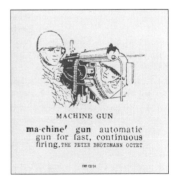

Perhaps the most savage and brutal recording in jazz history, *Machine Gun* is a landmark in the European avant garde. The reasoning behind the record's title becomes brutally clear within the its first five seconds, as the three saxophones front line of leader Peter Brötzmann, Willem Breuker and Evan Parker ruthlessly fire off round after round of thunderous musical ammunition, accompanied by pianist Fred Van Hove, bassists Buschi Niebergall and Peter Kowald and drummers Han Bennink and Sven Ake Johansson. Bordering on the unbearable, there is a sense of both the emotional and technical extreme that is a curiously addictive, if draining, experience.

Machine Gun (second take); Machine Gun (third take); Responsible (first take); Responsible (second take); Music For Man Bennick 1 (first take).

First released 1968
UK peak chart position: did not chart
USA peak chart position: did not chart

92. Soprano Sax
Steve Lacy

Soprano specialist Steve Lacy remains one of jazz's instantly recognisable soloists. His big, steady tone, matter-of-fact phrasing and lean, angular melodic conception make up a truly unique and refreshing sound. Originally inspired by Sidney Bechet, and playing predominately New Orleans jazz, he quickly propelled himself forward, becoming obsessed with the compositions of Thelonious Monk, working with piano rebel Cecil Taylor and eventually experimenting with jazz-and-spoken-word recordings. Soprano Sax dates from 1957, and features sparkling, exuberant pianist Wynton Kelly, and Cecil Taylor alumni Buell Niedlinger on bass and Dennis Charles on drums.

Day Dream; Alone Together; Work; Rockin' In Rhythm; Little Girl Your Daddy Is Calling You; Easy To Love.

First released 1957
UK peak chart position: did not chart
USA peak chart position: did not chart

93. A Day In The Life
Wes Montgomery

Another asrtist in the listing whose appearances in the pop charts had the jazz pusists crying 'sell out'. Montgomery moved from jazz to very accessible jazz music, very much like the sound today produced by GRP Records. The soulful and mantric opening with beautiful slip-note piano from Herbie Hancock, leads into the Beatles' 'A Day In The Life' but can only be properly recognised in brief snatches. A great deal of work went into this record and the accompanying musicians are too many for this review. Save to say that the main unit in addition to Wes and Hancock consists of Ron Carter, bass and Grady Tate, drums. Many Montgomery albums were nominated, indicating a healthy respect for easy jazz, this wins by a short head as the one to own.

A Day In The Life; Watch What Happens; When A Man Loves A Woman; California Nights; Angel; Eleanor Rigby; Willow Weep For Me; Windy; Trust In Me; The Joker.

First released 1967
UK peak chart position: did not chart
USA peak chart position: 13

94. Greens
Benny Green

A superbly talented young pianist out of the 80s bop revival, Benny Green always seemed like a name to watch during his stints with Betty Carter, Art Blakey's Jazz Messengers and Freddie Hubbard. He is an exciting but intelligent swinger with a clear, attractive articulation and a debt to the style of Bud Powell. On this, his second album for the Blue Note label, he is joined, in what has become a particularly productive partnership, by bassist Christian McBride and drummer Carl Allen, and plays a fine selection of standards and original tunes with panache and imagination.

Greens; Bish Bash; Captain Hook; You Don't Know What Love Is; Time After Time; Battle Hymn Of The Republic; Decidedly; Soon; Cute; I See Your Face Before Me; Second Time Around; Shiny Stockings.

First released 1991
UK peak chart position: did not chart
USA peak chart position: did not chart

95. STLL LIFE (TALKING)
Pat Metheny

The third Metheny album in the list is as hard to categorize as his previous efforts. This time around his south American influence is strong and the melody is more AOR than jazz. 'Last Train Home' is evocative of its title and has punishing timing throughout for Paul Wertico's drums. Throughout each track Lyle Mays creates a sheet of canvas, utilising various keyboards and synthesizers, for Metheny to paint his Brazilian excursions on. The group is completed by Steve Rodby, bass and the voices of Armando Marcal, David Blamires and Mark Ledford.

Minuano; So May It Secretly Begin; Last Train Home; It's Just Talk; Third Wind; Distance; In Her Family.

First released 1987
UK peak chart position: did not chart
USA peak chart position: 86

96. BLACK COFFEE
Peggy Lee

In 1952, Capitol Records wouldn't allow Peggy Lee to record 'Lover' because the label already had a big hit with Les Paul's version of the song. So she switched to Decca for the next five years and made a number of excellent recordings, including this set of standards on which she is accompanied by the cream of America's session musicians. It was originally issued as a 10-inch LP in 1953, and later extended to 12-inch with four additional tracks: 'It Ain't Necessarily So', 'Gee Baby, Ain't I Good To You', 'You're My Thrill' and 'There's A Small Hotel'. Forty years after it release, it is still regarded as one of the definitive jazz - tinged vocal albums of all time.

Black Coffee; I've Got You Under My Skin; Easy Living; My Heart Belongs To Daddy; It Ain't Necessarily So; Gee Baby Ain't I Good To You; Woman Alone With The Blues; I Didn't Know What Time It Was; When The World Was Young; Love Me Or Leave Me; You're My Thrill; There's A Small Hotel.

First released 1961
UK peak chart position: 20
USA peak chart position: did not chart

97. COOL BLUES
Jimmy Smith

Of all the album's recorded by Jimmy Smith for Blue Note, this is the best example of what he could do before he started to coast, both as a purveyor of orchestrated organ music, but more importantly becoming aware that you are the world's greatest, and most successful jazz organist. Both *House Party* and *The Sermon* are excellent albums but this is more worthy because it is captured live. Recorded at a New York club it features among others Lou Donaldson, alto, Art Blakey and Donald Bailey, drums. Smith plays as though he means it especially on 'Groovin' At Small's' and 'A Night In Tunisia'.

Dark Eyes; Cool Blues; A Night In Tunisia; What's New; Small's Minor; Once In A While; Groovin' At Small's.

First released 1958?
UK peak chart position: did not chart
USA peak chart position: did not chart

98. ELECTRIC BATH
Don Ellis

A man who is criminally ignored and one who will in time be seen as a pioneer. The late Don Ellis was signed to CBS in the late 60s and marketed with Blood, Sweat And Tears, Spirit and Moby Grape, rather like selling Take That records to John Lee Hooker fans. Had Ellis been promoted properly his standing would be much greater. This wonderful record is his best; rich full orchestration with short non-indulging solos, this is a recording by an orchestra whose charts were painstakingly and individually worked out by Ellis. He did find success writing film themes such as *The French Connection*.

Indian Lady; Alone; Turkish Bath; Open Beauty; New Horizons.

First released 1968
UK peak chart position: did not chart
USA peak chart position: did not chart

99. MING
David Murray Octet

Ayler-influenced tenor saxophonist and bass clarinettist David Murray has earned a reputation for releasing more albums in a year than other important jazz musicians manage to put out in a decade. But *Ming*, recorded in 1980, holds a special place in the Murray cannon, for the huge enthusiasm with which it was received by fans and critics alike, and the attention it brought Murray's superb compositional skills. Its star cast includes saxophonist Henry Threadgill, cornettist Butch Morris and trombonist George Lewis, blasting through Murray's intricate but daring arrangements and playing some intense, memorable solos. Check out the beautiful title track, and the chaotic 'Dewey's Circle'.

Fast Life; The Hill; Ming; Jasvan; Dewey's Circle.

First released 1981
UK peak chart position: did not chart
USA peak chart position: did not chart

100. THE PIED PIPER
Chico Freeman

One of the more talented and interesting of America's younger(ish) crop of saxophonists, Chico Freeman combines a Coltrane-influenced intensity on uptempo tunes, with a lush, romantic feel for ballads. Joined on the front-line here by fellow reedsman John Purcell, the pair utilise a vast array of instruments, including oboe, sopranino saxophone, flute and piccolo, to create a good range of sounds and textures. The title track is a complex but catchy composition combining two time signatures, and the rest of the material includes a jaunty blues, and a fast and exciting 'Softly, As In A Morning Sunrise'.

The Pied Piper; The Rose Tattoo; Blues On The Bottom; Monk 2000; Softly, As In A Morning Sunrise; Amor Soña Dor.

First released 1984
UK peak chart position: did not chart
USA peak chart position: did not chart

THE TOP 50
BLUES ALBUMS

THE BLUES APPEALS TO EVERYONE, NOT JUST THE PURIST, AND THIS LIST REFLECTS THAT FACT. THE BLUES BOOM OF THE LATE 60S AND EARLY 90S USHERED IN NEW BLOOD INTO A GENRE PREVIOUSLY DOMINATED BY NAMES SUCH AS MUDDY WATERS, HOWLIN' WOLF AND B.B. KING. THE FACT THAT MUDDY HAS ONLY ONE ALBUM IN THE LIST DOES NOT MEAN HE IS A LESSER FIGURE THAN JOHN MAYALL OR ROBERT CRAY, WHO BOTH HAVE MORE THAN ONE. COMPLETE WORKS (EXCEPT BY ROBERT JOHNSON) ARE NOT ALLOWED OTHERWISE MUDDY, WOLF AND B.B. WOULD WIPE THE FLOOR.

1. THE HEALER
John Lee Hooker

When popular culture embraced John Lee, purists turned up their noses. They should have been pleased that the world's greatest living Delta bluesman was going to make some money before he turned up his toes. Teaming up with Carlos Santana, Bonnie Raitt, Los Lobos, Canned Heat (not for the first time) and others, lent Hooker's blues a contemporary gloss. It took the album to the upper reaches of the album charts around the world, brought him a number of Grammy awards and a new career in advertising. The blues is not only a healer, it drinks brandy and wears jeans.

The Healer; I'm In The Mood; Baby Lee; Cuttin' Out; Think Twice Before You Go; Los Lobos; Sally Mae; That's Alright; Rockin' Chair; My Dream; No Substitute.

First released 1989
UK peak chart position: 63
USA peak chart position: 62

2. KING OF THE DELTA BLUES SINGERS
(ROBERT JOHNSON 1936-37)
Robert Johnson

If you're a mountain-climber you tackle Everest, if you're a blues lover you get to know this album very well. Very few had heard his music when this milestone album was first released in 1962, but it was evident that here was a body of work of fundamental importance to the development of postwar Chicago blues and blues in general. Little known in his lifetime, Johnson synthesised traditions represented by men like Charley Patton, Son House, Lonnie Johnson and Leroy Carr and refined them through his unique interpretative skills. An accomplished guitarist with finger and slide, Johnson matched his virtuosity with a tortured vocal style that added deeper resonance to his words.

Crossroads Blues; Terraplane Blues; Come On In My Kitchen; Walking Blues; Last Fair Deal Gone Down; 32-20 Blues; Kindhearted Woman Blues; If I Had Possession Over Judgment Day; Preaching Blues; When You Got A Good Friend; Rambling On My Mind; Stones In My Passway; Traveling Riverside Blues; Milkcow's Calf Blues; Me And The Devil Blues; Hellhound On My Trail

First released 1962
UK peak chart position: did not chart
USA peak chart position: did not chart

3. BLUESBREAKERS WITH ERIC CLAPTON
John Mayall

The principals may have regarded it as just a representation of their live work, but this album had as much to do with the British Invasion of America's musical dominance as the Beatles or the Stones. Mayall willingly assumed the mantle of father of British blues that he'd taken from Alexis Korner. Clapton was a blues purist who discovered other demons to drive his ambition, even if he could only emulate originals like Freddie King, Buddy Guy, Otis Rush and Jimi Hendrix. Some maintain that he has never played as well again, notwithstanding his current godlike status. Mayall has pursued a less notable but satisfying career, confident that this early achievement can never be bettered - by anyone.

All Your Love; Hideaway; Little Girl; Another Man; Double Crossin' Time; What'd I Say; Key To Love; Parchman Farm; Have You Heard; Ramblin' On My Mind; Steppin' Out; It Ain't Right.

First released 1966
UK peak chart position:6
USA peak chart position: did not chart

4. THE BLUES OF LIGHTNIN' HOPKINS
Lightnin' Hopkins

Hopkins had been a prolific recording artist in the decade from his first sessions in 1948. His stark, functional guitar style and rich Texas drawl made his work instantly recognisable. The inheritor of a blues tradition that went back to Blind Lemon Jefferson and Texas Alexander, he was an idiosyncratic musician, at his best when playing alone. His predecessor's work was reflected in his first album session, recorded by Sam Charters in January 1959. Not having recorded commercially for several years, Lightnin' was in serious mood, resulting in a set of masterful performances that carried more weight than his later, frequently arbitrary sessions.

Penitentiary Blues; Bad Luck And Trouble; Come Go Home With Me; Trouble Stay 'Way From My Door; See That My Grave Is Kept Clean; Goin' Back To Florida; Reminiscenses Of Blind Lemon; Fan It; Tell Me, Baby; She's Mine.

First released 1959
UK peak chart position: did not chart
USA peak chart position: did not chart

5. THE COMPLETE RECORDINGS
Bessie Smith

Bessie Smith was a legend before she died in a manner that merely added to a larger than life story. Since then, her records have never been out of catalogue. The four volumes of The Bessie Smith Story represented merely a portion of her recorded output, some 160 titles in the course of the decade from 1923-33. She rarely recorded with more than a small group, but whoever was with her, including at times, Louis Armstrong, Coleman Hawkins and Fletcher Henderson, was dominated by the power of her voice and the strength of her character. Many times she triumphed over her material but, as the 1929 film showed, she made W.C. Handy's St Louis Blues her own.

Down Hearted Blues; Gulf Coast Blues; Aggravatin' Papa; Beale Street Mama; Baby Won't You Please Come Home; Oh Daddy Blues; 'Tain't Nobody's Bizness If I Do; Keeps On A-Rainin' (Papa, He Can't Make No Time); Mama's Got The Blues; Outside Of That; Bleeding Hearted Blues; Yodling Blues; Lady Luck Blues; Midnight Blues; If You Don't, I Know Who Will; Nobody In Town Can Bake A Sweet Jelly Roll Like Mine; Jail-House Blues; St Louis Gal; Sam Jones Blues; Graveyard Dream Blues; Cemetery Blues; Far Away Blues; I'm Going Back To My Used To Be; Whoa, Tillie, Take Your Time; My Sweetie Went Away; Any Woman's Blues; Chicago Bound Blues; Mistreating Daddy; Frosty Morning Blues; Haunted House Blues; Eavesdropper's Blues; Easy Come, Easy Go Blues; Sorrowful Blues; Pinchback - Take 'Em Away; Rocking Chair Blues; Ticket Agent, Ease Your Window Down; Boweavil Blues; Hateful Blues.

First released 1989
UK peak chart position: did not chart
USA peak chart position: did not chart

6. COMPLETE LIBRARY OF CONGRESS RECORDINGS
Leadbelly

Huddie Ledbetter was a bull of a man, with a rock-hard physique and a bellowing voice. He wielded a 12-string guitar like it was a banjo, his dexterity with finger and slide lending a relentless rhythm to the songs that he'd learned from a wide variety of sources. The blues was just one of his disciplines, some of the songs learned from leading Blind Lemon Jefferson around the towns of Texas. Leadbelly was a songster with an encyclopaedic memory, anything from gospel and cowboy songs to children's ring games and sentimental popular ditties. All of this was recorded by John and Alan Lomax for the Library of Congress. The Leadbelly tapes are an indispensable microcosm of black musical life from the first decades of this century.

including; Mr Tom Hughes' Town; De Kalb Blues; Take A Whiff On Me; The Medicine Man; I'm Sorry Mama; Monologue: Square Dances, Sooky Jumps; Po' Howard; Monologue: Dance Calls, Dance Steps; Gwine Dig A Hole; Tight Like That; Green Corn; Becky Dean; Monologue: Prison Singing; Midnight Special; I Ain't Gonna Ring Dem Yellow Woman's Do' Bells; Rock Island Line; Governor Pat Neff; Irene Part I, Part II; Governor O.K. Allen; Git On Board; Hallelujah; Monologue: Joining The Church; Backslider, Fare You Well; Amazing Grace; Must I Be Carried To The Sky On Flowered Beds Of Ease; Amazing Grace, Flowered Beds Of Ease; Down In The Valley To Pray; Let It Shine On Me; Run Sinners; Ride On; Monologue: The Blues; Thirty Days In The Workhouse; Fo' Day Worry Blues; Matchbox Blues.

First released 1966
UK peak chart position: did not chart
USA peak chart position: did not chart

7. MOANIN' IN THE MOONLIGHT
Howlin' Wolf

Unlike Muddy Waters, Howlin' Wolf kept his Mississippi roots learnt from Charley Patton, the so-called Father of Delta blues, throughout his career. 'Smokestack Lightnin'', the song that epitomised the Wolf's roar, came from Patton, as did 'I Asked For Water (She Gave Me Gasoline)'. The howl was saved for 'Moanin' At Midnight' and 'Moaning For My Baby'. Although he'd started on guitar, he took up the harmonica, which he played with more force than virtuosity. Having spent time around Memphis, Wolf knew how to rock as well, and he got the best from his Chicago musicians. His later collaborations with Willie Dixon may have brought him wider recognition, but the meat of the matter was in these earlier songs.

Moanin' In The Moonlight; How Many More Years; Smokestack Lightning; Baby How Long; No Place To Go; Evil; I'm Leading You; Moanin' For My Baby; I Ask For Water; Forty Four; Somebody In My Home.

First released 1962
UK peak chart position: did not chart
USA peak chart position: did not chart

8. THE LATE-FANTASICALLY GREAT
Elmore James

It's easy to write Elmore James off as a one song man but his remains one of most distinctive voices in the whole of postwar blues. Like Jimmy Reed's boogie rhythms, Elmore's bottleneck guitar technique seemed to be simple. The insistent riff became almost a caricature, but no one, apart from perhaps Jeremy Spencer, came close to recreating his special sound. 'Dust My Blues' and 'Standing At The Crossroads' were taken from Robert Johnson's repertoire, but Elmore could also write a mean blues, as 'Dark And Dreary' proved. Elmore James died just as the 60s Blues Boom began; this was the album that provoked regret for the fact.

Dust My Blues; Sunnyland; Mean And Evil; Dark And Dreary; Standing At The Crossroads; Happy Home; No Love In My Heart; Blues Before Sunrise; I Was A Fool; Goodbye Baby.

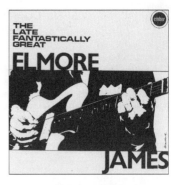

First released 1964
UK peak chart position: did not chart
USA peak chart position: did not chart

9. JUST JIMMY REED
Jimmy Reed

This wasn't vintage Reed by any stretch of the imagination, but it was one of the first of his albums to fuel the British Blues Boom. By 1962, the Jimmy Reed boogie groove had not yet become a rut and his accompanists, Lefty Bates, Jimmy Reed Jnr., Phil Upchurch and Al Duncan, knew exactly what was expected of them. They were at their best when they could rock out on something like 'Good Lover', which ought to be titled 'Natural Born Lover' since that's what Reed sings. 'Down In Mississippi' was more bucolic than J.B. Lenoir's song of the same name and bad habits were having a further effect on his already mumbled diction. No one believed it when he sang 'I'll Change My Style', because then it wouldn't have been the Jimmy Reed that everyone liked and no one could imitate.

Take It Slow; Good Lover; Too Much; I'll Change My Style; In The Morning; You Can't Hide; Back Home At Noon; Kansas City Baby; Oh John; Let's Get Together; Down In Mississippi.

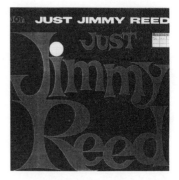

First released 1962
UK peak chart position: did not chart
USA peak chart position: 103

10. THE SKY IS CRYING
Stevie Ray Vaughan

Vaughan's death on 27 August 27 1990 brought to a tragic end the cresting wave of his popularity. The album he'd made with his brother Jimmie, *Family Style*, had just been released and when this album, prepared by Jimmie from the various album sessions, it wasn't expected to amount to much. In fact, this was at least as good as any of them - and better than *Live Alive*. 'Little Wing' was perhaps his best adaptation of a Jimi Hendrix song. His take on the Elmore James title song was also a fitting tribute to both the writer and the performer. There are bound to be further compilations and live recordings released, but these studio recordings are testimony to Stevie Ray's devotion to his craft.

Boot Hill; The Sky Is Crying; Empty Arms; Little Wing; Wham; May I Have A Talk With You; Close To You; Chittlins Con Carne; So Excited; Life By The Drop.

First released 1991
UK peak chart position: did not chart
USA peak chart position: 10

11. THE BEST OF LITTLE WALTER
Little Walter

At the time of its release, this was indeed the best of Chicago blues' finest harmonica player. Arriving in the city in the mid-40s, the teenage Walter Jacobs could already encompass the whole of John Lee 'Sonny Boy' Williamson's style. When he joined up with Muddy Waters and Jimmy Rogers, he became an integral part of a daring new blues style that made Muddy a star. 'Juke' was Walter's first hit, a dazzling exhibition of amplified harmonica playing that set the standard for other players. Other tracks like 'Mean Old World', 'Blues With A Feeling', 'Last Night' and 'My Babe' revealed he could sing, too. Before the end of the 50s, he'd slipped from the pedestal on which this work had placed him.

My Babe; Sad Hours; You're So Fine; Last Night; Blues With A Feeling; Can't Hold Out Much Longer; Juke; Mean Old World; Off The Wall; You Better Watch Yourself; Blue Light; Tell Me Mama.

First released 1964
UK peak chart position: did not chart
USA peak chart position: did not chart

12. DOWN AND OUT BLUES
Sonny Boy Williamson

Sonny Boy was a garrulous old rogue and he bitterly resented the down-and-out depicted on this album's cover. He'd endured a long and hard life before becoming the darling of the European blues circuit in the mid-60s, with his bowler hat and quarter-cut city suit. He was in his fifties when he cut these tracks in Chicago with Muddy Waters' band and worthies like Robert Lockwood, Luther Tucker and Fred Below. A decade later, these were the songs that delighted his new audiences. He rarely bettered 'Don't Start Me Talking', 'Your Funeral And My Trial' and 'Fattening Frogs For Snakes'. His harmonica playing never dazzled like Little Walter's, but the notes he chose beat a hot line to the heart.

Don't Start Me Talkin'; I Don't Know; All My Love In Vain; The Key (To Your Door); Keep It To Yourself; Dissatisfied; Fattening Frogs For Snakes; Wake Up Baby; Your Funeral And My Trail; 99; Cross My Heart; Let Me Explain.

First released 1962
UK peak chart position: did not chart
USA peak chart position: did not chart

13. MY KIND OF BLUES
B.B. King

By 1960, B.B. King was one of the most popular and prolific blues stars. Much of the time, he recorded with a full band, but this album features him in a quartet made up of himself, pianist Lloyd Glenn, bassist Ralph Hamilton and Jesse Sailes on drums. For the session, King drew on his deep appreciation of Doctor Clayton and recorded both 'Walking Dr Bill' and 'Hold That Train'. The session was a relaxed affair but the level of musicianship was uniformly high. The accent was on traditional themes such as 'Catfish Blues', 'Driving Wheel' and 'Someday Baby', all of which may have been sung more dramatically elsewhere but seldom performed with the ease and expertise on display here. King was in good voice and his guitar playing, in sharper focus in these surroundings, had never been better.

You Done Lost Your Good Thing Now; Walking Dr Bill; Catfish Blues; Hold That Train; Understand; Someday Baby; Mr Pawnbroker; Driving Wheel; My Own Fault Baby; Please Set A Date.

First released 1961
UK peak chart position: did not chart
USA peak chart position: did not chart

14. DAMN RIGHT I GOT THE BLUES
Buddy Guy

And in 1991, he had good reason. Guy hadn't made a studio album in a decade at that point. The fact that Eric Clapton, who made sure that Buddy was a regular guest on his Albert Hall Blues Nights, had called him the world's greatest guitarist still hadn't gained him a recording contract. Silvertone put that right with sessions that included the best session men from Britain and America, with guest appearances by Clapton, Jeff Beck and Mark Knopfler. The album showed all sides of Guy's talent, the blues singer, the soul man and the extravagantly gifted guitarist. A reluctant star, he has nevertheless taken full advantage of his new-found status as the uncrowned King of Chicago Blues.

Damn Right I Got The Blues; Where Is The Next One Coming From; Five Long Years; Missing Sally; There Is Something On Your Mind; Early In The Morning; Too Broke To Spend The Night; Let Me Love You Baby; Rememberin' Stevie.

First released 1991
UK peak chart position:43
USA peak chart position: 136

15. THE BLUES
John Lee Hooker

Although he made his records in Detroit, Hooker's music was firmly in the rhythmic Mississippi tradition. Nothing could have been simpler than 'Boogie Chillen', but the combination of bedrock boogie guitar and Hooker's declamatory vocal had an elemental appeal. The harsh distortion of his amplified guitar and the insistent tapping of his feet created a unique atmosphere, enhanced by a prolific ability to create powerful images with his lyrics. There was a dark undertone to songs like 'Wednesday Evening', 'Whistlin' and Moanin' Blues' and sexual bravado in his first million-seller, 'I'm In The Mood'. Forty years on, the power of Hooker's music is undiminished.

First released 1960
UK peak chart position: did not chart
USA peak chart position: did not chart

16. BIG MAYBELLE
Big Maybelle

Like so many before her, Mabel Smith learned to sing in the church, but she was discovered singing in a Kentucky bar and raising her capacious dress so that silver dollars could be stuck in the top of her stockings. Her legs remained covered after 'Gabbin' Blues' became her first hit. Others like 'Way Back Home' and 'My Country Man' put her on the road, where her drug addiction could not be ministered too quite so readily. Her recording career continued for another 15 years, but so did her habit. It killed her career and then it killed her, too. Her voice could bring to mind the classic blues singer, Bessie Smith but she was happiest when she was rocking out like Big Mama Thornton. There was indeed a Whole Lotta Shakin' Goin' On.

Just Want Your Love; So Good To My Baby; Gabbin' Blues; My Country Man; Rain Down Rain; Way Back Home; Stay Away From My Sam; Jinny Mule; Maybelle's Blues; I've Got A Feeling; You'll Never Know; No More Trouble Out Of Me; My Big Mistake; Ain't No Use; I'm Gettin' 'Long Alright; Hair Dressin' Women; One Monkey Don't Stop No Show; Don't Leave Poor Me; Ain't To Be Played With; New Kind Of Mambo; Whole Lotta Shakin' Goin' On.

First released 1958
UK peak chart position: did not chart
USA peak chart position: did not chart

17. MUDDY WATERS FOLK SINGER
Muddy Waters

The title was a contradiction in terms, of course. Muddy Waters had never been a folk singer but in 1963 producers Ralph Bass and Willie Dixon figured it wouldn't hurt to identify him with all the acoustic blues artists that were touring Europe on a regular basis. Muddy never made a bad record and here he sings impressively and plays acoustic slide better than his audience had a right to expect. Buddy Guy shows that he's no slouch on an unamplified instrument, either. The only drawback to the enterprise is the starkness of the sound, which implies conscious artistry and preciousness in a set of songs that should express a stronger range of emotions. This is Muddy without a tiger in his tank and with a mojo operating on half power.

My Home Is In The Delta; Long Distance; My Captain; Good Morning Little Schoolgirl; You Gonna Need My Help; Cold Weather Blues; Big Leg Woman; Feel Like Going Home.

First released 1964
UK peak chart position: did not chart
USA peak chart position: did not chart

18. GO BLOW YOUR HORN
Louis Jordan

Throughout the 40s, Louis Jordan was perhaps the best known black artist in America. With his Tympany Five, he'd had an unbroken succession of hit records for the Decca label, appeared in several films, some of which he was the principal star, and 'Soundies', an early form of video jukebox. In 1954, he changed labels to Aladdin and attempted to carry on. But the times were changing, rock 'n' roll was about to explode and his upbeat, good-time music began to sound old-fashioned. These 12 tracks were all recorded in the Spring of 1954 and none was a significant hit. He tried to keep up with musical trends for a while and then reverted to his original style, which brought a measure of success to his final years.

Yeah, Yeah Baby; Louis' Blues; I've Seen What You've Done; Fat Back And Corn Likker; Put Some Money In The Pot; Gotta Go; The Dripper; Times A Passin'; Whiskey Do Your Stuff; Gal, You Need A Whippin'; It's Hard To Be Good; Dollar Down.

First released 1957
UK peak chart position: did not chart
USA peak chart position: did not chart

19. GETTING READY
Freddie King

Despite hailing from Texas, Freddie King came to musical maturity on Chicago's West Side, along with Magic Sam, Otis Rush and Buddy Guy. During the early 60s, he made a groundbreaking series of records, vocal and instrumental, for Cincinnati's King and Federal labels. 'Have You Ever Loved A Woman' and 'Hideaway' later became standards during the British Blues Boom. Leaving King in 1966, he made a couple of lacklustre records for Cotillion, before signing with Leon Russell's Shelter label. Russell had a deep appreciation of King's music and knew how to combine traditional material with contemporary arrangements. *Getting Ready*, cut in the Chess studios in 1970, showed that Freddie's chops were still in good condition on a set of standard blues that included 'Five Long Years', 'Dust My Broom', 'Key To The Highway' and even Stevie Winwood's 'Gimme Some Lovin''.

Same Old Blues; Dust My Broom; Worried Life Blues; Five Long Years; Key To The The Highway; Going Down; Living On The Highway; Walking By Myself; Tore Down; Palace Of The King; Gimme Some Lovin'; Send Someone To Love.

First released 1971
UK peak chart position: did not chart
USA peak chart position: did not chart

20. BOSS OF THE BLUES
Joe Turner

Even as early as 1956, Big Joe Turner had nothing left to prove in a career that was already two decades old. His recording career had prospered since the late 40s; a move to the Atlantic label provided the impetus to achieve national acceptance. After several hits, including 'Chains Of Love' and 'Shake, Rattle & Roll', the label reunited him with pianist Pete Johnson and an all-star band of mostly Count Basie alumni. New versions of Turner/Johnson staples such as 'Low Down Dog', 'Roll 'Em Pete', 'Cherry Red', 'How Long Blues' and 'Morning Glories' re-introduced a young audience, weened on nascent rock 'n' roll, to the new music's storming antecedents. The album was so popular that even a bootleg of out-takes was issued and sold well.

Roll 'Em Pete; Cherry Red; Testing The Blues; Morning Glories; Low Down Dog; St. Louis Blues; You're Driving Me Crazy; How Long Blues.

First released 1956
UK peak chart position: did not chart
USA peak chart position: did not chart

21. THE LONDON HOWLIN' WOLF SESSIONS
Howlin' Wolf

Chess began to lose the thread as its natural audience for the blues deserted them. Wolf and Muddy had to suffer psychedelic torture before it occurred to their producers to transport them to London, new Home Of The Blues, and get some famous friends to put them through their paces. The results were better than they had a right to expect, for unlike their American counterparts, were honoured to share a recording studio with a living legend. Eric Clapton, Stevie Winwood, Bill Wyman, Ringo Starr and Charlie Watts knew how to make their changes and Wolf was grateful for the efforts they made to play the blues the way he liked them.

Rockin' Daddy; I Ain't Superstitious; Sitting On Top Of The World; Worries About My Baby; Built For Comfort; Who's Been Talkin'; The Red Rooster (Rehearsal); The Red Rooster; Do The Do; Highway 49; Wang Dang Doodle.

First released 1971
UK peak chart position: did not chart
USA peak chart position: 79

22. A HARD ROAD
John Mayall And The Bluesbreakers

Following Eric Clapton's departure, after the magnificent *Bluesbreakers* album Mayall plugged the gap with Peter Green. Little did anyone know (except Green) that he would almost equal Clapton with fans and the cogniscenti. Two instrumentals on this collection; Freddie King's 'The Stumble' and Green's 'The Super-Natural' clearly demonstrate a clean and sparing sound from his Les Paul. The line-up is completed by John McVie, bass and Aynsley Dunbar on drums. Ex-commercial artist Mayall also designed and painted the cover, which itself is a fine piece of work and is probably rotting in some printer's basement, long forgotten. The CD reissue/remaster is quite superb.

A Hard Road; It's Over; You Don't Love Me; The Stumble; Another Kinda Love; Hit The Highway; Leaping Christine; Dust My Blues; There's Always Work; The Same Way; The Super-Natural; Top Of The Hill; Someday After A While (You'll Be Sorry), Living Alone.

First released 1963
UK peak chart position: 10
USA peak chart position: did not chart

23. GANGSTER OF LOVE
Johnny 'Guitar' Watson

Watson began his career playing piano with tenorman Chuck Higgins. His own recording career began in 1953 but blossomed three years later with a series of records for RPM, including Hot Little Mama and Three Hours Past Midnight, that highlighted a guitar style likened by Frank Zappa to 'an icepick through the forehead'. The first version of the title track was recorded for Keen in 1957. Watson re-recorded it for King in 1963, but it was Steve Miller's idiosyncratic version that made it a pop hit. A long-term friendship with Larry Williams led to a well-remembered British tour and a number of records by the duo. In the 70s, Watson reinvented himself through the medium of funk, cutting a number of successful and well-regarded albums, in the course of which he was able to suitably recast his best-known song.

I Got Eyes; Motorhead Baby; Gettin' Drunk; Walkin' To My Baby; Highway; Space Guitar; Sad Fool; Half Pint Of Whiskey; No I Can't; Thinking; Broke And Lonely; Cuttin' In; What You Do To Me; Those Lonely, Lonely Nights; You Can't Take It With You; I Just Wants Me Some Love; Gangster Of Love; Space Guitar; Sweet Lovin' Mama.

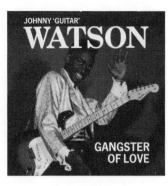

First released 1991
UK peak chart position: did not chart
USA peak chart position: did not chart

24. ITS MY LIFE BABY
Junior Wells

It was Junior Wells' hard luck to be the second-best harmonica player in Chicago; the only thing that he shared in full measure with Little Walter was a volatile temper. In the late 50s, he made a series of pop-oriented singles for Mel London's Chief and Profile labels, scoring with 'Little By Little' and 'Messin' With The Kid'. During the early 60s, he formed a loose partnership with Buddy Guy and *It's My Life Baby* was their third album collaboration in two years. Four songs, including the title track, were recorded live at Chicago's Pepper's Lounge; the remainder were studio cuts which indulged Wells' growing penchant for soul-based performances that would mar much of his later records. He's caught here on the cusp.

It's My Life Baby; Country Girl; Stormy Monday Blues; Checking On My Baby; I Got A Stomach Ache; Slow, Slow; It's So Sad To Be Lonely; You Lied To Me; Shake It Baby; Early In The Morning; Look How Baby; Everything's Going To Be Alright.

First released 1964
UK peak chart position: did not chart
USA peak chart position: did not chart

25. BORN UNDER A BAD SIGN
Albert King

The giant left-handed guitarist was no stranger to the recording studio by 1966, but Albert King had still to make his mark with the record-buying public. When he hooked up with the cream of Stax's Memphis musicians, including Booker T. & The MG's and the Memphis Horns, that connection was made. 'Laundromat Blues', 'Oh Pretty Woman' and 'Crosscut Saw' set the scene for *Born Under A Bad Sign* and 'The Hunter', which quickly found their way into the repertoires of Cream and Free. The convolutions of his guitar style were perfectly complimented by the trademark Stax funk rhythms. The team went on to make many more singles and albums, none of which really topped the achievements of their first meeting.

Laundromat Blues; Oh, Pretty Woman; Crosscut Saw; Down Don't Bother Me; Born Under A Bad Sign; Personal Manager; Kansas City; The Very Thought Of You; The Hunter; Almost Lost My Mind; As The Years Go Passing By.

First released 1967
UK peak chart position: did not chart
USA peak chart position: did not chart

26. THE BLUES OF OTIS SPANN
Otis Spann

Muddy and Otis Spann were touring England in the early summer of 1964 when this album was recorded at Decca's West Hampstead studios. Because of his Chess contract, Muddy had to be hide behind the pseudonym 'Brother' on the original release, but the disguise fooled nobody. Accompanied by bassist Ransom Knowling and Little Willie Smith on drums, and with the occasional help of Memphis Slim on a second, upright piano, Otis grasped the nettle and came up with a score of supremely accomplished blues. The original album contained just 12 tracks, ranging from his own 'Spann's Boogie' to Muddy's 'Country Boy', Big Boy Crudup's 'Rock Me Mama' and even Eugene Church's 'Pretty Girls Everywhere'. In the end, Muddy couldn't contain himself and turned in the chilling version of 'You're Gonna Need My Help' that was added to later reissues.

First released 1964
UK peak chart position: did not chart
USA peak chart position: did not chart

Rock Me Mama; I Came From Clarksdale; Keep Your Hand Out Of My Pocket; Spann's Boogie; Sarah Street; The Blues Don't Like Nobody; Meet Me In The Bottom; Lost Sheep In The Fold; I Got A Feeling; Jangleboogie; T.99; Natural Days.

27. THE LEGEND OF SLEEPY JOHN ESTES
Sleepy John Estes

Everyone believed him when Big Bill Broonzy told everyone that Sleepy John Estes was dead. But Estes was alive, albeit frail, and his music had lost little of its power. His first album featured new versions of his most famous blues, 'Someday Baby', 'Milk Cow Blues', and 'Drop Down Mama' among them. With 'I'd Been Well Warned' and 'Rats In My Kitchen', he also proved that his compositional powers were undiminished. Estes had always been noted for writing about the details of his life and the people around him. These new songs detailed the onset of blindness and the squalor in which he was living when he was rediscovered. That changed when he and longtime partner, harmonica/jug player Hammie Nixon, became popular on the international blues circuit.

First released 1962
UK peak chart position: did not chart
USA peak chart position: did not chart

Rats In My Kitchen; Someday Baby; Stop That Thing; Diving Duck Blues; Death Valley Blues; Married Woman Blues; Down South Blues; Who's Been Telling You, Buddy Brown; Drop Down Mama; You Got To Go; Milk Cow Blues; I'd Been Well Warned.

28. SECOND WINTER
Jonny Winter

The third album, not as this title suggests, was for many his best and one that appealed to lovers of rock and blues and even snuck into the conciousness of a few metal followers. Whilst Johnny's voice may not appeal to everyone, his fluid, fast and often astonishing guitar playing is his great strength. Blues is the closest genre even though the rock 'n' roll 'Slippin' And Sliding' and 'Johnny B. Goode' are included along with Dylan's 'Highway 61 Revisited. When originally issued the double album set had the fourth side completely blank. How many owners in a drunken stupor put side four on, and waited, and waited, and waited.

Memory Pain; I'm Not Sure; The Good Love; Slippin' And Slidin'; Miss Ann; Johnny B. Goode; Highway 61 Revisited; I Love Everybody; Hustled Down In Texas; I Hate Everybody; Fast Life Rider.

First released 1970
UK peak chart position: 59
USA peak chart position: 55

29. HOOKER 'N HEAT
Canned Heat/John Lee Hooker

Over the course of a double-album, the Boogie Man is joined by the members of Canned Heat, the only group to take the blues into the UK and US Top 20. When they weren't having hits like 'On The Road Again' or 'Goin' Up The Country', Canned Heat were boogin' up a storm. As Hooker had shown in his collaboration with Britain's John Lee and the Groundhogs, a vigorous rhythm section held no threat for him. When the full band weighed into 'Whiskey And Wimmen' and 'Let's Make It', he was just getting ready for a marathon stomp-off on 'Boogie Chillen No. 2'. In the next two decades, Alan Wilson, Bob Hite and Henry Vestine would die and John Lee just carried on with his endless boogie.

Messin' With The Hook; Drifter; You Talk Too Much; Burning Hell; Bottle Up And Go; I Got My Eyes On You; The Feelin' Is Gone; Send Me Your Pillow; You Talk Too Much; I Got My Eyes On You; Whiskey And Wimmen; Just You And Me; Let's Make It; Peavine; Boogie Chillen No. 2.

First released 1971
UK peak chart position: did not chart
USA peak chart position: 77

30. BLUES ALONE
John Mayall

John Mayall, the Father Of British Blues, was responsible for furthering the careers of several musicians, notably guitarists Eric Clapton and Peter Green. For this album, however, he abandoned a backing group, relying solely on ex-Artwoods' drummer, Keef Hartley, and accompanied himself with a variety of instruments, ranging from six and nine-string guitar, harmonica and bass to piano, organ and celeste. Mayall's plaintive voice is ideally suited for the sparse setting and brings a resonant depth to the self-composed material. Echoes of mentors J.B. Lenoir and Sonny Boy Williamson can be heard, but *The Blues Alone* is firmly Mayall's vision and, freed from association with stellar participants, becomes a unique and highly personal statement.

Brand New Start; Please Don't Tell; Down The Line; Sonny Boy Blow; Marsha's Mood; No More Tears; Catch That Train; Cancelling Out; Harp Man; Brown Sugar; Broken Wings; Don't Kick Me.

First released 1967
UK peak chart position:24
USA peak chart position: 128

31. BARE WIRES
John Mayall

One of Mayalls bravest and best change of style and line-ups. He enlisted the some of the cream of the British jazz movement (Henry Lowther, Dick Heckstall Smith, Chris Mercer) who together with drummer Jon Hiseman made a formidable brassy album. Mayall's lyrics although often obscured by the great musicianship were also notable, as this was a highly reflective time of his life. The album is best enjoyed complete as the links between songs are vital to its enjoyment especially the Bare Wires suite containing the sad but beautiful 'I Know Now'. Guitarist Mick Taylor added the obligatory nifty lead breaks.

Bare Wires Suite; Where Did I Belong; Start Walking; Open A New Door; Fire; I Know How; Look In The Mirror; I'm A Stranger; No Reply; Hartley Quits; Killing Time; She's Too Young; Sandy.

First released 1968
UK peak chart position:3
USA peak chart position: 59

32. ICE PICKIN'
Albert Collins

The 70s were a frustrating time for Albert Collins. Canned Heat had discovered him in Houston in 1968 and arranged a contract with Imperial which resulted in three rather formulaic hot guitar albums. In 1972, he made an album which few heard for Tumbleweed some months before the label closed. It took another six years of unrewarding hard work before another label took an interest in him. Bruce Iglauer surrounded him with first-rate musicians and chose material sympathetic to Collins' slyly humorous vocal style. *Ice Pickin'* set the tone for all the albums that followed, with tracks like 'Master Charge' and 'Cold, Cold Feeling', but they couldn't reproduce the hungry feeling an artist gets when he knows that success is just around the corner.

Talking Woman Blues; When The Welfare Turns Its Back On You; Ice Pick; Cold, Cold Feeling; Too Tired; Master Charge; Conversation With Collins; Avalanche.

First released 1978
UK peak chart position: did not chart
USA peak chart position: did not chart

33. COULDN'T STAND THE WEATHER
Stevie Ray Vaughan

Stevie Ray was already the hottest act in Austin, Texas before David Bowie used his guitar on 'Let's Dance'. Vaughan's 1983 debut album, *Texas Flood*, had alerted the world to a new guitar phenomenon which combined the blues power of Freddie and Albert King with the inspired ferocity of Jimi Hendrix. He made the Hendrix connection plain with his take on 'Voodoo Chile (Slight Return)', which rapidly became a concert highlight. At the other extreme was 'Tin Pan Alley', a slow blues made famous by Jimmy Wilson but now to be associated with the Texas hotshot. This was the time when Stevie Ray's celebrity and status among his peers was at least the equal of Eric Clapton. The pitfalls were beckoning.

Scuttle Buttin'; Couldn't Stand The Weather; Things That I Used To Do; Voodoo Chile (Slight Return); Cold Shot; Tin Pan Alley; Honey Bee; Stang's Swang.

First released 1984
UK peak chart position: did not chart
USA peak chart position: 31

34. THE BOSS MAN OF THE BLUES
Jimmy Reed

A curious compilation that falls between a greatest hits package and a career retrospective. As the title implies, it contains the hits 'Big Boss Man', 'Shame, Shame, Shame' and 'Baby What You Want Me To Do', as well as 'Roll And Rhumba' from his very first 1953 session and less immediately impressive material like 'My First Plea', 'Odds And Ends' and 'Caress Me Baby'. The most remarkable thing to note about a set that covers a decade of recording is how little Reed diverted from what was obviously a winning formula. That begs the question of whether he could have changed had it been deemed necessary. No matter how simple his music was and how many, particularly the Louisiana bluesmen that recorded for Excello, tried to imitate his style, he was in the end, unique.

Roll And Rhumba; Odds And Ends; Caress Me Baby; Baby, What You Want Me To Do; Big Boss Man; Baby What's Wrong; Down In Mississippi; Too Much; Oh John; Shame Shame Shame; Mary, Mary; The Outskirts Of Town; St Louis Blues; My First Plea.

First released 1964
UK peak chart position: did not chart
USA peak chart position: did not chart

35. BLUES FROM THE GUTTER
Champion Jack Dupree

The garrulous ex-boxer and New Orleans pianist had already recorded for a host of record labels, large and small, when he cut this album in New York in February 1958. The small band included alto player Pete Brown and guitarist Larry Dale. Their contributions helped to keep Dupree's music where the album title located it. There was a lot of humour in his music, heard here on 'Evil Woman', but here he concentrated on starkly honest themes. 'Junker's Blues' and 'Can't Kick The Habit' addressed drug addiction; 'Goin' Down Slow', 'T.B. Blues' and 'Bad Blood' were about decline and death. The album brought him recognition in Europe, where he would shortly make his home.

Walking The Blues; T.B. Blues; Can't Kick The Habit; Evil Woman; Nasty Boogie; Junker's Blues; Bad Blood; Goin' Down Slow; Frankie & Johnny; Stack-O-Lee.

First released 1958
UK peak chart position: did not chart
USA peak chart position: did not chart

36. STRONG PERSUADER
Robert Cray

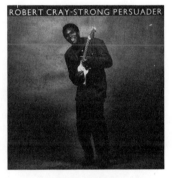

Although he discourages being identified too closely with the blues, it's undeniable that, along with the late Stevie Ray Vaughan, Robert Cray has been one of the prime movers of the recent resurgence of interest in the blues. *Strong Persuader* is perhaps the strongest exhibition of his particular talents. His songs inhabit a narrow universe of bitterness, deceit and morally questionable conduct. 'Right Next Door (Because Of Me)' and 'Smoking Gun' typify the pain, jealousy and guilt that are his stock-in-trade. He's also no mean guitarist, even if he doesn't always want to prove it. Allied to an expressive vocal style alert to every lyrical nuance, this makes Robert Cray an unequalled representative of the modern blues tradition.

Smoking Gun; I Guessed I Showed Her; Right Next Door (Because Of Me); Nothin' But A Woman; Still Around; More Than I Can Stand; Foul Play; I Wonder; Fantasized; New Blood.

First released 1986
UK peak chart position:34
USA peak chart position: 13

37. SHOWDOWN!
Albert Collins, Robert Cray, Johnny Copeland

What should have been a celebration of Texas blues was changed into something greater when Robert Cray stepped in to replace Clarence 'Gatemouth' Brown. The result was a Grammy-winning combination of three different but sympathetic talents. If both Collins and Copeland attacked their guitars as though their fingers were plugged into the electricity supply, Cray provided a contrasting note of balanced and thoughtful musicianship. It was inevitable that Albert Collins should dominate proceedings, having been an influence on the others. Playing in various duet and trio combinations, the protagonists never drew blood in a contest that wasn't designed to have a winner.

T-Bone Shuffle; The Moon Is Full; Lion's Den; She's Into Something; Bring Your Fine Self Home; Black Cat Bone; The Dream; Albert's Alley; Black Jack.

First released 1986
UK peak chart position: did not chart
USA peak chart position: 124

38. TAJ MAHAL
Taj Mahal

Bluesinger and ethnologist Taj Mahal began a long solo career with this impressive album. An aficionado of country blues, he drew on material by Robert Johnson, Willie McTell and Willie Johnson, but used electric instruments to enhance its subtleties and nuances. Slide guitarist Ry Cooder, who had played with Mahal in the Rising Sons, was among those supporting the singer whose relaxed, smoky intonation brought an authority to the album's content. A skilled and perceptive interpreter, Mahal brought an individuality to songs to often crushed elsewhere. His understanding of the genre is this album's abiding strength.

Leaving Trunk; Statesboro Blues; Checkin' Up On My Baby; Everybody's Got To Change Sometime; EZ Rider; Dust My Broom; Diving Duck Blues; Celebrated Walkin' Blues.

First released 1968
UK peak chart position: did not chart
USA peak chart position: did not chart

39. ICEMAN
Albert Collins

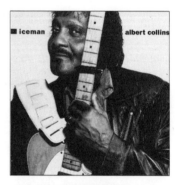

In what was to be his penultimate album, Albert Collins finally moved into the blues mainstream. In essence, the ingredients were no different from his Alligator albums, but a better promotional ensured significant success. Collins was renowned for straight-ahead, jazz-oriented blues, his guitar solos sharp and piercing, evoking the imagery that inspired his nickname. He also became a sardonic and humorous vocalist, aided by his wife Gwendolyn's knowing lyrics. Having struggled in the wasteland of endless club circuits, in his last years Collins took to the high ground, providing credibility for Gary Moore's 'rediscovery' of his blues roots and guesting on albums by John Lee Hooker and B.B. King. Death robbed him of the rewards he deserved.

Mr. Collins, Mr. Collins; Iceman; Don't Mistake Kindness For Weakness; Travelin' South; Put The Shoe On The Other Foot; I'm Beginning To Wonder; Head Rag; The Hawk; The Blues For Gabe; Mr. Collins, Mr. Collins (Reprise).

First released 1991
UK peak chart position: did not chart
USA peak chart position: did not chart

40. R & B FROM THE MARQUEE
Alexis Korner's Blues Incorporated

British blues would have been undeniably poorer - perhaps even non-existent - without Alexis Korner. His group was a catalyst for like-minded musicians and this seminal release featured Cyril Davies, Long John Baldry, Ronnie Jones and Dick Heckstall-Smith, each of whom would become respected performers in their own right. Sympathetic renditions of material drawn from Muddy Waters, Leroy Carr and Jimmy Witherspoon helped introduce these pivotal figures to a new audience and declare an agenda for the many groups which would follow in this album's wake. Without Blues Incorporated the possibility of a Rolling Stones or a Graham Bond Organization would have been greatly diminished - both were formed around ex-members - and by extension neither would the countless acts these two groups inspired. Few albums can claim such importance.

Gotta Move; Rain Is Such A Lonesome Sound; I Got My Brand On You; Spooky But Nice; Keep Your Hands Off Her; I Wanna Put A Tiger In Your Tank; I Got My Mojo Working; Finkle's Cafe; Hoochie Coochie; Down Town; How Long, How Long Blues; I Thought I Heard That Train Whistle Blow.

First released 1964
UK peak chart position: did not chart
USA peak chart position: did not chart

41. I WAS WARNED
Robert Cray

With this album, Cray said goodbye to bassist Richard Cousins, the last and staunchest survivor of his original band. At this point, the Memphis Horns were a regular part of the organisation. Inevitably, their presence had drawn the songwriting team into writing material that evoked the Stax era. Having previously kept a tight rein on both his singing and guitar playing, Cray was now becoming more adventurous, proved by the rhumba beat that propelled the title track. Many of the songs, including 'I'm A Good Man' and 'The Price I Pay', were written by Cray and producer Dennis Walker, but the album's one poignant note was struck with 'He Don't Live Here Anymore', written by keyboard man Jim Pugh.

Just A Loser; I'm A Good Man; I Was Warned; The Price I Pay; Won The Battle; On The Road Down; A Whole Lotta Pride; A Picture Of A Broken Heart; He Don't Live Here Anymore; Our Last Time.

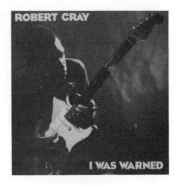

First released 1993
UK peak chart position:29
USA peak chart position: 103

42. MR LUCKY
John Lee Hooker

With the success of *The Healer* behind him, a newly-rich man who now had enough money to last out his years in some comfort, John Lee Hooker could only call himself Mr Lucky. He'd first recorded the song in 1967 and this time he had the Robert Cray Band giving him enthusiastic backing. Other guests included Ry Cooder, Albert Collins, John Hammond, Van Morrison, Carlos Santana, Johnny Winter and Keith Richards, none of whom could shake Hooker from his purpose. 'This Is Hip', with Cooder and Terry Evans, became the soundtrack for a Lee Jeans television advert. Most of the other songs revisited his huge song catalogue but 'Stripped Me Naked', with Carlos Santana's band, showed that he could still pen a powerful lyric.

I Want To Hug You; Mr. Lucky; Backstabbers; This Is Hip; I Cover The Waterfront; Highway 13; Stripped Me Naked; Susie; Crawlin' Kingsnake; Father Was A Jockey.

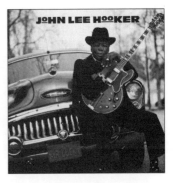

First released 1991
UK peak chart position:3
USA peak chart position: 101

43. THE LEGENDARY SON HOUSE
Son House

Few artists deserve the accolade, but Son House was very much a legend. His first recordings in 1930 exhibited a staggering power and intensity, and showed why he had been the mentor of both Robert Johnson and Muddy Waters. He recorded for the Library of Congress in 1941/2 and was thought to be dead prior to his rediscovery in 1964. His skills were somewhat depleted but the power of his performance could still amaze. Columbia A&R man John Hammond, himself something of a legend, produced this album in 1965. House's voice was magnificent in decay, as he roared out 'Death Letter', 'Levee Camp Moan' and 'Preachin' Blues' or laid down his guitar to sing 'John The Revelator'. His like will not be seen again.

Death Letter; Pearline; Louise McGhee; John The Revelator; Empire State Express; Preachin' Blues; Grinning On Your Face; Sundown; Levee Camp Moan.

First released 1966
UK peak chart position: did not chart
USA peak chart position: did not chart

44. INTO THE PURPLE VALLEY
Ry Cooder

Guitarist Cooder was a respected session musician prior to launching a solo career. His distinctive style blossomed fully on this, his second album, which is a brilliant compendium of American country/folk styles. Tight, but sparse accompaniment takes the artist through songs largely drawn from the Dustbowl Ballads of the Depression era. An unerring empathy is heard throughout, particularly on Woody Guthrie's 'Vigilante Man'. Cooder's ungamely voice captures the pervasive atmosphere, but it's his chilling side guitar work for which this album is renowned.

How Can You Keep On Moving; Billy The Kid; Money Honey; FDR In Trinidad; Teardrops Will Fall; Denomination Blues; On A Monday; Hey Porter; Great Dreams Of Heaven; Taxes On The Farmer Feeds Us All; Vigilante Man.

First released 1971
UK peak chart position: did not chart
USA peak chart position: 113

45. THE SOUND OF 65
Graham Bond Organisation

Of the many groups that developed from Blues Incorporated, this was probably the most musically talented. Led by the larger-than-life Graham Bond on organ, the Organisation consisted of Jack Bruce, Ginger Baker and Dick Heckstall-Smith. Every member of the band came from a jazz background and brought a much more open and improvisational approach to their blues playing, which had a harder edge than that heard from similar groups led by Georgie Fame and Brian Auger. Their repertoire ranged over crowd-pleasers like 'Hoochie Coochie Man' and 'Got My Mojo Working' to Ramsey Lewis' 'Wade In The Water'. Whether they were the sound of 65 or not, Bond never achieved the sort of success that Bruce and Baker did before his life ended under the wheels of an Underground train in May 1974.

Hoochie Coochie; Baby Make Love To Me; Neighbour Neighbour; Early In The Morning; Spanish Eyes; Oh Baby; Little Girl; I Want You; Wade In The Water; Got My Mojo Working; Train Time; Baby Be Good To Me; Half A Man; Tammy.

First released 1965
UK peak chart position: did not chart
USA peak chart position: did not chart

46. THE TRUTH
T-Bone Walker

The uncomfortable truth was that T-Bone hadn't made an album for several years and ill-health had reduced the fluent skill that had driven all his famous recordings decades earlier for Capitol and Imperial. But these tracks, recorded in Pasadena in 1966, revealed that he could still drive a guitar around the block. Producer Huey Meaux sat him down between a piano and organ in the studio and T-Bone would indulge himself whenever the mood took him. While his fingers may not obey his command, his voice had lost none of its smokey sensuality. Backed by local musicians, including Willard 'Piano Slim' Burton, guitarist Joey Long and tenorman Arnett Cobb, T-Bone testified to good effect just one more time.

Treat Your Daddy Well; Let Your Hair Down Baby; Old Time Used To Be; You Don't Love Me And I Don't Care; It Ain't No Right In You; You Ought To Know Better; I Ain't Your Fool No More; Don't Let Your Heartache Catch You; Hate To See You Go; It Takes A Lot Of Knowhow; I Don't Be Jiving.

First released 1968
UK peak chart position: did not chart
USA peak chart position: did not chart

47. PETER GREEN'S FLEETWOOD MAC
Fleetwood Mac

It's hard to believe now that such an out-and-out blues album could have remained in the album charts for almost a year. But that's what this one did. The blues was on a crest of a wave in 1968; Eric Clapton had left John Mayall for Cream, who never really lost sight of the blues; and his successor, Peter Green put his ideal band together with John McVie and Mick Fleetwood. Completing the band was the diminutive slide guitarist Jeremy Spencer. The album reflected their live appearances, with the 12 tracks shared between the two vocalists. At this remove, it's plain that Spencer's Elmore James imitations, while uncannily accurate, would quickly date. What hasn't are the sensitive songwriting and performances by the most accomplished blues musician this country has ever produced.

My Heart Beat Like A Hammer; Merry Go Round; Long Grey Mare; Shake Your Moneymaker; Looking For Somebody; No Place To Go; My Baby's Good To Me; I Loved Another Woman; Cold Black Night; The World Keep On Turning; Got To Move.

First released 1968
UK peak chart position:4
USA peak chart position: 198

48. ALABAMA BLUES!
J.B. Lenoir

JB had two careers, one as the extrovert R&B man in the leopard-skin jacket who chanted infectious trifles like 'Mama Talk To Your Daughter', the other as a thoughtful and intelligent writer of starkly honest blues songs. This album was recorded by Willie Dixon in Chicago before Lenoir embarked on the 1965 American Folk Blues Festival tour. He reprised the above hit and 'Mojo Boogie', but songs like 'Move This Rope', 'Down In Mississippi' and 'Born Dead' bore witness to the Civil Rights conflict of the time. Lenoir sang with dignity and compassion but the harshness of his message was not diminished by the method of its expression.

Alabama Blues; The Mojo Boogie; God's Word; The Whale Has Swallowd Me; Move This Rope; I Feel So Good; Alabama March; Talk To You Daughter; Mississippi Road; Good Advice; Vietnam; I Want To Go; Down In Mississippi; If I Get Lucky; Born Dead; Feeling Good.

First released 1965
UK peak chart position: did not chart
USA peak chart position: did not chart

49. THIS ONE'S A GOOD UN
Otis Rush

John Mayall had already included several of Rush's songs in his repertoire by the time Blue Horizon gathered together 18 originals and alternate takes for this release. Otis Rush has perhaps the most expressive voice in the blues, emphasised by his penchant for minor-key songs that accentuate the most telling aspects of his voice. Added to that is a guitar style that makes up with commitment what it lacks in originality. On one session that included 'Double Trouble', 'All Your Love' and 'Keep On Lovin' Me Baby', he was backed by the Ike Turner band. The results were some of the best music that either man ever produced. For many years, these tracks constituted the best of Otis Rush. Recent events suggest that he has returned to the form displayed here.

Double Trouble; Jump Sister Bessie; She's A Good 'Un (take A); Checking On My Baby; Sit Down Baby; Love That Woman; Keep On Loving Me Baby (take B); Keep On Loving Me Baby (take A); My Baby Is A Good 'Un; If You Were Mine; I Can't Quit You Baby (alternate take); All Your Love (I Miss Loving); Groaning The Blues (alternate take); It Takes Time; Violent Love; Three Times A Fool (alternate take); My Love Will Never Die (alternate take); She's A Good 'Un (take B).

First released 1969
UK peak chart position: did not chart
USA peak chart position: did not chart

50. EAST WEST
Paul Butterfield Blues Band

While the British Blues Boom was taking all the glory, harmonica player Butterfield and guitarist Mike Bloomfield were hanging out in the clubs and bars of Chicago, learning their blues technique from the originals. With ex-Howlin' Wolf sidemen, Sam Lay and Jerome Arnold, and keyboard player Mark Naftalin, they formed the most influential white blues band in America. Their first album had been aggressively blues-oriented, but East West reflected wider musical interests. Alongside Robert John's 'Walkin' Blues', there was Cannonball Adderley's 'Work Song' and the 13-minute title track, which adopted a raga-like structure and pointed the way for the marathon improvisation that became standard behaviour for groups formed in the wake of Cream. Both men were drawn into further experimentation but each returned to the blues before he died.

Walkin' Blues; Get Out Of My Life Woman; I Got A Mind To Give Up Living; All These Blues; Work Song; Mary Mary; Two Trains Running; Never Say No; East West.

First released 1966
UK peak chart position: did not chart
USA peak chart position: 65

THE TOP 50
COUNTRY ALBUMS

NEW COUNTRY, COUNTRY ROCK OR JUST PURE OL' TIMEY. THE RENAISSANCE AND ACCEPTANCE OF COUNTRY MUSIC IS A WELCOME EVENT. THE NEW TALENT IS EXCEPTIONAL, THE PIONEERING BRIDGE BUILDERS SUCH AS GRAM PARSONS OR THE BYRDS ARE UNDENIABLE AND THE QUALITY, THE WORK AND INFLUENCE OF HANK WILLIAMS OR PATSY CLINE IS FOREVER ETCHED IN TOMBSTONE.

1. MOANIN' THE BLUES
Hank Williams

The strong blues thread in Hank Williams' music is partially because he learnt guitar playing from a black musician, Tee-Tot. He also suffered a lot and maybe you can't write about misery without suffering. Songwriting doesn't come any better than the compact, aching poetry of 'I'm So Lonesome I Could Cry'. It's not all doom and gloom though on this 8-track, 10-inch album: there's the unusual chording of 'Honky Tonk Blues' and the playful yodels of 'Lovesick Blues' and 'Long Gone Lonesome Blues'. Hank Williams is the most influencial man Country music has ever produced, and is ever likely to. Essential.

Moanin' The Blues; I'm So Lonesome I Could Cry; My Sweet Love Ain't Around; Honky Tonk Blues; Lovesick Blues; The Blues Come Around; I'm A Long Gone Daddy; Long Gone Lonesome Blues.

First released 1952
UK peak chart position: did not chart
USA peak chart position: did not chart

2. COUNTRY MUSIC HALL OF FAME
Jimmie Rodgers

America's Blue Yodeller, Jimmie Rodgers, died at the age of 35 in 1933. Only shellac 78s, played on wind-up Victrolas, were issued in his day, but numerous collections have followed. This omits some of his best-known songs, but everyone is a gem. There are songs about trains, prisons, barrooms and cheating women, ie. not much different to today's country albums. Rodgers died of TB and he wrote about his illness in 'TB Blues'. The album was released after Jimmie Rodgers had been inducted as the first member of the Country Music Hall of Fame. His plaque reads, "Jimmie Rodgers' name stands foremost in the country music field as 'the man who started it all'." Amen to that.

Sweet Mama Hurry Home Or I'll Be Gone; I'm Lonesome Too; When The Cactus Is In Bloom; The Cowhand's Last Ride; Yodeling Cowboy; Dreaming With Tears In My Eyes; Roll Along Kentucky Moon; I'm Free From The Chain Gang Now; For The Sake Of Days Gone By; The Soldier's Sweetheart; Gambling Barroom Blues; The Sailor's Plea; Old Love Letters; She Was Happy Till She Met You; Mississippi River Blues; TB Blues.

First released 1962
UK peak chart position: did not chart
USA peak chart position: did not chart

3. RAMBLIN' MAN
Hank Williams

Many musicians overwrite, rather than write, their songs, but Hank Williams had the ability to hone his feelings and emotions into simple, direct images in everyday language. There's the wit of 'Why Don't You Love Me?' and 'Nobody's Lonesome For Me' and the melodrama of 'My Son Calls Another Man Daddy', although, in reality, Hank Williams Jnr. never lets us forget who his dad is. Also on this album is Hank's fine performance of another country classic, 'Take These Chains From My Heart', another swing at his strained relationship with his wife, Audrey.

Ramblin' Man; Lonesome Whistle; My Son Calls Another Man Daddy; I Just Don't Like This Kind Of Livin'; I Can't Escape From You; Nobody's Lonesome For Me; Take These Chains From My Heart; Why Don't You Love Me?; I Can't Help It (If I'm Still In Love With You); There'll Be No Teardrops Tonight; You're Gonna Change (Or I'm Gonna Leave); My Heart Would Know.

First released 1955
UK peak chart position: did not chart
USA peak chart position: did not chart

4. MEMORIAL ALBUM
Hank Williams

Hank Williams died on the road, on his way to a gig in Canton, Ohio on New Year's Day, 1953. The Grand Ole Opry had discredited him as a drunk and he was the first rock star, living a squalid life of amphetamines and whisky and putting family quarrels into his songs. This album, the first to cash in on a musician's death, was issued in 10-inch and 12-inch formats with eight and 12 songs, respectively. Country music doesn't come any better and Hank Williams' influence is immense: Elvis Presley, Buddy Holly and Bob Dylan have a lot to thank him for. Play 'Move It On Over' next to 'Rock Around The Clock' and you'll discover Bill Haley's listening habits.

You Win Again; Cold Cold Heart; I Could Never Be Ashamed Of You; Settin' The Woods On Fire; Hey, Good Lookin'; Kaw-Liga; Half As Much.

First released 1953
UK peak chart position: did not chart
USA peak chart position: did not chart

5. SLIM WHITMAN FAVORITES
Slim Whitman

This is one of the Top 1000 albums despite the cover portrait of Slim Whitman which is even worse than Bob Dylan's 'Self-Portrait'. Long playing records were still a novelty in 1956 so the fans were grateful for anything. (Bob Dylan had no excuse.) This collection contained the original versions of Slim's chief successes - 'Indian Love Call' and 'Rose Marie', both from the operetta 'Rose Marie'. Slim's yodelling on 'Love Song Of The Waterfall' still sounds remarkable and the combination of his tenor voice with Hoot Rains' steel guitar created many memorable tracks. According to Slim, Paul McCartney was so impressed at seeing him play the guitar left-handed in the 50s at the Liverpool Empire that he followed his style, but Slim is a southpaw guitarist because he lost part of a finger in an accident.

Beautiful Dreamer; I Went To Your Wedding; Marjie; I Remember You; Carolina Moon; Oh My Darlin (I Love You); Just An Echo In The Valley; If I Had My Life To Live Over; Silver Haired Daddy Of Mine; Ghost Riders In The Sky; Edelweiss; Take Good Care Of Her; Secret Love; Can't Help Falling In Love; When You Wore A Tulip; You Are My Sunshine; Rose Marie; Mr. Songman; Goodbye Little Darlin' Goodbye; Where Did Yesterday Go?; Indian Love Call; Love Song Of The Waterfall.

First released 1956
UK peak chart position: did not chart
USA peak chart position: did not chart

6. PATSY CLINE SHOWCASE
Patsy Cline

Astonishingly, only three albums were released during Patsy Cline's lifetime, the best one being *The Patsy Cline Showcase*. Although she was a competent up-tempo performer, she excelled with tear-jerking ballads like 'I Fall To Pieces' and Willie Nelson's 'Crazy'. Producer Owen Bradley bathed her throbbing vocals with echo, added a vocal group (the Jordanaires) and a gentle beat, sweetened by strings. Thus, they created the template for country music of the 60s. Patsy's male counterpart was Jim Reeves and in 1981, their versions of 'Have You Ever Been Lonely?' and 'I Fall To Pieces' were merged for duet recordings. Luckily they had sung the songs in similar keys and tempos but nothing would have deterred the Nashville entrepreneurs. Can't be long before we have the albums of Elvis duets.

I Fall To Pieces; Foolin' Round; The Wavering Wind; South Of The Border; I Love You So Much It Hurts; Seven Lonely Days; Crazy; San Antonio Rose; True Love; Walking After Midnight; A Poor Man's Roses.

First released 1962
UK peak chart position: did not chart
USA peak chart position: 73

7. WAYLON AND WILLIE
Waylon Jennings And Willie Nelson

Willie and Waylon moved to Austin, Texas and developed a rougher, looser form of country music. After the compilation, Wanted - The Outlaws, was a million-seller, they made the superb *Waylon And Willie*. Ed Bruce's 'Mammas, Don't Let Your Babies Grow Up To Be Cowboys' encompassed the new philosophy and the casual reference to drugs in 'I Can Get Off On You' was unique for country music. The album permeates with the feel of cheap digs, dingy dressing-rooms and one night relationships - 'Funny a woman can come so wild and so free/Yet insist I don't watch her undress or watch her watch me' is the killer opening of Lee Clayton's 'If You Can Touch Her At All'. That's one of Willie's solos and there's the same grits can be found in his versions of 'A Couple More Years' and 'It's Not Supposed To Be That Way'.

Mammas, Don't Let Your Babies Grow Up To Be Cowboys; The Year 2003 Minus 25; Pick Up The Tempo; If You Can Touch Her At All; Looking For A Feeling; It's Not Supposed To Be That Way; I Can Get Off On You; Don't Cuss The Fiddle; Gold Dust Woman; A Couple More Years; Wurlitzer Prize; Mr. Schuck 'N' Jive; Roman Candles; The Dock Of The Bay; The Year That Clayton Delaney Died; Lady In The Harbor; May I Borrow Some Sugar From You; The Last Cowboy Song; Heroes; Teddy Bear Song; Write Your Own Songs; The Old Mother's Locket Trick.

First released 1978
UK peak chart position: did not chart
USA peak chart position: 12

8. GUNFIGHTER BALLADS & TRAIL SONGS
Marty Robbins

Nowadays it is normal to take eight months over an album, so all credit to Marty Robbins who knocked off *Gunfighter Ballads And Trail Songs* in a day. Marty had had success with 'Singing The Blues' and 'A White Sport Coat' and loving the western part of C&W, he decided to cut an album of cowboy songs. It included his hit single, 'El Paso', which at four and a half minutes became, for a few brief years, the longest single to make the charts. Vocal accompaniment was by Tompall And The Glaser Brothers, who developed into a major country act in their own right. Its success prompted *More Gunfighter Ballads And Trail Songs* and two further songs about El Paso.

Big Iron; Cool Water; Billy The Kid; A Hundred And Sixty Acres; They're Hanging Me Tonight; The Strawberry Roan; El Paso; In The Valley; The Master's Call; Running Gun; Little Green Valley; Utah Carol.

First released 1959
UK peak chart position: 20
USA peak chart position: 6

9. ALWAYS ON MY MIND
Willie Nelson

Willie Nelson was so immersed in country music that he didn't know Elvis had recorded 'Always On My Mind'. Elvis sang it as an apology to Priscilla and even though it is among his best work, he was outclassed by Willie Nelson, whose performance ached with the regrets of a musician on the road. (Didn't stop his marriage breaking up though.) Producer Chips Moman realised that Willie could sing anything to perfection so he took songs from everywhere - soul, pop, psychedelia with a few country songs for good measure. If you want an aural definition of honesty and integrity in popular music, try this album.

Always On My Mind; Blue Eyes Crying In The Rain; Do Right Woman, Do Right Man; Whiter Shade Of Pale; Let It Be; Staring Each Other Down; Bridge Over Troubled Water; Old Fords And Natural Stone; Permanantly Lonely; Last Thing I Needed First Thing This Morning; Party's Over.

First released 1982
UK peak chart position: did not chart
USA peak chart position: 2

10. HANK WILLIAMS SINGS
Hank Williams

Like one Hank Williams album and you'll like the lot, and this 10-inch album was the first. All Williams' trademarks are in these eight songs: devotion to your mother, loveless marriages (his own is reflected in 'A House Without Love'), the deep religious convictions of the southern states and the problems of living up to those beliefs. Numerous interpretations have turned 'I Saw The Light' into a standard and far too many musicians have followed Hank down that 'Lost Highway'.

A House Without Love; Wedding Bells; The Mansion On The Hill; Wealth Won't Save Your Soul; I Saw The Light; Six More Miles To The Graveyard; Lost Highway; I've Just Told Mama Goodbye.

First released 1952
UK peak chart position: did not chart
USA peak chart position: did not chart

11. OKIE FROM MUSKOGEE
Merle Haggard

A chance remark on Merle Haggard's tour bus led to him writing the anthem against draft-dodgers and hippies, 'Okie From Muskogee'. Was it for real or was it a parody? Maybe we'll never know, but right-wing country fans were delighted to have a song that articulated their feelings. Haggard sided with blue collar America on 'Working Man Blues', and country fans loved his songs about prison life - 'Sing Me Back Home', 'Mama Tried', 'Branded Man' and 'I'm A Lonesome Fugitive'. Haggard was in the audience when Johnny Cash once played San Quentin. As John Stewart said in '18 Wheels', "Eight track's playing me 'Silver Wings', Like a razor's edge, Merle Haggard sings."

Opening Introduction And Theme; Mama Tried; No Hard Times; Silver Wings; Swinging Doors; I'm A Lonesome Fugitive; Sing Me Back Home; Branded Man; In The Arms Of Love; Workin' Man Blues; Introduction To Hobo Bill; Hobo Bill's Last Ride; Billy Overcame His Size; If I Had Left It Up To You; White Line Fever; Blue Rock; Okie From Muskogee.

First released 1970
UK peak chart position: did not chart
USA peak chart position: 46

12. RED HEADED STRANGER
Willie Nelson

Willie Nelson stopped shaving, grew his hair, ditched his suits and found acceptance with the hippies who bought the country/rock of the Flying Burrito Brothers. Like *Tommy*, *Red Headed Stranger* was a concept album, this time about a murderous preacher. His laidback voice-and-guitar revival of 'Blue Eyes Cryin' In The Rain' was a surprise US hit single, and Richard Thompson says, 'I like the fact that he plays these terrible solos and leaves them alone, which takes a lot of guts these days.'

Time Of The Preacher; I Couldn't Believe It Was True; Blue Rock Montana; Blue Eyes Crying In The Rain; Red Headed Stranger; Just As I Am; Denver; O'er The Waves; Down Yonder; Can I Sleep In Your Arms; Remember Me When The Candle Lights Are Gleaming; Hands On The Wheel; Bandera.

First released 1975
UK peak chart position: did not chart
USA peak chart position: 28

13. OL' WAYLON
Waylon Jennings

Although Waylon Jennings found fame as one of the country music outlaws, it is clear from 'Luchenbach, Texas' that he wasn't enjoying it much. (Luchenbach was a minute town owned by an 'imagineer' Hondo Crouch, to which the outlaws returned for solace.) Many of the songs reflected the darker side of Waylon's personality, notably 'Till I Gain Control Again', and a rock 'n' roll medley reminded us that he was around in the 50s and nearly took that 'plane with Buddy Holly. At times, he must have wished he was on it.

Luchenback, Texas (Back To The Basics Of Love); If You See Me Getting Smaller - with Larry Keith /Steve Pippin; Lucille; Sweet Caroline; I Think I'm Gonna Kill Myself; Belle Of The Ball; That's Alright; My Baby Left Me; Till I Gain Control Again; Brand New Goodbye Song; Satin Sheets - with Jesse Colter/Toni Wine; This Is Getting Funny (But There Ain't Nobody Laughing).

First released 1977
UK peak chart position: did not chart
USA peak chart position: 15

14. CITY OF NEW ORLEANS
Willie Nelson

Although only in his early fifties when he made this record, Willie Nelson was cultivating the image of being the ancient mariner, an old salt with the wisdom of the world on his face. Who better to sing of the misfits on the train, the City of New Orleans, than Willie Nelson? 'The Wind Beneath My Wings' was a successful attempt to recreate the mood of 'Always On My Mind' and he has not surpassed his tenderness on 'Please Come To Boston'. Willie Nelson's own songwriting had all but terminated, but this was a wonderful way around a writing-block.

City Of New Orleans; Just Out Of Reach; Good Time Charlie's Got The Blues; Why Are You Picking On Me?; She's Out Of My Life; Cry; Please Come To Boston; It Turns Me Inside Out; The Wind Beneath My Wings; Until It's Time For You To Go.

First released 1984
UK peak chart position: did not chart
USA peak chart position: 69

15. SONGS OUR DADDY TAUGHT US
Everly Brothers

Don and Phil walked right back to the songs of their youth for a delightful set of 12 plaintive, old-time melodies. They had been regular performers on their parents' radio show and this tribute to their father, Ike, was performed with warmth and affection. The only accompaniment came from Don's guitar and Floyd Chance's stand-up bass: Floyd remarked, 'Damn. You would put me on an album where everyone of my notes can be heard.' Their hit single, 'Take A Message To Mary', continued the mood of the album and to this day, the Everlys perform the songs, usually 'Long Time Gone' and 'Barbara Allen'.

Roving Gambler; Down In The Willow Green; Long Time Gone; Lightning Express; That Silver Haired Daddy Of Mine; Who's Gonna Shoe Your Pretty Little Feet?; Barbara Allen; Oh So Many Years; I'm Here To Get My Baby Out Of Jail; Rockin' Alone In My Old Rockin' Chair; Kentucky; Put My Little Shoes Away.

First released 1958
UK peak chart position: did not chart
USA peak chart position: did not chart

16. WHEN TRAGEDY STRUCK
Hank Snow

Hank Snow, who was born in Liverpool, Nova Scotia in 1914, recorded for RCA-Victor from 1936-81, the longest tenure of any entertainer with a recording company. He covered every style of country music, but he is best-known for his maudlin albums, *When Tragedy Struck* and *Songs Of Tragedy*, one of which had a noose, rather than a picture of the artist, on the cover. He brought his personal feelings to the tear-jerking 'Nobody's Child' as he had had an unhappy childhood. There's feeling and compassion in his performances and if you appreciate such titles as 'There's A Little Box Of Pine On The 7.29', this album's for you.

The Letter Edged In Black; Old Ship; The Prisoner's Prayer; The Drunkard's Child; Don't Make Me Go To Bed And I'll Be Good; The Convict And The Rose; Put My Little Shoes Away; Little Buddy; There's A Little Box Of Pine On The 7:29; Nobody's Child; I'm Here To Get My Baby Out Of Jail.

First released 1959
UK peak chart position: did not chart
USA peak chart position: did not chart

17. No Fences
Garth Brooks

Although he has yet to make a major impact on the British record market, Garth Brooks has been selling in Michael Jackson-style proportions in the US. He has become the biggest-selling country artist of all-time, so he has outsold all of Johnny Cash's work in five years. Whether he will make the lasting impression of Cash is open to debate because there is nothing radically new in this, his biggest-selling album. Having said that, *No Fences* is a superb collection of crossover country songs including the concert-stopping 'Friends In Low Places' and an uptempo revival of the Fleetwoods' 'Mr. Blue', both songs being written, 30 years apart, by Dewayne Blackwell. The concept of 'Unanswered Prayers' takes your breath away ("Some of God's greatest gifts are unanswered prayers'), not that Mr. Brooks has any prayers left to be answered. The British release of this album includes four songs from his first album, *Garth Brooks*.

If Tomorrow Never Comes; Not Counting You; Much Too Young (To Feel This Damn Old); The Dance; The Thunder Rolls; New Way To Fly; Two Of A Kind, Workin' On A Full House; Victim Of The Game; Friends In Low Places; Wild Horses; Unanswered Prayers; Same Old Story; Mr. Blue; Wolves.

First released 1990
UK peak chart position: did not chart
USA peak chart position: 3

18. Killin' Time
Clint Black

Although *Killin' Time* was Clint Black's debut album, many country fans thought they had been listening to him for years as his solid, honky-tonk style was modelled on Merle Haggard's. The title track, a drinking song, was a US country number 1 as was 'A Better Man', written about a broken romance he experienced. His second album, *Put Yourself In My Shoes*, was another million-seller but managerial disputes halted his career just as he was beginning to rival Garth Brooks.

Straight From The Factory; Nobody's Home; You're Gonna Leave Me Again; Winding Down; Live And Learn; A Better Man; Walkin' Away; I'll Be Gone; Killin' Time.

First released 1988
UK peak chart position: did not chart
USA peak chart position: 31

19. If There Was A Way
Dwight Yoakam

The packaging is designer country - Dwight attached to his large Stetson, torn jeans, lanky legs and James Dean posture. Forgetting the packaging, the music is very good, hillbilly deluxe, and Dwight's solid country voice makes no concessions to commerciality. Among the excellent tracks is Dwight's duet with Patty Loveless, 'Send A Message To My Heart', a revival of Wilbert Harrison/Bryan Ferry's 'Let's Work Together' and a joint composition with Roger Miller, 'It Only Hurts When I Cry'. Clearly the best place to hear him is a crowded honky-tonk.

The Distance Between You And Me; The Heart That You Own; Takes A Lot To Rock You; Nothing's Changed Here; Sad, Sad Music; Since I Started Drinkin' Again; If There Was A Way; Turn It On, Turn It Up, Turn Me Loose; It Only Hurts When I Cry; Send A Message To My Heart; I Don't Need It Done; You're The One.

First released 1990
UK peak chart position: did not chart
USA peak chart position: 96

20. ROPIN' THE WIND
Garth Brooks

Ropin' The Wind sold four million in its first month of release and kept on selling. 'Shameless', written by that up-and-coming country writer Billy Joel, was a US number 1, while 'Papa Loved Mama' has a classic chorus - 'Papa loved Mama/Mama loved men/Mama's in the graveyard/Papa's in the pen.' Even though Garth Brooks and his producer Allen Reynolds had sifted through 3,000 songs, the material is not as strong as *No Fences*. It didn't matter because Garth had transformed himself into the most exciting and energetic performer in America: not even Springsteen swings on a rope.

Against The Grain; Rodeo; What She's Doing Now; Burning Bridges; Papa Loved Mama; Shameless; Cold Shoulder; We Bury The Hatchet; In Lonesome Dove; The River; Alabama Clay; Everytime That It Rains; Nobody Gets Off In This Town; Cowboy Bill.

First released 1991
UK peak chart position: 41
USA peak chart position: 1

21. ALWAYS AND FOREVER
Randy Travis

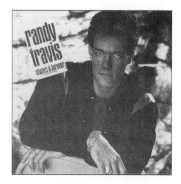

Couples everywhere have identified with Randy Travis's gorgeous love song, 'Forever And Ever, Amen' but it's a curious song with Randy telling his girl that it doesn't matter if her hair falls out. ('Well, honey, I don't care, I ain't in love with your hair.') The album's title is taken from a more conventional song, 'I Won't Need You Anymore'. For all that, the relationships in *Always And Forever* are not always so long-standing and Randy is at his best when he's sounding sad. Perfect 'cheatin'' songs for the 80s.

Too Gone Too Long; My House; Good Intentions; What'll You Do About Me?; I Won't Need You Anymore; Forever And Ever, Amen; I Told You So; Anything; The Truth Is Lyin' Next To You; Tonight We're Gonna Tear Down The Walls.

First released 1987
UK peak chart position: did not chart
USA peak chart position: 19

22. MY WORLD
Eddy Arnold

Country balladeer Eddy Arnold was recording before Hank Williams and was once managed by Colonel Parker. By 1965, he had a steady routine of three albums a year and regular touring. Because Jim Reeves' style was so popular, he had a worldwide hit in a similar vein with 'Make The World Go Away'. This album looks like a concept album of 'world' songs but there is only one other, 'What's He Doin' In My World?'. Apart from that, there are warm-voiced, intimate interpretations of 'Too Many Rivers', 'It Comes And Goes' and 'As Usual'. The album contains the most distinctive title from all the 1,000 here - 'Mary Claire Melvina Rebecca Jane'.

What's He Doin' In My World?; Too Many Rivers; It Comes And Goes; Make The World Go Away; The Days Gone By; Mary Claire Melvina Rebecca Jane; I'm Letting You Go; As Usual; I'm Walking Behind You; If You Were Mine; Taking Chances; You Still Got A Hold On Me.

First released 1965
UK peak chart position: did not chart
USA peak chart position: 7

23. STORMS OF LIFE
Randy Travis

Some long-standing country fans put down Randy Travis by saying that he copies Merle Haggard who in turn copied Lefty Frizzell. The comparison is true but the judgement is false because Randy Travis sings better than either and chooses his material with more care. There are no lightweight songs on Randy's albums and he started - with 'Storms Of Life' - as he intended to go on. The neat punning of 'But On The Other Hand' leads into a cheating song on a par with 'Almost Persuaded'. Another one is Randy's own 'Reasons I Cheat'.

But On The Other Hand; The Storms Of Life; My Heart Cracked; Diggin' Up Bones; No Place Like Home; 1982; Send My Body; Messin' With My Mind; Reasons I Cheat; There'll Always Be A Honky Tonk Somewhere.

First released 1986
UK peak chart position: did not chart
USA peak chart position: 5

24. TRIO
Dolly Parton, Linda Ronstadt, Emmylou Harris

Despite the third billing, Emmylou Harris was the strongest influence on making of *Trio* and its downhome feel makes it a companion to her own album, *Blue Kentucky Girl*. Dolly was still capable of singing country and Linda Ronstadt was comfortable with traditional material such as Jimmie Rodgers' 'Hobo's Meditation'. Emmylou sings lead on the best known track, an oh-so-sweet rendition of 'To Know Him Is To Love Him' . The superlative musicians include Mark O'Connor, Ry Cooder, Bill Payne and Britain's own country star, Albert Lee. Its success prompted Dolly to make a similar album with Loretta Lynn and Tammy Wynette, *Honky Tonk Angels*.

Pain Of Loving You; Making Plans; To Know Him Is To Love Him; Hobo's Meditation; Wilflowers; Telling Me Lies; My Dear Companion; Those Memories Of You; I've Had Enough; Rosewood Casket.

First released 1987
UK peak chart position:60
USA peak chart position: 6

25. HIGHWAYS AND HEARTACHES
Ricky Skaggs

Multi-instrumentalist Ricky Skaggs played traditional bluegrass with the Stanley Brothers, new bluegrass with J.D. Crowe and the new south and contemporary country with Emmylou Harris' Hot Band. All these influences combine on his albums, of which the best is his second for Epic, *Highways And Heartaches*. Among this 1982 album's many delights are Guy Clark's 'Heartbroke', Bill Monroe's 'Can't You Hear Me Callin'?' and Rodney Crowell's 'One Way Rider'. A great bluegrass album for people who didn't think they liked bluegrass.

Heartbroke; You've Got A Lover; Don't Think I'll Cry; Don't Let Your Sweet Love Die; Nothing Can Hurt You; I Wouldn't Change You If I Could; Can't You Hear Me Callin'?; Highway 40 Blues; Let's Love The Bad Times Away; One Way Rider.

First released 1982
UK peak chart position: did not chart
USA peak chart position: did not chart

26. GRIEVOUS ANGEL
Gram Parsons

Parsons' short life had already ended by the time his second album was released. An inevitable poignancy colours its content, but the singer's work was always charged with atmosphere. His subject matter followed accustomed country music precepts - broken hearts, stolen love and mortality - but Parsons' grasp of melody and lyrical intensity showed remarkable insight and ensured the lasting quality of his work. His duets with Emmylou Harris possess a heartfelt vulnerability and stand among the finest popular music has produced. Parsons' articulation of naked emotion is his final legacy.

Return Of The Grevious Angel; Hearts On Fire; I Can't Dance; Brass Buttons; $1000 Wedding; Medley: Cash On The Barrelhead/Hickory Wind; Love Hurts; Las Vegas; In My Hour Of Darkness.

First released 1974
UK peak chart position: did not chart
USA peak chart position: 195

27. SONGS OF TRAGEDY
Hank Snow

This album isn't as downbeat as *When Tragedy Struck* released five years earlier, but they are still songs that make Leonard Cohen sound like George Formby. Hank Snow covered all the bases you expect of country singers - old dogs, lonesome prisoners, patriotism and a mother who gives him a bible. Hank Snow sings in a distinctive Canadian baritone and is noted for his collection of ill-fitting toupees, so he was all too easy a target for Henry Gibson in Robert Altman's film, Nashville. Still indispensible in any comprehensive collection even though its tears in your beer throughout.

The Prisoner's Song; The Color Song; The Answer To Little Blossom; There's A Star Spangled Banner Waving Somewhere; Walking The Last Mile; Old Rover; The Prisoner's Dream; Put Your Arms Around Me; Your Little Band Of Gold; Rocking Alone In An Old Rocking Chair; Mother, I Thank You For The Bible You Gave; Little Joe.

First released 1964
UK peak chart position: did not chart
USA peak chart position: did not chart

28. THE SENSATIONAL CHARLEY PRIDE
Charley Pride

Charley Pride was the reverse of Elvis - a black man singing country - and he did it extremely well. Unlike today's country stars who record an album a year, Charley Pride was cutting three or four a year and the quality suffered, particularly when he selected songs he had published himself. Some tracks are bog standard country music and although the album does not contain 'Crystal Chandeliers', it does include some fine cajun music ('Louisiana Man', 'Billy Bayou') as well as one classic performance, 'Come On Home And Sing The Blues'.

Louisiana Man; She's Still Got A Hold On You; Let The Chips Fall; Come On Home And Sing The Blues; Never More Than I; Let Me Live; Take Care Of The Little Things; Even After Everything She's Done; (It's Just A Matter Of) Making Up My Mind; It's The Little Things; Billy Bayou; We Had All The Good Things Going.

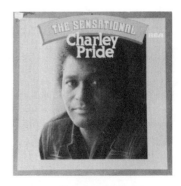

First released 1969
UK peak chart position: did not chart
USA peak chart position: 44

29. Same Train A Different Time
Merle Haggard

Merle Haggard has often recorded tributes to his heroes - Bob Wills, Lefty Frizzell and here Jimmie Rodgers. This album - a double-album in the US, a single album in the UK - showed his love for the Singing Brakeman and included such favourites as 'Waiting For A Train', 'Muleskinner Blues' and 'Miss The Mississippi And You'. This mesmerising album also serves as an obituary to the demise of passenger trains in America.

California Blues; Waiting For A Train; Train Whisle Blues; Why Should I Be Lonely; Blue Yodel Number Six; Miss The Mississippi And You; Muleskinner Blues; Frankie And Johnny; Hobo BIll's Last Ride; Travelin' Blues; Peach Picking Time Down In Georgia; No Hard Times; Down The Old Road To Home; Jimmie Rodger's Last Blue Yodel.

First released 1969
UK peak chart position: did not chart
USA peak chart position: 67

30. Salutes Hank Williams And Bob Wills
George Jones

To many, George Jones is the voice of country music, but all too often it has been wasted on schlock. Especially in the 60s when he was making four albums a year as well as touring extensively and appearing regularly on the Grand Ole Opry. *With My Favorites Of Hank Williams* and *George Jones Sings Bob Wills*, he was blessed with decent material and the records, subsequently combined on one album, stand up today. George Jones isn't associated with western swing but the Bob Wills collection matches the Hank Williams one.

Wedding Bells; I Just Don't Like This Kind Of Living; You Win Again; I Could Never Be Ashamed Of You; You're Gonna Change (Or I'm Gonna Leave); House Without Love; Your Cheatin' Heart; They'll Never Take Her Love From Me; Mansion On The Hill; Take These Chains From My Heart; (Last Night) I Heard You Crying In Your Sleep; Lonesome Whistle; Bubbles In My Beer; Faded Love; Roly Poly; Trouble In Mind; Take Me Back To Tulsa; The Warm Red Wine; Time Changes Everything; Worried Mind; Silver Dew On The Blue Grass Tonight; San Antonio Rose; Steel Guitar Rag; Big Beaver.

First released 1986
UK peak chart position: did not chart
USA peak chart position: did not chart

31. Chill Of An Early Fall
George Strait

The King of the White Stetson, George Strait acknowledged his honky tonk roots on this album by reviving both 'Lovesick Blues' and 'Milkcow Blues'. This is a very impressive collection with nothing better than the punning title song. One of the strangest songs that any country singer has ever recorded is 'You Know Me Better Than That': listen to it and think, is this a songwriter writing a really good song or having an off day?

The Chill Of An Early Fall; I've Convinced Everybody But Me; If I Know Me; You Know Me Better Than That; Anything You Can Spare; Home In San Antone; Lovesick Blues; Milk Cow Blues; Her Only Bad Habit Is Me; Is It Already Time.

First released 1991
UK peak chart position: did not chart
USA peak chart position: 45

32. Changes In Latitude, Changes In Attitudes
Jimmy Buffett

The sandy-haired, sunburnt Jimmy Buffett was the first musician to bring Caribbean rhythms to Nashville with warm, friendly albums about life in Florida or, in his words, 'drifting away in Margaritaville'. He describes his songs as '90% autobiographical' and, if so, life was a continuous party of wine, women, sailing and marijuana with a bit of smuggling thrown in. Even his band is called the Coral Reefers! All the ABC albums are good but this one includes his plaintive picture of Biloxi, the story of being run out of Tampico, thoughts on banana republics and his dismissive views on some surgeons ogling a stripper in 'Miss You So Badly'. It's okay for him, but not for the doctors.

Wonder Why We Ever Go Home; Banana Republic; Tampico Trauma; Lovely Cruise; Margaritaville; In The Shelter; Miss You So Badly; Biloxi; Landfall.

First released 1977
UK peak chart position: did not chart
USA peak chart position: 12

33. Joe Ely
Joe Ely

Hailing from Lubbock, Texas, Joe Ely had been working with Butch Hancock and Jimmie Dale Gilmore in the Flatlanders. His debut album included their songs ('She Never Spoke Spanish To Me', 'Treat Me Like A Saturday Night') as well as his own ('I Had My Hopes Up High', 'Mardi Gras Waltz'). The second album, *Honky Tonk Masquerade*, maintained the high standard and for a moment, it looked as though Joe Ely would be the new voice of American country music. He befriended the Clash and developed a hi-res country for his new audience, thereby leaving his country fans behind. Rockin' good stuff.

I Had My Hopes Up High; Mardi Gras Waltz; She Never Spoke Spanish To Me; Gambler's Bride; Suckin' A Big Bottle Of Gin; Tennessee's Not The State I'm In; If You Were A Bluebird; Treat Me Like A Staurday Night; All My Love; Johnny's Blues.

First released 1977
UK peak chart position: did not chart
USA peak chart position: did not chart

34. Garth Brooks
Garth Brooks

After several years as a small-time bar singer, Garth Brooks burst upon the American country scene in 1989 with this self-named album, produced by Don Williams' producer, Allen Reynolds. He sang songs with an old-time country feel ('Cowboy Bill') and revived a Jim Reeves' single ('I Know One'), but he was much too young to feel this damn old and the album had a solid, contemporary feel. One of the greatest love songs of recent years, if not of all-time, is his own composition, 'If Tomorrow Never Knows'. This album was the first in his on-going series of multi-platinum sales.

Not Counting You; I've Got A Good Thing Going; If Tomorrow Never Knows; Everytime That It Rains; Alabama Clay; Much Too Young (To Feel This Damn Old); Cowboy Bill; Nobody Gets Off In This Town; I Know One; The Dance.

First released 1989
UK peak chart position: did not chart
USA peak chart position: 13

35. WILL THE CIRCLE BE UNBROKEN
Nitty Gritty Dirt Band

The Nitty Gritty Dirt Band evolved as one of the long-haired country-rock bands in the late 60s, but they bridged the gap between the old music and the new with this brilliantly-packaged album featuring several traditional musicians that they admired - Doc Watson, Roy Acuff, Jimmy Martin, Maybelle Carter and Earl Scruggs. There's studio chat and you hear the performances coming together, the result being six sides - yes, a triple-album - of heavenly joy. In 1989 the band released a second volume featuring Emmylou Harris, Johnny Cash, Ricky Skaggs and a couple of Byrds that was almost as good.

Grand Ole Opry Song; Keep On The Sunny Side; You Are My Flower; The Precious Jewel; Dark As A Dungeon; Tennessee Stud; Black Mountain Rag; The Wreck Of The Highway; The End Of The World; I Saw The Light; Sunny Side Of The Mountain; Nine Pound Hammer; Losin' You (Might Be The Best Thing Yet); Honky Tonkin'; You Don't Know My Mind; My Walkin' Shoes; Lonesome Fiddle Blues; Cannonball Rag; Avalanche; Flint Hill Special; Togary Mountain; Earl's Breakdown; Orange Blossom Special; Wabash Cannonball; Lost Highway; Doc Watson and Merle Travis - First Meeting (dialogue); Way Downtown; Down Yonder; Pins And Needles (In My Heart); Honky Tonk Blues; Sailin' On To Hawaii; I'm Thinking Tonight Of My Blue Eyes; I Am A Pilgrim; Wildwood Flower; Soldier's Joy; Will The Circle Be Unbroken; Both Sides Now.

First released 1972
UK peak chart position: did not chart
USA peak chart position: 68

36. SWEETHEART OF THE RODEO
Byrds

Country music had always provided an intrigal influence on the Byrds, but the decision to record an entire album in that style was controversial. Despite contemporary disquiet, *Sweetheart Of The Rodeo* has since become a landmark release, popularising the notion of country-rock. Traditional songs, standards, Bob Dylan compositions and original material were drawn together in a seamless whole, its continuity enhanced by crack Nashville session musicians. New group member Gram Parsons proved an adept catalyst, his departure soon after the album's release ensured it remained a one-off experiment. The Byrds moved elsewhere stylistically, but the influence of this recording is immeasurable.

You Ain't Goin' Nowhere; I Am A Pilgrim; The Christian Eye; You Don't Miss Your Water; You're Still On My Mind; Pretty Boy Floyd; Hickory Wind; One Hundred Years From Now; Blue Canadian Rockies; Life In Prison; Nothing Was Delivered.

First released 1968
UK peak chart position: did not chart
USA peak chart position: 77

37. I STILL BELIEVE IN YOU
Vince Gill

Vince Gill wrote this album with eight songwriting partners, yet it still has a consistency and fluidity of its own. This is a truly great collection of love songs performed by a country singer with a beautiful tenor voice. Every track will make you weep but extra tissues are needed for 'One More Last Chance', I Still Believe In You' and 'Tryin' To Get Over You'. The care and attention lavished on this album is evident in every note, where nothing has been left to chance. The excellent musicians include Delbert McClinton, who played harmonica on Bruce Channel's 'Hey! Baby'.

Don't Let Our Love Start Slipping Away; No Future In The Past; Nothing Like A Woman; Tryin' To Get Over You; Say Hello; One More Last Chance; Under These Conditions; Pretty Words; Love Never Broke Anyone's Heart; I Still Believe In You.

First released 1992
UK peak chart position: did not chart
USA peak chart position: 10

38. LULLABYS LEGENDS AND LIES
Bobby Bare

When RCA gave Bobby Bare the freedom to make an album on his own terms, he decided to showcase the talents of one songwriter, Shel Silverstein. Silverstein, noted for his hit songs for Dr. Hook, gave Bare his best material - the shaggy dog story of 'The Winner', the whimsical story based around the Irish potato famine 'The Wonderful Soup Stone' and the eight-minute saga of 'Rosalie's Good Eats Cafe'. (The full lyric, reprinted in Playboy, runs to 40 verses!) Maybe the album could have been a bit more melodic, maybe the sentimentality should have been curbed, but, all in all, Shel had his 'Sure Hit Songwriters Pen' with this album and Bobby Bare, with his laconic, laidback delivery has never sounded better.

Lullabys, Legends And Lies; Paul; Marie Laveau; Daddy What If; The Winner; In The Hills Of Shiloh; She's My Ever Lovin' Machine; The Mermaid; Rest Awhile; Bottomless Well; The Wonderful Soup Stone; True Story; Sure Hit Songwriters Pen; Rosalie's Good Eats Cafe.

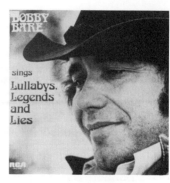

First released 1974
UK peak chart position: did not chart
USA peak chart position: did not chart

39. MOONLIGHT AND ROSES
Jim Reeves

It is fashionable to like Nat 'King' Cole but Jim Reeves is largely a voice from the past. It's hard to say why because they both were warm-voiced balladeers who specialised in intimate love songs. They hadn't started out that way: Cole had been a jazz pianist and Reeves a high-pitched singer of country novelties. Reeves' most romantic album, *Moonlight And Roses*, didn't contain any of his hit singles, but it almost topped the UK album charts. Recording songs about the moon or roses and calling it a concept is a bit twee but it works well and ironically, 'It's Only A Paper Moon' is associated with Nat.

Moonlight And Roses; Mexicali Rose; Carolina Moon; Rosa Rio; Oh What It Seemed To Be; What's In It For Me?; Roses; One Dozen Roses; Moon River; There's A New Moon Over My Shoulder; It's Only A Paper Moon; When I Lost You.

First released 1964
UK peak chart position: 2
USA peak chart position: 30

40. OLD No. 1
Guy Clark

Having retreated from Texas psychedelia to front a guitar repair shop, Guy Clark was saved from a journeyman life when several of his songs were covered by Jerry Jeff Walker. A recording deal ensued, which Clark embraced with this country/folk masterpiece. Mature lyricism and captivating melodies mark an intimate set enhanced by the singer's raspy, lived-in intonation. These largely autobiographical are never introverted and address scenarios of love, longing and ageing in a compelling, haunting manner. The evocative 'Desperadoes Waiting For A Train' exemplifies the skills of a crafted songsmith who reclaimed the art of the singer/songwriter at a time it seemed doomed to self-pity.

Rita Ballou; LA Freeway; She Ain't Goin' Nowhere; A Nickel For The Fiddler; Thjat Old Time Feeling; Texas 1947; Desperados Waiting For The Train; Like A Coat From The Cold; Instant Coffee Blues; Let Him Roll.

First released 1971
UK peak chart position: did not chart
USA peak chart position: did not chart

41. OCEAN FRONT PROPERTY
George Strait

George Strait, another country singer having tremendous success by developing Merle Haggard's sound, suffered personal tragedy when his daughter was killed in a car accident. With considerable composure, he managed to completed his magnificent album, *Ocean Front Property*, and perhaps the anguish in his voice is all too real. It's a very country album with George's western swing influences in evidence in 'You Can't Buy Your Way Out Of The Blues' and 'All My Ex's Live In Texas'. Veteran country writer Hank Cochran supplied the witty title song which is about ocean front property in Arizona!

All My Ex's Live In Texas; Someone's Walking Around Upstairs; Am I Blue; Ocean Front Property; Hot Burning Flames; Without You Here; My Heart Won't Wander Very Far From You; Second Chances; You Can't Buy Your Way Out Of The Blues; I'm All Behind You Now.

First released 1987
UK peak chart position: did not chart
USA peak chart position: 117

42. THE GILDED PALACE OF SIN
Flying Burrito Brothers

The Guilded Palace Of Sin allowed two former Byrds, Gram Parsons and Chris Hillman, to explore fully country music. Several selections, notably 'Christine's Tune' and 'Wheels', captured the joys of Nashville-inspired rock fully, but the group proved equally adept at interpreting southern soul standards. Parsons aching vocal on 'Dark End Of The Street' articulated the dilemmas of infidelity, while on his own composition, 'Hot Burrito No. 1', he revealed a vulnerability unusual in a male singer. 'Sneeky' Pete Kleinow explored the sonic possibilities of the pedal steel guitar, rather than employ orthodox embellishments, and this desire to question preconceptions gives this album its unique qualities.

Christine's Tune; Sin City; Do Right Woman, Do Right Man; Dark End Of The Street; My Uncle; Wheels; Juanita; Hot Burrito No. 1; Hot Burrito No. 2; Do You Know How It Feels; Hippie Boy.

First released 1969
UK peak chart position: did not chart
USA peak chart position: 164

43. POCKET FULL OF GOLD
Vince Gill

Vince Gill, a former member of Pure Prairie League, is the most popular of the country balladeers and this collection contains several tremendous examples - 'Look At Us', 'If I Didn't Have You In My World' and 'The Strings That Tie You Down'. The title song, which features harmonies from Patty Loveless, tells how cheaters will get their comeuppance, so watch out. Although Vince is known for his ballads, there are several excellent uptempo items here, notably 'Sparkle' and 'Lisa Jane'. You'll recognise Mark Knopfler's guitar on the album: Gill then added harmonies to Dire Strait's 'On Every Street'.

I Quit; Look At Us; Take Your Memory With You; Pocket Full Of Gold; The Strings That Tie You Down; Lisa Jane; If I Didn't Have You In My World; A Little Left Over; What's A Man To Do; Sparkle.

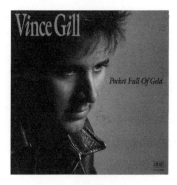

First released 1991
UK peak chart position: did not chart
USA peak chart position: 37

44. COPPERHEAD ROAD
Steve Earle

Steve Earle is one of the hip new stars who have given new country music acceptance with non honky tonkers. earle is a renegade who has been married almost as many times as the total albums he has released. His songs are new country-Springsteen and he is not frightened to rock. The Pogues give great support to this memorable album. His career has faltered commercially since this release as his music has taken on a harder edge. The title track is a highlight featuring some fine mandolin over an infectious beat, similar fare is 'You Belong To Me.' and 'Back To The Wall' Country purists may baulk, but this album is destined to last. Earle is the Lemmy Motorhead of new counrty.

Copperhead Road; Snake Oil; Back To The Wall; The Devil's Right Hand; Johnny Come Lately; Even When I'm Blue; You Belong To Me; Waiting On You; Once You Love; Nothing But A Child

First released 1988
UK peak chart position: 44
USA peak chart position: 56

45. THE PATSY CLINE STORY
Patsy Cline

This memorial album contained Patsy Cline's best-known singles and shared several tracks with the aforementioned *Showcase*. Her tender 'Sweet Dreams' became a country classic and 'Crazy' gave Patsy her first UK Top 20 hit in 1991. Listen to 'She's Got You' and wonder why it wasn't a hit at the time: maybe it was that cover version from Alma Cogan. It's hard to believe that Patsy died when she was only 30: she looks much older and her voice is so world-weary. Her small catalogue is destined to constantly be in print.

Heartaches; She's Got You; Walking After Midnight; Strange; Leavin' On Your Mind; South Of The Border; Foolin' Around; I Fall To Pieces; A Poor Man's Roses; Tra Le La Le La Triangle; True Love; Imagine That; Back In Baby's Arms; Crazy; You're Stronger Than Me; Seven Lonely Days; Sweet Dreams; Your Cheatin' Heart; San Antonio Rose; Why Can't He Be You; The Wayard Way; So Wrong; I Love You So Much It Hurts; You Belong To Me.

First released 1963
UK peak chart position: did not chart
USA peak chart position: 74

46. DON'T ROCK THE JUKEBOX
Alan Jackson

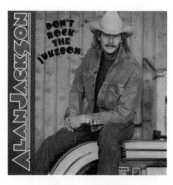

Another traditional-sounding country singer with a contemporary feel, Alan Jackson sounded his best on this, his second album. The title song was a tribute to his childhood hero, George Jones, and George himself makes a cameo appearance on 'Just Playin' Possum'. 'Midnight In Montgomery' is his homage to Hank Williams, but 'From A Distance' is not the standard but a new song, co-written with Randy Travis. Alan thanks God in the credits: maybe he was the Executive Producer.

Don't Rock The Jukebox; That's All I Need To Know; Dallas; Midnight In Montgomery; Love's Got A Hold On You; Someday; Just Playin' Possum; From A Distance; Walkin' The Floor Over Me; Working Class Hero.

First released 1992
UK peak chart position: did not chart
USA peak chart position: 17

47. QUARTER MOON IN A TEN CENT TOWN
Emmylou Harris

After Gram Parsons' death, Emmylou Harris continued his work by making her own albums with the Hot Band. Every album seemed to better the last, and this one was near perfection. The material is varied: Dolly Parton's sob-story with a bitter twist, 'To Daddy', Bill Haley's 'Burn That Candle' and Delbert McClinton's 'Two More Bottles Of Wine'. Rodney Crowell, a new Hot Bander, gave her the punchy rocker, 'I Ain't Livin' Long Like This'. Willie Nelson added his voice to 'One Paper Kid' and the Band helped out on the album's hottest cut, 'Leavin' Louisiana In The Broad Daylight'. Hard to believe that she became a country singer by accident.

Easy From Now On; Two More Bottles Of Wine; To Daddy; My Songbird; Leavin' Louisiana In The Broad Daylight; Defying; Gravity; I Ain't Livin' Long Like This; One Paper Kid; Green Rolling Hills; Burn That Candle.

First released 1978
UK peak chart position: 40
USA peak chart position: 29

48. GUITARS CADILLACS ETC ETC
Dwight Yoakam

Dwight Yoakam's driving music appealed to both rock and country fans. He wrote most of the songs, but the album contains excellent revivals of Johnny Cash's 'Ring Of Fire', Merle Travis' 'Miner's Prayer' and Johnny Horton's 'Honky Tonk Man', a perfect description of Yoakam himself and a significant country hit. Good taste in songs and great taste in hats. Country music for people who don't like country music.

Honky Tonk Man; It Won't Hurt; I'll Be Gone; South Of Cincinnati; Bury Me; Guitars, Cadillacs; 20 Years; Ring Of Fire; Miner's Prayer; Heartaches By The Number.

First released 1986
UK peak chart position: did not chart
USA peak chart position: 61

49. MODERN SOUNDS IN COUNTRY AND WESTERN
Ray Charles

Ray Charles had dabbled with country music at Atlantic, notably 'I'm Movin' On', but the move to ABC-Paramount prompted him to record a full album. His version of Don Gibson's 'I Can't Stop Loving You' was a transatlantic number 1 and not far behind his bitter-sweet performance of Eddy Arnold's 'You Don't Know Me'. Ray's own favourite was 'I Love You So Much It Hurts'. The album was so successful that he recorded a second volume and had hits with 'Take These Chains From My Heart' and 'Cryin' Time'. Although the album showed that black soul and white country could be merged, Ray Charles lost his momentum, tending to cruise along on the same theme and never again writing a song to equal 'What'd I Say'.

Bye Bye Love; You Don't Know Me; Half As Much; I Love You So Much It Hurts; Just A Little Lovin'; Born To Lose; Worried Mind; It Makes No Differnce Now; You Win Again; Careless Love; I Can't Stop Loving You; Hey; Good Lookin'.

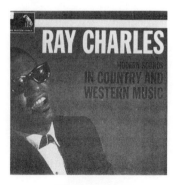

First released 1962
UK peak chart position: 6
USA peak chart position: 1

50. COME ON COME ON
Mary-Chapin Carpenter

As with so many of today's country stars, Mary-Chapin Carpenter has both folk and rock elements in her work - 'Labels are for soup cans,' she has said - and this cross-fertilisation makes for some very inventive albums. She writes both by herself and with Don Schlitz, who wrote 'The Gambler' for Kenny Rogers. The raunchy 'I Feel Lucky' is a witty expansion of Clint Eastwood's famous line, while 'He Thinks He'll Keep Her' owes much to John Hiatt's 'She Loves The Jerk'. She duets with Joe Diffie on 'Not Too Much To Ask' and does a fiery country version of Dire Straits' 'The Bug'. Judging the state of English cricket, this MCC has far more going for her, but a black mark for the fold-up CD booklet which quickly looks worn.

The Hard Way; He Thinks He'll Keep Her; Rhythm Of The Blues; I Feel Lucky; The Bug; Not Too Much To Ask; Passionate Kisses; Only A Dream; I Am A Town; Walking Through Fire; I Take My Chances; Come On Come On.

First released 1992
UK peak chart position: did not chart
USA peak chart position: 31

THE TOP 50
FOLK ALBUMS

IN MUCH THE SAME WAY THAT COUNTRY ROCK HAS BECOME THE PIVOT OF NEW COUNTRY MUSIC SO FOLK ROCK HAS ALTERED THE COURSE OF FOLK'S DEVELOPMENT. *LIEGE AND LIEF* IS PROBABLY THE MOST IMPORTANT ALBUM IN THIS SELECTION BECAUSE IT TOOK FOLK INTO PREVIOUSLY UNCHARTED WATERS. THIS IS NOT A LIST FOR FINGER-IN-THE-EAR-DERRY-DERRY-DOWN-O'S, IT IS NOW AS WIDE AS THE GENRE HAS BECOME.

1. THE TIMES THEY ARE A CHANGIN'
Bob Dylan

On his third album Bob Dylan both redefined and expanded his musical palate. Feted as a protest singer, a nomenclature he rejected, he brought new insight to the genre, particularly with 'Only A Pawn In Their Game', in which he paints a wider canvas relating to the murder of civil rights leader Medgar Evers. Dylan's love songs herein are particularly poignant, their stark, acoustic setting enhancing a graphic lyricism. The title songs boasts a wonderful ambiguity, managing to be political and personal, the latter aspect suggesting the changes Dylan would bring to his music. The last album as a folk artist per se, *The Times They Are A Changin'* is yet another essential Dylan collection.

Times They Are A Changin'; The Ballad Of Hollis Brown; With God On Our Side; One Too Many Mornings; North Country Blues; Only A Pawn In Their Game; Boots Of Spanish Leather; When The Ship Comes In; Lonesome Death Of Hettie Carroll; Restless Farewell.

First released 1964
UK peak chart position: 4
USA peak chart position: 20

2. LIEGE AND LIEF
Fairport Convention

Where so much began. The advertisements ran 'the first (literally) British folk rock LP ever.' It was also catharsis to Fairport reconvening after a traumatic road accident which killed drummer Martin Lamble. Once more focused and with redoubtable folk fiddler Dave Swarbrick now permanently involved they threw themselves into the electrification of ballads, myths and rollickin' jigs. The results were both innovative and stimulating. The union was blest. If you sat down and tried to think up a dream folk rock band it would still not match the potential here. From the lusting pace of 'Matty Groves' to the tender, cooing of 'Crazy Man Michael' Sandy Denny's voice is the perfect vehicle for a milestone. Imitated a thousand times, seldom equalled.

Come All Ye; Reynardine; Matty Groves; Farewell Farewell; The Deserter; The Lark In The Morning; Tamlin; Crazy Man Michael; Rakish Paddy; Foxhunters Jigs; Toss The Feathers.

First released 1970
UK peak chart position: 17
USA peak chart position: did not chart

3. THE FREEWHEELIN' BOB DYLAN
Bob Dylan

With this album Dylan emerged from the cloak of Woody Guthrie and proclaimed his own unique talent. No longer detached - the set was originally entitled Bob Dylan's Blues - he personalised his songs, famously rejecting four from the final draft in favour of others reflecting his newer muse. Protest songs were given a wider resonance - the text of 'Masters Of War' remains as relevant some 30 years on - while his love songs are haunting, but universal, statements. Dylan injected black humour into the talking blues and railed against injustice in all forms with a perception encompassing the anger of a generation. Freewheelin' is a landmark in the development of folk and pop music.

Blowin' In The Wind; Girl From The North Country; Masters Of War; Down The Highway; Bob Dylan's Blues; Hard Rain's Gonna Fall; Don't Think Twice; Bob Dylan's Dream; Oxford Town; Talking World War III Blues; Corina Corina; Honey, Just Allow Me One More Chance; I Shall Be Free.

First released 1964
UK peak chart position: 1
USA peak chart position: 22

4. LEGEND OF AMERICAN FOLK BLUES
WOODY GUTHRIE

Folksinger is too small a term to describe Woody Guthrie. Political activist, rambler, poet and commentator, he encapsulated the aura of Roosevelt's New Deal America. Guthrie spoke for the okie underclass in song the way Steinbeck chronicled their lives in novels and this superb selection compiles the best of his expansive output. The topical song was Guthrie's metier and his simple melodies and pungent lyrics left a huge impression on the 60s folk revival. Bob Dylan, Phil Ochs and Tom Paxton owe him a considerable debt, but Guthrie's importance lies in the lasting quality of his own work. This CD has replaced *This Land Is Your Land* as the definitive Guthrie album.

This Land Is Your Land; Pastures Of Plenty; Pretty Boy Floyd; Take A Whiff On Me; Do Re Mi; Put My Little Shoes Away; Washington Talkin' Blues; Hard Travelin'; Jesus Christ; Whoopee Ti Yi Yo, Get Along Little Dogies; Grand Coulee Dam; A Picture From Life's Other Side; Talkin' Hard Luck Blues; Philadelphia Lawyer; I Ain't Got No Home; The Wreck Of The Old '97; Keep Your Skillet Good And Greasy; Dust Pneumonia Blues; Going Down That Road Feeling Bad; Goodnight Little Arlo (Goodnight Little Darlin'); So Long It's Been Good To Know You.

First released 1992
UK peak chart position: did not chart
USA peak chart position: did not chart

5. SOLID AIR
John Martyn

He began as a folksy minstrel but seem drawn to experimental, free form improvisation. *Solid Air* is where John Martyn's love affair with effects and echoplex got serious. The title track dedicated to close friend Nick Drake became a eulogy, whilst the breezy 'Over The Hill' - one of the greatest songs ever written about a train journey - is a feathery delight. 'May You Never', 'Don't Want To Know' continued the simple, stoned ballad approach, though it's his interpretation of Skip James 'I'd Rather Be The Devil,' with hypnotic shifts, tidal echoes, a slurred growl and totally reshaped which broods over the whole album. A record that remains Martyn's youthful zenith.

Over The Hill; Don't Want To Know; I'd Rather Be With The Devil; Go Down Easy; Dreams By The Sea; May You Never; The Man In The Station; Easy Blues; Solid Air.

First released 1974
UK peak chart position: did not chart
USA peak chart position: did not chart

6. FIVE LEAVES LEFT
Nick Drake

Nick Drake's debut album encapsulates a marriage between folk music and the singer/songwriter genre. Part Donovan, part Jim Webb, he articulated an aching romanticism at a time progressive rock ran rampant. Beautiful melodies and fragrant accompaniment, in particular Robert Kirby's string arrangements, enhance the artist's sense of longing in which warm, but understated, vocals accentuate the album's passive mystery. An aura of existential cool envelops proceedings accentuated by Danny Thompson's sonorous bass lines and Drake's poetic imagery. The result is a shimmering, autumnal collection, reflective but never morbid.

Time Has Told Me; River Man; Three Hours; Day Is Done; Way To Blue; 'Cello Song; The Thoughts Of Mary Jane; Man In A Shed; Fruit Tree; Saturday Sun.

First released 1969
UK peak chart position: did not chart
USA peak chart position: did not chart

7. KATE & ANNA MCGARRIGLE
Kate & Anna McGarrigle

These Canadian sisters unknowingly recorded this album, which like Love's *Forever Changes* is a huge critic's favourite, yet deserves a much wider acceptance. Spotted and recorded by the canny Joe Boyd it is an album brimming with melancholy. Kate was formerly Mrs Loudon Wainwright, and the excellent 'Swimming Song'; was written by him. Elsewhere the evocative and anthemic '(Talk To Me Of) Mendocino' is a total joy in the way that it captures being resigned to homesickness. Those who have not discovered this album will not be disappointed with our hearty recommendation. Another quiet classic.

Kiss And Say Goodbye; My Town; Blues In D; Heart Like A Wheel; Foolish You; (Talk To Me Of) Mendocino; Complainte Pour Ste-Catherine; Tell My Sister; Swimming Song; Jigsaw Puzzle Of Life; Go Leave; Travellin' On For Jesus.

First released 1975
UK peak chart position: did not chart
USA peak chart position: did not chart

8. BRINGING IT ALL BACK HOME
Bob Dylan

Howls of rage greeted Dylan as he presented the world with folk rock - he was roundly booed at both The Newport Folk Festival and The Albert Hall. Yet here is one of those moments of cross influence which changed the course of popular music. 'Bringing It All Back Home' gave His Bobness an audience on a plate, it was a breakthrough. An album of two different sides, acoustic (his past) and electric (his future), the music - covered a thousand fold - has among it 'Maggie's Farm', 'Subterranean Home Sick Blues', 'Mr. Tambourine Man', 'Love Minus Zero' and the cosmopolitan political speak of 'It's Alright, Ma.' You can debate the is it folk or is it rock argument in a circle. The answer is it's Bob Dylan and nobody else is.

Subterranean Homesick Blues; She Belongs To Me; Maggie's Farm; Love Minus Zero; No Limit; Outlaw Blues; On The Road Again; Bob Dylan's 115th Dream; Mr. Tambourine Man; Gates Of Eden; It's Alright, Ma (I'm Only Bleeding); It's All Over Now, Baby Blue.

First released 1965
UK peak chart position: 1
USA peak chart position: 6

9. JACK ORION
Bert Jansch

Where Jansch's previous albums comprised largely of self-penned material, this third set was drawn from traditional songs, bar an instrumental reading of Ewan MacColl's 'First Time Ever I Saw Your Face'. The artist's highly-original guitar style underpins the lengthy title track and the enthralling 'Black Water Side'. Jimmy Page is only one of many musicians expressing a debt to Jansch and the latter track provided the template for 'Black Mountain Side' on *Led Zeppelin I*. Bert's languid interpretation of 'Nottamun Town' inspired a later version by Fairport Convention, but they struggled to match the enthralling atmosphere created here. Jack Orion is a mesmerising selection from a hugely influential performer.

First released 1966
UK peak chart position: did not chart
USA peak chart position: did not chart

10. HERE WE GO AGAIN
Kingston Trio

Admirers of left wing thinking songsters such as Guthrie and the Weavers, the Kingston Trio - Nick Reynolds, Bob Shane and Dave Guard - were the alternative. They cared enough but laced concern with commercial appeal. There was an intelligent market just waiting to sympathise, and for some four years The Trio were top dogs as far as folk singing was concerned. Successful with a campfire rendering of 'Tom Dooley' they rattled out albums at a hell of a lick. Have guitars will record? *Here We Go Again*, probably exactly how they felt in the liberal whirlwind that surrounded them is not only a fine slice of 50s American folkloric sound but a document of a period when acoustic music began spreading towards acceptance.

Molly Dee; Across The Wide Missouri; Haul Away; The Wanderer; 'Round About The Mountain; Oleanna; The Unfortunate Miss Bailey; San Miguel; (Inn Taton); Rollin' Stone; Goober Peas; A Worried Man.

First released 1959
UK peak chart position: did not chart
USA peak chart position: 1

11. WHAT WE DID ON OUR HOLIDAYS
Fairport Convention

An album that revels in an embarrassment of influences which the band bind making their own. This was the Fairport that ran with the psychedelic underground, flexing their muscles, a slumbering entity about to wake. This was their beatnick phase, producing such evergreens as Sandy Denny's beautiful 'Fotheringay' the first tangible examples of electrified trad in 'Nottamun Town' and 'She Moves Through The Fair' - neither song incidentally British. And more significantly Richard Thompson began to move in his own mysterious way gifting 'Meet On The Ledge' which has since become their signature. Variety as they say is the spice of life and this collection adroitly exploits just that.

Fotheringay; Mr. Lacey; Book Song; The Lord Is In His Place; No Man's Land; I'll Keep It With Mine; Eastern Rain; Nottamun Town; Tale In Hard Time; She Moves Through The Fair; Meet On The Ledge; End Of A Holiday.

First released 1969
UK peak chart position: did not chart
USA peak chart position: did not chart

12. THE BIG WHEEL
Runrig

Totally unique. The intention was to make an album which though rooted in something undeniably highland, reached out beyond and touched universal truisms. Runrig succeeded beyond the expectations of any involved, turning the band into Scotland's greatest live attraction, Loch Lomond summer 1991, silencing even the sternest critics. There is a spiritual wholeness, which lends cinematic overtones, Donnie Munro's voice becomes an almighty hammer for the gaels, whilst 'I'm Coming Home' showed what all Runrig felt at heart, 'Flower Of The West' captures their energy and essence in seven brief, glorious minutes. The Gaelic album which means everything, this is the big noise.

Headlights; Healer In Your Heart; Abyhainn An T-sluaigh; The Crowded River; Always The Winner; The Beautiful Pain; An Cuibhle Mor; The Big Wheel; Edge Of The World; Hearthammer; I'm Coming Home; Flower Of The West.

First released 1991
UK peak chart position: 4
USA peak chart position: did not chart

13. BERT JANSCH
Bert Jansch

Bert Jansch was the figurehead of the British 60s folk movement. An excellent composer and influential guitarist, he brought an earthy, blues-based perspective to the genre which took it out of the traditional circuit without sacrificing its strengths to commerciality. This album is little short of breathtaking. Jansch combines an arresting technique, as displayed on Davey Graham's 'Angie', with a gift for graphic lyricism, chillingly exhibited on 'Needle Of Death'. Artists as diverse as Jimmy Page and Donovan (who recorded 'Do You hear Me Now?') cited Jansch as an influence. Bert Jansch proves why.

Strolling Down The Highway; Smokey River; Oh How Your Love Is Strong; I Have No Time; Finches; Rambling's Gonna Be The Death Of Me; Veronica; Needle Of Death; Do You Hear Me Now?; Alice's Wonderland; Running From Home; Courting Blues; Casbah; Dreams Of Love; Angie.

First released 1965
UK peak chart position: did not chart
USA peak chart position: did not chart

14. UNHALFBRICKING
Fairport Convention

The transitional album before Fairport Convention invented folk/rock with Liege And Lief. On this they stretch out on longer numbers and introduce Dave Swarbrick, who plays some particularly fine fiddle on the lengthy 'A Sailor's Life'. Richart Thompson continued to mature with 'Genesis Hall' and 'Cajun Woman'. Equally impressive is Sandy's beautiful voice on her stellar composition 'Who Knows Where Time Goes'. Dylan abounds with three songs and 'Percy's Song' is a highlight. To round it up, a UK hit single, shock horror, with Dylan's 'Si Tu Dois Partir. A bold move also for a little known band was not to have their name on the album sleeve.

Genesis Hall; Si Tu Dois Partir; Autopsy; A Sailor's Life; Cajun Woman; Who Knows Where The Time Goes; Percy's Song; Million Dollar Bash.

First released 1969
UK peak chart position: 12
USA peak chart position: did not chart

15. THE KINGSTON TRIO AT LARGE
Kingston Trio

As if to prove a point this was the second album by the Trio that went to number one in the same year. But then back in America post McCarthyism folk song was far less complicated, more immediate. The era, where right students and town dwellers began to look to folk as a focal point and social credence. Recreators like the Kingstons as well as authentic rural performers opened up to an acceptance ever widening. If it wasn't rock 'n' roll it was folk which forced many later performers into the mainstream. It could be argued that with albums like this displaying an intimacy and yet all knowing awareness that folk for pop thinkers was being created and a whole movement had it's foundations in back to basics, quickly formulated recordings. At Large is a credit to its genre.

MTA; All My Sorrows; Blew Ye Winds; Carey, Carey; The Seine; I Bowled; Good News; Getaway John; The Long Black Rifle; Early Mornin'; Scarlet Ribbons (For Her Hair); Remember The Alamo.

First released 1959
UK peak chart position: did not chart
USA peak chart position: 1

16. RAMBLIN' BOY
Tom Paxton

Tom Paxton played an integral part of the 60s' folk revival. His topical songs and broadside-styled ballads owed a considerable debt to Pete Seeger, who in turn popularised this album's title song. A traditionalist, Paxton possessed acute songwriting skills, as evinced by this accomplished collection. Felix Pappalardi (guitarron) and Barry Kornfield (banjo, harmonica) provide sympathetic support to a diverse range of songs. Two selections, 'The Last Thing On My Mind' and 'Goin' To The Zoo', have become standards, the first as a tender love song, the second as a childrens' favourite. Such eclectic performances confirmed that Paxton truly was one of Woody Guthrie's heirs.

A Job Of Work; A Rumblin' In The Land; When Morning Breaks; Daily News; What Did You Learn In School Today?; The Last Thing On My Mind; Harper; Fare Thee Well, Cisco; I Can't Help But Wonder Where I'm Bound; High Sheriff Of Hazard; My Lady's A Wild, Flying Dove; Standing On The Edge Of Town; I'm Bound For The Mountains And The Sea; Goin' To The Zoo; Ramblin' Boy.

First released 1964
UK peak chart position: did not chart
USA peak chart position: did not chart

17. JOHN PRINE
John Prine

Discovered and championed by the unlikely combination of Paul Anka and Kris Kristofferson, John Prine was part of a new wave of singer/songwriters to emerge in the early 70s. Like his friend and contemporary Steve Goodman, Prine was feted as an ersatz Dylan, a tag, while flattering, tended to obscure the singer's gifts. An incisive composer and distinctive singer, he showcased such talents to best effect on this, his debut album, which deftly articulated a post-Woodstock, post-Vietnam perspective. Its best-known selection, 'Sam Stone', was recorded by several artists, notably Bonnie Raitt, but each song was strong, resulting in a mature collection which has easily stood the test of time.

Illegal Smile; Spanish Pipedream; Hello In There; Sam Stone; Paradise; Pretty Good; Your Flag Decal Won't Get You Into Heaven Anymore; Far From Me; Angel From Montgomery; Quiet Man; Donald And Lydia; Six O'clock News; Flashback Blues.

First released 1972
UK peak chart position: did not chart
USA peak chart position: 154

18. JOAN BAEZ No. 5
Joan Baez

A gifted interpreter of traditional song, Joan Baez quickly brought that skill to bear on contemporary folk material. Her version of Phil Ochs' cautionary 'There But For Fortune' brought the singer a rare hit single without sacrificing her art. Johnny Richard Farina, Bob Dylan and Johnny Cash were among the others Baez chose to record herein, her pure, virginal soprano investing their songs with a tender beauty. A cello section invests Heitor Villa Lobos' 'Bachianas Brasileiras' with added poignancy and shows the singer's grasp of international themes and languages is a sure as that of Childe ballads and broadsides.

There But For Fortune; Stewball; It Ain't Me Babe; The Death Of Queen Jane; Child Number 170; Bachianas Brasileiras Number 5 - Aria; Go 'Way From My Window; I Still Miss Someone; When You Here Them Cuckoos Hollerin'; Birmingham Sunday; So We'll Go No More A-roving; O'Cangaceiro; The Unquiet Grave; Child Number 78.

First released 1965
UK peak chart position:3
USA peak chart position: 12

19. HARD STATION
Paul Brady

An abrupt about turn from a man who up to this point was the blue eyed wonder of the traddies. Feeling he'd sung enough about maidens and transportation he decided to try rockin' out. Not only did he succeed, but he wrote in a subliminally Irish way. Originally the album was issued on WEA Eire and was powerful enough, but Brady dissatisfied switched his loyalties to 21 Records an arm of Polydor remixing and making a brilliant album downright superb. It remains a seminal work and Brady's writing is impressive enough to earn plaudits from the likes of Bonnie Raitt, Tina Turner and Bob Dylan.

Crazy Dreams; Road To The Promised Land; Busted Loose; Cold Cold Night; Hard Station; Dancer In The Fire; Night Hunting Time; Nothing But The Same Old Story.

First released 1981
UK peak chart position: did not chart
USA peak chart position: did not chart

20. SECOND ALBUM
Martin Carthy

One of the finest singers of the English folk revival, Martin Carthy brought a highly individual perspective to traditional songs. His work implied a contemporary viewpoint while retaining an authentic air. Although denied commercial acclaim until (briefly) joining Steeleye Span, Carthy enjoyed the respect of his peers. Both Bob Dylan and Paul Simon acquired melodies from his repertoire; the latter's version of 'Scarborough Fair' is the most obvious example. *Second Album* captures the singer at a creative peak, his resonant voice and excellent guitar playing injecting the material with startling originality. Fiddler Dave Swarbrick adds stellar support on a set which redefined British folk.

Two Butchers; Ball 'O' Yarn; Farewell Nancy; Lord Franklin; Ramblin' Sailor; Lowlands Of Holland; Fair Maid On The Shore; Bruton Town; Box On Her Head; Newlyn Town; Brave Wolfe; Peggy And The Soldier; Sailor's Life.

First released 1966
UK peak chart position: did not chart
USA peak chart position: did not chart

21. CHORDS OF FAME
Phil Ochs

Phil Ochs began his career as a topical folksinger. His compositions were highly literate, reflecting his journalistic studies, and they expressed a political dimension with pinpoint accuracy. As the focus changed from protest to counter-culture causes, so the singer's work increased in rage, still imbued with a desire for change, but proclaimed from a highly personal standpoint. Ochs' grasp of melody was always sure and his songs were charged with an emotion few peers could match. *Chords Of Fame* is an indispensable precis of the singer's entire career, one tragically cut short by his suicide in 1976. Early broadsides are balanced by later, introspective views and the set also contains the bulk of Ochs' seminal *In Concert* album. Unissued masters and rare recordings complete the consummate overview of a highly distinctive performer, whose crushed idealism would prove too much to bear.

I'm Going To Say It Now; Santo Domingo; Changes; Is There Anybody Here; Love Me, I'm A Liberal; When I'm Gone; Outside Of A Small Circle Of Friends; Pleasures Of The Harbor; Tape from California; Chords Of Fame; Crucifixion; War Is Over; Jim Dean Of Indiana; The Power And The Glory; Flower Lady; No More Songs.

First released 1976
UK peak chart position: did not chart
USA peak chart position: did not chart

22. GIVE A DAMN
The Johnstons

Following a line through Peter Paul And Mary/the Seekers by way of an Irish angle the Johnstons based on close harmony and family ties with sisters Adrienne and Luci, were a big noise in the folk scene of their own land. (Supporting was Mike Maloney and a young Paul Brady.) After doing just about everything there was to be done in Ireland during 1969 they relocated to London winning a contract with the then prestigious Transatlantic organisation. Their philosophy of homespun traditions began to balloon into a broader, international repertoire, sweeping through writers like Leonard Cohen, Jacques Brel, Joni Mitchell, Ralph McTell and Dave Cousins. Mirrored here that move into more serious music, reflected in the title foreshadowed and encouraged the writing chameleon within Brady.

Give A Damn; You Keep Going Your Way; Urge For Going; Port Of Amsterdam; Funny In A Sad Sad Way; Hey That's No Way To Say Goodbye; Both Sides Now; Julia; Sweet Thames Flow Softly; I Loved; I Don't Mind The Rain On Monday; Walking Out On Foggy Mornings.

First released 1969
UK peak chart position: did not chart
USA peak chart position: did not chart

23. BELOW THE SALT
Steeleye Span

Steeleye's two fingered salute to those who dismissed them as irrelevant after the departure of members with folksy cred. Taking aboard proven rockers in Rick Kemp and Bob Johnson their sound sharpened, toughened and became far more immediate. The music here is heading for the mainstream. 'Gaudete' was their first hit, though undeniably tracks like 'King Henry' with acid guitar solo meant more in terms of folk rock development. Closing is the melancholy 'Saucy Sailor' which Maddy Prior quotes as a favourite and sings still. A work which endures.

Spotted Cow; Rosebuds In June; Jigs; Sheepcrook And Black Dog; Royal Forester; King Henry; Gaudete; John Barleycorn; Saucy Sailor.

First released 1972
UK peak chart position: 43
USA peak chart position: did not chart

24. SWEET REVENGE
John Prine

Riding out the 'next Dylan' tag was tough if you had an ounce of roots in your voice and carried an acoustic guitar, during the early 70s. And indeed not long before this set the Bob himself was prone to wander on stage and strum along with Prine for a few numbers. However if any were going to avoid pigeon holes on a conscious level then John Prine was the man. His run of albums for Atlantic, whilst not commercial highs, marked creative ascendancy which saw him become a musician's musician. His compositions mixed elements of country and folk yet where characterised by a hard-nosed belief in the conventional American. Tales of ordinary people dominate and his use of backing, which was supportive never intrusive, is never better demonstrated than here where fellow strummer Steve Goodman is omnipresent along with the likes of Steve Burgh, Judy Clay and Cissie Houston. This is music for a thinking cognoscenti.

Sweet Revenge; Please Don't Bury Me; Christmas In Prison; Dear Abby; Blue Umbrella; Often Is A Word I Seldom Use; Onomatopoeia; Grandpa Was A Carpenter; The Accident (Things Could Be Worse); Mexican Home; A Good Time; Nine Pound Hammer.

First released 1973
UK peak chart position: did not chart
USA peak chart position: 135

25. PENGUIN EGGS
Nic Jones

One of the essential traditional folk records, like Martin Carthy - who he quotes as influential - Jones has a characteristic guitar style and approach to folk which marks him out for reverence and respect. In 1982 he was cruelly involved in a road accident which has removed him from an active musical life. His recovery is still not complete, but *Penguin Eggs* stands as his definitive work. *Melody Maker* Folk Album of the year, it's blessed with flawless selections and superb arrangements, that ensure whilst its creator maybe sadly absent from the scene his influence is not. Shades of Nic Jones can be seen in a whole new emerging generation of folk singers.

Canadee-i-o; The Drowned Lovers; The Humpback Whale; The Little Pot Stove; Courting Is A Pleasure; Barrack Street; Planxty Davis; The Flandyke Shore; Farewell To The Gold.

First released 1980
UK peak chart position: did not chart
USA peak chart position: did not chart

26. ENGLISH ROCK 'N' ROLL THE EARLY YEARS 1800-1850
Oyster Band

Bearing a brilliant sobriquet, this was where a new wave came on stream, that of the country dance acolytes. Not just a concert band, the Oysters were equally adept at playing village hops, and took the strain of the dance into more mainstream forms. This, the first step on that journey raised more than a few curious eyebrows, its origins obviously folksy, but its sights set higher. There is an altogether cheeky, boppy feel to which spry rhythms and jaunty melodies are welded in carefree spontaneity. Electric folk took a leap forward and the Oysters just kept on getting better.

The Prentice Boy; Rufford Park/Bobbing Joe; Sons Of Freedom; A Longport Hymn; Annan Water; Abroad A I Was Walking; Bold Wolfe; Old Molly Oxford; Slippin' & Slidin'; The Dockyard Gate; Holligrave/Wayfaring Stranger.

First released 1982
UK peak chart position: did not chart
USA peak chart position: did not chart

27. BASKET OF LIGHT
Pentangle

The Pentangle revolved around acoustic guitarists Bert Jansch and John Renbourne, vocalist Jacquie McShee and a jazz-based rhythm section, Danny Thompson (bass) and Terry Cox (drums). The understanding and interplay between these accomplished musicians brought new dimensions to folk music, blending improvisation and traditional songs with crisp, original material. 'Light Flight', the theme to a successful TV series, gave the group an unexpected hit single without sacrificing their strengths. Subtle, graceful and highly sophisticated, *Basket Of Light* retains the purity of the forms which influence it, but the way in which the Pentangle combined them resulted in a highly original set.

Light Flight; Once I Had A Sweetheart; Springtime Promises; Lyke Wyke Dirge; Train Song; Hunting Song; Sally Go Round The Roses; The Cuckoo; House Carpenter.

First released 1969
UK peak chart position: 5
USA peak chart position: 200

28. ALRIGHT JACK
Home Service

So much was expected of the Home Service, 'the greatest English band working with folk influences since Traffic' some wag said in print. No doubt their mixture of brass, rock, folk and the zealous nature of front man John Tams was loaded with potential. The trouble was converting all those credentials into something worthwhile in the way of recording. After a couple of stutters they hit top form with a deep booming mix, which thundered not only because of a hail of trumpets and saxophone, but also through the medieval fretwork of Graeme Taylor. Restyling classical influences like Grainger, Civil War celebratory bal. 's and composing their own bleak, folk music the Home Service took English music off at a tangent and vindicated the faith placed in them. Certainly the English roots band of the 80s.

Alright Jack; Rose Of Allandale; Radstock Jig; Sorrow; Scarecrow; Duke Of Marlborough Fanfare; A Lincolnshire Posy; Look Up Look Up; Babylon.

First released 1986
UK peak chart position: did not chart
USA peak chart position: did not chart

29. JOAN BAEZ
Joan Baez

Few debut albums are as assured and self-realised as this impressive set. Folksinger Baez possessed a voice of unrivalled purity, imbuing these recordings with a moving piquancy. She combined songs drawn from America's rich folk heritage with perceptive readings of Francis Childe ballads, bringing to them a haunting resonance. Her influence on a generation of woman singers, including Judy Collins and Joni Mitchell, is immeasurable and two of the selections herein, 'The House Of The Rising Sun' and 'Johnoa' were later taken up, respectively, by Bob Dylan then the Animals and the Byrds.

Silver Dagger; East Virginia; Ten Thousand Miles; The House Of The Rising Sun; All My Trails; Wildwood Flower; Donna Donna; John Riley; Rake And The Rambling Boy; Little Moses; Mary Hamilton; Henry Martin; El Preso Numero Nuevo; Johnoa.

First released 1962
UK peak chart position: 9
USA peak chart position: 15

30. THE CUTTER AND THE CLAN
Runrig

On which Runrig staked it all. Their Gaelic pride and passion was assured with the cognoscenti but they needed to do more than remain a Scottish phenomenon. Taking it's roots and drenching the whole album with intrinsic Highland values, Calum and Rory McDonald's writing took on a whole new class. Producer Chris Harley found the right wavelength and between them they lit the blue touch paper. The fireworks which ensued were spectacular; within weeks they'd signed to Chrysalis and the album was reissued and repromoted. It was goodbye to cosy parochialism and hello big wide world.

Alba; The Cutter; Hearts Of Olden Glory; Pride Of The Summer; Worker For The Wind; Rocket To The Moon; The Only Rose; Protect And Survive; Our Earth Was Once Green; An Aubhal As Airds.

First released 1987
UK peak chart position: did not chart
USA peak chart position: did not chart

31. BATTLE OF THE FIELD
Albion Country Band

Delayed some three years and with no band to herald release, nonetheless its place in the quest for an English sound is assured. The restless spirit of Ashley Hutchings urged him towards the strain of morris and ritual dance. His creation was a group plagued with baffling personnel shifts, each version lasting but months. Yet the final line-up including Steeleye and Fairport alumni held together long enough to deliver a big cheery sound full of pumping accordions, frail oboes and blocky, square endemic rhythms. All very rustic and earthy, the Albion beat found purpose here in Martin Carthy's yeoman vocal, John Kirkpatrick's haunting anglo concertina and the stately 'Battle Of The Somme.'

Albion Sunrise; Morris Medley; I Was A Young Man; New St. George/La Rotta; Gallant Poacher; Cheshire Rounds/The Old Lancashire Hornpipe; Hanged I Shall Be; Reaphook And Sickle; Battle Of The Somme.

First released 1989
UK peak chart position: did not chart
USA peak chart position: did not chart

32. WHO KNOWS WHERE TIME GOES
Judy Collins

On which Judy Collins took the step of unceremoniously dumping her previous orchestral balladeer approach and hiring herself a list of names which gelled in perfect style as a loose backing band. A move prompted no doubt by the fact that her paramour of the time was Stephen Stills, who along with Chris Ethridge, Van Dyke Parks and others gave the impressively wide selection of songs - among them Sandy Denny's wistful title track - an almost tactile vibrancy. Collins responded with a candour and tenacity in her vocal she never found again. This is her singular achievement.

Hello, Hooray; Story Of Isaac; My Father; Someday Soon; Who Knows Where The Time Goes; Poor Immigrant; The First Boy I Loved; Bird On The Wire; Pretty Polly.

First released 1968
UK peak chart position: did not chart
USA peak chart position: 29

33. AQABA
June Tabor

Status as a folk diva assured, June Tabor's dramatic, telling vocal haunts the listener. For many years she was associated with the nation's premier folk label Topic, for whom this was her last effort. She also had a reputation for making recordings which exceeded previous efforts quite considerably. Both selection of trusted musicians to provide the backing, and producer in mad professor Andy Cronshaw were inspired. She is never less than precise or passionate about the music and this, from the dramatic cover to the final note, is a challenge to the listener. At times it's stark, others it's a beast of taut control and dark joy. Even if you only listen once it is hard to remain aloof. State of the art female roots vocal.

Old Man's Song (Don Quixote); Searching For Lambs; The Banks Of Red Roses; Where Are You Tonight?; Aqaba; Bogie's Bonnie Belle; The Reaper; Verdi Cries; The Grazier's Daughter; Seven Summers; The King Of Rome; Mayn Rue Plats.

First released 1988
UK peak chart position: did not chart
USA peak chart position: did not chart

34. HANDFUL OF EARTH
Dick Gaughan

Fiercely political, this was the work which cemented Gaughan's reputation for outspoken topicality and burning Scots nationalism. It's a milestone and be in no doubt traditional music would be the poorer without it. The mix of vitriol and conciliation is startling. There are no punches pulled in 'The World Turned Upside Down' yet contrast that with the tender 'Snows They Melt The Soonest' or hands across the water brotherhood on 'Both Sides The Tweed.' The unobtrusive, atmospheric backing allows Gaughan to range free across the principles and influences which he still stands by as loyally to this day.

Erin Go Bragh; Now Westlin' Winds; Craigie Hill; The World Turned Upside Down; The Snows That Melt The Soonest; Lough Erne; First Kiss At Parting; Scojun Waltz; Randers Hopsa; A Song For Ireland; The Worker's Song; Both Sides The Tweed.

First released 1981
UK peak chart position: did not chart
USA peak chart position: did not chart

35. PLEASE TO SEE THE KING
Steeleye Span

If the early days of electric folk produced a lady to match the more waggish elements of Fairport then, here she is. She is both graceful and so well mannered. This Steeleye Span were folk darlings, they did things with reverence, creating a dense, forest of layered music in which rooted electric dulcimer, guitars, keyboards and violin wrap a blanket round Maddy Prior and Martin Carthy's harmony. Here was an ethnic wall of sound. 'The Blacksmith', 'The Lark In The Morning', 'Lovely On The Water,' all remain gemstones that ensure the whole album is untouched by the passing years. Truly timeless.

Blacksmith; Cold, Haily, Windy Night; Bryan O'Lynn; The Hag With The Money; Prince Charlie Stuart; Boys Of Bedlam; False Night On The Road; The Lark In The Morning; Female Drummer; The King; Lovely On The Water.

First released 1971
UK peak chart position: 45
USA peak chart position: did not chart

36. I GOT A NAME
Jim Croce

One of the most catastrophic stories in popular music. Croce, in the summer of 1973 was somewhere on the road to stardom, his style was balladic and it fell between James Taylor and Gordon Lightfoot, with a down to earth quality that probably came from his direct blue collar experience and despite the hits and exposure he never lost. Croce had just hit the top when his life was taken in a plane crash. This set completed before his demise, but released after, is ironically his most accomplished - what would have followed can only be guessed at, he was certainly stretching the accepted idea of folk singer/songwriters, and he was popular, in the afterglow both the title track and 'Time In A Bottle', a really achesome love song, rocketed up the American charts. His removal was tragically untimely.

I Got A Name; Lover's Cross; Five Short Minutes; Age; Workin' At The Car Wash Blues; I'll Have To Say I Love You In A Song; Salon And Saloon; Thursday; Top Hat Bar And Grille; Recently; The Hard Way Every Time.

First released 1973
UK peak chart position: did not chart
USA peak chart position: 2

37. THE THINGS I NOTICE NOW
Tom Paxton

Paxton's image is bound to be cast forever as commercialism for kiddies, this man is responsible for 'Goin' To The Zoo' and 'The Marvellous Toy' as well as 'The Last Thing On My Mind' the one song mauled by anyone hoping to master an acoustic guitar. What is less appreciated is that at one stage he was as much of an angry young man as Dylan or Ochs, it was just that he tempered protest with warmth and humour. In Britain his considerable standing was done no harm by a singalong set at The Isle Of Wight Festival in 1970. This was just after the release of 'The Things I Notice Now' which revealed a man and his music on the move and acknowledging the work of younger, less-driven writers like Tim Buckley. There's more to the man than meets the eye. The two highlights are the title track and the 15 minute 'The Iron Man'.

Bishop Cody's Last Request; Wish I Had A Troubadour; About The Children; I Give You The Morning; The Things I Notice Now; The Iron Man; All Night Long.

First released 1969
UK peak chart position: did not chart
USA peak chart position: 155

38. FOR PENCE AND SPICY ALE
Watersons

When it comes to close harmonies then there's nobody that can touch the Watersons, their a cappella, part singing is emotional, and gritty, which while not exactly in any classical choral idiom, is far more compelling. This set was the first to be recorded after Martin Carthy joined both group and family - he's married to Norma Waterson. 'Country Life' says as much about them as anything. Though they're steeped in tradition they remain maverick and have despite winning the undying adulation of the folk world cut rock albums and a whole collection of sacred hymn music! What you call versatile.

Country Life; Swarthfell Rocks; Barney; Swinton May Song; Bellman; Adieu, Adieu; Apple Tree; The Wassailing Song; Sheep Shearing; Three Day Millionaire; King Pharin; T Stands For Thomas; Malpas Wassail Song; Chickens In The Garden; The Good Old Way.

First released 1975
UK peak chart position: did not chart
USA peak chart position: did not chart

39. RISE UP LIKE THE SUN
Albion Band

By the latter end of the 70s most folk rock was stylistically redundant, the major players had mostly gone their separate ways. But then out came the Albions with this classic, which took English music into megadrive. Gathering a big band of varied experience around him - early music professors, jazzers, folkies, classical players, and rocksters - Ashley Hutchings diverse grouping was shaped further by vocalist John Tams for whom this album held particular vision. That ideal held true in a mixture of contemporary songs and traditional mutations, 'Ragged Heroes' was Tams own patriotic anthem, a call for a nation to awake, elsewhere religious lullabies, 'Lay Me Low' were counteracted against a cyclical jazz free for all as Ric Sanders 'Gresford Disaster' pushed electric folk into power and pathos. For along time no other band came so close to furthering English derived music.

Ragged Heroes; Poor Old Horse; Afro Blue/Danse Royale; Ampleforth I Lay Me Low; Time To Ring Some Changes; House In The Country; The Primrose; Gresford Disaster.

First released 1978
UK peak chart position: did not chart
USA peak chart position: did not chart

40. THE 5000 SPIRITS OR THE LAYERS OF THE ONION
Incredible String Band

The second album by the Incredible String Band broke down the barriers between folk and pop. Sitar, oud, gimbri and tamboura are employed to add texture to a collection of outstanding, original songs. The contrast between the duo's compositional styles is another important factor; where Mike Heron wrote crisp, structured songs, as exemplified by 'Painting Box', Robin Williamson contributed material which eschewed formal meter, freeing his voice to reflect his imaginative lyrics. Together they take folk music into uncharted territory with an album full of mystery and imagination.

Chinese White; No Sleep Blues; Painting Box; The Mad Hatter's Song; Little Cloud; The Eyes Of Fate; Blues For The Muse; The Hedgehog's Song; First Girl I Loved; You Know That You Could Be; My Name Is Death; Gently Tender; Way Back In The 1960's.

First released 1967
UK peak chart position: 26
USA peak chart position: did not chart

41. THE BOOK OF INVASIONS
Horslips

It was erratically brilliant Horslips who got their teeth into the serious question of giving the hallowed ancient music of Ireland a modern identity. This the first of an unintentional trilogy charting the course of Irish history was their commercial and creative zenith. What is pertinent to remember is that these guys weren't folkies, but out and out rockers with a love of acoustic reeling as well as Liffey falling over water. They dragged airs and old dance tunes kicking and howling into the backbeat, a technique never better demonstrated than on the driving 'King Of Morning, Queen Of Day' where 'KIFENORA' a Clare jig is used as a springboard. A superb album of acoustic atmosphere's and rock's grittier textures.

Daybreak; March Into Trouble; Trouble (With A Capital T); Power And The Glory; The Rocks Remain; Dusk; Sword Of Light; Warm Sweet Breath Of Love; Fantasia (My Lagan Love); King Of Morning, Queen Of Day; Sideways To The Sun; Drive The Cold Winter Away; Ride To Hell; The Dark.

First released 1977
UK peak chart position: 39
USA peak chart position: did not chart

42. DESERTERS
Oyster Band

The album with which the Oyster Band divested themselves of most lingering folkisms and went all out for leather, shades and rock. The fact that their lead vocalist plays a squeezebox is totally incidental, *Deserters* is hard nosed, thudding and mainstream. The songs mirror bleak, hard times where politically the only way to lighten the gloom is to hold hands, and dance. The flag waving and rallying aspects dominate, 'All That Way For This', and there's a hollow eyed rendering of 'The Bells Of Rhymney.' Live work and unceasing gigging had honed the Oysters into the likeness of a well oiled machine. Goes for the throat, not for the faint hearted, and it sort of makes sense that they drew as much inspiration from Joy Division as any old country dance players.

All That Way For This; The Deserter; Angels Of The River; We Could Leave Right Now; Elena's Shoes; Granite Years; Diamond For A Dime; Never Left; Ship Set Sail; Fiddle Or A Gun; Bells Of Rhymney.

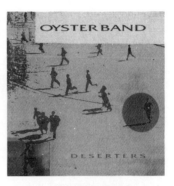

First released 1992
UK peak chart position: did not chart
USA peak chart position: did not chart

43. STEP OUTSIDE
Oyster Band

It's hard to imagine that this was the outfit (as Fiddler's Dram) responsible for the UK top 3 hit 'Day Trip To Bangor' in 1979, the vocalist Cathy Lesurf joined the Albion Band and the Oysters were formed. *Step Outside* is perfect middle period Oyster Band, and the third appearance in the listings which is conveniently represented by both early and late period pieces. This is the transitional album before they began to rock, and important in the development and perception of what folk music is or should be. The album, produced by Clive Gregson contains the indispensable 'Another Quiet Night In England' and like their publishing company the other songs are 'pukka music. Important for their progressive stance, just like Fairport or Steeleye Span but different.

Hal-An-Tow; Flatlands; Another Quiet Night In England; Molly Bond; Bully In The Alley; The Day That The Ship Goes Down; Gaol Song; The Old Dance; Bold Riley.

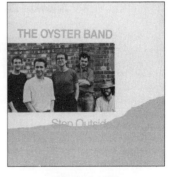

First released 1986
UK peak chart position: did not chart
USA peak chart position: did not chart

44. FULL HOUSE
Fairport Convention

With the departure of integral members and the new formed crown of folk rock on their head, these were difficult days for Fairport. They became a male five-piece concentrating their efforts on the Thompson/Swarbrick team who were emerging as writers of effective folk sentiment. They produced a more brittle, ringing style which ranged from impossibly dervish dance tunes to the divine blackness of the anti war tirade 'Sloth,' thence to continuing electric traditions in 'Sir Patrick Spens' or 'Flowers Of the Forest.' At seven tracks long it's a mite short but it is still a great album.

Walk Awhile; Dirty Linen; Sloth; Sir Patrick Spens; Flatback Caper; Doctor Of Physick; Flowers Of The Forest.

First released 1970
UK peak chart position: 13
USA peak chart position: did not chart

45. SHIFTING GRAVEL
Four Men And A Dog

This album pips their admirable debut by the dog's whisker. This followed and built upon the 1992 release *Barking Mad*. The varied selection can only help define and expand folk music in the 90s. Four Men And A Dog make a contribution in bringing folk music back to the masses by infusing their music with shots of rockabilly and zydeco ('I'm Walking'). The third track is a perfect example; 'Work Together' is an uptempo R&B number that only earns the folk label by having an accordion present. 'Joh' is a beautiful slow ballad that follows the traditional sounding 'Bertha's Goat'. Four Men And A Dog are bold and one of the (if not *the*) most refreshing folk/rock groups of the 90s. Much is promised and much is expected.

Another Irish Rover; Shifting Gravel; Work Together; Bertha's Goat; Joh; Newmarket Polkas; I'm Walking; The Mountain Road; Struggle On; Micho Russells Set; Where Has My Lady Gone; The Kilfenora Sexy Jig.

First released 1993
UK peak chart position: did not chart
USA peak chart position: did not chart

46. ANOTHER SIDE OF BOB DYLAN
Bob Dylan

Upon which moves were obvious that the almighty Zim was becoming bored with straight folk. Though acoustic his left thinking devotees began to raise an eye brow at subtle lyrical shifts, yet this album was to be raided time and again - especially by the Byrds - in 1965's folk rock boom. There's much free spirited music as if Dylan was somehow aware of the acceptance that was around the corner. And it has been noted that here were the first signs of the trademark vocal so prevalent through the rest of the 60s. take your pick really most of the offerings are striking. 'My Back Pages', 'All I Really Want To Do', 'It Ain't Me Babe' even a last nod to protest 'The Chimes Of Freedom.' How can one man make so much great music?

All I Really Want To Do; Black Crow Blues; Spanish Harlem Incident; Chimes Of Freedom; I Shall Be Free; To Ramona; Motorpsycho Nightmare; My Back Pages; I Don't Believe You; Ballads In Plain D; It Ain't Me Babe.

First released 1964
UK peak chart position: 8
USA peak chart position: 43

47. LAST OF THE TRUE BELIEVERS
Nanci Griffith

Bobbysox, homespun tunes and country meets folk on a back porch somewhere out west. Lost in a small town all of its own this slice of side track America spins tales of ordinary people in back to basics fashion. Nanci Griffith's appeal and charm found wider appreciation with clean cut music and cooing, prim vocals. If she never sang another note, 'Banks Of The Pontchatrain' would be enough. The music of a thousand pump boys and dinettes across a continent.

The Last Of The True Believers; Love At The Five And Dime; St. Olav's Gate; More Than A Whisper; Banks Of The Old Pontchatrain; Looking For The Time; Goin' Gone; One Of These Days; Love's Found A Shoulder; Fly By Night; Wing And The Wheel.

First released 1986
UK peak chart position: did not chart
USA peak chart position: did not chart

48. GRAVE NEW WORLD
Strawbs

Oh the excesses of the 70s! Somewhat peacock-like with triple gatefold sleeve and an outsized booklet, the music was in danger of being swamped by packaging. The Strawbs however were one of the few bands to ride from folk onto the coat tails of progressive rock successfully. Dave Cousins played the wandering minstrel to the full, leading his merry men as well as a whole array of guest stars into songs of deep consciousness, and pseudo religious images. 'Benedictus' is prime Strawbs, acoustic strumming balladry, swelling into a lead guitar and grandiose keyboard fill with climactic finale. Strong stuff, but if you were in any doubt you could always contemplate on the mind expanding quotes which decorated the sleeve.

Benidictus; Hey Little Man; Queen Of Dreams; Heavy Disguise; New World; The Flower And The Young Man; Tomorrow; On Growing Older; Ah Me, Ah My; Is It Today, Lord?; The Journey's End

First released 1972
UK peak chart position: 11
USA peak chart position: did not chart

49. HAND OF KINDNESS
Richard Thompson

Richard Thompson's position as Britain's premier chronicler of pain, loving and most things black was on the line here, his first album minus wife of a decade Linda - hers a voice guaranteed to lift any music - and lots to prove. He did it with considerable panache and a trusted band of old mates. The r in rock is R and the i in acoustic is for intimate, thus the collection is a two headed demon. The songs are of a vintage, 'Poisoned Heart And A Twisted Memory', 'Hand Of Kindness' itself and his greatest ever folksong, 'Devonside.' Hungry music which should be force fed.

A Poisoned Heart And A Twisted Memory; Tear Stained Letter; How I Wanted To; Both Ends Burning; Wrong Heartbeat; Hand Of Kindness; Devonside; Two Left Feet.

First released 1983
UK peak chart position: did not chart
USA peak chart position: 186

50. FAIRYTALE
Donovan

Folksinger Donovan began his career in the shadow of Bob Dylan, but with Fairytale he discarded the copyist mantle and emerged as a distinctive performer in his own right. His debt to the Woody Guthrie tradition was maintained in the style of several selections, notably 'Colours' and 'Jersey Thursday', but the singer brought to them a romanticism setting him apart from such peers. 'Sunny Goodge Street' boasts a charming string arrangement complimenting the picturesque vignettes of London it portrays and both it and the evocative 'Try For The Sun' were recorded by other artists, another crucial factor signalling Donovan's maturation as a composer. This confident album prepared a path for the sweeping commercial success which followed.

Colours; Try For The Sun; Sunny Goodge Street; Oh Deed I Do; Circus Of Sour; The Summer Day Reflection Song; Candy Man; Jersey Thursday; Belated Of A Crystal Man; Little Tin Soldier; The Ballad Of Geraldine.

First released 1965
UK peak chart position: 20
USA peak chart position: 85

THE TOP 50
HEAVY METAL ALBUMS

A NUMBER OF ITEMS HERE WOULD HAVE QUALIFIED FOR THE ROCK AND POP SECTION, ALBEIT HEAVY ROCK. METAL IS DESERVING OF ITS OWN CHART, EVEN IF THAT CHART RESTATES THE IMPORTANCE OF LED ZEPPELIN - A BAND THAT WAS AROUND BEFORE THE GENRE WAS DEFINED. METAL DEVOTEES ARE PARTISAN BUT THEY ARE NOT BEYOND RECOGNISING THE POWER OF THE EARLY HEAVY ROCKERS SUCH AS DEEP PURPLE AND BLACK SABBATH.

IT CONTINUES TO GROW AND DEVELOP AS THE PRESENCE OF GRUNGE AND OTHER SUBGENRES INDICATE.

1. LED ZEPPELIN II
Led Zeppelin

Having declared an individual brand of blues/rock on their debut album, Led Zeppelin significantly expanded musical horizons on its successor. The opening riff to 'Whole Lotta Love' declared a strength of purpose and excitement and the song quickly achieved anthem-like proportions. *Led Zeppelin II* personifies the entire heavy-metal spectrum, from guitar hero to virile vocalist. Sexual metaphor ('The Lemon Song') collides with musical dexterity ('Moby Dick') and the faintest whiff of sword and sorcery to create one of rock's most emphatic and celebratory albums.

Whole Lotta Love; What Is And What Should Be; The Lemon Song; Thank You; Heartbreaker; Livin' Lovin' Maid (She's A Woman); Ramble On; Moby Dick; Bring It On Home.

First released 1969
UK peak chart position: 1
USA peak chart position: 1

2. LED ZEPPELIN IV
Led Zeppelin

Its unscripted sleeve design suggested anonymity, but nothing was left to question over this album's content. Led Zeppelin were never so strident as on 'Rock 'n' Roll' and 'Black Dog', two selections of undiluted urgency. Blues' standard 'When The Levee Breaks' is recast as a piece of unremitting power, particularly through John Bonham's expansive drumming, and the group's love of folk forms surface on the graceful 'Battle Of Evermore', complete with cameo from Fairport Convention's Sandy Denny. 'Stairway To Heaven' has, of course, become the album's best-known track, but the anthem-like stature it has since assumed should not obscure its groundbreaking, companion selections. *Led 'Zeppelin IV* left much of heavy metal, and indeed rock itself, trailing in its wake.

Black Dog; Rock 'n' Roll; The Battle Of Evermore; Stairway To Heaven; Misty Mountain Hop; Four Sticks; Going To California; When The Levee Breaks.

First released 1971
UK peak chart position: 1
USA peak chart position: 2

3. PARANOID
Black Sabbath

The murderous riff on which the title track hinges set the tone for bruising album. Doom, death and destruction is Black Sabbath's staple diet, which they devoured with numbing intensity. Repetition is this album's hinge, sustained chords and ponderous bass often slowing tempos to crawling pace until, on 'War Pigs', they groan with suffocation. Guitarist Tony Iommi punctuates the sound with simple, but lengthy solos, leaving vocalist Ozzie Osbourne to inject a sly cockiness. Pretenders have often grasped at their crown, but *Paranoid* shows Black Sabbath remain the quintessential heavy metal band.

War Pigs; Planet Caravan; Iron Man; Electric Funeral; Hand Of Doom; Rat Salad; Fairies Wear Boots; Wicked World; Paranoid.

First released 1970
UK peak chart position: 1
USA peak chart position: 12

4. MACHINE HEAD
Deep Purple

From the heady intro of 'Highway Star', written in a couple of hours on a bus between shows, to the lazy beat of 'Space Truckin'', *Machine Head* would have remained one of the classic line-up's, Glover, Paice, Gillan, Blackmore, Lord, great albums. But, due to the hand of fate that took them to Montreux at the same time as Frank Zappa's Mothers Of Invention and the witnessing of the burning down of the Casino that was to be immortalised with, 'Smoke On The Water', Blackmore's plaintive riff, studied and dedicated to memory in a thousand guitar classes, and Gillan's simple retelling of events, elevated then and their record to legendary status.

Highway Star; Maybe I'm A Leo; Pictures Of Home; Never Before; Smoke On The Water; Lazy; Space Truckin'.

First released 1972
UK peak chart position: 1
USA peak chart position: 7

5. IN ROCK
Deep Purple

Formed by discontented pop musicians, Deep Purple embraced progressive rock through judicious cover versions which drew acclaim at the expense of original material. Sensing a stylistic blind alley, Jon Lord (keyboards) and Ritchie Blackmore (guitar) brought new vocalist Ian Gillan into the line-up, a decision which irrevocably changed their fortunes. *In Rock* is one of the genre's definitive albums, combining hard-edged riffs with virtuoso technique, topped by Gillan's full-throated roar. Few singers could survive the instrumental power beneath him, this he does with room to spare, reacting to and emphasising his colleagues' musical prowess. Chock-full of material destined to become Deep Purple anthems, later releases were evaluated against this trailblazing, heavy rock collection.

Speed King; Blood Sucker; Child In Time; Flight Of The Rat; Into The Fire; Living Wreck; Hard Lovin' Man.

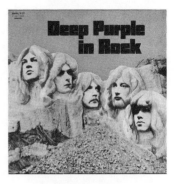

First released 1970
UK peak chart position: 4
USA peak chart position: 143

6. SLIPPERY WHEN WET
Bon Jovi

Bon Jovi took a few faltering steps with their promising self-titled debut album and its shoddy 7800 Fahrenheit follow up. Though, it was with this third record, a mixture of New Jersey storytelling and songwriter/collaborator Desmond Child's keen eye for any kind of commercial bent, that the perfect equation of songs and suss were found. The almost noble, 'Wanted Dead Or Alive', spawned a thousand copy cat monochrome, on-the-road videos. While the sure-fire snap of, 'Livin' On A Prayer' and 'You Give Love A Bad Name', simply elevated the banner that much the higher.

Let It Rock; You Give Love A Bad Name; Livin' On A Prayer; Social Disease; Wanted Dead Or Alive; Raise Your Hands; Without Love; I'd Die For You; Never Say Goodbye; Wild In The Streets.

First released 1986
UK peak chart position: 6
USA peak chart position: 1

7. BACK IN BLACK
AC/DC

After the untimely death of former, enigmatic vocalist Bon Scott, AC/DC finally chanced upon a worthy replacement in the shape of former Geordie frontman, Brian Johnson. The result was more than the formal pastiche some thought it might be. Johnson stamping his own personality, not to mention distinctive rasp, on the record. Though the band's staple lyrical diet of sex and the general pursuit of happiness remained very much intact. Highlights include the stomping, 'Hell's Bells', the quiet build of the title track and the chuckling insolence of, 'Rock And Roll Ain't Noise Pollution'. A winning return.

Back In Black; Hell's Bells; Shoot To Thrill; Give The Dog A Bone; What Do You Do For Money Honey?; Rock And Roll Ain't Noise Pollution; Let Me Put My Love Into You; You Shook Me All Night Long; Shake A Leg; Have A Drink On Me.

First released 1980
UK peak chart position: 1
USA peak chart position: 4

8. VAN HALEN
Van Halen

Quite simply put, no-one had seen or heard anything like it. Roth's flamboyant showmanship, the mic dangling provocatively between his legs on the cover, and Eddie Van Halen's monstrously inventive guitar playing, became a textbook for wannabes the world over. From the instrumental blow-out of, 'Eruption', the gritty, teen pop of, 'Feel Your Love Tonight', the strutting riff that, 'Ain't Talkin' Bout Love', was built around, to the grandiose reworking of The Kinks', 'You Really Got Me', Van Halen set their own absurd standards. One of the truly great rock and roll/metal debut albums.

You Really Got Me; Jamie's Cryin'; On Fire; Runnin' With The Devil; I'm The One; Ain't Talkin' Bout Love; Little Dreamer; Feel Your Love Tonight; Atomic Punk; Eruption; Ice Cream Man.

First released 1978
UK peak chart position: 34
USA peak chart position: 19

9. APPETITE FOR DESTRUCTION
Guns N'Roses

Already a legend in its own meagre lifetime. This startling debut shrouded itself in controversy, from its original Robert Williams artwork to Axl Rose's unblinking retelling of LA's underbelly. This mawkish storytelling combined with a brattish collective swagger and a surprisingly mature approach to their songs, guaranteed Guns N'Roses a speedy notoriety that was to serve their legend brilliantly. From the laconic, 'Paradise City', to the achingly beautiful, 'Sweet Child O' Mine', or the furious, 'Welcome To The Jungle', the record brims with a brutal integrity. One they're now unlikely ever to surpass.

Welcome To The Jungle; It's So Easy; Nightrain; Out Ta Get Me; Mr. Brownstone; Paradise City; My Michelle; Think About You; Sweet Child O' Mine; You're Crazy; Anyhting Goes; Rocket Queen.

First released 1987
UK peak chart position: 5
USA peak chart position: 1

10. LED ZEPPELIN
Led Zeppelin

Led Zeppelin emerged from the ashes of the Yardbirds, but their self-assured debut album immediately established them in their own right. Faultless musicianship combined with strong material to create an emphatic statement of purpose. Blues standards are extensively reworked and original songs either acknowledge pop/rock structures or allow the quartet to extend itself musically. Guitarist Jimmy Page explores the instrument's potential with dazzling runs or sonic inventiveness, while Robert Plant takes the notion of vocalist into new realms of expression. *Led Zeppelin* announced the arrival of one of rock's most important groups.

Good Times Bad Times; Babe I'm Gonna Leave You; You Shook Me; Dazed And Confused; Your Time Is Gonna Come; Black Mountain Side; Communication Breakdown; I Can't Quit You Baby; How Many More Times.

First released 1969
UK peak chart position: 6
USA peak chart position: 10

11. THE NUMBER OF THE BEAST
Iron Maiden

A creative zenith for Iron Maiden. Capitalising on new vocalist Bruce Dickinson and his rapturous wail, along with a keen eye for songwriting detail, *The Number Of The Beast*, was an uncompromising, though surprisingly subtle, great hard rock record. Displaying their Boys' Own Metal badge proudly, subject matter included The Prisoner television series as well as the plight of Indian in the Old West, they combined arch arrangements with a telling use of melody that, after the initial assault, lingered brilliantly in the mind.

The Invaders; Children Of The Damned; The Prisoner; 22, Acacia Avenue; The Number Of The Beast; Run To The Hills; Gangland; Hallowed Be Thy Name.

First released 1982
UK peak chart position: 1
USA peak chart position: 33

12. BLACK SABBATH
Black Sabbath

The archetypal heavy metal band, Black Sabbath unleashed a debut album marked by basic riffs, power chords and the faintest whiff of satanism. Its crushing atmosphere of doom proved intense and relentless, the cumulative effect was dubbed 'downer rock', but it proved immediately popular to a disaffected, often working-class, audience. Their fierce loyalty was inspired by the negative response this album garnered from many rock critics who proved immune to its single-minded power. Singer Ozzie Osbourne already possessed one of the most distinctive voices in rock and proved the ideal frontman for his group's unremitting attack.

Black Sabbath; The Wizard; Behind The Walls Of Sleep; NIB: Evil Woman; Sleeping Village; Warning.

First released 1970
UK peak chart position: 8
USA peak chart position: 23

13. METALLICA
Metallica

For the band who helped change the traditional face of contemporary heavy metal, Metallica were never found wanting in innovation. Though, 1991's album of the same name came as a telling blow of ideas, surprising even their most ardent of fans. Songs were stripped down to comparatively palatable lengths, subtle orchestration introduced, vocalist James Hetfield dropping his infamous growl for a warm accomplished vocal. While, 'Enter Sandman' and the lilting, 'Nothing Else Matters', showed both sides of their clever songwriting temperament. An unabashed master stroke of sincerity and overwhelming musical confidence.

Enter Sandman; Sad But True; Holier Than Thou; The Unforgiven; Wherever I May Roam; Don't Tread On Me; Through The Never; Nothing Else Matters; Of Wolf And Man; The God That Failed; My Friend Of Misery; The Struggle Within.

First released 1991
UK peak chart position: 1
USA peak chart position: 1

14. PHYSICAL GRAFFITI
Led Zeppelin

One of the greatest hard rock albums ever. Almost 20 years later it's still much imitated, more lately sampled and, quite rightly, the major contemporary reference point in rock music. The heavily stylised 'Kashmir', allegedly the starting point for a war of words between Plant and David Coverdale after a very similar refrain appeared in Whitesnake's, In The Heat Of The Night. The blissful, 'Bron-Yr-Aur', which followed their limo through New York during, 'The Song Remains The Same'. 'Custard Pie', with its legendary intro, and the innovative, 'In The Light'. All combined to create a truly credible musical landmark.

Houses Of The Holy; Trampled Under Foot; Kashmir; Custard Pie; The Rover; In My Time Of Dying; In The Light; Bron-Yr-Aur; Down By The Seaside; Ten Years Gone; Night Flight; The Wanton Song; Boogie With Stu; Back Country Woman; Sick Again.

First released 1975
UK peak chart position: 1
USA peak chart position: 1

15. FOR THOSE ABOUT TO ROCK WE SALUTE YOU
AC/DC

Brian Johnson's second album as AC/DC's frontman, and as such helped them create a phenomenal commercial success. Both singles, 'Let's Get It Up', and the title track charting on both sides of the Atlantic. While the album went on to sell over a million copies worldwide. With the latter becoming an immediate live favourite complete with a cannon fire salute stage show that became instant encore material. Elsewhere, their familiar rattle remained intact with, 'Night Of The Long Knives' and 'Breaking The Rules' hoeing a familiar row.

For Those About To Rock (We Salute You); Put The Finger On You; Let's Get It Up; Inject The Venom; Snowballad; Evil Walk; COD; Breaking The Rules; Night Of The Long Knives; Spellbound.

First released 1981
UK peak chart position: 3
USA peak chart position: 1

16. VAN HALEN II
Van Halen

Dismissed as the poor relation to their thrilling debut on its release, it has only been with the advent of time that Van Halen II, has been afforded any kind of classic stature. Roth's impertinent, sly humour's still in place, but it's Eddie Van Halen's easy experimentation that takes this record to another level. His daring and frantic switch in styles set him aside, ultimately, as any kind of player. He still worked the effusive pop for, 'Dance The Night Away', but his brush strokes, within, 'DOA', and 'You're No Good', especially, were now much more daring and wide.

You're No Good; Dance The Night Away; Somebody Get Me A Doctor; Bottoms Up; Outta Love Again; Light Up The Sky; DOA; Women In Love; Spanish Fly; Beautiful Girls.

First released 1979
UK peak chart position: 23
USA peak chart position: 6

17. BURN
Deep Purple

The first Deep Purple album to feature Glenn Hughes and David Coverdale, and as such, a much more bluesier effort all round. Coverdale's throaty roar combined with Hughes' soaring vocal made for a heartfelt, rootsy record. On that combined a commercial motif, 'Might Just Take Your Life' was a hit single, with a series of extended jams, working most spectacularly with the elongated, 'Mistreated'. Which Coverdale later resurrected as a live favourite with his Whitesnake. While the title track and, 'Lay Down, Stay Down' gave vent to their more familiar refrains and strength of songwriting.

Burn; Might Just Take Your Life; Lay Down, Stay Down; Sail Away; You Fool No-one; What's Goin' On Here?; Mistreated; 'A' Zoo.

First released 1974
UK peak chart position: 3
USA peak chart position: 9

18. THE SOUTHERN HARMONY AND MUSICAL COMPANION
Black Crowes

Given the sub-Stones boogie of their debut, Shake Your Money Maker, *The Southern Harmony*, came as a quietly accomplished body of work seemingly way beyond their relative youth and experience. The Exile On Main Street references were still intact, but the predominant swagger and sashay had been given over for a soulful interpretation of their roots, not merely a parody of their influences. Chris Robinson's Jagger pastiche given over for a more gutsy, honest strut, while brother Rich plays with an aplomb and spirit that struck darkly at the heart of their songs. A very grown up record indeed.

Sting Me; Remedy; Thorn In My Pride; Bad Luck Blue Eyes Goodbye; Sometimes Salvation; Hotel Illness; Black Moon Creepin'; No Speak, No Slave; My Morning Song; Time Will Tell.

First released 1992
UK peak chart position: did not chart
USA peak chart position: 1

19. ELIMINATOR
Z.Z. Top

1983 was the year Z.Z. Top went from everyone's favourite barroom boogie band to international superstars. Graced with mind boggling and incredibly photogenic beards, a very neat trilogy of videos and a collective ear for a quite distinct and highly stylised, if somewhat grizzled blues/pop, the sudden enormity of their success, in retrospect, now seems like no real surprise. MTV had never quite seen the like and the attention given to the excellent, 'Gimme All Your Lovin'' single was quickly repeated for both, 'Sharp-dressed Man', and the quite irreverent, 'Legs'. It still sounds fresh, innovative and fun today.

Gimme All Your Lovin'; Got Me Under Pressure; Sharp-dressed Man; I Need You Tonight; I Got The Six; Legs; Thug; TV Dinners; Dirty Dog; If I Could Only Flag Her Down; Bad Girl.

First released 1983
UK peak chart position: 3
USA peak chart position: 9

20. Screaming For Vengance
Judas Priest

Judas Priest's first platinum selling album, and the record that truly broke them in the US. With the success of their, You've Got Another Thing Comin', their consequent American tour became a huge arena draw. Rob Halford taking to the stage each night on his Harley-Davidson. The album, a consistent mixture of twin guitar work, Halford's piercing vocal range, a liberal twist of groove and an unrelenting thunderous backbeat, became a surprise teen sensation. A somewhat gruelling, but ultimately enlightened rock record. Worth more than a passing glance.

Hellion; Electric Eye; Riding On The Wind; Bloodstone; Pain And Pleasure; (Take These) Chains; Screaming For Vengance; You've Got Another Thing Comin'; Fever; Devil's Child.

First released 1982
UK peak chart position: 11
USA peak chart position: 17

21. Blizzard Of Oz
Ozzy Osborne

After the quiet implosion of Black Sabbath, the clever money wasn't on former vocalist , Ozzy, being the one to redeem himself musically. Though, with shrewd management and a hotshot Californian in the shape of ex-Quiet Riot guitarist, Randy Rhoads, he reinvented himself, his musical persona and created a startling debut album. Combining Rhoads' impetuous flurries of heavily stylised guitar and his own series of lyrical caricatures; 'Crazy Train', 'Revelation (Mother Earth)', and a healthy dose of controversy, sighting renowned Satanist Aleister Crowley as the subject matter for 'Mr. Crowley', he ensured himself acclaim and commerciality in equal measure.

I Don't Know; Crazy Train; Goodbye To Romance; Dee; Suicide Solution; Mr. Crawley; No Bone Movies; Revelation (Mother Earth); Steal Away (The Night).

First released 1980
UK peak chart position: 7
USA peak chart position: 21

22. Moving Pictures
Rush

The Canadian trio's new found technological musing, which infuriated their more traditionally minded audience, came to a glorious fruition with this record. The organic sensibilities of their quite excellent musicianship, combined with their dextrous inventiveness made for a diverse and compelling record. Adapting a surprise reggae beat for, 'Vital Signs', while drummer Neil Peart's literary leanings were much in evidence with a goggle eyed adaptation of John Dos Passos', 'USA Trilogy', for the mini epic, 'The Camera Eye'. Creating a rich mesh of styles that is somehow both restrained and wildly evocative in the same instant. Reassuringly mature stuff.

Tom Sawyer; Red Barchetta; YYZ; Limelight; The Camera Eye; Witch Hunt; (Part III Of Fear); Vital Signs.

First released 1981
UK peak chart position: 3
USA peak chart position: 3

23. PYROMANIA
Def Leppard

The album that elevated Def Leppard to their now familiar superstar status. The combination of Mutt Lange's lush vocal arrangements and Def Leppard's hard-bitten, riffing approach to their music, gave them an endearing and instantly accessible formula of sometimes furious rock/pop. Best typified with the excellent, 'Photograph', and the enigmatic, 'Comin' Under Fire'. While vocalist Joe Elliot's lyricism was developing with the thematic 'Vietnam War' backdrop for 'Die Hard The Hunter', and its effect on its veterans with, 'Billy's Got A Gun', hinting at their burgeoning songwriting maturity.

Rock Rock ('Til You Drop); Photograph; Stagefright; Too Late For Love; Die Hard The Hunter; Foolin'; Rock Of Ages; Comin' Under Fire; Action Not Words; Billy's Got A Gun.

First released 1983
UK peak chart position: 18
USA peak chart position: 2

24. PIECE OF MIND
Iron Maiden

That nice little chap in the padded cell on the cover of this spunky album is clearly distressed by what is contained within. He should not be worried, it is first division metal with the now departed Bruce Dickenson sounding in dynamic control. The CD version had the lead guitar strangely down in the mix, this was especially noticeable on the driving 'Flight Of Icarus'. The twin guitars of Dave Murray and Adrian Smith blend together magnificently on 'The Trooper'. Sales of this were boosted by crediting hundreds of people on the CD sleeve, including their many loyal early followers from east London.

Where Eagles Dare; Revelations; Flight Of Icarus; Die With Your Boots On; The Trooper; Still Life; Quest For Fire; Sun And Steel; To Tame A Land.

First released 1983
UK peak chart position: 3
USA peak chart position: 14

25. IRON FIST
Motorhead

From the moment it starts right up until 'Bang To Rights' there is no let up whatsoever, breakneck fast and powerful. Lemmy will always be figurehead for metal, both he and the band may not have invented the genre but they certainly define its style and attitude. Metal vocalist often have high voices (Plant, Axl and Bruce Dickenson), Lemmy is hoarse and shouts and sounds like he should be emblazoned across the back of a Lewis leather astride a Harley Davison. maybe a lyric sheet should be included for those who actually want to know what he is singing about, many others will just nod furiously to the breathtaking speed of the music. Have a lie down afterwards.

Iron Fist; Heart Of Stone; I'm The Doctor; Go To Hell; Loser; Sex And Outrage; America; Shut It Down; Speedfreak; (Don't Let 'Em) Grind Ya Down; (Don't Need) Religion; Bang To Rights.

First released 1982
UK peak chart position: 6
USA peak chart position: 174

26. RIDE THE LIGHTNING
Metallica

An album so zealously out of step with all things metal in 1984 that the music press could only look on and admonish Metallica's youthful creativity. After the heady bluster of their, *Kill 'Em All* debut, no-one expected, or seemed able to fully comprehend the restraint and comparative musical civility contained herein. From the understated, and at the time controversial suicide story, 'Fade To Black', to the heavy wings of, 'For Whom The Bell Tolls', or the incessant, 'Creeping Death', 'Ride The Lightning', remains a visionary masterpiece. One that was for years consigned to independent status. Oddly cherishable.

Fight Fire With Fire; Ride The Lightning; For Whom The Bell Tolls; Fade To Black; Trapped Under Ice; Escape; Creeping Death; The Call Of Ktulu.

RIDE THE LIGHTNING

First released 1984
UK peak chart position: 87
USA peak chart position: 100

27. STRANGERS IN THE NIGHT
UFO

Culled from their sell out 1977 tour of the USA, *Strangers In The Night* still remains an apt reminder of just what it was that made UFO such a great rock 'n' roll band. Their ear for a concise melody and their ability to truly excite as a live band was captured stunningly here. The blissful, 'Too Hot To Handle', or the escalating, 'Doctor Doctor', the thrilling, 'Out In The Streets'. Pick a point out of either of the twin albums and the result is an uncanny sense of musical clarity and powerful execution. Apart from the appalling multi-coloured, dot-to-dot sleeve, it's an exceptional package.

Natural Thing; Out In The Streets; Only You Can Rock Me; Doctor Doctor; Mother Mary; This Kid's; Love To Love; Lights Out; Rock Bottom; Too Hot To Handle; I'm A Loser; Let It Roll; Shoot Shoot.

First released 1979
UK peak chart position: 8
USA peak chart position: 42

28. MASTER OF REALITY
Black Sabbath

Black Sabbath's third album and their first real international breakthrough, peaking in the Top 10 in both the UK and US. Following on the heels of their much vaunted, *Paranoid* album, they surprised initially with the cool, 'Sweet Leaf', but retained their insightful, if not truly realising it themselves at the time, and unique stranglehold on what is now seen as the original and traditional sound of near classic heavy metal. Best sounded out in the eerie, 'Children Of The Grave' and the expressive reaches of, 'Into The Void'. A remarkable piece of work.

Sweet Leaf; After Forever; Embryo; Children Of The Grave; Lord Of This World; Solitude; Into The Void; Orchid.

First released 1971
UK peak chart position: 5
USA peak chart position: 8

29. 1984
Van Halen

Vocalist David Lee Roth's final record for the band and as such, stands as a testament of worth somewhere between high camp and high class. Eddie Van Halen's venerable, rolling guitar pulled immaculately into place, while his new found love of the keyboard gave them their first international smash with, 'Jump'. Though, it is the quite demented rush of, 'Panama', and the hilarious, 'Hot For Teacher', with Roth exuding a droll litany of school yard fantasies over a thunderous Alex Van Halen backbeat, that gives ultimate credence to the rock 'n' roll party that was the Roth/Van Halen vehicle.

Jump; Panama; Top Jimmy; Drop Dead Legs; Hot For Teacher; I'll Wait; Girl Gone Bad; House Of Pain.

First released 1984
UK peak chart position: 15
USA peak chart position: 2

30. DIVER DOWN
Van Halen

Rumoured at the time to be nothing more than a contractual obligation album, the Van Halen approach to what is in essence an album of cover tunes, turned it into an effortless party record. As tightly tuned as collections of their own material, but given an extra touch of recklessness with an indulgence that was simple, illicit fun. Showing off their roots without candour, their version of, 'Dancing In The Street', charting as a US single, pre-empting their, Hide Your Sheep tour. The album foregoing a planned UK tour, which although a major disappointment at the time, gave us in retrospect, one of the truly enjoyable, razzamatazz, rock 'n' roll albums.

Where Have All The Good Times Gone; Hang 'Em High; Cathedral; Secrets; Intruder; Oh Pretty Woman; Dancing In The Street; Little Guitar (Intro); Little Guitars; Big Bad Bill Is Sweet William Now; The Bull Bug; Happy Trails.

First released 1982
UK peak chart position: 36
USA peak chart position: 3

31. RAINBOW RISING
Rainbow

A mystical meeting of minds, Blackmore's egotistical antics juxtaposed with Dio's less than droll imagery of a Tolkeinesque nature, lead to a sweeping and quite mind-bogglingly great album. Their respective sense of the theatrical played out wilfully, from the immediate, and in this company, relatively concise, 'Tarot Woman', to the long and quite perfect stretch of, 'Stargazer'. They had, almost it seems as if by mistake, created a grandiose rock 'n' roll record that held sway with a creative and precise control that held pomposity and over self-indulgence at bay. Excellent.

Tarot Woman; Run With The Wolf; Starstruck; Do You Close Your Eyes; Stargazer; A Light In The Black.

First released 1976
UK peak chart position: 11
USA peak chart position: 48

32. LOVEDRIVE
Scorpions

The Scorpions unruly history of album artwork continued with the cover shot of this album. Gone was the implied fellatio with a Doberman pinscher, or the naked photograph of a pre-pubescent girl, Lovedrive, adopted a couple seated in the back of a car. His hand pulling what looked like a yard of bubble gum from her right breast. Thankfully, not a concept album Lovedrive's musical content was not, unlike its cover, left wanting. Their ramshackle, if faint-hearted misogyny was still intact. But their musical elegance; 'Coast To Coast', 'Always Somewhere', 'Loving You Sunday Morning', still shone brilliantly through.

Loving You Sunday Morning; Another Piece Of Meat; Always Somewhere; Coast To Coast; Can't Get Enough; Is There Anybody There?; Lovedrive; Holiday.

First released 1979
UK peak chart position: 36
USA peak chart position: 55

33. HYSTERIA
Def Leppard

Four years after their, *Pyromania* record, Def Leppard were a comparative write off. Dismissed by critics, seemingly dogged by bad luck, drummer Rick Allen losing an arm in a car accident. *Hysteria*, it seemed, had to be an album to turn heads. In retrospect, it sounded like the first true hard rock record for the CD generation. Ambitious arrangements and remixes on songs such as, Rocket, and, 'Armaggedon It', a crisp single in, 'Animal', and a dense paean to love with, 'Love Bites'. All bets were off, Def Leppard creating an intriguing language of ideas that still speaks volumes today.

Women; Rocket; Animal; Love Bites; Pour Some Sugar On Me; Armaggedon It; Gods Of War; Don't Shoot Shot Gun; Run Riot; Hysteria; Excitable; Love And Affection; I Can't Let You Be A Memory.

First released 1987
UK peak chart position: 1
USA peak chart position: 1

34. REIGN IN BLOOD
Slayer

Slayer's controversial gorefest of an album highlighted both their grasp of the extreme and the eye for an angle. Complimenting their brutal explosion of sound and bloody lyrics with artwork depicting a particularly gruesome hell, and a running controversy over the topic of, 'Angel Of Death'. Whether the song celebrated or berated the figure of Dr Josef Mengele, the infamous Auschwitz surgeon. It was, however, their taut musicianship and a sense of the absurd that made the record so great. 'Necrophobic', summing up its splendid lunacy, 'Limb dissection, amputation, from a mind deranged.' One to embalm and keep.

Angel Of Death; Piece By Piece; Necrophobic; Altar Of Sacrifice; Jesus Saves; Criminally Insane; Reborn; Epidemic; Postmortem; Raining Blood.

First released 1986
UK peak chart position: 47
USA peak chart position: 94

35. MASTER OF PUPPETS
Metallica

Metallica's irresistible rise to the top continued with their enigmatic 1986 album. A constant touring unit by this point, their combination of light and dark and their deft staccato delivery, especially on the title track, came brusquely through here. Their ever lengthening arrangements, three songs came in at over eight minutes, bolstered by the precise snap of Hetfield's vocals testified to their undeniable power. The striding, 'Battery', the darkly lit, 'Welcome Home (Sanitarium)', as well as the complex instrumental, 'Orion', all giving powerful testament to their ever developing skill and vision.

Battery; Master Of Puppets; The Thing That Should Not Be; Welcome Home (Sanitarium); Disposable Heroes; Leper Messiah; Orion; Damage Inc.

First released 1986
UK peak chart position: 41
USA peak chart position: 29

36. A VULGAR DISPLAY OF POWER
Pantera

The Texan four piece living up to all the earlier promise offered by their, *Cowboys From Hell* record. Though, it was with, *A Vulgar Display Of Power*, that their uniquely constructed components of sound and distinct aural power were tempered into more than a handful of songs. Creatively peaking with clever word play and a clear sense of sloganeering and songwriting that made them the most unlikely of singles bands. The dry rasp of 'Walk', the tight reproach of, 'Mouth For War' and the strangely anthemic and clear live favourite, 'Fucking Hostile', made them teen heroes overnight.

Mouth For War; New Level; Walk; Fucking Hostile; This Love; Rise; No Good For No One; Live In A Hole; Regular People; By Demons Be Driven; Hollow.

First released 1992
UK peak chart position: 64
USA peak chart position: 44

37. SEVENTH SON OF A SEVENTH SON
Iron Maiden

On this album Bruce Dickinson manages to sound like the late Alex Harvey on occasions and the album has very much a 70s hard rock feel about it. The playing as usual is tight exciting and quite immaculate. Whilst it looks like a traditional metal album this has enough gentle AOR moments to appeal to a much wider net. This is presumably why it topped the charts in the UK. Loads of cruifix's, tarots, demons and wonderful mumbo jumbo. Settle down with a big pile of Marvel comics, a bean bag and a pair of headphones and turn this up very very loud. You will not be disappointed.

Moonchild; Infinite Dreams; Can I Play With Madness; The Evil That Men Do; Seventh Son Of A Seventh Son; The Prophecy; The Clairvoyant; Only The Good Die Young.

First released 1988
UK peak chart position: 1
USA peak chart position: 12

38. ACE OF SPADES
Motorhead

Feted by bikers, respected by punks, Motorhead exemplified rock's outlaw chic. On *Ace Of Spades* their speed-metal attack exploded with unparalleled fury. Thrashing guitars and primitive drums underpinned vocalist/bassist Lemmy, whose blooded-throat roar enhances the trio's aggression. Mind-numbingly basic and deafeningly loud, they savage rock's pomp and circumstance, rivalling 'Louie Louie' for simplicity and excitement. Choc-full of anthems for the dispossessed (witness '(We Are) The Road Crew'), *Ace Of Spades* is a classic of its genre. Motorhead exude the same cartoon personae as the Ramones, and as a result inspire a similar affection.

Ace Of Spades; Bite The Bullet; The Chase Is Better Than The Catch; Dance; Fast And Loose; Fire Fire; The Hammer; Jailbait; Live To Win; Love Me Like A Reptile; (We Are) The Road Crew; Shoot You In The Back.

First released 1980
UK peak chart position: 4
USA peak chart position: did not chart

39. OPERATION: MINDCRIME
Queensryche

The idea in the late 80s that the concept album could attain any sort of artistic or commercial significance, was at best unfashionable. Though, Queensryche with their unlikely tale of subversion and mental manipulation (with full orchestration and choral backing) centred around prostitute turned nun, Mary, street punk, Nikki and the mysterious Dr X, brought the band to an entirely new audience. Geoff Tate's dramatic vocal swoops matched with the band's sublime eloquence, both lyrically and musically, ensured them a host of songs strong enough to stand in or out of context. Dazzling and complex, but worthy of closer inspection.

I Remember Now; Anarchy X; Revolution Calling; Operation: Mindcrime; Speak; Spreading The Disease; The Mission; Suite Sister Mary; The Needle Lies; Electric Requiem; Breaking The Silence; I Don't Believe In Love; Waiting For 22; My Empty Room; Eyes Of A Stranger.

First released 1988
UK peak chart position: 58
USA peak chart position: 50

40. TED NUGENT
Ted Nugent

With the steady decline of the Amboy Dukes and the reassuring flamboyant rise of band/guitarist, Ted Nugent, the arrival of his first solo album in 1975 came as no real surprise. His extravagant and somewhat gonzoid stage persona took full bloom on this debut. Unashamedly heavy metal in its approach, though with enough breadth to sustain interest. The stomping and still very listenable, 'Just What The Doctor Ordered', the reckless and quite wonderful loon antics of, 'Motor City Madhouse', and the vivacious, 'Stormtroopin'' all bear testament to his brash skills. Unfortunately, he's now a Damn Yankee, but this is Ted at his best, before the fire went out.

Stranglehold; Stormtroopin'; Hey Baby; Just What The Doctor Ordered; Snakeskin Cowboys; Motor City Madhouse; Where Have You Been All My Life; You Make Me Feel Right At Home; Queen Of The Forest.

First released 1975
UK peak chart position: 56
USA peak chart position: 28

41. IRON MAIDEN
Iron Maiden

The first appearance for the now infamous Eddie the 'Ead mascot for one of the most consistently successful British metal acts. It was this debut that set the tone for bassist Steve Harris' occasionally complex arrangements and a clever use of twin guitars borrowed from Judas Priest and Thin Lizzy. Though, it was Maiden's distinct use of concise rhythm changes and clever switches in tempo that set them apart. From the punky, 'Prowler', to 'Running Free', with its almost hypnotic hook, *Iron Maiden*, contained all the elements that was soon to elevate the band to Odeon status and ultimately farther still.

Prowler, Remember Tomorrow; Running Free; Phantom Of The Opera; Transylvania; Strange World; Charlotte The Harlot; Iron Maiden.

First released 1980
UK peak chart position: 4
USA peak chart position: did not chart

42. HOUSES OF THE HOLY
Led Zeppelin

Led Zeppelin at their most wilfully inventive. Displaying an eclectic irreverence for their recent history, they struck out with an assured astuteness that pretty much let them play what they felt. Consequently, the results were so genuinely original that the idea that they had any musical contemporaries suddenly seemed absurd. 'The Crunge', playing at funk rock years before the popular press had stumbled across and christened it. 'D'yer Mak'er', tossing reggae around for fun, while 'No Quarter' went on to be lifted wholesale by Pearl Jam predecessors, Mother Love Bone. At the heart and yet still ahead of their time.

The Song Remains The Same; The Rain Song; Over The Hills And Far Away; The Crunge; Dancing Days; D'yer Mak'er; No Quarter; The Ocean.

First released 1973
UK peak chart position: 1
USA peak chart position: 1

43. DR. FEELGOOD
Motley Crue

The late 80s were, like those of the World Bank, a boom time for Motley Crue. Their particular brand of trashy rock 'n' roll, teased hair and carefully manufactured sneer typified American ernomodome fodder. Bursting with irreverence, their over zealous brand of backstage antics, 'She Goes Down', 'Sticky Sweet', 'Rattlesnake Shake', combined with their newly toughened musical exterior, 'Kickstart My Heart' and the title track especially, easily ensured them a number one album in the USA. Their greatest good time moment and a guaranteed sleaze classic.

Same Old Situation; Slice Of Your Pie; Rattlesnake Shake; Kickstart My Heart; Without You; Don't Go Away Mad; She Goes Down; Sticky Sweet; Time For A Change; TNT; Dr. Feelgood; Terror In Tinseltown.

First released 1989
UK peak chart position: 4
USA peak chart position: 1

44. LOVE AT FIRST STING
Scorpions

Youthful delusion persisted in an ageing Scorpions camp with what was a quite reckless, strutting declaration of an album. A party atmosphere prevailing throughout the entire record. The same English-as-a-second-language and identikit sexuality prevailed with such dumb gems as, 'So give her inches, feed her well', 'Rock You Like A Hurricane'. 'Tie you up and you give it away', 'Bad Boys Running Wild'. But it's the heartfelt exuberance of their delivery that carries the whole thing along so well. A grand execution much in the style of contemporaries, Def Leppard, though without their deliberation or formality.

Bad Boys Running Wild; Rock You Like A Hurricane; I'm Leaving You; Coming Home; Same Thrill, The; Big City Nights; As Soon As The Good Times Roll; Crossfire; Still Loving You.

First released 1984
UK peak chart position: 17
USA peak chart position: 6

45. HEAVEN AND HELL
Black Sabbath

Probably the greatest of the attempted revampings of the Black Sabbath line-up, with Ronnie James Dio taking over as vocalist. Dio's mythological slant to his lyrics combined with a new found strictness in Butler and Iommi's writing, quickly gave them a hit single in the shape of 'Neon Knights'. While the album charted strongly on both sides of the Atlantic. The artwork also drawing attention to itself with its depiction of angels playing cards and smoking cigarettes. Strong indication at the time that there was life post-Ozzy, though one unfortunately that was not to come to any real fruition.

Neon Knights; Children Of The Sea; Lady Evil; Heaven And Hell; Wishing Well; Die Young; Walk Away; Lonely Is The World; Tomorrow's Dream.

First released 1980
UK peak chart position: 9
USA peak chart position: 28

46. BLACKOUT
Scorpions

Arguably the Scorpions finest moment. A creative crest best typified by the raucous title track. The persistent overloaded refrain of Rudolf Schenker's guitar and Klaus Meine's piercing vocal gave play to the crisp commerciality of songs such as, 'No One Like You', while still managing to uphold the death-rattle approach of, 'Can't Live Without You'. Contrary styles that sat comfortably in their engaging pan of highly polished rock 'n' roll. It comes as no surprise that on the strength of, Blackout, the Scorpions began their ascent out of Europe and into the American heartland. Still refreshingly bombastic.

Blackout; Can't Live Without You; You Give Me All I Need; Now; No One Like You; Dynamite; Arizona; China White; When The Smoke Is Going Down.

First released 1982
UK peak chart position: 11
USA peak chart position: 10

47. SHOUT AT THE DEVIL
Motley Crue

The Crue's first stab at major label stardom after the success of their independent Leathur Records debut, *Too Fast For Love*. Elektra went all out for infamy with a gatefold sleeve package complete with a translucent pentagram adorning their logo. Musically, it was more of the same, the anthemic title track, the instant clarity of, 'Looks That Kill', with its wasteland and warriors video. While their troubled history with the LAPD was raked over for, 'Knock 'Em Dead Kid' .All of this and a trashy cover of, 'Helter Skelter'. Their capacity for stardom seemed infinite.

In The Beginning; Shout At The Devil; Looks That Kill; Bastard; Knock 'Em Dead Kid; Danger; Too Young To Fall In Love; Helter Skelter; Red Hot; Ten Seconds 'Til Love; God Bless The Children Of The Beast.

First released 1983
UK peak chart position: did not chart
USA peak chart position: 17

48. LOOK WHAT THE CAT DRAGGED IN
Poison

A roving party waiting to happen on eight spindly legs was this Poison's first and finest moment. It was this record that set the standard for 80s, west coast, trash pop and big hair. No mean achievement for a band who valued eyeliner prices over devotion to their musical duties. At the end of the day however, it made no difference. 'Cry Tough', 'I Want Action', 'Talk Dirty To Me', helped them create a truly great glam album. Obviously because they were enjoying themselves as much as we were. These days, however, they keep talking about being taken seriously, unsurprisingly, the magic has all now gone.

Cry Tough; I Want Action; I Won't Forget You; Play Dirty; Look What The Cat Dragged In; Talk Dirty To Me; Want Some, Need Some; Blame It On You; No.1 Bad Boy ; Let Me Go To The Show.

First released 1986
UK peak chart position: did not chart
USA peak chart position: 3

49. BLACK SABBATH VOL 4
Black Sabbath

One of the great Heavy Metal albums. Their initial assault on the senses with their debut album may have surprised both critics and the public, but it was the creative flux of Vol 4 that really shaped and defined their vision and abilities. From the piano/vocal of, 'Changes' the driving, 'Snowblind', to the somewhat quirky, 'Laguna Sunrise', the mood was one of invention and without restriction. Afterwards, the wayward determination of their respective imaginations was to cause dissent and dissolution within the band. But for this moment, at least, their free rein of ideas was near perfect in execution.

Wheels Of Confusion; Tomorrow's Dream; Changes; FX; Supernaut; Snowblind; Cornucopia; Laguna Sunrise; St Vitas Dance; Under The Sun.

First released 1972
UK peak chart position:8
USA peak chart position: 13

50. THE REAL THING
Faith No More

The San Francisco five piece created, with the help of new vocalist, Mike Patton, a sound and approach to their music that was to turn any preconceptions of what hard rock should or should not be on its head. By turns whimsical and doggedly creative, even its lyrical slant confounded expectations. Patton adopting the first person with a baby's viewpoint for, 'Zombie Eaters', while for, 'Edge Of The World', he became the leering paedophile. While the music tumbled from expressionless jams to intricate piano work and a nagging grasp of the perfect hook. A surreal gem.

From Out Of Nowhere; Epic; Falling To Pieces; Surprise You're Dead; Zombie Eaters; Real Thing, The; Underwater Love; Edge Of The World; Morning After, The; Woodpecker From Mars.

First released 1990
UK peak chart position: 30
USA peak chart position: 11

THE TOP 50
INDIE ALBUMS

INDIE IS THE HARDEST CATEGORY TO DEFINE. THE OLD DEFINITION OF BEING INDEPENDENTLY PRODUCED AND DISTRIBUTED IS NOW OUTMODED AS THESE DAYS A MAJOR LABEL NEED ONLY WAVE A CHEQUE BOOK AND IT HAS ITS OWN INDIE BAND.
INDIE IS MAINLY GUITAR-BASED POP, AS SEEN FROM THIS LIST

1. STONE ROSES
Stone Roses

Manchester's most likely to, who escaped independent status after a lengthy court battle, signed to Geffen and then promptly disappeared. Rumours abound around the album's imminent release, with vocalist Ian Brown allegedly writing a brief terse, None of your business note to one magazine. Why the fuss and impatience? Quite simply put, their debut album had all the markings of greatness. A Byrds-like listlessness that caused listeners to swoon in wonder and slip quietly beneath the surface. 'Waterfall' and 'She Bangs The Drum', sublime and quietly brilliant, and, of course, creating incredible pressure for that all important second album. This was a winner by a mile.

I Wanna Be Adored; She Bangs The Drum; Waterfall; Don't Stop; Bye Bye Badman; Elizabeth My Dear; (Song For My) Sugar Spun Sister; Made Of Stone; Shoot You Down; This Is The One; I Am The Resurrection.

First released 1989
UK peak chart position: 19
USA peak chart position: 86

2. THE QUEEN IS DEAD
Smiths

Arguably the Smiths' masterpiece album, *The Queen Is Dead* shows a group expanding horizons without sacrificing their unique sound. Vocalist Morrissey retains his self-centred romanticism, but articulates his anguish through a successions of engaging melodies, notably 'The Boy With The Thorn In His Side'. The singer's flippant persona surfaces on 'Frankly, Mr. Shankly' and 'Vicar In A Tutu', while Johnny Marr's multi-layered guitar work is best heard on the abrasive title track. This album shows a group aware of its strengths, but unafraid to build and expand upon them.

Frankly, Mr. Shankly; I Know It's Over; Never Had No One Ever; Cemetery Gates; Big Mouth Strikes Again; Vicar In A Tutu; There Is A Light That Never Goes Out; Some Girls Are Bigger Than Others; The Queen Is Dead; The Boy With The Thorn In His Side.

First released 1986
UK peak chart position: 2
USA peak chart position: 70

3. PSYCHOCANDY
Jesus And Mary Chain

A love of classic pop songs and sonic terrorism conspire on this euphoric collection. Fuzz guitar, distortion and feedback drench almost every track, but beneath this assertive noise lies a gift for melody inspired by the Beach Boys and girl-group genre. The contrast is beguiling and if the constituent parts are not original, the audacity of such a combination is. Understated voices and nihilistic lyrics belie the intensity forged within. Created by passionate adherents of pop culture, *Psychocandy* is one of the 80s landmark releases, inspiring some to follow a similar course, while others took similar influences to forge a quite different perspective.

Just Like Honey; The Living End; Taste The Floor; Hardest Walk; Cut Dead; In A Hole; Taste Of Cindy; Never Understand; It's So Hard; Inside Me; Sowing Seeds; My Little Underground; You Trip Me Up; Something's Wrong.

First released 1985
UK peak chart position: 31
USA peak chart position: 188

4. THE SMITHS
Smiths

As great first albums go, *The Smiths*, remains a perfect bedsitter moment. Cultivated from a batch of Morrissey's diaries then uplifted and exonerated on Marr's guitar. Their juxtaposing of a lop sided grin of gloom and the light doodling of an almost always perfectly placed guitar was virtually unheard of. Reference points were rare, apart from Morrissey's adopted Oscar Wilde demeanour, which the press clung to with a morbid fascination. It remains a delicate set of knowing quiffs and rounded, innocent eyes, beguiling the listener with some wonderfully crafted pop. When they weren't laughing behind their hands.

Reel Around The Fountain; You've Got Everthing Now; Miserable Lie; Pretty Girls Make Graves; The Hand That Rocks The Cradle; Still Ill; Hand In Glove; What Difference Does It Make?; I Don't Owe You Anything; Suffer Little Children.

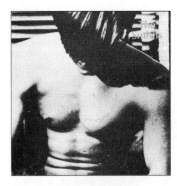

First released 1984
UK peak chart position: 2
USA peak chart position: 150

5. SCREAMADELICA
Primal Scream

Primal Scream's understanding of rock's varied vistas is encapsulated on this release. At its core are a series of dance-oriented tracks which broached several musical barriers. Samples, tape loops, dub and plangent chords gell together over various grooves, at time uplifting, at other ambient. Mixmasters Terry Farley and Andy Weatherall add different perspectives to individual tracks, with gospel choirs, pumping brass and spaceward basslines bubbling around several selections. Former Rolling Stones producer Jimmy Miller induced the spirit of Beggars' Banquet to the rousing 'Movin' On Up', while elsewhere the group imply acknowledgement to talismen the Beach Boys and Big Star. *Screamadelica* is the ultimate confluence of rock and rave cultures.

Movin' On Up; Slip Inside This House; Don't Fight It, Feel It; Higher Than The Sun; Inner Flight; Come Together; Loaded; Damaged; I'm Comin' Down; Higher Than The Sun (A Dub Symphony In Two Parts); Shine Like The Stars.

First released 1991
UK peak chart position: 8
USA peak chart position: did not chart

6. LIFE
Inspiral Carpets

The Inspiral Carpets emerged from Manchester's rave/club scene alongside the Stone Roses and Happy Mondays. Each of these groups fused a dance groove to 60s' styled pop, the Carpets' brand of psychedelia fashioned by Clint Boon's Vox-styled organ work. Taking inspiration from garage-bands and the Doors, he adds a distinctive flourish to the band's grasp of simple, commercial melodies. *Life* is the unit's first full-length album, following three EPs and a selection drawn from John Peel sessions. It captures their enthusiastic slant of a genre briefly in vogue, one to which they brought humour and a refreshing eclecticism.

Real Thing; Song For A Family; This Is How It Feels; Directing Traffik; Besides Me; Many Happy Returns; Memories Of You; She Comes In The Fall; Monkey On My Back; Sun Don't Shine; Inside My Head; Move; Sackville.

First released 1990
UK peak chart position: 2
USA peak chart position: did not chart

7. SUEDE
Suede

Suede played intellectual hi-jinks with this their debut album, provocative lyrics, a weighty, unknowing sexuality and the pointed angst of troubled teenagers the world over. The clever draw of their androgynous artwork combined tellingly with Bret Anderson's teasing flamboyance and dedicated, some might say studied, David Bowie air. Though, they would have remained a one trick pony were it not for their stirring ability to put together some unashamedly great singles and adapt a host of subtle mood swings and arrangements that took Anderson's vocals to soaring new heights. Another bedsitter classic for indie lovers.

So Young; Animal Nitrate; She's Not Dead; Moving; Pantomime Horse; The Drowners; Sleeping Pills; Breakdown; Metal Mickey; Animal Lover; The Next Life.

First released 1992
UK peak chart position: 1
USA peak chart position: did not chart

8. CLOSER
Joy Division

The news of singer Ian Curtis' suicide still hung in the air when this album was released. Given the deep introspective nature of Joy Division's music, his death invested *Closer* with an even greater pessimism. Yet there is a fragile beauty in its content and if Curtis' voice seems more distant, it compliments the sparse textures created by mesmerising synthesiser lines and occasional, highly effective, piano. Slow, hypnotic tempos increase the sense of brooding mystery and if the few faster songs provide musical relief, their lyrics prove equally tortured. Eerie, yet compulsive, *Closer* confirmed Joy Divison's pre-eminent place in rock's pantheon.

Heart And Soul; 24 Hours; Eternal; Decades; Atrocity Exhibition; Isolation; Passover; Colony; Means To An End.

First released 1980
UK peak chart position: 6
USA peak chart position: did not chart

9. RUM SODOMY & THE LASH
Pogues

The Elvis Costello produced, *Rum .Sodomy & The Lash*, a title taken from Winston Churchill's description of life in the Royal Navy apparently, was the creative apex of their lolling, folky output. Shane MacGowan's rolling lilt called to expound upon the rich lyrical tinge of, 'A Pair Of Brown Eyes' and 'Dirty Old Town'. While their ragged glory, dipping from a whisper to a powerful roar, shone through with 'The Old Main Drag' and 'I'm A Man You Don't Meet Every Day', utilising their sometime sumptuous rasp. A fiercely unique record alive with abandon and a carefree soul.

The Sick Bed Of Cúchulainn; The Old Main Drag; Wild Cats Of Kilkenny; I'm A Man You Don't Meet Every Day; A Pair Of Brown Eyes; Sally Maclennane; Dirty Old Town; Jesse James; Navigator; Billy's Bones; The Gentleman Solder; And The Band Played Waltzing Matilda.

First released 1985
UK peak chart position: 13
USA peak chart position: did not chart

10. COPPER BLUE
Sugar

Having disbanded the hugely influential Husker Du, guitarist/vocalist Bob Mould embarked on a solo career during which he completed two contrasting albums. He then founded this power-packed trio, which resurrected the tone of his earlier group. *Copper Blue* sees Mould still firmly in control of his art, his barking voice enveloped by loud, crushing guitar and a succession of exhilarating hooklines. The album possesses awesome power and drive, but beyond the speed and distortion lies an understanding of the mechanics of classic pop songs, short, sharp and highly memorable. Mould is a crafted composer, *Copper Blue* shows his grasp of dynamics is as sure as ever.

The Act We Act; A Good Idea; Changes; Helpless; Hoover Dam; The Slim; If I Can't Change Your Mind; Fortune Teller; Slick; Man On The Moon.

First released 1992
UK peak chart position: 10
USA peak chart position: did not chart

11. THE BEAST INSIDE
Inspiral Carpets

Never regarded as the artistic elite of the Madchester scene (although, of course, they were not actually from Manchester itself), the Inspiral Carpets have nevertheless produced a body of work which, if not paralleling the one-off impact of the Stone Roses, has marked them out as consistent achievers. The best of their albums are *Life* and this one, which maintains the group's traditions (a big organ sound, character-based lyrics, bad haircuts) yet also saw a bolder songwriting effort which had them reach inwards in furtherance of the reportage expressed on their debut album.

Caravan; Please Be Cruel; Born Yesterday; Sleep Well Tonight; Grip; Beast Inside; Niagara; Mermaid; Further Away; Dreams Are All We Have.

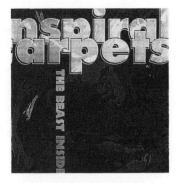

First released 1991
UK peak chart position: 5
USA peak chart position: did not chart

12. TALKING WITH THE TAXMAN ABOUT POETRY
Billy Bragg

Agitpop's aggrieved and finely humoured singer/songwriter, Billy Bragg gave full vent to his impassioned view of the world with the excellent, *Talking With The Taxman About Poetry*. Less fully blown in execution than, *Brewing Up*, or his mini, *Life's A Riot With Spy Vs Spy* album, his finally honed angst remained intact nevertheless. With his pungent and almost always topical material sitting comfortably alongside a new and instantly more accessible batch of songs. The wonderfully arch, 'Greetings To The New Brunette', and the uplifting, 'Levi Stubbs Tears', indicative of Bragg's quickly developing craft.

Greetings To The New Brunette; Train Train; The Marriage; Ideology; Levi Stubbs Tears; Honey I'm A Big Boy Now; There Is Power In A Union; Help Save The Youth Of America; Wishing The Days Away; The Passion; The Warmest Room; The Home Front.

First released 1986
UK peak chart position: 8
USA peak chart position: did not chart

13. PILLS THRILLS AND BELLYACHES
Happy Mondays

The sound of Madchester baggydom could be heard going to the wall with this album. A creative peak for the whole scene and the Mondays especially. Shaun Ryder's laconic vocal dips creating some real ambience and body for their swaying and almost graceful dancing backdrops. It was his clever, almost punning wordplay and sometimes wonderfully obscure vocal and lyrical chatter combined with Mark Day's surprisingly credible guitar work that helped create a stylish, if loose fitting album. 'Kinky Afro', 'Step On', 'Holiday', all charming and charmed, long before anyone could see them falling away.

Kinky Afro; God's Cop; Donovan; Grandbag's Funeral; Loose Fit; Dennis And Lois; Bob's Yer Uncle; Step On; Holiday; Harmony.

First released 1990
UK peak chart position: 4
USA peak chart position: 89

14. MEAT IS MURDER
Smiths

The second Smiths' album expanded upon the twin flight paths of its predecessor; singer Morrissey's unabashed solipsism and Johnny Marr's textured guitar playing. Opening with the plangent 'Headmaster's Ritual', *Meat Is Murder* brings both these facets into sharp focus with layers of sound supporting the singer's confessional, singsong style. Bittersweet humour and rampant profligacy mark the album's lyrical content, no more so than on the indignant, pro-vegetarian title track. Rhythm section Rouke and Joyce provide a supple spine for the group's two sparring partners, keeping both their potential excesses in check. Self-indulgent? Yes; but brilliantly so.

The Headmaster Ritual; Barbarism Begins At Home; Rusholme Ruffians; I Want The One I Can't Have; What She Said; Nowhere Fast; That Joke Isn't Funny Anymore; Well I Wonder; Meat Is Murder.

First released 1985
UK peak chart position: 1
USA peak chart position: 110

15. SURFER ROSA
Pixies

The Boston-based Pixies exploded into life with this abrasive selection. Produced by enfante-terrible Steve Albini, the album emphasised the quartet's scratchy tension. A vicious drum sound underpins the group's uncanny blend of urgency and melody, where Black Francis' rabid intonation contrasts Kim Deal's more gentle perspective. Obtuse lyrics and barely-controlled guitar accentuate the Pixies uncompromising visions and emphasis an approach that both excites and intrigues. Terse, exhilarating and single-minded, *Surfer Rosa* is an audacious collection.

Bone Machine; Something Against You; Gigantic; Where Is My Mind?; Tony's Theme; Vamos; Brick Is Red; Break My Body; Broken Face; River Euphrates; Cactus; Oh My Golly!; I'm Amazed.

First released 1988
UK peak chart position: did not chart
USA peak chart position: did not chart

16. THE WONDERFUL AND FRIGHTENING WORLD OF
Fall

The eighth Fall album consolidated the abrasive sextet's relationship with producer John Leckie, who helped expand their musical palate without sacrificing individuality. The presence of guitarist Laura Elise, better-known as Brix Smith, expanded the unit's tonal capabilities, but they remain firmly a vehicle in which singer Mark Smith vented his spleen. His vitriolic lyrics were as uncompromising as ever, even if now-accustomed dissonance is occasionally paired with neo-psychedelic nuances. *The Frightening World* captures the Fall as they expand their frame of reference and in the process gain recognition for their highly original music.

Lay Of The Land; 2 x 4; Copped It; Elves; Oh! Brother; Draygo's Guilt; God-box; Clear Off; C.R.E.E.P.; Pat-Trip Dispenser; Slang King; Bug Day; Stephen Song; Craigness; Disney's Dream Debased; No Bulbs.

First released 1984
UK peak chart position: 62
USA peak chart position: did not chart

17. YOU CAN'T HIDE YOUR LOVE FOREVER
Orange Juice

Orange Juice was the leading attraction on Glasgow's feted Postcard label. Critical plaudits followed the release of their first four singles and much was expected from this debut album. The insouciant charm of their windblown pop was emphasised by a clear production which focused on singer Edwyn Collins' sonorous croon. Songs echoing the strains of classic west coast pop deal with sorrow and rejection, a fragility matched by the group's still-untutored playing in which their aspirations outstripped technical abilities. Their continued desires to broach preconceived barriers is what gives this album its implicit strength.

Falling And Laughing; Untitled Melody; Wan Light; Tender Object; Dying Day; L.O.V.E.; Intuition Told Me; Upwards And Onwards; Satellite City; Three Cheers For Our Side; Consolation Prize; Felicity; In A Nutshell.

First released 1982
UK peak chart position: 21
USA peak chart position: did not chart

18. STUTTER
James

Yet another product of Manchester's impressive scene, James offered this brash, folk-styled pop selection as their debut album following acclaimed singles for the Factory label. Produced by former Patti Smith Group guitarist Lenny Kaye, it opened with the eccentric 'Skullduggery' and proceeded in a quirky, unconventional manner. Complex arrangements and unorthodox lyrics abound, while vocalist Tim Booth accentuates the loose arrangements with highly-stylised vocals which demand attention. An expanded line-up would gain commercial success with a much different sound. *Stutter* captures James during their formative, experimental era.

Skullduggery; Scarecrow; So Many Ways; Just Hipper; John Yen; Summer Songs; Really Hard; Billy's Shirts; Why So Close; Withdrawn; Black Hole.

First released 1986
UK peak chart position: 68
USA peak chart position: did not chart

19. BOSS DRUM
Shamen

The Shamen began their career as a retro-psychedelic band, but a combined love of technology and dance-floor beats brought them into the acid-house culture. Boss Drum exhibits the many styles making up their complex interests, from the irascible rap of 'Ebeneezer Goode' to the transcendalism of 'Re-Evolution', a lengthy slice of blissed-out sound which features narration from psychoactive lecturer Terrence McKenna. Compulsive rhythms, nagging tunes and a sense of spiritualised commitment bring together such disparate elements which express the many facets of 90s rave music without losing sight of the Shamen's own identity.

Boss Drum; LSI; Love Sex Intelligence; Space Time; Librae Solidi Denari; Ebeneezer Goode Beatmasters Mix; Comin' On; Phoever People; Fatman; Scientas; Re-Evolution.

First released 1992
UK peak chart position: 3
USA peak chart position: did not chart

20. LOW-LIFE
New Order

New Order evolved from the rump of Joy Division following the death of vocalist Ian Curtis. The course they followed contrasted that of their former incarnation, exploring a heady mix of techno-styled dance tracks and melodic soundscapes. *Low-Life* captured the quartet in eclectic mood, taking an electronic muse through diffuse material. It boasts two of New Order's finest-ever songs, the ballad-styled 'Love Vigilantes' and lush 'The Perfect Kiss', while elsewhere the quartet explore different facets of their sound without losing cohesion. This acclaimed release finally confirmed New Order as an act in its own right.

Sooner Than You Think; Sub Culture; Face Up; Love Vigilantes; Elegie; The Perfect Kiss; This Time Of NIght; Sunrise.

First released 1985
UK peak chart position: 7
USA peak chart position: 94

21. BANDWAGONESQUE
Teenage Fanclub

Teenage Fanclub emerged from a fraternal milieu centred on the Scottish town of Bellshill. A common love of pop tradition bound the quartet together and elements of their mentors abound on this collection. Neil Young and Big Star are obvious reference points, but the Fanclub are not merely copyist. Dizzy melodies, longhair guitar and unpretentiousness abound, the set's attraction ultimately resting in a cumulative, carefree charm. An impishness enhances the entire proceedings; only the churlish can resist its obvious attractions.

The Concept; Satan; December; What You Do To Me; I Don't Know; Star Sign; Metal Baby; Pet Rock; Sidewinder; Alcoholiday; Guiding Star; Is This Music?.

First released 1991
UK peak chart position: 22
USA peak chart position: 137

22. Brotherhood
New Order

A set which marked a departure in the New Order sound, their previous album, *Low-Life*, having seen them reach the pinnacle of the original vision. *Brotherhood* brought a more pop-orientated electronic vein, with the synthesizers being given ever greater prominence. The group maintained its fan base, thanks to songs like 'Bizarre Love Triangle', and 'Weirdo', but from here on in New Order were no longer the plaything of a handful of bedroom-based students, but the larger pop world, being placed back to back with the Pet Shop Boys in the field of intelligent electronic synth pop. Which in itself was a remarkable transition.

Paradise; Weirdo; As It Was When It Was; Broken Promise; Way Of Life; Bizarre Love Triangle; All Day Long; Angel Dust; Every Little Counts; State Of The Nation.

First released 1986
UK peak chart position: 9
USA peak chart position: 117

23. BOSSANOVA
Pixies

With a keen sense of the absurd, Black Francis', now Frank Black, Pixies were the consummate English press darlings. No surprise with their refreshing mix of overblown guitars, the old, discreet nod to the surreal and a vibrant grasp of pure pop that became a luscious blow to the senses on execution. 'Cecilia Ann', standing somewhere between spandex metal and 'Beach Blanket Bingo'. The deranged singalong of, 'Is She Weird', while the first single, 'Velouria', underlined their ability to write timeless singles that filled the head and sent your toes tapping incessantly out of time. Reformation now!

Cecilia Ann; Velouria; Is She Weird; All Over The World; Down To The Well; Blown Away; Stormy Weather; Rock Music; Allison; Ana; Dig For Fire; The Happening; Hang Wire; Havalina.

First released 1990
UK peak chart position: 3
USA peak chart position: 70

24. ISN'T ANYTHING
My Bloody Valentine

Where earlier recordings showed a group struggling to find its niche, Isn't Anything established My Bloody Valentine's uncompromising art. Layers of feedback and guitars laid a tapestry of sound into which they sank delicate harmonies. The final effect was not necessarily aggressive, although on '(When You Wake)' and 'Feed Me With Your Kiss' the quartet unveil a remarkable power. Elsewhere the combination results in a hypnotic wash of sound, punctuated by fevered drumming, heavy bass and hooks which take unexpected twists and turns. Isn't Anything is a highly inventive release.

Soft As ? (But Warm Inside); Lose My Breach; Cupid Come; (When You Wake) You're Still A Dream; No More Sorry; All I Need; Feed Me With Your Kiss; ?; Several Girls Galore; You Never Should; Nothing Much To Lose; I Can See It (But I Can't Feel It).

First released 1988
UK peak chart position: did not chart
USA peak chart position: did not chart

25. THE NATION'S SAVING GRACE
Fall

As stubbornly maverick as ever, the Falls' tenth album hinges on their now-accustomed dissonance, into which a tighter, commercial edge was introduced. New guitarist Brix Smith, wife of leader Mark E., added a partly-melodious sheen which brought an air of 60s subculture to the group's post-industrial rattle. Nothing was sacrificed in the process and while 'Bombast' hurtles with a vicious power, talismen Can were acknowledged in 'I Am Damo Suzuki', the name of the German band's Japan-born singer. Mark Smith towers over the proceedings, his voice prowling about the music, enhancing its intensity. This album shows the Fall extending stylistic barriers without sacrificing their individuality.

Mansion; Bombast; Barmy; What You Need; Spoilt Victorian Child; LA; Vixen; Couldn't Get Ahead; Gut Of The Quantifier; My New House; Paintwork; I Am Damo Suzuki; To NK Roachment: Yarbles; Petty (Thief) Lout; Rollin' Danyy; Cruisers Creek.

First released 1985
UK peak chart position: 54
USA peak chart position: did not chart

26. YOUNG AND STUPID
Josef K

This posthumous release collects material from one of Edinburgh's leading post-punk attractions. Matching Thin White Duke-period Bowie with abrasive pop, they joined Orange Juice on the cult Postcard label. Several tracks culled from that period are accompanied by recordings drawn from the John Peel Show, compilations and abandoned first draft's from sessions for the quartet's debut album. *Young And Stupid* also features one side from Josef K's first single and in doing so completes the definitive overview of a short-lived but fascinating act.

Heart Of Song; Endless Soul; Citizens; Variation Of Scene; It's Kinda Funny; Sorry For Laughing; Chance Meeting; Heaven Sent; Drone; Sense Of Guilt; Revelation; Romance.

First released 1989
UK peak chart position: did not chart
USA peak chart position: did not chart

27. DAYDREAM NATION
Sonic Youth

A double album that alerted Sonic Youth to a wider audience and the eager interest of a handful of major labels. *Daydream Nation*, with its sleepy single candle flickering silently on the gatefold cover, harnessed their reckless live favourite, 'Teenage Riot'. while they ran gloriously roughshod from, 'Rain King' to 'Silver Rocket', to the overtly camp glee of 'Trilogy' which came with parts a, b and z. Their assured ascension to festival billing and the giant Geffen label came as no surprise to anyone that had heard it.

Teenage Riot; Silver Rocket; The Sprawl; 'Cross The Breeze; Eric's Trip; Total Trash; Hey Joni; Providence; ?; Rain King; Kissability; Triology: a) The Wonder b) Hyperstation c) Eliminator Jr.

First released 1988
UK peak chart position: 99
USA peak chart position: did not chart

28. SHIFT WORK
Fall

Shift Work is divided into two parts, both exhuming the doom that was prevelent for the unprivelidged during Thatcher's reign. Mark Smith illuminates his feelings with some of his finest sneer/slur vocals. Part 1, Earth's Impossible Day and Part 2, Notebooks Out Plagiarists - both essential listening. The Fall churn out great albums, quickly and quietly, they need to be noisy so that the rest of the world can catch up with an incredible band that should be compared alongside The Smiths as giants of thinking persons irreverent music. Mark E. Smith's time will surely come, even though he is leaving it a bit late.

"Earths Impossible Day": So What About It?; Idiot Joy Showland; Edinburgh Man; Pittsville Direkt; The Book Of Lies; High Tension Line; The War Against Intelligence; "Notebooks Out Plagiarists": Shift-Work; You Haven't Found It Yet; The Mixer; White Lightning; A Lot Of Wind; Rose; Sinister Waltz.

First released 1991
UK peak chart position: 17
USA peak chart position: did not chart

29. Unknown Pleasures
Joy Division

Joy Division's music inhabits an eerie, twilight world. Decay and alienation envelop singer Ian Curtis, whose cavernous, but dispassionate, voice belied the intensity he brought to bear. Rolling drum patterns, thudding bass lines and uncluttered synthesiser create a dank, brooding atmosphere, chillingly supporting the songs' bleak lyrics. Yet listening to *Unknown Pleasures* is not a depressing experience. The group generate a terse excitement, honing in on individual strengths and avoiding unnecessary embellishment. Their sense of commitment is utterly convincing and few debut albums can boast such unremitting power.

Disorder; Day Of The Lords; Candidate; Insight; New Dawn Fades; She's Lost Control; Shadow Play; Wilderness; Interzone.

First released 1979
UK peak chart position: 71
USA peak chart position: did not chart

30. YOUR ARSENAL
Morrissey

Produced by the late Mick Ronson this record has incredible tension, long before the overblown and unnecessary Morrissey/Rogan fued started. Beat group echoes, doom-laden lyrics and a full atmosphere that conjures memories of Johnny Kidd And The Pirates, The Ventures and the Pretenders. Solo artists often mellow out and mature. On this superlative recording Morrissey paradoxically rocks more than ever and shows further creative maturity. 'You're Gonna Need Someone On Your Side' and 'Glamorous Glue are only two reasons to buy this album. How many more lyrical odes has he got left.

You're Gonna Need Someone On Your Side; Glamours Glue; We'll Let You Know; The National Front Disco; Certain People I Know; We Hate It When Our Friends Become Successful; You're The One For Me, Fatty; Seasick, Yet Still Docked; I Know It's Gonna Happen Someday.

First released 1993
UK peak chart position: 4
USA peak chart position: 21

31. DOOLITTLE
Pixies

The album which brought the Pixies commercial acclaim did so without self-sacrifice. Hammered chords, twisting melodies and obtuse lyrics still abound, pulled together and given new purpose by Gil Norton's incisive production. Black Francis and Kim Deal share the vocal spoils, providing the content with contrasting texture. The raw anger of 'Debaser' is offset by the aurally sweet 'Monkey Gone To Heaven', while elsewhere killer tunes confirm a collective love of pop. Where later releases showed increasing schizophrenia, *Doolittle* fully captures the Pixies' unified zeal.

Debaser; I Bleed; Wave Of Mutilation; Dead; Mr. Grieves; La La Love You; There Goes My Gun; Silver; Tame; Here Comes Your Man; Monkey Gone To Heaven; Crackity Jones; No. 13 Baby; Hey; Gouge Away.

First released 1989
UK peak chart position: 8
USA peak chart position: 98

32. PORNOGRAPHY
Cure

Before Cure founder Robert Smith drew up his archetype for eccentric pop and a fresh sense of lament that turned his band into an arena act in the USA, the Cure's leanings were more darkly felt. Pornography, a beautifully still and deep record is a room full of shadows. Ambient in part, and occasionally challenging, its vision, even down to the oddly distorted photo on the cover, was one darkly wrapped. smith's yelp of a vocal rising and falling in and out of the light. while 'Hanging Gardens' hinted at his yet untapped, but clearly commercial bent.

Pornography; The Hanging Gardens; One Hundred Years; Siamese Twins; Figurehead; A Strange Day; Cold; A Short Term Effect.

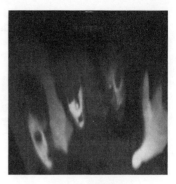

First released 1982
UK peak chart position: 8
USA peak chart position: did not chart

33. CROCODILES
Echo And The Bunnymen

Echo And The Bunnymen was formed by vocalist Ian McCulloch on sundering his partnership with Julian Cope in the Crucial Three. The singer's melange of Jim Morrison and Lou Reed is encapsulated on this engaging album, which matched persuasive melodies to a moody air of doom. It included a re-recording of the quartet's first single, 'Pictures On The Wall' and the anthem-like 'All That Jazz', but while the musicians invested each track with a taught precision, especially guitarist Will Sergeant, *Crocodiles*' strength is derived from McCulloch's stylish vocals. He adds a new dimension to already strong material, a factor investing the set with its lasting appeal.

Going Up; Stars Are Stars; Pride; Monkeys; Crocodiles; Rescue; Villiers Terrace; Pictures On The Wall; All That Jazz; Happy Death Man.

First released 1980
UK peak chart position: 17
USA peak chart position: did not chart

34. DRY
PJ Harvey

The West Country chanteuse with a credible line in extolling the virtues of sex and who came with a wealth of emotional baggage that she was more than willing to share. Her public persona, a mix of nudity wrapped in clingfilm, or draped with a feather boa and arch, accentuated sunglasses, while her songs bristle with fragility and pain and then, occasionally, a surly inner strength. Now more widely acknowledged with her excellent, 'Rid Of Me' and '4 Track Demo', *Dry* was the bedrock that she built her tower of emotions on. The gritty, 'Victory', the surprisingly light, 'Water' the evocative, 'Happy And Bleeding'. A crushing masterpiece.

Oh My Lover; O Stella; Dress; Victory; Happy And Bleeding; Rid Of Me; Hair; Joe; Plants And Rags; 4 Track Demo; Water.

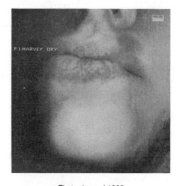

First released 1992
UK peak chart position: 11
USA peak chart position: did not chart

35. DEBUT
Bjork

One of the most pleasingly quizzical and quite unexpected first albums. Though, Bjork's animated meandering with the Sugarcubes hinted at a deeply singular approach to songwriting, the depth and inventiveness employed for *Debut*, went far beyond the imagined or expected. Bringing new meaning to the word unorthodox, 'There's More To Life Than This', recorded live in the toilet of a club, replete with slamming doors. While the fragility of the human condition was expounded on in reflections of love and sex, each point wonderfully adorned by the rise and fall of her yearning vocal. A true delight.

Human Behaviour; Crying; Venus As A Boy; There's More To Life Than This; Like Someone In Love; Big Time Sensuality; One Day; Aeroplane; Come To Me; Violently Happy; The Anchor Song.

First released 1993
UK peak chart position: 3
USA peak chart position: 61

36. KILIMANJARO
Teardrop Explodes

The Teardrop Explodes evolved from a nucleus of Liverpool musicians which also spawned Echo And The Bunnymen. Where the latter group explored a darker psyche, this particular unit, led by the eccentric Julian Cope, offered a brash brand of pop psychedelia. Cope's grand vision encompassed a range of mentors from Scott Walker to the Turtles, bound together by grasp of strong, exciting melodies. *Kilimanjaro* contains a succession of brilliant songs - several of which were re-recorded from early singles - marked either by ebullient passion or melancholic reflection. Cope's quirky sense of humour adds another perspective to a highly inventive album.

Ha Ha I'm Drowning; Sleeping Gas; Treason; Second Head; Reward Poppies; Went Crazy; Brave Boys Keep Their Promises; Bouncing Babies; Books; The Thief Of Baghdad; When I Dream.

First released 1980
UK peak chart position: 24
USA peak chart position: 156

37. HIGH LAND HARD RAIN
Aztec Camera

Aztec Camera emerged from the ruins of Glasgow's acclaimed Postcard label with this poignant, poetic collection. Group leader Roddy Frame possessed a precious talent, sculpting windblown melodies and honeyed arrangements in the manner of 60s Californian pop. Rippling acoustic guitars emphasise the album's fresh spirit while Frame invests his songs with a mature insight belying his comparative youthfulness. His astute lyrics result in wordplay that is knowing but never clever, resulting in a collection that shows bite behind its aural sweetness.

Oblivious; Boy Wonder; Walk Out To Winter; We Could Send Letters; The Bugle Sounds Again; Pillar To Post; Release; Lost Outside The Tunnel; Back On Board; Down The Dip.

First released 1983
UK peak chart position: 22
USA peak chart position: 129

38. HATFUL OF HOLLOW
Smiths

A composite of radio sessions and sundry early singles, *Hatful Of Hollow* provides an alternative snapshot of the Smiths' early career. Complied in the wake of their debut album, it exhibited all of their considerable strengths, in particular Johnny Marr's ringing, expressive guitarwork. The riff he creates on 'How Soon Is Now' is thoroughly captivating. Vocalist Morrissey's distinctive croon and solipsistic lyrics are already unique and give the group its originality. At times ironic, at others wistful (as on 'Back At The Old House'), he takes the Smiths into new areas of expression and his contrasting visions are fully expressed herein.

William, It Was Really Nothing; What Difference Does It Make?; These Things Take Time; This Charming Man; How Soon Is Now?; Handsome Devil; Hand In Glove; Still Ill; Heaven Knows I'm Miserable Now; This Night Has Opened My Eyes; You've Got Everything Now; Accept Yourself; Girl Afraid; Back At The Old House; Reel Around The Fountain; Please, Please, Please Let Me Get What I Want.

First released 1984
UK peak chart position: 2
USA peak chart position: did not chart

39. HEAVEN OR LAS VEGAS
Cocteau Twins

Long-time favourites of UK radio presenter John Peel and a band who have had to endure the term 'ethereal' being bandied about around their name more than any other. With their soulful and quite blissful meanderings, their music has a sustainable beauty free of regard for contemporaries or peers. *Heaven Or Las Vegas* saw vocalist Elizabeth Fraser substituting the occasional obscure lyric in place of her uniquely visionary wall of sound. While the single, 'Ice Blink Luck' had a near recognisable structure and a very tempting hook. They are now a part of the Phonogram catalogue and in the major league, but their unearthly wealth of ideas remains undiminished.

Cherry-coloured Funk; Pitch The Baby; Iceblink Luck; Fifty-fifty Clown; Heaven Or Las Vegas; I Wear Your Ring; Fotzepolitic; Wolf In The Breast; River, Road And Rail; Frou-frou Foxes In The Midsummer Fires.

First released 1990
UK peak chart position: 7
USA peak chart position: 99

40. HEAVEN UP HERE
Echo And The Bunnymen

On their debut album this Liverpool quartet unveiled a sound crossing post-punk with psychedelic pop. Rather than repeat the formula, the group teased out the constituent parts of their sound to create *Heaven Up Here*. Alternately dreamlike, then melancholically fragile, the set is marked by Ian McCulloch's arresting vocals which sweep across the textured sound with awesome confidence. The album exudes a cumulative power, building in atmosphere as it progresses, with Will Sergeant's plangent guitar emphasising and supporting the drift of the singer's nuances. It is the final icing on an exquisite collection.

Show Of Strength; With A Hip; Over The Wall; It Was A Pleasure; The Promise; Heaven Up Here; The Disease; All My Colours; No Dark Things; Turquoise Days; All I Want.

First released 1981
UK peak chart position: 10
USA peak chart position: 184

41. LIFE'S TOO GOOD
Sugarcubes

The album with an exclamation mark for a spine, gave more credence to Icelandic music in a moment that the unfortunately musical history that had gone before. Fronted by the now near legendary Björk and befuddled as a band by the whole thing, they were inconsistent too. That, or concentrating on higher things. They once wandered on to the Astoria stage a full two hours late, Björk taking a bite from an apple before telling the audience to stop complaining, I mean, they'd been there all day. A droll logic that endured in their musical cavalcade of wonder and high-jinks. If it wasn't for Björk's *Debut*, they'd still be sorely missed.

*Traitor; Motorcrash; Birthday; Delicious Demon; Mama; Coldsweat; Blue Eyed Pop; Deus; Sick For Toys; F***ing In Rhythm And Sorrow.*

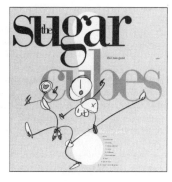

First released 1988
UK peak chart position: 14
USA peak chart position: 54

42. BUMMED
Happy Mondays

The Happy Mondays before the trappings of success had taken them off the council estates and lead then to sell-out shows at the G-Mex, exotic recording locations and their full and sumptuous groove of sound had been fully developed. *Bummed* held the very essence of their lazy, dry wit, their extolling of experience and experiences. The single , 'Wrote For Luck', the thin chuckle of, 'Fat Lady Wrestlers', or the very credible, 'Moving In With', gave credence to their dense plotting and pointed to a very bright future indeed. But didn't even hint at the notion that they'd be the band to almost single-handedly bring down the Factory Records empire.

Country Song; Moving In With; Mad Cyril; Fat Lady Wrestlers; Performance; Brain Dead; Wrote For Luck; Bring A Friend; Do It Better; Lazy Itis.

First released 1989
UK peak chart position: 59
USA peak chart position: did not chart

43. NEVER LOVED ELVIS
Wonderstuff

The Wonderstuff playing at pop stars and carrying the whole thing off with not some little style. Their folkier roots were encapsulated grandly in their bittersweet, and often flourishing, pop. They almost created the perfect single with, 'The Size Of A Cow', caught somewhere between 70s trash pop and real grown up stuff, while their weightier learnings were not forsaken with the sublime eloquence of, '38 Line Poem', or 'Caught In My Shadow'. Elsewhere, 'Welcome To The Cheap Seats, unearthed a wantonly frivolous moment that still somehow worked, much like the Wonderstuff, at a variety of levels.

Mission Drive; Play; False Start; Welcome To The Cheap Seats; The Size Of A Cow; Sleep Alone; Donation; Inertia; Maybe; Grotesque; Here Comes Everyone; Caught In My Shadow; 38 Line Poem.

First released 1991
UK peak chart position: 3
USA peak chart position: did not chart

44. GARLANDS
Cocteau Twins

Although they took their name from an early Simple Minds' song, the Cocteau Twins have pursued a musical path owing little to other acts. The Scottish trio sculpted an ambient mood with synthesiser and guitar over which Elizabeth Fraser floats ethereal vocals. Relying on atmosphere rather than structure, Garlands has the veneer of new age music, but is more than mere background music. The compositions entice and perplex in equal measure, refusing to fit any artistic straight-jacket. The album prepared a path for the Cocteau's subsequent work which developed themes and nuances first aired on this adventurous set.

Blood Bitch; Wax And Wane; But I'm Not; Blind Dumb Deaf; Gail Overfloweth; Shallow Than Hallow; The Hollow Men; Garlands.

First released 1982
UK peak chart position: did not chart
USA peak chart position: did not chart

45. WHAT DOES ANYTHING MEAN? BASICALLY?
Chameleons

The second album by Manchester's Chameleons developed the stylish pop of its predecessor. An edgy quality grips the quartet's melodies which are pieced together meticulously over layers of treated guitarwork and atmospheric keyboards. Mark Burgess sings in a moody, resigned manner, but this does not undermine the emotive qualities he brings to the group's imaginative material. Cut from a cloth inspiring Echo And The Bunnymen and the Psychedelic Furs, the Chameleons offer a plangent sound in which mystery pairs with tough beauty. What Does Anything Mean? Basically? captures this combination at is finest.

Silence, Sea And Sky; Perfume Garden; Inrigue In Tangiers; Return Of The Roughnecks; Singing Rule Britannia (While The Walls Close In); On The Beach; Looking Inwardly; One Flesh; Home Is Where The Heart Is; P.S. Goodbye.

First released 1985
UK peak chart position: 60
USA peak chart position: did not chart

46. PICTURES OF STARVING CHILDREN SELL RECORDS
Chumbawamba

Though in the 90s the group have largely dismissed their anarcho-punk roots, this first album was the perfect culmination of Crass aesthetics textured by a much greater musical palate. It is a record which seethes with resentment, and produces a number of observations which many will not find easy to accommodate. Among the targets are Band Aid (alluded to in the album title) - 'Paul McCartney - Come On Down! With crocodile tears to irrigate this ground, Make of Ethiopia a fertile paradise, where everyone sings Beatles' songs and buys shares in EMI'. Multinationals like Coca Cola and Unilever are taken to task for 'whitewashing' the world, alongside third world cash crops and industrial exploitation. While this is an arresting sequence of protest lyrics, what underpins it all is the musical and theatrical variety, from a cappella through to full blown thrash.

Prologue; 1. How To Get Your Band On Television; 2. British Colonialism And The BBC - Flicking Pictures Hypnotise; 3. Commercial Break; 4. Unilever; 5. More Whitwashing; 6. ...An Interlude Beginning To Take It Back; 7. Dutiul Servants And Political Masters; 8. Cocoa-Colanisation; 9. ...And In A Nutshell 'Food Aid Is Our Most Powerful Weapon'; 10. Invasion.

First released 1993
UK peak chart position: did not chart
USA peak chart position: did not chart

47. STRANGEWAYS HERE WE COME
Smiths

Allegedly, both Morrissey and Marr's favourite Smiths album. And it's not difficult to understand why. With its resounding, flexing songwriting strength. Marr's extraordinary grasp of styles combined with Morrissey's Wildean protestations and giggling stares make for one of the great English pop albums. Their quintessential grasp of the delightfully dramatic best captured by the rolling play of, 'Stop Me If You Think You've Heard This One Before'. Morrissey's indignant howl, 'And the pain was enough to make/A shy bald Buddhist reflect/And plan a mass murder'. A truly glorious moment among a host of glories.

A Rush And A Push And The Land Is Ours; I Started Something I Couldn't Finish; Death Of A Disco Dancer; Girlfriend In A Coma; Stop Me If You Think You've Heard This One Before; Last Night I Dreamt That Somebody Loved Me; Unhappy Birthday; Paint A Vulgar Picture; Death At One's Elbow; I Won't Share You.

First released 1987
UK peak chart position: 2
USA peak chart position: 55

48. LA'S
The La's

The perpetually disenchanted Liverpudlians grumbled their way through most of their interviews. Scathing perfectionist, they dismissed most of their output with a metaphorical wave of the hand, compliments bounced off them in all directions, for the La's, it was never enough. It's hard now to see why they were so dissatisfied, *The La's* is a graceful, sweeping and rather grand pop record. Utterly charming and filled with a meek beauty typified by the wonderful, 'There She Goes' single, the sincere, 'I Can't Sleep' and the shining, 'Timeless Melody'. Great moments.

Son Of A Gun; I Can't Sleep; Timeless Melody; Liberty Ship; There She Goes; Doledrum; Feeling; Way Out; IOU; Freedom Song; Failure; Lookin' Glass.

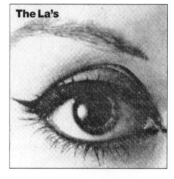

First released 1990
UK peak chart position: 30
USA peak chart position: 196

49. CHEMICRAZY
That Petrol Emotion

Formed in 1986 by two former members of the Undertones, brothers Damien and John O'Neill, That Petrol Emotion offered an exciting, guitar-based music, drawing on the anger of punk and the energy of R&B. *Chemicrazy* was issued in the wake of John O'Neill's departure and a resultant internal shuffle. Producer Scott Litt harnessed a previous disparate energy to create a unified sound which nonetheless bore the group's trademarks. Seattle-born singer Steve Mack adds fire to the proceedings, which confirms That Petrol Emotion's position as one of the most fascinating acts of the late 80s.

Hey Venus; Blue To Black; Mess Of Words; Sensitize; Another Day; Gnaw Mark; Scum Surfin'; Compulsion; Tingle; Head Staggered; Abandon; Sweet Shiver Burn.

First released 1990
UK peak chart position: 62
USA peak chart position: did not chart

50. SEARCHING FOR THE YOUNG SOUL REBELS
Dexy's Midnight Runners

Led by the abrasive/single-minded Kevin Rowland, Dexy's Midnight Runners spoke for an all-night culture immersed in northern soul. Searching For The Young Soul Rebels captures the original eight-piece group infusing passionate self-belief to songs based on 60s mentors Geno Washington and Jimmy James. Rowland's expressive voice is perfectly matched by pumping horns and punchy rhythms, but the intensity of their performance ensures the set never falls into pastiche. Each song bears the stamp of manifesto, one largely Rowland's, a myopic vision which brought this line-up to an acrimonious, premature end. His commitment, however, ensured the lasting qualities of this album.

Burn It Down; Tell Me When My Lights Turn To Green; Teams That Meet In The Caffs; I'm Just Looking; Geno; Seven Day's To Long; I Couldn't Help It If I Tried; Thankfully Not Living In Yorkshire, It Doesn't; Keep It; Love Part One; There, There My Dear.

First released 1980
UK peak chart position: 6
USA peak chart position: did not chart

THE TOP 50
LIVE ALBUMS

SOME ARTISTS CAN ONLY PERFORM WELL IN FRONT OF A LIVE
AUDIENCE. OTHERS HIT THE BUTTON BY CHANCE AND RECORD THE GIG,
PUT IT OUT AND YOU HAVE AN UNBEATABLE LIVE ALBUM. ERROLL
GARNER AND HENDRIX/REDDING ARE TWO EXAMPLES OF THE LATTER.
OTHERS LIKE GRATEFUL DEAD, B.B. KING AND KEITH JARRETT CAN
GIVE US LIVE ALBUMS TILL THE COWS COME HOME.
THE WINNER IS UNLIKELY TO EVER BE TOPPLED.

1. LIVE AT THE APOLLO
James Brown

Superlatives abound when considering this seminal set. It has been called 'the greatest live album of all time' while Brown's position as the Godfather of Soul is almost indisputable. The singer was largely unknown outside black music circles prior to the release of this million-seller which fully captured the power and intensity of Brown in concert. It contains the cream of his releases to that point, each of which is injected with a passionate fervour. Brilliantly paced, the set grows in stature, as the famed Apollo audience responds to and, indeed, adds to the excitement. Brown towers majestically over the proceedings; pleading, extolling, proving himself not just the finest R&B singer of his generation, but one of the most distinctive in the history of popular music.

I'll Go Crazy; Try Me; Think; I Don't Mind; Lost Someone (Part 1); Lost Someone (Part 2); Please, Please, Please; You've Got The Power; I Found Someone; Why Do You Do Me Like You Do; I Want You So Bad; I Love You Yes I Do; Why Does Everything Happen To Me; Bewildered; Please Don't Go; Night Train.

First released 1963
UK peak chart position: did not chart
USA peak chart position: 2

2. LIVE
Bob Marley

Nobody who likes music could fail to be emotionally moved by this album, and not because Marley is no longer with us. It was a special live treat before he died. The great thing about this record is the feeling that this is what it was like every night, unlike other live recordings which capture one or two gigs of a tour. Marley was extra special and a giant of popular music. Wallow in this vital record and listen to a man had something to say and yet had fun while he said it. Most of the tracks you would want on a record are here.

Trenchtown Rock; Burnin' And Lootin'; Them Belly Full (But We Hungry); Lively Up Yourself; No Woman No Cry; I Shot The Sheriff; Get Up, Stand Up.

First released 1975
UK peak chart position: 38
USA peak chart position: 90

3. UNLEASHED IN THE EAST
Judas Priest

The first real transatlantic breakthrough for Judas Priest came with this most unforgiving of live albums. Playing on their early success in the Far East, Judas Priest recorded a handful of shows in Tokyo on the back of their, *Hell Bent For Leather* album. Their magnanimous success there made for a brutal and excited showing of live favourites that translated as a riotous success with the Japanese. Their inspired covers of Joan Baez's, 'Diamonds And Rust' and Fleetwood Mac's, 'Green Manalishi,' as well as such gruelling standards as, 'Exciter' and 'Ripper', made for a convincing, sweatpit of a show. One to raise your hands to.

Exciter; Running Wild; Sinner; Ripper; Green Manalishi (With The Two-Pronged Crown); Diamonds And Rust; Victim Of Changes; Genocide; Tyrant.

First released 1979
UK peak chart position: 10
USA peak chart position: 70

4. THE KOLN CONCERT
Keith Jarrett

Albums that sell vast quantities are not always to be recommended. This exceptional example of solo piano is the biggest selling record in the 25 year history of the pioneering jazz label ECM. An almost perfect recording of the art of piano dynamics. Full of emotion and throughout the hour or so duration the listener is never bored. Jarrett has repeated his concerts of improvisation hundreds of times, many have been recorded, and presumably many routes of his spontaneity have led to blind alley's of jazz doodling. This is the best recorded example of the art, unlikely to be bettered.

Part I; Part II a; Part II b; Part I Ic.

First released 1975
UK peak chart position: did not chart
USA peak chart position: did not chart

5. JUDY AT CARNEGIE HALL
Judy Garland

The sleeve note begins: 'On the evening of April 23, 1961, 3,165 privileged people packed the world famous Carnegie Hall beyond its capacity, and witnessed what was to be probably the greatest evening in show business history.' This souvenir of that remarkable occasion is said to contain the complete concert during which Judy Garland sang 26 songs and mesmerized the audience with her sensational all-round performance. The album won Grammys for album of the year, best female vocal performance, best engineering and best cover. It was in the US chart for 73 weeks, 13 of them at number 1.

When You're Smiling; Almost Like Being In Love (medley); Who Cares?; Puttin' On The Ritz; How Long Has This Been Going On; Just You, Just Me; The Man That Got Away; San Francisco; That's Entertainment; Come Rain Or Come Shine; You're Nearer; A Foggy Day; If Love Were All; Zing Went The Strings Of My Heart; Stormy Weather; You Made Me Love You (medley); Rockabye Your Baby With A Dixie Melody; Over The Rainbow; Swanee; After You've Gone; Chicago; The Trolley Song (overture); Over The Rainbow (overture); The Man That Got Away (overture); Do It Again; You Go To My Head; Alone Together; I Can't Give You Anything But Love.

First released 1961
UK peak chart position: 13
USA peak chart position: 1

6. AT NEWPORT
Duke Ellington

This concert marked the so-called rebirth of Ellington. Of course, it was the jazz audience that had lost sight of the band. Newport saw the end of temporary obscurity. Irritated by the place on the programme and his musicians' habitual tardiness, Ellington began the second set in a do-or-die mood. They didn't die. Wonderful solos by the likes of Clark Terry and Johnny Hodges, propulsive drumming, and the incredible marathon solo by Paul Gonsalves which links the two parts of 'Diminuedo In Blue' and 'Crescendo In Blue', makes this an evening that will live forever in the annals of jazz.

Newport Jazz Festival Suite - a) Festival Junction b) Blues To Be There c) Newport Up; Jeep's Blues; Diminuendo And Crescendo In Blue.

First released 1957
UK peak chart position: did not chart
USA peak chart position: 14

7. RATTLE AND HUM
U2

The album of the movie, or the movie of the album? U2's trip into the America of myths and legends took them into the musical heartland of their heroes. Jamming and recording with both B.B. King and Bob Dylan respectively in Sun Studios. The Irish four-piece doffing their metaphorical hats in respect and not some little awe. Hendrix's, 'The Star Spangled Banner' standing alone, quietly dignified toward the end of their record. It now seems a long way from Mephisto's Zoo TV antics, and maybe, in retrospect, that's not such a bad thing.

Helter Skelter; Hawkmoon 269; Van Dieman's Land; Desire; Angel Of Harlem; I Still Haven't Found What I'm Looking For; When Love Comes To Town; God Part II; Bullet The Blue Sky; Silver And Gold; Love Rescue Me; Heartland; The Star Spangled Banner; All I Want Is You; Freedom For My People; All Along The Watchtower; Pride (In The Name Of Love).

First released 1988
UK peak chart position:1
USA peak chart position: 1

8. JOAN BAEZ IN CONCERT
Joan Baez

The 'queen of folk' was an accomplished live performer as this, the first of two In Concert albums proved. Accompanying herself on acoustic guitar, Baez brought her pure, virginal soprano to contrasting material. Her interpretations of Childe ballads 'Matty Groves' and 'The House Carpenter' are particularly moving, but an empathy with American folklore, including Woody Guthrie and the Carter Family is equally apparent. Baez's reading of Malvina Reynolds' protest song, 'What Have They Done To The Rain', is especially arresting and inspired a later pop hit for the Searchers. This album helped take folk music out of the coffeehouse circuit and into national consciousness.

Babe; I'm Gonna Leave You; Geordie; Copper Kettle; Kubaya; What Have They Done To The Rain; Black Is The Colour Of My True Love's Hair; Danger Water; Gospel Ship; The House Carpenter; Pretty Boy Floyd; Lady Mary; Ate Amanha; Matty Groves.

First released 1962
UK peak chart position: did not chart
USA peak chart position: 10

9. CONCERT BY THE SEA
Erroll Garner

Garner's place in the history of jazz piano is unusual. He shows no obvious influences of any other pianist, he appears to have influenced no-one. And yet his is such a thoroughly engaging, happy, always enjoyable style. Here, he deftly picks his way through a sprightly selection of songs. Throughout, the Elf happily indulges his love for lengthy introductions which defy listeners to identify the coming tune. Yet, when he finally arrives at the song as the composer wrote it, everything seems just right. Ageless music in an impishly droll style that defies categorization. It's just Erroll's way.

I'll Remember April; Teach Me Tonight; Mambo Carmel; It's Alright With Me; Red Top; April In Paris; They Can't Take That Away From Me; Where Or When; Erroll's Theme.

First released 1958
UK peak chart position: did not chart
USA peak chart position: 12

10. THE AUDIENCE WITH BETTY CARTER
Betty Carter

For Betty Carter, songs are vehicles for her talent. If something does not fit her conception of how her performance should go, then she changes it. Nothing is sacred; and yet, somehow, nothing is profaned. Standards from the Great American Songbook are reworked with seemingly dismissive ease. The album title says a lot. Woe betide any audience that risks not being 'with' Betty Carter. In command, on display, this tough, restless tigress of jazz singing overshadows her contemporaries, What is more, her statement, that she sees no-one coming along to challenge her superiority, looks increasingly true as the years pass by.

Sounds (Movin' On); I Think I Got It Now; Caribbean Sun; The Trolley Song; Everything I Have Is Yours; I'll Buy You A Star; I Could Write A Book; Can't We Talk It Over; Either It's Love Or It Isn't; Deep Night; Spring Can Really Hang You Up The Most; Tight; Fake; So; My Favourite Things; Open The Door.

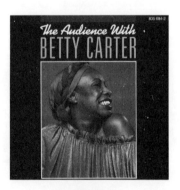

First released 1979
UK peak chart position: did not chart
USA peak chart position: did not chart

11. JOHNNY CASH AT SAN QUENTIN
Johnny Cash

One of country music's unequivocal stars, Johnny Cash retained respect for the travails of the audience elevating him to that position. Recorded live at one of America's most notorious prisons, this album displays an empathy bereft of condescension and captures a performer combining charisma with natural ease. The material is balanced between established favourites and new material, including 'Wanted Man', an unrecorded Bob Dylan song, and the lighthearted hit 'A Boy Named Sue'. It was not the first time Cash had recorded in a penal institution, but this appearance, at a time American values were vociferously questioned, suggested the artist's rebelliousness had not dimmed.

Wanted Man; Wreck Of Old 97; I Walk The Line; Darling Companion; Starkville City Jail; San Quentin; A Boy Named Sue; Peace In The Valley; Folsom Prison Blues.

First released 1969
UK peak chart position: 2
USA peak chart position: 1

12. STOP MAKING SENSE
Talking Heads

A live album made for the film of the same name, and one that deserves to survive as it is one of the finest concert recordings ever made. The quality is such that the listener can be lulled into forgetting it is live, only the up-front and un-overdubbed drums give the game away. Elsewhere Byrne perfroms majestically giving new life to old masters. Both 'Psycho Killer' and' Once In A Lifetime' benefit from fresher versions and the hypnotic lenghy finale 'Take Me To The River' is deliberate in that it is gaurenteed to stay in your head for days. The Talking Heads sound better on this than they do on record, if you get my drift.

Psycho Killer; Swamp; Slippery People; Burning Down The House; Girlfriend Is Better; Once In A Lifetime; What A Day That Was; Life During Wartime; Take Me To The River.

First released 1984
UK peak chart position: 37
USA peak chart position: 41

13. TRAVELS
Pat Metheny

A double album that flirts with rock, folk, country and latin - but is emphatically a jazz album. Metheny is equipped with probably his best ever live group; Steve Rodby, Dan Gottlieb, Nana Vasconcelos, and his right arm, keyboard virtuoso Lyle Mays. The recording exudes warmth, and often improves over those already issued on studio albums, for example 'Phase Dance' is played with more verve and 'Song For Bilbao' has sounds more passionate in a live context. The diamond in the mine however is the shortest track, the glorious and delicate title track. Worth the price of the album alone.

Are You Going With Me?; The Fields, The Sky; Goodbye; Phase Dance; Straight On Red; Farmer's Trust; Extradition; Goin' Ahead; As Falls Wichita, So Falls Wichita Falls; Travels; Song For Bilbao; San Lorenzo.

First released 1983
UK peak chart position: did not chart
USA peak chart position: 62

14. UNPLUGGED
Eric Clapton

The clear leader of the unplugged fashion and one of Clapton's finest efforts. A wonderful relaxed atmosphere oozes through the record as we read Eric's mind 'I don't have to do this, but I choose to do because I love it'. Beautifully played acoustic blues, strongly sung and well-supported by his regulars including second guitarist Andy Fairweather Low and acrobatic percussionist Ray Cooper. MTV probably didn't know what they were starting with this and when this 'sitting down' fashion fades, as it certainly will, this album will always be regarded as its vanguard.

Signe; Before You Accuse Me; Hey Hey; Tears In Heaven; Lonely Stranger; Nobody Knows You When You're Down And Out; Layla; Running On Faith; Walkin' Blues; Alberta; San Francisco Bay Blues; Malted Milk; Old Love; Rollin' And Tumblin'.

First released 1992
UK peak chart position: 2
USA peak chart position: 2

15. IT'S TOO LATE TO STOP NOW
Van Morrison

Having completed a sequence of peerless studio albums, Van Morrison encapsulated an expansive tour with this searing live set. Drawing sterling support from the Caledonia Soul Orchestra, the singer offers some of his most popular songs, acknowledges influences and even pays homage to his hit group, Them, with a medley of their two most successful singles. Not content with simply recreating material, Van uses his instinctive gifts to change inflections and bring new emphases, reshaping each piece according to the moment's mood, rather than rely on previously recorded versions. Such authoritative performances make *It's Too Late To Stop Now* one of rock's essential in-concert albums.

Ain't Nothing You Can Do; Warm Love; Into The Mystic; These Dreams Of You; I Believe To My Soul; Bring It On Home; Saint Dominic's Preview; Take Your Hand Out Of My Pocket; Listen To The Lion; I've Been Working; Help Me; Wild Children; Domino; I Just Wanna Make Love To You; Here Comes The Night; Gloria; Caravan; Cypress Avenue.

First released 1974
UK peak chart position: did not chart
USA peak chart position: 53

16. NO SLEEP TILL HAMMERSMITH
Motorhead

Unlike many heavy-metal contemporaries, Motorhead leader Lemmy possesses self-deprecating humour. Stripped of pretension, he goads the basic three-chord trick with a full-throated bellow, emphasising his trio's vicious racket. On this live selection the group reprise the cream of their back-catalogue with untrammelled venom, in the process destroying already power-packed studio counterparts. Continuing a line from the MC5 and Stooges, rather than gothic fantasy, the band understand the excitement of noise and exploit it to full potential. Thrash metal and hardcore owe them a debt but, as this album proves, there is only one Motorhead.

Ace Of Spades; Stay Clean; The Metropolis Hammer; Iron Horse; No Class; Overkill; The Road Crew; Capricorn; Motorhead.

First released 1981
UK peak chart position: 1
USA peak chart position: did not chart

17. MADE IN JAPAN
Deep Purple

Recorded on the Japanese tour of 1972, Deep Purple created the most effortless of great live albums. Labouring under the *Machine Head* tour and inter band relationships that saw both Gillan and Glover feuding with Blackmore and quitting the band early the following year. For its part though, the record shows none of its personnel inconsistencies, the band playing what would become in retrospect, a greatest hits set. The consistency of the material, 'Child In Time', 'Strange Kind Of Woman', 'Space Truckin'' was, and still is, astounding. Matched only by the arch standards of Purple's live performance.

Highway Star; Child In Time; Smoke On The Water; The Mule; Strange Kind Of Woman; Lazy; Space Truckin'.

First released 1973
UK peak chart position: 16
USA peak chart position: 6

18. MONTEREY INTERNATIONAL POP FESTIVAL
Jimi Hendrix/Otis Redding

'Yeah dig brother, its really outasite here, didn't even rain, no buttons to push'. The opening words from Jimi Hendrix at the legendary festival as he introduces 'Like A Rolling Stone' with great humour and plays it with casual ease. The two artists on this album are probably the greatest of their genre. Both are black, one plays rock, one sings soul, one charms as the other sweats. Both were outstanding stars at this festival, and although both are dead they remain towering giants of music. Even when first released in 1970 the subtitle *Historic Performances* already stated the importance of this album.

Like A Rolling Stone; Rock Me, Baby; Can You See Me; Wild Thing; Shake; Respect; I've Been Loving You Too Long; (I Can't Get No) Satisfaction; Try A Little Tenderness.

First released 1970
UK peak chart position: did not chart
USA peak chart position: 16

19. IF YOU WANT BLOOD YOU'VE GOT IT
AC/DC

From the bloody artwork, vocalist Bon Scott forcing a guitar through Angus Young's midriff, this, AC/DC's truly bombastic live album, was an unrepentant acclimation of attitude and boogie, rock 'n' roll that had combined to give this Australian outfit international notoriety. From Young's schoolboy outfit and antics, elongated soloing and an uproarious version, complete with full crowd backing, of, 'Whole Lotta Rosie' Bon Scott's lurid retelling of his encounter with a somewhat overweight and overwrought lady friend, *If You Want Blood You've Got It*, is a very live record indeed.

Riff Raff; Hell Ain't A Bad Place To Be; Bad Boy Boogie; The Jack; Problem Child; Whole Lotta Rosie; Rock 'N' Roll Damnation; High Voltage; Let There Be Rock; Rocker.

First released 1978
UK peak chart position: 13
USA peak chart position: 113

20. LIVE (X CERT)
Stranglers

It may not even be the definitive Stranglers live album - in that *X-Cert* draws on just three studio sets Yet it also carries the character and the colour (black) of the punk movement's most undesirables. From its dramatic cover, in itself more in keeping with the early 70s than the cut and paste of the Pistols, the Stranglers combined the movement's venom with an aggressive musicality and narcotic lyricism. This set also became legendary for Hugh Cornwall's onstage patter, deriding his audience for spitting ('I know you like spitting but I don't particularly like being spat at while I'm playing') and remonstrating with the audience member audacious enough to call him a wanker (anybody who did the same at subsequent gigs was hoisted up on stage and spanked).

Get A Grip On Yourself; Dagenham Dave; Burning Up Time; Dead Ringer; Hanging Around; Feel Like A Wog; Straight Out; Do You Wanna - Death And Night And Blood; Five Minutes; Go Buddy Go.

First released 1988
UK peak chart position: 7
USA peak chart position: did not chart

21. THE LAST WALTZ
Various/The Band

The Band turned their decision to retire into a gala occasion. Recorded live at San Francisco's Winterland auditorium, *The Last Waltz* not only documents their exceptional repertoire with telling versions of their best-known songs, it also featured a stellar cast of contemporary performers, including Ronnie Hawkins, with whom the Band first recorded, and Bob Dylan. Muddy Waters, Eric Clapton, Neil Young and Joni Mitchell are among the others paying tribute to this exemplary group, and by doing so the entire proceedings becomes not simply a farewell concert, but a celebration of a generation and era.

The Last Waltz; Up On Cripple Creek; Who Do You Love; Helpless; Stage Fright; Coyote; Dry Your Eyes; It Makes No Difference; Such A Night; The Night They Drove Old Dixie Down; Mystery Train; Mannish Boy; Further On Up The Road; The Shape I'm In; Down South In New Orleans; Ophelia; Tura Lura Larai (That's An Irish Lullaby); Caravan; Life Is A Carnival; Baby Let Me Follow You Down; I Don't Believe You (She Acts Like We Never Have Met); Forever Young; I Shall Be Released; The Last Waltz Suite; The Well; Evangeline; Out Of The Blue; The Weight.

First released 1978
UK peak chart position: did not chart
USA peak chart position: 16

22. UNPLUGGED
Neil Young

Recorded for MTV at the Universal Studios, Los Angeles and released soon after, this is the Unplugged phenomenon at its best. Young calmly eases us through almost 30 years of ever-changing, fresh and highly powerful songs. The strength of his catalogue is that with or without instrumentation, Crazy Horse, Stray Gators or Shocking Pinks the songs can be tackled at any pace in any way. Who would have thought that the blistering guitar rocker 'Like A Hurricane' could be pumped out on a tiny pedal harmonium. This man is another rare musical genius still producing great work.

The Old Laughing Lady; Mr. Soul; World On A String; Pocahontas; Stringman; Like A Hurricane; The Needle Damage Done; Helpless; Harvest Moon; Transformer Man; Unknown Legend; Look Out For My Love; Long May You Run; From Hawk To Hendrix.

First released 1993
UK peak chart position: 4
USA peak chart position: 23

23. MUDDY WATERS AT NEWPORT
Muddy Waters

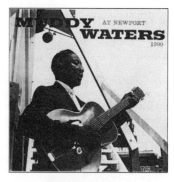

The cover photograph of Muddy clutching John Lee Hooker's guitar gave the impression that he was at a Folk Festival rather than the prestigious Newport Jazz Festival. But the record revealed the King of Chicago blues at his very best, shouting his music above the discordant wail of a band that included Otis Spann, James Cotton, Pat Hare and Francis Clay. Film of the event shows a sharply-dressed Muddy shimmying and jiving around the stage with the energy of a man half his age. Some of that atmosphere gets onto record, in a programme that includes 'Hoochie Coochie Man', Big Bill Broonzy's 'I Feel So Good', recent singles 'I Got My Brand On You' and 'Soon Forgotten', and a massive 'Got My Mojo Working'. The set ends in poignant mood with the announcement of the end of the Festival and Otis Spann's improvised 'Goodbye Newport Blues'.

I Got My Brand On You; I'm Your Hoochie Koochie Man; Baby, Please Don't Go; Soon Forgotten; Tiger In Your Tank; I Feel So Good; Got My Mojo Working; Got My Mojo Working Part 2; Goodbye Newport Blues.

First released 1960
UK peak chart position: did not chart
USA peak chart position: did not chart

24. LIVE AT THE REGAL
B.B. King

No matter how good the studio sessions were, B.B. King was at his best on stage in front of an appreciative, if not ecstatic, crowd. This set, recorded at Chicago's premier black theatre on 21 November 1964, delivered just that. Despite the less than perfect recording conditions, at a time when technology had yet to catch up with the demands placed upon it, the King of the Blues delivers a definitive performance on a programme that includes his recent single, 'Help The Poor', and a clutch of songs that were responsible for much of his success, 'Everyday I Have The Blues', 'Sweet Little Angel', 'It's My Own Fault', 'You Upset Me Baby' and 'Woke Up This Morning' among them. The band, including tenorman Johnny Board and organist Duke Jethro, is lean but tight, providing King with a springboard from which to leap into flights of immaculate guitar playing and singing.

Everyday I Have The Blues; Sweet Little Angel; It's My Own Fault; How Blue Can You Get; Please Love Me; You Upset Me Baby; Worry, Worry; Woke Up This Morning; You Done Lost Your Good Thing Now; Help The Poor.

First released 1965
UK peak chart position: did not chart
USA peak chart position: 78

25. LIVE AT LEEDS
Who

The Who forged their reputation as an exciting live attraction and elected to issue this set in the wake of the highly-successful *Tommy*. Selections from that ground-breaking rock opera formed the core of this concert, but the group equally used the opportunity to restate past glories and acknowledge influences. Rock 'n' roll star Eddie Cochran had inspired the Who's Pete Townshend; the former's 'Summertime Blues' exploded with new fury within. 'Young Man Blues', first recorded by jazz singer Mose Allison, was given a new dimension through power chords, pulsating drumming and Roger Daltrey's expressive vocal. *Live At Leeds* successfully captures a live performance for posterity.

Magic Bus; My Generation; Shakin' All Over; Substitute; Summertime Blues; Young Man Blues.

First released 1970
UK peak chart position: 3
USA peak chart position: 4

26. FRAMPTON COMES ALIVE
Peter Frampton

The real renegade album in the entire listing. Frampton sold goodness how many million copies making it the biggest selling double live album of all time. Nobody expected Frampton to become a superstar, least of all Frampton, and sadly in the wake of this album his career began to falter. In addition to some quite memorable songs there is also the famous plastic tube voice box that Frampton and Joe Walsh specialized in. This ultimately dates this album to the mid-70s, but it does sound pretty good, even though the unnecessary version of 'Jumpin' Jack Flash' is still included.

Something's Happening; Doobie Wah; Show Me The Way; It's A Plain Shame; All I Want To Be (Is By Your Side); Wind Of Change; Baby, I Love Your Way; I Wanna Go To The Sun; Penny For Your Thoughts; I'll Give You Money; Shine On; Jumpin' Jack Flash; Lines On My Face; Do You Feel Like We Do?.

First released 1976
UK peak chart position: 6
USA peak chart position: 1

27. FOUR WAY STREET
Crosby Stills Nash And Young

Often chided for their sickly banter onstage, CSN joined by 'our friend Neil Young' this double album was recorded at the height of their success. Other than one or two overlong efforts, 'Southern Man' and 'Carry On', the album is varied and exciting even with the chat. 'Sheer profundity', say's Crosby about Nash, 'go get it Stephen' says Nash about Stills and even Young delivers 'we've had our ups and downs, but we're still playing together'. Crosby is excellent on 'Triad', Nash passes on 'Chicago' and on the CD version Stills and Young delight respectively with 'Black Queen' and 'The Loner/Cinnamon Girl/Down By the River'.

On The Way Home; Cowgirl In The Sand; Southern Man; Teach Your Children; Don't Let It Bring You Down; Ohio; Triad; 49 Bye Byes; Carry On; Lee Shore; Love The One You're With; Find The Cost Of Freedom; Chicago; Pre Road Downs; Right Between The Eyes; Long Time Gone.

First released 1971
UK peak chart position: 5
USA peak chart position: 1

28. WHEELS OF FIRE
Cream

Wheels Of Fire solved Cream's artistic dilemma whereby studio work was largely concise but live appearances centred on improvisation. This double set successfully offered both facets and captures the trio at their most ambitious. Where the in-concert section, in particular, 'Crossroads', showed remarkable musical empathy, its counterpart offered a wide range of contrasting perspectives. Pop songs and blues standards nestled together while cellos, viola and trumpet embellish certain selections as the group, in tandem with producer Felix Pappalardi, expanded Cream's oeuvre. Lyricist Pete Brown enhanced this experimental vision which defined the unit's creative peak.

White Room; Sitting On Top Of The World; Passing The Time; As You Said; Pressed Rat And Warthog; Politician; Those Were The Days; Born Under A Bad Sign; Deserted Cities Of The Heart; Crossroads; Spoonful; Train Time; Toad.

First released 1968
UK peak chart position: 3
USA peak chart position: 1

29. LIVE AT THE BUDOKAN
Cheap Trick

A richly coloured bubblegum wrapper of a record that took Cheap Trick's reputation, not to mention their commercial appeal, to a much more exonerated level. Probably, now in retrospect, their greatest record, *Live At Budokan* set their majestic ear for four minute pop nuggets against the backdrop of a thousand plus screaming Japanese teens. Robin Zander's pin-up, suave playboy and Nielsen's and Carlos' endearingly wacked out image alongside the truly great, 'I Want You To Want Me', 'Surrender', 'Need Your Love', the occasional well groomed cover, and a handful of roof down, summertime blow-outs, ensured them a place in live album legend.

Hello There; Come On, Come On; Lookout; Big Eyes; Need Your Love; Ain't That A Shame; I Want You To Want Me; Surrender; Goodnight Now; Clock Strikes Ten.

First released 1979
UK peak chart position: 29
USA peak chart position: 4

30. WELD
Neil Young And Crazy Horse

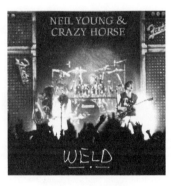

The *Arc Weld* version has been outvoted as all votes went for two albums instead of three. Young hit yet another peak in the 90s and this blisteringly distorted album was the best. He out-grunges everybody with the best support band in the world (ask Ian McNabb). 'Cortez The Killer' is given new life, as is his then gentle rocker 'Cinnamon Girl' from 1968. The excitement level of the double set is extraordinary as the gut wrenching volume of playing fails to irritate - only ignites the soul for more. The low point is the overlong and ponderour 'Farmer John', which should be left with the Searchers.

Hey Hey, My My (Into The Black); Crime In The City; Blowin' In The Wind; Welfare Mothers; Love To Burn; Cinnamon Girl; Mansion On The Hill; F*!#In' Up; Cortez The Killer; Powderfinger; Love And And Only Love; Rockin' In The Free World; Like A Hurricane; Farmer John; Tonight's The Night; Roll Another Number.

First released 1991
UK peak chart position: 20
USA peak chart position: 154

31. OTIS REDDING LIVE IN EUROPE
Otis Redding

Otis Redding was adored in Europe long before he bacame an international star. The Essex mods held him in high esteem, and that spread early on to Germany and Holland. The wonderful Stax tour of 1967 will remain in the hearts of everyone who were lucky enough to have seen it. The cream of the 60s soul movement came and played on our doorstep. This is living proof of what it was like - Otis shook, he shaked, he moaned, he cried, he sang his soul out and still didn't manage to split his blue mohair suit. This is a sweaty album worth the price alone for the emotional version of 'Try A Little Tenderness'.

Respect; I Can't Turn You Loose; I've Been Loving You Too Long; My Girl; Shake; (I Can't Get No) Satisfation; Fa-Fa-Fa-Fa-Fa (Sad Song); These Arms Of Mine; Day Tripper; Try A Little Tenderness.

First released 1967
UK peak chart position: 14
USA peak chart position: 32

32. JOHNNY CASH AT FOLSOM PRISON
Johnny Cash

Appearing at Glastonbury in 1994, it was clear that Johnny Cash has become an icon for the current generation. One reason is his alleged background of crime, although, in reality, Cash has only spent three days in jail - one of them for picking flowers. He is more like an old-time preacher, often finding his audiences in prisons. This classic album, which he had wanted to make for some years, brought out the best in his music. The audience is lively and unlike audiences anywhere else - listen to the applause when he sings, 'I shot a man in Reno just to watch him die.' There's the gallows humour of 'Twenty-Five Minutes To Go', the whimsy of 'Dirty Old Egg-Sucking Dog', a song written by one of the prisoners 'Greystone Chapel', and a duet of 'Jackson' with June Carter. But the real star of the record is the audience: other albums have been recorded in prisons, and Johnny Cash has recorded in other prisons, but this album is special.

Folsum Prison Blues; Dark As A Dungeon; I Still Miss Someone; Cocaine Blues; 25 Minutes To Go; Orange Blossom Special; The Long Black Veil; Send A Picture Of Mother; The Wall; Dirty Old Egg-Sucking Dog; Flushed From The Bathroom Of Your Heart; Jackson; Give My Love To Rose; I Got Stripes; Green Green Grass Of Home; Greystone Chapel.

First released 1968
UK peak chart position: 8
USA peak chart position: 13

33. SHADOWS AND LIGHT
Joni Mitchell

Although this incredible live unit never recorded a proper studio album we do have this as a reminder of just what is possible. Joni the folkie briefly became Ms Mitchell the jazz singer supported by the formidable talents of Pat Metheny, Lyle Mays, Jaco Pastorius, Michael Brecker and Don Alias. Many of Mitchell's jazz flirtations are given the full treatment with musicians who understood both her and the genre. It is a staggering marriage of talent and wholly successful. There is even an obligatory bonus solo from Pat and one from Don. They should have stayed together.

In France They Kiss On Main Street; Edith And The Kingpin; Coyote; Goodbye Pork Pie Hat; The Dry Cleaner From Des Moines; Amelia; Pat's Solo; Hejira; Black Crow; Don's Solo; Dreamland; Free Man In Paris; Band Intro; Furry Sings The Blues; Why Do Fools Fall In Love; Shadows And Light; God Must Be A Boogie Man; Woodstock.

First released 1975
UK peak chart position: 34
USA peak chart position: 2

34. LIVE AT SAN QUENTIN
B.B. King

Much gutsier than the Regal album, this is in harmony with the patrons as King plays to a to different audience; the inmates of one of America's toughest prisons. King devotes a lot of his time every year performing to prisoners, and he communicates on this album without patronising them. This is a fairly predictable B.B. set but the high level recording (presumably to block out any obscenities) makes it one of his most exciting live albums. Songs he has played a thousand times sound fresh and energetic, notably 'Everyday I Have The Blues and 'Let The Good Times Roll'.

BB King Intro; Let The Good Times Roll; Everyday I Have The Blues; Whole Lotta Lovein'; Sweet Little Angel; Never Make A Move To Soon; Into The Night; Ain't Nobody's Bizness If I Do; The Thrill Is Gone; Peace To The World; Nobody Loves Me But My Mother; Sweet Sixteen; Rock Me Baby.

First released 1990 rec.70s
UK peak chart position: : did not chart
USA peak chart position: did not chart

35. LIVE DEAD
Grateful Dead

As the archetypal west coast band, famed for lengthy improvisation, the Grateful Dead found it difficult to translate their in-concert fire on to record. The group addressed this dilemma by recording *Live Dead* live in the studio, allowing free rein for guitarist Jerry Garcia's liquid flights. The twin drumming of Mickey Hart and Bill Kreutzman provides an imaginative platform, bassist Phil Lesh takes his instrument into new dimensions, while organist Pigen provides a distinctive swirling sound which envelops and enhances his colleagues' interplay. The last-named takes a vocal cameo on 'Turn On Your Lovelight', a performance showing the Dead's R&B roots, while 'Dark Star' exposes new levels of musical empathy. Such factors ensure this album's prominence in the group's canon.

Dark Star; Death Don't Have No Mercy; Feedback; And We Bid You Goodnight; St. Stephen; Eleven; Turn On Your Lovelight.

First released 1970
UK peak chart position: did not chart
USA peak chart position: 64

36. LIVE WIRE/BLUES POWER
Albert King

Big Albert had been recording for Stax for two years, putting out a series of epochal contemporary blues records - 'Oh Pretty Woman', 'Crosscut Saw', 'Born Under A Bad Sign' and 'The Hunter' - when his label decided to record him live at San Francisco's Fillmore Auditorium. Later issues of material from the two nights that were recorded show that he performed most of his recent successes to his new-found hippy audience. By contrast on *Live Wire/Blues Power*, Albert's tortuously convoluted guitar style was given full and free rein. Despite his tetchy reputation, Albert responded gratefully to his new fans, but made no concessions to their initial ignorance of his music. The resulting record underlined his musical strengths and the vitality of the blues itself.

Watermelon Man; Blues Power; Night Stomp; Blues At Sunrise; Please Love Me; Lookout.

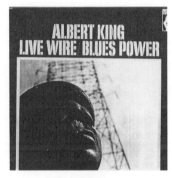

First released 1968
UK peak chart position: did not chart
USA peak chart position: 150

37. CONCERT FOR BANGLA DESH
Various

For a short while after the break up of the worlds most revered group, George Harrison was by far the most successful moptop. Unlike the others he was getting amongst other musicians, and generally having a much better time. This concert although blighted by some non-payment shenanigans remains an important milestone in rock history. It stands up very well 23 years on even though Ringo still forgets the words in 'It Don't Come Easy' and most people will skip through the Ravi Shankar section. Leon Russell sounds good, George carries his own numbers admirably, but it is Mr Dylan that made us cry.

Bangla Dhun; Wah-Wah; My Sweet Lord; Awaiting On You All; Ythat's The Way God Planned It; It Don't Come Easy; Beware Of Darkness; While My Guitar Gently Weeps; Jumpin' Jack Flash; Youngblood; Here Comes The Sun; A Hard Rain's Gonna Fall; It Takes A Lot To Laugh/It Takes A Train To Cry; Blowin' In The Wind; Mr. Tambourine Man; Just Like A Woman; Something; Bangla Desh.

First released 1972
UK peak chart position: 1
USA peak chart position: 2

38. BLUES IS KING
B.B. King

The mid-60s brought a crucial turning point in B.B. King's career. For the first time, he began to attract significant numbers of young white fans to his gigs. Through their interest, he was able to take his music beyond the 'chitlin' circuit' that had been his staple money-earner for more than a decade. He also acquired a new manager, Sid Seidenberg, who was able to open doors that had previously been closed against him. *Blues Is King* was King's second live album, enhanced by the inclusion of a version of his recent hit, 'Don't Answer The Door'. 'Sweet Sixteen Parts 1 & 2' also came from the same November 1966 gig. King's studio sessions were already leaning towards a more bland presentation, but his energy and charisma onstage revealed the true blues artist everyone knew he was.

Waitin' On You; Gambler's Blues; Tired Of Your Jive; Night Life; Buzz Me; Sweet Sixteen Part 1; Don't Answer The Door; Blind Love; I Know What You're Puttin' Down; Baby Get Lost; Gonna Keep On Loving You; Sweet Sixteen Part 2.

First released 1967
UK peak chart position: did not chart
USA peak chart position: did not chart

39. HAPPY TRAILS
Quicksilver Messenger Service

If the quintessential San Francisco Sound is defined by lengthy improvised guitar work and near-telepathic interplay, then *Happy Trails* crystallises the genre on record. Taking cues from two Bo Diddley songs, the quartet introduce new realms of expression to rock music. Guitarists John Cipollina and Gary Duncan offer contrasting textures and sound, goading each other to greater heights. Largely recorded live in concert, *Happy Trails* encapsulates an era of experimentation, employing images which embodied the outlaw chic of the hippie subculture. Its strengths are not, however, hidebound to an era, the album's mesmerising power remains as true as ever.

Who Do You Love (Part One); When You Love; Where You Love; How Do You Love; Which Do You Love; Who Do You Love (Part Two); Mona; Maiden Of The Cancer Moon; Calvary; Happy Trails.

First released 1968
UK peak chart position: did not chart
USA peak chart position: 27

40. CHUCK BERRY ON STAGE
Chuck Berry

Chuck Berry articulated teen culture better than any musician before or since and in doing so determined the progress of pop music. Time has not diminished the power of his work, the best of which appear on this (dubbed) live set. An erratic performer in later years, this album is powerful and concise, showcasing material which changed the notion of the pop song. Concise lyrics of near poetic simplicity are driven along by Berry's distinctive chord patterns and the artist also acknowledges his R&B roots with strong cover versions of material by Muddy Waters. *Chuck Berry On Stage* is an ebullient tribute to an artist and his music.

Go, Go, Go; Memphis Tennessee; Maybelline; Surfing Steel; Rocking On The Railroad; Brown Eyed Handsome Man; Still Got The Blues; Sweet Little Sixteen; Jaguar And The Thunderbird; I Just Want To Make Love To You; All Aboard; Trick Or Treat; The Man And The Donkey.

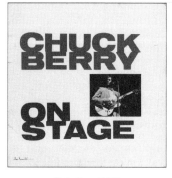

First released 1963
UK peak chart position: 6
USA peak chart position: 29

41. BELAFONTE AT CARNEGIE HALL
Harry Belafonte

Belafonte was just about at the peak of his popularity when he made this double-album set in a venue that, in the 50s, was usually the home of classical performers rather than pop artists. His magnetic personality and an impressive mixture of material which ranges from international folk songs such as 'Hava Nageela', 'Sylvie', 'Day-O', and 'Jamaican Farewell', to the traditional 'Danny Boy' and even a sea shanty, 'Shenandoah', ensured a stay of 86 weeks in the US chart and a Gold Disc award. The album also won a Grammy for Best Engineering Contribution.

Darlin' Cora; Sylvie; John Henry; Take My Mother Home; Jamaica/Farewell; Man Piaba, All My Trials, Man Smart; Matilda

First released 1959
UK peak chart position: did not chart
USA peak chart position: 3

42. My Funny Valentine
Miles Davis

Probably the finest live album in the history of jazz, *My Funny Valentine* presents the Miles Davis Quintet live at the Lincoln Centre's Philharmonic Hall in 1964. Surrounded by the vibrant and youthful rhythm section of Herbie Hancock (piano), Ron Carter (bass) and Tony Williams (drums), Davis was enjoying a strong new surge of creativity, and played at a stunning level of invention and passion throughout. The resonance of the long title track - one of those flawless performances that happens only very occasionally - dominates the record. Front-line partner George Coleman (tenor saxophone) chose a good evening to play some of the most beautiful solos in his life.

My Funny Valentine; All Of You; Stella By Starlight; All Blues; I Thought About You.

First released 1964
UK peak chart position: did not chart
USA peak chart position: 138

43. JOAN BAEZ IN CONCERT VOL 2
JOAN BAEZ

A year had passed between the release of the first In Concert album and its successor. The folk revival of the ensuing period introduced a new generation of performers, many of whom wrote their own material. Joan Baez continued to draw on Childe ballads, spirituals and Appalachian songs, but the inclusion of Bob Dylan's 'Don't Think Twice, It's Alright' signalled her move from traditional to contemporary styles. The singer's memorable soprano voice ensured the special nature of her interpretations and brought continuity to a seemingly disparate content.

Once I Had A Sweetheart; Jackaroe; Don't Think Twice, It's Alright; We Shall Overcome; Portland Town; Queen Of Hearts; Manha De Carnaval; Te Ador; Long Black Veil; Fennario; Ne Belle Cardillo; With God On Our Side; Three Fishers; Hush Little Baby; Battle Hymn Of The Republic.

First released 1964
UK peak chart position: 8
USA peak chart position: 7

44. ALIVE!
Kiss

A breakthrough record for Kiss, as well as being the first of their three live double albums. Culled from shows on their, Dressed To Kill tour, its wildly emblazoned antics, complete with full make up, blood letting and fire breathing and a collection of pop/rock anthems that revelled in their own glory. It came as no surprise that the band were beginning to exude a superstar mystique and status. The highlight being the plaintive, 'Black Diamond', which of all bands, the Replacements choose to cover on their, Let It Be album. Which gives you some indication of how widespread Kiss' influence on American youth was generally.

Deuce; Strutter; Got To Choose; Hotter Than Hell; Firehouse; Nothin' To Lose; C'mon And Love Me; Parasite; She; Watchin' You; 100,000 Years; Black Diamond; Rock Bottom; Cold Gin; Rock And Roll Nite; Let Me Go Rock n' Roll.

First released 1975
UK peak chart position: 49
USA peak chart position: 9

45. LENA HORNE AT THE WALDORF ASTORIA
Lena Horne

This album, which was made when on-site recording was very much in its infancy, has become a classic of its kind. It gives a tantalising insight into the ritzy world of New York cabaret and one of the supreme exponents of that art. The risqué 'New-Fangled Tango' got a lot of air-play at the time, but Miss Horne ran the gamut of musical emotions in a perfectly balanced programme which ranged from the witty 'How You Say It' through a storming version of 'Day In Day Out', to a medley of what she herself calls 'the surprising Cole Porter tunes'. Still as fresh as ever after nearly 40 years.

Today I Love Everybody; Let Me Love You; Come Running; How's Your Romance; After You; Love Of My Life; It's Alright With Me; Mood Indigo; I'm Beginning To See The Light; How You Say It; Honeysuckle Rose; Day In, Day Out; New-Fangled Tango; I Love To Love; From This Moment On.

First released 1957
UK peak chart position: did not chart
USA peak chart position: 24

46. IN CONCERT VOL. 1
Peter, Paul And Mary

Even though Bob Dylan and Joan Baez dominated the folk world and the album charts during 1964, there was still room for the gentle approach folkies. Peter Paul And Mary were able to regularly appear on peak television shows in the UK because they sounded harmless and the bite in their lyrics was overshadowed by overall goodness. This album stayed in the charts for months on both sides of the Atlantic and contains two essential Dylan protest songs; 'Blowin' In The Wind' and The Times They Are A Changin'' in addition to the mass market 'Puff The Magic Dragon'. Although important it now sounds dated.

The Times They Are A Changin'; A 'Soalin'; 500 Miles; Blue; Three Ravens; One Kind Favour; Blowin' In The Wind; Car, Car; Puff; Jesus Met The Woman.

First released 1964
UK peak chart position: 20
USA peak chart position: 4

47. LIVE AND DANGEROUS
Thin Lizzy

Phil Lynott's glorious call to arms; a heady mix of wry humour and wonderfully constructed vignettes of youthful indulgence and an intricate weave of Celtic moods. A soulful and stirring double album that captured evocatively the real show stopping sense that Thin Lizzy were adept at. Riding roughshod over a variety of styles; the woeful, 'I'm Still In Love With You', the frantic enthusiasm of the, 'Boys Are Back In Town' or the clever knitting of styles with, 'Rosalie/Cowgirl's Song', complete with giant mirror ball. Thin Lizzy were a band blessed with grace and fistful of ideas. All the evidence you need is here.

Boys Are Back In Town; Dancing In The Moonlight; Massacre; I'm Still In Love With You; Me And The Boys...; Don't Believe A Word; Warriors; Are You Ready?; Sha-la-la; Baby Drives Me Crazy; Rosalie/Cowgirl's Song.

First released 1978
UK peak chart position: 2
USA peak chart position: 84

48. FIVE LIVE YARDBIRDS
Yardbirds

Few British Beat groups attempted in-concert recordings, but this proved a natural vehicle for the Yardbirds. One of the era's most popular live attractions, the set captures their exciting interpretation of R&B. Their arrangements of material by Howlin' Wolf, Bo Diddley and Slim Harpo is exceptional and their prowess as musicians is immediately self-evident. Keith Relf proves himself an accomplished harmonica player while Eric Clapton's guitarwork lays the foundation for his future recordings. Where many contemporaries struggled to complete wholly satisfying albums, the Yardbirds did so with breath to spare.

Too Much Monkey Business; I Got Love If You Want It; Smokestack Lightning; Good Morning Little Schoolgirl; Respectable; Five Long Years; Pretty Girl; Louise; I'm A Man; Here 'Tis.

First released 1964
UK peak chart position: did not chart
USA peak chart position: did not chart

49. LIVE BULLET
Bob Seger

The double live album that, not unlike Kiss', truly opened the floodgates for Seger's real commercial success in the USA. A full blown gatefold sleeve affair recorded at two sold-out and enthusiastic shows in Detroit. Highlighting Seger's unpretentious and sometimes quietly profound take on small town living and its consequences. The sublime, 'Jody Girl', acts as a strong indication of his storytelling abilities. Though, it's on such nefarious blow-outs as the indulgent crowd pleasing, 'Heavy Music' and the stomping, honky-tonk of 'Katmandu' that this record really comes to life.

Nutbush City Limits; Travellin' Man; Beautiful Loser; Jody Girl; Looking Back; Get Out Of Denver; Let It Rock; I've Been Working; Turn The Page; UMC; Bo Diddley; Ramblin' Gamblin' Man; Heavy Music; Katmandu.

First released 1976
UK peak chart position: did not chart
USA peak chart position: 34

50. TURNING POINT
John Mayall

The almost all acoustic Mayall band was in stark contrast to the power and brass of his previous team during the *Bare Wires* period. Now a quiet quartet with finger style guitarist Jon Mark, Johnny Almond on sax and flute and bassist Stephen Thompson. Mayall stretches through some glorious jazz/blues fusion with some outstanding playing from Almond. There is the legendary chikka chikka harmonica solo on 'Room To Move', which Mayall still encores with. The only low point is the crass lyrics on 'The Laws Must Change' including, 'you're screaming at policeman, but they're only doing a gig'. Yuch!

The Laws Must Change; Saw Mill Gulch Road; I'm Gonna Fight For You JB; So Hard To Share; California; Thoughts About Roxanne; Room To Move.

First released 1969
UK peak chart position: 11
USA peak chart position: 32

THE TOP 50 PUNK ALBUMS

ANOTHER GENRE THAT HAS A MIXTURE OF STYLES. WE NOW LOOK BACK AT PUNK AS MUSIC THAT SHOOK THE RECORD INDUSTRY TO ITS ROOTS. IT CLEANED OUT, WOKE UP, SHOCKED AND PRODUCED A LOT OF SECOND-RATE MUSIC. THE RECORDS LISTED HERE HOWEVER WOULD AND SHOULD SIT WELL IN ANY DECENT RECORD COLLECTION AND ONCE AGAIN THE WINNER IS HEAD AND SHOULDERS ABOVE THE FOLLOWERS.

1. NEVER MIND THE BOLLOCKS HERE'S THE SEX PISTOLS
Sex Pistols

In the same way that Sgt Pepper... is unlikely to be toppled in the pop/rock category so this milestone stands atop any other record of its kind. Seen by some snobs at the time as musical illiterates, the Pistols legend continues as strong as ever. The music was in such stark contrast to what we had been enjoying that a backlash was inevitable. This will stay as a classic because it will not date. The power of tracks such as 'Pretty Vacant' or 'No Feelings' is as strong as 1977. This pivotal record has not mellowed with age, thankfully.

Holidays In The Sun; Bodies; No Feelings; Liar; God Save The Queen; Problems; Seventeen; Anachy In The UK; Submission; Pretty Vacant; EMI.

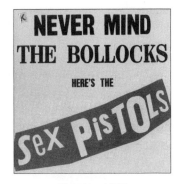

First released 1977
UK peak chart position: 1
USA peak chart position: 106

2. LONDON CALLING
Clash

If punk rejected pop history, *London Calling* reclaimed it, albeit with a knowing perspective. The scope of this double set is breaktaking, encompassing reggae, rockabilly and the group's own furious mettle. Where such a combination might have proved over-ambitious, the Clash accomplish it with swaggering panache. Guy Stevens, who produced the group's first demos, returns to the helm to provide a confident, cohesive sound equal to the set's brilliant array of material. Boldly assertive and superbly focused, *London Calling* contains many of the quartet's finest songs and is, by extension, virtually faultless.

London Calling; Brand New Cadillac; Jimmy Jazz; Hateful; Rudie Can't Fail; Wrong 'Em Boyd; Death Or Glory; Koka Kola; The Card Cheat; Spainsih Bombs; The Right Profile; Lost In The Supermarket; Clampdown; The Guns Of Brixton; Lover's Rock; Four Horsemen; I'm Not Down; Revolution Rock; Train In Vain.

First released 1979
UK peak chart position: 9
USA peak chart position: 27

3. RATTUS NORVEGICUS
Stranglers

Probably the most under-rated of the new wave/punk bands, these non-too youthful Guildford brutes simply didn't count according to pundits like Jon Savage, though that view may have been tempered by the fact that Jean Jaques Burnel gave him a kicking after a hostile review. The Stranglers combined a dark view of human nature with a musical legacy which stretched far beyond the year zero philosophy of others. *Rattus* offers a blend of cynicism, menace and antagonism unheard of since the Stooges (frequent comparisons to the Doors were misleading - they both had prominent keyboards). Standout tracks include the utterly venomous 'Ugly', the stage standard 'Hanging Around' and the elegiac 'Down In The Sewer'.

Sometimes; Goodbye Toulouse; London Lady; Princess Of The Streets; Hanging Around; Peaches; Get A Grip On Yourself; Ugly; Down In The Sewer: Falling; Down In The Sewer: Trying To Get Out Again; Rats Rally.

First released 1977
UK peak chart position: 4
USA peak chart position: did not chart

4. CLASH
Clash

The definitive punk statement, this album's power and authority have not diminished. It assails a variety of subjects; unemployment, imperialism and rebellion, deriding or lauding according to political stance. Joe Strummer's barking vocals expressed the anger of a disenfranchised generation, guitarist Mick Jones punctuating his ire with near telepathic precision. Almost every track is essential and in tackling Junior Murvin's 'Police And Thieves', the Clash show an empathy for reggae rarely heard in white rock. One of the finest first albums ever.

Janie Jones; Remote Control; I'm So Bored With The USA; White Riot; Hate And War; What's My Name; Deny; London's Burning; Career Opportunities; Cheat; Protex Blue; Police And Thieves; 48 Hours; Garage Land.

First released 1977
UK peak chart position: 12
USA peak chart position: 126

5. DAMNED DAMNED DAMNED
Damned

The first British punk band to release a single ('New Rose'), the Damned followed this achievement with the genre's debut album. *Damned Damned Damned* captured its furious rattle of basic chords and angry sentiments, delivered at amphetamine-like speed. Producer Nick Lowe ensured the quartet's primal scream was not modified by prevailing attitudes of musical correctness and the set's success is as due to his detached overview as the group's fevered nihilism. Their energy is exciting, the sense of freedom and mischief unrelenting, *Damned Damned Damned* defined punk both aurally and philosophically.

Neat Neat Neat; Fan Club; I Fall; Born To Kill; Stab Your Back; Feel The Pain; New Rose; Fish; See Her Tonite; 1 Of The 2; So Messed Up; I Feel Alright.

First released 1977
UK peak chart position: 36
USA peak chart position: did not chart

6. RAMONES
Ramones

Described alternately as minimalists or cartoon characters, the Ramones brought both elements to their metier. Drawing upon the undying appeal of simple 50s and 60s pop, the quartet reclaimed simplicity, adding to it a buzzsaw guitar and trash-culture values. Gore films, beach parties and solvent abuse are canonised in turn, but a sense of innocent self-deprecation prevents the charge of cheap sensationalism. Each track flirts around the two-minute watershed, the gaps between them barely discernible, the cumulative sense of fun and excitement as vital as ever.

Blitzrieg Bop; Beat On The Brat; Judy Is A Punk; I Wanna Be Your Boyfriend; Chain Saw; Now, I Wanna Sniff Some Glue; I Don't Wanna Go Down In The Basement; Loud Mouth; Havana Affair; Listen To My Heart; Fifty Third And Third; Let's Dance; I Don't Wanna Walk Around With You; Today Your Love, Tomorrow The World.

First released 1976
UK peak chart position: did not chart
USA peak chart position: 111

7. SINGLES GOING STEADY
Buzzcocks

The Buzzcocks emerged from Manchester's thriving punk enclave with a succession of startling pop singles. Tight melodies and highly memorable hooklines were enveloped in a breathless group sound full of purpose and drive which contrasted singer Pete Shelly's dispassionate, almost throw-away delivery. These eight singles, both a-sides and flips, encompassed a variety of subject matter, from masturbation ('Orgasm Addict') to 1981 nuspeak ('Everbody's Happy Nowadays'), without recourse to obfuscation. Such seminal recordings have ensured the Buzzcocks' place in a lineage between the Kinks and the Smiths as one of the greatest purveyors of the 45rpm.

Orgasm Addict; What Do I Get; I Don't Mind; Love You More; Ever Fallen In Love (With Someone You Shouldn't'ave); Promises; Everybody's Happy Nowadays; Harmony In My Head; Whatever Happened To; Oh Shit!; Autonomy; Noise Annoys; Just Lust; Lipstick; Why Can't I Touch It; Something's Gone Wrong Again; Love You More.

First released 1981
UK peak chart position: did not chart
USA peak chart position: did not chart

8. Germ Free Adolescents
X Ray Spex

Punk with a twist that was very nearly animated. Cartoon characters embroiled in the new wave, though the posturing, aggression and a collective two fingers to the world mentality that proliferated elsewhere, seemed to have passed X Ray Spex by. They were the deliberate underachievers, poking fun at the establishment as opposed to the heavy reprimands of their contemporaries. 'The Day The World Turned Dayglo', 'Warrior In Woolworths', the title track, all typifying their brash indulgences in punk/pop. A theme park equivalent to their more stern faced counterparts. A colourful explosion of sound.

The Day The World Turned Dayglo; Obsessed With You; Genetic Engineering; Identity; I Live Off You; Germfree Adolescents; Art-I-Ficial; Let's Submerge; Warrior In Woolworths; I Am A Poseur; I Can't Do Anything; Highly Inflammable; Age; Plastic Bag; I Am A Cliche; Oh Bondage Up Yours!.

First released 1978
UK peak chart position: 30
USA peak chart position: did not chart

9. Marquee Moon
Television

New York's 70s' punk was markedly different to that of Britain. Rather than reject the past, American groups deconstructed its forms to rebuilt with recourse to its strengths. Television's leader, Tom Verlaine, professed admiration for Moby Grape and the folk-rock of early Fairport Convention. Elements of the latter appear on this album's title track, which offers a thrilling instrumental break, built upon a modal scale. Verlaine's shimmering guitar style provides the set's focus, but his angular compositions are always enthralling. A sense of brooding mystery envelops the proceedings, and *Marquee Moon* retains its standing as one of the era's pivotal releases.

See No Evil; Venus; Friction; Marquee Moon; Elevation; Guiding Light; Prove It; Torn Curtain.

First released 1977
UK peak chart position: 28
USA peak chart position: did not chart

10. Pink Flag
Wire

Wire's furious interpretation of punk was encapsulated on this primitive, minimalist debut. Abrasive and disjointed, these 21 tracks exude a fury impossible to ignore and one enhanced by their very brevity. Tracks halt, sometimes abruptly, when the point has been made, creating an ever-changing melange of sound and texture. While generally aggressive, *Pink Flag* also boasts two wonderful pop songs ('Ex-Lion Tamer' and 'Mannequin'), suggesting that Wire would not be constrained by stylistic expectations. The album's mixture of polemics and pointedness would influence several US groups, including R.E.M., who later covered 'Strange'. Its perceptive urgency grows with time.

Reuters; Field Day For The Sundays; Three Girl Rhumba; Ex Lion Tamer; Lowdown; Start To Move; Brazil; It's So Obvious; Surgeon's Girl; Pink Flag; The Commercial; Straight Line; 106 Beats That; Mr. Suit; Strange; Fragile; Mannequin; Differnet To Me; Champs; Feeling Called Love; 12 X U.

First released 1977
UK peak chart position: did not chart
USA peak chart position: did not chart

11. LEAVE HOME
Ramones

Basic chords, furious tempos and moronic intensity had defined the Ramones' debut album. On their second, they simply repeated that mix. Despite appearances to the contrary, the quartet understood the attraction of primeval pop, grafting urgency to exciting hooklines which snapped shut when their appeal peaked. Brill Building ghosts hover around the commercial twists of 'Swallow My Pride', whereas gore films and cartoons inspired 'Gimme Gimme Shock Treatment' and 'Pinhead'. The latter's 'gabba gabba' refrain comes directly from Tod Browning's shocker, 'Freaks'. *Leave Home* shows the Ramones fully aware of their strengths the result is another unqualified classic.

Glad To See You Go; Gimme Gimme Shock Treatment; I Remember You; Oh, Oh I Love Her So; Carbona Not Glue; Suzy Is A Headbanger; Pinhead; Now I Wanna Be A Good Boy; Shallow My Pride; What's Your Game; California Sun; Commando; You're Gonna Kill That Girl; You Should Never Have Opened That Door.

First released 1977
UK peak chart position: 45
USA peak chart position: 148

12. CROSSING THE RED SEA WITH
Adverts

One of British Punk's archetypal acts, the Adverts blend rudimentary skills with self-deprecating irony. Indeed 'One Chord Wonders' is the perfect encapsulation of the movement inspiring it. Songwriter T.V. Smith articulated the frenzied anger of the period in a way that marked him both as participant and observer. Aware of his group's limitations, he wrote material which emphasised their strengths and as a result captured the spirit of the times few contemporaries could match. It would prove a passing moment, later releases were knowing where this was inspired, but *Crossing The Red Sea* is as vital a documentary as *The Clash* or *Never Mind The Bollocks*

One Chord Wonders; Bored Teenagers; New Church On The Roof; New Boys; Bombsite Boy; No Time To Be 21; Safety In Numbers; Drowning Man On Wheels; Great British Mistake.

First released 1978
UK peak chart position: 38
USA peak chart position: did not chart

13. THE UNDERTONES
Undertones

Having announced their arrival with the thrilling 'Teenage Kicks', one of pop's most perfect singles, the Undertones completed a debut album possessing all the charm of that first single. Innocent to the point of naiveté, the group deftly combine punk and pop with songs which articulate the angst of adolescence from within. Feargal Sharkey's braying voice cuts through the band's gutsy playing like a knife through butter, where simple, energetic hooklines emphasises the bubblegum charm of 'Jimmy Jimmy' and 'Here Comes Summer'. Only the churlish could fail to be moved by this album's simplicity and verve.

Family Entertainment; Girl's Don't Like It; Male Model; I Gotta Getta; Teenage Kicks; Wrong Way; Jump Boys; Here Comes Summer; Get Over You; Billy's Third; Jimmy Jimmy; True Confessions; She's A Runaround; I Know A Girl; Listening In.

First released 1979
UK peak chart position: 13
USA peak chart position: 154

14. NO MORE HEROES
Stranglers

Punk's parents terribles, the Stranglers courted controversy throughout their early career. Bileful lyrics brought charges of misogyny, although the group suggested that outrage was merely part of the genre's tenet. They answered such criticism of their debut album with the even more uncompromising *No More Heroes*, a vengeful collection echoing the nihilism of its title. Role playing apart, there was no denying a musical prowess compressing savage guitar, throbbing bass and swirling organ into vicious, driving sound. Hugh Cornwell's sneering intonation matched the aggression of his accompaniment, but the album also offered indications of the lighter pop style which the quartet would later follow.

I Feel Like A Wog; Bitching; Dead Ringer; Dagenham Dave; Bring On The Nubiles; Something Better Change; No More Heroes; Peasant In The Big Shitty; Burning Up Time; English Towns; School Mam; In The Shadows.

First released 1977
UK peak chart position: 2
USA peak chart position: did not chart

15. CHAIRS MISSING
Wire

A euphemism for insanity, *Chairs Missing* is an apt summation of Wire's disturbing music. A product of London's punk scene, the quartet nonetheless owed a debt to the art-school experimentation of the mid-60s, a contrast which gave their craft originality. Oblique pop songs, including 'Outdoor Miner' and 'I Am The Fly', exemplify Wire's development from the abrasive minimalists of earlier releases, while their widening musical perspectives are reflected in the edgy 'Practice Makes Perfect'. Producer Mike Throne adds keyboards and synthesiser to the group's guitar-based attack as *Chairs Missing* establishes Wire as one of the most innovative of their era.

Practice Makes Perfect; French Film Blurred; Another The Letter; Men Second; Marooned; Sand In My Joints; Being Sucked In Again; Heartbeat; Mercy; Outdoor Miner; I Am The Fly; I Feel Mysterious Today; From The Nursey; Used To; Too Late.

First released 1978
UK peak chart position: 48
USA peak chart position: did not chart

16. ROCKET TO RUSSIA
Ramones

Credible American punk with a sloppy grin and fringe to match. The Ramones, unblinking eyes, quizzical expressions and masters of the studied state and an eloquence that ran to '1-2-3-4', or 'Gabba-Gabba-Hey' at its most revealing. To the mythical Ramones brothers it didn't matter one bit, the closest New York's CBGB's club came to a house band, had made good with the excellent throwaway pop/punk of, *Rocket To Russia*. While punk was exploding all over, the Ramones kept their nonchalance and unaddressed humour intact. 'Rockaway Beach', a near perfect summertime anthem. While, 'Teenage Lobotomy', revelled in their legend pure unadulterated joy.

Cretin Hop; Rockaway Beach; Here Today, Gone Tomorrow; Locket Love; I Don't Care; Sheena Is A Punk Rocker; We're A Happy Family; Teenage Lobotomy; Do You Wanna Dance?; I Wanna Be Well; I Can't Give You Anything; Ramona; Surfin' Bird; Why Is It Always This Way?.

First released 1977
UK peak chart position: 60
USA peak chart position: 49

17. BLACK ALBUM
Damned

The Damned completing this album was markedly different to that which recorded *New Rose* three years earlier. Captain Sensible had switched from bass to lead to replace Brian James, while ex-Hot Rod Paul Gray took up the former instrument. A double set, *The Black Album* included live material and an extended gothic workout, but at its core was a series of highly-charged power pop songs crammed with exotica ranging from mellotron to synthesiser. The ghost of 60s psychedelia wraps itself around these compositions, but the Damned's irreverence ensures their individuality remains intact.

Wait For The Blackout; Lively Arts; Silly Kids Games; Drinking About My Baby; Hit And Miss; Doctor Jekyll And Mr. Hyde; 13th Floor Vendetta; Twisted Nerve; Sick Of This And That; History Of The World (Part One); Therapy.

First released 1980
UK peak chart position: 29
USA peak chart position: did not chart

18. ALL MOD CONS
Jam

Tagged punk by default, the Jam preferred 60s iconography, particularly the Mod movement, to the rattle of safety-pins. But if the uniform was different, the sense of commitment was identical, and on *All Mod Cons*, the trio fused references and individuality. The spectre of the Who and Kinks remained, but songwriter Paul Weller restructured such influences to proclaim his own voice. Thus a version of the latter's 'David Watts' introduces intent, rather than summarising it and the set successfully explores several avenues postulated by the Jam's craft. Social comment, personal reflection and assured musicianship bind the album into a cohesive whole and laid down the contrasting paths the group would later follow.

All Mod Cons; To Be Someone (Didn't We have A Nice Time); Mr. Clean; David Watts; English Rose; In The Crowd; Billy Hunt; It's Too Bad; Fly 3.18; The Place I Love; 'A' Bomb In Wardour Street; Down In The Tube Station At Midnight.

First released 1978
UK peak chart position: 6
USA peak chart position: did not chart

19. THE SCREAM
Siouxsie And The Banshees

Despite evolving from a group of Sex Pistols' fans, Siouxsie And The Banshees eschewed the cliches of punk, offering instead an austere and bleak music. Bassist Steve Severin and drummer Kenny Morris provide simple, Teutonic-style patterns over which Siouxsie Sioux wails in the manner of former Velvet Underground chanteuse Nico. Unremitting original songs are joined by a version of the Beatles' 'Helter Skelter', which the Banshees interpret with the full knowledge of how it helped inspire the Charles Manson murders. *The Scream* is an apt title for such desolate music.

Pure; Jigsaw Feeling; Overground; Carcass; Helter Skelter; Mirage; Metal Postcard; Nicotine Stain; Surburban Relapse; Switch.

First released 1978
UK peak chart position: 12
USA peak chart position: did not chart

20. A Different Kind Of Tension
Buzzcocks

The Buzzcocks' third album was their last release until regrouping in 1989. Tiring of their mantle as purveyors of perfect pop songs, they used this album to attack musical barriers and preconceptions. Although vocalist Pete Shelley continued to write the bulk of the material, guitarist Steve Diggle makes several telling contributions, providing contrast in the process. The highlights, however, belong to the former, notably 'You Say You Don't Love Me' and the extended closing track, 'I Believe'. A superb album in its own right, *A Different Kind Of Tension* also completes the first inception of a truly fascinating act.

Paradise; Sitting 'Round At Home; You Say You Don't Love Me; You Know You Can't Help It; Mad, Mad July; Raison D'etre; I Don't Know What To Do With My Life; Money; Hollow Inside; Different Kind Of Tension; I Believe; Radio Nine.

First released 1979
UK peak chart position: 26
USA peak chart position: 163

21. In The City
Jam

Although bracketed with punk, the Jam were, in many ways, its apotheosis. Their unashamed love of 60s Mod culture was fully exposed on this nerve-tingling collection which drew on style icons the Who and Tamla/Motown, yet articulated frustration for a different generation. Anger and alienation explode from Paul Weller's crisp, well-sculpted compositions, the group's tight playing contrasting his barely-checked emotion. Although unambiguous lyrically, it's on guitar that Weller really sets his ire free, in particular on 'Bricks And Mortar', which bursts into a pop-art frenzy. A highly-charged debut album.

Art School; I've Changed My Address; Slow Down; I Got By In Time; Away From The Numbers; Batman; In The City; Sounds From The Street; Non Stop Dancing; Time For Truth; Takin' My Love; Bricks And Mortar.

First released 1977
UK peak chart position: 20
USA peak chart position: did not chart

22. Black And White
Stranglers

b. Punk's sophisticates, the Stranglers making good on their laconic reputation, sitting somewhere between, aesthetically, a host of lounge room lizards, and aurally, as shrewd engineers with a brash punk mentality and a delivery that was very nearly that of a quite demented roomful of crooners. *Black And White* played on these elements perfectly. From the corrupting lilt of 'Nice 'N' Sleazy', to the much favoured live, 'Toiler On The Sea', the Stranglers showed an irascible fervour for their dark and glistening art. A very cultivated and cultured punk rocker.

Tank; Nice 'N' Sleazy; Outside Tokyo; Mean To Me; Sweden (All Quiet On The Eastern Front); Hey (Rise Of The Robots); Toiler On The Sea; Curfew; Threatened; Do You Wanna; In The Shadows; Enough Time; Walk On By.

First released 1978
UK peak chart position: 2
USA peak chart position: did not chart

23. 154
Wire

The much revered and influential punk outfit that had a complexity and sense of original thought that could have easily outlived the self-destructive punk boom. Articulate but truly anarchic in their vision, they had a wry sense of cynicism tempered by a glorious abandon in their music. *154*, their third album, showed them in a truly innovative light. Guitarist Bruce Gilbert estimated the songs as nothing more than, coffee table polaroids. Saying they were larger observations. Whatever. The final result is a magnificent work of wordplay, wit, texture and some occasional brevity. Definitely at the upper reaches of punk's legacy.

I Should Have Known Better; Two People In A Room; The 15th; Other Window; Single KO; Touching Display; On Returning; Mutual Friend; Blessed State; Once Is Enough; Map Ref 41 Degrees N. 95 Degrees SW; Indirect Enquiries; 40 Versions.

First released 1979
UK peak chart position: 39
USA peak chart position: did not chart

24. WILD GIFT
X

While the East Coast was ably represented by the starker but less musical vision of Darby Crash and the Germs, X were central to the emergence of the Los Angeles punk scene. Fronted by the twin vocals of John Doe and Exene Cervanka, and boosted by the guitar adrenalin of Billy Zoom, this was a compelling second album. The short sharp blasts of songs articulated both the excitement and decay of the inner city, with an urgency that steamrollered sacred cows (notably some none too printable references to Elvis Presley on 'Back 2 Base') and wrestled with their hometown's varied reference points ('White Girl', 'Adult Books', 'We're Desperate'). Afterwards Black Flag brought the region hardcore but X remain the godfathers to the whole movement.

The Once Over Twice; We're Desperate; Adult Books; Universal Corner; I'm Coming Over; It's Who You Know; In This House That I Call Home; Some Other Time; White Girl; Beyond And Back; Back 2 The Base; When Our Love Passed Out On The Couch; Year 1.

First released 1981
UK peak chart position: did not chart
USA peak chart position: 165

25. METAL BOX
Pil

Determined to deny musical preconceptions, former Sex Pistols' singer John Lydon undertook a radical path with his next venture. On *Metal Box* he unleashed a torrent of vocal styles, alternately pleading, moaning or wailing over a sound drawn equally from Jamaican dub or German experimentalists Can. Bassist Jah Wobble provides the fluid skeleton with throbbing, sinewy lines and patterns, while Keith Levene adds instinctive flourishes on both guitar and keyboards. Impressionistic rather than defined, the material owes its strength to the quartet's determination to challenge and their disavowal of compromise.

Albatross; Memories; Swan Lake; Poptones; Careeing; No Birds; Graveyard; The Suit; Bad Baby; Socialist; Chant; Radio 4.

First released 1978
UK peak chart position: 22
USA peak chart position: did not chart

26. ANOTHER MUSIC IN A DIFFERENT KITCHEN
Buzzcocks

Opening, unannounced, with the briefest snatch of 'Boredom' from the Buzzcocks' first EP, this debut album shows how much the group had developed. They are the best exponents of the pop song to emerge from the punk explosion and herein the Buzzcocks marry thrilling hooklines with tense, propulsive energy. Vocalist Pete Shelley delivers his lines in a casual, but effective, manner, articulating hope and despair with equal unanimity. The set's intensity increases as it progresses, culminating in the seven-minute closing track in which jagged chords are propelled by a rollicking, Bo Diddley-styled drum pattern.

Fast Cars; No Reply; You Tear Me Up; Get On Our Own; Love Battery; Sixteen; I Don't Mind; Fiction Romance; Autonomy; I Need; Moving Away From The Pulsebeat.

First released 1978
UK peak chart position: 15
USA peak chart position: did not chart

27. GIVE 'EM ENOUGH ROPE
Clash

Sensing the emollient rattle of punk was an artistic dead end, the Clash took an abrupt volte-face and invited American Sandy Pearlman to produce their second album. Respected for his work with Blue Oyster Cult and the Dictators, Pearlman introduced a sheen which disturbed purists but introduced the Clash to a wider audience. The clear sound brought new emphasis to the quartet's internal interplay and allowed the material to stand up in its own right. *Give 'Em Enough Rope* contains several of the band's most popular songs, which range from the defiant 'Tommy Gun' to the sensitive 'Stay Free', a contrast confirming the Clash's wider musical ambitions.

Safe European Home; English Civil War; Tommy Gun; Julie's Been Working For The Drug Squad; Last Gang In Town; Guns On The Roof; Drug-stabbing Time; Stay Free; Cheapstakes; All The Young Punks (New Boots And Contracts).

First released 1978
UK peak chart position: 2
USA peak chart position: 128

28. LAMF
Heartbreakers

The Heartbreakers revolved around two former members of the New York Dolls, Johnny Thunders and Jerry Nolan. Having decamped to London in 1976, they became an integral part of the early punk circuit, before their solitary studio album. Although hampered by an insubstantial mix, the set contains some of the era's most expressive songs, notably 'Born Too Loose' and 'Chinese Rocks', the latter a chilling account of heroin addiction co-written with Dee Dee Ramone. Tight, unfussy playing emphasises the power of material which proved pivotal in the development of the new music in both the UK and USA. Sadly, the featured line-up disintegrated soon afterwards and numerous permutations failed to recreate its strengths.

Born Too Loose; Baby Talk; All By Myself; I Wanna Be Loved; It's Not Enough; Chinese Rocks; Get Off The Phone; Pirate Love; One Track Mind; I Love You; Goin' Steady; Let Go.

First released 1977
UK peak chart position: 55
USA peak chart position: did not chart

29. I'M STRANDED
Saints

Formed in 1975 in Brisbane, Australia, the Saints were endeavouring to punk glory before the Sex Pistols had even taken up their instruments. Fronted by the guttural sneer of vocalist, Chris Bailey and the enigmatic guitar work of Ed Kuepper, the Saints had a swagger that was pure Stooges, but a lyrical bent that was almost Dylan with a sneer. Ramshackle, but consistently profound, this, their first album was full of high glories and damning asides. The biting title track, the uproarious, 'Demolition Girl', and the insistent and quite brilliant, 'Erotic Neurotic'. Buy it.

(I'm) Stranded; One Way Street; Wild About You; Messin' With The Kid; Erotic/Neurotic; No Time; Kissin' Cousins; Story Of Love; Demolition Girl; Nights In Venice.

First released 1977
UK peak chart position: did not chart
USA peak chart position: did not chart

30. FRESH FRUIT FOR ROTTING VEGETABLES
Dead Kennedys

Where most American groups formed in the Sex Pistols' wake adopted their image but none of their substance, the Dead Kennedys brought a new perspective to punk's storm and drang. Group leader Jello Biafra attacked hypocrisy with a series of virulent anthems and, by extension, fought a tireless campaign against censorship. Bitter sarcasm is unleashed on 'Kill The Poor' and 'Holiday in Cambodia' while 'California Uber Alles' savages the 'new age' politics of contemporary governor Jerry Brown. Furious tempos and gunshot guitar emphasise the album's anger and frustration, and set a pattern for the ensuing hardcore movement. A hugely influential set.

Kill The Poor; Forward To Death; When Ya Get Drafted; Let's Lynch The Landlord; Drug Me; Your Emotions; Chemical Warfare; California Uber Alles; I KIll Children; Stealing People's Mail; Funland At The Beach; Ill In The Head; Holiday In Cambodia; Viva Las Vegas.

First released 1980
UK peak chart position: 33
USA peak chart position: did not chart

31. SOUND AFFECTS
Jam

The most eloquent of punk rockers, the Jam may have had the energy and youthful fury of their musical contemporaries, but they also had the spirit, insight and wit of one Paul Weller. From the punning title to the easy storytelling that harboured an ingrained bitterness and a quiet desperation that was to earmark much of Weller's work with the Jam. Lifting the Beatles' 'Taxman' almost wholesale for 'Start' may have seemed unforgiveable, but having written the flawless, 'That's Entertainment' quite rightly absolved him of any blame. A great, great record.

Pretty Green; Monday; But I'm Different Now; Set The House Ablaze; Start; That's Entertainment; Dreamtime; Man In The Cornershop; Music For The Last Couple; Boy About Town; Scrape Away.

First released 1980
UK peak chart position: 2
USA peak chart position: 72

32. HORSES
Patti Smith

Poet/playwright Patti Smith embraced rock as a critic and performer during New York Punk's formative era. These different elements gelled to startling effect on *Horses*, which attacked preconceptions and declared innovation to great effect. Her untutored voice provides raw realism while a refusal to compromise took music into uncharted territory. Smith's splicing together of her own 'Horses' to the standard 'Land Of 1000 Dances' simultaneously declared pop history and its future. John Cale's production inevitably suggests comparison's with the Velvet Underground, but despite a sense of shared commitment, Smith's music is powerful and exciting on its own terms. Few debut albums are as intense or as fully-formed.

Gloria: In Excelsis Deo; Gloria (Version); Redondo Beach; Birdland; Free Money; Kimberly; Break It Up; Land: Horses/Land Of A 1000 Dances/La Mer (De); Elegie.

First released 1975
UK peak chart position: did not chart
USA peak chart position: 47

33. MOVING TARGETS
Penetration

Press acclaim and the patronage of Radio One's John Peel wasn't enough to sustain this female lead five-piece. Their debut single, the excellent, 'Don't Dictate', which came out in the autumn of 1977, set the tone and a widely regarded reputation for their punky enthusiasm. With this, their debut album, that appeared the following year, cementing their critical acclaim. Though, their much vaunted appeal never truly translated into record sales. Both their albums never managing to break into the UK Top 20. Pauline Murray eventually going solo but suffering a much similar fate.

Future Daze; Life's A Gamble; Lovers Of Outrage; Vision; Silent Community; Stone Heroes; Movement; Too Many Friends; Reunion; Nostalgia; Freemoney.

First released 1978
UK peak chart position: 22
USA peak chart position: did not chart

34. KICK OUT THE JAMS
MC5

A true explosion of a record. Unfeasibly heady in its approach and delivery, it still stands today as one of the great, unabashed maws of raw, musical energy. Vocalist Rob Tyner crawling from a whisper to a scream, the tunnel of sound put around him both desperate and admirable. The title track a manifestation of sound threatening to stumble and fall in on itself. The simply great, 'Motor City Is Burning', the unsurprisingly monikered guitarist, Fred 'Sonic' Smith proving the power of a well chosen nickname. While the eager sentiment of, 'I Want You Right Now' speaks volumes about the tone of the album. One to blow your speaker covers off to.

Ramblin' Rose; Kick Out The Jams; Come Together; Rocket Reducer Number 52; Borderline; Motor City Is Burning; I Want You Right Now; Starship.

First released 1969
UK peak chart position: did not chart
USA peak chart position: 30

35. TIME'S UP
Buzzcocks

Originally one of the punk era's most notorious 'bootleg' albums, *Time's Up* eventually gained this legitimate release. The Manchester group grabbed immediate attention with their debut EP *Spiral Scratch*, a home-made artefact fulfilling the genre's do-it-yourself ethos. Culled from the same early studio sessions, this album rings with the same sense of purpose, amateurish, but wholly compelling. In 'Boredom' the quartet articulated punk's raison d'etre with pinpoint accuracy, its tow-note refrain a nagging reminder of frustration. The set also features original vocalist Howard Devoto, who later left to form Magazine, and in doing so is a valuable testament historically and musically. Not just a chronicle of the formative stage of an important act, *Time's Up* encapsulates the emotion of a movement.

You Tear Me Up; Breakdown; Friends Of Mine; Orgasm Addict; Boredom; Time's Up; Lester Sands (Drop In The Ocean); Love Battery; I Can't Control Myself; I Love You, You Big Dummy; Don't Mess Me 'Round.

First released 1991 rec. 1976
UK peak chart oposition: did not chart
USA peak chart position: did not chart

36. PURE MANIA
Vibrators

One of the great London bands at the latter end of the 70s, the Vibrators were a massive jangle of punk and a shakedown of great songs. John Ellis, latterly of the Stranglers, gave a raspy backbone to their pure and quite driven catalogue of three-minute-plus dementia. The firm live favourite, 'Baby Baby', the well crafted rush of, 'Into The Future' and the clearly homegrown, 'London Girls'. Reports in the mid-90s indicate that they've been spotted playing live again, how well remains to be seen.

Into The Future; Yeah Yeah Yeah; Sweet Sweet Heart; Keep It Clean; Baby Baby; No Heart; She's Bringing You Down; Petrol; London Girls; You Broke My Heart; Whips And Furs; Stiff Little Fingers; Wrecked On You; I Need A Slave; Bad Time.

First released 1977
UK peak chart position: did not chart
USA peak chart position: did not chart

37. CAN'T STAND THE REZILLOS
Rezillos

One of the finest groups to emerge from Scotland's punk scene, the Rezillos created a wonderful hybrid of pop culture and attitude. Their love of Merseybeat, girl-groups and garage bands was matched only by a similar affection for related ephemera, be it Doctor Who, Thunderbirds or Marvel comics. Exuberant almost to the point of hysteria, they created a body of work full of verve, style and humour, which this album encapsulates to perfection. From the pubescent sting of 'No' to the irony of 'Top Of The Pops', the set bubbles with mischief and invention, qualities undiminished by time.

Flying Saucer Attack; No; Someone's Gonna Get Their Head Kicked In Tonight; Top Of The Pops; 2000 AD; It Gets Me; Can't Stand My Baby; Glad All Over; My Baby Does Good Sculptures; I Like It; Gettin' Me Down; Cold Wars; Bad Guy Reaction.

First released 1978
UK peak chart position: 16
USA peak chart position: did not chart

38. THE ONLY ONES
Only Ones

The closest thing the UK had to Johnny Thunder's Heartbreakers, a laconic, shamble of a band who were, at moments, touched by a creative greatness that made you want to get out of the glare. This, their debut, was of course graced with, 'Another Girl, Another Planet', but it's the sheer excitement generated by the entire record itself that still bites. Shambolic, but proud and somehow fully tangled up in the band themselves. Perrit, after numerous attempts, making some sort of comeback in London earlier this year. But it's highly unlikely that he or a host of impersonators will ever capture this record's ragged glory.

Trouble In The World; The Beast; Lovers Of Today; Why Don't You Kill Yourself; As My Wife Says; Big Sleep; City Of Fun; Programme; No Peace For The Wicked; Miles From Nowhere; Another Girl, Another Planet; Me And My Shadow.

First released 1978
UK peak chart position: 56
USA peak chart position: did not chart

39. LIVE AT THE WITCH TRIALS
Fall

One of rock's most original and distinctive acts, the Fall have consistently refused to brook compromise. Led by the irascible Mark E. Smith, they declared a pungent individuality on a debut album indebted to Punk's freedom, yet one which rejected its trappings. Smith's bitter wit is crucial to their metier; half speaking, half singing, he savages insincerity, implying political statements without overtly expressing them. The group support his rant with rudimentary dissonance, creating scratchy pulses of sound that are both invigorating and exciting. Terse and combative, *Live At The Witch Trials* is a radical statement, the power of which remains undiminished.

Frightened; Crap Rap 2 - Like To Blow; Rebellious Jukebox; No Xmas For John Quays; Mother-Sister?; Industrial Estate; Underground Medecin; Two Steps Back; Live At The Witch Trials; Futures And Pasts; Music Scene.

First released 1979
UK peak chart position: did not chart
USA peak chart position: did not chart

40. WHAT'S THIS FOR
Killing Joke

Killing Joke at their most powerful. Unrelenting in their stark outlook, their particular brand of agitprop idealism and fiery musical bombast was best captured here. Chillingly adept in their remoteness, their dark, musical heart came alive with *What's This For*. The remarkable texture of their music; jagged then remotely sullen, was paraded through the enigmatic, 'Follow The Leaders'. Jaz Coleman's sense of bloody purpose lifting 'The Fall Of Because', while 'Who Told You How?' remains enigmatic and disdainful. It's little wonder that their return has been greeted with such enthusiasm.

The Fall Of Because; Tension; Unspeakable; Butcher; Who Told You How?; Follow The Leaders; Madness; Exit.

First released 1981
UK peak chart position: 42
USA peak chart position: did not chart

41. NOBODY'S HEROES
Stiff Little Fingers

Irish pop punk that took real flight after the original provocation and hastily fanned flames of punk's initial bravura and sometime carefully engineered hype had died down. Stiff Little Fingers were a provocative strand of punk rock and flaming youth caught up in the day to day living with the Troubles in Ireland. Consequently, they had the vision and wit of folk musicians in their stories. Their punk ethos intact, but still managing to suffuse their music with a strength of melodies and some memorable playing. Forget the comeback, this is surly testimony of their strength enough.

Gotta Gettaway; Wait And See; Fly The Flag; At The Edge; Nobody's Hero; Bloody Dub; No Change; Suspect Device; Tin Soldiers.

First released 1980
UK peak chart position: 8
USA peak chart position: did not chart

42. DAMAGED
Black Flag

Henry Rollins, more recently seen concocting a brew of ferocious hard rock alongside some wry spoken word work, helped create a truly abandoned hardcore record with his former band Black Flag. *Damaged* was evoked, in part, through his youthful, unbridled psyche. Brimming with energy, angst and tense, fiery lyrics of betrayal and anger, *Damaged* became a cornerstone of American hardcore with its ebullient, uncompromising musical stances. 'Rise Above' still frequently covered today, though it was the stark intensity of songs like, 'Police Story' and 'Life Of Pain' that typified their commitment.

Rise Above; Spray Paint; Six Pack; What I See; TV Party; Thirsty And Miserable; Police Story; Gimmie Gimmie Gimmie; Depression; Room 13; Damaged II; No More; Padded Cell; Life Of Pain; Damaged I.

First released 1981
UK peak chart position: did not chart
USA peak chart position: did not chart

43. POWER IN THE DARKNESS
Tom Robinson Band

Tom Robinson's first outspoken album of many. Complete with liner notes detailing the impetus behind the songs. While the rear sleeve gives vent to Robinson's political angst and a roundabout call to arms at the barricades. The record, however, is profound in its enduring self-belief. A great amalgam of punk/pop, ethics and all, translated as an exciting, visceral album in a style since much imitated, but rarely bettered for fury and genuine loathing. The fiery, 'Ain't Gonna Take It', with its impassioned and smoking sense of betrayal encapsulates the mood and the time perfectly. A ludicrously good debut.

Up Against The Wall; Grey Cortina; Too Good To Be True; Ain't Gonna Take It; Long Hot Summer; Winter Of '79; Man You Never Saw; Better Decide Which Side You're On; You Gotta Survive; Power In The Darkness.

First released 1978
UK peak chart position: 4
USA peak chart position: 144

44. VENGEANCE
New Model Army

Subsequently derided by the UK music press (seemingly because of little else than their Yorkshire roots), New Model Army were nevertheless in magnificent form for this debut mini-album, recorded before the departure of maestro bass player Stuart Morrow. Other efforts over the next decade or so have all had merit, often offering more in the way of considered songwriting. But it was *Vengeance* which really gave NMA its huge fan base. The lynchpin title-track blew a whole straight through the side of traditional left wing liberal tastes of protest rock music: 'I believe in justice, I believe in vengeance, I believe in GETTING the bastards'. Accusations of machismo were diffused by the stark questions posed in 'A Liberal Education', which honed in just as effectively on the lack of natural justice in the world.

Christian Militia; Notice Me; Smalltown England; A Liberal Education; Vengeance; Sex (The Black Angel); Running; Spirit Of The Falklands.

First released 1984
UK peak chart position: 73
USA peak chart position: did not chart

45. CYCLEDELIC
Johnny Moped

It's not quite a punk album in the truest sense, nor would it sit happily with a collection of conventional psychedelia, but this is the perfect combination of the two traditions. Rare, in rock 'n' roll terms, has been the 'genius' of Johnny Moped. If we were as fond as our American cousins of coining the term 'loser', Johnny would surely have terminal recorded as his own personal prefix. The sessions for this were only achieved when the rest of Moped's band (who included alumni like Captain Sensible) kidnapped him from Brenda, his wife. Brenda didn't take too kindly to Johnny, otherwise an intellectually challenged, moped-driving factory worker, doing the rock star business. Though a second album came years later, this is the perfect demonstration of Moped's pre-care in the community rock chic.

VD Boiler; Panic Button; Little Queenie; Maniac; Darling, Let's Have Another Baby; Groovy Baby; 3D Time; Wee Wee; Make Trouble; Wild Breed; Hell Razor; Incendiary Device.

First released 1978
UK peak chart position: did not chart
USA peak chart position: did not chart

46. FEEDING OF THE 5000
Crass

Perhaps the only truly anarchic band to come out of the punk movement. Uncompromising in their approach and execution, their sloganeering and lifestyle, communal, once quite rightly described as Underground, now has more familiar reference points with the New Age Travellers. The band, formed by Penny Rimbaud earned its reputation through near constant live work and released is material on its own Crass records. A truly singular exponent of the punk ideals and idealism that was given a full and bloody hearing on, *Feeding Of The 5000* 'Fight War, Not Wars', 'Punk Is Dead', 'Reject Of Society', all inflammatory, all brightly burning. A statement of real intent.

Asylum; Do They Owe Us A Living?; End Result; They've Got A Bomb; Punk Is Dead; Reject Of Society; General Bicardi; Banned From The Roxy; G's Song; Fight War, Not Wars; Women; Securicor; Sucks; You Pay; Angels; What A Shame; So What; Well?...Do They?.

First released 1978
UK peak chart position: did not chart
USA peak chart position: did not chart

47. ROCK FOR LIGHT
Bad Brains

One of the most accomplished and electrifying live bands ever. Bad Brains managed to match their ferocious sprawl of punk, theology and philosophical tenderness in a rare instant for this record. More a way of life than simply a band, Bad Brains utilised a knowledge of the inner self with a wonderfully bombastic approach to their music that often belied belief. Cultivating an occasional reggae backbeat with a stomping thrash and infrequent hard rock blow out, they were without equal. From the frantic title track to the expert shudder of, 'Banned In DC' they were, quite simply put, as vibrant as hell.

Big Takeover; Attitude; Right Brigade; Joshua's Song; I And I Survive; Banned In DC; Supertouch; Destroy Babylon; FVK; The Meek; I; Coptic Times; Sailin' On; Rock For Light; Rally Round Jah Throne; At The Movies; Riot Squad; How Low Can A Punk Get; We Will Not; Jam.

First released 1986
UK peak chart position: did not chart
USA peak chart position:

48. THE CRACK
Ruts

Ebullient punksters who strayed, intentionally or otherwise, into a less than dignified rock 'n' roll. Brash, but not without an understanding of terse vignettes of striding pop and a sometimes underplayed anger. 'Babylon's Burning', later covered by the Little Angels among others, brought them to notoriety with its tight rattle, but their depth of songwriting was prevalent elsewhere. Obviously, not just a bunch of dumb punks, they provided the cool, 'Dope For Guns', the cutting, 'It Was Cold', and the beat up, 'Something That I Said'. Surprisingly intoxicating.

Babylon's Burning; Dope For Guns; SUS; Something That I Said; You're Just A...; It Was Cold; Savage Circle; Jah War; Criminal Mind; Backwater; Out Of Order; Human Punk.

First released 1979
UK peak chart position: 16
USA peak chart position: did not chart

49. GENERATION X PERFECT HITS
Generation X

Suddenly the possessors of a most contemporary moniker. Though, the band had taken the name from a 1964 paperback on disaffected youth that they'd found on Idol's mum's bookshelves, it's suddenly become the catchword for the generation following the Baby Boomers. So much for style journalists everywhere. The band themselves, while denouncing musical history were only too happy to employ Ian Hunter to produce two of their singles. Though, it was their initial enthusiasm and carefully constructed attitude that held their career in brief stead. Idol eventually going solo and taking their rather ironically titled, 'Dancing With Myself' successfully with him. *Perfect Hits* replaces the debut.

Dancing With Myself; Your Generation; Ready, Steady, Go; Untouchables; Day By Day; Wild Youth; Wild Dub; One Hundred-Punks; King Rocker; Kiss Me Deadly; Gimme Some Truth; New Order; English Dream; Triumph; Youth, Youth, Youth.

First released 1991
UK peak chart position: did not chart
USA peak chart position: did not chart

50. HYPNOTISED
Undertones

Often neglected next to the Undertones' debut, *Hypnotised* has huge merit of its own. Prior to the more ragged experimentalism of Positive Touch, *Hypnotised* saw the Undertones rampantly expanding on their favourite subjects (as declared by the self-explanatory title-track, 'Here's More Songs About Chocolate And Girls'). It was the latter which always proved a mystery to the Derry five-piece: practically every song makes mention of females either collectively or singularly, yet never mentions them by name. The feel is one of schoolyard chaps bemused by the opposite sex, treating them with a reverence one would associate with an alien culture. Psychology aside, the tracks are without exception rip-roaring efforts, especially the mighty 'Tearproof'. However, you'll have to buy the CD to pick up the superb 'You've Got My Number'.

First Released 1980
UK peak chart position: 6
USA peak chart position: did not chart

More Songs About Chocolate And Girls; There Goes Norman; Hypnotised; See That Girl; Whizz Kids; Under The Broadwalk; The Way Girls Talk; Hard Luck; My Perfect Cousin; Boys Will Be Boys; Tearproof; Wednesday Week; Nine Times Out Of Ten; Girls That Don't Talk; What's With Terry?; You've Got My Number (Why Don't You Use It); Hard Luck (Again); Let's Talk About Girls; I Told You So; I Don't Wanna See You Again.

THE TOP 50
RAP ALBUMS

WE ALLOCATED 50 ALBUMS TO THIS COMPARATIVELY NEW PHENOMENON BECAUSE WE RECOGNISE ITS IMPORTANCE IN THE 90S. IT WILL BE INTERESTING TO SEE ONCE THE GENRE HAS COME INTO ITS OWN HOW MANY OF THE FRONT RUNNERS WILL BE STICKING TO THEIR CHOSEN STYLE OR IF THEY MOVE INTO OTHER CLEARLY DEFINED AREAS.

1. IT TAKES A NATION OF MILLIONS TO HOLD US BACK
Public Enemy

The title says it all. In 1988, when this album was released, Public Enemy's music cut with a wholly revolutionary edge. Rarely has fear, anger, paranoia and anxiety been so masterfully compressed onto a record's grooves. The Bomb Squad's artistry is the keynote to the hard, lean delivery, while Chuck D's supremely pointed lyrics leave no stone of the black experience unturned. It is not comfortable listening, but on tracks like 'Don't Believe The Hype', 'Night Of The Living Baseheads' and 'Rebel Without A Pause' the listener is left in no doubt that they are facing a fantastically potent force.

Countdown To Armageddon; Bring The Noise; Don't Believe The Hype; Cold Lampin With Flavor; Terminator X To The Edge Of Panic; Mind Terrorist; Louder Than A Bomb; Caught, Can We Get A Witness?; Show Em Whatcha Got; She Watch Channel Zero?!; Night Of The Living Baseheads; Black Steel In The Hour Of Chaos; Security Of The First World; Rebel Without A Pause; Prophets Of Rage; Party For Your Right To Fight.

First released 1988
UK peak chart position: 8
USA peak chart position: 42

2. HIPHOPRISY IS THE GREATEST LUXURY
Disposable Heroes Of Hiphoprisy

Often berated as the group its OK for non rap fans to like, the Disposable Heroes' solitary album proper represents much more than that might imply. Shades of Michael Franti and Rono Tse's previous incarnation, as part of the Beatnigs, resurface in the collision of samples, noise and breakbeats. Tse's technique is exemplary. However, it is Franti's fiercely intelligent narratives that carry the day. Where bombast and finger-pointing had been the order of the day in hip hop, Franti includes his own inadequacies (notably calling himself a 'jerk' in 'Music And Politics') in his diagnosis of the problem.

Satanic Reverses; Famous And Dandy (Like Amos 'N' Andy); Television, The Drug Of The Nation; Language Of Violence; The Winter Of The Long Hot Summer; Hypocrisy Is The Greatest Luxury; Everyday Life Has Become A Health Risk; Ins Greencard A-19 191 500; Socio-Genetic Experiment; Music And Politics; Financial Leprosy; California Über Alles; Water Pistol Man.

First released 1992
UK peak chart position: 40
USA peak chart position: did not chart

3. FEAR OF A BLACK PLANET
Public Enemy

If Public Enemy's two previous albums had ruffled feathers, *Fear Of A Black Planet* set out its stall to exploit mainstream fears. Again, the title spoke volumes. This time they raged just as hard, but their political consciousness had grown. Professor Griff had been ejected from the band for his anti-Semitic stance, and much of the album's atmosphere is created by the bunker-mentality of resultant clashes with the press. The siege mentality only underscores the group's hard-nosed cut and paste sample technique and the eloquence of Chuck D. And 'Fight The Power' still bites harder than just about any other track in rap's history.

Contract On The World Love Jam; Brothers Gonna Work It Out; 911 Is A Joke; Incident At 66.6 FM; Welcome To The Terrordome; Meet The G That Killed Me; Polywanacraka; Anti-nigger Machine; Burn Hollywood Burn; Power To The People; Who Stole The Soul; Fear Of A Black Planet; Revolutionary Generation; Can't Do Nuttin' For Ya Man; Reggie Jax; Leave This Off Your F***in' Charts; B Side Wins Again; War At Thirty Three And A Third; Final Count Of The Collision Between Us And Them.

First released 1990
UK peak chart position: 4
USA peak chart position: 10

4. STRAIGHT OUTTA COMPTON
NWA

They might have lacked Chuck D's dexterity, but when Ice Cube, Dr Dre, MC Ren, Eazy-E *et al* arrived on the scene in 1988 they did so with irresistible force. The intensity of the music, the brutality of the rhymes and the explicit violence of the lyrics single-handedly triggered gangsta rap. There had been historical precedents, notably Schooly D, but we have *Straight Outta Compton* to blame for everything from the Geto Boys to Snoop Doggy Dogg (whom Dre would produce). Unlike Public Enemy, NWA were unable to maintain the momentum, and after this album their influence would dissipate with the defection of chief lyricist Cube. But this album even got the FBI interested.

Straight Outta Compton; Fu** The Police; Gangsta Gangsta; If It Ain't Rough It Ain't Me; Parental Discretion Is Advised; Express Yourself; I Ain't The One; Dopeman; Compton's In The House; 8 Ball.

First released 1989
UK peak chart position: 41
USA peak chart position: 37

5. 3 Years, 5 Months, And 2 Days In The Life Of
Arrested Development

Titled after the length of time it took them to win a recording contract, this debut album from the Atlanta hip hop team arrived as a breath of fresh air in the 90s. Urban rap's appetite for self-aggrandisement and 'my Uzi's bigger than your Uzi' mentality was given short shrift by the highly articulate Speech and colleagues, who acted on a community basis and included in their ranks a 60-year-old spiritual advisor. The affirmation of the black experience was dealt with in terms of self respect and integrity, rather than advancement via the gun, while the music was a splendid feast of cool funk and R&B.

Man's Final Frontier; Mama's Always On Stage; People Everyday; Blues Happy; Mr. Wendal; Children Play With Earth; Raining Revolution; Fishin' For Religion; Give A Man A Fish; U; Eave Of Reality; Natural; Dawn Of The Dreads; Tennessee; Washed Away.

First released 1992
UK peak chart position: 3
USA peak chart position: 13

6. THE MESSAGE
Grandmaster Flash & The Furious Five

Built around the cornerstone of the title track, this album could legitimately have been included in such a listing had it featured 'The Message' alone. No MC has yet equalled Melle Mel's ominous poise in his delivery of 'Don't push me, 'cos I'm close to the edge'. It was the first record to provide rap with a conscience and, to some extent, an identity. Unlike much of the pioneering material by Sugarhill, and even Grandmaster Flash himself, 'The Message' has not been dated by the passage of time. And everything that came in rap thereafter, from Public Enemy to Arrested Development, owes it a debt.

She's Fresh; It's Nasty (Genius Of Love); Scorpio; It's A Shame; Dreamin'; You Are; The Message; Adventures Of Grandmaster Flash On The Wheels Of Steel.

First released 1982
UK peak chart position: 77
USA peak chart position: 53

7. ONE FOR ALL
Brand Nubian

From the Bronx, New York, and led by Grand Puba Maxwell, Brand Nubian's debut album was as cool and classy as anything in the genre. Backed by Lord Jamar, Sadat X and DJ Alamo, Puba kicked out reams of Muslim-influenced thinking, backed by steals from some of the great moments of soul music. Despite the creed of the Five Percent Nation, which was so manifest within its grooves, it was by no means humourless (highlighted by namechecks for characters like Englebert Humperdink), while samples of James Brown and Roy Ayers spiced up the backing tracks. In 1991 Puba split to go solo, taking DJ Alamo with him, and although Brand Nubian have persevered with a new line-up and recorded two well-received albums, they have yet to match this achievement.

All For One; Feels So Good; Concerto In X Minor; Ragtime; To The Right; Dance To My Ministry; Drop The Bomb; Wake Up; Step To The Rear; Slow Down; Try To Do Me; Who Can Get Busy Like This Man; Grand Puba, Positive And LG; Brand Nubian; Wake Up; Dedication.

First released 1991
UK peak chart position: did not chart
USA peak chart position: 130

8. RAISING HELL
Run DMC

Raising Hell is an appropriate title, for that is exactly what Joe Simmons, Darryl McDaniels and Jam Master Jay achieved on this, their third album. By the end of 1987 it had sold over three million copies in the US alone, primarily through the success of their MTV-friendly collaboration with Aerosmith on 'Walk This Way'. Suddenly every young black man on the block (and a fair few white ones too) was wearing B-boy attire and Adidas footwear. The evocation of street culture and language is uniformly superb, and while this was re-created elsewhere on subsequent albums, Run DMC never again captured the timeless immediacy of this set.

Peter Piper; It's Tricky; My Adidas; Walk This Way; Is It Live; Perfection; Hit It Run; Raising Hell; You Be Illin'; Dumb Girl; Son Of Byford; Proud To Be Black.

First released 1986
UK peak chart position: 41
USA peak chart position: 3

9. STRAIGHT OUT OF THE JUNGLE
Jungle Brothers

If the Jungle Brothers never became quite as huge as they deserved to be, it had nothing whatsoever to do with any flaws in this, their debut album. While De La Soul and PM Dawn would fine tune the sound and image, the Jungle Brothers were the first to popularise the 'Afrocentricty' vibe, which they had in turn inherited from Afrika Bambaataa. Perhaps the Native Tongues Posse could sometimes appear to be a cosy closed shop, but on this evidence, we could forgive Mike G, Sammy B and Baby Bam anything for their loose, funky aggregation of beats and rhymes, and succinct lyricism.

Straight Out Of The Jungle; What's Going On; Black Is Black; Jimbrowski; I'm Gonna Do You; I'll House You; On The Run; Behind The Bush; Because I Like It Like That; Braggin' And Boastin'; Sounds Of The Safari; Jimmy's Bonus Beats.

First released 1989
UK peak chart position: did not chart
USA peak chart position: did not chart

10. GHETTO MUSIC: THE BLUEPRINT OF HIP HOP
Boogie Down Productions

Hugely influential to modern rappers, both in delivery and integrity, KRS-1 (by this time his original partner Scott La Rock had been murdered) placed some of his greatest work on this, the third BDP album. Featuring mainly live musicians, it cut deep with tracks like the anti-police tirade, 'Who Protects Us From You?', or the dub rap, 'Jah Rulez'. The force of KRS-1's conviction and intelligence is undeniable, in a distillation of the formula he would later term 'edutainment'. This squeaks ahead of other BDP product for the consistency of the overall presentation.

The Style You Haven't Done Yet; The Blueprint; Jah Rulez; Who Protects Us From You?; Hip Hop Rules; Gimme, Dat, (Woy); World Peace; Why Is That?; Jack Of Spades; Breath Control; You Must Learn; Bo! Bo! Bo!; Ghetto Music.

First released 1989
UK peak chart position: 32
USA peak chart position: 36

11. THREE FEET HIGH AND RISING
De La Soul

The closest the rap world would come to the cartoon quality of Madness, with a similar musical integrity lurking beneath, De La Soul were warmly embraced both by hip hop fans and chart-followers for their infectious, uninhibited blend of laconic rhymes and buoyant humour. Posdnous, Trugoy and Pasemaster Mase emerged from Long Island with an entirely different slant on rap's place in the scheme of things, piecing together this 1989 debut around the concept of a game show. The vitality of the single, 'Me Myself And I', was merely an appetiser for a carefree creative feast. Daisy Age Soul (Da Inner Sound, Y'all) had arrived, and we liked it very much.

Intro; The Magic Number; Change In Speak; Cool Breeze On The Rocks; Can You Keep A Secret; Jenifa (Taught Me); Ghetto Thang; Transmitting Live From Mars; Eye Know; Take It Off; A Little Bit Of Soap; Tread Water; Say No Go; Do As De La Does; Plug Tunin'; De La Orgee; Buddy; Description; Me Myself And I; This Is A Recording For Living In A Fulltime Era; I Can Do Anything; D.A.I.S.Y. Age; Potholes In My Lawn.

First released 1989
UK peak chart position: 13
USA peak chart position: 24

12. PEOPLE'S INSTINCTIVE TRAVELS AND THE PATHS OF RHYTHM
A Tribe Called Quest

Treading a similarly off-kilter approach to De La Soul, Q-Tip, Ali Shaheed Muhammed and Phife were also members of the Native Tongues posse. They filtered their rhymes through a seductive platform of soul and jazz on this, their excellent debut album. Their humour proved the equal of De La Soul, with wonderful narratives like 'I Left My Wallet In El Segundo', while 'Can I Kick It?' practically defined new age rap cool.

Push It Along; Luck Of Lucien; After Hours; Footprints; I Left My Wallet In El Segundo; Public Enemy; Bonita Applebum; Can I Kick It?; Youthful Expression; Rhythm (Devoted To The Art Of Moving Buts); Mr Muhammad; Ham N' Eggs; Go Ahead In The Rain; Description Of A Fool.

First released 1990
UK peak chart position: 54
USA peak chart position: 91

13. ALL HAIL THE QUEEN
Queen Latifah

The undisputed first lady of rap, each of Dana Owens' albums, as Queen Latifah's parents know her, are thoroughly enterprising and worthwhile purchases. However, *All Hail The Queen* wins through for its timing and conviction. Although she was not the first female MC *per se*, her entrance on the scene was a powerful rebuke to the rappers who saw women purely as cannon fodder for their spurious sexual claims. 'Mama Gave Birth To The Soul Children', in particular, is a delicious manifesto on an album devoid of weak links, with no small debt to producers Daddy-O, KRS-1, DJ Mark the 45 King and De La Soul.

Dance For Me; Mama Gave Birth To The Soul Children; Come Into My House; Latifah's Law; Wrath Of My Madness; Inside Out; The Pros; Ladies First; A King And Queen Creation; Queen Of Royal Badness; Evil That Men Do; Princess Of The Posse; The Pros.

First released 1989
UK peak chart position: did not chart
USA peak chart position: 124

14. YO! BUM RUSH THE SHOW
Public Enemy

Hindsight may sometimes reduce the import of Public Enemy's debut set, particularly in the light of brilliant subsequent outings, but *Bum Rush The Show*'s impact was devastating. It introduced one of the most fearsome rhythmic talents in Terminator X and the Bomb Squad, carrying enough musical ballast to sink a battleship. 'Miuzi Weighs A Ton' is a key track here. By looping James Brown's 'Funky Drummer' break Public Enemy gave birth to the most over-used musical convention in rap. The ideology was not quite there (notably on 'Sophisticated Bitch'), though there were definite hints of greatness in 'Rightstarter (Message To A Black Man)'.

You're Gonna Get Yours; Sophisticated Bitch; Miuzi Weighs A Ton; Time Bomb; Too Much Posse; Rightstarter (Message To A Black Man); Public Enemy Number 1; MPE; Yo, Bum Rush The Show; Raise The Roof; Megablast; Terminator X Speaks With His Hands.

First released 1988
UK peak chart position: did not chart
USA peak chart position: 125

15. MAMA SAID KNOCK YOU OUT
LL Cool J

It might not include any of the earlier classics like 'I Can't Live Without My Radio', but *Mama Said Knock You Out* is undoubtedly James Todd Smith's finest album. Producer extraordinaire Marley Marl provided the beats for this 1990 set, where LL's familiar braggadocio was tempered with new-found wisdom. Never before had LL suggested himself capable of calm reflection on the development of anything other than his sexual conquests. Here he waxed lyrical on the hip hop tradition and its current trajectory. Notable not least because it arrived at a time when he had been largely written off, it would deservedly go triple platinum in the US.

The Boomin' System; Around The Way Girl; Eat Em Up L Chill; Mr. Good Bar; Murdergram (Live At Rapmania); Cheesy Rat Blues; Farmer Boulevard (Our Anthem); Mama Said Knock You Out; Milky Cereal; Jingling Baby; To Da Break Of Dawn; Six Minutes Of Pleasure; Illegal Search; The Power Of God.

First released 1990
UK peak chart position: 49
USA peak chart position: 16

16. BY ALL MEANS NECESSARY
Boogie Down Productions

The first post-Scott La Rock BDP release, *By All Means Necessary* is a fitting testament to his former partner. With KRS-1's brother Kenny Parker and D-Nice taking over the musical backdrop, samples ran from familiar funk to Deep Purple. KRS-1 was again in supreme form, boasting a more sharply politicised edge, predicted by the cover image of the artist holding an Uzi in homage to the familiar Malcolm X image. Most pleasing of all was 'Stop The Violence', a call to inner city youth to stop destroying themselves, which rapidly became a movement.

My Philosophy; Ya Slippin'; Stop The Violence; Illegal Business; Nervous; I'm Still Number 1; Part Time Success; Jimmy; P'Cha; Necessary.

First released 1988
UK peak chart position: 38
USA peak chart position: 75

17. OG (ORIGINAL GANGSTER)
Ice-T

The hardest Tracey ever. Ice-T had a longer history than most on the west coast, having even appeared in an early 80s breakdancing film. His 'party rhymes' on earlier excursions saw him permanently walking the good taste tightrope, but this was his most forceful statement so far. The sustained intensity of his delivery was familiar, but there was greater finesse on display too. It was this set that formed the platform for his elevation to black spokesman of the 90s, and the first to provide real evidence of substance behind the stance.

Home Of The Bodybag; First Impression; Ziplock; Mic Contract; Mind Over Matter; New Jack Hustler; Ed; Bitches 2; Straight Up Nigga; OG Original Gangster; The House; Evil E - What About Sex?; Fly By; Midnight; Fried Chicken; MVP's; Lifestyles Of The Rich And Infamous; Body Count; Prepared To Die; Escape From The The Killing Fields; Street Killers; Pulse Of The Rhyme; The Tower; Ya Shoulda Killed Me Last Year.

First released 1991
UK peak chart position: 38
USA peak chart position: 15

18. CYPRESS HILL
Cypress Hill

If a strict diet of guns and ganja runs contrary to your sensibilities, then this, the work of Los Angeles' premier Latin hip hop coalition, is an album to avoid. If not, then the musical strengths of DJ Muggs are hard to ignore. Escapism via pot was the message (and the medium). It did contain the odd street missive, but generally B-Real and Sen Dogs' rhymes were somehow secondary to a choking blend of beats and bass. A thousand immitators followed, including a 'rehabilitated' Vanilla Ice.

Pigs; How I Could Just Kill A Man; Hand On the Pump; Hole In The Head; Ultraviolet Dreams; Light Another; The Phunky Feel One; Break It Up; Real Estate; Stoned In The Way Of The Walk; Psycobetabuckdown; Something For The Blunted; Latin Lingo; The Funky Cypress Hill Shit; Tres Equis; Born To Get Busy.

First released 1993
UK peak chart position: did not chart
USA peak chart position: 31

19. BIGGER AND DEFFER
LL Cool J

This 1987 set, his second album, was distinguished by the first ever 'ballad rap', 'I Need Love'. The B-boy phenomenon was in full swing, with LL's popularity only eclipsed by the Run DMC boys, and he proves himself in fine fettle here. Without the contribution of Rick Rubin, which had dominated his debut, there is a diversity of musical scope and signature which, whilst hardly breaking rap's shackles, shows him capable of spanning several of its conventions. Moreover, it is performed with a highly individualistic, personable charm

I'm Bad; Get Down; The Bristol Hotel; My Rhyme Ain't Done; 357 Break It On Down; Go Cut Creator Go; Breakthrough; I Need Love; Ahh, Let's Get Ill; The Doo Wop; On The Ill Tip.

First released 1987
UK peak chart position: 54
USA peak chart position: 3

20. WANTED: DEAD OR ALIVE
Kool G. Rap & Polo

New York-based Kool G is one of the East Coast's most underrated rappers. This despite singles like 'Streets Of New York' (contained on the album), which set a new benchmark for hardcore hip hop. With production by Eric B and Large Professor and featuring guest appearances from Big Daddy Kane and Biz Markie, there is much more to the album than merely that (though it is by no means a consistent effort). It preceded the band's problems with censorship on the follow-up set, which featured the duo in baraclavas feeding steak to a pair of rotweilers, while two white males stood on chairs with nooses around their necks in the background. That sense of sensationalist drama and resentment, though, is best represented on this album, which when it hits the target is utterly convincing.

First released 1990
UK peak chart position: did not chart
USA peak chart position: did not chart

Streets Of New York; Wanted Dead Or Alive; Money In The Bank; Bad To The Bone; Talk Like Sex; Play It Again, Polo; Erase Racism; Kool Is Back; Play It Kool; Death Wish; Jive Talk; The Polo Club.

21. APOCALYPSE 91- THE ENEMY STRIKES BLACK
Public Enemy

Proving that all PE albums are requisite listening, this set was the band's fourth, and attained a similar quality threshold to its forerunners. The conceptual high watermark achieved on *The Enemy Strikes Black* was its focus on inner black society. Tracks like '1 Million Bottlebags', with its overview of the waste and degradation of empty lives filled by substance abuse, had a direct forerunner in *It Takes A Nation Of Millions...* 'Night Of The Living Baseheads'. And it was difficult to imagine a more strident stance than that adopted on 'I Don't Wanna Be Called You Niga'. It also included the thrash-rap crossover, 'Bring The Noise', performed with Anthrax.

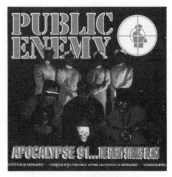

First released 1991
UK peak chart position: 8
USA peak chart position: 4

Lost A Birth; Rebirth; Can't Truss It; I Don't Wanna Be Called Yo Niga; How To Kill A Radio Consultant; By The Time I Get To Arizona; Move!; 1 Million Bottlebags; More News At 11; Shut Em Down; A Letter To The New York Post; Get The F*** Outta Dodge; Bring The Noize.

22. AMERIKKKA'S MOST WANTED
Ice Cube

Like Ice-T, Cube has often been the subject of impassioned argument over his merits as an artist. Certainly those in the PC lobby could hardly have been offered more incendiary evidence than this album's 'You Can't Fade Me', on which he struggles over the moral question of whether he should end his girlfriend's pregnancy by kicking her in the stomach. Throughout, Cube conducts himself with a sense of his own presence that marks him out as the clear talent of the original NWA. And when he isn't busy offending your sensibilities, he emerges as one of the most supremely gifted commentators on the modern urban black experience.

First released 1990
UK peak chart position: did not chart
USA peak chart position: 48

Better Off Dead; The Nigga You Love To Hate; Amerikkka's Most Wanted; What They Hittin' Foe?; You Can't Fade Me; JD's?; Once Upon A Time In The Projects; Turn Off The Radio; Endangered Species (Tales From The Darkside); A Gangster's Fairytale; I'm Only Out For One Thing; Get Off My Dick And Tell Yo Bitch To Come Here; The Drive-By; Rollin' With The ? Mob; Who's The Mack?; It's A Man's World; The Bomb.

23. SLEEPING WITH THE ENEMY
Paris

Paris, alongside Brand Nubian/Grand Puba, is the most enduring of the hardcore black Muslim rappers. While his work has been widely shunned by the mainstream for its militant stance, his MC abilities and musical soundscapes deserve their place in a book of this type. Based in San Francisco, this was his second 'independent' album, recorded after touring with Public Enemy. It injected a focused, reasoning intelligence alongside the openly inflammatory 'Bush Killa', a revenge fantasy on the US president which was taken rather too seriously in some quarters. On other tracks like 'Make Way For A Panther' and 'Coffee, Donuts & Death' this came across more as an introduction to civil war rather than civil disobedience. As he pointedly states in 'Bush Killa', alluding to Ice T's problems: 'My brother down south said fuck the police, I'm saying no justice no peace'.

The Enemy (Live At The Whitehouse); Make Way For A Panther; Sleeping With The Enemy; House Niggas Bleed Too; Bush Killa; Coffee, Donuts & Death; Thinka Bout It; Guerillas In The Mist; The Days Of Old; Long Hot Summer; Conspiracy Of Silence; Funky Lil' Party; Check It Out Ch'All; Rise; Assata's Song.

First released 1992
UK peak chart position: did not chart
USA peak chart position: 182

24. STRICTLY BUSINESS
EPMD

Erick 'E' Sermon and Parrish 'P' Smith hailed from Brentwood, Long Island, and revitalised the rap scene with this, their 1988 debut. Taking their samples from rock as well as dance and funk sources, they provided plenty of lyrical scope with their inventive, loosely-ordered routines. Subsequent albums refined, rather than improved upon, their solid, slightly understated formula. As their acronym inferred, Erick and Parish were, indeed, starting to make dollars.

Strictly Business; Because I'm Housin'; So Let The Funk Flow; You Gots To Chill; It's My Thing; You're A Customer; The Steve Martin; Get Off The Bandwagon, DJ K La Boss; Jane.

First released 1988
UK peak chart position: did not chart
USA peak chart position: 80

25. I WISH MY BROTHER GEORGE WAS HERE
Del Tha Funkee Homosapien

With its title a reference to George Clinton, something of a godhead figure to west coast rap squads, Del introduced himself properly to the record-buying public via this, his debut album. Previously he had played a minor role in his cousin Ice Cube's backing band, Da Lench Mob. A long way from the hardcore gang narratives of his better known relation, Del offered a more detached viewpoint, and one which came laced with humour. Artistically, it was an unqualified success, providing a blueprint which Del's own Hieroglyphic crew would follow.

What Is Booty; Mistadobalina; The Wacky World Of Rabid Transit; Pissin' On Your Steps; Dark Skin Girls; Money For Sex; Ahonetwo, Ahonetwo; Prelude; Dr. Bombay; Sunny Meadowz; Sleepin' On My Couch; Hoodz Come In Dozens; Same Ol' Thing; Ya Lil' Crumbsnatchers.

First released 1991
UK peak chart position: did not chart
USA peak chart position: did not chart

26. Return Of Da Boom Bap
KRS-1

The first time KRS-1 had reverted to his own name following his work with Boogie Down Productions, though *Return Of Da Boom Bap* was not widely perceived as a success. However, there was still much to admire, particularly a set of reference points which alluded to his early career. 'KRS-One Attacks', for example, looped part of *Criminal Minded*'s title-track, while 'P Is Free' updates his own 1986 anti-crack opus, 'P Is Free'. KRS-1 was still with us, and still very much the 'edutainer'.

KRS-ONE Attacks; Outta Here; Black Cop; Mortal Thought; I Can't Wake Up; Slap Them Up; Sound Of Da Police; Mad Crew; Uh Oh; Brown Skin Woman; Return Of The Boom Bap; P Is Still Free; Stop Frontin'; Higher Level.

First released 1993
UK peak chart position: did not chart
USA peak chart position: 37

27. Blacks' Magic
Salt 'n Pepa

The pop charts, never mind the rap/R&B variants, would be a much duller place without Cheryl 'Salt' James and Sandra 'Pepa' Denton. The two former telephone sales girls united in the mid-80s to score several singles successes. This, their third album, confirmed both their commercial ascendency and their growing songwriting craft. The best example of which is undoubtedly 'Let's Talk About Sex', which brought frank discussion of post-AIDS relationships to the dancefloor. Hardcore hip hop fans may scoff, but the talents of Salt 'n Pepa are there for all but those without gangsta myopia to see.

Expression; Doper Than Dope; Negro Wit' And Ego; You Showed Me; Do You Want Me; Swift; I Like To Party; Blacks' Magic; Start The Party; Let's Talk About Sex; I Don't Know; Live And Let Die; Independent.

First released 1990
UK peak chart position: 70
USA peak chart position: 38

28. Sex Packets
Digital Underground

No group has more thoroughly looted the P-Funk cupboard than Oakland, California's Digital Underground. They have also injected a good deal of revelry and humour into proceedings in the process, notably on this debut album. There is a concept, of sorts, to *Sex Packets*. The narrative was the ruse of a mad scientist marketing a drug which causes the recipients to have wet dreams. Group rappers Shock-G (Gregory Jacobs) and Humpty Hump (Eddie Humphrey) adopted the characters of two dealers, and, despite the threadbare plot, it actually works. Sort of. It is buoyed up in no small part by the live piano and musicians orchestrated by Chopmaster J.

The Humpty Dance; The Way We Swing; Rhymin' On The Funk; The New Jazz (One); Underwater Rimes (remix); The Danger Zone; Gutfest '89; Freaks Of The Industry; Doowutchyalike; Packet Prelude; Sex Packets; Street Scene; Packet Man; Packet Reprise.

First released 1990
UK peak chart position: did not chart
USA peak chart position: did not chart

29. CRIMINAL MIND
Boogie Down Productions

Many fans of hip hop would automatically select this as BDP's greatest moment. It is, after all, the only document of KRS-1's time with Scott La Rock, and it includes genuine genre classics like the title-track and '9mm Goes Bang'. It is also a stunning debut, and a clear signpost in the development of gangsta rap (though few of that scene's proponents would ever address the issues with a similar level of sincerity and humanity). Perhaps Parker's delivery is not as fully developed as on later works, but the musical interface is deeply invigorating. The saddest part of the equation is the cover, picturing both partners holding guns, shortly before La Rock's murder.

Poetry; South Bronx; 9mm Goes Bang; Word From My Sponsor; Elementary; Dope Beat; The Remix For The P Is Still Free; Bridge Is Over; Super Ho; Criminal Minded.

First released 1987
UK peak chart position: did not chart
USA peak chart position: did not chart

30. NATURE OF A SISTA
Queen Latifah

Another unimpeachable set from the Queen of East Orange, and a second long playing treatise on enlightened female perspective. This saw soul and ragga tunes dominate, taking over from the rawer hip hop tones on her debut. This results in a dilution of impact, though this is partially compensated for by the classy, dancefloor-aimed cuts like 'Give Me Your Love' and 'How Do I Love Thee?'. It is a lesser album, indeed, but one which should not be overlooked, as it still blows the majority of Latifah's competition out of the water.

Latifah's Had It Up 2 Here; Nuff Of The Ruff Stuff; One Mo' Time; Give Me Your Love; Love Again; Bad As A Mutha; Fly Girl; Sexy Fancy; Nature Of A Sister; That's The Way We Flow; If You Don't Know; How Do I Love Thee?.

First released 1991
UK peak chart position: did not chart
USA peak chart position: 117

31. GANGSTER CHRONICLES
London Posse

Rodney and Bionic's Cockney take on gangsta rap, which was practically the first worthwhile long player in the rap field to emerge from the UK. The fusion of rap and reggae, the indigenous black music of most second generation English blacks, as opposed to the R&B of America, proved an engaging formula. There was a downpoint, notably the sadly non-ironic 'Sexy Gale', but elsewhere tracks like 'Live Like The Other Half Do' more than compensated.

Mad Money; Livin' Pancoot; Original London Style; Remedy For Black Ash Blues; Jump Around; Sexy Gal; Gangsta Chronicle; Live Like The Other Half Do; Oversize Idiot; Tell Me Something; Money Mad Bonus Beats.

First released 1990
UK peak chart position: did not chart
USA peak chart position: did not chart

32. MIDNIGHT MARAUDERS
A Tribe Called Quest

A second take on A Tribe Called Quest's lush formula. This time there was a rejection of purely Afrocentric rhymes, picking up on the chill breeze of gangsta rap that was blowing through hip hop in 1993. They did, however, maintain their allegiances to 'positivity', rather than empty braggadocio or gun-slinging rhetoric. It saw them maintain their high profile in rap, as members variously siphoned time off to build film and production careers.

Midnight Marauders Tour Guide; Steve Biko (Stir It Up); Award Tour; 8 Million Stories; Sucka Nigga; Midnight; We Can Get Down; Electric Relaxation; Clap Your Hands; Ooh My God; Keep It Rollin'; The Chase, Part II; Lyrics To Go; God Lives Through; Hot Sex.

First released 1993
UK peak chart position: 70
USA peak chart position: 8

33. AND NOW THE LEGACY BEGINS
Dream Warriors

The first commercial outpouring from Canada's nascent rap scene, the Dream Warriors were made up of two expatriate West Indians who shared a similar line to A Tribe Called Quest in beautifully crafted, jazz-tinged hip hop. The lyrics, such as they are, may have been utterly inscrutable, acting more as an added percussion dimension, but that hardly lessened the effect. Both 'Wash Your Face In My Sink' and 'My Definition Of A Boombastic Jazz Style' deservedly took them into the charts, but the album worked well in its entirety.

Mr Bubbunut Spills His Guts; My Definition Of A Boombastic Jazz Style; Follow Me Not; Ludi; U Never Know A Good Thing Till U Lose It; And Now The Legacy Begins; Tune From The Missing Channel; Wash Your Face In My Sink; Voyage Through The Multiverse; U Could Get Arrested; Journey On; Face In The Basin; Do Not Feed The Alligators; Twelve Sided Disc; Maximum 60 Lost In A Dream.

First released 1991
UK peak chart position: 18
USA peak chart position: did not chart

34. GANG STARR
Step In The Arena

Gang Starr were not the first to experiment with the jazz tradition, but they rivalled A Tribe Called Quest and the Dream Warriors in melding it successfully within a hip hop superstructure. Of course, Guru and Premier were equally adept at hardcore stylings, but it was on this album that they pushed jazz rap to its logical conclusion. An obvious forerunner of Guru's collaborations with Jazzamatazz, which spawned a highly successful album, *Step In The Arena* itself is a deeply satisfying set.

Name Tag (Premier And The Guru); Step In The Arena; Form Of Intellect; Execution Of A Chump (No More Mr Nice Guy Part 2); Who's Gonna Take The Weight?; Beyond Comprehension; Check The Technique; Love Sick; Here Today, Gone Tomorrow, Game Pain; Take A Rest; What You Want This Time?; Street Ministry; Just To Get A Rep; Say Your Prayers; As I Read My S-A; Precisely The Right Rhymes; The Meaning Of The Name.

First released 1991
UK peak chart position: 36
USA peak chart position: 121

35. INNER CITY GRIOTS
Freestyle Fellowship

Hailing from South Central Los Angeles, Freestyle Fellowship are definitely not of the gangsta rap persuasion. Their superior old school rhyming abilities and dextrous word play (learnt at the famed Good Life Center) dominate this set. Despite comparisons to De La Soul and Dream Warriors (for their freeform word association), the Fellowship proved themselves unique by employing rhymes which consciously employed poetry devices like alliteration to emphasise effect. But the dizzy speed of their delivery and appetite for innovation is the real key, notably on cuts like 'Inner City Boundary', which carries as much weight as any territorial claim made by gangsta rap but with a much greater sense of propriety and skill.

Bully Of The Block; Everything's Everything; Shammy's; Six Tray; Danger; Inner City Boundaries; Corn Bread; Way Cool; Hot Potato; Mary; Park Bench People; Heavyweights; Respect Due; Pure Thought.

First released 1993
UK peak chart position: did not chart
USA peak chart position: did not chart

36. X VERSES THE WORLD
Overlord X

The most popular hardcore hip hop album in Europe, Brit rapper Overlord X represented his clan and creed well on this debut album. The lynchpin in the album's assembly is 'You Can't Do It In London', which took NWA and the gangsta rappers to task (though there was 'nuff respect for Public Enemy, who were sampled and/or paraphrased on many other cuts). Next to London Posse, this was the first evidence that UK hip hop could hold its own against all comers. A series of continuity links for *Def II* beckoned.

Prologue 1990; The Predator; You Oughta Get Rushed; Planet Hackney; X Versus The World; Tell Yer Crew; Prelude; Definition; Suppression; The Untouchable; Powerhouse; Lyrical Turmoil; You Can't Do It In London; X Keeps Turning; O.X. Corral.

First released 1990
UK peak chart position: did not chart
USA peak chart position: did not chart

37. INTELLIGENT HOODLUM
Intelligent Hoodlum

The influence of Public Enemy is obvious, Percy Chapman (aka the Intelligent Hoodlum) having spent several months in jail listening to nothing else. However, his largely autobiographical self-titled debut album is much more than a carbon copy. It saw him reunited with childhood friend Marley Marl who provided one of his most persuasive musical suites to bedeck the set. The ferocious protest of 'Black And Proud', or, more poignantly, 'Arrest The President', announced the Hoodlum as a major new talent.

Intelligent Hoodlum; Back To Reality; Trag Invasion; No Justice, No Peace; Party Animal; Black And Proud; Game Type; Microphone; Keep Striving; Party Pack; Arrest The President; Your Tragedy.

First released 1990
UK peak chart position: did not chart
USA peak chart position: did not chart

38. JAZZAMATAZZ
Guru

This jazz rap collision had been anticipated by earlier Gang Starr efforts like 'Jazz Thing', a collaboration with Branford Marsalis which Spike Lee has used to theme his film, *Mo' Better Blues.*. This 'side-project' saw Guru reproducing that winning formula which others, notably Us3, have subsequently attempted to emulate. However, the latter's approach (that of ram-raiding the Blue Note vaults with a sampler) can hardly compare to the assembled cast which make up the Jazzamatazz ranks: the exponents including N'Dea Davenport (Brand New Heavies), Carleen Anderson, Courtney Pine, Marsalis, Roy Ayers, Donald Byrd, Lonnie Liston Smith and French rapper MC Solaar. Rap had many times been called the rock 'n' roll of the 90s, but this album saw critics retrace its heritage back to its own black traditions.

Introduction; Loungin'; When You're Near; Transit Ride; No Time To Play; Down The Backstreets; Respectful Dedications; Take A Look (At Yourself); Trust Me; Slicker Than Most; Le Bien, Le Mal; Sights In The City.

First released 1993
UK peak chart position: 58
USA peak chart position: 3

39. FOLLOW THE LEADER
Eric B & Rakim

A New York team who met in 1985 and have gone on to become rap's prime duo (with EPMD a close second). Their debut album, *Paid In Full*, caused great legal waves via its explicit use of samples (Eric B is often credited with putting the funk back into rap music via his James Brown signatures). Rakim was responsible for introducing a more relaxed, intuitive delivery which was a distinct advance on the thumping bravado of Run DMC and LL Cool J, and is best sampled on this influential and instructive album. The title-track, 'Lyrics Of Fury' and 'Microphone Fiend' provided the fullest possible evidence of the duo's skill.

Follow The Leader; Microphone Fiend; Lyrics Of Fury; Eric B Never Scared; Just A Beat; Put Your Hands Together; To The Listeners; No Competition; The R; Musical Massacre; Beats For The Listeners.

First released 1988
UK peak chart position: did not chart
USA peak chart position: 22

40. THE CHRONIC
Dr Dre

The rap producer with the golden touch in the 90s, before Dre fell out with Eazy E he had provided Ruthless Records with an almost uninterrupted sequence of major sellers. He is no great rapping talent himself, and does not profess to be, but this album, recorded with the aid of Snoop Doggy Dogg and the Pound, gave a clear indication of what the world could expect when Dogg's much heralded debut dropped. In truth *The Chronic* is the greater effort, setting the standard for gangsta rap by slowing the pace and taking a largish toke on the weed celebrated in its title. Musically it was flawless, lyrically it left a lot to be desired.

The Chronic; Fuck Wit Dre Day; Let Me Ride; The Day The Niggaz Took Over; Nuthin' But A G Thang; Dreeez Nuuuts; Bitches Ain't Shit, Lil' Ghetto Boy; A Nigga Witta Gun; Rat-Tat-Tat-Tat; The $20 Sack Pyramid; Lyrical Gangbang; High Powered; The Doctor's Office; Stranded On Death Row. The Roach.

First released 1993
UK peak chart position: did not chart
USA peak chart position: 3

41. MAKE WAY FOR THE MOTHERLODE
Yo Yo

Often quoted in Ice Cube's defence when that rapper suffers accusations of misogyny, Yo Yo (Yolanda Whitaker) is his female MC protégé, who had previously contributed to Cube's *AmeriKKKa's Most Wanted*, duetting on 'It's A Man's World', representing her gender with admirable gusto. This, her 1991 debut album, played it as rough and rugged as her male counterparts, but amid the assertive, abrasive lyrics lurked a dexterity which might not have been envisaged. The keynote is 'Sisterland', a rallying call to fellow female MCs proffered with sincerity and conviction.

Stand Up For Your Rights; Stompin' To Tha 90's; You Can't Play With My Yo-Yo; Cube Gets Played; Put A Lid On It; What Can I Do?; Dedication; Sisterland; The IBWC National Anthem; Make Way For The Motherlode; Tonight's The Night; I Got Played; Girl, Don't Be No Fool; Ain't Nobody Better; Outro; More Of What I Can Do.

First released 1991
UK peak chart position: did not chart
USA peak chart position: 74

42. GUERILLAS IN THA MIST
Da Lench Mob

Another of Ice Cube's spin-off groups, Da Lench Mob also double as his backing band. When *Guerillas In The Mist* emerged in 1992 it surpassed Cube's own recordings of the period. Front person Shorty (Jerome Washington) proved to be among the most gifted of rap's inner city spokesmen. They looked absolutely fearsome on their press shots, and the sound itself was not far short of terrifying. Yet there was a moral tone struck on several songs which pulled it about the usual ghetto reportage syndrome which has dogged rap music.

Capitol Parliament In America; Back The Devil; Lost In The System; Yout Yar Heroes; All On My Nut Sac; Guerillas In The Mist; Lenchmob Also In Tha Group; Ain't Got No Class; Freedom Got An AK; Ankle Blues; Who Ya Ganna Shoot Wit That, Lord Have Mercy; Inside Tha Head Of A Black Man.

First released 1992
UK peak chart position: did not chart
USA peak chart position: 24

43. 19NAUGHTY3
Naughty By Nature

New Jersey residents Treach, Vinnie and DJ Kay Gee were initially heavily influenced by the patronage of Queen Latifah, with their rhymes drenched in the atmosphere of the street and ghetto vernacular. Unlike other hardcore outfits, however, they were not afraid of injecting a touch of soul into the mix, which makes the best of their work all the more endearing. Their debut set had provided the huge crossover hit, 'OPP', the largest-grossing authentic rap single in the US in 1990. This, their second album, was preceded by another big single, 'Hip Hip Hooray', (with a Spike Lee-filmed video) and is a more seamless collection.

19 Naughty III; Hip Hop Hooray; Take It To Ya Face; Daddy Was A Street Corner; The Hood Comes First; The Only Ones; It's On; Cruddy Clique; Knock 'Em Out Da Box; Hot Potato; Sleepin; On Jersey; Written On Ya Kitten; Sleepwalkin' II; Shout Outs.

First released 1993
UK peak chart position: 40
USA peak chart position: did not chart

44. HEAVY RHYME EXPERIENCE VOL. ONE
Brand New Heavies

Together with N'Dea Davenport, Heavies Simon Bartholomew and Andrew Levy created an indelible selection of hip hop on this, their debut album. The group had been picked up by smart US label Delicious Vinyl, who saw genuine possibilities in their dusky rhythms. There was no shortage of takers to offer their services, and with talent like Jamal-Ski, Master Ace, Pharcyde and Grand Puba on display next to the Heavies' astute songwriting, it is little wonder that the sessions for this album have passed into legendary status in hip hop.

Bonafied Funk; It's Gettin' Hectic; Who Makes The Loo?; Wake Me When I'm Dead; Jump N' Move; Death Threat; State Of Yo; Do Watta I Gotta Do; Whatgoabouthat; Soul Flower.

First released 1992
UK peak chart position: 38
USA peak chart position: did not chart

45. OF THE HEART, OF THE SOUL AND OF THE CROSS
THE UTOPIAN EXPERIENCE
PM Dawn

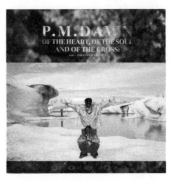

They don't have many friends in hardcore hip hop circles (just ask KRS-1), but anybody who wilfully ignores this set in is denying themselves a treat. Boosted by the hugely impressive singles, 'Reality Used To Be A Friend Of Mine' and the Spandau Ballet-sampling 'Set Adrift On Memory Bliss', PM Dawn fused pop sentiments with knowing lyrics in a manner which saw them draw comparisons to De La Soul and the Daisy Age Soul tag. But Prince Be and DJ Minute Mix employed more than copycat tactics, with fully-blown song structures which betrayed the former's musical heritage (his father was a member of Kool & The Gang).

Intro; Reality Used To Be A Friend Of Mine; Paper Doll; To Serenade A Rainbow; Comatose; A Watcher's Point Of View (Don't 'Cha Think); Even After I Die; In The Presence Of Mirrors; Set Adrift On Memory Bliss; Shake; If I Wuz U; On A Clear Day; The Beautiful.

First released 1991
UK peak chart position: 8
USA peak chart position: 48

46. DOGGY STYLE
Snoop Doggy Dogg

The most widely anticipated album in rap history, arguably in modern music *per se*. Doggy Style could hardly have been expected to live up to the momentous hype which surrounded it. Doubtless sales were boosted by news of Snoop (Calvin Broadus)'s arrest for his part in a gang-related murder, not to mention the legions of converts to the Dogg Pound via producer Dre's previous megaseller, *The Chronic*. However, dubious lyrical imagery and awful cover art aside, this was another successful instalment in Dre's crusade to popularise the gangsta format.

Bath Tub; G Funk Intro; Gin And Juice; The Shiznit; Lodi Doctor; Murder Was The Case (Death/Revisualizing Eternity); Serial Killer; Who Am I (What's My Name?); For All My Niggaz And Bitches; Ain't No Fun (If The Homies Can't Have None); Doggy Dogg World; GZ And Hustlas; Pump Pump.

First released 1993
UK peak chart position: 38
USA peak chart position: 1

47. ENTA DA STAGE
Black Moon

One of the biggest rap breakthroughs of the 90s happened in Brooklyn, New York (or 'Crooklyn', as Black Moon preferred to call it). Housed on the impressive new Wreck subsidiary, *Enta Da Stage* brought the world the superb 'Who Got The Props', via 5ft Excelerator, DJ Evil Dee and Buckshot. Musically it was a throwback to rap's old school, with bleak bass and beatbox counterpointing their articulate, considered observations on life in the 'hood. When onlookers like KRS-1 were forced to concede that *Enta Da Stage* was 'the phattest shit I've heard in a long time', it was obvious that something special was brewing.

(First Stage) Powaful Impak!; Niguz Talk S—t; Who Got The Props?; Ack Like U Want It; Buck Em Down; Black Snif-N-Wessum; Son Get Wrec; (Second Stage) Make Minne; Slave; I Got Cha Opin; S—t Iz Real; Enta Da Stage; How Many MC's...; U Da Man.

First released 1993
UK peak chart position: did not chart
USA peak chart position: did not chart

48. DEATH CERTIFICATE
Ice Cube

Something of a return to the Neanderthal misogyny of earlier releases, *Death Certificate* nevertheless has its saving graces. From its portentous cover shot onwards, the vehemence of this record is its outstanding feature. Despite throwing venom at everyone from 'white devils' to gays and Asians, the set is rescued by superior selections like 'Steady Mobbin'' and 'True To The Game'. It is this album which gives rap's critics most of their evidence when they confront Cube, yet it is also one of his most musically stellar creations.

The Funeral; The Wrong Nigga To Fuck Wit; My Summer Vacation; Steady Mobbin'; Robin Lench; Givin' Up The Nappy Dug Out; Look Who's Burnin'; A Bird In The Hand; Man's Best Friend; Alive On Arrival; Death; The Birth; I Wanna Kill Sam; Horny Lil' Devil; True To The Game; Color Blind; Doing Dumb...; Us.

First released 1991
UK peak chart position: did not chart
USA peak chart position: 2

49. TRICKS OF THE SHADE
Goats

Oatie Kato, Madd and Swayzack of the Philadelphia-based Goats did much to inherit the tarnished crown of De La Soul with this debut set from 1993. Alter-egos Chickenlittle and his lil' bro' Hangerhead acted as tour guides through this collection, a skewed snapshot of tales from 90s America. Instead of polemic they hit targets like Dan Quayle with such unforgettable couplets as 'A Quayle is a bird, and bird's have bird brains'. They even pulled off a hardcore rap parody in 'Drive By Bumper Cars', although there was genuine substance in the civil rights protest, 'Do The Digs Dug?'.

Got Kinda Hi; Tricks Of The Shade; ?Do The Digs Dug?; Hip-Hopola; Aaaah D. Yaaa; Watcha Got Is Watcha Getin; R U Down Wit Da Goats; TV Cops; Wrong Pot 2 Piss In; Cumin' In Ya Ear; Typical American; Unodostresquattro; Burn The Flag.

First released 1993
UK peak chart position: did not chart
USA peak chart position: did not chart

50. In Full Gear
Stetsasonic

Elder statesmen of rap who afforded De La Soul and the Jungle Brothers much of their 'Afrocentric' philosophical viewpoint. Rarely have two such talented individuals as Daddy-O and Prince Paul been housed in a single group, as they would prove in their subsequent solo/production careers. However, this set captures Stetsasonic at the height of their powers. It set other another huge precedent with 'Talkin' All That Jazz', which predicted the jazz-rap boom, and converted the energy of their renowned stage act to posterity. Cuts like the Floaters' cover 'Float On' and 'Miami Bass' remain enthralling, several years from release, in a musical environment in which shelf life is notoriously short.

This Is It, Y'all (Go Stetsa II); Sally; It's In My Song; The Odad; Rollin' Wit Rush; Miami Bass; In Full Gear; DBC Let The Music Play; Float On; Pen And Paper; Stet Troop '881.

First released 1988
UK peak chart position: did not chart
USA peak chart position: did not chart

THE TOP 50
ROCK 'N' ROLL ALBUMS

OTHER THAN ELVIS, THE GENRE THAT STARTED IT ALL HAS OFTEN BEEN OVERLOOKED. THERE WAS A STIGMA ATTACHED TO ROCK 'N' ROLL IN THE 50S AND SURPRISINGLY FEW OF THESE ALBUMS CHARTED. IT WAS OFTEN DIFFICULT TO PRODUCE A CONSISTENT ALBUM BUILT UP AROUND ONE FAMILIAR RIFF. THE NAMES IN THIS CHART ARE LEGENDARY WITH ELVIS PREDICTABLY DOMINATING, BUT THE IMPORTANCE OF DUANE EDDY AND JOHNNY AND THE HURRICANES CAN NOW BE ACKNOWLEDGED.

1. SUN COLLECTION
Elvis Presley

Elvis Presley's recordings for the Sun label almost venture beyond the realms of description. They not only define rockabilly's blend of country and R&B, but expose a singer whose unbridled style burst with freedom and sexual excitement. Material drawn from Arthur Crudup, Junior Parker and Arthur Gunter joins songs popularised by Bill Monore, Bob Wills and the Carter Family in a fervid melting pot which changed the course of pop forever. Rare masters from the same era join the five compelling singles Presley cut for Sun before leaving for RCA. Rarely has history sounded so alive.

That's Alright; Blue Moon Of Kentucky; I Don't Care If The Sun Don't Shine; Good Rockin' Tonight; Milk Cow Blues Boogie; You're A Heartbreaker; I'm Left, You're Right, She's Gone; Baby Let's Play House; Mystery Train; I Forgot To Remember To Forget; I'll Never Let You Go; I Love You Because (first version); Tryin' To Get To You; Blue Moon; Just Because; I Love You Because (second version).

First released 1975
UK peak chart position: 16
USA peak chart position: did not chart

2. ELVIS PRESLEY
Elvis Presley

Although 5 tracks remained from the Sun cellar this is usually known as Elvis' first RCA album, and what a lucky company they were, probably unaware that they had signed the greatest ever doner to their company pension scheme. No rock afficionado should be unaware of the tracks, although the album has long been replaced with compilations. It still is nominated by the majority of the cogniscenti who are old enough to remember this album plopping down on their Dansettes. It was a vitally important album although now doomed by the age of CD.

Blue Suede Shoes; I Love You Because; Tutti Frutti; I'll Never Let You Go; Money Honey; I'm Counting On You; I Got A Woman; One-Sided Love Affair; Just Because; Tryin' To Get To You; I'm Gonna Sit Right Down And Cry Over You; Blue Moon.

First released 1956
UK peak chart position: did not chart
USA peak chart position: 1

3. HERE'S LITTLE RICHARD
Little Richard

The enigmatic Little Richard turned rock 'n' roll inside out with a succession of highly expressive recordings during the mid-50s. Fuelled by an unfettered New Orleans backbeat, he combined gospel fervour and orgasmic delight in equal doses, singing without recourse to convention, hammering the piano keys with barely-checked passion. *Here's Little Richard* abounds with essential performances which define an era and few collections offer such unremitting excitement. The pace barely relents, while almost every track has become an integral part of pop history, either in its own right, or through the countless cover versions they have inspired. It is an exceptional album from an exceptional talent.

Tutti Frutti; True, Fine Mama; Ready Teddy; Baby; Slippin' And Slidin'; Long Tall Sally; Miss Ann; Oh Why?; Rip It Up; Jenny Jenny; She's Got It; Can't Believe You Wanna Leave.

First released 1957
UK peak chart position: did not chart
USA peak chart position: 13

4. FABULOUS
Little Richard

Little Richard's third album captured a singer building on his acknowledged style. He had forged a reputation based on undiluted R&B, typified on such expressive recordings as 'Tutti Frutti', 'Long Tall Sally' and 'Good Golly Miss Molly'. *Fabulous* offered a wider musical perspective, although there was no denying the frantic fervour surrounding his readings of 'Kansas City' and 'Whole Lotta Shakin' Goin' On'. Such performances contrast the more conciliatory 'Directly From My Heart', but the opportunity to broaden musical horizons suggested by this set was never fully taken up. In 1957 Richard denounced his work and joined the Church, but although he later reversed this decision, this album closes his most creative period.

Shake A Hand; Chicken Little Baby; All Night Long; The Most I Can Offer; Lonesome And Blue; Wonderin'; Whole Lotta Shakin' Goin' On; She Knows How To Rock; Kansas City; Directly From My Heart; Maybe I'm Right; Early One Morning; I'm Just A Lonely Guy.

First released 1958
UK peak chart position: did not chart
USA peak chart position: did not chart

5. EDDIE COCHRAN MEMORIAL ALBUM
Eddie Cochran

Eddie Cochran was part of an immediate post-Elvis group of rock 'n' roll singers. Drawing on rockabilly influences, he invested such roots with a technological edge and some incisive electric guitar runs. He shared, with Chuck Berry, an ability to articulate teenage frustration, a talent heard to perfection on 'Summertime Blues'. This album was issued in the wake of Cochran's premature death, and comprises of his best-known recordings. As such, it not only contains the cream of the singer's output, but also shows 50s rock maturing, developing a sound which would, in turn, inspire many musicians during the subsequent decade.

C'mon Everybody; Three Steps To Heaven; Cut Across Shorty; Jeannie, Jeannie, Jeannie; Pocketful Of Hearts; Hallelujah, I Love Her So; Don't Ever Let Me Go; Summertime Blues; Teresa; Something Else; Pretty Girl; Teenage Heaven; Boll Weevil; I Remember.

First released 1960
UK peak chart position: 9
USA peak chart position: did not chart

6. THE BUDDY HOLLY STORY
Buddy Holly

Few artists have enjoyed such a profound influence in such a short space of time. Holly's untimely death robbed pop of a performer adept as a solo act or as leader of his group, the Crickets. He wrote, or co-wrote, most of his own material at a time many singers relied on outside material, while a sparse, but effect, guitar style proved highly influential, particularly on British Beat groups. *The Buddy Holly Story* abounds with songs now indisputably pop classics and confirms Holly's status as a major figure. The Beatles, Tex-Mex music and the singer/songwriter genre each owe Holly a debt, which is itself a lasting tribute to the quality of his work.

Raining In My Heart; Early In The Morning; Peggy Sue; Maybe Baby; Everyday; Rave On; That'll Be The Day; Heartbeat; Think It Over; Oh Boy; It's So Easy; It Doesn't Matter Any More.

First released 1959
UK peak chart position: 2
USA peak chart position: 11

7. LOVING YOU
Elvis Presley

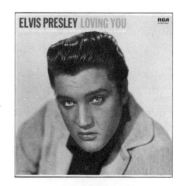

Elvis Presley's first film, *Love Me Tender*, included music as an afterthought, but music was the priority in his next, 'Loving You'. Four of the seven songs were hits, while 'Mean Woman Blues' has been recorded by Jerry Lee Lewis, Roy Orbison and many others. '(Let's Have A) Party' at 90 seconds is the shortest single ever to make the charts, a peculiar achievement as Elvis has an additional verse in the film. Fans used to send Elvis Presley teddy bears, hence the song of the same name. Jerry Leiber and Mike Stoller wrote one of their finest ballads with 'Loving You', a song comparable to Cole Porter's 'True Love' which, in turn, completed this 8-track, 10-inch album. In the US, the album was issued in 12-inch format and the four additional tracks, including 'Blueberry Hill', were released on an EP here.

Mean Woman Blues; (Let Me Be Your) Teddy Bear; Got A Lot O' Livin' To Do; Lonesome Cowboy; Hot Dog; (Let's Have A) Party; Blueberry Hill; True Love; Don't Leave Me Now; Have I Told You Lately That I Love You?; I Need You So; Loving You.

First released 1957
UK peak chart position: 24
USA peak chart position: 1

8. ROCK AND ROLLIN' WITH
Fats Domino

Antoine 'Fats' Domino's brand of New Orleans R&B had scarcely changed since his first record, 'The Fat Man', in 1949 but with the advent of rock 'n' roll, his record label encouraged him to push the rhythm, drop the blues, beef up the saxes, write teenage lyrics and call it rock 'n' roll. Fats didn't mind: he simply loved playing music. This collection included older material like 'Please Don't Leave Me', but could still justify the rock 'n' roll tag. Fats' wife is the subject of 'Rosemary' and they had eight children, each of which was christened with a name beginning with 'A'. Maybe Fats' records had plenty of bounce because he used to work in a bedsprings factory.

Tired Of Crying; Rosemary; All By Myself; You Said You Love Me; Ain't It A Shame; The Fat Man; Poor Me; Bo Weevil; Don't Blame It On Me; Goin' Home; Going To The River; Please Don't Leave Me.

First released 1956
UK peak chart position: did not chart
USA peak chart position: 17

9. EXPLOSIVE! FREDDY CANNON
Freddy Cannon

Vocalist Freddie Cannon encapsulated a period in American pop sandwiched between rock 'n' roll and the British Invasion. It was the era of DJ Dick Clark and *American Bandstand*, where the well-scrubbed features of Bobby Vee, Fabian and Bobby Rydell replaced the menace of Little Richard or Jerry Lee Lewis. Cannon's singles, the cream of which are included here, were unabashed pop, but there was no denying the exuberant charm of 'Palisades Park' or the exciting simplicity of 'Tallahassie Lassie'. Cannon's recordings walked a fine tightrope between bubblegum and novelty, the latter style apparent on 'If You Were A Rock 'n' Roll Record', but together they forge an album which extols an innocent era.

Abigail Beecher; Action; Buzz Buzz A-Diddle-It; Chattanooga Shoe Shine Boy; The Dedication Song; For Me And My Gal; Happy Shades Of Blue; If You Were A Rock And Roll Record; Muskrat Ramble; Okefenokee; Palisades Park; Tallahassee Lassie; Teen Queen Of The Week; Transistor Sister; Way Down Yonder In New Orleans; The Urge.

First released 1960
UK peak chart position: 1
USA peak chart position: did not chart

10. THIS IS FATS DOMINO
Fats Domino

Despite the cheapo-cheapo cover, this is one of the most potent rock 'n' roll albums of the 50s. Fats' revival of Louis Armstrong's 'Blueberry Hill' was so successful that nearly everyone now regards it as Fats' song. He and his producer Dave Bartholomew wrote straightforward, conversational rock 'n' roll songs including 'Ain't It A Shame', now known as 'Ain't That A Shame'. Pat Boone, an English graduate, originally hadn't wanted to cover a song with the word 'Ain't' in the title. 'Blue Monday', which Fats sang in 'The Girl Can't Help It', is one of the first songs about the drudgery of the working week. He sent himself up in 'The Fat Man's Hop'. Why were people so concerned when Elvis put on weight? Fats Domino always looked the same and was always heavier than Elvis.

Blueberry Hill; Honey Chile; What's The Reason I'm Not Pleasing You; Blue Monday; So Long; La La; Troubles Of My Own; You Done Me Wrong; Reeling And Rocking; The Fat Man's Hop; Poor Poor Me; Trust In Me.

First released 1957
UK peak chart position: did not chart
USA peak chart position: 19

11. ONE DOZEN BERRIES
Chuck Berry

Popular music is almost unthinkable without the influence of Chuck Berry. He combined the economy of R&B with a brilliant gift for lyricism which encapsulated adolescent spirit in manner no other performer has matched. The three opening tracks on this album define Berry's gifts; each one is now an integral part of pop's lexicon. Intriguingly these compositions can be heard in the early work of the Beach Boys, Rolling Stones and Beatles, which itself is a tribute to Berry's enormous influence. His unique guitar style is showcased on 'Blue Ceiling' and 'Guitar Boogie', resulting in a set which expresses the artist's talent to the full.

Sweet Little Sixteen; Blue Feeling; La Jaunda; Guitar Boogie; Oh Baby Doll; In-Go; Rock At The Philharmonic; Reelin' And Rockin; Rock & Roll Music; It Don't Take But A Few Minutes; Low Feeling; How You've Changed.

First released 1958
UK peak chart position: did not chart
USA peak chart position: did not chart

12. ELVIS
Elvis Presley

While Private Elvis Presley was gaining his stripes in Germany, RCA was desperate for new material. They kept the pot boiling with by taking his first UK album, *Rock 'n' Roll No.1*, substituting three tracks and adding two more. Although critics sometimes regard his Sun tracks in a different light to his RCA ones, they sit well together. 'I Was The One', the b-side of 'Heartbreak Hotel' and one of Elvis' favourite songs, could easily have been recorded at Sun. 'Lawdy, Miss Clawdy', written and originally recorded by Lloyd Price, remains one of Presley's best-ever performances: the lyrics don't mean much but there's tremendous commitment from Elvis. Lloyd Price's original version had Fats Domino on piano: this one had Elvis himself. Elvis always enjoyed his recording sessions and you can sense this in the good-natured 'Money Honey'.

That's All Right; Lawdy, Miss Clawdy; Mystery Train; Playing For Keeps; Poor Boy; Money Honey; I'm Counting On You; My Baby Left Me; I Was The One; Shake, Rattle And Roll; I'm Left, You're Right, She's Gone; You're A Heartbreaker; Trying To Get You; Blue Suede Shoes.

First released 1959
UK peak chart position: did not chart
USA peak chart position: 1

13. JERRY LEE'S GREATEST!
Jerry Lee Lewis

Jerry Lee Lewis's UK tour collapsed when it was revealed that he had married his 13 year old cousin. His sales plummeted but Sun Records persevered, hoping for a single that was so good that rock 'n' rollers would just have to buy it. Unfortunately, Jerry Lee had lost his impetus, so Sam Phillips taunted him by saying, "You couldn't cover Ray Charles for shit." Jerry Lee immediately tore into a take-no-prisoners version of 'What'd I Say' which restored him to the charts. The resulting album came from all periods of his Sun career and included his singles, 'Great Balls Of Fire', 'Let's Talk About Us' and Charlie Rich's 'Breakup'. 'Cold Cold Heart', from 1957, shows that Jerry Lee was always a fine country singer. When a researcher asked Jerry Lee who played on his records, he replied, "I played on them - what the hell else do you need to know?"

Money; As Long As I Live; Hillbilly Music; Breakup; Hello, Hello Baby; Home; Let's Talk About Us; Great Balls Of Fire; Frankie And Johnny; Cold Cold Heart; What'd I Say; Hello Josephine.

First released 1962
UK peak chart position: 14
USA peak chart position: did not chart

14. SINGIN' TO MY BABY
Eddie Cochran

Singin' To My Baby was the only album to be issued during Eddie Cochran's lifetime, so it's sad that it wasn't a better reflection of his talent - and it certainly would have sounded better without the Johnny Mann Singers. A dichotomy raged within Cochran: with his astonishing good looks, should he concentrate on being a teenage idol or should be a top rate guitarist and rough rock 'n' roller? (He told Brian Mathew on the BBC Radio's *Saturday Club* that his ambition was 'to be successful', so make what you will of that.) His first successes were with the innocent teenage pop of 'Sittin' In The Balcony' and 'Drive-In Show' - but does he say 'I bet my penis to a candy bar' in 'Drive-In Show'?! He toughened his approach with 'Twenty Flight Rock', which was featured, to great effect, in 'The Girl Can't Help It'.

Sittin' In The Balcony; Completely Sweet; Undying Love; I'm Alone Because I Love You; Lovin' Time; Proud Of You; Am I Blue; Twenty Flight Rock; Drive In Snow; Mean When I'm Mad; Stockin's 'N' Shoes; Tell Me Why; Have I Told You Lately That I Love You; Cradle Baby; One Kiss.

First released 1957
UK peak chart position: did not chart
USA peak chart position: did not chart

15. ROCKIN' WITH WANDA
Wanda Jackson

Wanda Jackson's career has combined country, gospel and rock, and many regard her as the finest female rockabilly singer. Few singers had the nerve to cover one of Elvis Presley's hits, but she made the US charts with a wild, wild '(Let's Have A) Party'. Her record had been two years earlier, so Capitol trawled through her sessions for an album of her most rocking sides. 'I Gotta Know', 'Hot Dog! That Made Him Mad' and the raving 'Mean Mean Man' showed that she could be as dynamic as Brenda Lee, and 'Baby Loves Him' contains Elvis references - and Wanda had been dating the King. She was backed by the finest guitarists in Hollywood - Merle Travis, Buck Owens and Joe Maphis. *Rockin' With Wanda* includes 'Fujiyama Mama' and Wanda says, 'Here I was, an American singing about those tragedies, 'I've been to Nagasaki, I've been to Hiroshima'. It was a number 1 record in Japan for three months. I did a seven week tour over there on the strength of that song.'

Hot Dog! That Made Him Mad; Baby Loves Him; Mean Mean Man; You've Turned To A Stranger; Don'a Wan'a; I Gotta Know; Yakety-Yak; (Let's Have A) Party; Rock Your Baby; Fujiyama Mama; You're The One For Me; Did You Miss Me?; Cool Love; Honey Bop; Whole Lotta Shakin' Goin' On; Savin' My Love.

First released 1960
UK peak chart position: did not chart
USA peak chart position: did not chart

16. Rock Around The Clock
Bill Haley And His Comets

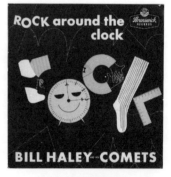

Bill Haley was not an overnight success: he had been working as a country performer since the 40s and 'Rock Around The Clock' was his 28th single. He had even recorded rock 'n' roll before but it was 'Rock Around The Clock', used in the film *Blackboard Jungle*, that became the international teenage anthem. The only thing Bill dropped was his yodel - somewhat reluctantly as he had been the champion yodeller in Indiana. 'Shake, Rattle And Roll' was an expurgated version of a R&B hit by Big Joe Turner. Haley's perception of his audience can also be gleaned from 'Rock-a-beatin' Boogie', which, like a lot of his songs, seems intent on teaching his audience to spell.

Rock Around The Clock; Shake, Rattle And Roll; ABC Boogie; Thirteen Women; Razzle-dazzle; Two Hound Dogs; Dim, Dim The Lights; Happy Baby; Birth Of The Boogie; Mambo Rock; Burn That Candle; Rock-a-beatin' Boogie.

First released 1956
UK peak chart position: 34
USA peak chart position: 12

17. RICKY
Ricky Nelson

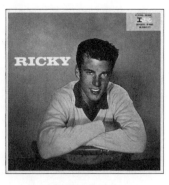

When 17 years old, Ricky Nelson became the youngest person to top the US album charts and he owed his success, not just to a fine album but to regular appearances in a television soap. He attempted to bring the sound of Sun Records to California by covering Carl Perkins' 'Your True Love' and 'Boppin' The Blues' and recording several pieces in a similar vein. Ricky knew his limitations - he didn't take on the excesses of Little Richard - and he created a fine rockabilly sound with the help of guitarists Joe Maphis and James Burton. 'Be-bop Baby' was a US Top 10 hit and the UK issue of this album included both sides of the follow-up single, 'Stood Up' and 'Waitin' In School', two definitive rockabilly songs. Ricky Nelson always produced good albums and his later hit, 'Garden Party', showed that he was not too comfortable as being regarded as an oldies performer.

First released 1957
UK peak chart position: did not chart
USA peak chart position: 1

Honeycomb; Boppin' The Blues; Be-bop Baby; Have I Told You Lately That I Love You; Teenage Doll; If You Can't Rock Me; Whole Lotta Shakin' Goin' On; Baby I'm Sorry; Am I Blue; I'm Confessin'; Your True Love; True Love.

18. BLUEJEAN BOP
Gene Vincent

In May 1956, the two-and-a-half minutes of 'Be Bop A Lula' marked the astonishing recording debut of Gene Vincent, and the following month Gene was back in Owen Bradley's studio in Nashville for his first album, *Bluejean Bop*. Producer Ken Nelson flipped the echo switch to maximum and created a space age sound for 'Who Slapped John?', in particular. Gene's voice was softer than most rock 'n' rollers and his tender versions of 'Ain't She Sweet?' and 'Up A Lazy River' display an inkling to become an all-round entertainer. His country roots are covered in ''Waltz Of The Wind' but it is the extraordinary rock 'n' roll numbers like 'Bluejean Bop' and 'Bop Street' (don't be fooled by the slow start!) that make the album so remarkable and created a guitar hero out of Cliff Gallup. Gene Vincent rocks, the Bluecaps roll and the result is uninhibited magic.

First released 1956
UK peak chart position: did not chart
USA peak chart position: 16

Bluejean Bop; Jezebel; Who Slapped John?; Ain't She Sweet?; I Flipped; Waltz Of The Wind; Jump Back, Honey, Jump Back; That Old Gang Of Mine; Jumps, Giggles, And Shouts; Up A Lazy River; Bop Street; Peg O' My Heart.

19. SOLID AND RAUNCHY
Bill Black

Double-bass player Bill Black left Elvis Presley in 1957 in a dispute over money: Elvis, usually so generous, was only paying him $100 a week. He formed the Bill Black Combo and recorded for another Memphis company, Hi. They developed an R&B instrumental sound with a touch of jazz. *Solid And Raunchy* was his first, big-selling album, the title being a dig at his old label, Sun, who had had success with Bill Justis' 'Raunchy'. Bill Black died in 1965 by which time the group was on its eleventh album, called *More Solid And Raunchy*.

First released 1960
UK peak chart position: did not chart
USA peak chart position: 23

Don't Be Cruel; Singing The Blues; Blueberry Hill; I Almost Lost My Mind; Cherry PInk; Mona Lisa; Honky Tonk; Tequila; Raunchy; You Win Again; Bo Diddley; Mack The Knife; Movin'; What I'd Say?; Hey Bo Diddley; Witchcraft; Work With Me Annie; Be Bop A Lula; My Babe; 40 Miles Of Bad Road; Ain't That Loving You Baby; Honky Train; The Walk; Torquay.

20. DREAMIN'
Johnny Burnette

Although highly regarded as part of the Rock & Roll Trio ('Honey Hush', 'The Train Kept A-Rollin''), Johnny Burnette's explosive work had only limited appeal at the time. He and his brother Dorsey had success writing for Ricky Nelson and then Johnny pursued a career alongside other beat-balladeers like Bobby Vee and Bobby Rydell, although, as a former boxer, he never shared their 'pretty boy' looks. He found success with the romantic 'Dreamin'' (the strings, surprisingly, were his own idea), although the powerhouse b-side 'Cincinnati Fireball' was more in keeping with his earlier work. The resulting album found him in a country mood, doing presentable versions of country standards such as 'Lovesick Blues' and 'Settin' The Woods On Fire', which was banned by one radio station as it might encourage pyromaniacs. Johnny had further hits with 'You're Sixteen' and 'Little Boy Sad' before a fatal boating accident in 1964. His son, Rocky Burnette, had his own success with 'Tired Of Toein' The Line'.

First released 1960
UK peak chart position: did not chart
USA peak chart position: did not chart

Dreamin'; Lovesick Blues; Please Help Me, I'm Falling; Haul Off And Love Me One More Time; Love Me; Kaw-Liga; Settin' The Woods On Fire; I Want To Be With You Always; Cincinnati Fireball; My Special Angel; Finders Keepers; I Really Don't Want To Know.

21. KING CREOLE
Elvis Presley

One of the very few Elvis films with good music, and recorded when he was a rock 'n' roll singer first and foremost. Although crudely recorded, the dated sound gives the album great bounce - thin guitar recorded in the bathroom, pudding drums and soggy stand-up bass but the instrumentation complimented the King's quite magnificent voice. 'Hard Headed Woman' remains one of his liveliest tracks and the title track still has incredible moodyness, and even with 50s dance band brass it still works. The CD reissue announces a playing time of 21.12, the only negative thing about the record.

King Creole; As Long As I Have You; Hard Headed Woman; Trouble; Dixieland Rock; Don't Ask Me Why; Lover Doll; Crawfish; Young Dreams; Steadfast, Loyal And True; New Orleans.

First released 1958
UK peak chart position: 4
USA peak chart position: 2

22. THIS IS BRENDA
Brenda Lee

This album contained two of Brenda Lee's ballad hits, 'I'm Sorry' and 'I Want To Be Wanted' and she sounds so mature that the French maliciously exposed her as a 32-year-old midget (she wasn't). Her singles were noted for having two good sides - one ballad, one beat - and, similarly, her albums were equally mixed and equally strong. The rocking 'Just A Little' was a b-side hit and she also paid tribute to Fats Domino and Ray Charles. The emotional 'We Three (My Echo My Shadow And Me)' is one of her best performances. Says Brenda, 'I had a great run but I always knew I couldn't keep having hit after hit after hit. There are so many other entertainers out there.'

When My Dreamboat Comes Home; I Want To Be Wanted; Just A Little; Pretend; Love And Learn; Teach Me Tonight; Hallelujah I Love Him So; Walkin' To New Orleans; Blueberry Hill; We Three (My Echo My Shadow And Me); Build A Big Fence; If I Didn't Care.

First released 1960
UK peak chart position: did not chart
USA peak chart position: 4

23. ELVIS IS BACK
Elvis Presley

Recorded immediately after completing his spell in the US Army, *Elvis Is Back* is a massive sigh of relief and a restatement of talent. Elvis takes these blues songs and shreds them, reclaiming his role as interpreter nonpareil, proving his art had not faltered through abstinence. Pleading, assertive or simply exuberant, he made each selection his own, the exhortations enhanced by sterling support from Scotty Moore (guitar) and Boots Randolph (saxophone). 'Such A Night' and 'Reconsider Baby' are among the finest tracks the singer ever recorded, but from here Elvis slid into film and soundtrack work. Yet if nothing else, this marvellous, unified album damns the lie that national service killed Presley's talent.

Make Me Know It; Fever; The Girl Of My Best Friend; I Will Be Home Again; Dirty, Dirty Feeling; Thrills Of Your Love; Soldier Boy; Such A Night; It Feels So Right; Girl Next Door Went A'walking; Like A Baby; Reconsider Baby.

First released 1960
UK peak chart position: 1
USA peak chart position: 2

24. THE TWANGS THE THANG
Duane Eddy

Duane Eddy didn't put his hit singles on his third album and instead created an atmospheric work, which might rank as an early concept album. The sleeve notes convey the setting for each instrumental: 'The minute before your first goodnight kiss . . . The minute between happiness and the blues . . . These are the last minutes of innocence' convey the mood of 'The Last Minute Of Innocence'. The best-known track is Duane's version of Chet Atkins' lazy, insidious 'Trambone' and his new Danelectro six-string bass on 'Tiger Love And Turnip Greens'. 'It is about an octave lower than a regular guitar,' says Duane, 'and even though it is cheap and inexpensive, it has a great sound.' The album includes 'You Are My Sunshine', which Duane later recorded with his wife (Deed), his ex-wife (Jessi Colter), his ex-wife's husband (Waylon Jennings) and an old friend (Willie Nelson).

My Blue Heaven; Tiger Love And Turnip Greens; The Last Minute Of Innocence; Route No. 1; You Are My Sunshine; St. Louis Blues; Night Train To Memphis; The Battle; Trambone; Blueberry Hill; Rebel Walk; Easy.

First released 1959
UK peak chart position: 2
USA peak chart position: 18

25. THE BUDDY HOLLY STORY VOL 2
Buddy Holly

Buddy Holly's memorial album, *The Buddy Holly Story*, was so successful that a second was issued a year later. Six songs, including 'Peggy Sue Got Married' and 'Crying, Waiting, Hoping', had been recorded by Buddy in his New York apartment a few weeks before he died. Studio backings were added to make them sound more professional, although most Holly fans prefer the voice-and-acoustic-guitar originals which were eventually released. The album was completed by two songs from his final recording session ('True Love Ways', 'Moondreams'), three b-sides and one album track. Although the result is something of a ragbag, Holly's presence is so sure and so strong that it works as an excellent album.

Peggy Sue Got Married; Well...All Right; What To Do; That Makes It Tough; Now We're One; Take Your Time; Crying, Waiting, Hoping; True Love Ways; Learning The Game; Little Baby; Moondreams; That's What They Say.

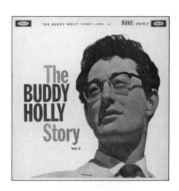

First released 1960
UK peak chart position: 7
USA peak chart position: did not chart

26. JOHNNY BURNETTE AND THE ROCK 'N' ROLL TRIO
Johnny Burnette

Although chiefly recalled for pop hit singles, notably 'Only Sixteen', Johnny Burnette began his career as a rockabilly singer. The genre's speedball crossing of blues and country was brilliantly expressed on this ground-breaking album in which the trio allow themselves unfettered musical expression. 'Train Kept A-Rollin'' is the archetypal selection; Tiny Bradshaw's big band classic is stripped down and supercharged with fervour, almost rendering the original version meaningless. Only Elvis Presley's Sun recordings match this collection for exuberance, it is the standard by why which all rockabilly is judged.

Tear It Up; You're Undecided; Oh Baby Babe; Midnight Train; Shattered Dreams; Train Kept A Rollin'; Blues Stay Away From Me; All By Myself; Drinkin' Wine Spo-Dee-O-Dee; Chains Of Love; Honey Hush; Lonesome Tears In My Eyes; I Just Found Out; Please Don't Leave Me; Rock Therapy; Rockabilly Boogie; Lonesome Train (On A Lonesome Track); Sweet Love On My Mind; My Love You're A Stranger; I Love You So; Your Baby Blue Eyes; Touch Me; If You Want It Enough; Butterfingers; Eager Beaver Baby.

First released 1957
UK peak chart position: did not chart
USA peak chart position: did not chart

27. HATS OFF TO DEL SHANNON
Del Shannon

Del Shannon disproves the fallacy that the immediate pre-Beatles era was a musical backwater. His often self-penned singles combined melodrama with sizzling hooklines and many are rightly regarded as pop classics. *Hats Off To Del Shannon*, which was only issued in Britain, compiles both sides of the singer's first seven releases, bar his debut single. Four reached the UK Top 10, giving Shannon greater commercial success than he enjoyed in his native USA. His distinctive voice was capable of switching from passivity to fully-animated falsetto but this was a style as opposed to a gimmick. This eclectic intonation gives an added edge to this highly crafted selection.

The Swiss Maid; Cry Myself To Sleep; Ginny In The Mirror; You Never Talked About Me; Don't Gild The Lily, Lily; If Won't Be There; Hats Off To Larry; The Answer To Everything; Hey! Little Girl; I'm Gonna Move On; I Don't Care Anymore; So Long Baby.

First released 1963
UK peak chart position: 9
USA peak chart position: did not chart

28. THE SOUND OF FURY
Billy Fury

Arguably Britain's finest singer from the pre-Beatles age, Billy Fury enjoyed commercial success with a series of impassioned ballads. *The Sound Of Fury*, however, was markedly different and showed the singer equally comfortable with rock 'n' roll and rockabilly. Guitarist Joe Brown played Scotty Moore to Fury's Elvis Presley in a set brimming with purpose and unfettered joy. Although musical debts are apparent, the verve with which the participants approach the project is exciting and highly influential. The collection stands beside 'Shakin' All Over', 'Move It' and 'Brand New Cadillac' as crucial lynchpins in the evolution of British pop.

That's Love; My Advise; Phone Call; You Don't Know; Turn My Back On You; Don't Say It's Over; Since You've Been Gone; It's You I Need; Alright Goodbye; Don't Leave Me This Way.

First released 1960
UK peak chart position: 18
USA peak chart position: did not chart

29. FROM ELVIS IN MEMPHIS
Elvis Presley

Years trapped making facile films and equally poor soundtrack albums dented Presley's popularity without tarnishing the myth. Convincing material would rekindle his reputation. *From Elvis In Memphis* was issued in the wake of the spellbinding *Elvis' TV Special* and it offered a similar sense of musical adventure. Recorded at Chips Moman's American Recording Studio, it featured the crack houseband behind hits for the Box Tops, Aretha Franklin and Sandy Posey. Presley's first sessions in Memphis for 14 years result in a thrilling set which captures the singer at his finest. Like *Elvis Is Back*, his immediate post-army release, this spirited album proves that Presley could turn on his talent when the mood or opportunity took him.

Wearin' That Loved On Look; Only The Strong Survive; I'll Hold You In My Heart; Long Black Limousine; It Keeps Right On A-Hurtin'; I'm Moving On; Power Of My Love; Gentle On My Mind; After Loving You; True Love Travels On A Gravel Road; Any Day Now; In The Ghetto.

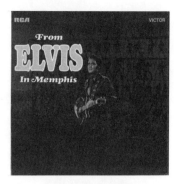

First released 1969
UK peak chart position: 1
USA peak chart position: 13

30. STORMSVILLE
Johnny And The Hurricanes

The tenor saxophonist, Johnny Paris, had his first success with 'Crossfire' under the name of the Orbits in 1959. They changed it to Johnny And The Hurricanes and the main instruments were Johnny's sax and Paul Tesluk's organ. They had a hit with 'Red River Rock' and then 'Reveille Rock': remember that conscription was still around. They cut two minute instrumentals with simple riffs and little variation, but they still acquired a large following. Trivia buffs: extrovert Merseybeat performer, Rory Storm, called his group, the Hurricanes, and his house, Stormsville.

Reveille Rock; Milk Shake; Cyclone; Travelin'; Beanbag; Rockin' 'T'; The Hungry Eye; Hot Fudge; Time Bomb; Corn Bread; Catnip; The 'Hep' Canary (The Hot Canary).

First released 1960
UK peak chart position: 18
USA peak chart position: 34

31. COMPELLING PERCUSSION
Sandy Nelson

Named after Sandy Nelson's ongoing obsession with drums and much more satisfying than the hastily put together *Teen Beat '65*. Nelson was the first (and only) rock 'n' roll drummer who took his art seriously, even though he continued to re-work his major hit 'Let There Be Drums' under many different titles. On this album we have 'And Then There Were Drums'. Nelson's forte had remained largely the same since his first hit, 'Teen Beat' in 1959. Propulsive musicianship from a tight band, which included Richie Podolor, later producer of Steppenwolf, takes its cue from Nelson's percussive interludes. Never flashy, he simply emphasises the beat, forging a sound epitomising mid-60s discotheques and parties.

Civilization; And Then There Were Drums; Alexes; Chicka Boom; Jump Time; Drums, For Drummers Only; Drums, For Strippers Only.

First released 1965
UK peak chart position: did not chart
USA peak chart position: 141

32. ALL THE WAY
Brenda Lee

Although only 16, Brenda Lee had the audacity to cover Frank Sinatra's 'All The Way' and make it the title track of her album. Her singles were released with one beat side and one ballad, and this album had a similar format. Here, the beat numbers are more uptempo pop than rock 'n' roll and the indications were that Brenda was moving away from the sounds that made her famous. The exception is 'Dum Dum', a nonsense song that Cliff Richard selected as one of his favourite records. Her wonderful rasping voice is exhilarating on this, one of her best recordings. When you consider that it is such a simple song, it is perhaps surprising that there was a dispute over its authorship - no, perhaps not, anyone of 100 songwriters could have written it, but only Brenda could have done it justice.

Lover Come Back To Me; All The Way; Dum Dum; Kansas City; On The Sunny Side Of The Street; Talkin' 'Bout You; Someone To Love Me (The Prisoner's Song); Eventually; Do I Worry (Yes I Do); Tragedy; Speak To Me Pretty; The Big Chance.

First released 1961
UK peak chart position: 20
USA peak chart position: 17

33. ROCK THE JOINT!
Bill Haley And His Comets

Bill Haley had first recorded 'Rock The Joint' in 1952 and a new, more rocking version was recorded for this album. Haley's rock 'n' roll was not threatening like Little Richard's: compare their versions of 'Rip It Up'. It was brave of Haley to cover Hank Williams' 'Move It On Over': play it next to 'Rock Around The Clock' and it's easy to see where Haley derived his inspiration. By 1957, though, most of the inspiration had left: hence, the embarrassing 'Rock Lomond'. For the next few years, most of Haley's material would be novelty material, although he had a moment of splendour with 'Skinny Minnie'.

Rocket 88; Tearstains On My Heart; Green Tree Boogie; Jukebox Cannonball; Sundown Boogie; Icy Heart; Rock The Joint; Dance With A Dolly; Rockin' Chair On The Moon; Stop Beatin' Around The Mulberry Bush; Real Rock Drive; Crazy Man Crazy; What Cha' Gonna Do; Pat-a-cake; Fractured; Live It Up; Farewell, So Long, Goodbye; I'll Be True; Ten Little Indians; Chattanooga Choo Choo; Straight Jacket; Yes Indeed.

First released 1957
UK peak chart position: did not chart
USA peak chart position: did not chart

34. CHERISHED MEMORIES
Eddie Cochran

How ironic that Sharon Sheeley, Eddie Cochran's fiancée, should write him a song called 'Cherished Memories' and that he should record it at his final session in 1960. It was the perfect title for a tribute album, but the best material had appeared on *The Eddie Cochran Memorial Album*. Of particular interest is 'Let's Get Together' - the original version of 'C'mon Everybody' before Eddie changed the title. Much of the rock 'n' roll sounds second-hand: 'Pink Peg Slacks' is a feeble rewrite of 'Blue Suede Shoes', but the mumbling 'Sweetie Pie' has real rock 'n' roll presence.

Cherished Memories; I've Waited So Long; Never; Skinny Jim; Half Loved; Weekend; Nervous Breakdown; Let's Get Together; Rock And Roll Blues; Dark Lonely Street; Pink Peg Slacks; That's My Desire; Sweetie Pie; Think Of Me.

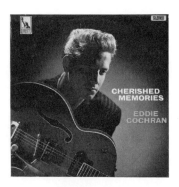

First released 1963
UK peak chart position: 15
USA peak chart position: did not chart

35. LET'S TWIST-HER
Bill Black

By 1962 everyone (Elvis, Frank Sinatra, Zsa Zsa Gabor) wanted to cash in on the twist but for the Bill Black Combo, the sound was pretty much the same as before. The album included rock 'n' roll standards and his first US hit, 'Smokie (Part 2)', from 1959. Of the new material, 'Twist-Her' was a US Top 30 single. Bill Black died of a brain tumour in 1965, but the group continued playing. His double-bass was bought by Paul McCartney and Paul plays it on 'Baby's Request'.

Twist Her; High Train; Corrine Corrina; The Hucklebuck; Royal Twist; Yogi; My Girl Josephine; Twistaroo; Johnny B. Goode; Twist With Me Baby; Slippin' And Slidin'; Smokey (Part 2).

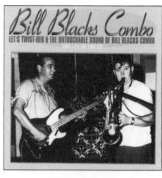

First released 1962
UK peak chart position: did not chart
USA peak chart position: 35

36. SINGS THE MILLION SELLERS
Connie Francis

Connie Francis was one of the most successful singers of the late 50s and early 60s. Her pseudo-operatic voice brought an individuality to teen melodrama, notably on her singles, 'Who's Sorry Now' and ' Stupid Cupid'. Her own million-seller, 'Lipstick On Your Collar' is on this collection, where Francis brings her distinctive timbre to songs originally recorded by, among others, Elvis Presley, Fats Domino and Conway Twitty. This was not, however, a stop-gap release, born of an artistic malaise. Her interpretations were carefully recorded, bringing new slants to already well-known material, confirming both its abiding strength and the memorable quality of Francis' singing.

Heartbreak Hotel; Tweedlee Dee; I Almost Lost My Mind; I Hear You Knocking; Just A Dream; Don't Be Cruel; Lipstick On Your Collar; Sincerely; Ain't That A Shame; Silhouettes; I'm Walkin'; It's Only Make Believe.

First released 1960
UK peak chart position: 12
USA peak chart position: did not chart

37. WHY DO FOOLS FALL IN LOVE?
Frankie Lymon

There were numerous street corner doo-wop groups before Frankie Lymon And The Teenagers and indeed their record label, Gee, was named after the Crows' US hit. However, it was the Teenagers that made the major breakthrough onto the US charts. Who could resist the nonsense opening to 'Why Do Fools Fall In Love?' which was followed by 13 year old Frankie's soaring falsetto? They followed up their success with 'I Want You To Be My Girl', 'Baby Baby' and 'I'm Not A Juvenile Delinquent', although Lymon was precisely that. After splitting with the Teenagers, he was involved in drugs, sex and precious little rock 'n' roll, eventually OD'ing in 1968. Smokey Robinson, Diana Ross, the Ronettes have acknowledged his influence, and someone, someday is bound to film his story.

Why Do Fools Fall In Love?; I Want You To Be My Girl; I Promise To Remember; ABC's Of Love; I'm Not A Juvenile Delinquent; Baby Baby; Teenage Love; Love Is A Clown; Thumb Thumb; I Put The Bomp; Little Bitty Pretty One; Buzz Buzz Buzz; Waitin' In School; Jailhouse Rock; Silhouettes; Next Time You See Me; Send For Me; It Hurts To Be In Love; Searchin'; Short Fat Fannie.

First released 1979
UK peak chart position: did not chart
USA peak chart position: did not chart

38. BRENDA LEE
Brenda Lee

The whispers at the start of 'Sweet Nothin's' are so appealing that if the record had ended there and then, Brenda Lee would still have had a smash hit. The rasping, growling 'Let's Jump The Broomstick' had been recorded when she was only 13, but her first US successes, 'Jambalaya' and 'Dynamite', were re-made because her voice had matured. Mostly, though, this was a solid set of new rock 'n' roll songs - Jackie de Shannon wrote 'My Baby Loves Western Guys' and John D. Loudermilk, the Fats Domino-styled 'Weep No More My Baby', featuring Boots Randolph on tenor sax. The surprise song on the album was one recorded, at her request, at the end of a session: it was the ballad, 'I'm Sorry', which included an Inkspots-styled narration. It became a US number 1 and set the pattern for several hit records. Says Brenda, "The song really wasn't long enough. That's why we did the narration."

First released 1960
UK peak chart position: did not chart
USA peak chart position: 5

Sweet Nothin's; Let's Jump The Broomstick; Jambalaya; Dynamite; My Baby Loves Western Guys; Weep No More My Baby; I'm Sorry.

39. A DATE WITH THE EVERLY BROTHERS
Everly Brothers

At a time when albums were often an adjunct to hit singles, the Everly Brothers created collections which stood on their own terms. With 'Cathy's Clown' the pair introduced a fuller, richer sound to their recordings and such elements are apparent on this album. It combines six songs by Felice and Boudleaux Bryant, the Everlys' favoured collaborators, a handful of cover versions and two new original compositions, 'That's Just Too Much' and 'Made To Love'. 'So How Come' became a part of the Beatles' live set and the Everly Brothers' harmonies left an undoubted mark on the vocal interplay between Lennon and McCartney. This album confirms the special talent of one of pop's most enduring acts.

First released 1960
UK peak chart position: 3
USA peak chart position: 9

Made To Love; That's Just Too Much; Stick With Me Baby; Baby What You Want Me To Do; Sigh Cry Almost Die; Always It's You; Love Hurts; Lucille; So How Come; Donna Donna; A Change Of Heart; Cathy's Clown.

40. DIAMONDS
Diamonds

The Diamonds, invariably dressed in dinner-jackets and bowties, had such overblown vocal arrangements that you wonder whether their rock 'n' roll was serious or a parody. Indeed, their version of the Gladiolas' 'Little Darlin'' could have passed for one of Stan Freberg's fun-filled records and Elvis later used it as a comedy number for stage appearances. Nevertheless, the Diamonds were a top rock 'n' roll group and their album contains such doo-wop favourites as 'The Stroll' (actually, a slow dance), 'A Thousand Miles Away' and 'Daddy Cool'.

The Stroll; You Baby You; Ev'ry Night About This Time; Ka-Ding-Dong; A Thousand Miles Away; Ev'ry Minute Of The Day; Little Darlin'; Faithful And True; Straight Skirts; Silhouettes; Passion Flower; Daddy Cool.

First released 1956
UK peak chart position: did not chart
USA peak chart position: did not chart

41. CHIRPIN'
Crickets

Another great classic that failed to chart on both sides of the Atlantic. Maybe the name Crickets on the cover fooled deterred purchasers not realising this featured Mr Holly. The tracks speak for themselves, timeless pop-flavoured rock 'n' roll songs which still take some beating, 'Maybe Baby', That'll' Be The Day', 'Oh Boy' were the main hit singles but the inclusion of 'Not Fade Away', 'It's Too late' and 'Send Me Some Lovin'' make this collection essential. The cover is a priceless timepeace, before real graphic designers were used, a wonderful false sky is dropped in behind four 'senior citizen' looking men uncomfortably posing with guitars.

Oh Boy; Not Fade Away; You've Got Love; Maybe Baby; It's Too Late; Tell Me How; That'll Be The Day; I'm Looking For Someone To Love; An Empty Cup (And A Broken Date); Send Me Some Lovin'; Last Night; Rock Me My Baby.

First released 1958
UK peak chart position: did not chart
USA peak chart position: did not chart

42. FOR TEENAGERS ONLY
Bobby Darin

They were the kind of people Bobby Darin was singing to when he cut most of these mono-only tracks in 1958, but, by the time the album was released late in 1960, he had moved on to a more hip, adult audience. His reading of the well-known standard 'That Lucky Old Sun', which is surrounded here by teeny-bopper material such as 'I Ain't Sharin' Sharon' and 'Pretty Miss Kitty', sign-posted his immediate future as a sophisticated swinger. As an insight into a man about to eschew sweat shirt and jeans for sharp suits, this is a fascinating album.

I Want You With Me; Hush, Somebody's Coming; Keep A' Walkin'; Somebody To Love; I Ain't Sharin' Sharon; Pretty Miss Kitty; That Lucky Old Sun; All The Way Home; You Never Called; A Picture No Artist Could Paint; Here I'll Stay; You Know How.

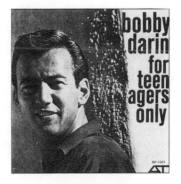

First released 1960
UK peak chart position: did not chart
USA peak chart position: did not chart

43. LET THERE BE DRUMS
Sandy Nelson

The rock 'n' roll drummer, Sandy Nelson, made numerous albums, but the best-known is the one riding on his hit single, 'Let There Be Drums'. Sandy, who lives in the Mohave Desert, says, 'Let There Be Drums was done with a lot of love and sincerity. When it was a hit, we had to put out an album and some of the sessions were dreadful because they were done after a night's drinking with Bruce Johnston in Tijuana. I got to bed at five in the morning and I had to get up at nine. I was hungover and the producer did some terrible arrangements for 'My Girl Josephine', 'Slippin' And Sliding' and 'Tequila'. He never even finished the phrase on 'Tequila!'. I am ashamed of those sessions but I messed up own career. I was often drunk when I made my records."

Slippin' And Sliding; Tequila; My Girl Josephine; The Big Noise From Winnetka; Let There Be Drums; Bouncy; The Birth Of The Beat; Quite A Beat; Get With It.

First released 1962
UK peak chart position: did not chart
USA peak chart position: 6

44. HAVE TWANGY GUITAR WILL TRAVEL
Duane Eddy

Duane Eddy, the most self-effacing of all rock 'n' roll stars, was also the first to give credits to his fellow musicians on the sleeve of an album. This, his first album, was made in Phoenix and produced by Lester Sill and Lee Hazlewood, who made a homemade echo chamber from a water-tank in the parking lot. Duane's first hits - 'Moovin' 'n Groovin'' (sic), 'Rebel-Rouser' and 'Cannon Ball' - are included. Many may think that an album featuring the bass strings of an electric guitar, albeit a Gretsch 6120, would be boring. The producers Lester Sill and Lee Hazlewood circumvent this by allowing the various Rebels, notably Steve Douglas on sax, to take solos and by varying the material, especially the atmospheric 'Three-30-Blues'.

Lonesome Road; I Almost Lost My Mind; Rebel-Rouser; Thirty-30-Blues; Cannon Ball; Moovin' 'n Groovin'; The Lonely One; Detour; Stalkin'.

First released 1959
UK peak chart position: 6
USA peak chart position: 5

45. THE PLATTERS
Platters

Buck Ram was one of the first managers to own the name of a group, so that he could always promote his act as the original Platters, even if none of the hit-making line-up were present. It was deserved as he developed their sound, produced their records and wrote several of their hits ('Only You', 'The Great Pretender'). The Platters themselves, four guys and a girl, had a recognisable sound, not quite old-fashioned, not quite rock 'n' roll. Tony Williams' lead vocals captured the attention of their revival of Jerome Kern's 'Smoke Gets In Your Eyes' or Buck Ram's former success, 'Twilight Time', possibly the first rock 'n' roll record to use strings. The Platters were out of favour by the mid-60s but they turned their career around with the disco hits, 'With This Ring' and 'Washed Ashore'.

The Great Pretender; Only You; Smoke Gets In Your Eyes; Red Sails In The Sunset; Harbor Lights; I'll Be Home; My Prayer; Twilight Time; I'm Sorry; Pledging My Love; With This Ring; Washed Ashore (On A Lonely Island In The Sea).

First released 1965
UK peak chart position: did not chart
USA peak chart position: 7

46. FABULOUS STYLE OF
Everly Brothers

Issued as the Everly Brothers switched labels from Cadence to Warners, this excellent album served as a partial overview of the duo's 50s' recordings. Aided by excellent compositions, chiefly from Felice and Boudleaux Bryant, the pair helped define the innocence of a passing era. Their close harmonies brought an immediate richness to material either sad or celebratory. Elements of rock 'n' roll, country and bluegrass can be gleaned from this work, a tapestry enhancing the special nature of the duo's recordings. Traces of the Everly Brothers is heard in the Beatles, Byrds and Simon and Garfunkel and without them the course of harmony pop would have been much poorer.

Claudette; Like Strangers; Since You Broke My Heart; Let It Be Me; Oh What A Feeling; Take A Message To Mary; Devoted To You; When Will I Be Loved; Bird Dog; 'Til I Kissed You; Problems; Love Of My Life; Poor Jenny (2nd Version); All I Have To Do Is Dream.

First released 1960
UK peak chart position: 4
USA peak chart position: 23

47. ROCK 'N ROLL STAGE SHOW
Bill Haley And His Comets

Although this album features studio recordings, it gives you an idea of what Bill Haley And His Comets sounded like on stage. Haley led a showband who just happened to find fame with rock 'n' roll. When they had success, he wanted the Comets to show their versatility and he did not mind if he was not the centre of attraction. There are instrumentals, notably 'Rudy's Rock' featuring Rudy Pompilli's sax and 'Goofin' Around' featuring Franny Beecher's lead guitar, and an old-style vocal number, 'Hey Then, There Now', with the Comets who were shortly to leave him for the Jodimars. Accordionist Johnny Grande takes the lead vocal on 'A Rockin' Little Tune' and steel guitarist Billy Williamson takes lead vocals on 'Tonight's The Night' and 'Hide And Seek'. It's as though Bill Haley is making a guest appearance on his own record.

Calling All Comets; Rockin' Through The Rye; A Rockin' Little Tune; Hide And Seek; Hey Then, There Now; Goofin' Around; Hook, Line And Sinker; Rudy's Rock; Choo Choo Ch'boogie; Blue Comet Blues; Hot Dog, Buddy Buddy; Tonight's The Night.

First released 1956
UK peak chart position: did not chart
USA peak chart position: 18

48. ESPECIALLY FOR YOU
Duane Eddy

What could be more exciting than the way Duane Eddy transforms Henry Mancini's theme from the TV series, *Peter Gunn*, into pile-driving rock 'n' roll? Duane had been encouraged to record it by his sax player Steve Douglas. He did for the album but it was released as a single first in Australia and then in the UK, thereby creating his best-known record. The b-side, also from the album, was the whooping and hollering 'Yep!'. (That rebel yell is 'Leaping lizards', a phrase from 'Little Orphan Annie') The album was designed to show Duane's versatility: there's a tribute to Les Paul with 'Lover' and personal favourites like 'Along The Navajo Trail' and 'Tuxedo Junction'. 'Quiniela', written by Duane and producer Lee Hazlewood, is a term used in dog-racing and features an upright bass solo from Jimmy Simmons and a piano solo from Al Casey. It's all good, but 'Peter Gunn' alone would qualify it for one of the best albums.

Peter Gunn; Only Child; Lover; Fuzz; Just Because; Trouble In Mind; Tuxedo Junction; Hard Times; Along Came Linda; Quiniela; Yep; Along The Navajo Trail.

First released 1959
UK peak chart position: 6
USA peak chart position: 24

49. TEQUILA
Champs

The singing cowboy, Gene Autry, started the Challenge label in 1957 and signed the Texas singer-guitarist Dave Burgess. Working in the now-famed Goldstar studios, he developed an instrumental sound with his fellow musicians and the Champs - the name being a derivative of Gene Autry's horse, Champion - were born. One of their first recordings, 'Train To Nowhere', was developed by overdubbing, a rarity at that time. Danny Flores, a Mexican-American, had been using a riff in-between his songs on club dates and this was developed into 'Tequila'. The take used on the hit single was the one in which they testing the microphones - first the acoustic guitar, then the bass, then the electric guitar and then the drums. The musicians went their separate ways, little realising they had cut a classic instrumental hit. They continued the Mexican feel by reviving the standard, 'El Rancho Rock', while the b-side, 'Midnighter', is still popular in rock 'n' roll clubs. This reissue replaces *Go Champs Go*.

Tequila; Train To Nowhere; Sombrero; Sky High; Experiment In terror; La Cucaracha; The Shoddy Shoddy; Jumping Bean; Too Much Tequila; Turnpike; The Caterpillar; Beatnik; El Rancho Rock; Midnighter; Chariot Rock; Bandido; Limbo Rock; Subway; Red Eye; Gone Train; Caramba.

First released 1992
UK peak chart position: did not chart
USA peak chart position: did not chart

50. IT'S EVERLY TIME
Everly Brothers

It's Everly Time was the duo's first album under their million-dollar deal with Warner Brothers, the first in pop's history. Having repaid some of the company's faith with the riveting 'Cathy's Clown', the brothers continued to show an adventurous approach with this selection. Of the 12 songs. Six were written by longtime associates Felice and Boudleaux Bryant, including the poignant 'Some Sweet Day'. The highlight, however, is Don Everly's 'So Sad', a haunting ballad tailor-made for the pair's woven harmonies which captures all that was special in their work. Released at a time when pop albums were largely an adjunct to hit singles, the consistency offered on *It's Everly Time* helped establish the 12-inch long player as an entity in its own right.

So Sad (To Watch Good Love Go Bad); Just In Case; Memories Are Made Of This; That's What You Do To Me; Sleepless Nights; What Kind Of Girl Are You; Oh, True Love; Carol Jane; Some Sweet Day; Nashville Blues; You Thrill Me (Through And Through); I Want You To Know.

First released 1960
UK peak chart position: 2
USA peak chart position: 9

THE TOP
50 SOUL ALBUMS

SOUL MUSIC IS NOW REFERRED TO IN *BILLBOARD* MAGAZINE AS R&B. THE SOUL MAGAZINES THAT NOW FLOOD THE MARKET ENCOMPASS RAP, DANCE, FUNK, HIP HOP AND JAZZ WITHIN THIS MUCH ABUSED GENRE. OUR WRITERS HAVE TAKEN THE COMPASS POINT THAT STARTS WITH 'MUSIC OF A SOULFUL NATURE', WHICH CHRONOLOGICALLY MEANS RAY CHARLES, OTIS REDDING AND ARETHA FRANKLIN. DUSTY SPRINGFIELD'S INCLUSION IS NOT A MISTAKE, HERS IS THE BEST WHITE SOUL ALBUM OF ALL TIME.

1. WHAT'S GOING ON
Marvin Gaye

Prior to this seminal release, albums recorded for Tamla/Motown were largely adjuncts to successful singles, rather than independent projects. Despite pressure to conform, Gaye was determined not only to break with tradition but also to comment on social topics. Through a seamless suite of songs the singer addressed issues including ecology, poverty and the Vietnam War, yet polemics did not deflect his artistic strengths, and 'Inner City Blues' and 'Mercy Mercy Me' boast hypnotic melodies and vocals. Gaye's sinewy voice retained its distinctive qualities and his vision was rewarded with both critical and commercial success. In turn the course of Black Music was irrevocably changed.

What's Going On; What's Happening Brother; Flyin' High (In The Friendly Sky); Save The Children; God Is Love; Mercy Mercy Me (The Ecology); Right On; Wholy Holy; Inner City Blues (Make Me Wanna Holler).

First released 1971
UK peak chart position: did not chart
USA peak chart position: 6

2. OTIS BLUE
Otis Redding

The man who bought classic soul music to the white masses at the Monterey Pop Festival died later that year, just as he was really gearing up for creative burst that included 'Dock Of The Bay'. This is the first of many Otis albums in the soul listings and an automatic recommendation for anyone's playlist. Redding could make you dance and scream and the next minute have you crying yourself to sleep, such was his wide range. Compare the power of 'Respect' and 'Shake' to the emotion of 'I've Been Loving You Too Long' and 'My Girl'. Untouchable.

Ole Man Trouble; Respect; Change Gonna Come; Down In The Valley; I've Been Loving You Too Long; Shake; My Girl; Wonderful World; Rock Me Baby; Satisfaction; You Don't Miss Your Water.

First released 1966
UK peak chart position: 6
USA peak chart position: 75

3. SONGS IN THE KEY OF LIFE
Stevie Wonder

An ambitious double set (plus a further freebie EP) which was the culmination of Wonder's second golden period which started with *Music In My Mind*. Now firmly established as a musical genius Wonder gave us longer songs and stronger songs. Although the hits such as 'Sir Duke', 'Another Star' and 'I Wish' are more often remembered, it is the overall incredibly high standard of all songs that make this such an outstanding achievement. Beautiful gems such as 'Joy Within My Tears', the brassy and funky 'Black Man', the cloying but unforgettable 'Isn't She Lovely'. Stevie packed it all in for us.

Love's In Need Of Love Today; Have A Talk With God; Village Ghetto Land; Confusion; Sir Duke; Isn't She Lovely; Joy Inside My Tears, Black Man; I Wish; Knocks Me Off My Feet; Pastime Paradise; Summer Soft; Ordinary Pain; Ngiculela Es Una Historia - I Am Singing; If It's Magic; As; Another Star.

First released 1976
UK peak chart position: 2
USA peak chart position: 1

4. TALKING BOOK
Stevie Wonder

Hot on the heals is grown up Stevie again, with the album that confirmed everything promised in *Music Of My Mind*. Although he came dangerously close to AOR the quality of songs and the remarkable choice of running order makes this an all-important Wonder album. Even if you chose to skip the first track 'You Are The Sunshine Of My Life' the beautifully relaxing sound will eventually get you to admit your romantic vulnerability. Jeff Beck sneaks in some subtle guitar on 'Lookin' For Another True Love' and Stevie plays some innovative Arp and Moog Sythesizers throughout.

You Are The Sunshine Of My Life; Maybe Your Baby; You And I; Tueday Heartbreak; You've Got It Bad Girl; Superstition; Big Brother; Blame It On The Sun; Lookin' For Another True Love; I Believe (When I Fall In Love It Will Be Forever).

First released 1972
UK peak chart position: 16
USA peak chart position: 3

5. STAND
Sly And The Family Stone

Sly Stone was too busy having a good time and living life to the excess to begin to realise how influential his brand of funky soul would become. Early signs of rap also prevailed on this album. Confident, hard rocking and marvellously arrogant, the band were outrageous and exciting, even five minutes of a cappella handclapping was riveting. Two classics appear on this , 'I Want To Take You Higher' and 'Everyday People', but the whole album is a necessary purchase for students of good time soul, dance, rap and funk. This family is the acknowledged leader.

Stand!; Don't Call Me Nigger, Whitey; I Want To Take You Higher; Somebody's Watching You; Sing A Simple Song; Everday People; Sex Machine; You Can Make It If You Try.

First released 1969
UK peak chart position: did not chart
USA peak chart position: 13

6. CAN'T SLOW DOWN
Lionel Richie

Mr Richie's brand of silky smooth macho soul was the butt of some critics during the early 80s. A plethora of handsome studs with great voices, who just wanted to lurve all night long followed Richie. Yet another album crammed with hit singles, it was one of the 80s sales phenomenons both in the USA and the UK - as was 'Hello'. Corny but delicious, unashamedly romantic and consequently more couples have danced to this 'All Night Long (All Night)', than any other - and then 16 million couples went out and bought it.

Can't Slow Down; All Night Long (All Night); Penny Lover; Stuck On You; Love Will Find A Way; The Only One; Running With The Night; Hello.

First released 1983
UK peak chart position: 1
USA peak chart position: 1

7. GENIUS + SOUL = JAZZ
Ray Charles

It has to appear somewhere, and soul would seem the closest category. It is big band swing, jazz, soul, R&B, pop and blues but mostly it is 'the genius'. This man has managed to stay hip for succeeding generations and also appeal to middle class America. This superb recording was made in 1961 shortly before he hit his commercial peak. Don't be put off by the big band it is dynamic stuff, for example 'Moanin'' and 'Strike Up The Band'. The CD reissue adds three live tracks from his *Genius Hits The Road* album to make this even more necessary and vital.

From The Heart; I've Got News For You; Moanin'; Let's Go; One Mint Julep; I'm Gonna Move To The Outskirts Of Town; Stompin' Room Only; Mister; Strike Up The Band; Birth Of The Blues.

First released 1961
UK peak chart position: did not chart
USA peak chart position: 4

8. LADY SOUL
Aretha Franklin

Aretha's Franklin's position as soul music's premier woman vocalist was consolidated by this album. Her strident reading of Don Covay's 'Chain Of Fools' set the tone for a collection in which the singer unveiled several stellar original compositions and reinterpreted a batch of classic songs. Franklin's gospel roots were clearly displayed on the anthem-like 'People Get Ready' while her interpretation of 'Natural Woman' showed both vulnerable and assertive qualities. *Lady Soul* captures a performer at the peak of her power, retating her ability to take material and make it uniquely her own.

Chain Of Fools; Money Won't Change You; People Get Ready; Niki Hoeky; (You Make Me Feel Like) A Natural Woman; Since You've Been Gone (Sweet Sweet Baby); Good To Me As I Am To You; Come Back Baby; Groovin'; Ain't No Way.

First released 1968
UK peak chart position: 25
USA peak chart position: 2

9. THE GENIUS OF RAY CHARLES
Ray Charles

Neither pop nor jazz, once again Charles is hard to categorize even though many of the musicians have string jazz credentials; Paul Gonsalves, Clark Terry, Zoot Sims and Bob Brookmeyer. The album's strength (in addition to Brother Ray) are the choice of classic songs matched with lush orchestration. Ray's soulful voice will break hearts on 'Don't Let The Sun Catch You Cryin'', 'Just For A Thrill' and the ultimate for hopeless romantics Johnny Mercer and Harold Arlen's starry-eyed 'Come Rain Or Come Shine'. The excellent recording, particularly with Ray's up-front vocals is due to Jerry Wexler, Tom Dowd and Bill Schwartau.

Let The Good Times Roll; It Had To Be You; Alexander's Ragtime Band; Two Years Of Torture; When Your Lover Has Gone; Deed I Do; Just For A Thrill; You Won't Let Me Go; Tell Me You'll Wait For Me; Don't Let The Sun Catch You Cryin'; Am I Blue; Come Rain Or Come Shine.

First released 1959
UK peak chart position: did not chart
USA peak chart position: 17

10. DUSTY IN MEMPHIS
Dusty Springfield

Not only is this Dusty's finest work it is unanimously recognised as one of the great soul albums. The secret is in the production; Jerry Wexler, Tommy Dowd and Arif Mardin who enlisted the Sweet Inspirations for vocal support and the best Memphis session boys. Dusty's choice of material is exemplary choosing songs by Randy Newman, Mann/Weill, Goffin King and Bacharach/David. This should have made her an international megastar, instead it scratched the US Top 100, failed to, chart in the UK and started her slow decline. It is a faultless record that we have thankfully now recognised she was years ahead of her time.

Just A Little Lovin'; So Much Love; Son Of A Preacher Man; I Don't Want To Hear It Anymore; Don't Forget About Me; Breakfast In Bed; Just One Smile; The Windmills Of Your Mind; In The Land Of Make Believe; No Easy Way Down; I Can't Make It Alone.

First released 1969
UK peak chart position: did not chart
USA peak chart position: 99

11. THE DOCK OF THE BAY
Otis Redding

Compiled in the wake of Redding's premature death, *Dock Of The Bay* is a suitable testimony to a highly popular performer. The melancholic title track inferred a new musical blueprint and elements of the previously unissued 'Open The Door' show a similarly muted perspective. Tracks culled from *Otis Blue* and *The Soul Album* sit beside the playful 'Tramp', which represents the singer's brief partnership with Carla Thomas. The remaining material is drawn from various sources, including flipsides and compilations and, taken together, the album provides a précis of Redding's past, as well as implying what was sadly lost.

Shake; Mr. Pitiful; Respect; Love Man; (I Can't Get No) Satisfaction; I Can't Turn You Loose; Hard To Handle; Fa-Fa-Fa-Fa-Fa (Sad Song); My Girl; I've Been Loving You Too Long; Try A Little Tenderness; My Lover's Prayer; That's How Strong My Love Is; Pain In My Heart; A Change Is Gonna Come; (Sittin' On) The Dock Of The Bay.

First released 1968
UK peak chart position: 1
USA peak chart position: 4

12. WHEN A MAN LOVES A WOMAN
Percy Sledge

Had it not been for two highly memorable singles this album may have stayed outside the listings. 'When A Man Loves A Woman' and 'Warm And Tender Love' are still classic radioplay fodder. They established Sledge as a master soul balladeer and the voice for teenage romantics. DJ Johnny Walker broadcasting from the pirate ship Radio Caroline used both songs regularly for his 'Frinton flashers'; couples parked on the Essex coast would flash car lights in anticipation of Percy Sledge being played. Other highlights on this underrated album are 'It Tears Me Up' and 'Take Time To Know Her, both great examples of southern soul.

I'll Be Your Everything; If This Is the Last Time; Hard To Be Friends; Blue Water; Love Away People; Take Time To Know Her; Out Of Left Field; Warm And Tender Love; It Tears Me Up; When A Man Loves A Woman; Walkin' In The Sun; Behind Closed Doors; Make It Good And Make It Last; The Good Love; I Believe In You; My Special Prayer.

First released 1966
UK peak chart position: did not chart
USA peak chart position: 37

13. COMPLETE & UNBELIEVABLE. . . THE DICTIONARY OF SOUL
Otis Redding

Soul singer Otis Redding crossed over into the pop charts with a version of the Temptations' 'My Girl'. This album followed that achievement and showed him bringing a wider perspective to R&B. Working in tandem with guitarist Steve Cropper, Redding tore up the blueprints of Beatles' songs and standards, making them as much his own as the original songs the pair contributed. Never a subtle singer, Otis possessed a raw intensity, charging the material through the force of his personality. *Dictionary Of Soul* was the last album issued before the singer's untimely death, the artistic challenges it posed were sadly left unrealised.

Fa-Fa-Fa-Fa-Fa (Sad Song); I'm Sick Y'all; Tennessee Waltz; Sweet Lorene; Try A Little Tenderness; Day Tripper; My Lover; Prayer; She Put The Hurt On Me; Ton Of Joy; You're Still My Baby; Hawg For You; Love Have Mercy.

First released 1966
UK peak chart position: 23
USA peak chart position: 73

14. THERES A RIOT GOING ON
Sly And The Family Stone

During the late 60s Sly And The Family Stone changed the nature of soul music by infusing it with elements of psychedelic pop. Their exciting, effervescent singles included 'Dance To The Music', 'Stand' and 'I Want To Take You Higher', but with the release of this album group leader Sly Stone exorcised personal and cultural psychoses. Its brooding funk was distilled through a deep, somnambulist sound in which even the lightest of songs, 'Runnin' Away' or 'Family Affair', were tinged with discomfort. The set culminates with bitter, twisted rhythms, disembodied vocals and a ravaged intensity quite unlike anything heard before in black music.

Luv 'N' Haight; Just Like A Baby; The Poet; Family Affair; Africa Talks To You; The Asphalt Jungle; There's A Riot Goin' On; Brave And Strong; (You Caught Me) Smilin'; Time; Spaced Cowboy; Runnin' Away; Thank You For Talking To Me Africa.

First released 1971
UK peak chart position: 31
USA peak chart position: 1

15. ARETHA NOW
Aretha Franklin

Aretha Now opens with the explosive 'Think', an ecstatic performance propelled by the singer's gospel-like fervour and punchy piano playing. It set the tone for yet another self-assured selection, in which Franklin brought her expressive voice to bear on a series of excellent songs. She brings new authority to material first recorded by Sam Cooke ('You Send Me'), Don Covay ('See-Saw') and Dionne Warwick ('I Say A Little Prayer'), investing each with a ferocious pride and zeal. The original songs are equally strong, resulting in one of 60s soul most accomplished albums.

Think; I Say A Little Prayer; See-Saw; Night Time Is The Right Time; You Send Me; You're A Sweet Sweet Man; I Take What I Want; Hello Sunshine; A Change; I Can't See Myself Leaving You.

First released 1968
UK peak chart position: 6
USA peak chart position: 3

16. YOU GOT MY MIND MESSED UP
James Carr

For lovers of vintage soul James Carr is God. Totally underrated with only odd compilation albums available it is a mystery why this man is so overlooked. Carr like Johnny Taylor was also a member of the legendary Soul Stirrers until he went solo for the Goldwax label. His deep and powerful 'You've Got My Mind Messed Up' was a huge R&B hit in the USA and this album followed it. There is not a bad track on the album, but one further high point is the definitve reading of Dan Penn and Spooner Oldham's 'Dark End Of The Street'. The greatest ever country meets soul song. This album begs reissue.

Pouring Water On A Drowning Man; Love Attack; Coming Back To Me Baby; I Don't Want To Be Hurt Anymore; That's What I Want To Know; These Ain't Raindrops; Dark End Of The Street; I'm Going For Myself; Lovable Girl; Forgetting You; She's Better Than You.

First released 1965
UK peak chart position: did not chart
USA peak chart position: did not chart

17. TELL MAMA
Etta James

Having already been an established leading soul singer for 13 years and having 18 R&B hits to her name, Etta went to record in Alabama at the legendary Muscle Shoals studio in 1967. The result was her most accomplished album, on which her voice had been mixed to perfection allowing her to sound string on the previously distorted high notes. James was rightly seen in a different light as one of the great soul voices of all time as she belted out powerful tracks such as "The Love Of My Man' and 'Watch Dog'. Her slower numbers were equally arresting, including the wonderful 'I'd Rather Go Blind'.

Tell Mama; I'd Rather Go Blind; Watch Dog; The Love Of My Man; I'm Gonna Take What He's Got; The Same Rope; Security; Steal Away; My Mother-In-Law; Don't Lose Your Good Thing; It Hurts Me So Much; Just A Little Bit.

First released 1968
UK peak chart position: did not chart
USA peak chart position: 82

18. INNERVISIONS
Stevie Wonder

Uplifting and rolling, continuing a sequence of outstanding albums, Stevie Wonder again stamped his seal of importance during the early 70s. Twenty years on 'Living For the City' does sound a bit crass, especially rhyming pollution with solution, but that is a small carp when placed against the magnificence of 'He's Misstra Know-It-All' the out and out cleverness of 'Too High' and the graceful 'Golden Lady'. Stevie has an amazing conception of what vision is, something we take for granted when listening to the lyrics of 'Golden Lady' for example. Quite uncanny.

Too High; Visions; Living For The City; Golden Lady; Higher Ground; Jesus Children Of America; All In Love Is Fair; Don't You Worry 'Bout A Thing; He's Misstra Know-It-All.

First released 1973
UK peak chart position: 8
USA peak chart position: 4

19. I NEVER LOVED A MAN THE WAY I LOVE YOU
Aretha Franklin

Aretha Franklin emerged from years of often inappropriate recordings with 'I Never Loved A Man', one of soul music's definitive performances. The song's simple, uncluttered arrangement allowed the singer free expression and her sense of artistic relief is palpable. The attendant album captured all of Franklin's gifts as she brings gospel fervour and individuality to a peerless collection of songs. Material drawn from Sam Cooke, Otis Redding and Ray Charles are infused with a rampant spirituality and given new perspectives when sung by a woman. The set also provides a showcase for Aretha's own compositional skills, as well as her propulsive piano playing which employs the forcefulness of her singing. This album unleashed a major talent.

Respect; Drown In My Own Tears; I Never Loved A Man (The Way I Love You); Soul Serenade; Don't Let Me Lose This Dream; Baby, Baby, Baby; Dr. Feelgood (Love Is A Serious Business); Good Times; Do Right Woman Do Right Man; Save Me; A Change Is Gonna Come.

First released 1967
UK peak chart position: 36
USA peak chart position: 2

20. THE EXCITING WILSON PICKETT
Wilson Pickett

Wilson Pickett's career was moribund until Jerry Wexler signed him to Atlantic Records. Within months he had secured an international hit with 'In The Midnight Hour', one of several highly successful singles featured on this album. Recorded at two legendary studios, Stax and Fame, it showcased the artist's often overlooked strengths as a songwriter, which he pursued with various partners, including Eddie Floyd and Steve Cropper. Elsewhere Pickett's powerful, rasping voice brought new meaning to a clutch of soul standards, resulting in what is his finest album and, indeed, one of the best soul sets of the 60s.

Barefootin'; Danger Zone; I'm Drifting; In The Midnight Hour; It's All Over; Land Of A 1000 Dances; Mercy, Mercy; Ninety-Nine And A Half (Won't Do); She's So Good To Me; 634-5789; Something You Got; You're So Fine.

First released 1966
UK peak chart position: did not chart
USA peak chart position: 21

21. FOUR TOPS REACH OUT
Four Tops

The dramatic 'Reach Out, I'll Be There' brought the Four Tops their first international chart-topper. Songwriters/producers Holland/Dozier/Holland sculpted a massive sound with flutes, oboes and pounding drums, emphasising the pulsating rhythm with a stop-start interlude prior to its chorus. The same sense of adventure permeated the original material included on this album, which was counterbalanced by stylish reinterpretations of contemporary hits. Levi Stubbs' impassioned vocals encapsulates the urgency of much of this imaginative selection which helped expand what constituted the 'Tamla/Motown' sound.

Reach Out I'll Be There; Walk Away Renee; Seven Rooms Of Gloom; If I Were A Carpenter; Last Train To Clarksville; I'll Turn To Stone; I'm A Believer; Standing In The Shadows Of Love; Bernadette; Cherish; Wonderful Baby; What Else Is There To Do (But Think About You).

First released 1967
UK peak chart position: 4
USA peak chart position: 11

22. SUPERFLY
Curtis Mayfield

As leader of the Impressions, Curtis Mayfield brought a lyricism to soul music. As a solo artist he chronicled and society's travails and 'street' culture which in turn inspired *Superfly*, the soundtrack to one of the era's most popular 'blaxploitation' movies. Mayfield's gift for combining light melody with simple, but chilling, wordplay ensured that the album stood up on its own terms without visual images and its lynchpin selection, 'Freddy's Dead', was a million selling single in its own right. Sympathetic but not sentimental, *Superfly* set new standards for Black music.

Little Child Runnin' Wild; Freddy's Dead; Give Me Your Love; Nothing On Me; Superfly; Pusherman; Junkie Chase; Eddie You Should Know; Think.

First released 1972
UK peak chart position: 26
USA peak chart position: 1

23. LETS GET IT ON
Marvin Gaye

Relishing the artistic freedom afforded by the success of *What's Goin' On*, Marvin Gaye recorded this sultry paean to sex. Where its predecessor relied on complex arrangements, the unfussy sound of *Let's Get It On* focused attention on its tight rhythms, strong melodies and Gaye's expressive singing. Either celebratory, as on the explicit title track, or reflective ('Distant Lover'), he encompasses a range of emotion with equal ease and intensity. Seductive sound matches seductive lyrics and attitude at a time Al Green, Barry White and Isaac Hayes laid claim to the 'lover-man' sobriquet. *Let's Get It On* showed Marvin Gaye its undoubted master.

Let's Get It On; Please Don't Stay (Once You Go Away); If I Should Die Tonight; Keep Gettin' It On; Come Get To This; Distant Lover; You Sure Know How To Ball; Just To Keep You Satisfied.

First released 1973
UK peak chart position: 39
USA peak chart position: 2

24. AMAZING GRACE
Aretha Franklin

The fourth Aretha album in this listing shows a non-secular mother seated and at peace with herself. The music within although pure gospel certainly is not peaceful. Aretha's voice cuts through the pulpit like lightning striking, try playing this at high volume in the dark and you will get the message. It was recorded in a Baptist Church and therefore has superb natural acoustics. Her father, the famous minister Rev. C.L. Franklin adds comment to the record, a proud father no doubt. For non-believers this is a dynamite album and as one reviewer said 'its enough to turn me religious'.

Mary, Don't You Weep; Precious Lord; Take My Hand; You've Got A Friend; Old Landmark; Give Yourself To Jesus; How I Got Over; What A Friend We Have In Jesus; Amazing Grace; Precious Memories; Climbing Higher Mountains; God Will Take Care Of You; Wholy Holy; You'll Never Walk Alone; Never Grow Old.

First released 1972
UK peak chart position: did not chart
USA peak chart position: 7

25. LET'S STAY TOGETHER
Al Green

The evocative title track that opens this glorious record sets a paradox. Al Green's remarkable voice, one that is hidden in the back of his throat, makes you constantly feel good. The subject matter of many of the songs on this album are of sadness, lost love and frustration and confusion. Green was to popular soul in the 70s what Otis was in the 60s, it was refreshing to see him performing and recording again in 1993. Maybe the good reverend already knew in 1972 that he would be called to the church, because this collection has amazing healing powers.

Let's Stay Together; I've Never Found A Girl; You're Leaving; It Ain't No Fun To Me; Talk To Me, Talk To Me; Old Time Lovin'; Judy; What Is This Feelin'; Tomorrow's Dream; How Can You Mend A Broken Heart; La La For You.

First released 1972
UK peak chart position: did not chart
USA peak chart position: 8

26. Breezin'
George Benson

Benson earned his reputation as a superior jazz guitarist through his partnership with organist Brother Jack McDuff. Seceral solo albums for the CTI label ensued before a switch to Warner Brothers resulted in chart success with this release. Benson's remake of the title track, originally a hit for fellow guitarist Gabor Szabo, set the tone for the entire set wherein mellifluous funk underscores the artist's sweet voice and soft-touch technique. Like Nat 'King' Cole before him, Benson left jazz to court a wider audience and with *Breezin'* did so with considerable aplomb.

This Masquerade; Six To Four; Breezin'; So This Is Love; Lady; Affirmation.

First released 1976
UK peak chart position: did not chart
USA peak chart position: 1

27. The Soul Album
Otis Redding

The Soul Album is often over-looked when examining Redding's output. No singles were culled from its content, but this does not diminish the excellent songs it contains. The original material reveals the strength of the singer's partnership with guitarist Steve Cropper, and the cover versions show Redding's gift for reinterpretation. Sam Cooke, the Temptations and Wilson Pickett are each acknowledged in turn, while Otis also took shots at two contemporary hits, Roy Head's 'Treat Her Right' and Slim Harpo's 'Scratch My Back'. *The Soul Album* is a strong as any issued by the singer during his short lifetime.

Just One More Day; It's Growing; Cigarettes And Coffee; Chain Gang; Nobody Knows You (When You're Down And Out); Good To Me; Scratch My Back; Treat Her Right; Everybody Makes A Mistake; Any Ole Way; 634-5789.

First released 1966
UK peak chart position: 22
USA peak chart position: 54

28. Cloud Nine
Temptations

One of Tamla/Motown's leading attractions, the Temptations undertook a shift in musical direction with this pivotal release. Former Contours' vocalist Dennis Edwards replaced lead baritone David Ruffin as the quintet embraced socially-conscious material. Taking inspiration from Sly Stone, producer/songwriter Norman Whitfield wrapped the group's sumptuous harmonies with a heavier, more complex sound which acknowledged rock influences without sacrificing soul roots. The title track - a brave anti-drugs' song - reached the US Top 10, rekindling the Temptations' career as a commercial force. This album opened new artistic possibilities both for the group and those they influenced.

Cloud Nine; I Heard It Through The Grapevine; Runaway Child Running Wild; Love Is A Hurtin' Thing; Hey Girl (I Like Your Style); Why Did She Have To Leave Me (Why Did She Have To Go?); I Need Your Lovin'; Don't Let Them Take Your Love From Me; I Gotta Find A Way (To Get You Back); Gonna Keep On Tryin' Till I Win Your Love.

First released 1969
UK peak chart position: 32
USA peak chart position: 4

29. KNOCK ON WOOD
Eddie Floyd

Eddie Floyd began his career as a member of gospel act the Falcons, before embarking on a solo career which was initially ill-starred. Having joined the Stax label as a songwriter and performer, he struck gold with 'Knock On Wood', one of soul music's immutable anthems. The album it inspired is equally strong with its judicious cross-section of original songs and cover versions. Floyd reclaims '634-5789', which he wrote for Wilson Pickett and breathes new life into material first recorded by James Ray, Tommy Tucker and Jerry Butler. The label's crack houseband provides supple, rhythmic support to an under-rated singer, whose strengths are displayed on this excellent album.

Knock On Wood; Something You Got; But It's Alright; I Stand Accused; If You Gotta Make A Fool Of Somebody; I Don't Want To Cry; Raise Your Hand; Got To Make A Comeback; 634-5789; I've Just Been Feeling Bad; High Heel Sneakers; Warm And Tender Love.

First released 1967
UK peak chart position: 36
USA peak chart position: did not chart

30. GOING TO A GO-GO
Miracles

One of the finest composers in pop, Smokey Robinson possessed a gift for simple, precise lyricism and dizzy, memorable melodies. Mary Wells, the Temptations and Marvin Gaye are among the acts he wrote for, but the best was saved for his own group. The title song on this album is one of Motown's greatest dance tracks, while 'Ooh Baby Baby' and 'The Tracks Of My Tears' are starkly beautiful love songs. Robinson's pleading voice is ably supported by the Miracles' harmonies, investing already emotional material with a poignant vulnerability. Bob Dylan once declared Robinson as 'America's greatest living poet'. This album shows that statement is not necessarily far-fetched.

The Tracks Of My Tears; Going To A Go-Go; Ooh Baby Baby; My Girl Has Gone; In Case You Need Love; Choosey Beggar; Since You Won My Heart; From Head To Toe; All That's Good; My Baby Changes Like The Weather; Let Me Have Some; A Fork In The Road.

First released 1965
UK peak chart position: did not chart
USA peak chart position: 8

31. I AM
Earth Wind And Fire

Very possibly the most uplifting album in the entire book. The combination of brass and quite immaculate harmonies induce a feeling of warmth and big cheesy grins. Earth Wind And Fire sound like a family, they sound like they know what they are doing and mostly they sound as if they like it. Every track is a rush of adrenalin, even the one weepie 'After The Love Has Gone' still manages to retain the atmosphere of overall happiness. Supported by the Emotions and a cast of hundreds of violins, trumpets, trombones, cellos and french horns, this is popular soul music at its very very best.

In The Stone; Can't Let Go; After The Love Has Gone; Let Your Feelings Show; Boogie Wonderland; Star; Wait; Rock That; You And I.

First released 1979
UK peak chart position: 5
USA peak chart position: 3

32. 3+3 FEATURING THAT LADY
The Isley Brothers

The day Ernie Isley picked up his electric guitar with a fuzzbox was the day the Isley's fortunes changed for the better. The slick besuited Tamla/Motown soul was replaced by funky stuff with some truly spectacular guitar solos. The title track is here in its full lenth glory as is the lengthy workout on 'Summer Breeze'. Ernie became a guitar hero with those two tracks and had a host of second rate imitators. Other highlights are 'The Highways Of My Life' and James Taylor's 'Don't let Me Be Lonely Tonight. The version of the Doobies 'Listen To the Music' can be dispensed with. Almost a rock album, but not quite.

That Lady; Don't Let Me Be Lonely Tonight; If You Were There; You Walk Your Way; Listen To The Music; What It Comes Down To; Sunshine (Go Away Today); Summer Breeze; The Highways Of My Life.

First released 1973
UK peak chart position: did not chart
USA peak chart position: 8

33. WANTED ONE SOUL SINGER
Johnnie Taylor

Johnny taylor had one of the best voices in soul music, quite why he failed to make the impact made by Redding, Pickett and Burke will remain a mystery. Taylor was the man who replaced Sam Cooke in the legendary Soul Stirrers having served in numerous gospel bands. Sadly the excellent 'Who's Making Love' came a year after this debut album - but the rest will suffice. Supported by the regular Stax musician's this is yet another classic album from that highly influential label. Two outstanding tracks are 'I Had A Dream' and 'I Got To Love Somebody's Baby'.

I Got To Love Somebody's Baby; Just The One I've Been Lookin' For; Watermelon Man; Where Can A Man Go From Here; Toe-Hold; Outside Love; Ain't That Loving You (For More Reasons Than One); Blues In The Night; I Had A Dream; Sixteen Tons; Little Bluebird.

First released 1967
UK peak chart position: did not chart
USA peak chart position: did not chart

34. DOUBLE DYNAMITE
Sam And Dave

Sam Moore and Dave Prater were soul music's definitive male duo. Signed by Atlantic in 1965, they were taken to the legendary Stax studio and teamed with writers/producers Isaac Hayes and David Porter. *Double Dynamite* showed the combination to great effect, and the pair proved equally adept with up-tempo material ('You Got Me Hummin'') or ballads ('When Something Is Wrong With My Baby'). Houseband the Memphis Horns enrich Sam And Dave's impassioned criss-crossing voices with a tight, economical punch, the resultant energy produced as effective on the ear as it is on the dancefloor.

You Got Me Hummin'; Said I Wasn't Gonna Tell Nobody; That's The Way It's Gotta Be; When Something Is Wrong With My Baby; Soothe Me; Just Can't Get Enough; Sweet Pains; I'm Your Puppet; Sleep Good Tonight; I Don't Need Nobody (To Tell Me 'Bout My Baby); Home At Last; Use Me.

First released 1967
UK peak chart position: 28
USA peak chart position: 118

35. BACKSTABBERS
O'Jays

With its in-house staff and recognisable sound, the Philadelphia International label was an early 70s' equivalent of 60s' Tamla/Motown. Flagship harmony act the O'Jays revelled in its sumptuous arrangements and flowing rhythms as this excellent album testifies. Producers/songwriters Kenny Gamble and Leon Huff sculpted brilliant scenarios for the group; cautionary, in the case of the exhilarating title track, or clarion-calls for universal brotherhood, as exemplified in 'Love Train'. The O'Jays brought many years of experience to these recordings, and on *Backstabbers* found a spiritual home for their considerable talents.

When The World's At Peace; Back Stabbers; Who Am I; (They Call Me) Mr. Lucky; Time To Get Down; 992 Arguments; Listen To The Clock On The Wall; Shiftless, Shady, Jealous Kind Of People; Sunshine; Love Train.

First released 1972
UK peak chart position: did not chart
USA peak chart position: 10

36. HOT BUTTERED SOUL
Isaac Hayes

A staff songwriter with the legendary Stax label, Issac Hayes, with partner David Porter, composed material for many of the company's artists, including Sam And Dave, Carla Thomas and Johnnie Taylor. Frustrated with this backroom role, he began recording in his own right and with *Hot Buttered Soul*, redefined the notion of soul music. Although the tracks were lengthy, there was no sense of self-indulgence, each one evolving over sensual rhythms and taut arrangements. Hayes' vocal anticipated the 'rap' genre of Barry White and Millie Jackson without slipping into self-parody, lending an air of sophistication to a highly influential collection.

Walk On By; Hyperbolicsyllacisescesquedalymistic; One Woman; By The Time I Got To Pheonix.

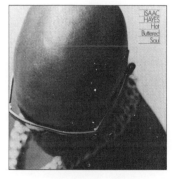

First released 1969
UK peak chart position: did not chart
USA peak chart position: 8

37. CELEBRATE!
Kool And The Gang

Just a whisker ahead of *Something Special*, this album surprisingly failed to sell in the UK outside the bands circle of followers. Kool And The Gang brilliantly blended jazz, pop, funk and soul into a sound that was a celebration itself, much in the way Sly Stone had done a decade earlier. Album sales were further increased when 'Celebration', already a US number 1, was adopted by the media to welcome home the American hostages from Iran. This album was strengthened by the addition of vocalists Earl Toon Jr and James J.T Taylor, who became frontmen during the 80's. *Celebrate* is driving happy soul/funk that has rarely been surpassed.

Celebration; Jones VS Jones; Take It To The Top; Morning Star; Love Festival; Just Friends; Night People; Love Affair.

First released 1980
UK peak chart position: did not chart
USA peak chart position: 10

38. WILL DOWNING
Will Downing

Highly regarded and purchased in considerable quantities by the UK soul cogniscenti, yet strangely ignored in his homeland. New York born Downing has an exceptional voice that is combined with strong songs for this, his debut and his best album. Downing was formerly a member of Arthur Baker's Wally Jump Jr And The Criminal Element and Baker produced this album. One highlight is a clever interpretation of John Coltrane's classic work 'A Love Supreme'. Sadly Downing has not repeated this winning formula on his two other solo albums and at the time of writing a fourth album is long overdue.

In My Dreams; Do You/; Free; A Love Supreme; Security; Set Me Free; Sending Out An S.O.S.; Dancin' In The Moonlight; Do You RememberLove?; So You Wanna Be My Lover.

First released 1988
UK peak chart position: 20
USA peak chart position: did not chart

39. GREEN ONIONS
Booker T. And The MGs

The debut, and still the best, from the legendary Memphis group. Just a bunch of session musicians who happened to be able to play together, better than most. In addition to the timeless standard 'Green Onions' there is 'Mo' Onions, a slightly reworked version that is almost as great. Booker T. gets into his Jimmy Smith mood with the sultry 'Behave Yourself' and 'Lonely Avenue' and Steve Cropper picks his Telecaster hard on 'You Can't Sit Down' and 'I Got A Woman'. The remastered CD is exquisite even though 'Stranger On The Shore'; has not stood the test of time.

Green Onions; Rinky-Dink; I Got A Woman; Mo' Onions; Twist And Shout; Behave Yourself; Stranger On The Shore; Lonely Avenue; One Who Really Loves You; You Can't Sit Down; A Woman, A Lover, A Friend; Comin' Home Baby.

First released 1964
UK peak chart position: 11
USA peak chart position: 33

40. GIVE ME THE REASON
Luther Vandross

Vandross together with Lionel Ritchie put their blend of 'up' soul/pop firmly in the hearts and minds of the masses during the 80s. Vandross was more soul than Richie and spent an eternity in the UK chart with this album. The familiar Marcus Miller production inflections are present and the sound, although occasionally clinical, especially with overdone syn drums, is ultimately right for the style. The choice of the Bacharach and David classic 'Anyone Who Had A Heart' was a nice touch but the appeal of Vandross remains in the beautiful big soul ballad such as 'So Amazing'. Great music for Belgium chocolates and candlelit dinner.

Stop To Love; See Me; I Gave It Up (When I Fell In Love); So Amazing; Give Me The Reason; There's Nothing Better Than Love; I Really Didn't Mean It; Because It's Really Love; Anyone Who Had A Heart.

First released 1986
UK peak chart position: 3
USA peak chart position: 14

41. SINGS SOUL BALLADS
Otis Redding

Otis Redding epitomised 60s soul, proving equally adept at uptempo styles and reflective ballads. By devoting an entire album to the latter mode, the singer created a measured, inspirational collection. Burning versions of songs from R&B's past are adapted an infused with elegant intensity, in particular his hypnotic reading of O.V. Wright's 'That's How Strong My Love Is'. 'Mr. Pitiful', co-written with guitarist Steve Cropper, offers Redding a slightly faster perspective without breaking the mood of reflection. *Soul Ballads* is an emotional highpoint in the singer's sadly foreshortened career.

That's How Strong My Love Is; Chained And Bound; A Woman, A Lover, A Friend; Your One And Only Man; Nothing Can Change This Love; It's Too Late; For Your Precious Love; I Want To Thank You; Come To Me; Home In Your Heart; Keep Your Arms Around Me; Mr. Pitiful.

First released 1965
UK peak chart position: 30
USA peak chart position: 147

42. SOUL MEN
Sam And Dave

A run of classic singles, including 'Hold On I'm Comin'' and 'You Got Me Hummin'', established Sam And Dave as one of soul music's premier attractions. Stax houseband Booker T. And The MGs fired up their expressive voices, epitomising the genre's excitement. *Soul Men* was their third album for Atlantic and the title track alone, replete with Steve Cropper's ringing guitar, is worth the price of admission. Material from Issac Hayes and David Porter, who wrote the duo's best-known songs, sits beside equally well-sculpted originals from the supporting musicians and a searing take of the 'standard', 'Let It Be Me'. *Soul Men* is one of the genre's definitive albums.

Soul Man; May I Baby; Broke Down Piece Of Man; Let It Be Me; Hold It Baby; I'm With You; Don't Knock It; Just Keep Holding On; The Good Runs The Bad Way; Rich Kind Of Poverty; I've Seen What Loneliness Can Do.

First released 1967
UK peak chart position: 32
USA peak chart position: 62

43. FIRST TAKE
Roberta Flack

Originally billed as *Les McCann Presents Roberta Flack*, this album reflects the jazz heritage of the singer's mentor, but deftly combines it with other musical styles. Flack brings together soft soul and the singer/songwriter tradition, creating a seamless whole in the process. A crafted interpreter, she takes the nuances of chosen material and invests it with a quiet strength. Flack's superb reading of Ewan MacColl's 'First Time Ever I Saw Your Face' exemplifies this skill, rendering superfluous almost ever other version. *First Take* is a measured, confident collection, showcasing the art of a highly sensitive talent.

Compared To What; Angelitos Negros; Our Ages Or Our Hearts; I Told Jesus; Hey, That's No Way To Say Goodbye; First Time Ever I Saw Your Face; Trying Times; Ballad Of The Sad Young Man.

First released 1970
UK peak chart position: 47
USA peak chart position: 1

44. MAKE TIME FOR LOVE
Keith Washington

Washington is one of the post Vandross soul singers who have taken the smooth romantic approach to its orgasmic extreme. Quite apart from the fact that he possesses a fantastic vocal range and has one of the best voices in 'new soul' he is able to confidently make love (or sing about it0 throughout the length of this superb album. This is the album for late night dancing before the inevitable happens. Those who thought that romance stopped with Frank Sinatra in the 50s and thought Barry White was soppy should be force fed this music. It would appear that Keith Washington gave too much on this album, and now lies exhausted. Try 'Make Time For Love' and 'Kissing You'; for starters.

All Night; Make Time For Love; Kissing You; Are You Still In Love With Me; When You Love Somebody; Ready Willing And Able; I'll Be There; When It Comes To You; Lovers After All; Closer.

First released 1991
UK peak chart position: did not chart
USA peak chart position: 48

45. UNDER THE BOARDWALK
Drifters

The Drifters had been one of Black music's leading harmony groups since the 50s, but defections and managerial tussles undermined their career. In 1964 they came under the guidance of producer/songwriter Bert Berns, who brought a contemporary edge to their work. *Under The Boardwalk* overspills with influential material and several British acts, including the Rolling Stones, Paramounts and Cliff Bennett, drew from its content. The Drifters' versions were definitive, whether on the lilting title track, the majestic 'Up On The Roof' or evocative 'On Broadway'. A balance between soul and R&B was deftly struck, sweeping Latin-inspired arrangements supported their endearing voices and in the process imbued this veteran group with a new lease of life.

One Way Love; Didn't It; Up On The Roof; I Feel Good All Over; Under The Boardwalk; Via Condias; In The Land Of Make Believe; If You Don't Come Back; On Broadway; Let The Music Play; I'll Take You Home; Rat Race.

First released 1964
UK peak chart position: did not chart
USA peak chart position: 40

46. HOLD ON I'M COMIN'
Sam And Dave

Sam Moore and Dave Prater began singing together in 1958 and commenced recording two years later. Their gospel-tinged work for the Roulette label made little commercial impact but, having switched to Atlantic in 1965, they proceeded to cut some of soul music's finest singles. *Hold On I'm Comin'* captures their searing vocal interplay, Moore's high lead brilliantly offset by Prater's deeper register. Songwriters Isaac Hayes and David Porter contribute material playing to the duo's strengths, resulting in a collection which encapsulates one of the genre's most exciting acts.

Hold On, I'm Comin'; If You Got The Loving; I Take What I Want; Ease Me; I Got Everything I Need; Don't Make It So Hard On Me; It's A Wonder; Don't Help Me Out; Just Me; You Got It Made; You Don't Know Like I Know; Blame Me (Don't Blame My Heart).

First released 1967
UK peak chart position: 35
USA peak chart position: 45

47. SOUL DRESSING
Booker T. And The MGs

The two albums either side of this release both made the USA Top 40, yet *Green Onions* and *Hip Hug-Her* were similarly great records containing the best Memphis soul music by the best Memphis soul group. *Soul Dressing* is less cocktail lounge than the debut, probably because the band had turned into a formidable writing unit, astonishingly this classic album failed to chart. Even though they often 'borrowed' heavily the sound was unmistakeable and irresistible. 'Big Train' is a steal from 'My Babe' and shades of 'Green Onions' inflect 'Home Grown'. No criticism is intended because a quadruple box set of 'Green Onions' soundalikes would be manna from heaven.

Soul Dressing; Tic-Tac-Toe; Big Train; Jellybread; Aw'Mercy; Outrage; Night Owl Walk; Chinese Checkers; Home Grown; Mercy Mercy; Plum Nellie; Can't Be Still.

First released 1965
UK peak chart position: did not chart
USA peak chart position: did not chart

48. DIANA ROSS PRESENTS THE JACKSON FIVE
Jackson Five

Many laid claim to 'discovering' the Jackson Five, but the association with Motown's premier artist signalled the label's commitment to this act. Their first single for the company, the million-selling 'I Want You Back', established the quintet's early style, wherein commercial pop soul was ignited by Michael Jackson's unfettered enthusiasm. Although still not a teenager, he invested each song he recorded with an understanding and empathy beyond mere charm. The group's first album contains material ideally suited to his singing style, showing that Motown wished to develop his talent, rather than simply exploit it.

Zip A Dee Doo Dah; Nobody; I Want You Back; Can You Remember; Standing In The Shadows Of Love; You've Changed; My Cherie Amour; Who's Loving You?; Chained; I'm Losing You; Stand; Born To Love You; The Love You Save; One More Chance; ABC; 2-4-6-8; Come 'Round Here I'm The One You Need; Don't Know Why I Love You; Never Had A Dream Come True; True Love Can Be Beautiful; La La Means I Love You; I'll Bet You; I Found That Girl; The Young Folks.

First released 1970
UK peak chart position: 16
USA peak chart position: 5

49. KING AND QUEEN
Otis Redding And Carla Thomas

The Stax label 'crowned' their leading male and female singers following the pair's charming version of Lowell Fulsom's 'Tramp'. Taking a cue from 50s 'sweethearts' Shirley And Lee, the duo's verbal sparrings were lighthearted, but accomplished, playing on both vocalist's strengths. 'Ooh Carla, Ooh Otis' and 'Lovey Dovey' rock with an engaging innocence, while the pair bring an emotive resonance to Aaron Neville's 'Tell It Like It Is'. Redding's premature death ended any prospects of a reprise and Thomas sadly failed to retain her regal position. *The King And Queen* is a beguiling snapshot in time.

Knock On Wood; Let Me Be Good To You; Tramp; Tell It Like It Is; When Something Is Wrong With My Baby; Lovey Dovey; New Year's Resolution; It Takes Two; Are You Lovely For Me Baby; Bring It On Home To Me; Ooh Carla, Ooh Otis.

First released 1967
UK peak chart position: 18
USA peak chart position: 36

50. PROUD MARY
Solomon Burke

In Peter Guralnick's excellent book *Sweet Soul Music* he opens with a piece on Soloman Burke, and how he regards him as the king of soul music. Many vintage soul fans share this view although commercially the mantle has long been owned by Otis Redding and James Brown. Solomon Burke continues to work hard and released a fine album in 1993 but it is this album that stands as his greatest collection and is rightly applauded as a classic of southern soul music. *The Bishop Rides South* is also recommended as it is this album plus four extra tracks. Purists will no doubt want the original cover.

Proud Mary; These Arms Of Mine; I'll Be Doggone; How Big A Fool (Can A Fool Be); Don't Wait Too Long; That Lucky Old Sun; Uptight Good Woman; I Can't Stop; Please Send Me Someone To Love; What Am I Living For.

First released 1969
UK peak chart position: did not chart
USA peak chart position: 140

THE TOP 25 GREATEST HITS & COMPILATION ALBUMS

THE SECOND MOST SUBJECTIVE LIST IN THE BOOK HAS BEEN COMPILED BY CONSIDERING ARTISTS WHOSE GREATEST WORK WAS IN THE POP CHARTS WITH A STRING OF UNFORGETTABLE HIT SINGLES. BOB MARLEY WINS HANDS DOWN BECAUSE HIS SELECTION IS THE MOST PERFECT REPRESENTATION OF HIS WORK. THE HOLLIES AND ABBA ARE BOTH MASTERS OF OUTSTANDING THREE-MINUTE HIT SINGLES. THE MOST SURPRISING OMISSION IS THE KINKS, SURELY DESERVING OF A DEFINITIVE PACKAGE - MAYBE THEIR CATALOGUE IS TOO BIG. HUGELY INFLUENTIAL COMPILATIONS ARE ALSO REPRESENTED. TWO NOTABLE SETS ARE: *THIS IS SOUL* AND *THE ROCK MACHINE TURNS YOU ON*. BOTH ACTED AS PIVOTAL INTRODUCTORY SAMPLERS AT A BARGAIN PRICE.

1. LEGEND
Bob Marley

Although reggae is still perceived as a minor specialist genre, when it hits the button right, the music captures the hearts of the masses. Marley is a giant similar to Elvis Presley: both continue to sell vast numbers of records long after their death and both are clear leaders of their genre. This album is the most perfect selection of hits. The running order is unbeatable, each track is made for the next. There is a superb four CD box set available for serious collectors, but for those who want to chuck on a CD at any time of the day this will always satisfy.

Is This Love; Jamming; No Woman No Cry; Stir It Up; Get Up And Stand Up; Satisfy My Soul; I Shot The Sheriff; One Love; People Get Ready; Buffalo Soldier; Exodus; Redemption Song; Could You Be Loved; Want More.

First released 1984
UK peak chart position: 1
USA peak chart position: 54

2. BEATLES
1967-70

The famous red and blue double albums were finally released on CD this year to a public outcry, complaining that the price was too high. The record company argued that it was the high royalty negotiated with the artists that hiked the price of a double CD. It made no difference whatsoever, both albums zoomed into the charts as we forked our £20 for the pleasure of buying tracks we already own in some other shape or form. Such is the power of the greatest pop group that ever was and will ever be. No discussion of the tracks is necessary, they are already part of our national heritage.

Strawberry Fields Forever; Penny Lane; Sgt. Pepper's Lonely Hearts Club; With A Little Help From My Friends; Lucy In The Sky With Diamonds; A Day In The Life; All You Need Is Love; I Am the Walrus; Hello Goodbye; The Fool On The Hill; Magical Mystery Tour; Lady Madonna; Hey Jude; Revolution; Back In The USSR; While My Guitar Gently Weeps; Ob La Di Ob La Da; Get Back; Don't Let Me Down; Ballad Of John And Yoko; Old Brown Shoe; Here Comes The Sun; Come Together; Something; Octopus's Garden; Let It Be; Across The Universe; The Long And Winding Road.

First released 1973
UK peak chart position: 2
USA peak chart position: 1

3. GREATEST HITS
Queen

The other group, excluding Abba because they were not a 'beat combo', who rightly deserve our automatic love and support. A series of real quality singles over 20 years make them one group to rival the fab four who would settle as the second greatest pop group of all time. The word pop is deliberately used, even though their heavy metal support is considerable. These hits stormed the pop charts and were loved by all ages and social denominations. Freddy Mercury was truly loved and the remaining members know they could not continue to use the name without him. An exceptional group that nobody could or should dislike.

Bohemian Rhapsody; Another One Bites The Dust; Killer Queen; Fat Bottomed Girls; Bicycle Race; You're My Best Friend; Don't Stop Me Now; Save Me; Crazy Little Thing Called Love; Now I'm Here; Good Old-fashioned Lover Boy; Play The Game; Flash; Seven Seas Of Rhye; We Will Rock You; We Are The Champions; Somebody To Love.

First released 1981
UK peak chart position: 1
USA peak chart position: 14

4. THIS IS SOUL
Various

The finest sampler of soul music ever released, in terms of track selection. Quite apart from the giveaway price of twelve shillings and sixpence. It opened doors to the magnificent artists of Stax and Atlantic Records of the 60s. Every track could have topped the charts, and this album played end to end could still form the basis of any programme on soul music. Ben E King asks on one track 'what is soul?', the answer as if you didn't know, is on this album. Only Aretha and Otis are missing from the original but thankfully added to the repackaged reissue.

Mustang Sally - Wilson Pickett; B-A-B-Y - Carla Thomas; Sweet Soul Music - Arthur Conley; When A Man Loves A Woman - Percy Sledge; I Got Everything I Need - Sam And Dave; What Is Soul? - Ben E. King; Fa Fa Fa Fa Fa (Sad Song) - Otis Redding; Knock On Wood - Eddie Floyd; Keep Looking - Solomon Burke; I Never Loved A Man (The Way I Love You) - Aretha Franklin; Warm And Tender Love - Percy Sledge; Land Of A Thousand Dances - Wilson Pickett.

First released 1968
UK peak chart position: 16
USA peak chart position: 146

5. BEATLES
1962-66

Of the pair of famous red and blues, this one was always the poor relative, being one or two positions behind in the charts and selling one or two million less copies. Quite why will never be known as the singles contained on this one were bigger hits and make for a better greatest hits package. This editor cannot tamper with the general opinion, although if *you* have any doubts, go for this one. Having said that, if you had any doubts about the Beatles in the first place you should not be holding this book, let alone contemplating buying it. They were the greatest popular 'beat combo' in the world.

Love Me Do; Please Please Me; From Me To You; She Loves You; I Want To Hold Your Hand; All My Loving; Can't Buy Me Love; A Hard Day's Night; And I Love Her; Eight Days A Week; I Feel Fine; Ticket To Ride; Yesterday; Help; You've Got To Hide Your Love Away; We Can Work It Out; Day Tripper; Drive My Car; Norwegian Wood; Nowhere Man; Michelle; In My Life; Girl; Paperback Writer; Eleanor Rigby; Yellow Submarine.

First released 1973
UK peak chart position: 3
USA peak chart position: 3

6. GREATEST HITS 1971-1975
Eagles

The recent tour undertaken by (probably) America's most successful band, excluding the Dead and the Beach Boys, grossed millions of dollars every night. The Eagles had to re-form one day and during the hiatus this album stayed in the charts as a stock back catalogue item. As the band became softer and lost their hard edge desperado image their sales shot up, peaking with *Hotel California*. Those who preferred Poco and Firefall must now concede; this band is seriously popular, and obscenely successful and actually pretty good after all.

Take It Easy; Witchy Woman; Lyin' Eyes; Already Gone; Desperado; One Of These Nights; Tequila Sunrise; Take It To The Limit; Peaceful Easy Feeling; Best Of My Love.

First released 1976
UK peak chart position: 2
USA peak chart position: 1

7. THAT'LL BE THE DAY
Various

How was it that a film and compilation album released during one of rock 'n' roll's serious lulls become so popular. Was it simply the presence of David Essex in the film? Was it Ringo or Dave Edmunds' cameo appearances? We shall never know, but whoever chose the tracks (it may have been Edmunds) deserves a medal. Quite apart from the fact that it saved hours of locating scratched singles, putting them on one by one and then taping them to make the ultimate party tape, it is also a history of rock 'n' roll in two albums. Even the David Essex/Edmunds/Billy Fury tracks are fitting.

Bye Bye Love; Poetry In Motion; Little Darlin'; Smoke Gets In Your Eyes; Chantilly Lace; Runaround Sue; Devoted To You; Great Balls Of Fire; Running Bear; Tequila; Tutti Frutti; (Till) I Kissed You; I Love How You Love Me; Runaway; Bony Maronie; Honeycombe; Why Do Fools Fall In Love; Party Doll; Linda Lou; Red River Rock; That'll Be The Day; Born Too Late; Wake Up Little Suzy; Sealed With A Kiss; Book Of Love; (You've Got) Personality; Well All Right; At The Hop; Ally Oop; Raunchy; Rock On; A Thousand Stars; Real Leather Jacket; Long Live Rock; What In The World (Shoop); That's All Right Mama; Slow Down; Get Yourself Together; What Did I Say; It'll Be Mine.

First released 1973
UK peak chart position: 1
USA peak chart position: did not chart

8. GREATEST HITS
Abba

Everybody likes Abba, or at least no one wishes to say anything against Sweden's greatest export since the Volvo. Abba appeal to the widest section of music critics and this album spent two and a half years in the UK chart. Since their well documented personal break up and professional parting Abba's reputation has continued to grow. Television comedy sketches, Abba lookalikes and a further reissued collection, which also went to no 1, enhanced their reputation. This is the famous cover that graced a million homes, but only now do we realise that 'Knowing Me Knowing You', 'Dancing Queen' and 'Take A Chance On Me' are contained on volume 2, which of course nobody voted for. CD's only next edition, this omission is a crime.

SOS; He Is Your Brother; Ring Ring; Hasta Manana; Nina; Pretty Ballerina; Honey Honey; So Long; I Do I Do I Do; People Need Love; Bang A Boomerang; Another Town Another Train; Mamma Mia; Dance (While The Music Still Goes On); Waterloo; Fernando.

First released 1976
UK peak chart position: 1
USA peak chart position: 48

9. THE SINGLES 1969-1973
Carpenters

The most difficult album in the whole book to own up to liking. Abba sounded positively anarchic compared to Karen and Richard, and yet just look at the sales and the position it gained. This book represents the public as well as reviewers and music biz types. The Carpenters' success was extraordinary and without explanation. The reissued/re-compiled CD also had incredible success when released three years ago. This will go on selling for as long as the record company keeps it in print. The lead guitar solo on 'Goodbye To Love' is still amazing though.

We've Only Just Begun; Top Of The World; Ticket To Ride; Superstar; Rainy Days And Mondays; Goodbye To Love; Yesterday Once More; It's Going To Take Some Time; Sing; For All We Know; Hurting Each Other; (They Long To Be) Close To You.

First released 1974
UK peak chart position: 1
USA peak chart position: 1

10. THE ALL TIME GREATEST HITS
Elvis Presley

A suitable replacement for the often cited *Worldwide Greatest Hits* package that takes advantage of the benefits of CD. The chronological listing is highly useful especially for those who, like John Lennon, felt Elvis died when he went into the army. Much of the second CD can be ignored if you share that belief. CD one however is almost absolute perfection, almost because the omission of 'Don't Be Cruel' is a serious error. Still, in a five year journey from 1956 to 1961 you can experience 'Heartbreak Hotel' to 'Good Luck Charm'. Nobody can deny the massive importance of this man.

Heartbreak Hotel; Blue Suede Shoes; Hound Dog; Love Me Tender; Too Much; All Shook Up; Teddy Bear; Paralysed; Party; Jailhouse Rock; Don't; Wear My Ring Around Your Neck; Hard Headed Woman; King Creole; One Night; A Fool Such As I; A Big Hunk O' Hunk; Stuck On You; The Girl Of My Best Friend; It's Now Or Never; Are You Lonesome Tonight?; Wooden Heart; Surrender; (Marie's The Name) His Latest Flame; Can't Help Falling In Love; Good Luck Charm; She's Not You; Return To Sender; (You're The) Devil In Disguise; Crying In The Chapel; If I Can Dream; Love Letters; In The Ghetto; Suspicious Minds; Don't Cry Daddy; The Wonder Of You; I Just Can't Help Believin'; An American Trilogy; Burning Love; Always On My Mind; My Boy; Suspicion; Moody Blue; Way Down; It's Only Love.

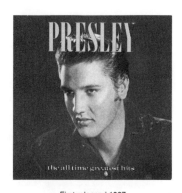

First released 1987
UK peak chart position: 4
US peak chart position: did not chart

11. GREAT BALLS OF FIRE!
Jerry Lee Lewis

It is astonishing to note that this record failed to make the charts on both sides of the Atlantic. Although the singles have become classics, this album was released at a time when Lewis' country roots were taking over. Fortunately his rock 'n' roll material is now back in favour and most of the vital piano bashing gems are included here. Lewis was the first white rock 'n' roller to give new meaning to the word 'sweat'. At live performances as he progressed further into his greatest hits catalogue his hair would curl, as buckets of the stuff poured onto his keyboard. Unbeatable.

Whole Lotta Shakin' Going On; It'll Be Me; Lewis Boogie; Drinkin' Wine Spo-Dee-O-Dee; Rock 'N' Roll Ruby; Matchbox; Ubangi Stomp; Great Balls Of Fire; You Win Again; Mean Woman Blues; Milkshake Mademoiselle; Breathless; Down The Line; Good Rockin' Tonight; Jambalaya (On The Bayou).

First released 1964
UK peak chart position: did not chart
US peak chart position: did not chart

12. GREATEST HITS
Hollies

Some of the finest pop music of the 60s came from the Hollies, Manchester's answer to the fab four. Both bands even collided when the Hollies recorded Harrison's 'If I Needed Someone'. The record stalled at the top 20 and Lennon 'blasted Hollies' in a slanging match. Although CD packages eclipse this record in content, both the familiar cover and often played track sequence makes this album an old friend. There was a time however when this record was hidden from view, during the heavy underground prog scene of the late 60s. The Hollies had the last laugh, this is timeless quality pop back in fashion.

I Can't Let Go; Bus Stop; We're Through; Carrie Anne; Here I Go Again; King Midas In Reverse; Yes I Will; I'm Alive; Just One Look; On A Carousel; Stay; Look Through Any Window; Stop Stop Stop; Jennifer Eccles.

First released 1967
UK peak chart position: 1
US peak chart position: 11

13. THROUGH THE PAST DARKLY
Rolling Stones

The Stones went from being a great R&B band to the world's greatest rock 'n' roll band. Both titles are slightly dubious because much of the material on this vital package are simply good pop songs. This will also probably be the last time this record, and its sister, *High Tide & Green Grass*, get in any listings. The recent CD packages have a bigger and better selection. This book is about 'all time' and CD does not yet have age on its side, unlike this record. This is the Stones (mostly) in transition with Brian Jones still present. The hexagonal cover was brilliant but a severe pain to own.

Paint It, Black; Ruby Tuesday; She's A Rainbow; Jumpin' Jack Flash; Mother's Little Helper; Let's Spend The Night Together; Honky Tonk Woman; Dandelion; 2000 Light Years From Home; Have You Seen Your Mother Baby, Standing In The Shadows; Street Fighting Man.

First released 1969
UK peak chart position: 2
USA peak chart position: 2

14. GREATEST HITS
Aretha Franklin

Where 'greatest hits' can sometimes be a loose description, here it is particularly apt. These recordings capture an extraordinary talent, a vocalist capable of wrenching emotion from the slightest phrase. Building on gospel roots, Aretha Franklin took each song she recorded and recast it into an inimitable style; impassioned, tender or ebullient. She redefined the notion of woman singer, proclaiming fiery independence ('Respect') or aching vulnerability ('I Never Loved A Man') but in each case on her own terms and with the control of a consummate artist. This peerless selection contains the cream of Franklin's work and as such is essential. And this did not chart in the UK?

Spanish Harlem; Chain Of Fools; Don't Play That Song; I Say A Little Prayer; Dr. Feelgood; Let It Be; Do Right Woman-Do Right Man; Bridge Over Troubled Water; Respect; Baby I Love You; (You Make Me Feel Like) A Natural Woman; I Never Loved A Man (The Way I Love You); You're All I Need To Get By; Call Me.

First released 1971
UK peak chart position: did not chart
USA peak chart position: 19

15. LONELY AT THE TOP
Randy Newman

A criminally underrated man who has been writing poetical songs of American life for four decades. This is his greatest hits offering with the reality that he only hit once with the misunderstood 'Short People'. Many of his early songs recorded by the likes of Dusty Springfield and Gene Pitney are still overlooked on this compilation, but we do have heartfelt ramblings and powerful understatements. To think that Newman can move us to tears of emotion with a lyric that merely states 'I think its going to rain today' is remarkable. Please note the section 'did not chart'! Maybe the next century will discover this man's genius.

Love Story; Living Without You; I Think Its Going To Rain Today; Mama Told Me Not To Come; Sail Away; Simon Smith And The Amazing Dancing Bear; Political Science; God's Song; Rednecks; Birmingham; Louisiana 1927; Marie; Baltimore; Jolly Coppers On Parade; Rider In The Rain; Short People; I Love L.A.; Lonely At The Top; My Life Is Good; In Germany Before The War; Christmas In Capetown; My Old Kentucky Home

First released 1987
UK peak chart position: did not chart
USA peak chart position: did not chart

16. THE BEST OF VAN MORRISON
Van Morrison

They very wisely opted against calling this Greatest Hits for obvious reasons, yet such a good package of songs only highlights the fact that they all could have been massive hits. Maybe it's because Van is a very private man and unlike Phil Collins or Eric Clapton, does not grant interviews often. Yet he is up there with the greatest of all time. His catalogue is one of the finest in popular music, and in choosing a best of CD the choice will be ultra subjective. This gets near to the mark, even though there is no 'Madame George', 'Listen To The Lion' or 'Tupelo Honey'. There we are again, purely subjective. The alternative is to have a standing order made out to purchase one Van Morrison album for the next 24 months.

Bright Side Of The Road; Gloria; Moondance; Baby Please Don't Go; Have I Told You Lately; Brown Eyed Girl; Sweet Thing; Warm Love; Wonderful Remark; Jackie Wilson Said; Full Force Gale; And It Stoned Me; Here Comes The Night; Domino; Did Ye Get Healed; Wild Night; Cleaning Windows; Whenever God Shines His Light; Queen Of The Slipstream; Dweller On The Threshold.

First released 1990
UK peak chart position: 4
USA peak chart position; 41

17. GREATEST HITS
Simon And Garfunkel

This has now been overtaken in terms of content by other packages, but the success and the familiarity that the cover brings, makes this album, together with Carole King's *Tapestry*, the album that everybody had that particular year, whenever it was. Simon neatly covered up his thinning hair with a daft woolly hat and Artie smiled benignly. They were the most successful duo of all time and this is the best possible selection for a single album, none of your favourites are missing. Nowadays we have the even better *Simon And Garfunkel Collection* beats this hands down because of the space on a single CD. The songs are all exquisite but this time around pay special attention to the quality of 'America' and recall Annie Nightingales' classic gaff.

Mrs Robinson; For Emily, Whenever I Find Her; The Boxer; The 59th Street Bridge Song; The Sound Of Silence; I Am A Rock; Scarborough Fair/Canticle; Homeward Bound; Bridge Over Troubled Water; America; Kathy's Song; El Condor Pasa (If I Could); Bookends; Cecilia.

First released 1972
UK peak chart position: 2
USA peak chart position: 5

18. BIG HITS HIGH TIDE AND GREEN GRASS
Rolling Stones

Through The Past Darkly was ahead by a whisker, even though there is little to choose between them. This is more bluesy. Mercifully the Stones are still with us and their recent album found favourable reviews, which is a remarkable feat to be able to keep the critics happy after 30 or more years. 'Hey you get offa mah cloud' in Jagger's best Sidcup dialect still sounds magnificent, as does Brian's booming Vox pearl guitar on 'The Last Time' and Keef's opening chords to 'Not Fade Away'. To be handed down to your children.

Have You Seen Your Mother, Baby, Standing In The Shadow; Paint It Black; It's All Over Now; The Last Time; Heart Of Stone; Not Fade Away; Come On; Satisfaction; Get Off My Cloud; As Tears Go By; 19th Nervous Breakdown; Lady Jane; Time Is On My Side; Little Red Rooster.

First released 1966
UK peak chart position: 4
USA peak chart position: 3

19. PHIL SPECTOR'S CHRISTMAS ALBUM
Various

Also known as *A Christmas Gift For You*, this album has grown in stature over the years and has been reissued countless times. If you have to own a record to play half a dozen times during the festive season this is the one and only. Featuring the amazing Spector production together with Darlene Love, The Crystals, The Ronettes, Bob B. Soxx And The Blue Jeans and even Leon Russell on piano and Sonny Bono on percussion. Another timeless record that is unlikely to ever be surpassed as the greatest Christmas compilation of all time.

White Christmas; Frosty The Snowman; The Bells Of St. Marys; Santa Claus Is Coming To Town; Sleigh Ride; Marshmallow World; I Saw Mommy Kissing Santa Claus; Rudolph The Red Nosed Reindeer; Winter Wonderland; Parade Of The Wooden Soldiers; Christmas (Baby Please Come Home); Here Comes Santa Claus; Silent Night.

First released 1963
UK peak chart position; 19
USA peak chart position: 6

20. THE MAN AND HIS MUSIC
Sam Cooke

Although Cooke never made an individually great album, this collection demonstrates his enormous catalogue of sweet soul music. The age of CD gave us this selection which is unbeatable in choice, ranging from his early days of gospel right through to near the time he was tragically killed. The fresh faced man on the cover looks exactly as you imagine his music to sound, his voice was like cream in coffee. Most songs have been covered dozens of time by artists such as Cat Stevens, Rod Stewart, Aretha Franklin, Steve Miller and Otis Redding. None have succeeded in interpreting any Cooke song as anything more than a humble tribute. Rod Stewart would be the first to admit this.

Touch The Hem Of His Garment; That's Heaven To Me; I'll Come Running Back To You; You Send Me; Win Your Love For Me; Just For You; Chain Gang; When A Boy Falls In Love; Only Sixteen; Wonderful World; Cupid; Nothing Can Change This Love; Rome Wasn't Built In A Day; Love Will Find Away; Everybody Loves To Cha Cha Cha; Another Saturday Night; Meet Me At Mary's Place; Having A Party; Good Times; Twistin' The Night Away; Shake; Somebody Have Mercy; Sad Mood; Ain't That Good News; Bring It On Home To Me; Soothe Me; That's Where It's At; A Change Is Gonna Come.

First released 1986
UK peak chart position: 8
USA peak chart position: 175

21. SHAVED FISH
John Lennon

Once again the age of CD has surpassed this 1975 release with *The John Lennon Collection*, but at the time it was novel to have a greatest hits record from an ex-Beatle, such was his talent. His appalling death prompted an uncomfortable jump in sales of his back catalogue, and a reissue of many of the hits contained here. His anthems seemed to come alive when we came to terms with the reality of losing him. And he was right all along, just read the titles out aloud to yourself. John was a difficult man, sometimes cruel and always determined to march out of time with the orchestra, but he was worth it and he *was* right about so many things.

Give Peace A Chance; Cold Turkey; Instant Karma!; Power To The People; Mother; Woman Is The Nigger Of the World; Imagine; Whatever Gets You Through The Night; Mind Games; No9 Dream; Happy Xmas (War Is Over); Reprise, Give Peace A Chance.

First released 1975
UK peak chart position: 8
USA peak chart position: 12

22. ENDLESS SUMMER
Beach Boys

Just as everybody had written off the Beach Boys as passé, we were reminded of the colossal contribution that Brian Wilson had made to popular music with this inspired choice. New Beach Boys' albums were selling badly at the time of this release, and then somebody had the idea of packaging this superb collection of surf and car songs that reeked of sand, sea, sun and innocence. There is something special about 'catching a wave and you're sitting on top of the world' even though most of us have never been near a surfboard in our lives.

Surfin' Safari; Surfer Girl; Catch A Wave; Warmth Of The Sun; Surfin' USA; Be True To Your School; Little Deuce Coup; In My Room; Shut Down; Fun Fun Fun; I Get Around; Girls On The Beach; Wendy; Let Him Run Wild; Don't Worry Baby; California Girls; Girl Don't Tell Me; Help Me Rhonda; You're So Good To Me; All Summer Long; Good Vibrations.

First released 1974
UK peak chart position: did not chart
USA peak chart position: 1

23. THE ROCK MACHINE TURNS YOU ON
Various

Somebody at CBS Records had the inspiration to introduce their new progressive or 'underground' music through this affordable sampler. Little did they realise that the tracks selected would still form the core of every late 60s rock music lovers collection. Sandwiched in between Simon And Garfunkel and the Byrds we had our ears opened to the mercurial Spirit, the legendary Moby Grape, the powerful Tim Rose and the wonderfully obscure Peanut Butter Conspiracy. The marketing worked for this writer and many others. We changed our buying habits until all the albums, from which the tracks were selected, were purchased and displayed, while we hid our Hollies records. The complete albums were even better than the one track selected from each.

I'll Be Your Baby Tonight; Can't Be So Bad; Fresh Garbage; I Won't Leave My Wooden Wife For You, Sugar; Time Of The Season; Turn On A Friend; Sisters Of Mercy; My Days Are Numbered; Dolphins Smile; Scarborough Fair/Canticle; Statesboro Blues; Killing Floor; Nobody's Got Any Money In The Summer; Come Away Melinda; Flames.

First released 1969
UK peak chart position: 18
USA peak chart position: did not chart

24. ANTHOLOGY
Miracles

The lasting music of the great Motown era has not been from the ones most likely to. The Supremes have been eclipsed by Diana Ross. Stevie Wonder took another direction with *Music Of My Mind* and has never returned to the 'Uptight' era and the Four Tops catalogue is not big enough. It is left to the greatest of them all; Smokey Robinson and his priceless Miracles. This contains some of the richest, warmest most uplifting music ever made, and deserves to be played end to end to end to end three times. On a recent album by John Sebastian one line of the song dedicated to Mr Robinson reads; 'Oh Smokey please don't go, I don't wanna fall in love without the Miracles'. A very important record.

including; Bad Girl; Way Over There; (You Can) Depend On Me; Shop Around; Who's Lovin' You; Ain't It Baby; Brokenhearted; Everybody's Gotta Pay Some Dues; What's So Good About Goodbye; I'll Try Something New; You've Really Got A Hold On Me; A Love She Can Count On; Mickey's Monkey; I Like It Like That; That's What Love Is Made Of; Come On Do The Jerk; Ooo Baby Baby; The Tracks Of My Tears; My Girl Has Gone; Going To A Go-Go; Whole Lot Of Shakin' In My Heart (Since I Met You); (Come 'Round Here) I'm The One You Need; The Love I Saw In You Was Just A Mirage; More Love; I Second That Emotion; If You Can Want; Yester Love; Special Occasion; Baby Baby Don't Cry; Doggone Right; Abraham, Martin & John; Darling Dear; The Tears Of A Clown; Who's Gonna Take The Blame; I Don't Blame You At All; Satisfaction.

First released 1986
UK peak chart position: did not chart
USA peak chart position: did not chart

25. NICE ENOUGH TO...JOIN IN
Various

The Rock Machine, released by CBS in 1968, redefined the notion of the pop sampler. Part primer, part manifesto, several such collections assumed a significance outside commercial expediency thanks to the excellence of its content. Two further samplers are now combined on CD as *Nice Enough To ... Join In* , drawn from the Island label's roster, including Jethro Tull, Free, and Spooky Tooth. It spans progressive rock, folk, blues and pop; contrasting elements held together by the high quality of the acts on offer. Established names were set beside new signings and successful samplers naturally promoted further purchases of the artists on display. This particular set fulfilled that purpose, but the care lavished upon its content also provides an aesthetic enjoyment. (*Nice Enough To Eat* and *You Can All Join In*)

A Song For Jeffrey; Sunshine Help Me; I'm A Mover; What's That Sound; Pearly Queen; You Can All Join In; Meet On The Ledge; Rainbow Chaser; Dusty; I;ll Go Girl; Somebody Help Me; Gasoline Alley; Sing A Song That I Know; Forty Thousand Headmen; Time Has Told Me; Gungamai; Strangely Strange But Oddly Normal; At The Crossroads; Better By You Better Than Me; Woman; I Keep Singing That Same Old Song.

First released 1992
UK peak chart position: did not chart
USA peak chart position: did not chart

THE TOP 25
REGGAE ALBUMS

THE RECENT BOOM IN REGGAE CLEARLY MERITS HAVING THE FIRST EVER REGGAE LIST FOR THE MASS MARKET. BOB MARLEY AND THE WAILERS ARE RIGHTLY AT THE TOP BUT FOR THOSE STUDENTS WANTING TO LOOK BEYOND, THERE IS THE VITALLY IMPORTANT *MARCUS GARVEY*. PLEASE NOTE FOR POPOPHILES THERE IS NO DESMOND DEKKER OR MUSICAL YOUTH.

1. CATCH A FIRE
The Wailers

One of the biggest regrets of the CD age is the lack of potential for the covers. The original issue of this necassary album was in the shape of a Zippo lighter, that opened with a rivetted flip top(eventually) to reveal the flame. Beyond the flame was the real fire; a superb collection of songs that stand up to repeated play 20 years on. Even with the huge commercial success that Marley enjoyed with big selling albums the Wailers followers and critics come back to this record time and time again. The first proper reggae album for any new collecter.

Concrete Jungle; 400 Years; Stop That Train; Baby We've Got A Date; Stir It Up; Kinky Reggae; No More Trouble; Midnight Ravers.

First released 1973
UK peak chart position: did not chart
USA peak chart position: 171

2. MARCUS GARVEY
Burning Spear

One of reggae's most distinctive and original talents, Burning Spear - nee Winston Rodney - was launched internationally with this striking album. His deep, preaching vocal is immediately arresting, a characteristic enhanced by a dense and brooding accompaniment. Taking cues from Rastfarian chants, Spear subtly builds an intensity, locking each track into a seamless whole. His knowledge of Black history brings a chilling realism to the album's lyrics, resulting in what is incontestably a milestone in the development of reggae.

Marcus Garvey; Slavery Days; Invasion; Live Good; Give Me; Old Marcus Garvey; Tradition; Jordan River; Red, Gold And Green; Resting Place.

First released 1975
UK peak chart position: did not chart
USA peak chart position: did not chart

3. BURNIN'
Bob Marley And The Wailers

Catch A Fire launched Jamaica's Wailers into international prominence with a brilliant cross of reggae and rock. Purists did fault its emphasis on the latter, a criticism answered with the earthier *Burnin'*. Stripped of session musicians, the group's frontline harmonies were supported by the sinewy Barrett brothers rhythm section which provided a dry counterpoint. Although Bob Marley was fully in control, the support of Bunny Livingston and Peter Tosh was crucial to the overall sound. Their vocal interplay mirrored that of the Impressions, but lyrically the Wailers proclaimed a vibrant militancy instantly heard on 'Get Up Stand Up'. Eric Clapton helped popularise 'I Shot The Sherrif', but this album is noteworthy for its uncompromising blend of polemics and tough melodies.

Get Up Stand Up; Hallelujah Time; I Shot The Sheriff; Burnin' And Lootin'; Put It On; Small Axe; Pass It On; Duppy Conqueror; One Foundation; Rastaman Chant.

First released 1975
UK peak chart position: did not chart
USA peak chart position: 151

4. GUSSIE PRESENTING
I Roy

Following (as he did) in the wake of U Roy it would be far too simplistic to write off Roy Reid as a mere U Roy impersonator. Apart from his more measured and reasoned delivery his forte was his razor sharp humour and acute intelligence which he turned on anyone or anything that took his fancy or didn't in many cases. In the introduction to 'Black Man Time' he admonishes a beggar and tells him that if it's food he wants I Roy will give food for thought. Producer Gussie Clarke was only a young man too and he knew exactly what the youth audience wanted - he wasn't afraid to experiment and the choice of rhythms (or backing tracts) is faultless and I Roy is given enough space to work all the way through. A name a bit too readily forgotten nowadays I Roy's contribution to the DJ school was prodigious and the balance against him needs to be redressed quite urgently.

Red Gold And Green; Pusher Man; Black Man Time; Smile Like An Angel; Peace Coxsone Affair; Screw Face; First Cut Is The Deepest; Melinda; Tourism Is My Business; Tripe Girl; Cow Town Skank.

First released 1973
UK peak chart position: did not chart
USA peak chart position: did not chart

5. KING TUBBY'S MEETS ROCKERS UPTOWN
Augustus Pablo

Pablo's 'Far East' melodies and approach to building rhythms were hugely influential on the whole of reggae music in the early and mid-70s. This set features the mixing talents of King Tubby let loose on some of Pablo's finest rhythming. Tubbys, ostensibly a studio engineer but so much more, not only transformed reggae but the sound of popular music as we know it and his work here brings out the depth and mystery of Pablo's music without ever sacrificing its inherent qualities. This album is a timeless showcase of his mixing skills and Pablo's singular musicianship.

Keep On Dubbing; Stop Them Jah; Young Generation Dub; Each One Dub; Braces Tower Dub; King Tubby's Meets Rockers Uptown; Corner Crew Dub; Say So; Skanking Dub; Frozen Dub; Satta.

First released 1975
UK peak chart position: did not chart
USA peak chart position: did not chart

6. SATTA MASA GANA
Abyssinians

Widely recognised as *the* roots vocal group the Abyssinians ethereal/harmonies and beautiful songs put them head and shoulders above their contemporaries. Bernard Collins, Donald and Lynford Manning shared songwriting, lead vocals and harmony roles and the results were never less than quite, quite beautiful. Included here are recuts of their first two anthems 'Satta Masa Gana' (a self production) and 'Declaration Of Rights' (for Studio One) plus more songs of the same calibre which serve as definitions of roots music - moral and uplifting yet without ever resorting to sermonising or serving up the same old truisms. The Abyssinians never strayed far from this particular party and after some internal dissent it's heartening to see them together again in the mid-90s, making records and live appearance that do much more than echo former glories.

Declaration Of Rights; Good Lord; Forward On To Zion; Know Jah Today; Abendigo; Yim Mas Gan; Black Man Strain; African Race; I And I; Satta Masa Gana.

First released 1993
UK peak chart position: did not chart
USA peak chart position: did not chart

7. NATTY DREAD
Bob Marley

Out on his own following the defection of Bunny Wailer and Peter Tosh, this album saw Marley utilising the talents of the I-Threes for the first time. There was still a nod to his past in the inclusion of a cover of Wailers' tune 'Lively Up Yourself', but elsewhere he revelled in his new found freedom on 'Revolution' and most particularly 'No Woman, No Cry', which has practically become a Jamaican national anthem since its release. If that song had an instantly universal appeal, Rasta themes were also brilliantly conveyed via 'Them Belly Full (But We Hungry)' and 'Rebel Music (Three O'Clock Roadblock)'. Marley had announced himself as one of the greats of modern music.

Lively Up Yourself; No Woman No Cry; Them Belly Full (But We Hungry); Rebel Music (3 O'clock Roadblock); So Jah Seh; Natty Dread; Bend Down Low; Talkin' Blues; Revolution.

First released 1975
UK peak chart position: 75
USA peak chart position: 28

8. WAILING WAILERS
The Wailers

Although just one of many excellent harmony groups to emerge from Jamaica in the mid-60s, the Wailers' subsequent success inspired interest in their early work. *The Wailing Wailers* shows that the unit's core trio - Bob Marley, Neville Livingston (aka Bunny Wailer) and Peter McIntosh - already possessed an intuitive understanding. The Studio One houseband support their close-knit voices with a hypnotic ska beat and although Marley emerges as the principal songwriter, Livingston also makes telling contributions, in particular with the homage-like 'Rude Boy'. Indeed the group would later revive some of this material - 'One Love' is a prime example of this - which itself is a tribute to the lasting quality of this exceptional album.

Put It On; I Need You; Lonesome Feeling; What's New Pussycat; One Love; When The Well Runs Dry; Ten Commandments Of Love; Rude Boy; It Hurts To Be Alone; Love Or Affection; I'm Still Waiting; Simmer Down.

First released 1965
UK peak chart position: did not chart
USA peak chart position: did not chart

9. SCREAMING TARGET
Big Youth

Big Youth could do no wrong in Jamaica during 1973, his fruity rich voice was the best of the DJ phenomenon, Scotty's voice was too high. When you hear Youth say 'going down town as I will tell you' you realise he ain't joking. Downtown Kingston was particularly volatile that year ,and Youth recognised it and preached his blend of 'chill out' music with great subtlety. The bass is particularly rich and begs to tear your sopeakers apart. The CD reissue stops the distortion of Youth's primal scream on the title track.

Screaming Target; Pride And Joy Rock; Be Careful; Tippertong Rock; One Of These Fine Days; Screaming Target (version 2); The Killer; Solomon A Gundy; Honesty; I Am Alright; Lee A Low; Concrete Jungle.

First released 1973
UK peak chart position: did not chart
USA peak chart position: did not chart

10. EXODUS
Bob Marley

Marley's consistent (certainly by reggae standards) album career has proffered many great songbooks, of which Exodus is just one good example. The singles 'One Love' and 'Jamming' will be familiar to anyone with even a passing acquaintance with Jamaican music, but just as vital are the touchingly vulnerable love song 'Waiting In Vain', the title-track and the splendid 'Guiltiness'. This was the first album to feature Junior Marvin on guitar, while the expressive use of horns adds new texture to the established quality of the Wailers backing.

Natural Mystic; So Much Things To Say; Guiltiness; The Heathern; Exodus; Jamming; Waiting In Vain; Turn Your Lights Down Low; Three Little Birds; One Love - People Get Ready.

First released 1977
UK peak chart position: 8
USA peak chart position: 20

11. SOON FORWARD
Gregory Isaacs

The Cool Ruler, The Lonely Loves, Mr Isaacs, Gregory has maintained his position as reggae music's most popular vocalist by virtue of his distinctive style, his ability to stay ahead of the pack at all times and his uncompromising attitude *Soon Forward* is a near perfect blend of love songs such as the insistent 'Mr Brown' and reality/cultural tunes such as the chilling 'Universal Tribulation' where he points out that we're all suffering in one way or another. A self production (apart from the massive 'Soon Forward' hit for Sly And Robbie) he manages with the aid of Dennis Brown and Junior Delgado on harmonies to sing out the best within himself every time without fail.

Universal Tribulation; Mr Brown; Down The Line; Lonely Girl; Bumping And Boring; My Relationship; Slave Market; Black Liberation Struggle; Jah Music; Soon Forward.

First released 1979
UK peak chart position: did not chart
USA peak chart position: did not chart

12. FUNKY KINGSTON
Toots And The Maytals

This Jamaican trio began recording in 1963 as the Vikings. They embraced bluebeat, rocksteady and finally reggae styles, firstly as the Maytals, before adopting the above name after lead singer, Toots Hibbert. *Funky Kingston* was issued to great fanfare following the group's successful appearance in *The Harder They Come* and in the wake of the Wailers' *Catch A Fire*. It focuses on the trio's expressive voices, in particular Hibbert's excited delivery which resembles Otis Redding but with a greater range. The production left enough rough edges to appease purists, but the album was one of a handful of collections introducing Reggae to the wider rock audience.

Sit Right Down; Pomp And Pride; Louie Louie; I Can't Believe; Redemption Song; Daddy's Home; Funky Kingston; It Was Written Down.

First released 1976
UK peak chart position: did not chart
USA peak chart position: 164

13. DREADLOCKS DREAD
Big Youth

This is the perfect Big Youth pop album, gone is the thundering sparse bass and in its place is a more orchestrated effort with shades of Marley and Burning Spear. 'Lightning Flash (Weak Heart Drop)' is a killer whilst the happy go lucky 'Some Like It Dread' in addition to great humour should have been a national hit. Only the power of his *Screaming Target* can top this album. He recorded output in recent years is meagre but the two albums in this listing will keep Youth's name alive, long after the current reggae boom has faded.

Train To Rhodesia; House Of Dreadlocks; Lightning Flash; Weak Heart; Natty Dread She Want; Some Like It Dread; Marcus Garvey; Big Youth Special; Dread Organ; Blackman Message; You Don't Care; Moving Away.

First released 1975
UK peak chart position: did not chart
USA peak chart position: did not chart

14. VERSION GALORE
U Roy

The man who almost single handedly invented the entire DJ phenomenon (and all that came afterwards) on his debut long player where he laid down all the grand rules for the genre. Live DJs had been essential to reggae's development throughout the 60s and had already made it on to record on a number of occasions most notably with King Stiff in the late 60s and early 70s but it was U Roy who woke the town and told the people. At one stage he held the top three places in the Top 10 for weeks at a stretch. Here he argues and agrees with some of Duke Reid's finest rocksteady vocals, hollering and whooping along and an infectious joy runs from every groove of this record. A perceptive critic once noted that 'no one will make a better album than this . . . ever' and as time goes by his words (and U Roy's) ring more and more true true true . . .

Your Ace From Space; On The Beach; Version Galore; True Confession; Tide Is High; Things You Love; The Same Song; Happy Go Lucky Girl; Rock Away; Wear You To The Ball; Don't Stay Away; Hot Pop.

First released 1971
UK peak chart position: did not chart
USA peak chart position: did not chart

15. WOLF AND LEOPARDS
Dennis Brown

That the 'boy wonder', Dennis Brown, was able to release an album of this calibre gathering together only some of his hits from the previous couple of years at the age of 20 seems almost unbelievable. The whole set demonstrates a maturity both in content and delivery that is quite staggering. From the intense spirituality of 'Emanuel God Is With Us' and 'Created By The Father' to the vengeful 'Whip Them Jah' every track oozes authority and class and nothing Brown has done in the time subsequent to this release has lessened his impact or his appeal. He remains one of the music's most popular and influential performers.

Wolves And Leopards; Emanuel God Is With Us; Here I Come; Whip Them Jah; Created By The Father; Party Time; Rolling Down; Boasting; Children Of Israel; Lately Girl.

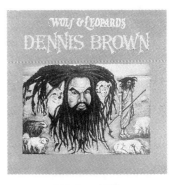

First released 1978
UK peak chart position: did not chart
USA peak chart position: did not chart

16. TEASE ME
Chaka Demus And Pliers

Both Chaka Demus and Pliers enjoyed huge success in the reggae market as solo acts in their own right before teaming up in a combination style ie live DJ and live singer as opposed to live DJ working over pre-recorded singing tracks. Their first huge worldwide smash 'Tease Me' was built around a sample from the Skatalites 60s hit 'Ball Of Fire' and Chaka's 'rockstore' voice proved the perfect counterpoint for Pliers youthful sweet voiced tones. Much more than mere one hit wonders as the subsequent follow ups proved their willingness to share the limelight was underpinned at all times by producers Sly Dunbar's and Robbie Shakespeare's understanding of reggae music which managed to look both backwards and forwards simultaneously. Ragga music had finally arrived.

Tease Me; She Don't Let Nobody; Nuh Betta Nuh Deh; Bam Bam; Friday Evening; Let's Make It Tonight; One Nation Under A Groove; Tracy; Sunshine Day; Murder She Wrote; Roadrunner; I Wanna Be Your Man; Twist And Shout; Gal Wine.

First released 1993
UK peak chart position: 26
USA peak chart position: did not chart

17. FLESH OF MY SKIN, BLOOD OF MY BLOOD
Keith Hudson

Totally unlike anything that had gone before (or followed after) Hudson had already established his reputation as one of Jamaica's most consistently inventive and innovative record producers before unleashing this set of meditative songs with their accompanying instrumental versions which completely defy classification. The inclusion of Dylan's 'I Shall Be Released' as a sole concession to outside influences perhaps goes some way towards explaining the appeal of this album with its world weary resignation yet ever hopeful yearning for something better. Even the most kind hearted would be hard pressed to describe Hudson as a singer yet his near vocals in this context radiate a quiet dignity that is beyond criticism.

Hunting; Flesh Of My Skin; Blood Of My Blood; Testing My Faith; Fight Your Revolution; Darkest Night; Talk Some Sense (Gamma Ray); Treasures Of The World; My Nocturne; I Shall Be Released; No Friends Of Mine; Stabiliser.

First released 1974
UK peak chart position: did not chart
USA peak chart position: did not chart

18. IN THE DARK/ROOTS REGGAE
Toots And The Maytals

Released at the time when reggae was first making inroads on the 'rock' consciousness and was for the first time being viewed as a 'serious' music by many who had previously scorned its 'monotony' and 'lack of variation'. 'Toots' Hibbert's voice had a power and strength achieved from over 10 years at the top as lead singer in one of Jamaica's most popular vocal groups ever - the Maytals - along with 'Jerry' Mathias and 'Raleigh' Gordon whose harmonies ensured that nothing was ever missing from this Jamaican wall of sound. Toots And The Maytals were poised for the big time. The clean, sharp rhythms from the Dynamic house band - the Dynamites - were the perfect setting for Toots' hoarse style and the team even managed to transform 'Take Me Home Country Roads' into a Jamaican *tour de force*. Sadly the big break never came their way although Toots demonstrated in some UK shows in the summer of 1994 that he never lost it and still had just what it takes.

Got To Be There; In The Dark; Having A Party; Time Tough; I See You; Take A Look In The Mirror; Take Me Home Country Roads; Fever; Love Gonna Walk Out On Me; Revolution; 54-46 Was My Number; Sailing On.

First released 1974
UK peak chart position: did not chart
USA peak chart position: did not chart

19. BLACKHEART MAN
Bunny Wailer

Bunny's first solo album after leaving the Wailers set the kind of standards that everyone, everywhere had to work towards for ever more. Personal, fused throughout with Biblical imagery and references, the entire set is imbued with Bunny's deep Rastafarian faith while the gentle pastoralism of the songs is strengthened by harmonies from fellow Wailers Bob Marley and Peter Tosh and complemented by Jamaican musicians of the highest order. There's no more complete testament to the Rastafarian influence on reggae music.

Blackheart Man; Fighting Against Conviction; The Oppressed Song; Fig Tree; Dreamland; Rasta Man; Reincarnated Souls; Amagideon (Armagedon); Bide Up; This Train.

First released 1975
UK peak chart position: did not chart
USA peak chart position: did not chart

20. HEART OF THE CONGOS
Congos

One of the handful of near perfect albums ever made this one really does have it all. Produced by Lee Perry the Upsetter (one of Jamaica's true musical geniuses) at the height of his powers when the sounds and ideas coming from his own Black Ark Studio were at a mind boggling pitch of creativity. He set Cedric Myton and Roy Johnson, whose voices had a purity that has to be experienced to be believed, against some of his most innovative ever rhythms. Their songwriting was firmly based in the Kingston Biblical tradition and the results were stupendous - this set can still raise the little hairs at the nape of the neck every time it's played.

Fisherman; Congo Man; Open Up The Gate; Children Crying; La La Bam Bam; Can't Come In; Sodom And Gomorrah; The Wrong Thing; Ark Of The Covenant; Solid Foundation.

First released 1981
UK peak chart position: did not chart
USA peak chart position: did not chart

21. RIGHT TIME
Mighty Diamonds

The Diamonds borrowed from a number of sources most notably the cool classical three part harmonies of the best rock steady vocal groups and the then current (mid-70s) vogue for reality or Rastafarian songs. However, the teaming of these elements with Channel One's young band the Revolutionaries (led by Sly Dunbar) militant 'rockers' rhythms was nothing short of inspired and the Diamonds sound was to dominate reggae music for years to come. They managed, somehow, to sound incredibly involved and disinterested observers at the same time. This collection catches like them at their first peak - there were many more to follow. An interesting comparison get to this is Channel One's (almost) dub counter part - Vital Dub - also on Well Charge and released later the same year.

The Right Time; Why Me Black Brother Why?; Shame And Pride; Gnashing Of Teeth; Them Never Love Poor Marcus; I Need A Roof; Go Seek Your Rights; Have Mercy; Natural Natty. Africa.

First released 1976
UK peak chart position: did not chart
USA peak chart position: did not chart

22. LOVE ME FOREVER
Carlton And His Shoes

One of the purest ever to grace vinyl Carlton Manning's Carlton And His Shoes - the Shoes comprised brothers Donald and Lynford Manning, sometimes Alexander Henry and sometimes Carlton double and treble tracking his own harmonies on to his lead vocal - provided one of reggae music's most popular (and versioned) songs ever 'Love Me Forever' which was originally released on Coxsone Dodd's Supreme label. The b-side 'Happy Land' formed the basis of the Abyssinians' (Donald and Lynford Manning with Bernard Collins) anthem 'Satta Masa Gana' another key work in the history of Jamaican music. Their rock steady into reggae hits are here and although they never repeated the success of 'Love Me Forever' they continued to record throughout the 70s and their entire output for Studio One (apart from their late 70s 12-inch release 'Let Me Love You') is here. The album is a beauty and the heart rending purity of 'Never Give Your Heart Away' still tears the listener apart. Under rated and under recorded they remain a legendary outfit.

First released 1978
UK peak chart position: did not chart
USA peak chart position: did not chart

Love Me Forever; Never Give Your Heart Away; Love Is All; Sincerely Yours; Just Me; This Feeling; I've Got Soul; Love To Share; Me And You; Forward Jerusalem.

23. SKYLARKING
Horace Andy

Horace Hinds was re-named Andy due to his ability to write songs in the Bob Andy tradition by Studio One controller Coxsone Dodd. His other distinguishing feature is his eerie, haunting vocal style which has been widely imitated over the years. Ironically enough many of the pretenders have achieved far more fame and financial success than Horace during his long career. The superb Studio One rhythms complement Sleepy's thoughtful songs and many of these songs and rhythms have been endlessly recycled and this set remains the definitive Horace Andy collection - any album that contains 'Skylarking' has got to be a classic!

Where Do The Children Play; Just Say Who; Love Of A Woman; Skylarking; Mammie Blue; Please Don't Go; Every Tongue Shall Tell; Something's On My Mind; See A Man's Face; Don't Cry; I'll Be Gone; Got To Be Sure.

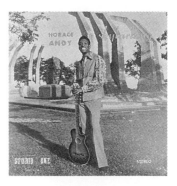

First released 1972
UK peak chart position: did not chart
USA peak chart position: did not chart

24. ON TOP
Heptones

The transformation from ska to rock steady during the mid-60s took Jamaican music away from the brazen, fast-tempos of the former to the more measured, lilting drift of the latter. This evolution allowed greater emphasis on vocal groups. The Heptones were one of several superb acts, including the Paragons and the Melodians, to rise to prominence at this time. Their superb close three-part harmonies were inspired by the Impressions and a similar spirituality marked their work. *On Top* is the Heptones' second album for the fabled Studio One label. Its empathic houseband provides subtle support to the trios gorgeous voices, which weave together with mesmerising sweetness. This is a lynchpin collection in the development of Jamaican music.

Equal Rights; Pure Sorrow; Heptones Gonna Fight; I Hold The Handle; My Baby Is Gone; Soul Power; Take Me Darling; We Are In The Mood; Sea Of Love; Pretty Looks Isn't All; Party Time; I Love You.

c.60s
UK peak chart position: did not chart
USA peak chart position: did not chart

25. AS RAW AS EVER
Shabba Ranks

A title that lives up to its contents both lyrically and rhythmically too as Rexton Gordon led the way into the main stream and opened up the floodgates for Jamaican DJs to emulate his astonishing success. Shabba's gruff ranting, with the emphasis firmly on slack (or sexually explicit) lyrics, had already earned him a reputation second to none within the confines of reggae music as the reggae audience stayed with him as he moved up into the international market. They're still with him now - no compromises have been made along the way. With his debut set for a major label he stayed with producers who knew reggae music back to front and inside out. Digital Bobby, Steely And Clevie, Clifton Dillon and Mikey Bennet share the credits here - and it shows. The first ragga DJ to achieve lasting success Shabba has proved just how much more there is to reggae/ragga (or whatever this week's name for the genre happens to be) than mere novelty value.

Trailor Load Of Girls; Where Does Slackness Come From; Woman Tangle; Gun Pon Me; Gone Up; Ambi Get Scarce; Housecall; Flesh Axe; A Mi Di Girls Dem Love; Fist A Ris; The Jame; Park Yu Benz.

First released 1991
UK peak chart position: 51
USA peak chart position: 89

THE TOP 20
BEDSITTER ALBUMS

THOSE OF US WHO ARE NOT TOO PROUD TO ADMIT TO OUR EMOTIONS HAVE ALL SAT ALONE AT SOME TIME IN BEDSITTERS OR BEDROOMS LISTENING TO THESE ALBUMS. USUALLY IT IS DURING OR AFTER A RELATIONSHIP PROBLEM. MANY OF THESE ARTISTS HAVE SUCCEEDED IN MAKING US FEEL WORSE, BUT THE SELF-INFLICTED PUNISHMENT IS WONDERFUL AND GOOD FOR THE SOUL.
OWN UP THOSE WHO NEEDED LEONARD COHEN TO TAKE THEM ONE STEP AWAY FROM SUICIDE, OR WHO REVELLED IN THE SOLITARY NATURE OF CAT STEVENS' ACOUSTIC MUSIC!

1. SONGS OF LEONARD COHEN
Leonard Cohen

Leonard Cohen's debut album encapsulated the performer's artistry. A successful poet and novelist, he came to music through the folk idiom and this set combines the aural simplicity and visual clarity of these two passions. Cohen's lugubrious voice brought an intensity to a haunting collection bound together by beautiful melodies and deeply personal lyrics. Members of contemporary group Kaleidoscope join producer John Simon in creating a delicate backdrop for some of pop's most memorable love songs. Cohen's ability to be both intimate and universal is a rare gift and results in a body of work that is both timeless and enthralling.

Suzanne; Master Song; Winter Lady; The Stranger Song; Sisters Of Mercy; So Long, Marianne; Hey, That's No Way To Say Goodbye; Stories Of The Street Teachers; One Of Us Cannot Be Wrong.

First released 1968
UK peak chart position: 13
USA peak chart position: 83

2. SWEET BABY JAMES
James Taylor

Taylor had already 'seen and been' enough by the time this album was released - having survived drug addiction and mental institutions not to mention broken relationships. There was much for the listener to relate to during those heady days and this album made him a star which he tried to recoil from. Two tracks from this album have been performed at every Taylor gig for 25 years - the irritating but necessary 'Steamroller' and probably his greatest song 'Fire And Rain' which tells the story of his first 20 years in just over three minutes. Headphone and bean bag friendly.

Sweet Baby James; Lo And Behold; Sunny Skies; Steam Roller; Country Roads; Oh Susannah; Fire And Rain; Blossom; Anywhere Like Heaven; Oh Baby Don't You Lose Your Lip On Me; Suite For 20G.

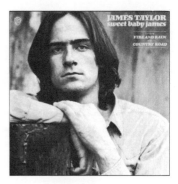

First released 1970
UK peak chart position: 7
USA peak chart position: 3

3. TEA FOR THE TILLERMAN
Cat Stevens

The series of album's Yusuf Islam (formerly Mr. Stevens) made following this magnificent introspective set were all of similar but gradual declining quality. What was totally original became less so even though his voice retained its sad quality and his acoustic guitar was as wooden as ever. This record has been played hundreds of times so that the running order is automatic. The long intro into 'Where Do The Children Play' into 'Hard Headed Woman' and then on track three wait for the middle eight 'oh baby baby its a wild world'. turn over and you've still 'Father And Son' to come.

Where Do The Children Play; Hard Headed Woman; Wild World; Sad Lisa; Miles From Nowhere; But I Might Die Tonight; Longer Boats; Into White; On The Road To Find Out; Father And Son.

First released 1970
UK peak chart position: 20
USA peak chart position: 8

4. TRACY CHAPMAN
Tracy Chapman

Although she must be tired of the comparisons Tracy did look like Joan Armatrading, and at times sounded like her. She also debuted with an impressive album. Her career was given an irregular shot in the arm when she appeared at the Nelson Mandela concert. Her solo spot was extended at short notice because Stevie Wonder was unable to come on. She won over the crowd who loved her brave vulnerability and rose to it and played an immaculate and memorable set. This album leaped into the charts the following day and refused to be budged for many months.

Talkin' 'Bout A Revolution; Fast Car; Across The Lines; Behind The Wall; Baby Can I Hold You; Mountains O' Things; She's Got Her Ticket; Why?; For My Lover; If Not Now...; For You.

First released 1988
UK peak chart position: 1
USA peak chart position: 1

5. BEDSITTER IMAGES
Al Stewart

Stewart achieved commercial success during the 70s with a AOR-style exemplified on *Year Of The Cat*. Yet he began his career as a folk singer, aiding the early work of Paul Simon and John Martyn, and recording several excellent albums, of which this was his first. Taking a cue from Donovan, Stewart sang in a light, restrained manner, describing scenes in meticulous detail and with a keenly romantic eye. Stewart's grasp of simple melody is always true and if the orchestrations are a shade overblown, they do not undermine the material's quiet strength. British folk-rock took many cues from this engaging collection.

Bedsitter Images; Swiss Cottage Manoeuvres; Scandinavian Girl; Pretty Golden Hair; Denise At 16; Samuel, Oh How You've Changed!; Cleave To Me; A Long Way Down From Stephanie; Ivich; Beleeka Doodle Day.

First released 1967
UK peak chart position: did not chart
USA peak chart position: did not chart

6. TIM HARDIN II
Tim Hardin

Tim Hardin's beguiling brand of jazz/folk, unveiled on his debut album, is equally prevalent on its follow-up. Although many of its songs last less than two minutes, they each possess a resonant beauty enhanced by the singer's smoky intonation. Always an introspective composer, Hardin takes the opportunity to extol pleasures discovered through family life and few writers can expose such emotions without resorting to cliche. Sweet melodies and tinkling accompaniment reinforces the songs' fragility, underscoring the aura of gracefulness Hardin's best work generates.

If I Were A Carpenter; Red Balloon; Black Sheep Boy; Lady Came From Baltimore; Baby Close Its Eyes; You Upset The Grace Of Living When You Lie; Speak Like A Child; See Where You Are And Get Out; It's Hard To Believe In Love For Long; Tribute To Hank Williams.

First released 1967
UK peak chart position: did not chart
USA peak chart position: did not chart

7. GRACE AND DANGER
John Martyn

Martyn shared the break-up of his marriage to Beverly by tearing open his heart and exposing all his emotions to us. Those listeners who were experiencing similar problems found it torturously listenable. The three emotional killers run consecutively - 'Sweet Little Mystery', 'Hurt In Your Heart' and 'Baby Please Come Home'. Each one pleads, begs and reasons and inevitably you ask, how on earth could she leave him? The answer is in the penultimate track where our John announces 'I saved some for me' and 'I didn't give it all'. If you survived this album you can survive anything in later life.

Some People Are Crazy; Grace And Danger; Lookin' On; Johnny Too Bad; Sweet Little Mystery; Hurt In Your Heart; Baby Please Come Home; Save Some For Me; Our Love.

First released 1980
UK peak chart position: 54
USA peak chart position: did not chart

8. SONGS FROM A ROOM
Leonard Cohen

Leonard Cohen's second album maintained the haunting strengths of its predecessor. His hypnotic, murmured voice retains its compelling power and the content on *Songs From A Room* proves equally resonant. Where another pensive singer/songwriter might warp his craft in bathos, Cohen injects his work with mature insight, using metaphor and poetic insight to enhance his craft. Superb acoustic guitar work weaves a path throughout the bewitching melodies, enhancing the singer's spell, although Cohen's self-deprecating humour is equally prevalent, particularly on the singalong 'Tonight Will Be Fine'. *Songs From A Room* captures every facet of Cohen's inestimable talent.

Bird On A Wire; Story Of Isaac; A Bunch Of Lonesome Heroes; Seems So Long Ago; Nancy; The Old Revolution; The Butcher; You Know Who I Am; Lady Midnight; Tonight Will Be Fine.

First released 1969
UK peak chart position: 2
USA peak chart position: 63

9. BROKEN ENGLISH
Marianne Faithfull

Marianne Faithfull returned to recording after a lengthy hiatus with this starkly personal release. The tremulous high register of her 60s recordings was lost forever, replaced by a husky realism where the baggage of personal disaster is apparent in every intonation. The power of this association is matched by a brilliant cast of songs, in which original material co-exists with seemingly surprising cover versions. Faithfull brings a chilling resonance to Dr. Hook's 'The Ballad Of Lucy Jordan' while the depth of feeling apparent on 'Why Did Ya Do It' and the title song matches anger with knowing resignation. Such emotional dilemmas run throughout this deeply hypnotic set.

Working Class Hero; What's The Hurry; The Ballad Of Lucy Jordan; Why Did Ya Do It; Broken English; Witches' Song; Guilt; Brain Drain.

First released 1979
UK peak chart position: 57
USA peak chart position: 82

10. TEASER AND THE FIRECAT
Cat Stevens

Following in the tradition of his previous effort, with similar cover design and feel Cat continued his painful journey through life. Even then there was a sadness linked to his happy songs such as 'Moonshadow', 'How Can I Tell You' and 'Tuesday's Dead'. Our favourite school hymn was also given the treatment - how did he manage to make such a happy verse sound sad. The answer as we all have seen was in himself, he was a rare songwriter but he was mostly a very troubled soul, something he seems to have sorted out by his conversion to the Muslim faith.

The Wind; Rubylove; If I Laugh; Changes IV; How Can I Tell You; Tuesday's Dead; Morning Has Broken; Bitterblue; Moonshadow; Peace Train.

First released 1971
UK peak chart position: 3
USA peak chart position: 2

11. THE PAUL SIMON SONGBOOK
Paul Simon

Having begun his singing career as half of be-bop duo Tom And Jerry, Paul Simon embraced folk music during a spell domiciled in the UK and returned there in 1965 to record this haunting solo album. Fellow singer Al Stewart produced the set on which Simon accompanied himself solely on acoustic guitar. This simple setting enhances the self-penned compositions, many of which would be re-recorded when the artist rejoined his erstwhile partner, Art Garfunkel. The pair gained early success with new renditions of 'The Sound Of Silence' and 'I Am A Rock', but these first versions are equally persuasive, possessing a quiet maturity which permeates this entire album.

I Am A Rock; Leaves That Are Green; A Church Is Burning; April Come She Will; The Sound Of Silence; A Most Peculiar Man; He Was My Brother; Kathy's Song; The Side Of A Hill; A Simple Desultory Philippic; Flowers Never Bend With The Rainfall; Patterns.

First released 1965
UK peak chart position: did not chart
USA peak chart position: did not chart

12. JOAN ARMATRADING
Joan Armatrading

The anchor hymn for this album is the gorgeous 'Love And Affection', a song that never fails to capture the ears when it is played two decades on. Joan exposes herself with a collection of desperately honest tracks which never lapse into sentimentality. Her naturally bass inflected voice is made in heaven for acoustic guitar - the combination is like gin and tonic especially on 'Water With The Wine'. This may explain why her rock/guitar based material of late is of average quality. There is no driftwood on this album, one introspective story follows another.

Down To Zero; Help Yourself; Water With The Wine; Love And Affection; Save Me; Join The Boys; People; Somebody Who Loves You; Like Fire; Tall In The Saddle.

First released 1976
UK peak chart position: 12
USA peak chart position: 67

13. LADIES OF THE CANYON
Joni Mitchell

a. No longer the wistful folkie, Joni had by now joined the late 60s rock fraternity through her association with Graham Nash. Her lyrics had acquired an originality which she expanded on *Blue* and *For The Roses* but it was the quality of the songs that made them classics of the era. 'For Free' was recorded by David Crosby and the reformed Byrds and CSNY turned 'Woodstock' into a full blown rock number. Joni's own definitive stamp remains on the much covered 'The Circle Game' the ecology conscious 'Big Yellow Taxi' and 'Willy', her song for Nash.
b. Joni Mitchell's third album encapsulates the personalisation of the singer/songwriter genre. She unabashedly chronicles her relationships; graphically so on 'My Old Man' and 'Willy', and elsewhere relays momentary encounters with penetrative insight. The ecologically-sound 'Big Yellow Taxi' brought commercial success as a single, while the anthem-like 'Woodstock' served as a celebration and eulogy for the generation she address.

First released 1970
UK peak chart position: 8
USA peak chart position: 27

Morning Morgan Town; For Free; Conversation; Ladies Of The Canyon; Willy; The Arrangement; Rainy Night House; The Priest; Blue Boy; Big Yellow Taxi; My Old Man; Woodstock; The Circle Game.

14. SUZANNE VEGA
Suzanne Vega

A latecomer to the art of bedsitter albums, especially as Vega was probably one of those American girls crying over James Taylor or Leonard Cohen. This is an assured debut that lends itself to the populist market. Suzanne crafted the songs over a period of time and delivered a very controlled series of song while managing to make herself sound totally vulnerable and insecure especially in 'Cracking' and 'Small Blue Thing'. The mood is briefly broken by the slightly up tempo 'Marlene On The Wall' but its back to the cracks in the ceiling and broken kettle for 'Undertow' and 'Some Journey'.

Cracking; Freeze Tag; Marlene On The Wall; Small Blue Thing; Straight Lines; Undertow; Some Journey; The Queen And The Soldier; Night Movies; Neighborhood Girls.

First released 1985
UK peak chart position: 11
USA peak chart position: 91

15. TIM HARDIN I
Tim Hardin

Normally classed as a folksinger, Tim Hardin brought a jazz/blues perspective to the genre. His relaxed, languid voice mirrored the ease of his stylish compositions, the strongest of which showcased a highly original talent. Fragile lyrics, romanticism, tender melodies and haunting instrumentation combine to perfection on a collection of enchanting songs, several of which have become pop standards, notably 'Reason To Believe'. Although known for wistful ballads, Hardin was equally adept with up-tempo material, a combination fully exploited herein. His highly personal reflections left its mark on a generation of singer/songwriters.

Don't Make Promises; Green Rocky Road; Smugglin' Man; How Long; While You're On Your Way; It'll Never Happen Again; Reason To Believe; Never Too Far; Part Of The Wind; Ain't Gonna Do Without; Misty Roses; How Can We Hang On To A Dream.

First released 1966
UK peak chart position: did not chart
USA peak chart position: did not chart

16. SONGS OF LOVE AND HATE
Leonard Cohen

Leonard Cohen was already established as a denizen of 'bedsitter music' by the time this third album was issued. Deftly balanced between newly-written material and older songs, it contains several of the singer's most graphic and literate compositions. Allegory vies with personal recollection to create a set of unparalleled depth while Cohen's grasp of melody stays as secure as ever. His unconventional voice remains fixedly morose, but its individuality ensures a bewitching resonance, particularly on 'Famous Blue Raincoat' and 'Joan Of Arc'. Cohen's poetic imagery was never as striking or as moving.

Avalanche; Last Year's Man; Dress Rehearsal Rag; Diamonds In The Mine Field; Love Calls You By Your Name; Famous Blue Raincoat; Sing Another Song, Boys; Joan Of Arc.

First released 1971
UK peak chart position: 4
USA peak chart position: 145

17. NEW YORK TENDABERRY
Laura Nyro

Laura Nyro found fame when her compositions were covered by other artists, including Blood, Sweat And Tears, Barbra Streisand and the Fifth Dimension. Drawing inspiration from Broadway's Tin Pan Alley, R&B and Brill Building acolytes Carole King and Ellie Greenwich, she wrote material echoing these elements without ever sounding derivative. *New York Tendaberry* shows her skills to full effect, combining brassy, up-tempo pop with plaintive, introspective musings. Nyro's emotional voice swoops and dives at will, emphasising the intensity of her songwriting. Uncompromising and challenging, this album showcases the art of superior performer.

You Don't Love Me When I Cry; Captain For Dark Mornings; Tom Cat Goodby; Mercy On Broadway; Save The Country; Gibsom Street; Time And Love; Sweet Lovin Baby; Capatain Saint Lucifer; New York Tendaberry.

First released 1969
UK peak chart position: did not chart
USA peak chart position: 32

18. THE CIRCLE GAME
Tom Rush

A product of Boston's thriving folk enclave, Tom Rush embraced contemporary singer/songwriter material with this exceptional collection. Jackson Browne, James Taylor and Joni Mitchell had not recorded and were largely unknown prior to this album which introduced their work to a wider audience. Rush's sympathetic interpretations of 'Tin Angel', 'Shadow Dream Song' and 'Sunshine Sunshine' were enhanced by Paul Harris' imaginative arrangements, but the highlight, undoubtedly, was his own composition, 'No Regrets'. This moving eulogy to a broken relationship became a hit for the Walker Brothers and Midge Ure, but neither matched the tenderness of the original herein. It closes one of rock's most moving releases.

Tin Angel; Something In The Way She Moves; Urge For Going; Sunshine Sunshine; The Glory Of Love; Shadow Dream Song; The Circle Game; So Long; Rockport Sunday; No Regrets.

First released 1970
UK peak chart position: did not chart
USA peak chart position: 76

19. HAPPY SAD
Tim Buckley

Two previous albums established Tim Buckley as an imaginative folk singer. On this release he extended his musical range, incorporating jazz structures into his repertoire. Formal meter was broken down to allow the artist's voice fuller expression, a freedom he embraced with relish. Vibes and conga drums provide a rhythmic pulse on material ranging from intense reflection to scat-singing association, the latter encapsulated on the extended *tour de force*, 'Gypsy Woman'. The contrast between its stridency and the beautiful melancholia of the remaining selections is the album's abiding strength.

Strange Feeling; Buzzin' Fly; Love From Room 109 At The Islander; Dream Letter; Gypsy Woman; Sing A Song For You.

First released 1969
UK peak chart position: did not chart
USA peak chart position: 81

20. COME OUT FIGHTING GHENGIS SMITH
Roy Harper

Roy Harper was, alongside Al Stewart and John Martyn, part of a second wave of British folk singers who largely eschewed traditional forms in favour of a more introspective style. Harper's biting, personal lyrics and superb guitar work are to the fore on this, his second album, but producer Shel Talmy, famed for his work with the Kinks and Who, brings a crisp discipline to the set. A whiff of Summer of Love optimism is also apparent, a dimension not usually apparent in Harper's work and a facet which gives this set such a distinctive place in the artist's extensive catalogue.

Freak Street; You Don't Need Money; Ageing Raver; In A Beautiful Rambling Mess; All You Need Is; What You Have; Circle; Highgate Cemetary; Come Out Fighting Ghengis Smith; Zaney Janey; Ballad Of Songwriter; Midspring Dithering; Zenjem; It's Tomorrow And Today Is Yesterday; Francesca; She's The One; Nobody's Got Any Money In The Summer.

First released 1967
UK peak chart position: Did not chart
USA peak chart position: Did not chart

The Top 20 Brilliantly Unlistenable Classics

Many listed would have appeared in other genres while others have rotted in collections for years without being played. Why did we buy them in the first place, what made us punish ourselves with Tiny Tim, Sid Vicious or David Peel? Can we truthfully sit down now and wallow in the pomp of Rick Wakeman or the lengthy *In-A-Gadda-Da-Vida*? Of course we can, they are magnificently wretched.

1. Trout Mask Replica
Captain Beefheart And The Magic Band

Head and shoulders above every other album in this section, this Frank Zappa produced extravaganza remains a classic of lyrical malarkey. Accompanied by his finest ever Magic Band, the Captain entered the recording studio with a few ideas for songs. What came out is still to this day, quite astonishing. Ornette Coleman wildness, guitars thrashing in tune but deliberately off key. At times, it was alleged, Beefheart was singing in another studio. Beefheart's retirement from the music world to take up painting is a great loss. This record is living proof of his bizarre genius. A difficult but outstanding record. Fast and bulbous.

Frownland; The Dust Blows Forward 'N The Dust Blows Back; Dachau Blues; Ella Guru; Hair Pie: Bake 1; Moonlight On Vermont; Hair Pie: Bake 2; Pena; Well; When Big Joan Sets Up; Fallin' Ditch; Sugar 'N Spikes; Ant Man Bee; Pachuco Cadaver; Bills Corpse; Sweet Sweet Bulbs; Neon Meate Dream Of A Octafish; China Pig; My Human Gets Me Blues; Dali's Car; Orange Claw Hammer; Wild Life; She's Too Much For My Mirror; Hobo Chang Ba; The Blimp; Steal Softly Thru Snow; Old Fart At Play; Veteran's Day Poppy.

First released 1969
UK peak chart position: 21
USA peak chart position: did not chart

2. AN EVENING WITH WILD MAN FISCHER
Wild Man Fischer

A well-known figure on Sunset Strip in Los Angeles, Larry Fischer earned a living singing impromptu songs in return for small change. His eccentricity found favour with Frank Zappa, who produced this album in unadulterated fashion. Fischer's compositions were largely modelled on 50s doo-wop, although his lyrics were genuinely off-beat, reflective of the artist's perilous mental state. Alternately funny, then disturbing, this sometimes unaccompanied set is often an uncomfortable experience as the listener struggles with voyeurism. Ultimately Fischer's naive optimism is the album's attraction.

First released 1968
UK peak chart position: did not chart
USA peak chart position: did not chart

Merry Go Round; New Kind Of Songs For Sale; I'm Not Shy Anymore; Are You From Claris?; The Madness And Ecstacy; Which Way Did The Freaks Go?; I'm Working For The Federal Bureau Of Narcotics; The Leaves Are Falling; 85 Times; Cops And Robbers; Monkeys Vs Donkeys; Start Life Over Again; The Mope; Life Brand New; Who Did It Johnny?; Think Of Me When Your Clothes Are Off; Jennifer Jones; The Taster; The Story Of The Taster; The Rocket Rock; The Rocket Rock Explanation And Dialogue; Dream Girl; Dream Girl Explanation; Serrano (Sorrento?) Beach; Success Will Not Make Me Happy; Wild Man On The Strip Again; Why Am I Normal; The Wild Man Fischer Story; Balling Isn't Everything; Ugly Beautiful Girl; Larry And His Guitar; Circle; Larry Under Pressure.

3. GOD BLESS TINY TIM
Tiny Tim

A Greenwich Village eccentric, Tiny Tim sang 20s' songs in a high falsetto, accompanying himself on the ukulele. His version of 'Tiptoe Through The Tulips' was a minor hit but this attendant album suggested he was more than a mere novelty. Producer Richard Perry bathed the singer in imaginative arrangements and chose material which extended his repertoire. Sonny Bono, Irving Belrin and Biff Rose were among those whose songs were covered while a hint of psychedelic pop permeated 'The Other One' and 'Strawberry Tea'. A genuine original, Tiny Tim brings these elements together by sheer force of personality.

First released 1968
UK peak chart position: did not chart
USA peak chart position: 7

Welcome To My Dream; Tiptoe Through The Tulips With Me; Livin' In The Sunlight, Lovin' In The Moonlight; On The Old Front Porch; The Viper; Stay Down Here Where You Belong; Then I'd Be Satisfied With Life; Strawberry Tea; The Other Side; Ever Since You Told Me That You Love Me; (I'm A Nut); Daddy, Daddy What Is Heaven Like?; The Coming Home Party; Fill Your Heart; I Got You Babe; This Is All I Ask.

4. IN-A-GADDA-DA-VIDA
Iron Butterfly

For many years this late 60s heavyish extravaganza was the biggest selling record in Atlantic's history. The reason was the title track, a wonderful but ponderous 17 minute slice of self indulgence. Its all here, drum solo; takka takka ding ding boom boom, guitar solo that is good, but ultimately a bore, and finally a sluggish overlong organ solo, that needed the beef of a hammond instead of a Vox Farfisa sound. The vocals are great, but in a strange sort of way so is the whole album. We may never play it, but it is there in our collection.

Most Anything You Want; My Mirage; Termination; Are You Happy; In-A-Gadda-Da-Vida; Flowers And Beads.

First released 1968
UK peak chart position: did not chart
USA peak chart position: 4

5. JOURNEY TO THE CENTRE OF THE EARTH
Rick Wakeman

Choosing between this album and the similarly now unlistenable The Six Wives Of Henry VIII was a difficult task. The former one because it is that much more grandiose a perfect example of 'pomp rock'. The quality of the music is good, the arrangements faultless and Wakeman is (no pun intended) a master of his organ. Rick attempted to put this project on the stage and for ten minutes we all loved it. Wakeman is now producing some fine new age inspired piano music and appears on television displaying his great sense of humour. Maybe this was an early practical joke he worked on us.

The Journey; Recollection; The Battle; The Forest.

First released 1974
UK peak chart position: 1
USA peak chart position: 3

6. UNFINISHED MUSIC NO 1: TWO VIRGINS
John Lennon

Controversy raged when the sleeve for this album was first seen as it featured both performers naked. An equally vociferous furore surrounded its content. Those expecting Beatle-style melodies and a passive woman singer were thrown into disarray by its uncompromising, *avant garde* material where found-sound and improvised instrumentation supported Yoko's strident, braying, largely wordless vocals. Borrowing the John Cage dictum that all noise is music, the pair demanded a response, suggesting art is confrontation and that confrontation is art. The first of three similarly unequivocal statements, *Two Virgins* still retains an ability to bewilder, animate or enthral.

Two Virgins.

First released 1969
UK peak chart position: did not chart
USA peak chart position: 124

7. WONDERWALL
George Harrison

The first official release on the Beatles' Apple label, *Wonderwall* was the soundtrack to an elliptical film of the same name. The 'quiet' Beatles' love of Indian music was already well-chronicled and here, freed from the constraints of commercial consideration, he fused raga and rock in innovatory fashion. Members of ex-Merseybeat group the Remo Four joined guitarist Eric Clapton in providing occidental perspectives, but the selections hinge on Eastern sounds and scales resulting in a serene, hypnotic selection. Harrison directs proceedings, rather than leads them, but nonetheless creates a unique and highly personal statement.

Microbes; Red Lady Too; Table And Pakavaj; In The Park; Drilling A Home; Guru Vandana; Greasy Legs; Ski-ing; Gat Kirwani; Dream Scene; Party Seacombe; Love Scene; Crying; Cowboy Music; Fantasy Sequins; On The Bed; Glass Box; Wonderwall To Be Here; Singing Om.

First released 1969
UK peak chart position: did not chart
USA peak chart position: 49

8. LICK MY DECALS OFF BABY
Captain Beefheart And The Magic Band

Beefheart's second recording for Frank Zappa's Straight label consolidated the artistic freedom expressed on its predecessor *Trout Mask Replica*. Avant garde rock and free jazz melt into a seamless whole, jagged guitars and ravaged saxophone splinter through the mix while ex-Mothers Of Invention drummer Artie Tryp, herein renamed Ed Marimba, brings new rhythmic possibilities to the Captain's heady brew. Beefheart prowls around the proceedings with consummate ease, his expressive voice, which echoes bluesman Howlin' Wolf, emphasising the adventurism of both music and lyrics. By demolishing previous notions of tonality and structure, Captain Beefheart inspired a whole generation of post-punk disciples, from Pere Ubu to Sonic Youth.

Lick My Decals Off, Baby; Doctor Dark; I Love You, You Big Dummy; Peon; Bellerin' Plain; Woe-Is-Uh-Me-Bop; Japan In A Dishpan; I Wanna Find A Women That'll Hold My Big Toe Till I Have To Go; Petrified Forest; One Rose That I Mean; The Buggy Boogie Woogie; The Smithsonian Institute Blues (Or The Big Dig); Space-Age Couple; The Clouds Are Full Of Wine (Not Whiskey Or Rye); Flash Gordon's Ape.

First released 1970
UK peak chart position: 20
USA peak chart position: did not chart

9. PREFLYTE
Byrds

Before they were the Byrds they were the Beefeaters. The Beefeaters tried to get a recording contract on the strength of their songs . . . I hope. This is fascinating for Byrdologists like myself but quite wretched. The version of 'Mr Tambourine Man' is worth the price of the album. Never has a Dylan song sounded so bad, never have the Byrds sounded so sloppy. The military two-step drumming was reputedly played on packing cases. Rest in peace Michael Clarke, you won't have to listen to this travesty ever again. The rest of the material is better . . . slightly.

You Showed Me; Here Without You; She Has A Way; The Reason Why; For Me Again; Boston; You Movin'; The Airport Song; You Won't Have To Cry; I Knew I'd Want You; Mr. Tambourine Man.

First released 1969
UK peak chart position: did not chart
USA peak chart position: 84

10. HAVE A MARIJUANA
David Peel And The Lower East Side

Although it sold less copies than any other record in this particular list, those of us who own it will never part with it. It is totally unlistenable. Wonderfully sloppy songs underneath the other Mr Peel's heavy Bronx or Brooklyn accent. Apparently recorded on the streets of New York, the record's objective is to make us smoke dope, and clearly it fails because we cannot take this man seriously, even though John Lennon later befriended him. Other ditty's such as 'I Do My Balling In The Bathroom' are equally forgettable but irreplaceable in any comprehensive record collection.

Mother Where Is My Father?; I Like Marijuana; Here Comes A Cop; I've Got Some Grass; Happy Mother's Day; Up Against The Wall; I Do My Balling In The Bathroom; The Alphabet Song; Show Me The Way To Get Stoned; We Love You.

First released 1969
UK peak chart position: did not chart
USA peak chart position: 186

11. SID SINGS
Sid Vicious

A cruel, cruel record that took advantage of a tragic icon at a time when he was not in control of his life. The feeling of 'the emperor's new clothes' that permeates throughout is tasteless. Sid was told that he could sing and play bass, neither are strictly true. The record's long-time favourite is a rendition of 'My Way' made famous by his diametrically opposite role model Frank Sinatra. It is wretched, sad and brilliant in the way it manages to debase a whole style of music built up over many years. Paul Anka, the song's author presumably allowed it to be recorded, although Eddie Cochran was not alive to grant permission for 'Something Else'.

Born To Lose; I Wanna Be Your Dog; Take A Chance On Me; Stepping Stone; My Way; Belsen Was A Gas; Something Else; Chatterbox; Search And Destroy; Chinese Rocks; I Killed The Cat.

First released 1979
UK peak chart position: 30
USA peak chart position: did not chart

12. THE TRANSFORMED MAN
William Shatner

Famed for his role as Captain William T. Kirk in television's enduringly popular *Star Trek* series, William Shatner joined fellow-star Leonard Nimoy (Mr. Spock) in recording a highly idiosyncratic album. *The Transformed Man* encompasses a quite breathtaking range of material, ranging from Shakespearian verse to songs drawn from the Beatles and Bob Dylan. Shatner tackles 'Lucy In The Sky With Diamonds' and 'Mr. Tambourine Man' with the humourless portentiousness of his Star Trek character and the listener is ultimately left baffled, wondering if the entire selection is tongue-in-cheek or serious. If the latter, then the results are unintentionally hilarious, cementing it's reputation as a cult classic.

King Henry The Fifth; Elegy For The Brave; Theme From Cyrano; Mr. Tambourine Man; Hamlet; It Was A Very Good Year; Romeo And Juliet; How Insensitive (Insensatez); Spleen; Lucy In The Sky With Diamonds; The Transformed Man.

First released 1972
UK peak chart position: did not chart
USA peak chart position: did not chart

13. METAL MACHINE MUSIC
Lou Reed

One of rock's most controversial releases, *Metal Music Machine* was viewed as artistic suicide by most contemporary reviewers. Fierce electronic passages converge with wailing feedback in a cascade of noise echoing the *avant garde* compositions of Stockhausen, Xenakis and LaMonte Young. The reaction the album generated reflected Reed's position as a 'rock star' - its release followed a period of considerable commercial success - but to interpret determinism as mere self-indulgence is misleading. Reed's work from the Velvet Underground onwards invariably operated at the cutting edge and this departure, however radical, simply showed another facet of a performer who refutes compromise.

Metal Machine Music Parts 1-4.

First released 1975
UK peak chart position: did not chart
USA peak chart position: did not chart

14. LORD SUTCH AND HEAVY FRIENDS
Screaming Lord Sutch

The Rolling Stone review of this record stands as one of the funniest ever published. Permission is not granted for use here, but I agree totally with its content. This is a truly diabolical record full of nifty lead guitar breaks from heavy friends such as Jimmy Page. The track titles speak for themself, 'Gutty Guitar', sounds like a gutty guitar, 'as for 'Wailing Sounds', well. Sutch has built a considerable career on being a chirpy character with brilliant self-publicity. He continues to perform with his Savages and would benefit from a long tour of the USA, where this album made an astonishing no. 84. Maybe if he goes he could make the tour last about 25 years, or thereabouts.

Wailing Sounds; 'Cause I Love You; Flashing Lights; Gutty Guitar; Would You Believe; Smoke And Fire; Thumping Beat; Union Jack Car; One For You, Baby; L-O-N-D-O-N; Brightest Light; Baby, Come Back.

First released 1970
UK peak chart position: did not chart
USA peak chart position: 84

15. UNFINISHED MUSIC NO 2: LIFE WITH THE LIONS
John Lennon & Yoko Ono

The second collaborative album by pop's premier couple exemplified their *avant garde* aspirations. On 'Cambridge 69', recorded live at the city's Lady Mitchell Hall, Lennon's feedback guitar and Yoko's spontaneous vocals were accompanied by free music acolytes John Tchikai (saxophone) and John Stevens (drums). Other, deeply personal, selections chronicled the pairs travails. 'Baby's Heartbeat' was a tangible momento of a child later miscarried, while on 'No Bed For Beatle John', Yoko reads a newspaper story relating Lennon's subsequent stay in hospital beside his partner. Once derided as self-indulgent *Life With The Lions* is now perceived as a brave, experimental statement. Still unlistenable.

Cambridge 1969; No Bed For Beatle John; Baby's Heartbeat; 2 Minutes Silence; Radio Play.

First released 1969
UK peak chart position: did not chart
USA peak chart position: 174

16. JOURNEY THROUGH THE PAST
Neil Young

Taking its title from one of his most introspective compositions, *Journey Through The Past* is the soundtrack to Neil Young's first foray into film work. This highly personal documentary came hard on the heels of the singer's success with *Harvest*, but in now-customary fashion, he refused to court the easy option. The album included a mesmerising pot pourri of material, ranging from rough live performances with his first group, Buffalo Springfield, to background sound drawn from the Beach Boys and Handel's Messiah. In between were some raging in-concert appearances with Crosby, Stills And Nash, notably the lengthy 'Words' and apocalyptic 'Ohio'. Although not an official album per se, *Journey Through The Past* is as revealing and intense as anything else in the artist's canon, but not as good.

For What It's Worth/Mr. Soul; Rock & Roll Woman; Find The Cost Of Freedom; Ohio; Southern Man; Are You Ready For The Country; Let Me Call You Sweetheart; Alabama; Words; Relativity Invitation; Handel's Messiah; King Of Kings; Soldier; Lets's Go Away For Awhile.

First released 1972
UK peak chart position: did not chart
USA peak chart position: 45

17. TRANSFIGURATION OF BLIND JOE DEATH
John Fahey

Drawing inspiration from ethnic American music, notably rural blues, guitarist John Fahey has recorded a succession of superb instrumental albums of which this was his fifth. Never simply a revivalist, Fahey brought elements of classical, folk, Episcopalian and Appalachian styles to his recordings, fusing them together with a distinctive sound and unorthodox tuning patterns. He brought an intense beauty to the form, no more so than on the aching 'Death Of A Clayton Peacock', while simultaneously throwing down a gauntlet for other aspiring acoustic guitarists. William Ackerman, Michael Hedges and Leo Kottke, whom Fahey 'discovered', are among the many musicians who owe him a considerable debt. Lots of late 60s hippies bought this album because it was hip. And have never played it since.

Beautiful Linda Getchell; Orinda-moraga; I Am The Resurrection; On The Sunny Side Of The Ocean; Tell Her To Come Back To Me; My Station Will Be Changed After A While; 101 Is A Hard Road To Travel; How Green Was My Valley; Bicycle Built For Two; Death Of A Clayton Peacock; Brenda's Blues; Old Southern Medley; Come Back Baby; Poor Boy; St. Patrick's Hymn.

First released 1959
UK peak chart position: did not chart
USA peak chart position: did not chart

18. LORD OF THE RINGS
Bo Hansson

For many years, the big fat dog-eared yellow cover paperback of this book was standard baggage at festivals. Millions were sold, and rightly so, it is a major work of considerable importance. It also spawned dozens of Tolkeinesque bands and songs, too many for this entry. Scandinavian composer and keyboardist Bo Hansson went whole hog. He retired to an island off Stockholm and doodled with his synthesizer, probably while reading the book. He then doodled some more, made some interesting sounds, doodled some more, read the book again and doodled some more. The cover is nice, and there is a photo of Tolkein inside the sleeve. The review ends now.

Leaving Shire; The Old Forest; Tom Bombardil; Fog On The Barrow; Downs; The Black Riders; Flight To The Ford; At The House Of Elrond; The Ring Goes South; A Journey In The Dark; Lothlorien; The Horns Of The Pelennor Fields; Dreams In The House Of Hearing; Homeward Bound; The Scouring Of The Shire; The Grey Havens.

First released 1973
UK peak chart position: did not chart
USA peak chart position: 154

19. APPROXIMATELY INFINITE UNIVERSE
Yoko Ono

Often cited as the first true feminist album, although Yoko upset a lot of her sisters with some of the lyrics, notably on the Elephants Memory accompanied 'What A Bastard The World Is' in which she chucks her man out only to bemoan the fact. The vicious anti-male 'Catman' threatens to castrate while on 'What A Mess' she compares anti-abortion with no more masturbation (for men). The one rocker is a joy; 'Move On Fast' and this for all its faults is a mainstream pop album.

Yang Yang; Death Of Samantha; I Want My Love To Rest Tonight; What Did I Do; Have You Seen The Horizon Lately; Approximately Infinite Universe; Peter The Dealer; Song For John; Catman; What A Bastard The World Is; Waiting For The Sunrise; I Felt Like Smashing My Face In A Clear Glass Window; Winter Song, Kite Song; What A Mess, Shirankatta; Air Talk; I Have A Woman Inside My Soul; Move On Fast; Now Or Never; Is Winter Here To Stay; Looking Over From My Window.

First released 1973
UK peak chart position: did not chart
USA peak chart position: did not chart

20. LIVE AT MAX'S KANSAS CITY
Velvet Underground

'Excuse me can I have a Pernod, get me a Pernod'. Whoever he is, wherever he his he must realise by now, his boorish demands for a bloody Pernod ruined the illegal cassette taping of this ramshackle gig. Had it been proffessionally recorded, the sound would be much better, although the guitars would still be out of tune and the drums would be playing a different song. Wonderful but unlistenable because every time it is played the desire to punch the Pernod charecter on the nose manifests itself. Will the offender please own up.

I'm Waiting For The Man; Sweet Jane; Lonesome Cowboy Bill; Beginning To See The Light; I'll Be Your Mirror; Pale Blue Eyes; Sunday Morning; New Age; Femme Fatale; After Hours.

First released 1974
UK peak chart position: did not chart
USA peak chart position: did not chart

THE TOP 20 FILM SOUNDTRACKS

IN RECENT YEARS IT IS THE 'GREAT COMPILATION' THAT MAKES FILM MUSIC SO MEMORABLE. IN THE PAST IT WAS THE FILM OF THE MUSICAL, TRANSFERRED FROM A WOODEN STAGE TO THE WONDERS OF WIDE-SCREEN TODD AO. *THE BLUES BROTHERS* AND *EASY RIDER'S* GREATNESS WAS ENHANCED BY THE MUSICAL CONTENT, BUT *OKLAHOMA!* AND *SOUTH PACIFIC* STOLE OUR HEARTS.

1. WEST SIDE STORY
Various

Electrifying on stage and screen - and just as exciting in superb stereo on this sensational album featuring Natalie Wood, Richard Beymer, Rita Moreno, Russ Tamblyn and George Chakiris. The singing voices of the first three of those artists were dubbed at various times by Marni Nixon, Jim Bryant and Betty Wand respectively, and they more than lived up to the challenge of Leonard Bernstein and Stephen Sondheim's dynamic and breathtaking score. The figures are staggering: US: 144 weeks in the Top 40, 54 of them at number 1; UK: 175 weeks in the Top 20, including 13 at number 1. Plus a US Grammy for best soundtrack album.

West Side Story - Prologue; Jet Song; Something's Coming; Dance At The Gym (Blues Promenade Jump); Maria; Tonight; America; Cool; One Hand, One Heart; Tonight; The Rumble; I Feel Pretty; Somewhere; Gee Officer Krupke; A Boy Like That; I Have A Love; West Side Story - Finale.

First released 1962
UK peak chart position: 1
USA peak chart position: 1

2. OKLAHOMA!
Various

Twelve years after it opened on Broadway, Richard Rodgers and Oscar Hammerstein II's first musical burst on to the screen in the Todd-AO wide-screen process with a fine cast which included Gordon MacRae, Shirley Jones, Charlotte Greenwood, Rod Steiger, Gloria Grahame, Gene Nelson and James Whitmore. All the marvellous songs heard in the stage production are here, with the highlights being 'Oh, What A Beautiful Mornin'', 'The Surrey With The Fringe On Top'. 'People Will Say We're In Love', and the rousing title number. A spell of over four years in the US charts (four weeks at number 1) says it all.

Oklahoma Overture; Oh What A Beautiful Morning; Surrey With The Fringe On Top; Kansas City; I Can't Say No; Many A New Day; People Will Say We're In Love; Poor Jud Is Dead; Out Of My Dreams; Farmer And The Cowman; All Er Nothin'; Oklahoma.

First released 1955
UK peak chart position: 4
USA peak chart position: 1

3. WOODSTOCK
Various

There will be a CD box set of all the Woodstock albums, plus many previously unreleased items. Until that arrives this album stands as the best live rock festival soundtrack. The story behind the festival is well known but the suggestion by Atlantic's marketing man Johnny Bienstock that 'you should put it out as a triple' was brave and bold. It worked of course, and thankfully CD allows us to listen instead of changing sides. The best moments are here; Santana, 'Evil Ways', John Sebastian charming the crowd and the cataclysmic Joe Cocker with his stunning 'With A Little Help From My Friends'

At The Hop; Coming Into Los Angeles; Dance To The Music; Drug Store Truck Drivin' Man; The Fish Cheer (medley); Freedom; Going Up The Country; I-Feel-Like-I'm-Fixin'-To-Die Rag (medley); I Had A Dream; I Want To Take You Higher; I'm Going Home; Joe Hill; Love March; Music Lover (medley); Purple Haze (medley); Rainbows All Over Your Blues; Rock And Soul Music; Sea Of Madness; Soul Sacrifice; Star Spangled Banner (medley); Suite: Judy Blue Eyes; Wooden Ships; We're Not Gonna Take It; With A Little Help From My Friends; Crowd Rain Chant; Volunteers.

First released 1970
UK peak chart position: 35
USA peak chart position: 1

4. SOUTH PACIFIC
Various

The blockbuster film starring Mitzi Gaynor, Rossano Brazzi and John Kerr spawned this record-breaking album full of some of Richard Rodgers and Oscar Hammerstein II's most popular songs. Opera singer Giorgio Tozzi dubbed for Brazzi's singing voice on the beautiful 'Some Enchanted Evening' and others, but Mitzi Gaynor provided her own vocals on songs such as the famous 'I'm Gonna Wash That Man Right Outa My Hair', 'I'm In Love With A Wonderful Guy', and the delightful 'Honey Bun'. The statistics are frightening: US: 161 weeks in the chart, 31 of them at number 1; UK: a total of 115 weeks at number 1, 70 of them consecutively. The UK figures are (to date) a record.

South Pacific Overture; Dites Moi; Cockeyed Optimist; Twin Soliloquies; Some Enchanted Evening; Bloody Mary; There Is Nothin' Like A Dame; Bali Ha'i; I'm Gonna Wash That Man Right Outa My Hair; I'm In Love With A Wonderful Guy; Younger Than Springtime; This Is How It Feels; Entr'acte; Happy Talk; Honey Bun; You've Got To Be Carefully Taught; This Nearly Was Mine.

First released 1958
UK peak chart position: 1
USA peak chart position: 1

5. THE SOUND OF MUSIC
Various

A massive hit around the world, this album from the soundtrack of the multi Oscar-winning film was especially successful in the USA (165 weeks in the chart), and in the UK, where it spent an incredible 381 weeks among the top albums - 70 of them in the number 1 spot. Julie Andrews and Christopher Plummer are the stars, and two songs on this recording, 'I Have Confidence In Me' and 'Something Good', were written especially for the film by Richard Rodgers following the death of Oscar Hammerstein II with whom he wrote the original stage score.

Prelude; Overture And Preludium; Morning Hymn And Alleluia; Maria; I Have Confidence In Me; Sixteen Going On Seventeen; My Favourite Things; Climb Every Mountain; The Lonely Goatherd; Do-re-mi; Something Good; Processional And Maria; Climb Every Mountain; Edelweiss.

First released 1965
UK peak chart position: 1
USA peak chart position: 1

6. EASY RIDER
Various

a. Several films have captured the mood of a generation; *Easy Rider* chronicled the dying embers of the hippie dream. Plot and characterisation apart, its appeal is also due to a carefully structured soundtrack which not only enhanced the celluloid imagery, but stands as a strong collection in its own right. Material is drawn from a wide range of artists and musical styles, be it the Byrds' superior folk-rock, the proto-heavy metal of Steppenwolf, the orchestrated Mass of the Electric Prunes or the hallucinogenic madness of the Holy Modal Rounders. Late-60s rock in microcosm, the set is a brilliant snapshot in time. The only gripe remains in choosing McGuinn's solo 'Ballad Of Easy Rider' over the superior band effort. Easily the best album of its type.

The Pusher - Steppenwolf; Born To Be Wild - Steppenwolf; The Weight - Band; I Wasn't Born To Follow - Byrds; If You Want To Be A Bird - Holy Modal Rounders; Don't Bogart Me - Fraternity Of Man; If Six Was Nine - Jimi Hendrix Experience; Kyrie Eleison Mardi Gras - Electric Prunes; It's Alright Ma (I'm Only Bleeding) - Roger McGuinn; Ballad Of East Rider - Roger McGuinn.

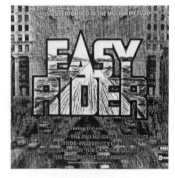

First released 1969
UK peak chart position: 2
USA peak chart position: 6

7. SATURDAY NIGHT FEVER
Various

One of these days there will be an early 70s disco revival and white suits with massive flares will be the order of the day. Whilst this album's success drove people mad as punk's enemy in the late 70s it is now seen as a great piece of musical history. The Bee Gees did write some excellent songs on this but there is further perfect disco soul from Yvonne Elliman ('If I Can't Have You'), Tavares and Kool And The Gang. This is one soundtrack that is better than the film, in that it is easier to listen to than watch.

Stayin' Alive; How Deep Is Your Love; Night Fever; Jive Talkin'; You Should Be Dancing; More Than A Woman; Calypso Breakdown; If I Can't Have You; A Fifth Of Beethoven; Open Sesame; Boogie Shoes; MFSB; K. Jee; Disco Inferno; Manhattan Skyline; Night On Disco Mountain; Salsation.

First released 1978
UK peak chart position: 1
USA peak chart position: 1

8. THE HARDER THEY COME
Various

a. The soundtrack to the groundbreaking film about Jamaican subcultures, this superb selection is also a synthesis of late 60s and early 70s reggae. Recordings by Jimmy Cliff, the movie's star, form the album's core and his contributions, notably 'Many Rivers To Cross', show his understated power to great effect. An important figure in the development of reggae, Cliff at last secured deserved acclaim with this collection. His work is ably supported by 'Pressure Drop', one of the finest songs the Maytals ever cut, while the Melodians and Slickers prove equally strong. The latter's 'Johnny Too Bad' perfectly encapsulates the film's plot, one which helped launch Reggae into the international arena.

You Can Get It If You Really Want It- Jimmy Cliff; Many Rivers To Cross - Jimmy Cliff; The Harder They Come - Jimmy Cliff; Sitting In Limbo - Jimmy Cliff; Draw Your Brakes - Scotty; Rivers Of Babylon - Melodians; Sweet And Dandy - Maytals; Pressure Drop - Maytals; Johnny Too Bad - Slickers; Shanty Town - Desmond Dekker.

First released 1972
UK peak chart position: did not chart
USA peak chart position: 140

9. A CLOCKWORK ORANGE
Various

The most difficult album in the book; is it pop or is it classical? The Editor rules that because it was a popular culture film and it does at least include one pop classic - Gene Kelly with 'Singin' In The Rain' it must qualify. Quite apart from the fact that it was to be found on the shelves of every rock fan in the early 70s it is mainly classical with an interlude of 'I Want To Marry A Lighthouse Keeper' and the fitting synthesizer work of Wendy (formerly Walter) Carlos. Beethoven's sales picked up after this film.

Title Music From A Clockwork Orange; The Thieving Magpie (Abridged); Theme From A Clockwork Orange (Beethoviana); Ninth Symphony, Second Movement (Abridged); March From A Clockwork Orange (Ninth Symphony, Fourth Movement) (Abridged); William Tell Overture (Abridged); Pomp And Circumstance March No. I; Pomp And Circumstance March No. IV (Abridged); Timesteps (Excerpt); Overture To The Sun; I Want To Marry A Lighthouse Keeper; William Tell Overture (Abridged); Suicide Scherzo (Ninth Symphony, Second Movement) (Abridged); Ninth Symphony, Fourth Movement) (Abridged); Singin' In The Rain.

First released 1972
UK peak chart position: 4
USA peak chart position: 34

10. OLIVER!
Various

Ron Moody recreates his magnificent stage performance as Fagin on this soundtrack album of what must be the best British musical film ever. Shani Wallis replaced Georgia Brown as Nancy, and, together with Mark Lester (Oliver), Jack Wild (Artful Dodger) and Oliver Reed (the sinister Bill Sikes), gives Lionel Bart's marvellous score the full treatment. Highlights are impossible to select, but Oliver's tender 'Where Is Love?' and Fagin's 'You've Got To Pick A Pocket Or Two' linger in the memory, but the complete set is as fresh now as when it was released over 25 years ago.

Overture; Food Glorious Food; Boy For Sale; Where Is Love?; You've Got To Pick A Pocket Or Two; Consider Yourself; I'd Do Anything; Be Back Soon; As Long As He Needs Me; Who Will Buy; It's A Fine Life; Reviewing The Situation; Oom Pah Pah; Finale.

First released 1968
UK peak chart position: 4
USA peak chart position: 20

11. BLUES BROTHERS
Various

A film that stands up to repeated viewing is complimented by an album that has the same effect. The musical stars make cameos to perform one track each, Aretha as the waitress in a diner tears into 'Think' while Cab Calloway dons his best white suit for a spectacular 'Minnie The Moocher'. The 'brothers' are supported by most of Booker T. And The MG's and they deliver some rousing numbers including a bottle throwing 'Rawhide' and a loose 'Gimme Some Lovin''. Ackroyd and Belushi could have become the Sam And Dave of the 80s.

Shake A Tail Feather; Think; Minnie The Moocher; Rawhide; Jailhouse Rock; She Caught The Katy; Gimme Some Lovin'; Old Landmark; Sweet Home Chicago; Peter Gunn; Everybody Needs somebody To Love.

First released 1980
UK peak chart position: 4
USA peak chart position: 13

12. GREASE
Various

Three of the first four tracks on this double album, 'Summer Nights', 'Hopelessly Devoted To You' and 'You're The One That I Want', all went on to become big hits in the US and UK for the new disco sensation John Travolta and his co-star Olivia Newton-John. Frank Valli also took the title song into the upper reaches of charts all over the world. As for this album, it lingered for 12 weeks at number 1 in America, and topped the British chart for a lucky 13. Even in the 90s several of these tracks are still guaranteed floor-fillers at many a party night.

Grease - Frankie Valli; Summer Nights - John Travolta/Olivia Newton-John; Hopelessly Devoted To You - Olivia Newton-John; Sandy - John Travolta; Look At Me, I'm Sandra Dee - Stockard Channing; Greased Lightning - John Travolta; It's Raining On Prom Night - Cindy Bullens; You're The One That I Want - John Travolta/Olivia Newton-John; Beauty School Dropout - Frankie Avalon; Alone At The Drive In Movie - Ernie Watts; Blue Moon - Sha Na Na; Rock 'N' Roll Is Here To Stay - Sha Na Na; Those Magic Changes - Sha Na Na; Hound Dog - Sha Na Na; Born To Hand Jive - Sha Na Na; Tears On My Pillow - Sha Na Na; Mooning - Cindy Bullens; Rock 'N' Roll Party Queen - Louis St. Louis; Freddy My Love - Cindy Bullens; There Are Worst Things I Could Do - Stockard Channing; Look At Me, I'm Sandra Dee (Reprise) - Olivia Newton-John; We Go Together - John Travolta/Olivia Newton-John; Love Is A Many Spendid Thing - Studio Orchestra; Grease (Reprise) - Frankie Valli.

First released 1978
UK peak chart position: 1
USA peak chart position: 1

13. BREAKFAST AT TIFFANY'S
Various

The film starred Audrey Hepburn and George Peppard, but it is Henry Mancini's music that lingers in the memory, particularly the haunting 'Moon River' (lyric by Johnny Mercer). That song won three Grammys (record and song of the year, best arrangement) and the album itself won two more. Mancini also received two Oscars, for 'Moon River' and the film score. The composer's well-known sense of humour is evident in some of the other numbers on this enormously successful set which spent 12 weeks at the top of the US chart and launched Mancini on his distinguished career as one of Hollywood's top music men.

Moon River; Something For Cat; Sally's Tomato; Mr. Yunioshi; The Big Blow-out; Hub Caps And Tail Lights; Breakfast At Tiffany's; Latin Golightly; Loose Caboose; The Big Heist; Moon River Cha Cha.

First released 1962
UK peak chart position: did not chart
USA peak chart position: 1

14. THE KING AND I
Various

Considered by many to be an improvement on the Original Cast album which followed the show's 1951 Broadway production, this record features the unmistakable tones of the definite 'King', Yul Brynner, but his co-star Deborah Kerr's singing voice is skilfully dubbed by one of the undisputed mistresses of that art, Marni Nixon. It's difficult to spot the point at which Kerr stops speaking and Nixon begins singing on lovely songs such as 'Shall We Dance?' and 'Getting To Know You', but, after listening to the score again on the 1993 CD reissue, it's easy to understand the album's long tenure in the UK (103 weeks) and US (178 weeks) best-sellers.

I Whistle A Happy Tune; My Lord And Master; Hello, Young Lovers; March Of The Siamese Children; A Puzzlement; Getting To Know You; We Kiss In A Shadow; I Have Dreamed; Shall I Tell You What I Think Of You?; Something Wonderful; Song Of The King; Shall We Dance?; Something Wonderful.

First released 1956
UK peak chart position: 4
USA peak chart position: 1

15. DOCTOR ZHIVAGO
Various

Having won one of the film's five Oscars for his glorious theme music, Maurice Jarre beat off fierce opposition from fellow composers Henry Mancini and John Barry to grab the Grammy Award for Best Original Score as well. 'Lara's Theme' ('Somewhere My Love') is the piece mostly associated with the album, but every one of the tracks evokes the dramatic events which unfolded during David Lean's superb film of Boris Pasternak's Nobel Prize-winning novel. Just a year after its release, *Doctor Zhivago* had become the best-selling MGM soundtrack of all time - quite an achievement in view of the studio's previous domination in the area of movie musicals.

At The Student Cafe; The Funeral; Komarovsky And Lara's Rendevous; Lara Leaves Yuri; Lara's Theme; Doctor Zhivago; Overture; Revolution; Sventyski's Waltz; Tonya Arrives At Varykino; Yuri Escapes; Yuri Writes A Poem For Lara.

First released 1966
UK peak chart position: 3
USA peak chart position: 1

16. THE BODYGUARD
Various

Not quite a Whitney Houston album, but almost. Few can deny being affected by her cover of Dolly Parton's 'I Will Always Love You', which stayed at the top of the worlds charts for what seemed like years. Kevin Costner and Whitney starred in an unremarkable film that was given strength by the quality of its music. In addition to Houston and the romantic electric piano intros, there are among others, Curtis Stigers blowing madly on Nick Lowe's 'Peace Love And Understanding' and Joe Cocker in fine from with Sass Jordan on the formula rocker 'Trust In Me'.

I Will Always Love You; I Have Nothing; I'm Every Woman; Run To You; Queen Of The Night; Jesus Loves Me; Even If My Heart Would Break; Someday (I'm Coming Back); It's Gonna Be A Lovely Day; (What's So Funny 'Bout) Peace, Love And Understanding; Waiting For You; Trust In Me.

First released 1992
UK peak chart position: 1
USA peak chart position: 1

17. DIRTY DANCING
Various

In the 90s the fashion of selecting a broad palette of songs as a soundtrack reached overkill, it seemed as if directors and producers were equally concerned that their personal favourites were included in addition to having a decent script. *Dirty Dancing* became hugely popular as an album because the choice of oldies was both inspired and varied. Never before (and never again) had Bruce Channel's 'Hey Baby' shared a stage with the Blow Monkeys. In breaking down musical barriers this album deserved a Grammy instead of just the nominated Warnes/Medley theme 'I've Had The Time Of My Life'.

I've Had The Time Of My Life - Bill Medley/Jennifer Warnes; Be My Baby - Ronettes; She's Like The Wind - Patrick Swayze/Wendy Fraser; Hungry Eyes - Eric Carmen; Stay - Maurice Williams And The Zodiacs; Yes - Merry Clayton; You Don't Own Me - Blow Monkeys; Hey Baby - Bruce Channel; Overload - Zappacosta; Love Is Strange - Mickey And Sylvia; Where Are You Tonight? - Tom Johnston; In The Still Of The Night - Five Satins.

First released 1987
UK peak chart position: 4
USA peak chart position: 1

18. GIGI
Various

This rare and beautiful film, which contained Alan Jay Lerner and Frederick Loewe's only original score for the screen, not only won a record-breaking nine Oscars, but its soundtrack album was also the recipient of the first National Academy of Recording Arts and Sciences' (NARAS) 'best original cast' award - more popularly known as a Grammy. Ten weeks at number 1 in the US and a spell of 88 weeks in the UK chart was a fitting tribute to the fine cast headed by Maurice Chevalier, Leslie Caron and Louis Jourdan - and those immortal songs.

Overture; Thank Heaven For Little Girls; Parisians; Waltz At Maxim's; The Night They Invented Champagne; I Remember It Well; Say A Prayer For Me Tonight; I'm Glad I'm Not Young Anymore; Gigi; Finale.

First released 1958
UK peak chart position: 2
USA peak chart position: 1

19. PAINT YOUR WAGON
Various

Several of the songs which survived from Alan Jay Lerner and Frederick Loewe's 1951 stage show were supplemented by others with music by André Previn for this 1969 screen version. Clint Eastwood was in surprisingly good vocal form on two lovely ballads, 'I Still See Elisa' and 'I Talk To The Trees', while Lee Marvin's mumbling, grumbling version of 'Wand'rin' Star' was pulled from the album and shot straight to the top of the UK singles chart. Ace arranger Nelson Riddle was responsible for the orchestral music score, and album won a Gold Disc within a few months of its release.

I'm On My Way; I Still See Elisa; The First Thing You Know; Hand Me Down That Can 'O Beans; They Called The Wind Maria; Million Miles Away Behind The Door; There's A Coach Comin' In; Whoop-ti-ay (Shivaree); I Talk To The Trees; The Gospel Of No Name City; Best Things; Wand'rin' Star; Gold Fever; Finale.

First released 1969
UK peak chart position: 2
USA peak chart position: 28

20. AROUND THE WORLD IN 80 DAYS
Various

Producer Mike Todd persuaded more than 40 major stars, including Frank Sinatra, Marlene Dietrich and Ronald Colman, to contribute cameo roles to this wide-screen treatment of Jule Verne's classic story in which David Niven as Phileas Fogg and his 'man', Passepartout, played by the Mexican comedian Cantiflas, circumnavigate the globe. They were accompanied by veteran composer Victor Young's breathtakingly beautiful musical themes which thrilled record-buyers to such an extent that this album stayed at number 1 in the US for 10 weeks. The composer's Academy Award for his work was a fitting end to a distinguished career which ended a few months after the film's release.

Around The World (main theme); Around The World Part II; Entrance Of The Bull March (medley); Epilogue; India Country Side; Invitation To A Bull Fight (medley); Land Ho; Pagoda Of Pillagi; Paris Arrival; Passepartout; Prairie Sail Car; Sky Symphony.

First released 1957
UK peak chart position: did not chart
USA peak chart position: 1

The Top 20
Stage Musical Albums

Never considered that important in the scheme of things, Stage Musicals are often viewed as the runt of the litter. The lasting appeal of many of the top selections is likely to outlive some of the more contemporary genres. Admittedly many in the list found favour with our American contributors, where 'Musical Theater' is much more popular. There are no surprises in the list, either critically acclaimed with good songs (Mack And Mable or Stop the World I Want To Get Off) or commercially successful with outstanding songs (West Side Story). Only 25% of the list is down to Andrew Lloyd Webber!

1. West Side Story
Original Broadway Cast

Record buyers who hadn't seen the show which opened on Broadway in 1957, could hardly believe their ears when this dramatic, early stereo album reached the stores soon afterwards. Classical composer Leonard Bernstein and newcomer Stephen Sondheim's spellbinding score combined exquisite ballads such as 'Maria' and 'Tonight' with street-wise numbers such as 'Gee, Officer Krupke' and the exhilarating 'America'. Carol Lawrence, Larry Kert and Chita Rivera led the superb young cast, and the album stayed for 120 weeks in the US chart but faired poorly on its UK release. In 1991 it was inducted into the NARAS Hall of Fame.

West Side Story Prologue; Jet Song; Something's Coming; Dance At The Gym (Blues Promenade Jump); Maria; Tonight; America; Cool; One Hand, One Heart; Tonight; The Rumble; I Feel Pretty; Somewhere; Gee, Officer Krupke; A Boy Like That; I Have A Love; West Side Story Finale.

First released 1958
UK peak chart position: 3
USA peak chart position: 5

2. MY FAIR LADY
Original Broadway Cast

In the early 90s this superb album of what some still consider to be the most perfect stage musical ever, had spent a record-breaking 292 weeks in US Top 40 - 15 of them at number 1. It also stayed in the upper reaches of the UK chart for 129 weeks. The album was recorded in mono, and Alan Jay Lerner and Frederick Loewe's wonderful score, and a cast headed by Rex Harrison, Julie Andrews and Stanley Holloway, were not nearly so effective in the subsequent stereo version. Just 10 years after its initial release sales were estimated to be well over six million, and the album was inducted into the NARAS Hall of Fame in 1977.

Overture; Why Can't The English; Wouldn't It Be Loverly?; With A Little Bit Of Luck; I'm An Ordinary Man; Just You Wait; The Rain In Spain; I Could Have Danced All Night; Ascot Gavotte; On The Street Where You Live; You Did It; Show Me; Get Me To The Church On Time; Hymn To Him; Without You; I've Grown Accustomed To Her Face.

First released 1956
UK peak chart position: 2
USA peak chart position: 1

3. THE SOUND OF MUSIC
Original Broadway Cast

Multi-million sales, a spell of 16 weeks at the top of the US chart, and winner of Gold Disc and Grammy Awards, were fitting rewards for this memorable recording of Richard Rodgers and Oscar Hammerstein II's much-loved musical which opened on Broadway in November 1959. The show's stars, Mary Martin and Theodore Bikel, were in fine vocal form, and led the excellent cast through the score's highlights which included 'My Favourite Things', 'Do-Re-Mi', and 'Edelweiss' - the last song that Rodgers and Hammerstein wrote together before the latter's death in 1960.

Preludium; The Sound Of Music; Maria; A Bell Is No Bell; I Have Confidence In Me; Do-Re-Mi; Sixteen Going On Seventeen; My Favourite Things; The Lonely Goatherd; How Can Love Survive; So Long, Farewell; Climb Every Mountain; Something Good; Wedding Sequence; Maria (Reprise); Concert Do-Re-Mi (Reprise); Edelweiss; So Long, Farewell (Reprise); Climb Every Mountain (Reprise).

First released 1960
UK peak chart position: 4
USA peak chart position: 1

4. OLIVER!
Original London Cast

A perfect souvenir of Lionel Bart's celebrated stage musical which was a smash hit in London and on Broadway in the early 60s. All the drama and exuberance of Peter Coe's breathtaking original production is captured perfectly on this album, with stand-out performances from Ron Moody (Fagin), Georgia Brown (Nancy) and Keith Hamshere (Oliver Twist). The 1989 re-issue on CD is a timely reminder that, although there have been many stage revivals over the past 30 years - and an excellent film version in 1968 - this cast laid down the definitive version of Bart's masterpiece.

Food Glorious Food; Oliver; I Shall Scream; Boy For Sale; That's Your Funeral; Where Is Love?; Consider Yourself; You've Got To Pick A Pocket Or Two; It's Fine Life; Be Back Soon; Oom Pah Pah; My Name; As Long As He Needs Me; I'd Do Anything; Who Will Buy?; Reviewing The Situation; Finale.

First released 1960
UK peak chart position: 4
USA peak chart position: did not chart

5. STOP THE WORLD I WANT TO GET OFF
Original London Cast

It wasn't a 'coach party' show, and this album only stayed in the UK chart for 14 weeks, but *Stop The World* proved to be the launching pad for authors and songwriters Anthony Newley and Leslie Bricusse, and remains a remarkable piece of work. Newley and his co-star Anna Quayle share some marvellous songs on this recording, including 'Typically English' and 'Someone Nice Like You', but it's the enormous hits such as 'What Kind Of Fool Am I?', 'Once In A Lifetime', and 'Gonna Build A Mountain', for which the show is inevitably remembered. After more than 30 years, worn-out copies can now be replaced by the 1989 CD reissue.

ABC; I Wanna Be Rich; Typically English; Lumbered; Gonna Build A Mountian; Glorious Russian; Melinki Meilchick; Typische Deutsche; Nag Nag Nag; All-American; Once In A Lifetime; Mumbo Jumbo; Someone Nice Like You; What Kind Of Fool Am I?.

First released 1961
UK peak chart position: 8
USA peak chart position: did not chart

6. THE PHANTOM OF THE OPERA
Original London Cast

As with *Cats*, Andrew Lloyd Webber's Really Useful Group issued a single album of highlights from this show, but that didn't seem to affect sales of this two-CD/LP set which went double platinum shortly after its release. The stars of the show, Michael Crawford, Sarah Brightman and Steve Barton, reprised their roles in the Broadway production, and this album was successful in the US as well as spending more than 100 weeks in the upper reaches of the UK chart. Crawford also had a singles hit with 'The Music Of The Night'.

Phantom Of The Opera (Overture); Think Of Me; Angel Music; Little Lotte; The Mirror; The Phantom Of The Opera; The Music Of The Night; I Remember; Stranger Than You Dreamt It; Magical Lasso; Prima Donna; Poor Fool, He Makes Me Laugh; All I Ask Of You; Entr'acte; Masquerade; Why So Silent; Twisted Every Way; Wishing You Were Somehow Here Again; Wandering Child; The Point Of No Return; Down Once More; Phantom Of The Opera (Finale).

First released 1987
UK peak chart position: 1
USA peak chart position: 33

7. FUNNY GIRL
Original Broadway Cast

The performance of almost overpowering range and depth by Barbra Streisand in her first Broadway starring role as the legendary entertainer Fanny Brice, is captured perfectly on this immensely entertaining album. Jule Styne and Bob Merrill's first score together includes a devastating blend of outrageous comedy numbers and spine-tingling ballads, one of which, 'People', went on to become a singles hit. The song won Streisand a Grammy for best vocal performance, and this album was awarded another Grammy for best cast recording. It also spent a total of 40 weeks in the US Top 40.

Funny Girl Overture; If A Girl Isn't Pretty; I'm The Greatest Star; Cornet Man; Who Taught Her Everything; His Love Makes Me Beautiful; I Want To Be Seen With You Tonight; Henry Street; People; You Are Woman; Don't Rain On My Parade; Sadie Sadie; Find Yourself A Man; Rat-tat-tat-tat; Who Are You Now; The Music That Makes Me Dance; Finale.

First released 1964
UK peak chart position: did not chart
USA peak chart position: 2

8. FIDDLER ON THE ROOF
Original Broadway Cast

A legendary show - still the sixth longest-running Broadway musical in history with a remarkable total of 3,242 performances, and this album does it full justice. The special atmosphere created in the theatre by the stars, Zero Mostel, Maria Karnilova, Beatrice Arthur and Joanna Merlin, comes across strongly here via Jerry Bock and Sheldon Harnick's immortal score with highlights such as 'If I Were A Rich Man', 'Matchmaker, Matchmaker' and 'Sunrise, Sunset'. Sixty weeks in the US Top 40, this album was awarded a Gold Disc in 1965, and eventually sold well in excess of a million.

Tradition; Matchmaker, Matchmaker; If I Were A Rich Man; Sabbath Prayer; Sunrise, Sunset; To Life; Miracle Of Miracles; Tevye's Dream; Now I Have Everything; Do You Love Me?; Far From The Home I Love; Anatevka.

First released 1964
UK peak chart position:did not chart
USA peak chart position: 7

9. HAIR
Original Broadway Cast

The first musical of the hippie peace and love generation, with a score by Gerome Ragni, James Rado and composer Galt MacDermot. The show and the album were quite different to the usual Broadway fare, but songs such as 'Aquarius', 'Good Morning Starshine', 'Let The Sunshine In' and the title number, soon went on to have a life of their own. The album spent 59 weeks in the US Top 40, 13 of them at number 1, and did well in the UK, too. It was also awarded a Grammy for 'best score from an Original Cast album'.

Aquarius; Donna; Hashish; Sodomy; Colored Spade; Manchester, England; I'm Black; Ain't Got No; Air; Initials; I Got Life; Hair; My Conviction; Don't Put It Down; Frank Mills; Be-In; Where Do I Go?; Black Boys; White Boys; Easy To Be Hard; Walking In Space; Abie Baby; Three-Five-Zero-Zero; What A Piece Of Work Is Man; Good Morning Starshine; Flesh Failures (Let The Sunshine In).

First released 1968
UK peak chart position: 29
USA peak chart position: 1

10. THE MUSIC MAN
Original Broadway Cast

Meredith Willson's charming and amusing score benefited from early stereo ('also available in regular monophonic', according to the sleeve), and inspired singing performances, especially from Robert Preston and Barbara Cook. The latter's thrilling voice is particularly effective on 'Goodnight, My Someone' and 'Till There Was You', and Preston has a ball with his *tour de force*, 'Ya Got Trouble'. It all added up to a spell of 123 weeks in the US Top 40, 12 of them at number 1, and the 1958 Grammy award for best Original Cast album.

Overture & Rock Island; Iowa Stubborn; Ya Got Trouble; Piano Lesson; Goodnight, My Someone; Seventy-six Trombones; Sincere; Sadder But Wiser Girl For Me; Pick-a-little, Take-a-little & Goodnight Ladies; Marian The Librarian; My White Knight; Wells Fargo Wagon; It's You; Shipoopi; Lida Rose & Will I Ever Tell You; Gary, Indiana; Till There Was You; Finale.

First released 1958
UK peak chart position:did not chart
USA peak chart position: 1

11. JOSEPH AND THE AMAZING TECHNICOLOR DREAMCOAT
1991 London Cast

Seventy three minutes of playing time from a show that originally ran for some 15-20 minutes, means that this album must be a recording of a contemporary production of Andrew Lloyd Webber and Tim Rice's biblical musical. In fact, it is from the highly successful 1991 London Palladium revival which starred Australian actor and pop star Jason Donovan as Joseph and Linzi Hateley as the Narrator. Donovan had a UK number 1 with 'Any Dream Will Do', and the album itself also topped the chart. Nine months after its release it was reported to have sold 500,000 copies.

Jacob And Sons; Joseph's Dreams; Poor, Poor Joseph; One More Angel In Heaven; Potiphar; Close Every Door; Go Go Go Joseph; Pharaoh Story; Poor Poor Pharaoh; Pharaoh's Dreams Explained; The Brothers Come To Egypt; Benjamin Calypso; Joseph All The Time; Jacob In Egypt; Stone The Crows; Those Canaan Days; Any Dream Will Do; Grovel Grovel; Song Of The King; Who's The Thief?.

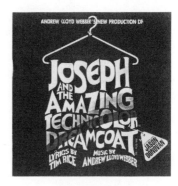

First released 1991
UK peak chart position: 1
USA peak chart position: did not chart

12. HELLO, DOLLY!
Original Broadway Cast

Carol Channing had her greatest Broadway role (to date) in this hit Broadway show, and her scatty style and unmistakable squeaky voice came over perfectly on this album. The many highlights from Jerry Herman's stunning score included the tender 'It Only Takes A Moment' and 'Put On Your Sunday Clothes', but it was the title number, a good old fashioned rouser, which won the Grammy for song of the year - in the middle of the beat boom! The album itself lingered for 58 weeks in the US Top 40, peaking at number 1.

I Put My Hand In; It Takes A Woman; Put On Your Sunday Clothes; Ribbons Down My Back; Dancing; Motherhood March; Before The Parade Passes By; Elegance; Hello, Dolly!; It Only Takes A Moment; So Long Dearie; Hello Dolly Finale.

First released 1964
UK peak chart position: did not chart
USA peak chart position: 1

13. SHOW BOAT
Broadway Cast

Some acclaimed recordings were made of the 1932 Broadway production of Jerome Kern and Oscar Hammerstein II's masterpiece which reunited most of those who were in the 1927 original, with the important addition of Paul Robeson. However, this album features the cast of the 1946 revival, which, according to Hammerstein's sleeve note, was 'as fine a group as in the first company'. Kenneth Spencer plays the Robeson role and gives an inspired rendering of the classic 'Ol' Man River'. The principals include Carol Bruce, Charles Fredericks, and Jan Clayton who introduces a new song, the delightful 'Nobody Else But Me'. Felicitations to Sony Broadway for re-releasing the set on CD in 1993.

Tracks: Overture; Cotton Blossom; Make Believe; Ol' Man River; Can't Help Lovin' Dat Man; Life Upon The Wicked Stage; You Are Love; Why Do I Love You?; Bill; Nobody Else But Me.

First released 1946
UK peak chart position: did not chart
USA peak chart position: did not chart

14. CAMELOT
Original Broadway Cast

Alan Jay Lerner and Frederick Loewe's follow-up to their enormously successful *My Fair Lady*, a musical adaptation of the Arthurian legend, was full of amusing and romantic numbers which are recreated perfectly on this album. Highlights include Julie Andrews' 'I Loved Him Once In Silence', Richard Burton's 'How To Handle A Woman', and a lovely version 'If Ever I Would Leave You' by Robert Goulet. Although unable to match the dizzy heights of *My Fair Lady*, this record spent a worthy 151 weeks in the US Top 40, six of them at number 1, and sold more than the London cast version in the UK.

Camelot Overture; I Wonder What The King Is Doing Tonight?; The Simple Joys Of Maidenhood; Camelot; Follow Me; The Lusty Month Of May; C'est Moi; Then You May Take Me To The Fair; How To Handle A Woman; If Ever I Would Leave You; Parade; Before I Gaze At You Again; The Seven Deadly Virtues; What Do You Simple Folk Do?; Fie On Goodness; I Loved Him Once In Silence; Guenevere; Camelot Finale.

First released 1961
UK peak chart position: 10
USA peak chart position: 1

15. FLOWER DRUM SONG
Original Broadway Cast

Record producer Goddard Lieberson, who was responsible for so many fine Columbia Original Cast recordings in the early days, supervised this superb recording of the hit Broadway show. Miyoshi Umeki, Larry Blyden, Juanita Hall and Pat Suzuki head the cast, and Richard Rodgers and Oscar Hammerstein's lovely score contains the memorable 'Sunday', 'Love, Look Away', and the joyful 'I Enjoy Being A Girl'. The album spent 67 weeks in the US Top 40, three of them at number 1, and also did well in the UK when the show opened there in 1960.

Overture; You Are Beautiful; A Hundred Million Miracles; I Enjoy Being A Girl; I Am Going To Like It Here; Like A God; Chop Suey; Don't Marry Me; Grant Avenue; Love, Look Away; Fan Tan Fannie; Gliding Through My Memoree; The Other Genberation; Sunday; Finale.

First released 1960
UK peak chart position: 2
USA peak chart position: 1

16. EVITA
Studio Cast

After their tremendous success with the concept album of *Jesus Christ Superstar* in the early 70s, Andrew Lloyd Webber and Tim Rice did it again with this double album set which spent 35 weeks in the upper reaches of the UK chart in 1977. Paul Jones, Barbara Dickson, Tony Christie and Julie Covington were the star singers, and the latter had a UK number 1 with her dramatic version of the haunting 'Don't Cry For Me Argentina'. Dickson also made the Top 20 with the poignant ballad, 'Another Suitcase In Another Hall'.

Actress Hasn't Learned The Lines (You'd Like To Hear); And The Money Kept Rolling In (And Out); Another Suitcase In Another Hall; Art Of The Possible Buenos Aires; Charity Concert (medley); Cinema In Buenos Aires, 26 July 1952; Dice Are Rolling; Don't Cry For Me Argentina; Eva And Magaldi; Eva Beware Of The City; Eva's Final Broadcast; Goodnight And Thank You; High Flying, Adored; I'd Be Surprisingly Good For You; Lament; Montage; New Argentina; Oh What A Circus; On The Balcony Of The Casa Rosada; On This Night Of A Thousand Stars; Peron's Latest Flame; Rainbow High; Rainbow Tour; Requiem For Evita; Santa Evita; She Is A Diamond; Waltz For Eva And Che.

First released 1976
UK peak chart position: 4
USA peak chart position: did not chart

17. MACK AND MABEL
Original Broadway Cast

As so often is the case, this was an appealing score from a flop show. At least it gives some indication of Robert Preston and Bernadette Peters' fine performances as Mack Sennett and Mabel Normand, and preserves Jerry Herman's lovely songs which included 'I Won't Send Roses', 'When Mabel Comes Into The Room', and 'I Wanna Make The World Laugh'. In the 80s ice dancers Torvill and Dean used the (partly edited) overture for their Olympic programme, and that exposure, coupled with repeated plays on BBC Radio 2, caused the album to enter the UK Top 40.

Overture; Movies Were Movies; Look What Happened To Mabel; Big Time; I Won't Send Roses; I Wanna Make The World Laugh; Wherever He Ain't; Hundreds Of Girls; When Mabel Comes Into The Room; My Heart Leaps Up; Time Heals Everything; Tap Your Troubles Away; I Promise You A Happy Ending.

First released 1974
UK peak chart position: 38
USA peak chart position: did not chart

18. GODSPELL
Original Broadway Cast

This light folk-rock musical based upon the gospel according to St. Matthew was highly successful in the 70s in London and New York. This recording is from the Broadway production which starred Stephen Nathan and David Haskell. Stephen Schwartz's score included the appealing 'Day By Day' which became a singles hit in the US for the show's cast with lead vocal by Robin Lamont. The album itself, which was produced by Schwartz, stayed in the US Top 40 for 12 weeks and won a Grammy for best score from an original cast.

Prepare Ye The Way Of The Lord; Save The People; Day By Day; Learn Your Lessons Well; Bless The Lord; All For The Best; All Good Gifts; Light Of The World; Turn Back O Man; Alas For You; By My Side; We Beseech Thee; On The Willows; Finale; Day By Day/Prepare Ye (reprise).

First released 1972
UK peak chart position: did not chart
USA peak chart position: 34

19. THE PAJAMA GAME
Original Broadway Cast

Broadway newcomers Richard Adler and Jerry Ross wrote the marvellous score for this show which ran for well over 1,000 performances in New York. Who could have foreseen that the subject of a strike in a pajama factory would produce great songs such as 'Hey, There', 'I'm Not At All In Love', 'Small Talk', and 'Hernando's Hideaway'. That fine singer, John Raitt, leads the cast which includes Janis Paige, Carol Haney, and Eddie Foy Jnr. Every track, whether witty, romantic, or down-right hilarious, is appealing on this enduring and memorable album.

Overture; The Pajama Game; Racing With The Clock; A New Town Is A Blue Town; I'm Not At All In Love; I'll Never Be Jealous Again; Hey, There; Her Is; Once A Year Day; Small Talk; There Once Was A Man; Steam Heat; Think Of The Time I Save; Hernando's Hideaway; Seven And A Half Cents; Finale.

First released 1955
UK peak chart position: did not chart
USA peak chart position: did not chart

20. Cats
Original London Cast

Andrew Lloyd Webber's longest-running show to date in London and on Broadway even merited a record containing just highlights from his intriguing and popular score. However, this one is the real McCoy - the double album full of those songs mostly named after poet T.S. Eliot's marvellous feline characters. The odd one out, with a more conventional title, is 'Memory', which provided a spine-tingling moment in the theatre each night when it was sung by Elaine Paige, and has the same effect here. She took it into the UK Top 10, and the album itself went platinum not long after release.

Jellicle Songs For Jellicle Cats; Old Gumbie Cat; Naming Of Cats; The Rum Rum Tugger; Grizabella; Bustopher Jones; Memory; Mungojerrie And Rumpleteazer; Old Deuteronomy; Moments Of Happiness; Gus, Theatre Cat; Cats; Overture/Prologue; Invitation To The Jellicle Ball; The Jellicle Ball; The Journey To The Heavy Side; The Ad-dressing Of Cats; Growltiger's Last Stand; The Ballad Of Billy McCaw's Skimbleshanks; Macavity; Mr. Mistoffolees.

First released 1981
UK peak chart position: 6
USA peak chart position: did not chart

10 ALBUMS DESTINED TO BECOME CLASSICS

THE MOST SUBJECTIVE LIST IN THE BOOK. IT ATTEMPTS TO REFLECT WHAT HAS BEEN ACCLAIMED IN RECENT MONTHS. MANY OF THESE ALBUMS ARE LIKELY TO GAIN STRENGTH BEFORE THE NEXT EDITION IS PREPARED. THIS LIST ALSO HIGHLIGHTS THE FACT THAT THE DINOSAUR ALBUM IS NOT NECESSARILY SACRED AS THE NEW GENERATION NOW LISTEN BEFORE THEY DECIDE.

1. IN UTERO
Nirvana

IN UTERO

First released 1993
UK peak chart position: 1
USA peak chart position: 1

And now he has gone and done his final act Cobain will now assume Morrison like status, which is a little out of balance with only three proper albums under their belt to the Doors output. Taken as a rock band they are the phenomenon of the 90s both important and successful. Their penchant for romanticising death is being followed with pied piper regularity. Their ability to shock was far better than any of the new wave followers. It was only the troubled Cobain who could write songs such as 'Rape Me' (an anti rape song!) and 'Heart-Shaped Box' with real conviction.

Serve The Servants; Scentless Apprentice; Heart-Shaped Box; Rape Me; Frances Farmer Will Have Her; Revenge On Seattle; Dumb; Very Ape; Milk It; Pennyroyal Tea; Radio Friendly Unit Shifter; Tourette's; All Apologies; Gallons Of Rubbing Alcohol Flow Through The Strip.

2. WHATEVER
Aimee Mann

Maybe the end of her relationship with Jules Shear gave Ms Mann a real kick to her songs, certainly the energy and the powerful lyrics succeed where *'Til Tuesday* failed. This won many critics over in 1993 both old and young - those of us who love anything that sounds like the Byrds and others who see guitar indie pop as an extension of punk. Whatever, the album is a corker and memorable tracks such as 'I Should Have Known', 'Fifty Years After The Fair' and 'Stupid Thing' are classic quality guitar pop. P.S. Roger McGuinn guests on guitar as well.

I Should've Known; Fifty Years After The Fair; 4th Of July; Could've Been Anyone; Put Me On Top; Stupid Thing; Say Anything; Jacob Marley's Chain; Mr Harris; I Could Hurt You Now; I Know There's A Word; I've Had It; Way Back When.

First released 1993
UK peak chart position: 39
USA peak chart position: did not chart

3. IN PIECES
Garth Brooks

The phenomenon that is Garth Brooks makes a substantial showing in the country list, this is his latest album which is destined to walk into those lists in time. This is irresistible popular country that reaches out beyond the C&W market. The press have tried to find something negative to say about Brooks, but other than the fact that he's a bit overweight and slightly religious they have no scam on him. He is as clean as his superb voice which tackle a country rocker like 'The Night I Called The Old Man Out' or the tearjerker ballad 'One Night A Day'.

Standing Outside The Fire; The Night I Called The Old Man Out; American Honky-Tonk Bar Association; One Night A Day; Kickin' And Screamin'; Ain't Going Down (Til The Sun Comes Up); The Red Strokes; Callin' Baton Rouge; The Night Will Only Know; The Cowboy Song.

First released 1993
UK peak chart position: 2
USA peak chart position: 1

4. Vs
Pearl Jam

The second album from Pearl Jam saw them break attempt to establish their own identity - previously they had trailed in the wake of Nirvana as 'Seattle's other band'. If *Ten* had seen them arrive from nowhere, then by the advent of this follow-up everyone knew who they were. The album entered the US chart at number 1, and recorded the highest one week sales total in history. After which a critical commentary on the merits or otherwise of the album is rendered utterly irrelevant. It was, however, another rock solid performance, substituting *Ten*'s verve for greater coherence.

Go; Animal; Daughter; Glorified G; Dissident; WMA; Blood; Rearviewmirror; Rats; Elderly Woman Behind The Counter In A Small Town; Leash; Indifference.

First released 1993
UK peak chart position: 2
USA peak chart position: 1

5. COME ON AND FEEL THE LEMONHEADS
Lemonheads

The darlings of the music press for 1993 along with the late Kurt Cobain, specifically their leader Evan Dando who definitely has that 'yes' factor that makes people want to write about him. This album was greatly anticipated after the promising signs shown with *Its A Shame About Ray*, and it lives up to expectations with a collection of short, mostly happy, well played but deadly infectious melodies. Some of Dando's riffs stay with you for weeks which like the Undertones, Buzzcocks and early Jam make this kind of pop so damn good. It is hoped that Dando never gets too complicated.

The Great Big No; Into Your Arms; It's About Time; Down About It; Paid To Smile; Big Gay Heart; Style; Rest Assured; Dawn Can't Decide; I'll Do It Anyway; Rick James Style; Being Around; Favorite T; You Can Take It With You; The Jello Fund.

First released 1993
UK peak chart position: 5
USA peak chart position: 56

6. GOD SHUFFLED HIS FEET
Crash Test Dummies

Out of Canada came a band with originality, something often lacking in the 90s. The band's two great strengths are the remarkable deep, resonant voice of Brad Roberts, one to make wine glasses walk off tables. The second is the seemingly flippant but brilliantly thought provoking lyrics. On the title track for example 'After seven days God said "let there be a day just for picnics with wine and bread"' or other gems like 'someday I'll have a disappearing hairline, someday I'll wear pyjamas in the daytime'. And they even get away with a chorus that goes 'mmmm mmmm mmmm mmmm'.

God Shuffled His Feet; Afternoons And Coffeespoons; Mmm Mmm Mmm Mmm; In The Days Of The Caveman; Swimming In Your Ocean; Here I Stand Before Me; I Think I'll Disappear Now; How Does A Duck Know?; When I Go Out With Artists; The Psychic; Two Knights And Maidens.

First released 1994
UK peak chart position: 2
USA peak chart position: 9

7. WILD WOOD
Paul Weller

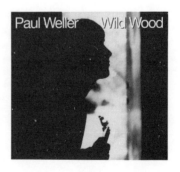

Long-standing Weller fans were overjoyed with this, the album he has been threatening to make for years. Taking his punk/pop roots and mixing it together with a late 60s prog/pop (Traffic spring to mind) not only put him back in the charts but once again he was courted favourably by the fickle pop press. Weller plays with anger and energy but never loses the melody, for example the opener 'Sunflower' which is held together by the repeated 'I miss you so' hook. The strong feeling that comes over is that the wonder from Woking knew this was a great album.

Sunflower; Can You Heal Us (Holy Man); Wild Wood; Instrumental (part 1); All The Pictures On The Wall; Has My Fire Really Gone Out?; Country Instrumental Two; 5th Season; The Weaver; Instrumental (part 2); Foot Of The Mountain; Shadow Of The Sun; Holy Man (Reprise); Moon On Your Pyjamas.

First released 1993
UK peak chart position: 2
USA peak chart position: did not chart

8. TEN SUMMONERS TALES
Sting

Mr 'sheer profundity' delivered a stunning fourth solo album that probably surprised himself as well as the critics who were prepared to watch his fall from grace after the seeming failure of the intense *The Soul Cages*. Right from the opener 'If I Ever Lose My Faith In You' the album holds its pace. That track will be seen as a classic in years to come as will the beautiful 'Fields Of Gold' and 'Shape Of My Heart'. Sting is established as a major artist with a solo career that has now eclipsed his former supergroup.

Prologue (If I Ever Lose My Faith In You); Love Is Stronger Than Justice (The Munificent Seven); Fields Of Gold; Heavy Cloud No Rain; She's Too Good For Me; Seven Days; Saint Augustine In Hell; It's Probably Me; Everybody Laughed But You; Shape Of My Heart; Something The Boy Said; Epilogue (Nothing 'Bout Me).

First released 1993
UK peak chart position: 2
USA peak chart position: 2

9. TUESDAY NIGHT MUSIC CLUB
Sheryl Crow

Her previous credentials included co-writing with Eric Clapton and suddenly she steps forward and delivers an album of breathtaking maturity that it sounds as if she has been making albums forever. Furthermore she also sounds like we have been listening to her for 20 years. Not so, this is a debut and one that will last; from full bodied anguish of 'Run, Baby, Run' to the cutesy Ricky Lee Jones voice on 'All I Wanna Do'. Her lyrics are honest, original and never dull wrapped around immediate songs. She is a notable 'new' talent being willed to succeed.

Run, Baby, Run; Leaving Las Vegas; Strong Enough; Can't Cry Anymore; Solidify; No One Said It Would Be Easy; What I Can Do For You; All I Wanna Do; We Do What We Can; I Shall Believe.

First released 1993
UK peak chart position: did not chart1
USA peak chart position: 94

10. AUGUST & EVERYTHING AFTER
Counting Crows

The Michael Stipe of this exciting new outfit from California is Adam Duritz whose dreadlocks and pained expressions belie his youth. He does sing and write some pretty good and intense songs. This album is still high on the US chart at the time of writing but it can only be a matter of before irresistible tracks such as 'Omaha' and 'Mr Jones' find wider acceptance. Duritz is clearly a major talent but it is hoped that this sparkling debut is not his best shot. For the record this is a better debut than R.E.M. and look what happened to them.

Round Here; Omaha; Mr. Jones; Perfect Blue Building; Anna Begins; Time And Time Again; Rain King; Sullivan Street; Ghost Train; Raining In Baltimore; A Murder Of One.

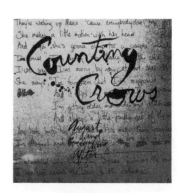

First released 1994
UK peak chart position: 16
USA peak chart position: 4

THE TOP 10
NEW AGE ALBUMS

THE COMMERCIAL SUCCESS OF WINDHAM HILL RECORDS AND THE POPULARIST ENYA DOMINATE THIS SMALL LIST. NEW AGE DID NOT QUITE FULFIL THE FAITH THE MAJOR RECORD LABELS HAD IN IT AND THE DEDICATED SECTIONS IN THE RECORD STORES ARE NOW TUCKED AWAY. ONE UNKIND CRITIC CALLED IT MUSIC FOR EMBALMING TO, IF THAT MEANS IT IS RELAXING, THEN ITS INTENTION WAS WHOLLY SUCCESSFUL.

1. AUTUMN
George Winston

Not only does the Gandalf figure of Winston top this listing he dominates the rest of the list. His success at Windham Hill is a phenomenon and sales are likely to continue as long as the market for new age music remains. Winston takes the art of solo piano and strips it naked - every pause, every space and every note is used to the record's advantage. His style is the direct opposite of Keith Jarrett, yet at times this sparse music is as emotional. The stand out tracks on *Autumn* are 'Longing/Love' and 'Colors/Dance', both are around ten minutes in length allowing Winston even more space.

Colors/Dance; Woods; Longing/Love; Road; Moon; Sea; Stars.

First released 1984
UK peak chart position: did not chart
USA peak chart position: 139

2. SHEPHERD MOONS
Enya

The follow-up to *Watermark*, *Shepherd Moons*, is much the same but more so. The angel choirs shimmer more, the plucked synth melodies chime brighter and the incomprehensible lyrics are yet more sweetly sung. On balance, *Shepherd Moons* is the more consistent of the two, but *Watermark* boasts the incomparable 'Orinoco Flow'. You probably don't need both, so the decision is yours.

Shepherd Moons; Caribbean Blue; How Can I Keep From Singing?; Ebudae; Angeles; No Holly For Miss Quinn; Book Of Days; Evacuee; Lothlórien; Marble Halls; Afer Ventus; Smaointe.

First released 1991
UK peak chart position: 1
USA peak chart position: 17

3. WATERMARK
Enya

Enya's place in rock history is assured. She's the one who first melded New Agey synthesisers with pop song lyrics to create the elusive crossover pop chart 'Orinoco Flow', with its curious echoes of Andy Williams' 'Can't Get Used To Losing You' and it's closing ad libs evoking the name of WEA label boss Rob Dickins. Folksy memories of her roots as a member of Clannad diminish the impact of some cuts on *Watermark*, but the powerfully building 'Storms In Africa' is in a ghostly style that barely existed before Enya breathed multi-tracked vocal life into it.

Watermark; Cursum Perfico; On Your Shore; Storms In Africa; Exile; Miss Clare Remembers; Orinoco Flow; Evening Falls; River; The Longships; Na Laetha Geal M'óige; Storms In Africa (Part II).

First released 1988
UK peak chart position: 5
USA peak chart position: 25

4. WINTER INTO SPRING
George Winston

The second part of Winston's seasons series of albums opens by playing ten piano notes in 17 seconds. This is a very spacious record that allows each track time to build. Like much of this genre's music its own lethargy allows you in turn, to be creative. Authors with writers block could do worse than to put on the beautiful 'January Stars' and dream. The quality of this and Winston's other 'seasons' albums is truly exceptional and really does place a piano in the front room. His music is the ultimate sound of understatement.

January Stars; February Sea; Ocean Waves (O Mar); Reflection; Rain/Dance; Blossom Meadow; The Venice Dreamer; Introduction (Part One); Part Two.

First released 1984
UK peak chart position: did not chart
USA peak chart position: 127

5. EQUINOXE
Jean-Michel Jarre

Oxygene (1976) was the album that unexpectedly, in the face of the punk revolution, catapulted Jarre to fame, but *Equinoxe* was a more robust creation. The eight parts of this continuously unfolding synthesised crescendo are richer in traditional melodic development and elaboration than *Oxygene*, frequently suggesting the baroque and early classical periods, while occasionally nodding to film-music, perhaps in quiet homage to his celebrated film-scoring father, Maurice Jarre. *Equinoxe* drifts languidly for the first quarter hour, so that when gentle beats and swirling climaxes kick in during the fourth movement, their effect is magnified. You'd have to be deaf not to hear the future (in the shape of OMD, Depeche Mode, Pet Shop Boys, the Orb and the Shamen) in the electro-bop of 'Part 6', and the only possible excuse for not dancing amid the sweeping arpeggios of 'Part 7' is that you can't get the lid off your coffin.

First released 1978
UK peak chart position: 2
USA peak chart position: 126

Equinoxe Part 1; Equinoxe Part 2; Equinoxe Part 3; Equinoxe Part 4; Equinoxe Part 5; Equinoxe Part 6; Equinoxe Part 7; Equinoxe Part 8.

6. DECEMBER
George Winston

Winston's solo piano is rooted in the season of winter as he offers a new age Christmas album. In keeping with all his other works it is sparsely beautiful. Unlike Slade or Roy Wood's perennials Winston's clean music will almost certainly stop you drinking or smoking that sneaky panatella. Whilst this album does not preach it does at least make you think. Even in mid-summer, when this recording was reappraised it has the ability to capture your ears exclusively. His interpretation of 'Kanon' is glorious but 'Thanksgiving' and 'Peace' are indispensable. Recommended out of season music.

First released 1983
UK peak chart position: did not chart
USA peak chart position: 54

Thanksgiving; Jesus, Jesus Rest Your Head; Joy; Prelude; Carol Of The Bells; Night; Midnight (Part 2); Minstrels (Part 3); Variations On The Kanon, By Johann Pachelbel; The Holly And The Ivy; Some Children See Him; Peace; Snow (Part 1).

7. AERIAL BOUNDRIES
Michael Hedges

This is spectacular solo acoustic guitar, unlike anything else. Hedges could be sitting in the next room, such is the recording excellence. Every note of every string seems to be lovingly cared for. New age is the nearest category although folkies should investigate the secrets of this record. Supervised by Windham Hill's William Ackerman, himself a notable acoustic player, it displays a diverse choice from the descriptive title track to the string slapping 'Hot Metal', even throwing in a highly original version of Neil Young's 'After The Gold Rush'. You will be shocked and rewarded by this outstanding album.

First released 1985
UK peak chart position: did not chart
USA peak chart position: did not chart

Aerial Boundaries; Bensusan; Rickover's Dream; Ragamuffin; After The Goldrush; Hot Type; Spare Change; Menage A Trois; The Magic Farmer.

8. SUMMER
George Winston

After a lengthy break of nine years, during which time Winston left Windham Hill only to return again, comes *Summer* - the final album in his seasons series. Although less immediate than its predecessors it remains a recommended album. It would also be churlish to not have this the sequence as the completist trait is in all of us. Seen as a body of work, Winston can feel justifiably proud of his achievement in producing some of the most timeless, evocative piano music ever recorded. And yes it can be played between the Stone Roses and Frank Sinatra and succeed.

Living In The Country; Loreta And Desiree's Bouquet Part 1; Loreta And Desiree's Bouquet Part 2; Fragrent Fields; The Garden; Spring Creek; Lullaby; Black Stallion; Hummingbird; Early Morning Range; Living Without You; Goodbye Montana Part 1; Corrina, Corrina; Goodbye Montana Part 2; Where Are You Now.

First released 1991
UK peak chart position: did not chart
USA peak chart position: 55

9. VAPOUR DRAWINGS
Mark Isham

Having cut his teeth with the Beach Boys, Van Morrison and the San Francisco Opera Company the multi talented Isham started to play some serious jazz with Art Lande in the late 70s. His Windham Hill material coincided with some scoring for films, notably *Mrs Soffell*. *Vapour Drawings* is a blissful album of trumpet, flugelhorn, piano, saxophone, drum machines and synthesizers; all played by Isham. The hypnotic repeat loops are similar to those used by John Adams and Steve Reich, but in the context of popular music. If you loved Oldfield's *Tubular Bells* and didn't know where to go beyond *Hergest Ridge*, this is the album for you.

Many Chinas; Sympathy And Acknowledgement; On The Threshold Of Liberty; When Things Dream; Raffles In Rio; Something Nice For My Dog; Men Before The Mirror; Mr Moto's Penguin (who'd be an Eskimo's wife?); In The Blue Distance.

First released 1983
UK peak chart position: did not chart
USA peak chart position: did not chart

10. NOUVEAU FLAMENCO
Ottmar Liebert

The flamenco old guard will tell you this is not really flamenco, much as the members of stodgy progressive combos like Barclay James Harvest and Camel would have told you that punk wasn't rock. Essentially, Liebert reduces the flamenco format to its rhythmic and melodic basics, and pulls them into shape with a rhythm section that wouldn't be out of place on one of Santana's better albums. When it works, which is about half of the time, Liebert's tense, hard-plucked gipsy melodies are irresistible, and even when it doesn't work they're still rich and vibrant. The Santa Fe-based 'nouveau-flamenco movement', of which Liebert was claimed to be a leading light, has failed to materialise, but the man himself has undeniably contributed something unique in the annals of new age. Ole!

Barcelona Nights; Heart Still/Beating; 3 Women Walking; 2 The Night; Passing Storm; Sante Fe; Surrender 2 Love; Waiting 4 Stars 2 Fall; Road 2 Her/Home; After The Rain; Flowers Of Romance; Moon Over Trees; Shadows.

First released 1990
UK peak chart position: did not chart
USA peak chart position: 134

THE TOP 1000 CHART OF CHARTS

IN COMPILING THE OVERALL CHART, IT IS CLEAR THAT ROCK & POP IS EASILY THE LEADING CATEGORY. OTHER STRONG CONTENDERS WERE HEAVY METAL, LIVE ALBUMS, GREATEST HITS & COMPILATIONS, INDIE AND SOUL.

THE OTHER SPECIALIST GENRES MADE UP MOST OF THE LAST 100, WITH FOLK, RAP AND SOME COUNTRY FINDING IT TOUGH TO COMPETE WITH THE MORE MARKETABLE MAINSTREAM ALBUMS. LATIN, WORLD AND GRUNGE MAY APPEAR NEXT TIME.

1	*Sgt. Peppers Lonely Hearts Club Band*	Beatles	Rock & Pop
2	*Highway 61 Revisited*	Bob Dylan	Rock & Pop
3	*Pet Sounds*	Beach Boys	Rock & Pop
4	*Blonde On Blonde*	Bob Dylan	Rock & Pop
5	*Revolver*	Beatles	Rock & Pop
6	*Dark Side Of The Moon*	Pink Floyd	Rock & Pop
7	*Astral Weeks*	Van Morrison	Rock & Pop
8	*Let It Bleed*	Rolling Stones	Rock & Pop
9	*What's Going On*	Marvin Gaye	Soul
10	*Rubber Soul*	Beatles	Rock & Pop
11	*Sticky Fingers*	Rolling Stones	Rock & Pop
12	*Never Mind The Bollocks Here's The Sex Pistols*	Sex Pistols	Punk
13	*Out Of Time*	R.E.M.	Rock & Pop
14	*Thriller*	Michael Jackson	Rock & Pop
15	*White Album*	Beatles	Rock & Pop
16	*Born To Run*	Bruce Springsteen	Rock & Pop
17	*Rumours*	Fleetwood Mac	Rock & Pop
18	*Unforgettable Fire*	U2	Rock & Pop
19	*The Rise And Fall Of Ziggy Stardust*	David Bowie	Rock & Pop
20	*Velvet Underground And Nico*	Velvet Underground	Rock & Pop
21	*Otis Blue*	Otis Redding	Soul
22	*Songs For Swinging Lovers*	Frank Sinatra	Rock & Pop
23	*Bad*	Michael Jackson	Rock & Pop

24	*Beggars Banquet*	Rolling Stones	Rock & Pop
25	*Private Dancer*	Tina Turner	Rock & Pop
26	*Led Zeppelin II*	Led Zeppelin	Heavy Metal
27	*Automatic For The People*	R.E.M.	Rock & Pop
28	*Kind Of Blue*	Miles Davis	Jazz
29	*Legend*	Bob Marley	Greatest Hits & Compilations
30	*Goodbye Yellow Brick Road*	Elton John	Rock & Pop
31	*The Blanton-Webster Years*	Duke Ellington	Jazz
32	*Forever Changes*	Love	Rock & Pop
33	*Sun Collection*	Elvis Presley	Rock 'n' Roll
34	*Hunky Dory*	David Bowie	Rock & Pop
35	*The Band*	The Band	Rock & Pop
36	*Live At The Apollo*	James Brown	Live Albums
37	*Imperial Bedroom*	Elvis Costello	Rock & Pop
38	*IV*	Led Zeppelin	Heavy Metal
39	*Are You Experienced*	Jimi Hendrix	Rock & Pop
40	*A Love Supreme*	John Coltrane	Jazz
41	*The Times They Are A Changin'*	Bob Dylan	Folk
42	*Birth Of The Cool*	Miles Davis	Jazz
43	*Crosby Stills And Nash*	Crosby Stills And Nash	Rock & Pop
44	*Purple Rain*	Prince	Rock & Pop
45	*Songs In The Key Of Life*	Stevie Wonder	Soul
46	*My Aim Is True*	Elvis Costello	Rock & Pop
47	*Stone Roses*	Stone Roses	Indie
48	*The Joshua Tree*	U2	Rock & Pop
49	*Elvis Presley*	Elvis Presley	Rock 'n' Roll
50	*Stars*	Simply Red	Rock & Pop
51	*Talking Book*	Stevie Wonder	Soul
52	*Songs Of Leonard Cohen*	Leonard Cohen	Bedsitter Albums
53	*New Boots And Panties*	Ian Dury And The Blockheads	Rock & Pop
54	*London Calling*	Clash	Punk
55	*West Side Story*	Various	Film Musical
56	*Swing Easy*	Frank Sinatra	Rock & Pop
57	*Nevermind*	Nirvana	Rock & Pop
58	*Abbey Road*	Beatles	Rock & Pop
59	*Stand*	Sly And The Family Stone	Soul
60	*Can't Slow Down*	Lionel Richie	Soul
61	*Liege And Lief*	Fairport Convention	Folk
62	*The Queen Is Dead*	Smiths	Indie
63	*Doors*	Doors	Rock & Pop
64	*Live*	Bob Marley	Live Albums
65	*Disraeli Gears*	Cream	Rock & Pop
66	*Imagine*	John Lennon	Rock & Pop
67	*This Years Model*	Elvis Costello	Rock & Pop
68	*Brothers In Arms*	Dire Straits	Rock & Pop
69	*Electric Warrior*	T. Rex	Rock & Pop
70	*Born In The USA*	Bruce Springsteen	Rock & Pop
71	*Face Value*	Phil Collins	Rock & Pop
72	*Electric Ladyland*	Jimi Hendrix	Rock & Pop
73	*Charlie Parker On Dial Vols 1-6*	Charlie Parker	Jazz
74	*Psychocandy*	Jesus And Mary Chain	Indie
75	*The Smiths*	Smiths	Indie

76	Genius + Soul = Jazz	Ray Charles	Soul
77	1967-70	Beatles	Greatest Hits & Compilations
78	So	Peter Gabriel	Rock & Pop
79	The Stranger	Billy Joel	Rock & Pop
80	The Freewheelin' Bob Dylan	Bob Dylan	Folk
81	Oklahoma!	Various	Film Musical
82	Greatest Hits	Queen	Greatest Hits & Compilations
83	In Utero	Nirvana	Destined To Become A Classic
84	Sign O' The Times	Prince	Rock & Pop
85	Lady Soul	Aretha Franklin	Soul
86	Lady In Autumn	Billie Holiday	Jazz
87	The Genius Of Ray Charles	Ray Charles	Soul
88	Once Upon A Time	Simple Minds	Rock & Pop
89	Blue	Joni Mitchell	Rock & Pop
90	Bat Out Of Hell	Meat Loaf	Rock & Pop
91	Genius Of Modern Music Vols 1 & 2	Thelonious Monk	Jazz
92	Off The Wall	Michael Jackson	Rock & Pop
93	Graceland	Paul Simon	Rock & Pop
94	Paranoid	Black Sabbath	Heavy Metal
95	Transformer	Lou Reed	Rock & Pop
96	Roxy Music	Roxy Music	Rock & Pop
97	Bridge Over Troubled Water	Simon And Garfunkel	Rock & Pop
98	Blood On The Tracks	Bob Dylan	Rock & Pop
99	With The Beatles	Beatles	Rock & Pop
100	West Side Story	Original Cast	Stage Musical
101	Elton John	Elton John	Rock & Pop
102	Like A Virgin	Madonna	Rock & Pop
103	Machine Head	Deep Purple	Heavy Metal
104	Miles Smiles	Miles Davis	Jazz
105	War	U2	Rock & Pop
106	After The Goldrush	Neil Young	Rock & Pop
107	Come Fly With Me	Frank Sinatra	Rock & Pop
108	Parallel Lines	Blondie	Rock & Pop
109	Hot Fives And Sevens 1-7	Louis Armstrong	Jazz
110	Pretzel Logic	Steely Dan	Rock & Pop
111	L.A. Woman	Doors	Rock & Pop
112	Help	Beatles	Rock & Pop
113	Synchronicity	Police	Rock & Pop
114	Exile On Main Street	Rolling Stones	Rock & Pop
115	Harvest	Neil Young	Rock & Pop
116	The Healer	John Lee Hooker	Blues
117	In Rock	Deep Purple	Heavy Metal
118	Be Yourself Tonight	Eurythmics	Rock & Pop
119	Slippery When Wet	Bon Jovi	Heavy Metal
120	Abraxis	Santana	Rock & Pop
121	Legend Of American Folk Blues	Woody Guthrie	Folk
122	A Swingin' Affair	Frank Sinatra	Rock & Pop
123	Morrison Hotel	Doors	Rock & Pop
124	Ten	Pearl Jam	Rock & Pop
125	Solid Air	John Martyn	Folk
126	Rust Never Sleeps	Neil Young	Rock & Pop
127	Wish You Were Here	Pink Floyd	Rock & Pop

128	*Making Movies*	Dire Straits	Rock & Pop
129	*Aja*	Steely Dan	Rock & Pop
130	*Five Leaves Left*	Nick Drake	Folk
131	*Surrealistic Pillow*	Jefferson Airplane	Rock & Pop
132	*Love Is The Thing*	Nat 'King' Cole	Rock & Pop
133	*Notorious Byrd Brothers*	Byrds	Rock & Pop
134	*Here's Little Richard*	Little Richard	Rock 'n' Roll
135	*Remain In Light*	Talking Heads	Rock & Pop
136	*Dusty In Memphis*	Dusty Springfield	Soul
137	*Pretenders*	Pretenders	Rock & Pop
138	*Layla And Other Assorted Love Songs*	Derek And the Dominos	Rock & Pop
139	*The River*	Bruce Springsteen	Rock & Pop
140	*Who's Next*	Who	Rock & Pop
141	*Catch A Fire*	The Wailers	Reggae
142	*This Is Soul*	Various	Greatest Hits & Compilations
143	*World Machine*	Level 42	Rock & Pop
144	*Fly Like An Eagle*	Steve Miller Band	Rock & Pop
145	*Court And Spark*	Joni Mitchell	Rock & Pop
146	*Traffic*	Traffic	Rock & Pop
147	*1962-66*	Beatles	Greatest Hits & Compilations
148	*Younger Than Yesterday*	Byrds	Rock & Pop
149	*Kate & Anna McGarrigle*	Kate & Anna McGarrigle	Folk
150	*Bringing It All Back Home*	Bob Dylan	Folk
151	*Outlandos D'Amour*	Police	Rock & Pop
152	*Moondance*	Van Morrison	Rock & Pop
153	*Trout Mask Replica*	Captain Beefheart And The Magic Band	Brilliantly Unlistenable Classic
154	*Diva*	Annie Lennox	Rock & Pop
155	*New Gold Dream (81,82, 83, 84)*	Simple Minds	Rock & Pop
156	*Diamond Life*	Sade	Rock & Pop
157	*Deja Vu*	Crosby, Stills, Nash And Young	Rock & Pop
158	*Milestones*	Miles Davis	Jazz
159	*Moby Grape*	Moby Grape	Rock & Pop
160	*Bookends*	Simon And Garfunkel	Rock & Pop
161	*Body And Soul*	Coleman Hawkins	Jazz
162	*Achtung Baby*	U2	Rock & Pop
163	*Music From Big Pink*	The Band	Rock & Pop
164	*A Night At The Opera*	Queen	Rock & Pop
165	*Woodstock*	Various	Film Musical
166	*Complete Benny Goodman Vol 1-7*	Benny Goodman	Jazz
167	*Woodface*	Crowded House	Rock & Pop
168	*King Of The Delta Blues Singers*	Robert Johnson	Blues
169	*Can't Buy A Thrill*	Steely Dan	Rock & Pop
170	*John Wesley Harding*	Bob Dylan	Rock & Pop
171	*Hotel California*	Eagles	Rock & Pop
172	*Damn The Torpedoes*	Tom Petty And The Heartbreakers	Rock & Pop
173	*Back In Black*	AC/DC	Heavy Metal
174	*Swordfishtrombones*	Tom Waits	Rock & Pop
175	*Stranger In Town*	Bob Seger	Rock & Pop
176	*The Wall*	Pink Floyd	Rock & Pop
177	*Van Halen*	Van Halen	Heavy Metal
178	*The Black Saint And the Sinner Lady*	Charles Mingus	Jazz
179	*Surfs Up*	Beach Boys	Rock & Pop

180	*Parade*	Prince	Rock & Pop
181	*Greatest Hits 1971-1975*	Eagles	Greatest Hits & Compilations
182	*Don't Shoot Me I'm Only The Piano Player*	Elton John	Rock & Pop
183	*Tapestry*	Carole King	Rock & Pop
184	*The Low Spark Of High Heeled Boys*	Traffic	Rock & Pop
185	*Fabulous*	Little Richard	Rock 'n' Roll
186	*Rattus Norvegicus*	Stranglers	Punk
187	*Get Happy!*	Elvis Costello	Rock & Pop
188	*Eddie Cochran Memorial Album*	Eddie Cochran	Rock 'n' Roll
189	*Greatest Hits*	Abba	Greatest Hits & Compilations
190	*The Buddy Holly Story*	Buddy Holly	Rock 'n' Roll
191	*Nice 'n Easy*	Frank Sinatra	Rock & Pop
192	*Desperado*	Eagles	Rock & Pop
193	*Green*	R.E.M.	Rock & Pop
194	*Unleashed In The East*	Judas Priest	Live Albums
195	*Hot Rats*	Frank Zappa	Rock & Pop
196	*Gerry Mulligan Meets Ben Webster*	Gerry Mulligan & Ben Webster	Jazz
197	*There Goes Rhymin' Simon*	Paul Simon	Rock & Pop
198	*Axis Bold As Love*	Jimi Hendrix	Rock & Pop
199	*In The Wee Small Hours*	Frank Sinatra	Rock & Pop
200	*Screamadelica*	Primal Scream	Indie
201	*Calypso*	Harry Belafonte	Rock & Pop
202	*Velvet Underground*	Velvet Underground	Rock & Pop
203	*Revenge*	Eurythmics	Rock & Pop
204	*Marcus Garvey*	Burning Spear	Reggae
205	*Avalon Sunset*	Van Morrison	Rock & Pop
206	*Appetite For Destruction*	Guns N'Roses	Heavy Metal
207	*Pet Shop Boys Actually*	Pet Shop Boys	Rock & Pop
208	*Waiting For The Sun*	Doors	Rock & Pop
209	*Led Zeppelin*	Led Zeppelin	Heavy Metal
210	*Bluesbreakers With Eric Clapton*	John Mayall	Blues
211	*All Things Must Pass*	George Harrison	Rock & Pop
212	*The Koln Concert*	Keith Jarrett	Live Albums
213	*Fleetwood Mac*	Fleetwood Mac	Rock & Pop
214	*Clash*	Clash	Punk
215	*Loving You*	Elvis Presley	Rock 'n' Roll
216	*Low*	David Bowie	Rock & Pop
217	*Pretenders II*	Pretenders	Rock & Pop
218	*The Dock Of The Bay*	Otis Redding	Soul
219	*Out Of The Blue*	Electric Light Orchestra	Rock & Pop
220	*Tubular Bells*	Mike Oldfield	Rock & Pop
221	*Freak Out*	Frank Zappa/Mothers Of Invention	Rock & Pop
222	*Today*	Beach Boys	Rock & Pop
223	*Judy At Carnegie Hall*	Judy Garland	Live Albums
224	*Strange Days*	Doors	Rock & Pop
225	*Everybody Knows This Is Nowhere*	Neil Young	Rock & Pop
226	*Touch*	Eurythmics	Rock & Pop
227	*Again*	Buffalo Springfield	Rock & Pop
228	*Suede*	Suede	Indie
229	*The Number Of The Beast*	Iron Maiden	Heavy Metal
230	*Stage Fright*	The Band	Rock & Pop
231	*Life*	Inspiral Carpets	Indie

232	Black Sabbath	Black Sabbath	Heavy Metal
233	Come Dance With Me	Frank Sinatra	Rock & Pop
234	Metallica	Metallica	Heavy Metal
235	Darkness At The Edge Of Town	Bruce Springsteen	Rock & Pop
236	Armed Forces	Elvis Costello	Rock & Pop
237	The Complete Savoy Sessions	Charlie Parker	Jazz
238	A Day At The Races	Queen	Rock & Pop
239	White Light White Heat	Velvet Underground	Rock & Pop
240	Giant Steps	John Coltrane	Jazz
241	St Dominic's Preview	Van Morrison	Rock & Pop
242	Reggatta De Blanc	Police	Rock & Pop
243	Feats Don't Fail Me Now	Little Feat	Rock & Pop
244	Reckless	Bryan Adams	Rock & Pop
245	Document	R.E.M.	Rock & Pop
246	My Fair Lady	Original Cast	Stage Musical
247	At Newport	Duke Ellington	Live Albums
248	South Pacific	Various	Film Musical
249	Alf	Alison Moyet	Rock & Pop
250	Aftermath	Rolling Stones	Rock & Pop
251	Smiley Smile	Beach Boys	Rock & Pop
252	Hello I Must Be Going	Phil Collins	Rock & Pop
253	The Lexicon Of Love	ABC	Rock & Pop
254	Rock And Rollin' With	Fats Domino	Rock 'n' Roll
255	American Beauty	Grateful Dead	Rock & Pop
256	September Of My Years	Frank Sinatra	Rock & Pop
257	Rattle And Hum	U2	Live Albums
258	Physical Graffiti	Led Zeppelin	Heavy Metal
259	Plastic Ono Band	John Lennon	Rock & Pop
260	Young Americans	David Bowie	Rock & Pop
261	The Last Record Album	Little Feat	Rock & Pop
262	Burnin'	Bob Marley And The Wailers	Reggae
263	Sound Of Music	Various	Film Musical
264	Sailin' Shoes	Little Feat	Rock & Pop
265	461 Ocean Boulevard	Eric Clapton	Rock & Pop
266	Closer	Joy Division	Indie
267	Viva Hate	Morrissey	Rock & Pop
268	Easy Rider	Various	Film Musical
269	When A Man Loves A Woman	Percy Sledge	Soul
270	Aladdin Sane	David Bowie	Rock & Pop
271	For Your Pleasure	Roxy Music	Rock & Pop
272	A Kind Of Magic	Queen	Rock & Pop
273	Rum Sodomy & The Lash	Pogues	Indie
274	Complete & Unbelievable. . . The Dictionary Of Soul	Otis Redding	Soul
275	The Kick Inside	Kate Bush	Rock & Pop
276	Rock 'n' Roll Animal	Lou Reed	Rock & Pop
277	Theres A Riot Going On	Sly And The Family Stone	Soul
278	Arc Of A Diver	Steve Winwood	Rock & Pop
279	Autobahn	Kraftwerk	Rock & Pop
280	Sweet Baby James	James Taylor	Bedsitter Albums
281	Escape	Journey	Rock & Pop
282	Heart	Heart	Rock & Pop
283	For Those About To Rock We Salute You	AC/DC	Heavy Metal

284 *In My Tribe*	**10,000 Maniacs**	Rock & Pop
285 *Blood And Chocolate*	**Elvis Costello**	Rock & Pop
286 *Dire Straits*	**Dire Straits**	Rock & Pop
287 *The Pretender*	**Jackson Browne**	Rock & Pop
288 *If Only I Could Remember My Name*	**David Crosby**	Rock & Pop
289 *Damned Damned Damned*	**Damned**	Punk
290 *Sings For Only The Lonely*	**Frank Sinatra**	Rock & Pop
291 *The Explosive Freddy Cannon*	**Freddy Cannon**	Rock 'n' Roll
292 *Rain Dogs*	**Tom Waits**	Rock & Pop
293 *Saturday Night Fever*	**Various**	Film Musical
294 *Joan Baez In Concert*	**Joan Baez**	Live Albums
295 *Stephen Stills*	**Stephen Stills**	Rock & Pop
296 *That'll Be The Day*	**Various**	Greatest Hits & Compilations
297 *Bad Company*	**Bad Company**	Rock & Pop
298 *Tea For The Tillerman*	**Cat Stevens**	Bedsitter Albums
299 *The Harder They Come*	**Various**	Film Musical
300 *Like A Prayer*	**Madonna**	Rock & Pop
301 *Lets Dance*	**David Bowie**	Rock & Pop
302 *Pearl*	**Janis Joplin**	Rock & Pop
303 *Sailor*	**Steve Miller Band**	Rock & Pop
304 *Close To The Edge*	**Yes**	Rock & Pop
305 *The Singles 1969-1973*	**Carpenters**	Greatest Hits & Compilations
306 *Daydream*	**Lovin Spoonful**	Rock & Pop
307 *A Clockwork Orange*	**Various**	Film Musical
308 *Stranded*	**Roxy Music**	Rock & Pop
309 *Oliver!*	**Various**	Film Musical
310 *Night And Day*	**Joe Jackson**	Rock & Pop
311 *Band On The Run*	**Wings**	Rock & Pop
312 *Pocket Full Of Kryptonite*	**Spin Doctors**	Rock & Pop
313 *The Sound Of Music*	**Original Cast**	Stage Musical
314 *Some Girls*	**Rolling Stones**	Rock & Pop
315 *Out To Lunch*	**Eric Dolphy**	Jazz
316 *I Want To See The Bright Lights Tonight*	**Richard And Linda Thompson**	Rock & Pop
317 *Cliff Sings*	**Cliff Richard**	Rock & Pop
318 *Our Man In Paris*	**Dexter Gordon**	Jazz
319 *Toys In The Attic*	**Aerosmith**	Rock & Pop
320 *Every Picture Tells A Story*	**Rod Stewart**	Rock & Pop
321 *Queen 2*	**Queen**	Rock & Pop
322 *This Is Fats Domino*	**Fats Domino**	Rock 'n' Roll
323 *Concert By The Sea*	**Erroll Garner**	Live Albums
324 *The Audience With Betty Carter*	**Betty Carter**	Live Albums
325 *The All Time Greatest Hits*	**Elvis Presley**	Greatest Hits & Compilations
326 *Johnny Cash At San Quentin*	**Johnny Cash**	Live Albums
327 *Stop Making Sense*	**Talking Heads**	Live Albums
328 *Travels*	**Pat Metheny**	Live Albums
329 *Jack Orion*	**Bert Jansch**	Folk
330 *12 Dreams Of Dr Sardonicus*	**Spirit**	Rock & Pop
331 *Fire And Water*	**Free**	Rock & Pop
332 *Copper Blue*	**Sugar**	Indie
333 *My Favorite Things*	**John Coltrane**	Jazz
334 *Shoot Out The Lights*	**Richard And Linda Thompson**	Rock & Pop
335 *Great Balls Of Fire!*	**Jerry Lee Lewis**	Greatest Hits & Compilations

336	Unplugged	Eric Clapton	Live Albums
337	The Original American Decca Recordings	Count Basie	Jazz
338	Full Moon Fever	Tom Petty	Rock & Pop
339	One Dozen Berries	Chuck Berry	Rock 'n' Roll
340	Ramones	Ramones	Punk
340	It's Too Late To Stop Now	Van Morrison	Live Albums
341	Van Halen II	Van Halen	Heavy Metal
342	Burn	Deep Purple	Heavy Metal
343	Breakfast In America	Supertramp	Rock & Pop
344	Greatest Hits	Hollies	Greatest Hits & Compilations
345	The Beast Inside	Inspiral Carpets	Indie
346	Elvis	Elvis Presley	Rock 'n' Roll
347	Duke	Genesis	Rock & Pop
348	Avalon	Roxy Music	Rock & Pop
349	Green River	Creedence Clearwater Revival	Rock & Pop
351	Me And My Shadows	Cliff Richard	Rock & Pop
352	Sweet Dreams	Eurythmics	Rock & Pop
353	No Sleep Till Hammersmith	Motorhead	Live Albums
354	Sonny Rollins Vol 2	Sonny Rollins	Jazz
355	Cheap Thrills	Big Brother And The Holding Company	Rock & Pop
356	Face To Face	Kinks	Rock & Pop
357	Talking With The Taxman About Poetry	Billy Bragg	Indie
358	Jerry Lee's Greatest!	Jerry Lee Lewis	Rock 'n' Roll
359	Blood Sweat And Tears	Blood Sweat And Tears	Rock & Pop
360	Ingenue	k d lang	Rock & Pop
361	Here We Go Again	Kingston Trio	Folk
362	Cosmo's Factory	Creedence Clearwater Revival	Rock & Pop
363	East Side Story	Squeeze	Rock & Pop
364	Pills Thrills And Bellyaches	Happy Mondays	Indie
365	Holland	Beach Boys	Rock & Pop
366	Ogdens Nut Gone Flake	Small Faces	Rock & Pop
367	Village Green Preservation Society	Kinks	Rock & Pop
368	Scott 2	Scott Walker	Rock & Pop
369	Singin' To My Baby	Eddie Cochran	Rock 'n' Roll
370	Rocks	Aerosmith	Rock & Pop
371	Made In Japan	Deep Purple	Live Albums
372	The Shape Of Jazz To Come	Ornette Coleman	Jazz
373	12 Songs	Randy Newman	Rock & Pop
374	Aretha Now	Aretha Franklin	Soul
375	Coltrane Jazz	John Coltrane	Jazz
376	Dare	Human League	Rock & Pop
377	Singles Going Steady	Buzzcocks	Punk
378	Meat Is Murder	Smiths	Indie
379	What We Did On Our Holidays	Fairport Convention	Folk
380	Whatever	Aimee Mann	Destined To Become A Classic
381	Tracy Chapman	Tracy Chapman	Bedsitter Albums
382	The Yes Album	Yes	Rock & Pop
383	The B-52's	B-52's	Rock & Pop
384	Monterey International Pop Festival	Jimi Hendrix/Otis Redding	Live Albums
385	Hounds Of Love	Kate Bush	Rock & Pop
386	Jailbreak	Thin Lizzie	Rock & Pop
387	The Blues Of Lightnin' Hopkins	Lightnin' Hopkins	Blues

388	*Time Out*	Dave Brubeck	Jazz
389	*Germ Free Adolescents*	X Ray Spex	Punk
390	*Oliver!*	Original Cast	Stage Musical
391	*Surfer Rosa*	Pixies	Indie
392	*Rockin' With Wanda*	Wanda Jackson	Rock 'n' Roll
393	*The Monkees*	Monkees	Rock & Pop
394	*Bedsitter Images*	Al Stewart	Bedsitter Albums
395	*The Rolling Stones*	Rolling Stones	Rock & Pop
396	*Gussie Presenting*	I Roy	Reggae
397	*The Wonderful And Frightening World Of*	Fall	Indie
398	*The Louis Armstrong Story 1-7*	Louis Armstrong	Jazz
399	*Jesus Of Cool*	Nick Lowe	Rock & Pop
400	*You Can't Hide Your Love Forever*	Orange Juice	Indie
401	*No Jacket Required*	Phil Collins	Rock & Pop
402	*If You Want Blood You've Got It*	AC/DC	Live Albums
403	*Starsailor*	Tim Buckley	Rock & Pop
404	*The Southern Harmony And Musical Companion*	Black Crowes	Heavy Metal
405	*Art Blakey's Jazz Messengers With Thelonious Monk*	Art Blakey	Jazz
406	*5th Dimension*	Byrds	Rock & Pop
407	*Tim Hardin II*	Tim Hardin	Bedsitter Albums
408	*Through The Past Darkly*	Rolling Stones	Greatest Hits & Compilations
409	*Eliminator*	Z.Z. Top	Heavy Metal
410	*Screaming For Vengance*	Judas Priest	Heavy Metal
411	*Moanin' The Blues*	Hank Williams	Country
412	*Impressions*	John Coltrane	Jazz
413	*Here Come The Warm Jets*	Brian Eno	Rock & Pop
414	*Stutter*	James	Indie
415	*More Of The Monkees*	Monkees	Rock & Pop
416	*Electric Music For The Body And Mind*	Country Joe And The Fish	Rock & Pop
417	*Live X Cert*	Stranglers	Live Albums
418	*Rock Around The Clock*	Bill Haley And The Comets	Rock 'n' Roll
419	*Boss Drum*	Shamen	Indie
420	*Nick Of Time*	Bonnie Raitt	Rock & Pop
421	*Tango In The Night*	Fleetwood Mac	Rock & Pop
422	*Greatest Hits*	Aretha Franklin	Greatest Hits & Compilations
423	*Tommy*	Who	Rock & Pop
424	*Scott*	Scott Walker	Rock & Pop
425	*Saxophone Colossus*	Sonny Rollins	Jazz
426	*David Ackles*	David Ackles	Rock & Pop
427	*Funhouse*	Stooges	Rock & Pop
428	*The Complete Recordings*	Bessie Smith	Blues
429	*The Big Wheel*	Runrig	Folk
430	*Blizzard Of Oz*	Ozzy Osborne	Heavy Metal
431	*The Last Waltz*	Various	Live Albums
432	*Anthem Of The Sun*	Grateful Dead	Rock & Pop
433	*Steve McQueen*	Prefab Sprout	Rock & Pop
434	*The Captain And Me*	Doobie Brothers	Rock & Pop
435	*Grace And Danger*	John Martyn	Bedsitter Albums
436	*You Got My Mind Messed Up*	James Carr	Soul
437	*Moving Pictures*	Rush	Heavy Metal
438	*Hejira*	Joni Mitchell	Rock & Pop
439	*Pyromania*	Def Leppard	Heavy Metal

440 Complete Library Of Congress Recordings	Leadbelly	Blues
441 Iron Fist	Motorhead	Heavy Metal
442 Argybargy	Squeeze	Rock & Pop
443 Ricky	Ricky Nelson	Rock 'n' Roll
444 Happy Sad	Tim Buckley	Rock & Pop
445 Moanin' In The Moonlight	Howlin' Wolf	Blues
446 Low-Life	New Order	Indie
447 Piece Of Mind	Iron Maiden	Heavy Metal
448 Bandwagonesque	Teenage Fanclub	Indie
449 The Late Fantastically Great	Elmore James	Blues
450 Just Jimmy Reed	Jimmy Reed	Blues
451 Songs From A Room	Leonard Cohen	Bedsitter Albums
452 The Thundering Herds 1945-1947	Woody Herman	Jazz
453 Bluejean Bop	Gene Vincent	Rock 'n' Roll
454 Blues Brothers	Various	Film Musical
455 Brotherhood	New Order	Indie
456 The Sky Is Crying	Stevie Ray Vaughan	Blues
457 Jazz Giant	Benny Carter	Jazz
458 Lonely At The Top	Randy Newman	Greatest Hits & Compilations
459 Ride The Lightning	Metallica	Heavy Metal
460 Bert Jansch	Bert Jansch	Folk
461 Coleman Hawkins Encounters Ben Webster	Coleman Hawkins	Jazz
462 Bossanova	Pixies	Indie
463 The Best Of Little Walter	Little Walter	Blues
464 In A Silent Way	Miles Davis	Jazz
465 Grease	various	Film Musical
466 Isn't Anything	My Bloody Valentine	Indie
467 Marquee Moon	Television	Punk
468 The Nation's Saving Grace	Fall	Indie
469 Greatest Hits	Simon And Garfunkel	Greatest Hits & Compilations
470 King Tubby Meets Rockers Uptown	Augustus Pablo	Reggae
471 Unplugged	Neil Young	Live Albums
472 Down And Out Blues	Sonny Boy Williamson	Blues
473 Tell Mama	Etta James	Soul
474 Young And Stupid	Josef K	Indie
475 Solid And Raunchy	Bill Black	Rock 'n' Roll
476 Dreamin'	Johnny Burnette	Rock 'n' Roll
477 Strangers In The Night	UFO	Heavy Metal
478 Daydream Nation	Sonic Youth	Indie
479 Innervisions	Stevie Wonder	Soul
480 Unhalfbricking	Fairport Convention	Folk
481 In Pieces	Garth Brooks	Destined To Become A Classic
482 Muddy Waters At Newport	Muddy Waters	Live Albums
483 Live At The Regal	B.B. King	Live Albums
484 King Creole	Elvis Presley	Rock 'n' Roll
485 Breakfast At Tiffany's	Various	Film Musical
486 The Best Of Van Morrison	Van Morrison	Greatest Hits & Compilations
487 Country Music Hall Of Fame	Jimmie Rodgers	Country
488 Shift Work	Fall	Indie
489 This Is Brenda	Brenda Lee	Rock 'n' Roll
490 Live At Leeds	Who	Live Albums
491 Out Of The Cool	Gil Evans	Jazz

492	*Big Hits High Tide And Green Grass*	Rolling Stones	Greatest Hits & Compilations
493	*Unknown Pleasures*	Joy Division	Indie
494	*Autumn*	George Winston	New Age
495	*Vs*	Pearl Jam	Destined To Become A Classic
496	*Pink Flag*	Wire	Punk
497	*My Kind Of Blues*	B.B. King	Blues
498	*Elvis Is Back*	Elvis Presley	Rock 'n' Roll
499	*Phil Spector's Christmas Album*	Various	Greatest Hits & Compilations
500	*The Bluebird Sessions*	Sidney Bechet	Jazz
501	*Your Arsenal*	Morrisey	Indie
502	*Heliocentric Worlds Of Sun Ra Vol 1*	Sun Ra	Jazz
503	*Satta Massa Gana*	Abyssinians	Reggae
504	*The Twangs The Thang*	Duane Eddy	Rock 'n' Roll
505	*Someday My Prince Will Come*	Miles Davis	Jazz
506	*Frampton Comes Alive*	Peter Frampton	Live Albums
507	*Damn Right I Got The Blues*	Buddy Guy	Blues
508	*Shepherd Moons*	Enya	New Age
509	*Fear Of A Black Planet*	Public Enemy	Rap
510	*Natty Dread*	Bob Marley	Reggae
511	*Doolittle*	Pixies	Indie
512	*Leave Home*	Ramones	Punk
513	*The Buddy Holly Story Vol 2*	Buddy Holly	Rock 'n' Roll
514	*The Man And His Music*	Sam Cooke	Greatest Hits & Compilations
515	*Crossing The Red Sea With*	Adverts	Punk
516	*Watermark*	Enya	New Age
517	*The Complete Chess Folk Blues Sessions*	John Lee Hooker	Blues
518	*Modern Art*	Art Farmer	Jazz
519	*The King And I*	Various	Film Musical
520	*Ramblin' Man*	Hank Williams	Country
521	*Four Way Street*	Crosby Stills Nash And Young	Live Albums
522	*Pornography*	Cure	Indie
523	*Bitches Brew*	Miles Davis	Jazz
524	*Doctor Zhivago*	Various	Film Musical
525	*Johnny Burnette And The Rock 'n' Roll Trio*	Johnny Burnette	Rock 'n' Roll
526	*Wheels of Fire*	Cream	Live Albums
527	*Hiphoprisy Is The Greatest Luxury*	Disposable Heroes Of Hiphoprisy	Rap
528	*Big Maybelle*	Big Maybelle	Blues
529	*Crocodiles*	Echo And The Bunnymen	Indie
530	*The Bodyguard*	Various	Film Musical
531	*Shaved Fish*	John Lennon	Greatest Hits & Compilations
532	*Dry*	PJ Harvey	Indie
533	*Master Of Reality*	Black Sabbath	Heavy Metal
534	*Hats Off To Del Shannon*	Del Shannon	Rock 'n' Roll
535	*1984*	Van Halen	Heavy Metal
536	*Mingus Ah Um*	Charles Mingus	Jazz
537	*Muddy Waters Folk Singer*	Muddy Waters	Blues
538	*Wailing Wailers*	The Wailers	Reggae
539	*Debut*	Bjork	Indie
540	*Blues And The Abstract Truth*	Oliver Nelson	Jazz
541	*It Takes A Nation Of Millions To Hold Us Back*	Public Enemy	Rap
542	*Endless Summer*	Beach Boys	Greatest Hits & Compilations
543	*Go Blow Your Horn*	Louis Jordan	Blues

544 *Screaming Target*	Big Youth	Reggae
545 *Diver Down*	Van Halen	Heavy Metal
546 *The Sound Of Fury*	Billy Fury	Rock 'n' Roll
547 *New Tijuana Moods*	Charles Mingus	Jazz
548 *Getting Ready*	Freddie King	Blues
549 *Memorial Album*	Hank Williams	Country
550 *The Rock Machine Turns You On*	Various	Greatest Hits & Compilations
551 *Kilimanjaro*	Teardrop Explodes	Indie
552 *Slim Whitman Favorites*	Slim Whitman	Country
553 *I Never Loved A Man The Way I Love You*	Aretha Franklin	Soul
554 *The Sidewinder*	Lee Morgan	Jazz
555 *Come On And Feel The Lemonheads*	Lemonheads	Destined To Become A Classic
556 *From Elvis In Memphis*	Elvis Presley	Rock 'n' Roll
557 *Spirits Rejoice*	Albert Ayler	Jazz
558 *Boss Of The Blues*	Joe Turner	Blues
559 *ESP*	Miles Davis	Jazz
560 *The Exciting Wilson Pickett*	Wilson Pickett	Soul
561 *Straight Outta Compton*	NWA	Rap
562 *The London Howlin' Wolf Sessions*	Howlin' Wolf	Blues
563 *Four Tops Reach Out*	Four Tops	Soul
564 *High Land Hard Rain*	Aztec Camera	Indie
565 *Offramp*	Pat Metheny	Jazz
566 *The Undertones*	Undertones	Punk
567 *Rainbow Rising*	Rainbow	Heavy Metal
568 *Broken English*	Marianne Faithfull	Bedsitter Albums
569 *No More Heroes*	Stranglers	Punk
570 *Live At The Budokan*	Cheap Trick	Live Albums
571 *Stop The World I Want To Get Off*	Original Cast	Stage Musical
572 *3 Years 5 Months And 2 Days In The Life Of*	Arrested Development	Rap
573 *Patsy Cline Showcase*	Patsy Cline	Country
574 *Weld*	Neil Young And Crazy Horse	Live Albums
575 *The Phantom Of The Opera*	Original Cast	Stage Musical
576 *A Hard Road*	John Mayall And The Bluesbreakers	Blues
577 *Hatful Of Hollow*	Smiths	Indie
578 *Big Band Bossa Nova*	Stan Getz	Jazz
579 *White Lines And Other Messages*	Grandmaster Flash & The Furious Five	Rap
580 *Waltz For Debby*	Bill Evans	Jazz
581 *Otis Redding Live In Europe*	Otis Redding	Live Albums
582 *Heaven Or Las Vegas*	Cocteau Twins	Indie
583 *Gangster Of Love*	Johnny 'Guitar' Watson	Blues
584 *Belonging*	Keith Jarrett	Jazz
585 *Winter Into Spring*	George Winston	New Age
586 *One For All*	Brand Nubian	Rap
587 *The Kingston Trio At Large*	Kingston Trio	Folk
588 *Diz And Getz*	Dizzy Gillespie & Stan Getz	Jazz
589 *Heaven Up Here*	Echo And The Bunnymen	Indie
590 *Stormsville*	Johnny And The Hurricanes	Rock 'n' Roll
591 *Raising Hell*	Run DMC	Rap
592 *Its My Life Baby*	Junior Wells	Blues
593 *Equinoxe*	Jean-Michel Jarre	New Age
594 *Jazz Samba*	Stan Getz	Jazz
595 *Teaser And The Firecat*	Cat Stevens	Bedsitter Albums

596	Superfly	Curtis Mayfield	Soul
597	Lets Get It On	Marvin Gaye	Soul
598	Life's Too Good	Sugarcubes	Indie
599	Waylon And Willie	Waylon Jennings And Willie Nelson	Country
600	New Concepts Of Artistry In Rhythm	Stan Kenton	Jazz
601	Gunfighter Ballads & Trail Songs	Marty Robbins	Country
602	Exodus	Bob Marley	Reggae
603	Lovedrive	Scorpions	Heavy Metal
604	Johnny Cash At Folsom Prison	Johnny Cash	Live Albums
605	Amazing Grace	Aretha Franklin	Soul
606	Bummed	Happy Mondays	Indie
607	Hysteria	Def Leppard	Heavy Metal
608	Let's Stay Together	Al Green	Soul
609	Joan Armatrading	Joan Armatrading	Bedsitter Albums
610	Anthology	Miracles	Greatest Hits & Compilations
611	Never Loved Elvis	Wonder Stuff	Indie
612	Chairs Missing	Wire	Punk
613	Straight Out Of The Jungle	Jungle Brothers	Rap
614	Born Under A Bad Sign	Albert King	Blues
615	Free Jazz	Ornette Coleman	Jazz
616	Always On My Mind	Willie Nelson	Country
617	December	George Winston	New Age
618	The Blues Of Otis Spann	Otis Spann	Blues
619	Reign In Blood	Slayer	Heavy Metal
620	All The Way	Brenda Lee	Rock 'n' Roll
621	Ghetto Music: The Blueprint Of Hip Hop	Boogie Down Productions	Rap
622	Ramblin' Boy	Tom Paxton	Folk
623	Soon Forward	Gregory Isaacs	Reggae
624	Conference Of The Birds	Dave Holland	Jazz
625	Master Of Puppets	Metallica	Heavy Metal
626	Compelling Percussion	Sandy Nelson	Rock 'n' Roll
627	Funky Kingston	Toots And The Maytals	Reggae
628	Rock The Joint	Bill Haley And The Comets	Rock 'n' Roll
629	The Legend Of Sleepy John Estes	Sleepy John Estes	Blues
630	Three Feet High And Rising	De La Soul	Rap
631	Second Winter	Johnny Winter	Blues
632	John Prine	John Prine	Folk
633	Change Of The Century	Ornette Coleman	Jazz
634	Cherished Memories	Eddie Cochran	Rock 'n' Roll
635	People's Instinctive Travels And The Paths Of Rhythm	A Tribe Called Quest	Rap
636	Midnight Blue	Kenny Burrell	Jazz
637	Vulgar Display Of Power, A	Pantera	Heavy Metal
638	God Shuffled His Feet	Crash Test Dummies	Destined To Become A Classic
639	The Paul Simon Songbook	Paul Simon	Bedsitter Albums
640	All Hail The Queen	Queen Latifah	Rap
641	Hooker 'n Heat	Canned Heat/John Lee Hooker	Blues
642	Seventh Son Of A Seventh Son	Iron Maiden	Heavy Metal
643	Ella Fitzgerald Sings The Cole Porter Song Book	Ella Fitzgerald	Jazz
644	Ace Of Spades	Motorhead	Heavy Metal
645	Hank Williams Sings	Hank Williams	Country
646	Operation: Mindcrime	Queensryche	Heavy Metal
647	Aerial Boundries	Michael Hedges	New Age

648 *Garlands*	Cocteau Twins	Indie
649 *Ted Nugent*	Ted Nugent	Heavy Metal
650 *And His Orchestra*	Dizzy Gillespie	Jazz
651 *Breezin'*	George Benson	Soul
652 *Yo! Bum Rush The Show*	Public Enemy	Rap
653 *Blues Alone*	John Mayall	Blues
654 *Funny Girl*	Original Cast	Stage Musical
655 *Return To Forever*	Chick Corea	Jazz
656 *The Soul Album*	Otis Redding	Soul
657 *Guitar Forms*	Kenny Burrell	Jazz
658 *Iron Maiden*	Iron Maiden	Heavy Metal
659 *Okie From Muskogee*	Merle Haggard	Country
660 *Houses Of The Holy*	Led Zeppelin	Heavy Metal
661 *Bare Wires*	John Mayall	Blues
662 *Fiddler On The Roof*	Original Cast	Stage Musical
663 *Rocket To Russia*	Ramones	Punk
664 *Dr. Feelgood*	Motley Crue	Heavy Metal
665 *Cloud Nine*	Temptations	Soul
666 *Meditations*	John Coltrane	Jazz
667 *Joan Baez No. 5*	Joan Baez	Folk
668 *Ella Fitzgerald Sings The Rodgers And Hart Songbook*	Ella Fitzgerald	Jazz
669 *Love At First Sting*	Scorpions	Heavy Metal
670 *Red Headed Stranger*	Willie Nelson	Country
671 *What Does Anything Mean Basically?*	Chameleons	Indie
672 *Ten Summoners Tales*	Sting	Destined To Become A Classic
673 *Heaven And Hell*	Black Sabbath	Heavy Metal
674 *Ol' Waylon*	Waylon Jennings	Country
675 *Black Album*	Damned	Punk
676 *Ice Pickin'*	Albert Collins	Blues
677 *Hair*	Original Cast	Stage Musical
678 *All Mod Cons*	Jam	Punk
679 *The Scream*	Siouxsie And The Banshees	Punk
680 *Shadows And Light*	Joni Mitchell	Live Albums
681 *Wild Wood*	Paul Weller	Destined To Become A Classic
682 *A Different Kind Of Tension*	Buzzcocks	Punk
683 *In The City*	Jam	Punk
684 *Couldn't Stand The Weather*	Stevie Ray Vaughan	Blues
685 *Unity*	Larry Young	Jazz
686 *Pictures Of Starving Children Sell Records*	Chumbawamba	Indie
687 *Blackout*	Scorpions	Heavy Metal
688 *City Of New Orleans*	Willie Nelson	Country
689 *The Boss Man Of The Blues*	Jimmy Reed	Blues
690 *Dirty Dancing*	Various	Film Musical
691 *Knock On Wood*	Eddie Floyd	Soul
692 *Shout At The Devil*	Motley Crue	Heavy Metal
693 *Organ Grinder Swing*	Jimmy Smith	Jazz
694 *Songs Our Daddy Taught Us*	Everly Brothers	Country
695 *Birds Of Fire*	John McLaughlin and the Mahavishnu Orchestra	Jazz
696 *The George And Ira Gershwin Songbook*	Ella Fitzgerald	Jazz
697 *Live At San Quentin*	B.B. King	Live Albums
698 *Look What The Cat Dragged In*	Poison	Heavy Metal
699 *Strangeways Here We Come*	Smiths	Indie

700	*Live Dead*	Grateful Dead	Live Albums
701	*Mama Said Knock You Out*	LL Cool J	Rap
702	*Going To A Go-Go*	Miracles	Soul
703	*Blues From The Gutter*	Champion Jack Dupree	Blues
704	*Dreadlocks Dread*	Big Youth	Reggae
705	*By All Means Necessary*	Boogie Down Productions	Rap
706	*When Tragedy Struck*	Hank Snow	Country
707	*I Am*	Earth Wind And Fire	Soul
708	*No Fences*	Garth Brooks	Country
709	*Hard Station*	Paul Brady	Folk
710	*Head Hunters*	Herbie Hancock	Jazz
711	*Live Wire/Blues Power*	Albert King	Live Albums
712	*OG (Original Gangster)*	Ice-T	Rap
713	*Summer*	George Winston	New Age
714	*Let's Twist Her*	Bill Black	Rock 'n' Roll
715	*Killin' Time*	Clint Black	Country
716	*Second Album*	Martin Carthy	Folk
717	*Blue Train*	John Coltrane	Jazz
718	*3+3*	Isley Brothers	Soul
719	*Version Galore*	U-Roy	Reggae
720	*Strong Persuader*	Robert Cray	Blues
721	*Cypress Hill*	Cypress Hill	Rap
722	*Sings The Million Sellers*	Connie Francis	Rock 'n' Roll
723	*Soulville*	Ben Webster	Jazz
724	*Concert For Bangla Desh*	Various	Live Albums
725	*If There Was A Way*	Dwight Yoakam	Country
726	*Showdown!*	Albert Collins, Robert Cray, Johnny Copeland	Blues
727	*Ropin' The Wind*	Garth Brooks	Country
728	*The Big Gundown*	John Zorn	Jazz
729	*Bigger And Deffer*	LL Cool J	Rap
730	*Why Do Fools Fall In Love?*	Frankie Lymon	Rock 'n' Roll
731	*Black And White*	Stranglers	Punk
732	*Maiden Voyage*	Herbie Hancock	Jazz
733	*Wanted One Soul Singer*	Johnny Taylor	Soul
734	*Song For My Father*	Horace Silver Quintet	Jazz
735	*Always And Forever*	Randy Travis	Country
736	*Double Dynamite*	Sam And Dave	Soul
737	*Brenda Lee*	Brenda Lee	Rock 'n' Roll
738	*Tuesday Night Music Club*	Sheryl Crow	Destined To Become A Classic
739	*154*	Wire	Punk
740	*Taj Mahal*	Taj Mahal	Blues
741	*Backstabbers*	O'Jays	Soul
742	*The Fifth Power*	Lester Bowie	Jazz
743	*My World*	Eddy Arnold	Country
744	*Wild Gift*	X	Punk
745	*Idle Moments*	Grant Green	Jazz
746	*Diamonds*	Diamonds	Rock 'n' Roll
747	*August & Everything After*	Counting Crows	Destined To Become A Classic
748	*Wolf And Leopards*	Dennis Brown	Reggae
749	*Hot Buttered Soul*	Isaac Hayes	Soul
750	*American Garage*	Pat Metheny	Jazz
751	*Storms Of Life*	Randy Travis	Country

752	*Tutu*	Miles Davis	Jazz
753	*Blues Is King*	B. B. King	Live Albums
754	*Trio*	Dolly Parton, Linda Ronstadt, Emmylou Harris	Country
755	*A Date With The Everly Brothers*	Everly Brothers	Rock 'n' Roll
756	*Celebrate*	Kool And the Gang	Soul
757	*Portrait Of Sheila*	Sheila Jordan	Jazz
758	*Another Music In A Different Kitchen*	Buzzcocks	Punk
759	*Iceman*	Albert Collins	Blues
760	*Highways And Heartaches*	Ricky Skaggs	Country
761	*Evidence*	Steve Lacy	Jazz
762	*Chirpin'*	Crickets	Rock 'n' Roll
763	*Tease Me*	Chaka Demus & Pliers	Reggae
764	*Ladies Of The Canyon*	Joni Mitchell	Bedsitter Albums
765	*Happy Trails*	Quicksilver Messenger Service	Live Albums
766	*Black Sabbath Vol 4*	Black Sabbath	Heavy Metal
767	*Metal Box*	Pil	Punk
768	*Open Sesame*	Freddie Hubbard	Jazz
769	*Give 'Em Enough Rope*	Clash	Punk
770	*Grievous Angel*	Gram Parsons	Country
771	*Will Downing*	Will Downing	Soul
772	*Suzanne Vega*	Suzanne Vega	Bedsitter Albums
773	*Chuck Berry On Stage*	Chuck Berry	Live Albums
774	*Creative Orchestra Music 1976*	Anthony Braxton	Jazz
775	*For Teenagers Only*	Bobby Darin	Rock 'n' Roll
776	*Green Onions*	Booker T And The MGs	Soul
777	*Songs Of Tragedy*	Hank Snow	Country
778	*LAMF*	Heartbreakers	Punk
779	*The Real Thing*	Faith No More	Heavy Metal
780	*Tim Hardin I*	Tim Hardin	Bedsitter Albums
781	*Chords Of Fame*	Phil Ochs	Folk
782	*Give Me The Reason*	Luther Vandross	Soul
783	*Belafonte At Carnegie Hall*	Harry Belafonte	Live Albums
784	*Flesh Of My Skin, Blood Of My Blood*	Keith Hudson	Reggae
785	*Sings Soul Ballads*	Otis Redding	Soul
786	*The Sensational Charley Pride*	Charley Pride	Country
787	*Dialogue*	Bobby Hutcherson	Jazz
788	*My Funny Valentine*	Miles Davis	Live Albums
789	*Songs Of Love And Hate*	Leonard Cohen	Bedsitter Albums
790	*Jazz In Silhouette*	Sun Ra	Jazz
791	*Same Train A Different Time*	Merle Haggard	Country
792	*I'm Stranded*	Saints	Punk
793	*Empyrean Isles*	Herbie Hancock	Jazz
794	*The Music Man*	Original Cast	Stage Musical
795	*Give A Damn*	The Johnstons	Folk
796	*Soul Men*	Sam And Dave	Soul
797	*Joan Baez In Concert Vol 2*	Joan Baez	Live Albums
798	*Soul*	Coleman Hawkins	Jazz
799	*Fresh Fruit For Rotting Vegetables*	Dead Kennedys	Punk
800	*First Take*	Roberta Flack	Soul
801	*Below The Salt*	Steeleye Span	Folk
802	*Still Warm*	John Scofield	Jazz
803	*Sound Affects*	Jam	Punk

804	*Salutes Hank Williams And Bob Wills*	George Jones	Country
805	*Horses*	Patti Smith	Punk
806	*Joseph And The Amazing Technicolor Dreamcoat*	Original Cast	Stage Musical
807	*Moving Targets*	Penetration	Punk
808	*Make Time For Love*	Keith Washington	Soul
809	*R & B At The Marquee*	Alexis Korner	Blues
810	*We Free Kings*	Roland Kirk	Jazz
811	*Chill Of An Early Fall*	George Strait	Country
812	*Under The Boardwalk*	Drifters	Soul
813	*I Was Warned*	Robert Cray	Blues
814	*Escalator Over The Hill*	Carla Bley	Jazz
815	*Sweet Revenge*	John Prine	Folk
816	*Kick Out The Jams*	MC5	Punk
817	*Mr Lucky*	John Lee Hooker	Blues
818	*Changes In Latitude, Changes In Attitudes*	Jimmy Buffett	Country
819	*There Goes The Neighbourhood*	Gary Bartz	Jazz
820	*In The Dark/Roots Reggae*	Toots And The Maytals	Reggae
821	*Penguin Eggs*	Nic Jones	Folk
822	*Joe Ely*	Joe Ely	Country
823	*Gigi*	Various	Film Musical
824	*Wanted: Dead Or Alive*	Kool G. Rap & Polo	Rap
825	*Kelly Blue*	Wynton Kelly	Jazz
826	*Garth Brooks*	Garth Brooks	Country
827	*Time's Up*	Buzzcocks	Punk
828	*Facing You*	Keith Jarrett	Jazz
829	*New York Tenderberry*	Laura Nyro	Bedsitter Albums
830	*Will The Circle Be Unbroken*	Nitty Gritty Dirt Band	Country
831	*Alive!*	Kiss	Live Albums
832	*Sweetheart Of The Rodeo*	Byrds	Country
833	*Blackheart Man*	Bunny Wailer	Reggae
834	*Pure Mania*	Vibrators	Punk
835	*Hello Dolly*	Original Cast	Stage Musical
836	*I Still Believe In You*	Vince Gill	Country
837	*Lost And Found*	Sheila Jordan	Jazz
838	*Lullabys Legends And Lies*	Bobby Bare	Country
839	*English Rock 'n' Roll The Early Years 1800-1850*	Oyster Band	Folk
840	*Moonlight And Roses*	Jim Reeves	Country
841	*Show Boat*	Original Cast	Stage Musical
842	*Can't Stand The Rezillos*	Rezillos	Punk
843	*Old No. 1*	Guy Clark	Country
844	*Basket Of Light*	Pentangle	Folk
845	*Lena Horne At The Waldorf Astoria*	Lena Horne	Live Albums
846	*Ocean Front Property*	George Strait	Country
847	*The Legendary Son House*	Son House	Blues
848	*Hold On I'm Comin'*	Sam And Dave	Soul
849	*The Gilded Palace Of Sin*	Flying Burrito Brothers	Country
850	*Machine Gun*	Peter Brotzman	Jazz
851	*La's*	The La's	Indie
852	*In Concert Vol. 1*	Peter Paul And Mary	Live Albums
853	*Camelot*	Original Cast	Stage Musical
854	*The Only Ones*	Only Ones	Punk
855	*Pocket Full Of Gold*	Vince Gill	Country

856 *Into The Purple Valley*	Ry Cooder	Blues
857 *Soprano Sax*	Steve Lacy	Jazz
858 *Live And Dangerous*	Thin Lizzy	Live Albums
859 *Live At The Witch Trials*	Fall	Punk
860 *Copperhead Road*	Steve Earl	Country
861 *The Sound Of 65*	Graham Bond Organisation	Blues
862 *A Day In The Life*	Wes Montgomery	Jazz
863 *Chemicrazy*	That Petrol Emotion	Indie
864 *The Patsy Cline Story*	Patsy Cline	Country
865 *Alright Jack*	Home Service	Folk
866 *Nice Enough To Join In*	Various	Greatest Hits & Compilations
867 *Don't Rock The Jukebox*	Alan Jackson	Country
868 *Paint Your Wagon*	Various	Film Musical
869 *AmeriKKKa's Most Wanted*	Ice Cube	Rap
870 *Quarter Moon In A Ten Cent Town*	Emmylou Harris	Country
871 *Greens*	Benny Green	Jazz
872 *The Truth*	T-Bone Walker	Blues
873 *Still Life (Talking)*	Pat Metheny	Jazz
874 *Guitars Cadillacs Etc Etc*	Dwight Yoakam	Country
875 *Modern Sounds In Country And Western*	Ray Charles	Country
876 *Joan Baez*	Joan Baez	Folk
877 *What's This For*	Killing Joke	Punk
878 *Searching For The Young Soul Rebels*	Dexy's Midnight Runners	Indie
879 *Come On Come On*	Mary-Chapin Carpenter	Country
880 *Peter Green's Fleetwood Mac*	Fleetwood Mac	Blues
881 *Sleeping With The Enemy*	Paris	Rap
882 *Nobody's Heroes*	Stiff Little Fingers	Punk
883 *The Cutter And The Clan*	Runrig	Folk
884 *Soul Dressing*	Booker T. And The MGs	Soul
885 *Black Coffee*	Peggy Lee	Jazz
886 *Flower Drum Song*	Original Cast	Stage Musical
887 *Battle Of The Field*	Albion Country Band	Folk
888 *Around The World In 80 Days*	Various	Film Musical
889 *Cool Blues*	Jimmy Smith	Jazz
890 *Five Live Yardbirds*	Yardbirds	Live Albums
891 *Damaged*	Black Flag	Punk
892 *Strictly Business*	EPMD	Rap
893 *Diana Ross Presents The Jackson Five*	Jackson Five	Soul
894 *Who Knows Where Time Goes*	Judy Collins	Folk
895 *Live Bullet*	Bob Seger	Live Albums
896 *King And Queen*	Otis Redding & Carla Thomas	Soul
897 *Happy Sad*	Tim Buckley	Bedsitter Albums
898 *Aqaba*	June Tabor	Folk
899 *I Wish My Brother George Was Here*	Del Tha Funkee Homosapien	Rap
900 *Handful Of Earth*	Dick Gaughan	Folk
901 *Electric Bath*	Don Ellis	Jazz
902 *Return Of Da Boom Bap*	KRS One	Rap
903 *Please To See The King*	Steeleye Span	Folk
904 *Black's Magic*	Salt 'n Pepa	Rap
905 *Evita*	Studio Cast	Stage Musical
906 *Alabama Blues!*	J.B. Lenoir	Blues
907 *Sex Packets*	Digital Underground	Rap

908	Let There Be Drums	Sandy Nelson	Rock 'n' Roll
909	Vapour Drawings	Mark Isham	New Age
910	Apocalypse 91- The Enemy Strikes Black	Public Enemy	Rap
911	I Got A Name	Jim Croce	Folk
912	Nouveau Flamenco	Ottmar Liebert	New Age
913	The Things I Notice Now	Tom Paxton	Folk
914	Have Twangy Guitar Will Travel	Duane Eddy	Rock 'n' Roll
915	For Pence And Spicy Ale	Watersons	Folk
916	Power In The Darkness	Tom Robinson Band	Punk
917	Vengeance	New Model Army	Punk
918	The Platters	Platters	Rock 'n' Roll
919	Heart Of The Congos	Congos	Reggae
920	Criminal Mind	Boogie Down Productions	Rap
921	Rise Up Like The Sun	Albion Band	Folk
922	The 5000 Spirits Or The Layers Of The Onion	Incredible String Band	Folk
923	The Book Of Invasions	Horslips	Folk
923	Fabulous Style Of	Everly Brothers	Rock 'n' Roll
924	Nature Of A Sista	Queen Latifah	Rap
926	Rock 'n' Roll Stage Show	Bill Haley And the Comets	Rock 'n' Roll
927	Right Time	Mighty Diamonds	Reggae
928	Gangster Chronicles	London Posse	Rap
929	Deserters	Oyster Band	Folk
930	Especially For You	Duane Eddy	Rock 'n' Roll
931	Step Outside	Oyster Band	Folk
932	Tequila	Champs	Rock 'n' Roll
933	Love Me Forever	Carlton And His Shoes	Reggae
934	Full House	Fairport Convention	Folk
935	Midnight Marauders	A Tribe Called Quest	Rap
936	Shifting Gravel	Four Men And A Dog	Folk
937	It's Everly Time	Everly Brothers	Rock 'n' Roll
938	Another Side Of Bob Dylan	Bob Dylan	Folk
939	Last Of The True Believers	Nanci Griffith	Folk
940	And Now The Legacy Begins	Dream Warriors	Rap
941	Step In The Arena	Gang Starr	Rap
942	Grave New World	Strawbs	Folk
943	Skylarking	Horace Andy	Reggae
944	Hand Of Kindness	Richard Thompson	Folk
945	Inner City Griots	Freestyle Fellowship	Rap
946	X Verses The World	Overlord X	Rap
947	On Top	Heptones	Reggae
948	As Raw As Ever	Shabba Ranks	Reggae
949	Intelligent Hoodlum	Intelligent Hoodlum	Rap
950	Circle Game	Tom Rush	Bedsitter Albums
951	Jazzamatazz	Guru	Rap
952	Follow The Leader	Eric B & Rakim	Rap
953	Turning Point	John Mayall	Live Albums
954	Living Large	Heavy D & The Boyz	Rap
955	Make Way For The Mother	Yo Yo	Rap
956	Pajama Game	Original Cast	Stage Musical
957	Guerillas In Tha Mist	Da Lench Mob	Rap
958	This One's A Good Un	Otis Rush	Blues
959	Ming	David Murray	Jazz

960	Cycledelic	Johnny Moped	Punk
961	19 Naughty 3	Naught By Nature	Rap
962	Proud Mary	Solomon Burke	Soul
963	The Pied Piper	Chico Freeman	Jazz
964	Heavy Rhyme Experience Vol. 1	Brand New Heavies	Rap
965	Feeding Of The 5000	Crass	Punk
966	Godspell	Original Cast	Stage Musical
967	Of The Heart Of The Soul And Of The Cross	PM Dawn	Rap
968	Rock For Light	Bad Brains	Punk
969	Cats	Original Cast	Stage Musical
970	The Crack	Ruts	Punk
971	Doggy Style	Snoop Doggy Dogg	Rap
972	Mack & Mabel	Original Cast	Stage Musical
973	Come Out Fighting Ghengis Smith	Roy Harper	Bedsitter Albums
974	Generation X Perfect Hits	Generation X	Punk
975	Enta Da Stage	Black Moon	Rap
976	East West	Paul Butterfield Blues Band	Blues
977	Death Certificate	Ice Cube	Rap
978	Hypnotised	Undertones	Punk
979	Fairytale	Donovan	Folk
980	Down To Earth	Monie Love	Rap
981	An Evening With Wild Man Fischer	Wild Man Fischer	Brilliantly Unlistenable Classic
982	In Full Gear	Stetasonic	Rap
983	God Bless Tiny Tim	Tiny Tim	Brilliantly Unlistenable Classic
984	In-A-Gadda-Da-Vida	Iron Butterfly	Brilliantly Unlistenable Classic
985	Journey To The Centre Of The Earth	Rick Wakeman	Brilliantly Unlistenable Classic
986	Unfinished Music No 1: Two Virgins	John Lennon	Brilliantly Unlistenable Classic
987	Wonderwall	George Harrison	Brilliantly Unlistenable Classic
988	Lick My Decals Off Baby	Captain Beefheart And The Magic Band	Brilliantly Unlistenable Classic
989	Preflyte	Byrds	Brilliantly Unlistenable Classic
990	Have A Marijuana	David Peel And The Lower East Side	Brilliantly Unlistenable Classic
991	Sid Sings	Sid Vicious	Brilliantly Unlistenable Classic
992	The Transformed Man	William Shatner	Brilliantly Unlistenable Classic
993	Metal Machine Music	Lou Reed	Brilliantly Unlistenable Classic
994	Lord Sutch And Heavy Friends	Screaming Lord Sutch	Brilliantly Unlistenable Classic
995	Unfinished Music No 2: Life With The Lions	John Lennon	Brilliantly Unlistenable Classic
996	Journey Through The Past	Neil Young	Brilliantly Unlistenable Classic
997	Transfiguration Of Blind Joe Death	John Fahey	Brilliantly Unlistenable Classic
998	Lord Of The Rings	Bo Hansson	Brilliantly Unlistenable Classic
999	Approximately Infinite Universe	Yoko Ono	Brilliantly Unlistenable Classic
1000	Live At Max's Kansas City	Velvet Underground	Brilliantly Unlistenable Classic